1968

rpt

1968

MASTERPIECES OF
GREEK SCULPTURE

Frontispiece: Lansdowne Herakles, J. Paul Getty Museum, Malibu, California

MASTERPIECES OF GREEK ✢ ✢ ✢ SCULPTURE ✢

A SERIES OF ESSAYS ON THE HISTORY OF ART ✤ BY ADOLF FURTWÄNGLER ✤ EDITED BY AL. N. OIKONOMIDES ✤ WITH 24 FULL-PAGE PLATES AND MORE THAN 280 TEXT ILLUSTRATIONS

NEW AND ENLARGED
EDITION

CHICAGO : ARGONAUT PUBLISHERS : MCMLXIV

EDITOR'S PREFACE

ANY unprejudiced attempt to form, from the text books now in use, an estimate of the state of our knowledge of the history of art among the Greeks will force us to own with shame that we appear to know and to utilize the monuments for less than did Winckelmann in his day." Thus wrote Adolph Furtwängler in the introductory paragraph of his Preface to the first English edition of this book in 1895.

What can be said of the state of our study of Greek art today? Can anyone deny that the above statement is no less true today? Is there anyone bold enough to state that we have attained a level of knowledge in this field in recent years of which we can be proud?

"Our more recent histories of art are wont to take into consideration only one and the same group of monuments, an accidental selection of the mass of what has been preserved," Furtwängler continues. Does not this quotation describe exactly the "manuals" and "textbooks" in use today? It is a well accepted fact that specialists in the field agree that most authors and editors of works published in recent years appear to know and utilize the monuments for less than did Furtwängler in his day.

And what of these luxurious publishing efforts of the twentieth century? With few exceptions, the study of Greek art seems to have become confused with the study of photographic, typographic and printing improvements. It would appear that the editors and publishers of the "big books" on the subject believe that the best and most complete views of Greek art can be presented simply by the use of color, more color, dramatic photographs, exotic bindings, scholarly titles, and the names of experts who apparently have little more to do with the books than to approve picture captions. Some creators of these works have lately become more progressive in accepting the idea of inserting appendices with limited texts in order to distinguish their books from those of the competition, but details such as footnotes and bibliographies, are for the most part, anathema.

A book reviewer for the *New York Times* recently awarded praises to an expensive and elaborate new book on ancient art, rich in color illustrations and properly impressive in size. The book, however, was lacking an index, noted the reviewer, but it is presumed that this feature is not a requirement for a coffee table ornament.

In an effort to provide a book worthy of its title for willing readers and students of the history of art, I have prepared this new edition of "Masterpieces of Greek Art," by Adolph Furtwängler. This book still heads the list of classics in the field of Greek sculpture, with only a few others such as Bieber's "Sculpture of the Hellenistic Age," Pickard's "Manuel de l' archeologie grecque," Richter's "Kouroi" and "Archaic Greek Art," deserving places beside it.

Furtwängler's masterpiece has received the praises of reviewers since its first appearance. Surely no other book in its field has been more widely acknowledged for its greatness, nor more extensively used for research and study by laymen, students and scholars alike, year after year.

The second edition of a book with such a reputation is bound to follow the original form; it would be presumptuous to do otherwise. Were an editor to comment in footnotes or other statements upon the original theories of the author, the result would be a monstrous product of nineteenth century text with twentieth century embroidery. Also, due to the scarcity of the original, this new edition will doubtless be the one most used for research, following references given by other authors, so I was reluctant to alter the pagination, which would have been necessary in any attempt to update or improve the original text. While maintaining the original text form, I made every effort to correct the one weakness of the original — the illustrations. Every possible source was contacted for both replacement and new photographs and I used my best judgment as to positioning in the available space. The full-page plates of Miss Sellers' edition were used as text blocks, with the exception of one which was omitted, and due to the text and note references to these, they are still labelled with the original

Plate numbers preceded with asterisks (*Plate I—XVIII).   A numbering problem ensued with the addition of new photographs which was solved by using Roman numerals again, without asterisks and with the designation, Figure (Fig. I—LXXXVII). In some cases photographs had to be added after the original numbering had been completed. These have been listed as Fig.—a. Due to printing vagaries, even this was impossible in four cases and these are simply called Fig. #, followed in the list of illustrations, by their page numbers. In order to best utilize the available space for illustrations, some of the original figures are not in numerical order, but each of them has been used as closely as possible to its original position.

Much of the new photographic material was printed in three eight page sections of plates (A through X). For distinction from the rest of the book these were printed in sepia ink on Embassy coated stock, with captions in a different typeface.

Miss Sellers' preface has been reprinted at the end of the text (Pages 413—416) for the benefit of those who wish a more complete understanding of the original plan of the first English edition. Miss Sellers was well advised to remove the two passages of German text dealing with archaic art, and I have taken the liberty of deleting the appendix of her edition dealing with the topography and temples of the Acropolis, due to the fact that much of the information therein has been revised and corrected by later study and discovery. The scholar who will use the indices I and II concerning Sculptors and Museums can verify that this appendix did not contain any important basic infomation relative to the great masters of Greek sculpture. In the general index, references to the appendix were removed.

So that the readers of this new edition will not be deprived of the knowledge of several masterpieces and copies discovered, published or identified since the first English edition, the most important have been illustrated and may be found, whenever possible, where I believe the author himself would have placed them, had they been available, in the sections treating the pertinent artists and the theories pertaining thereto. The reader is expected to find the present illustrations to be more than adequate for his studies on Greek sculpture of the fifth and fourth centuries B.C. While many other photographs could have been added, surely the most important ones illustrating the masterpieces around which Furtwängler's theories were established are included. For those wishing further reading, a bibliography has been added on pages 425 to 427 which should provide the necessary sources for the desired inquiries.

It is my hope that this improved reissue of a renowned reference book will help new students and scholars in their efforts to appreciate and study the works of the great masters of Greek sculpture as the original served to guide and enlighten those who are considered authorities in the field today. The study of classical sculpture has been neglected to a certain extent in the modern era of classical research due to an apparent lack of enthusiasm on the parts of educators, with the result that even the most fundamental passages of ancient authors necessary for research and productive study of the subject are still to be found only in the "Schriftquellen" by Overbeck first published in 1868 and reprinted without change or addition in 1959. Although great quantities of relative texts have been discovered since from papyri, inscriptions and manuscripts, apparently no college or university professor, no scholar and no student has had enough enthusiasm and historical reasoning ability to produce a new and comprehensive work, being occupied instead with worthless conventional and repetitive research projects.

Archaeology is the youngest and most vigorous of the historical sciences. However, stagnant scholastics and grammarians on the one hand, and pseudo"historians" and "esthetes" on the other, are so stifling its study that it is fast becoming a minor educational element in most institutions of higher learning. This must not be permitted to happen! In few areas of historical scholarship is there more opportunity for discovery, original work, extended research and even, if you will, excitement and adventure. It is hoped that the reappearance of this classical reference book in the field will inspire an awakened interest in classical sculpture, which in turn will affect the study of archaeology in general, bringing to it the new blood it so well deserves; thus, the new edition of "Masterpieces of Greek Sculpture."

Chicago, November 25, 1963   AL. N. OIKONOMIDES

AUTHOR'S PREFACE

ANY unprejudiced attempt to form, from the text-books now in use, an estimate of the state of our knowledge of the history of art among the Greeks will force us to own with shame that we appear to know and to utilize the monuments far less than did Winckelmann in his day. Winckelmann's History of Art is wholly based upon a fresh and personal observation of the monuments, of which he makes a constant and extensive use. Our more recent histories of art are wont to take into consideration only one and the same small group of monuments, an accidental section of the mass of what has been preserved. Ever since Brunn laid with a master hand the foundation for the history and the characterization of the Greek artists, so far as these can be gathered from the traditions of the ancients, writers have for the most part been content to repeat what he established, only perhaps adding an occasional 'selected' monument to trim, as it were, the fabric of his weaving. Still it was quite justifiable to be thus prudent and cautious in dealing with the monuments, so long as we only painfully groped our way amidst the wealth of remains, without knowing how they should be utilized: it was certainly better to limit investigation to the little which was ascertained, than to venture without stay or support upon the ocean of what actually exists.

Modern science, however, has afforded us a stay which enables us to keep steadily in the direction of our goal. Any one who understands how to observe the monuments, and who is willing, with indefatigable ardour, to test afresh and compare all forms, may nowadays, by means of photography, which helps to fix the individual objects, obtain a picture of Greek art far more richly coloured than the pale and meagre image we have hitherto possessed.

I know that many fellow-scholars are engaged upon these lines, and it is only by combined effort that we shall be able to advance. Each must bring what contributions he can. The investigations which I publish here are all closely interconnected ; their ultimate object is to gain from the monuments a new and solid foundation on which to build a history of statuary among the Greeks, for, before undertaking to draw from the monuments—as has long been my ambition—a new presentment of this history, the way must be smoothed by isolated inquiries.

The first of the essays, that on Pheidias—containing the identification of the Lemnia—was the external inducement to the publication of the other sections, most of which had been written previously. Starting from the Lemnia, the inquiry extends to the whole circle of Pheidias and to the Akropolis, the chief scene of his activity ; thence it passes on to his more independent contemporary Kresilas, and from him harks back to Myron. Myron affords a transition to Peloponnesian art, and the inquiry passes naturally on to Polykleitos. The powerful effect exercised by the creations of the latter upon the Attic artists of the fourth century leads accordingly to Skopas, Praxiteles, and Euphranor, and finally to a glance at Lysippos. Some special tendencies of Skopas and Praxiteles are followed out more in detail in the next section on the Venus of Milo, while the chapter on the Belvedere Apollo reverts from the creations of the fourth century to those of the Pheidian epoch. The method of investigation is throughout the inductive, which passes step by step from one conclusion to another. Much which belonged together has thus inevitably been wrenched apart ; but this fault may be rectified by the index, which will enable the student readily to put the material together in its systematic historical order. The museographic index will also be welcome to the reader.

The material treated in this book consists for the most part of antique copies, since, except for the well-known few though splendid exceptions, the best creations of antiquity survive only in copies. True, to the number of these exceptions—original works of first-rate artists—I add one at least (Plate XVII.) ; yet the multitude of other masterpieces whose traces are here followed are still known only at second hand.

The increasingly rich discoveries of original works on Greek soil have lately somewhat thrown into the shade the study of the copies, for which we are mainly indebted to Italy, not to the advantage of our science. The original sculptures from Greece are, with those rare exceptions to which I have already alluded, works of the second or even inferior rank. The Roman copies, on the other hand, have preserved that pick from the masterpieces of the classical epoch which pleased ancient taste and connoisseurship in the times of highest culture. It is the pick of the best and the most famous that antiquity possessed. Among these copies it is that we must look for the masterpieces mentioned by the authors, for the statues that made epochs or initiated movements. Were we to possess only copies of the noble creations of a Raphael, a Michelangelo, or a Rembrandt, these would certainly be better worth one's study than the hosts of other originals of the time.

It is manifest from this that our first duty is accurate examination and criticism of the extant copies. This kind of study is as yet only in its infancy ; but it is precisely here that photography is of invaluable assistance, and by its aid we may hope to make rapid progress. Above all, an almost painful accuracy is required. The older works dealing with our store of copies suffer almost throughout from obscurity as to what is to be really regarded as a copy. No adequate distinction is drawn between copies and adaptations or even figures which are merely similar. Formerly, indeed, relatively little was known of the existence of actual close copies, and for the most part only few late reproductions or variants were believed in. Two mistakes in particular were very frequently made: either actual copies of one and the same original were taken for different modifications or variants of one 'type'; or else copies of quite different originals were taken for later copyists' variations of one original.

As regards principles and method in the criticism of copies, many rules might be laid down—yet I have never been able to see any use in talk about method, much less in boasting about it. Rules would never embrace, even remotely, the whole range of possibilities presented by reality. Method can be shown only by application. The researches in this book show by numerous instances what are the requisitions I think necessary for the criticisms of copies, and how I think copies should be dealt with (cf. Index under COPIES). Just a few remarks may however be in place.

In the more delicate appreciation of the copies, all of course depends on a right discrimination between what is derived from the original and what is added by the copyist. This point will always be a rich mine of error in inquiries of this kind; yet a long familiarity with the monuments, and a sense sharpened thereby, will preserve one from at least gross mistakes. Further, it is above all important that the monuments should not be torn out of their setting. Any inquiry concerning the masterpieces of antiquity must, if we would avoid error, be made only in a wide connexion. The individual work must be replaced in the environment which conditioned it, and through which alone it can become intelligible; and in our inquiry concerning any single monument we must keep all the others to which it is akin steadily in view. This procedure alone can guard us from the errors which must necessarily arise from the dilettante habit of isolating works, and connecting them arbitrarily with the names of artists. Finally, I may add, I have made it my first and most natural rule to discuss only those works of art which I have myself examined. In the relatively few cases where this was not possible I have specially noted the fact. Ocular examination can, however, be at times replaced by good photographs; but the illustrated works, and the large one by Clarac in particular, are as good as useless for our purpose. It is of course my wish that my readers should be in a position to compare for themselves as many originals, casts, and photographs as possible. The illustrations in the book reproduce the most important and least accessible monuments.

At first many will doubtless think I have been too bold in my attributions of extant works to celebrated artists. But on deeper familiarity with the actual objects these doubts will vanish more and more. I can at any rate say for myself that I have, I believe, been sufficiently critical of my own conjectures, and that I have scarcely allowed one to stand that has not been practically laid aside and tested by repeated trials, and has approved itself in a wider connexion. But it may be further objected that it is not yet time, while we are still so behindhand in the knowledge of the general development of the separate forms, to inquire into the individualities of the several artists. The study of these forms, however—in so far as it touches upon the efflorescence of plastic art and so soon as it enters into more delicate distinctions—is inseparable from—nay, even identical with—the inquiry into the individualities to whom precisely this or that particular development of form is due. Only the general pervading features of this development must be assumed throughout as the solid basis of the inquiry. It were indeed much to be desired that this basis should be effectively laid down once and for all in some special treatise, since unanimity even in this respect is still lacking among scholars.

The more deeply we penetrate into that selection of antique masterpieces which undoubtedly survives in our extant copies, the more forcibly are we impressed by the individuality of the great artists of the best period. I venture to hope that, beyond the circle of specialists, the general reader—for the book is intended for him also—will see reason to modify his conception of the antique, and will grant that it includes a far greater range of individual development than has hitherto been supposed. It is true that the great distinction between ancient and modern culture still holds good: the untrammelled, free individuality, at once the strength and the weakness of modern artists, was quite foreign to antiquity. The ancient artist clung to established types of far-reaching influence. He obeyed laws and rules in his treatment of bodily forms and of attitude—and for this the book affords evidence step by step—which he modifies and alters, extends and fashions after new inspiration, but which yet impart to his whole production a something inevitable, typical, known by rule. It is this that brings about that unique effect of the antique which Goethe sums up in the words, ' These great works of art have been brought about in the same wise as the operations of nature. Everything arbitrary, everything self-conscious, disappears : there is Necessity, there is God.' But to penetrate into the whole mystery of individuality, and to learn to recognize there also the divine necessity—this was reserved for the moderns.

A. FURTWÄNGLER.

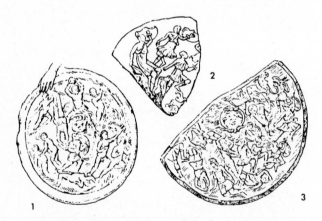

1. Amazonomachia on the shield of Athena Parthenos, Lenorman statuette, Athens, National Museum (cf. E3, Pl. E). 2. Fragment of Parthenos shield, copy in Vatican Museum. 3. The Strangford Shield, British Museum (cf. D1, D2, Pl. D).

CONTENTS

LIST OF TEXT ILLUSTRATIONS

LIST OF PLATES (FIRST EDITION)

*NOTE: The full-page plates of the original edition have been incorpo-
rated into the current edition and are marked as Plate with an asterisk.*

INITIAL AND TAIL-PIECES

LIST OF FULL-PAGE PLATES

INDEX
OF ILLUSTRATIONS

AAM -Athens Acropolis Museum
ANM -Athens National Museum
BM -British Museum
MNY -Metropolitan Museum ,New York
NCG -Ny Carlsberg Glyptotek, Copenhagen
NNM -Naples National Museum
OM -Olympia Museum
PM -Piraeus Museum

PLM -Paris Louvre Museum
RCM -Rome Capitoline Museum
RNM -Rome National Museum
SAM -Stoa of Attalos Museum ,Athens
UF -Uffizi Gallery, Florence
VM -Vatican Museum, Rome
st. - statue   stte. - statuette
br. - bronze   c. - copy

Conventional names have been placed between quotation marks. Figure numbers appear in parentheses, followed by their page numbers. Plates A -H appear between pages 48-49 ; Plates I-P appear between pp.112-113; Plates Q-X appear between pages 304 - 305.

Fig. I—Athena Parthenos, Varvakeion Statuette. Athens,
National Museum. (See pp. 3, 10 spp. 33 seq.,
47, 49 seq., 105, 107, 143—Plates D and E)

PHEIDIAS

OF the works of those sculptors whom antiquity esteemed as its greatest, one masterpiece, the Hermes of Praxiteles, has come down to our times in the undoubted original, while others, such as the Doryphoros of Polykleitos and the Apoxyomenos of Lysippos, are known to us in good and faithful copies, executed probably on the scale of the originals. But Pheidias, most famous of all who wrought the images of the gods, is represented so far neither by any ascertained original nor by any efficient copy. For of only two of his works, the Olympian Zeus and the Athena Parthenos, do we possess reproductions acknowledged to be such: the Zeus is reproduced chiefly on coins, and the Athena in statues and statuettes, so much reduced in size that they are rather abstracts or *résumés* than real transcripts; they differ totally from the faithful copies alluded to above. Though sufficient to give a general notion of the composition, of the arrangement and fall of the drapery, they are inadequate for all finer distinctions. Above all they give no exact idea of the head, which, as being the seat of intellectual life, is naturally of the highest interest. The various replicas exhibit differences so marked as to convey the impression that not one of them is accurate. And this is very natural, for the head of a colossal statue in ivory and gold must have offered unusual difficulties to the copyist. Those who had access to the original itself could only make drawings or small models, and in so doing each artist would follow his own style. Other and freer imitations of widely varying dimensions were derived from these sketches. It is small wonder, then, that the finer modelling of the head of the Parthenos has been lost to us in spite of its numberless reproductions.

Yet even if we possessed an exact copy of the head of the Parthenos or of the Zeus in the original size, I do not believe that we should thus gain a complete conception of the best that Pheidias could achieve. An artist cannot show the finest and most spiritual qualities of his treatment of form in a colossal head. Besides, the complicated ivory and gold technique must have placed many obstacles in the way of free artistic conception. An artist was much less trammelled in executing the clay model for a bronze statue, and even Pheidias must have found in this technique a purer and more exquisite medium for his genius.

Bronze statues by famous artists were usually, when of normal dimensions, copied in the original size. The copyists probably made use of casts,[1] which was of course

---

[1] The passage in Lucian (*Jup. Trag.* 33) concerning the Hermes Agoraios in Athens shows that it was quite usual for artists to take casts of famous works of art.

impossible in the case of gold and ivory images. Yet even so copyists allowed themselves a freedom which occasionally amounted to almost complete remodelling of details. Nevertheless, copies exist which can be proved to be perfectly accurate. Such a copy of a bronze work by Pheidias would be the first step towards an exact appreciation of his artistic personality.

I. *Discovery of the Lemnian Athena.*

It is this need—this deficiency in our knowledge—which, I believe, I have been able to fill. The two statues reproduced on Plates I. and II. can be shown to be faithful replicas of a bronze work by Pheidias—a work which ancient connoisseurship preferred to all others by the artist, which roused the enthusiasm of the subtle critic Lucian, and which even the matter-of-fact Pausanias admits to be the best worth seeing of all the creations of Pheidias. *This work is the Lemnian Athena.*

The two statues belong to the Dresden Museum, and have long been known: one of them had a head foreign to it, while the head of the other, though genuine, was disguised by inaccurate restoration. The statue given on Pl. I. is published in Becker's *Augusteum*, i. Pl. 14, and in Clarac's *Musée de Sculpt*. Pl. 464, 868. The head is antique, but has been broken and put on again. The whole upper part of the head, from the fillet, is restored ; an ugly modern helmet was formerly placed upon it. In 1894 Becker pronounced that it was impossible to decide with certainty whether the head belonged to the statue or not.[1] On the other hand, L. Schorn (1822),[2] while acknowledging that the head had been joined on again and the face worked over, added that there was nothing to prove that it might not have belonged to the statue. Hettner, in his catalogue of the Dresden antiques,[3] declared that the correspondence of the marble, and the fact that the turn of the head fitted the remaining portion of neck, showed the head to be genuine. More recently it was recognized by Flasch that the head was a replica of the beautiful Bologna head which Conze[4] had published as that of a young man, while Flasch[5] had interpreted it as an Amazon. It was accordingly taken for granted that the head did not belong to the statue,[6] and therefore, when Treu began his admirable and useful task of freeing the Dresden statues from their modern restorations, he removed the head from the statue, set it up separately, and restored it from the Bologna replica—*i.e.* he took away the helmet, and supplied the place of the missing upper part of the head by a cast taken from the Bologna head.

The statue and the head were thus separated when I saw them in 1891. At first it did not occur to me that they might belong together. It was only in the course of a protracted inquiry into the type of head appropriate to this statue of Athena that, to my own great astonishment, I came to the conclusion that the head which had been removed actually did belong to the statue, and that consequently the Bologna head also represented Athena, and came from another replica of the same statue. The portion of neck still attached to the torso and turned vigorously to the right, as well as the shape of the nude part of the chest, answered down to the minutest details to the corresponding parts of the Bologna bust. Further, head and torso are of the same marble. Probability became certainty when Treu, at my request, placed the

---

[1] *Augusteum*, i. p. 95. [2] In Bötticher's *Amalthea*, ii. 206 *sqq.*

[3] *Bildwerke d. Königlichen Antikensammlung*, 4th ed. No. 69.

[4] *Beiträge zur Geschichte d. Griechischen Plastik*, Taf. I. p. 1. Cf. Friederichs-Wolters, *Gipsabgüsse*, 519.

[5] *Bull. d. Inst.* 1872, 66. Brizio declared the head to be modern (*ibid.* p. 65 ; cf. Heydemann, *Mittheilungen aus den Antikensammlungen, in Ober- u. Mittelitaliens*, p. 60, 206), but was immediately refuted by Flasch.

[6] Cf. Puchstein in *Jahrb. d. Inst.* 1890, p. 96, note 36.

head upon the torso ; the two fitted together fracture for fracture, of course not in front where the edges are broken off, but in the core of the neck.

Pl. I. shows the statue in its present state. The missing parts in front of the neck, the nose, mouth, and upper part of the head are restored in plaster. The face, as Schorn correctly noticed, has been worked over, and has lost much of its beauty in the process ; but the hair, as far as it is preserved in the marble—*i.e.* the portion under the fillet—is uninjured, and corresponds exactly to the hair of the Bologna head, except for a few variations in the curls, which show that the copyist in this case was rather less careful. Yet the correspondence between these two copies is more exact than is usual in antiquity, and goes to prove that each is a fairly accurate rendering of a common original.

The other statue (Pl. II.) is published by Clarac, Pl. 464, 866.[1] The head was not made in one piece with the body, as in the preceding example, but was worked separately and inserted, with the nude part of the breast, into the draped torso. The head has been restored by using up an antique fragment of a replica of the head of the Farnese Athena in Naples,[2] which, placed on a hideous thick neck, looked curious enough when set upon the statue. This restoration has now been removed, and a cast of the Bologna bust has been inserted into the empty space cut out in the torso. Pl. II. represents the statue thus restored. The Bologna bust fitted into the hollowed torso, as exactly as if it had been made for it, hardly a *millimetre* of alteration being necessary. This bust is wonderfully well preserved,[3] the only injury it has suffered being the loss of the eyes, which were inserted separately. The exact correspondence of the hair with the Dresden head, and indeed the remarkably careful execution of the whole work, show the accuracy of the copy. Rather less care has been bestowed upon the hair above and behind the right ear, the head being so much turned that this part comes at the back.

The right breast and right shoulder of this statue were lost, and have now been restored by a piece cast from the other figure ; the left arm-stump, likewise, has been added, in accordance with the other figure where it is antique. The bodies, except for a few unimportant variations,[4] are exact replicas. On the whole, however, the statue reproduced in Pl. II. deserves the preference for its fresher and more refined workmanship, though it is evident from the close resemblance of the body to that of Pl. II. and of the head to the Bologna head that the statue on Pl. I. is also a very careful copy.

A third replica in the Museum of Cassel contributes nothing to our knowledge of the original, in spite of its careful workmanship. The head is missing (it is replaced by a replica of the Athena Giustiniani), and the body is not a copy, but a complete transformation of the original of the two Dresden statues.

---

[1] Hettner, *Bildw.* No. 72. A cast of it is in Berlin, Fried.-Wolters, *Gipsabg.* 478. Published in Sandrart, *Teutsche Academie,* ii. (1679), 2, ee, as being in the Palace Caesii in Rome.

[2] Published in Becker's *Augusteum,* i. cap. 15. B. Gräf (*Aus der Anomia,* p. 65) has already noticed that it belongs to a replica of the Athena Farnese.

[3] It has been supposed that the face was worked over in modern times (Fried.-Wolters, *Gipsabg.* 519) (cf. Heydemann, *Mitt. aus d. Antikens. Ober- u. Mittelitaliens,* p. 50). After repeated examination of the original I am able to state that this is not the case, though it is true that in certain parts acid has been used in order to remove incrustation (this was noticed by Brizio, *Bull. d. I.* 1872, 65), but without injuring the face in the least.

[4] Slight differences are to be observed in the hair and tongue of the Gorgoneion. The scales of the aegis also differ slightly : in the one statue (Pl. II.) they are lighter, flatter, and all turned downwards, while in the other (Pl. I.) they are harder, more plastic, and do not all follow the same direction. The first rendering (Pl. II.) is the more severe, and certainly the most correct. The ends of the snakes knotted in front also vary somewhat in arrangement in the two statues. [Pl. II.* shows the left side of the statue ; it is taken from the cast exhibited in the Pheidian room of the Dresden Cast Museum ; the body is that of statue Pl. I., on which has been placed a cast of the Bologna head.—E. S.]

The artist's aim evidently was to get rid of the severe simplicity of the folds, and to substitute for them a rich mass of petty details more suited to later taste.[1] This copyist shows himself unable to appreciate the greatness of the older manner ; he tried to correct and to improve, and only succeeded in becoming feeble, futile, and artificial.

There is still another copy of the head alone (probably part of a fifth replica), in the Vatican. The head is set on a female statue, to which it does not belong ; it was once a good copy, but it is now so broken and restored as to be almost unrecognizable.[2]

The position of the arms in the original can be made out from the Dresden statue (Pl. I.) The left upper arm is raised horizontally. The goddess must have held with her left hand a lance that rested on the ground. The right upper arm is lowered, but it is plain that the right forearm must have been extended somewhat forwards and sideways, so as to bring the right hand into the direction towards which the goddess is looking.

It would be impossible to say what this hand held, were it not for another copy of the original, which is fortunately preserved on an engraved gem (Fig. 1),[3] and

FIG. 1.—Athena on Gem (Cades, i. H, 17).

which confirms in the most satisfactory manner our reconstruction of the Dresden statues. It is quite evident that both statues and gem are derived from the same original. The gem-cutter has copied, as faithfully as was possible within so small a space, the bare head with the short knotted-up hair, leaving the ear free, the fillet, the neck, the opening of the drapery on the breast, even the folds falling over the left breast, the transverse aegis, and the raised left upper arm. He chose to represent the left side of the statue, so that the breast appears somewhat foreshortened, and the head in profile (cf. Pl. II.) In the field in front of the left shoulder is a helmet. Such objects on gems are never mere 'symbols' as they are on coins, therefore I think it quite certain that the artist, who had not room in the picture for the right arm, wished at least to indicate that the goddess bore a helmet in her right hand. This trait completes our conception of the original statue.

The composition which we have thus won back had been brought into connexion with Pheidias even before its design was thoroughly clear. L. Schorn[4] was the first to associate the statue with the Athena Parthenos of Pheidias, of which at that time no copies were known. This was no vague hypothesis, but the result of a careful and penetrating appreciation of the 'grand style'[5] of the Dresden statue. He describes the simple treatment and rich effect of the drapery ; the transverse aegis seems to him to indicate peaceful possession, the tranquil watch over the beloved city. And of the head he says that it has 'the features and solemn expression appropriate to the maiden goddess,' and that the beautiful turn towards the right completes the 'exalted image, which captivates the beholder as much by its godlike majesty as by

---

[1] Cf. Schreiber, *Athena Parthenos,* p. 583 ; my article in Roscher's *Lexikon,* i. 699 ; and Puchstein's remarks in *Jahrb. d. Inst.* 1890, 93. Wolters's view (*Gipsabg.* 477, 478) is obviously incorrect.

[2] Vatican, *Gall. delle Statue,* 400.

[3] According to Raspe, No. 1651, a nicolo, 'a beautiful engraving'; the owner is not named ; badly reproduced on Plate 25 of the same work. A cast is in the Cades Collection, i. H, 17, from which our illustration is taken. To the left is the inscription HEIOϒ, badly written and certainly modern, which made me formerly doubt the genuineness of the gem (*Jahrb. d. Inst.* iv. 1889, p. 71). But the inscription has nothing whatever to do with the stone, which is beyond suspicion, and is a beautiful and carefully executed work of about the time of Augustus.   [4] Bötticher's *Amalthea,* ii. (1822), 206 *sqq.*

[5] W. G. Becker (*Augusteum,* i. p. 93 *sqq.*) has likewise well appreciated this style.

the freedom and naturalness of the pose.' What judgment would he not have passed could he have seen the head freed from the ugly modern helmet and the statue completed by the finer head from Bologna! Recently the extraordinary likeness of the torso to the Parthenos caused Puchstein[1] to reckon it as distinctly Pheidian. The head belonging to it was unknown to him; but since an Athena from Pergamon (see p. 27) which he showed to be dependent on the Dresden type was bareheaded, he concluded that the Dresden statues also had worn no helmet, and pronounced it not impossible that we have in them good copies of the Lemnian Athena by Pheidias.[2]

The discovery of the head gives to this hypothesis a certainty which is only less than absolute in a case where there is neither the evidence of provenance nor of inscription to shut out the last doubts. The premises which lead to the conclusion that our statues are copies of the Lemnia consist in the following observations. The original must have been a famous work of classical antiquity, witness the marble replicas which have been enumerated and the small accurate copy on the engraved gem. Again, the body of the statue comes nearest in style, of any known work, to the Parthenos of Pheidias, and possesses all its most characteristic and personal qualities: this has already been pointed out by Puchstein, and we shall presently prove it more in detail. If any work is to be taken as Pheidian, surely this must be. Now the famous Lemnian Athena of Pheidias also wore no helmet, and was moreover the only famous bareheaded Athena known to literary tradition. And what is said of this work[3] corresponds in the most striking manner to our marbles, in fact has been made clear by them. The Lemnia was noted for exceptional charm; Lucian describes her as undoubtedly the masterpiece of Pheidias, and borrows for his ideal beauty the outline of her face, the delicacy of her cheeks, and the fine proportions of her nose (*Imagines*, 6). Applied to the Bologna head these words are no empty phrases (indeed, so far as we can verify, Lucian is never a mere phrase-maker): on the contrary, they emphasize peculiar merits which must strike any one who looks at this head and which distinguish it from other works of antiquity. The *eximia pulchritudo* of the Lemnia of Pheidias is possessed in a very high degree by the head which belongs to the statue acknowledged as Pheidian.

Finally, the Lemnia was a work in bronze, and, as nothing is said to the contrary, it was probably life-size. Now it is from a life-size figure that our statues derive, for, since they accurately reproduce their original in other respects, they presumably also reproduce its scale. It seems likely from the great distance at which the arms are held out from the body, and from the treatment of the hair, that this original was in bronze, while the extraordinary wealth of motive in the separate locks and the subtlety of the execution point emphatically to the same conclusion.[4] True, artists before Pheidias employed for marble the same technique that we consider characteristic of bronze—as for instance in the Aegina marbles and in the boy's head from the Akropolis[5]—*i.e.* they imitated bronze technique in an inferior material; but within the circle of Pheidias we can no longer suppose that this was the case, although the complete separation between marble and bronze technique, which manifested itself especially in

---

[1] *Jahrb. d. Inst.* 1890, p. 93 *sqq.*, 96, note 36.

[2] Michaelis, *Athen. Mitt.* 1876, p. 287, had previously tried to refer this type to the Athene Hygieia of Pyrrhos; his theory was however refuted by the discovery of the footmarks of the statue on the actual basis. Cf. *Ath. Mitth.* 1891, 163, Taf. 6.

[3] For the most recent discussion of the passages see Studniczka, *Vermutungen z. Kunstgeschichte*, p. 1 *sqq.*, and Weizsaecker, *Neue Jahrb. f. Philologie*, Bd. 133 (1886), p. 14 *seq.*

[4] Cf. Flasch in *Bull. d. Inst.* 1872, 66.   [5] Ἐφημερὶς ἀρχαιολ. 1888, Taf. 3.

the hair, was not effected till the fourth century.   As regards the treatment of hair, we may compare the head of the Lemnia with the fragment of the head of Nemesis from Rhamnus,[1] by Agorakritos, the closest pupil of Pheidias.   The enormous contrast between them is certainly due to differences not only of date but of material ; the pupil working in marble having contented himself with the broadest and most general reproduction of the principal outlines.   Bronze technique involves a previous modelling in clay and chisel work after the casting ; all this brings out the form in a sharp and detailed manner, and accounts for the totally different treatment of our Athena head. Lastly, the hollow eyes afford another proof, as they occur principally in copies from bronze works.

We are now justified, I think, in claiming to possess exact copies after a bronze work by Pheidias, and to have thereby gained for the first time a full conception of this artist's achievements in the round.   All through the fifth century, apparently, bronze casting was the method most in esteem ; artists found in it a vehicle for the finest execution of which their mastery was capable, whereas ivory and gold technique imposed on them an over rigid restraint, and the secrets of marble work, as Praxiteles understood them, were as yet undiscovered.

II. *Site of the Lemnia on the Akropolis.—Date and Dedication.*

The Lemnian Athena of Pheidias was named ἀπὸ τῶν ἀναθέντων.   As votive gifts of foreign states do not occur on the Akropolis of Athens, at least in the fifth century, the dedicators were not the Lemnians, but, as is universally agreed, the Attic kleruchs on Lemnos.   As to the occasion of the dedication, Löschcke has made the plausible suggestion[2] that it was set up by the kleruchs on their departure in order to secure for themselves, even when far away, the potent protection of the city goddess. Löschcke cites two votive gifts on the Akropolis with inscriptions which prove that they were set up by departing kleruchs ;[3] since they belong approximately to the same period as the statue by Pheidias, they afford a good analogy.   The objection that such a votive gift would not be offered before some success had been attained is without weight, for according to the ideas of the time 'the permanent holy offering was intended to remind the god constantly of the pious intentions of the giver, and of the consequent obligation to grant him protection and help in return for his gift.'[4]   Just as at the departure of the kleruchs a great sacrifice, ὑπὲρ τῆς ἀποικίας, was offered (as we know from the inscription concerning the kleruchs of Brea),[5] so it appears to have been the custom for the colonists to leave behind some more lasting symbol of sacrifice in the form of a votive gift.   Löschcke's suggestion is, I think, confirmed by the fact that the two inscriptions were found in the very part of the Citadel where, according to the *periegesis* of Pausanias, the Lemnia must have stood.   The inscriptions were found near the Propylaia ; I remember seeing one of them at the eastern end of the northern half of the principal structure. The Lemnia stood on the same part of the Akropolis.   If these three monuments, then, have a local connexion, we have the more reason for concluding that they

---

[1] Cf. Rossbach in *Athen. Mitt.* 1890, p. 64.
[2] *Tod des Phidias* in Histor. Unters. dedicated to A. Schäfer (Bonn, 1882), p. 43
[3] *C. I. A.* i. 339, Τῆς ἀποι[κίας] τῆς ἐς Ἐρ[έτριαν ; 340, Ἐποίκων ἐς Ποτείδαιαν.
[4] Emil Reisch, *Griechische Weihgeschenke*, p. 5.
[5] *C. I. A.* i. 31 ; Dittenberger, *Sylloge*, 12.

were presented on similar occasions. Plainly the statues dedicated by departing kleruchs, of which the Lemnia was one, all stood together.

This place needs however to be more exactly defined. Pausanias, whose evidence we take first, so arranged his *periegesis* of the Akropolis that after coming through the Propylaia he went to the right to view the south side of the Citadel and then by way of the Erechtheion along the north side back to the gates. He begins his account by describing the Propylaia and all that was to be seen in connexion with them, and does not mention them again at the end. We only find out that he has left the Akropolis by his reference to the Pelargikon below the Akropolis and to the grotto of Apollo. Of the four monuments which close his description of the Citadel, one, the so-called Promachos of Pheidias, is fixed, if not actually by remains of the basis,[1] yet at least by well-known coins,[2] as having stood between the Erechtheion and the Propylaia, just where we should have placed it in reliance on the account of Pausanias. Here too must have stood in the time of Pausanias the four-horsed chariot which he mentions together with the Promachos; and close by, nearer the gates, the Perikles and the Lemnia; Pausanias passed them on his way from the Promachos to the gate.[3] They cannot have been within the Propylaia or in front of them, for the gates are not mentioned again, and a complete description of them, including their north and south wings, had been given at the beginning. The statues more probably stood to the north of the principal road which led from the Propylaia along the top of the Citadel, and would therefore correspond to the other statues, south of the same road, which are named at the beginning of the actual *periegesis* of the Citadel. These other statues are not, it is true, clearly marked off from the description of the Propylaia, on account of the eloquent transition which Pausanias devised from the wisdom of Sokrates to the wisdom of Peisistratos and Hippias, and so on to the mistress of the murderer of Hippias. But the exact place of the Athena Hygieia, one of a group of works expressly mentioned as standing near together,[4] is definitely known through the basis found *in situ* on the Akropolis outside the Propylaia on the east. Hence we may conclude that the other works associated with it—*i.e.* the Lioness, the Aphrodite of Kalamis, the Diitrephes, and the 'Hygieia'—were also outside. From the circumstance that Pausanias mentions the Athena Hygieia last among them, we may presume that this statue, standing in front of the last pillar to the right, would not be noticed until the others had been passed. To suppose that these statues were in the porch itself, and to reason from this that the other statues—or at least the Perikles and the Lemnia—stood opposite them in the northern part of the porch,[5] is entirely mistaken. Neither the one series of statues nor the other was within the porch. No traces whatever of any such monuments have been found on the floor of the Propylaia. The two bases belonging to the statues were found not within, but

---

[1] Cf. Löschcke, *loc. cit.* p. 45, note. Lolling in Iwan Müller's *Handbuch d. Alterthumswissenschaft*, vol. iii. p. 352.

[2] Imhoof-Blumer and Gardner, *Num. Comm. on Pausanias*, Pl. Z, iii.—vii.

[3] The assumption that Pausanias is here, contrary to his usual custom, enumerating works of art without reference to their locality (Curtius, *Stadtgeschichte*, p. 300) is entirely without foundation. Cf. Michaelis, *Athen. Mitt.* ii. 95.

[4] After the express mention of the Hermes Propylaios and the Charites as κατὰ τὴν ἔσοδον αὐτὴν ἤδη τὴν ἐς ἀκρόπολιν, follows the mention of the lioness (the transition is effected by means of the *wisdom*), no definite place being given; παρὰ αὐτὴν stands the Aphrodite; πλησίον the Diitrephes, and again πλησίον to this the Hygieia and the Athena Hygieia.

[5] Cf. especially P. Weizsaecker, *Neue Jahrbücher f. Philologie* (Fleckeisen), vol. 133 (1886), p. 1 *sqq.*

immediately without the Propylaia,[1] in the locality where they once stood, though they were no longer *in situ*. Besides, all the statues, the northern as well as the southern,[2] with the single exception of the Athena Hygieia,[3] and possibly also of the hitherto unidentified ' Hygieia,' are older than the Propylaia, and therefore, supposing they were within the Propylaia, they must have been moved there from some other position. No possible reason for such a transfer can be discovered, for not only were all the statues in bronze and made for the open air, but the corridor of the Propylaia was the most unsuitable place that could be conceived for the reception of votive gifts. The narrow space was doubtless kept as free as possible and not crowded up with monuments.[4]

The Lemnia of Pheidias, then, stood on the way from the Promachos and the *quadriga* to the Propylaia; close to it were placed other monuments set up by the departing kleruchies, and here also stood the portrait of Perikles. It is quite evident how appropriately all these works were placed together, for the kleruchies, so often a godsend to the poorer citizens, were the work of this statesman.

The position which we have shown the Lemnia to have occupied explains the motive of the statue very simply. It stood on the left of the road, and would naturally face it. But as the gates were so near, it was natural that the figure should look towards them. With a kindly glance which promised peace and prosperity, the goddess followed the departing kleruchy, while the colonist returning to his native land and coming up to worship would be met and welcomed by the same protecting gaze.[5] Plate II. gives the view of the statue as I imagine it to have appeared to any one entering the Citadel.

According to Kirchhoff[6] the kleruchy to Lemnos must be dated between Ol. 82, 1 and Ol. 83, 2, *i.e.* between 451 and 448—7. It was at this time therefore—in the middle of the fifth century, roughly—that Pheidias made the statue. On the basis was inscribed not only the dedication, but, as tradition expressly states, the artist's signature.[7] Thus it is an absolutely authentic work by Pheidias, and not merely one that was ascribed to him, which survives in the beautiful Dresden copies.

III. *Comparison between Lemnia and Parthenos.*

The chronology which shows the Lemnia to have been a little older than the gold-ivory Parthenos executed in B.C. 447—438 receives important confirmation from a comparison of the style of the two figures. One external detail, the snake-border of the aegis, is specially important in this connexion. The Lemnia follows an old fashion taken over from the archaic period; the rolled edge of the aegis is worked in round scollops, each point terminating in the upper part of a snake. In the Parthenos the system is quite different: here whole snakes form the trimming, the scollops of

---

[1] The Kallias basis, *C. I. A.* i. 392, which supported the Aphrodite of Kalamis, and the Hermolykos basis, *C. I. A.* i. 402, on which the Diitrephes probably stood (see *infra*, p. 122).

[2] For Perikles and the Diitrephes cf. the section on Kresilas.

[3] Wolters (*Athen. Mitt.* 1891, p. 153 *sqq.*) has pointed out that this statue is more recent than the Propylaia.

[4] The much-disputed passage of Herodotos about the four-horsed chariot need cause no confusion. Herodotos had the old Propylaia before his eyes, and it was only at the building of the new Propylaia that the four-horsed chariot was set up where Pausanias saw it. Cf. Miller, *Amer. Journ. of Arch.* 1893, 504 *seq.*

[5] The Athena Hygieia too, to judge by the footmarks, turned slightly towards those entering from the gates; she did not stand exactly in front of the pillar.

[6] *Abhandl. d. Berliner Akademie*, 1875, 33.

[7] Lucian, *Imag.* 4 : τὴν Λημνίαν ᾗ καὶ ἐπιγράψαι τοὖνομα Φειδίας ἠξίωσε.

the older aegis being approximately imitated by the winding of the snakes, and by making the tail of the one curl round the neck of the next.[1] The statues on which this new manner occurs are almost without exception later than the Parthenos, and it is quite possible that the fashion was derived from this statue. The innovation presupposes an artist of bold and original temper; it is just what we should expect of Pheidias, who, it seems, also invented the motive of the girdle composed of two real snakes tied in a bow in front. We already find this girdle given to the Lemnia; it is directly derived from that archaic motive in which two snake-coils coming from the long aegis at the back are twisted together in front, to keep not the drapery but the aegis together.[2]

Another certain mark for the earlier date of the Lemnia lies in the rendering of the free leg (*Spielbein*). The first thing that distinguishes it from the Parthenos is that this foot, instead of being set considerably farther back than that of the supporting foot, is on a line with it. One result of this position is that the heel of the foot at ease is not raised as in the Parthenos, but seems, from a side view, to be placed flat on the ground, although in reality it presses less heavily than the ball of the foot. This attitude of the Lemnia is one stage nearer the old severe position (in which the foot is quite flat on the ground) than is the Parthenos. Again, in the Parthenos, the free leg is much more emphasized. In the Lemnia the drapery conceals the outline of the leg; in the Parthenos it clings closer, revealing the full rounded contour of the thigh, and in a lesser degree the shape of the leg below the knee. There is a sharper distinction between body and drapery. The fold which falls down on the outer side of the left shin of the Parthenos is missing in the Lemnia, where the treatment on the outer side is excessively simple; the garment is heavy, almost like leather, and shrouds the leg without forming any larger folds. The treatment of the Lemnia is evidently a survival of an older manner, in the Parthenos the transition is already being made to the development, which ended in the Caryatids of the Erechtheion, whose light clinging drapery reveals the bent leg, almost as if it were nude.

A consideration of the manner in which the garment terminates at the bottom leads to the same result. In the Parthenos it falls over the feet and touches the ground.[3] In the Lemnia the garment is shorter, and its lower hem touches neither the ground nor the supporting foot, but falls free, thus forming a simple horizontal line without the richness and variety shown in the corresponding part of the Parthenos. In this particular the Parthenos has the form which occurs in all more recent statues, while the Lemnia finds analogies only in earlier works.[4]

Although these details seem to indicate that the Lemnia is earlier than the Parthenos, the difference in date must have been slight, because the two statues correspond so closely in other respects. This conclusion is in harmony with the result arrived at in another way—namely, that the Lemnia must have been produced immediately before the first designs for the Parthenos (447).

Having thus gained a firm foothold whence to review the development of one of the greatest artists of antiquity, we may now proceed to examine these two fixed

---

[1] The border of snakes is best preserved in the replicas D. F. G. enumerated by Schreiber, *Athena Parthenos*.

[2] Cf. the copies of archaic Athenas in the Villa Albani and in Dresden, Clarac, 462 D, 842 B; 460, 855; for the bronze see A. S. Murray, *History of Greek Sculpture*, ii. Pl. 10.

[3] It does not seem likely that the folds of the drapery were bunched up over the right foot in the original as they are in the copy of the Louvre (*Minerve au collier*). The Varvakion statuette, which only shows a slight bend in the drapery over the instep, is probably correct.

[4] Cf. *e.g.* the Athena of the Akropolis, Ἐφημ. ἀρχ. 1887, Taf. 8, 7. See *infra*, p. 21 *sqq*.

points, the Lemnia and the Parthenos, more in detail.[1]   To begin with the
dress : there is no essential distinction between them in the treatment of folds.
Too much stress must not be laid on the difference of material in the originals—
bronze in one case, gold and ivory in the other ; its only consequence would be to
prevent Pheidias from weakening the wooden core of the gold-ivory statue by bringing
deep furrows from opposite directions towards the same point, a caution unnecessary
in the casting of bronze.   Otherwise in his conception of drapery Pheidias appears in
general to be independent of technique.   And, given the precaution mentioned, there
was nothing to check a free and rich arrangement of folds in the drapery of the
Parthenos.   Ivory and gold statues were in all probability executed in their complete
form in wood, and the draped parts would then be covered with thin plates of gold,
while for the nude parts flat slices of wood would be removed from the surface
(already completely modelled) and replaced by plates of ivory cut to the same size
and shape.[2]   The wood technique, while imposing the form, offers not the smallest
obstacle to the execution of deeply cut folds.

Other differences in the drapery of the two statues have nothing to do with
technique ; they may arise partly from the difference in date, but most of them exist
on internal grounds, and express the different character of the two statues ; the
Lemnia is as a whole simpler and more severe, the Parthenos richer and more
majestic.   The drapery of the Lemnia gives an impression of magnificence by its
severe reality, by the large, almost coarse simplicity of its rendering ; there is
no trace of the artificial or the intentional ; the folds fall as they must, without
regard to symmetrical arrangement, and equally unsymmetrical is the aegis
thrown obliquely across the breast.   The Parthenos is in festal attire, all is
arranged carefully, soberly, and of intention ; especially so are the folds above and below
the girdle.   Here the goddess steps forward to meet her worshippers in her holiday
robe disposed with delicate precision, but the Lemnia is in her everyday dress.   This
distinction must arise from the different conception which underlies the two statues.
In the temple the goddess appears in full majesty and splendour, as a queen
giving audience in her throne-room ; the figure in the open air has laid aside
outward marks of dignity, and meets her worshippers unadorned, on the footing
of everyday life, ready with friendly sympathy, advice, and aid.

This accounts for the stiffness and regularity of the folds in the *diploïs* of the
Parthenos, in contrast to the more natural and fresher rendering of the drapery of
the Lemnia.   The difference in the lower part of the body may be explained much
in the same way.   In the Parthenos this lower portion consists of two distinct halves,
owing to the different treatment of the free leg, and of the supporting leg which is
covered by regular perpendicular folds resembling the flutings of a pillar.   Pheidias
found this type ready to hand ;[3] he elaborated it, and in the period after the
Parthenos it came into great vogue.   But what we see in the Lemnia was never a
'type' either at the time it was produced or afterwards ; it is something quite
individual and unique.   The artist has broken away from tradition and scheme, from
rule and symmetry ; in a happy hour he has gone straight to nature, and expressed

---

[1] My remarks on the style of the Parthenos are based exclusively on the good copies, from which we must
exclude the torso from the Akropolis taken by Puchstein, *Jahrb. d. Inst.* v. (1890), p. 85, as the starting-point of
his inquiry.   P. was further misled in his observations by an inaccurate cast of the Varvakion statuette, in which
the depth of the folds had been smoothed down, so that his section (*loc. cit.* p. 84) is not exact.

[2] I owe this convincing argument to an experienced sculptor.

[3] It occurs for instance on the Athena of the Olympian metope representing the cleansing of the Augean
stables.

what he felt in a large and forcible manner. This work keeps the spontaneity of the first conception : it might be copied, but could not serve as a type or be further developed, while statues in the type of the Parthenos might exist in numbers.

What we have learnt from a comparison of the bodies of the statues doubtless applied in a far higher degree to the heads. But an exact comparison of these is impossible, because, as we remarked before, none of the extant copies of the head of the Parthenos are anything like as reliable and exact as the copies of the Lemnia. They differ among themselves so completely in the finer details of form and expression that they afford no fixed basis for argument. We can only judge of the superficial effect and the general character.[1] The head seems to have differed markedly from that of the Lemnia. The Parthenos appeared (as was appropriate to the conception) fully adorned, with necklace and earrings, with richly decorated helmet, and stately ringlets falling on the breast in severe symmetry. She was standing upright and looking straight out with joyful and victorious countenance. Carrying out this fundamental idea, Pheidias gave the goddess a somewhat broad, full face ; it was to express radiant health and well-nourished vigour, for the goddess was the personification of the great and brilliant Attic Empire. This was no place for the severe and thoughtful Athena, with the delicate cheeks. The deeper intellectual expression must make way for the representation of joyous wealth and splendour.

All this is an admirable testimony to the fact that the great artists of antiquity did not repeat the same type again and again, as modern critics would fain have us believe, but, like artists of more recent times, indefatigably created new forms to embody new ideas.

IV. *Analysis of the Lemnia.*

It is now time to examine more closely the individual peculiarities of the Lemnia, and in particular of the head, as being the grandest and most noteworthy part of the statue. The Bologna replica is reproduced alone on Pl. III.

The two most striking qualities of our Athena are the absence of helmet and the short hair combed up at the back. The goddess has wavy and curly hair parted in the middle and confined with a fillet tied in a simple knot behind ; in front, above the forehead, the full hair is combed back towards the ears in a manner which occurs only on female heads, and which is alone sufficient to decide the sex. The hair leaves the ears free, or only just touches their upper edge, and disappears under the fillet ; behind the ears the wavy ends are combed straight up, and likewise tucked into the fillet.

Was this conception of Athena, with bare head and short gathered-up hair, and carrying her helmet in her hand, an invention of Pheidias, or did he only follow an existing model ? A glance at the monuments will show us that the latter was the case.

If we look back into early archaic art we shall become aware that side by

---

[1] For heads of the Parthenos see Löschcke, *Festschrift d. Vereins v. Altert.-Fr. im Rheinlande z. 50 Jubil.* 1891, p. 1 *sqq.*; the list omits, however, the best of the heads, that of the statue by Antiochos in the Mus. Boncompagni (Helbig, *Museums*, 870). On the other hand, the head in Naples, published by B. Gräf (*Aus der Anomia*, p. 61) cannot, on account of its great variations from the ascertained copies, be reckoned among them. The most important copies of the Parthenos head are : the Varvakion statuette, the *Minerve au collier*, the statue by Antiochos, the Cologne head, the Berlin head ; of smaller monuments, a marble head from the Akropolis Museum (No. 647, unpublished) ; also the Aspasios gem and the corresponding head on Athenian bronze coins (Imhoof-Blumer and Gardner, *Num. Comm.* Pl. Y, xxiv. Specially good example in the collection of U. Köhler, Berlin). The St. Petersburg gold medallions are only free imitations.

side with the ordinary warlike conception of Athena there was another equally independent and original type, which presented the goddess entirely unarmed.[1] This conception, it is true, fell gradually into the background; it did not disappear, but it took a secondary place beside the dominant image of the armed warlike goddess, the only one recognized by the national poetry. To represent the peaceful Athena later archaic art invented a new motive: the goddess takes off her helmet and holds it in her hand. She appears frequently in this attitude on the later black-figured Attic vases, e.g. in peaceful colloquy with Herakles or in procession to the unwarlike competition before Paris on Ida.[2] On the earlier red-figured vases, too, this type sometimes appears; it seems to be a special favourite on vases belonging to the transition from the severe to the fine style or to the earlier fine style, i.e. to the period circa B.C. 480—450. Here Athena appears holding her helmet in her hand,[3] sometimes alone, sometimes in a peaceful assembly of divinities. From these paintings we gather that just in the period immediately preceding the Lemnia of Pheidias the Athenians had a fancy for representing their goddess with her helmet off and armed only with the lance. Probably the kleruchs who emigrated to Lemnos had expressly ordered just such an image, for their undertaking could be successful only if times were peaceful, and therefore a goddess of peace must be their patroness.

FIG. 2.—Athena from an Attic Vase (*Élite Céram.* i. 80).

In the period after the Lemnia this type outlived its popularity: it occurs rarely,[4] and after a time disappears altogether.

By a kind of extension of this type the helmet is sometimes entirely left out, i.e. it is not even carried in the hand. This modification in the representation of their goddess also enjoyed its own popularity among the Athenians just in the decades preceding the Lemnia, as we learn from vases.[5] It occasionally occurs later, but

[1] Roscher's *Lexikon*, i. 687 *sqq.*; 693, Z. 63 *sqq.*

[2] *Élite Céram.* i. 81; Millingen, *Vases Coghill*, 34; Roulez, *Choix*, Pl. 7, 2.

[3] Especially on the slender 'Nolan' amphorae, with as a rule only one figure on each side; cf. *Élite Céramogr.* i. 76 and 76 A, style about 480. Somewhat more recent, *ibid.* Pl. 80, 82, 86; cf. *Mus. Gregor.* ii. 52, 2; 21, 1; Klein, *Lieblingsinschriften*, p. 63, 80; Berlin, 2377, 2378; *Samm. Sabouroff*, Pl. 61; Roulez, *Choix de Vases*, Pl. 8; *Mon. d. Inst.* 6, 58; Benndorf, *Vasenbilder*, Pl. 27, 3 (Berlin, 2251). The seated figure on the coin (Gardner, *Types*, Pl. 3, 44) is certainly not Athena, but the nymph Thebe (so also Head, *Historia Num.* p. 296).

[4] Cf. the fine Attic relief of the end of the fifth century, in Lansdowne House (Michaelis, *Anc. Marbles in Gt. Britain*, p. 450, 59). The gem Brit. Mus. *Catal.* 649, Cades, i. K, 66 (for the forged inscription cf. *Jahrb. d. Inst.* iii. 214), and a similar one in Berlin (4651), probably reproduce a prototype of the later fifth century. The same is probably true of the beautiful Cyprian terra-cotta (*Ath. Mitth.* vi. 250; *J.H.S.* Pl. 16; A. S. Murray, *Hist. of Gr. Sculpture*, ii. Pl. 17).

[5] Athena pouring libation, Berlin vases, 2162; in an attitude of triumph with a ship's akroterion, *Élite Céram.* i. 75; pouring wine for Herakles, *Wiener Vorlegeb.* Ser. A, 2 (Kylix in style of Duris); Millingen, *Vases Peints*, ii. 41; receiving Erichthonios, *Mon. d. Inst.* i. 10, x. 38; receiving a fillet from Nike, *Élite Céram.* i. 68; before Paris, *Élite Céram.* ii. 28; with Perseus, Dumont-Chaplain, *Céram. Gr.* ii. Pl. suppl. A; with Pandora, *J. H. S.* xi. Taf. ii.; Roscher's *Lexikon*, i. 2051; alone, leaning on a lance, on a white lekythos from Eretria (Athens), similar to the relief (*infra*, fig. 4). Even in a fighting scene Athena appears without a

apparently only on monuments belonging to the fifth century or deriving from fifth-century originals.[1]   Thus we find Athena without a helmet in the peaceful festal assembly on the Parthenon frieze and on reliefs inscribed with treaties or decrees.[2]   It is interesting to note that the head of Athena without a helmet and wreathed with olive occurs in the first coin-types of the city of Herakleia in Lower Italy, founded about 433—432 (Plate VI. 18).   An aegis is given as background to the head in order to characterize it as Athena.[3]   The founding of the city was the result of an understanding arrived at after long conflicts between Thurii and Tarentum concerning the Siritis : the Tarentines were the actual founders,[4] but the choice of Athena in the attitude of peace for the coin-type was evidently a concession on their part to the Attic colony of Thurii—a concession typical of the peaceful understanding between the two states.   At this period even Tarentum for a short time stamped on her smaller coinage (on the obols) the head of Athena without helmet, against an aegis.[5]   This peaceful Athena, then, like the Lemnia, is closely bound up with historical events.   Some later monuments which represent the goddess bareheaded are apparently derived from Attic prototypes of the fifth century,[6] so that on the whole the type may be said to belong to the great period of Attic supremacy within which it took its rise.

The Athena who holds the helmet in her hand or has no helmet at all almost always wears a fillet or diadem, which is frequently of stately dimensions.[7] This is her festal ornament as goddess of peace.   In giving the Lemnia a fillet Pheidias was again following a firmly established tradition.

helmet on the krater, Millingen, *Div. Coll.* 49.   These vases all belong to *circa* 480—450 B.C.   The Olympian metope with the bareheaded Athena (Overbeck, *Gesch. d. Plastik,* 3rd ed. i. 442) belongs to the same period, and so does a Greek bronze of the Iran Collection in Vienna.

[1] The so-called Kodros Kylix is contemporary with, or only a little later than, the Lemnia.

[2] Studniczka, *Vermuthungen z. Kunstgeschichte*, p. 12, A. B.   The head of a statue representing the bareheaded Athena seems preserved in a copy : see *Mon. d. Inst.* ix. 49 ; cf. *Annali*, 1872, 5 *sqq.* (Flasch).   The gorgoneion and the snakes on the diadem seem enough to justify the interpretation as Athena.   The head probably reproduces an Attic original from the second half of the fifth century.   The snakes have nothing to do with Hygieia.

[3] Good illustrations Gardner (who wrongly interprets the head as Nike), *Types*, Pl. 5, 22 ; Head, *Guide*, Pl. 24, 11.   The type appears on the obol of the city as well as on the stater.   From their style these coins must be dated immediately after the founding of the city.   The usual assumption that they belong to the fourth century (Head, *Hist. Num.* p. 59, dates them *circa* 380—300), and that only the small obols with the Herakles head and the inscription **HE** (according to Head the only coins stamped between 432—380) are older, is untenable.   The style of these obols is exactly the same as that of staters ; especially is this the case in the fight with the lion (also with the inscription **HE**) which occasionally appears on the reverse.   The inscription **HE** affords no proof of date, for among these coins are some inscribed **HP** (Berlin) which differ in no other respect from those marked **HE**. The variation in epigraphy only marks a period of transition ; **HPAK...** and **⊦ HPAK...** occur side by side on the staters.   The staters with the Athena type of Thurii follow very closely on those with the bareheaded Athena.

[4] Cf. Antiochos, *frag.* 12, Müller (Strabo, 6, p. 264) ; Diod. 12, 36, 3 ; Busolt, *Griech. Gesch.* 2, 592.

[5] Examples in the Berlin Cabinet ; reverse Kantharos.

[6] So the Lower-Italy Kyknos vase, *Bull. Napol.* n. s. i. 6, from an Attic prototype of the end of the fifth century (cf. Roscher's *Lexikon*, i. 2231, 54) ; *Mon. d. Inst.* ix. 32.   The Ficoroni Cista (where Athena appears among the Argonauts without a helmet) is derived, I believe, from a mural painting of the Polygnotan cycle (cf. *infra*).   The Athena of the Tarentine vase, *Mon. d. Inst.* vi. 71, 1 ; *Wiener Vorlegeb.* Ser. A, 10, 1 (Judgment of Paris), seems to be dependent on the Lemnia, *e.g.* the hair, the helmet on the hand, the transverse aegis, and the drapery correspond.   A Florentine gem which belonged to the Medici family and is undoubtedly genuine (Gori, *Mus. Flor.* ii. 55, 1 ; Müller-Wieseler, *Denkm.* ii. 200ᵃ ; Impression, Cades, i. H, 30) is remarkable : the goddess appears here bareheaded with short hair.   A plume and snakes on the drapery designate her as Athena ; no aegis ; free fifth-century style.   An analogous work is the Berlin paste of Solon, *Jahrb. d. Inst.* iii. Taf. 3, 8.   Both are free 'fantasias' by artists of the Augustan age on themes of the Pheidian epoch.

[7] Long fillet twice bound round, *Élite Céram.* i. 76.   For flowers or zigzags on the diadem cf. *Élite Céram.* i. 68, 75.   For Pegasoi on diadem see the krater Millingen, *Div. Coll.* 49.   Cf. in addition to the Parthenos the earlier coin of Methymna (Head, *Guide*, Pl. II. 27) ; from this evidence it follows that the magnificent head on a fragment of pottery, known only from Tischbein's drawing (*Élite*, i. 29), may be named Athena ; the goddess wears a diadem crowned with Pegasoi, and no helmet.

Nor was the short bound-up hair invented by Pheidias. It is quite unknown in the archaic period, but in the transition style, when hair was more plainly dressed and more closely tied, the change of fashion influences the type of Athena. We find it for the first time in some helmeted Athenas belonging to the early decades of the fifth century. These show the simple round roll of hair on the nape of the neck,[1] introduced by Peloponnesian art and freely adopted for male and female figures of every kind.[2] It seems, then, that these monuments are Peloponnesian in style and perhaps in origin. In Attic art proper the bound-up hair occurs almost exclusively in the bareheaded Athena, just in the period immediately preceding the Lemnia, but the mass of hair is richer and fuller than in the Lemnia.[3] The coiffure of the Lemnia in its extreme simplicity and restraint recalls the plain roll of hair of Peloponnesian art. In the period after the Lemnia the bareheaded Athena with bound-up hair sometimes occurs.[4] The short hair, not rolled up, worn by the goddess on the Parthenon frieze, is practically unique.[5]

Another emblem of peace is the transverse aegis of the Lemnia: it is not intended as a protection, and therefore leaves part of the breast free. The girdle passes above it. Pheidias found the essential part of this arrangement ready to hand: it occurs more especially in the artistic cycle to which the Olympian sculptures belong; on one of the Olympian metopes, for instance, representing Athena, bareheaded, seated on a rock and receiving from Herakles the birds he has slain,[6] the goddess wears the transverse aegis fastened, just as in the Lemnia, on the right shoulder. The only difference is that the aegis on the Olympian metope covers the left shoulder and the left arm, which is pressed close to the body, while in the Lemnia the left arm is raised and the aegis passes under it. The same transverse aegis and manner of wearing it occur on an Athena rather under life-size lately found in Rome; the work is an original belonging to the same cycle as the Olympian sculptures.[7] The transverse aegis frequently appears in later art, but only in the narrow contracted form which it assumed in the second half of the fifth century. Even the Parthenos no longer wears the mighty aegis retained by Pheidias for the Lemnia, while the Athena on the west pediment of the Parthenon wears a very narrow transverse aegis.

Thus the external characteristics of the Lemnia—the uncovered head, the closely bound-up hair, the festal fillet, the helmet carried in the hand, and the transverse aegis—

---

[1] 1. Staters from Corinth; severe style. A poor example in Brit. Museum, *Catalog. Corinth*, Pl. 2, 20; three better in the Berlin Cabinet.—2. Staters from Side; fine severe style, hair short and curly or rolled up (Berlin); Hunter, Pl. 49, 3, quoted by Head, *Hist. Num.* p. 586, is a different type.—3. Bronze statuette from Magna Graecia in the British Museum, Coll. Castellani, badly reproduced in *Mon. d. Inst. Suppl.* Tav. 26, 6; good severe style; Athena striding.—4. Small silver coin of Kyme in Italy; severe, not fine (illus. Brit. Mus. *Catal. Italy*, p. 88).—5. Relief from the Akropolis (*infra*, Fig. 4). In all these monuments the helmet has the Corinthian shape. The same simple roll of hair, but with the Attic helmet, is seen on 6, the Olympian metope, Augean stables (*Ausgr. von Ol.* ii. 26 A), and 7, Athena head of severe style, wrongly placed on a statue of the Capitol (*Jahrb. d. Oesterr. Kunsts.* xii. p. 73).

[2] Cf. 50th *Berl. Winckelmannsprogramm* (1890), p. 128.

[3] Cf. *Élite Céram.* i. 75, 80, 82; *Mon. d. Inst.* x. 38; Overbeck, *Gallerie*, Taf. 10, 3 (Berlin, 2536); Benndorf, *Vasenbilder*, Taf. 27, 3 (Berlin, 2251); also Berlin, 2378; *J. H. S.* xi. Taf. ii.

[4] Cf. the coins already referred to Herakleia and Tarentum, the Kodros Kylix, the Kyknos vase, the Ficoroni Cista, the gem in the Brit. Museum *Catal.* 649, the similar one in Berlin, 4651, and the Pergamene statue, *Jahrb. d. Inst.* v. 1890, p. 95 (*infra*, p. 27). The Berlin carnelian (Tölken, iv. 245), showing head of Athena (*not* Achilles) wearing helmet, with hair rolled up behind, is influenced by an earlier work.

[5] The hair, now much defaced, is wound round with a broad fillet as on the Kyknos vase. Similar short hair for Athena on the Anesidora Kylix (Roscher's *Lex.* i. 2058, date *circa* B.C. 460).

[6] Overbeck, *Plastik*, 3rd ed. i. 442; Fried.-Wolters, *Gipsabg.* 273. The aegis is absolutely certain, and the figure (sometimes interpreted as a nymph) is certainly Athena.

[7] In the Museo delle Terme; Parian marble; head missing.

were borrowed by Pheidias from works already in existence. But the working out of these characteristics and the whole inner conception of his Athena is the master's very own. His intention is sufficiently clear. He wishes to present the ideal maiden, in her purity and strength. The forms of the body are slightly masculine in contour, the hips are narrow and the abdomen is almost flat, the chest is broad and powerful but the breasts undeveloped. The head was formerly supposed to be male ; the mistake was recognized even before the head was found to represent Athena, for not only the dressing of the hair but the forms, especially of the throat and cheeks, are undoubtedly female ; yet a right instinct lay below this wrong interpretation, for there is in the head a strong dash of boyishness combined with feminine charm. The maiden still shows the delicate austerity of early youth, the woman in her is not yet awake, and she is still intent on the occupations and sports proper to boy and girl alike. Modern art has tried to reach a similar goal by similar means ; the type of the full-grown angel shows the same mingling of boyish and maidenly characteristics. Finally, we may remember Preller's beautiful comparison,[1] made as if in anticipation of our statue, between the Lemnia of Pheidias and Schiller's Maid of Orleans, who lays down her arms when war is over.

We now pass from general impression to a close examination of the head and body of the statue.

The profile of the skull (Fig. 3) forms a perfect curve from the forehead to the nape of the neck. On the frieze and pediments of the Parthenon this line rises more perpendicularly above the forehead, and runs more horizontally on the top, as in the Doryphoros of Polykleitos. The skull of the Lemnia is rather elongated, and remarkably uniform ; looked at from above it has the shape of a regular oval equally developed in front and at the back—a shape usually supposed to betoken an harmonious disposition.

The face viewed from the front forms an elongated and regular oval to correspond with the skull. The forehead, cheek-bones, and chin are not prominent, but are bounded by softly curved lines. This is what Lucian means when he praises the 'contour of the face' and 'delicacy of the cheeks' in the Lemnia, and adopts them for his ideal beauty. The nose (no less admired by Lucian), although marked off from the forehead only by a very slight depression, is yet set at a more marked angle to the forehead than in the heads of the Parthenon frieze and other works of the same period ; the profile line finds its nearest parallel in the Olympian sculptures, the *Spinario* and the Massimi Diskobolos, as well as on vases of the earlier fine style. This is a fresh confirmation of our dating of the Lemnia at about 450 B.C. The lower part of the face is delicate, and recedes rather than projects, without however appearing weak ; the chin, seen in profile, forms an exquisite curve.

The forehead does not, as might appear from a cursory glance, form a simple plane surface. Placed in a good light or felt with the hand, it proves to swell gently and gradually towards the middle ; shallow depressions separate this central part from the rise over the eyebrows. The modelling of these parts is executed with extraordinary measure and restraint. The eyebrow itself has a very sharp edge and is finely arched, the eyelids are delicate, the bridge of the nose is narrow, the sides steep, the nostrils are full and living, though treated with moderation. The transition from the nose to the cheek is effected with peculiar beauty. The nose of the Lemnia differs totally from the Polykleitan nose, the sides of which

---

[1] *Hallische Encyklopädie*, iii. Vol. 22, p.186.

slope much more gradually.[1]   In the Bologna head the furrow between nose and upper lip is strongly accentuated, in evident imitation of the sharp contour of the bronze original.   The lips are closed, a feature of frequent occurrence in works of the first half of the fifth century, but rarer afterwards.   The mouth is modelled with indescribable grace ; every trace of hardness and severity such as still clings to the Olympian sculptures has disappeared ; and, further, Pheidias has succeeded in representing the very breath of life in a manner at once refined, measured, and reserved.   The unknown artist who made the head of Antinous Mondragone in the Louvre[2] for Hadrian seems to have attempted to bring some of the charm

Fig. 3.—Profile of the Bologna head. (From a photograph after the original.)

and beauty of the Lemnia into the face of the Emperor's favourite.   It was probably just this Pheidian quality in the Antinous that aroused Winckelmann's enthusiasm.[3]

The ears of the Lemnia are worthy of independent study : they are carefully

[1] This Polykleitan nose is also to be seen on the bronze head from Beneventum in the Louvre (*infra*, Plate XIV.), which offers many other analogies to the Lemnia.

[2] Fried. Wolters, *Gipsabg.* 1661 ; Brunn-Bruckmann, *Denkm.* No. 70.   Cf. mouth, cheeks, and parts below the eyes.

[3] *History of Anc. Art*, xii. 1, 17 (tr. Lodge, vol. ii. p. 335).

worked, and only just touched by the hair at their upper edge. The ear is slenderly formed with a long narrow lobule distinctly marked off from the upper cartilage. The copies of the Parthenos head, as far as they allow comparison, seem to have a similar ear: we may therefore conclude that this shape was the one preferred by Pheidias. This is interesting, because on Attic monuments of the Periklean epoch we find a broader, shorter type of ear, with a wide hollow and a short lobe; in this type the distance from the end of the lobe to the upper edge of the hollow is usually very small, if at all greater than the whole width of the ear. This is the shape of ear in the Massimi copy of Myron's Diskobolos, and Myron probably learned it from Kritios;[1] we also find it employed by the artist of the east pediment of Aegina,[2] but it does not occur earlier. Later it appears in the Aphrodite of the Louvre[3] (probably a copy after Alkamenes); on the Parthenon frieze[4] and in other works of the period[5] it is the common type, although the other more slender form also occurs;[6] in the Hegeso-relief, for instance, the ear of the mistress has the one shape, and that of the maid the other.

The hair of the Lemnia, finally, deserves a closer examination. It is parted in the middle from the crown (not merely in front as in earlier times), and combed to either side straight from the parting. The Lemnia appears to be the earliest female head with this arrangement of hair; following immediately on it come the famous Amazon heads. In the severe style the hair was invariably combed forwards from the crown without any parting, and only parted to the sides over the forehead.[7] The hair is thick and full, rising in a plastic ridge on each side the line of parting; just towards the back of the head it lies somewhat flatter. The smooth fillet presses deep into this soft abundant mass, which is subdivided into a multitude of separate meshes, each with a movement of its own. Not least charming are the little curls that cannot follow the track of the rest, but lie separate in front of the ear and at the back against the neck. Pheidias, however, was not the first to employ this motive. It was known to the artist (Kritios, as I believe) who made the statue of a boy, from the Akropolis,[8] and to the artist of the Apollo of Mantua;[9] in whose works the motive, which seems quite foreign to archaic art, apparently occurs for the first time.

Despite the marvellous wealth of form and movement displayed by the hair of the Lemnia on forehead and cheeks, the treatment distinctly follows an earlier tradition. The general form of the front hair is that of an undulating mass, with a regular rise and fall. Upon this full mass and in subordination to it the separate meshes of hair are carved. They start from the parting in almost parallel lines, but soon lose themselves in a rich tangle. This manner had its rise in a fashion, already invented in earlier archaic art, of long front hair[10] rendered by a solid undulating

---

[1] See the head, Ἐφημ. ἀρχ. 1888, Pl. 3 (cf. 50th Berl. Winckelmannsprogr. p. 150).

[2] This pediment belongs to the early fifth century, as can no longer be doubted after the discovery of the Athenian Treasury in Delphi.

[3] Gazette Archéol. 1887, Pl. 30. Cf. infra, p. 82.   [4] Cf. the beautiful head of the so-called 'Peitho.'

[5] E.g. the horseman-relief in the Villa Albani (Helbig, Museums, 759); the statue of the Coll. Jacobsen (Arch. Anz. 1891, p. 70); the Barberini Suppliant, etc.

[6] E.g. in the head of Iris on the Parthenon frieze.

[7] This older manner still appears on the Barberini Suppliant, which in other respects is a work of the free style, and at a much later date on the Artemis head wrongly placed on the Artemis Colonna in Berlin (Skulpt. 59).

[8] Cf. 50th Berl. Winckelmannsprogr. p. 150. The head, Ἐφημ. ἀρχ. 1888, Pl. 3.

[9] The replicas are quoted 50th Berl. Winckelmannsprogr. p. 139, Note 61.

[10] Cf. e.g. Ath. Mitth. 1889, Pl. 3 to the left. Sometimes only the mass was given plastically, and the lines of hair were painted upon it, e.g., Ath. Mitth. 1879, Pl. 5, 6, 1.

mass with parallel inner wave-lines.   In the later archaic period, this type of headdress was supplemented by one more artificial, but only to be taken up again with greater energy in the period of the severe style at the beginning of the fifth century.   It remained very popular for female figures both then and down to the early stages of the fine style, about the middle of the century, as is testified by numerous Attic vases,[1] Greek terra-cottas, bronzes,[2] and coins.[3]   Among larger works of art are to be named the foremost of the Charites on the famous Akropolis relief of severe style and the Athena seated upon a rock on one of the Olympia metopes ;[4] the undulating mass, with its regular rise and fall, is perfectly distinct in the Athena, though the separate lines of hair, which once were painted, are now obliterated.   This whole system disappears from Greek art in the second half of the fifth century ; the rendering of the front hair as a solid mass was gradually given up, and the separate meshes were made freer and more independent.   Undulating front hair was still in favour, but it was rendered quite differently ; it was compounded of loose separate masses, as may be seen on heads of the Parthenon frieze, in the Aphrodite of Alkamenes, the Barberini Suppliant,[5] and others.   The earlier formation was retained only, as on certain coins,[6] when older types were expressly copied.

Later artists must have studied the hair of the Lemnia, for its influence makes itself felt in many works, as for instance in the hair of the beautiful bronze *Camillus* of the Capitol,[7] which would be executed just at a time when Pheidias appears to have been held in special honour.

The proportions of the body still have to be touched upon.   They have a peculiarity, which has already been accurately observed by L. Schorn,[8] who recognized that the legs of the Dresden statue were somewhat too short.   According to normal proportions (in the Doryphoros, for instance) the length of leg from the upper edge of the knee-cap to the sole is just three times that of the face, measured from the root of the hair ; thus, while the upright leg of the Lemnia ought to measure 0·582, it is, as the measurements show, some centimetres too short.   Schorn has already suggested that the statue was originally placed rather high, so that, the upper part being seen foreshortened, the statue would appear in the right proportion. This supposition is borne out by the forward bend of the head, which would produce an excellent effect if viewed from below.   It must therefore be assumed that the

---

[1] In the severe style exceedingly common ; *e.g.*, *Wiener Vorlegeblätter*, v. 2, 5 (Athena) ; 7, 1 (Hetaira) ; vii. 6, Benndorf, *Griech. Vasenb.* Pl. 19, 3, 36, 8.   In the earlier fine style, *e.g.* in the bride of the Sabouroff marriage vase (*Coll. Sab.* Pl. 58), the Athena of the Kadmos-hydria (Berlin, 2634), and others.

[2] Examples in terra-cottas of the severe style are very common.   For bronzes cf. *B.C.H.* 1891, Pl. 9, 10 ; Fröhner, *Bronzes Gréau*, Pl. 27.

[3] *E.g.* Syracuse the Demareteia (Head, *Guide*, 17, 33 ; *Coinage of Syracuse*, Pl. I. 10), and the succeeding severe and severe-fine coins of the so-called transitional style, Head, *Coinage of Syracuse*, Pl. 2, 2, 6, 7 ; 3, 2 = *Guide*, 17, 37.   Also the female heads of the severe-fine style in Segesta (*Wiener Numism. Zeitschr.* 1886, Pl. 7, 11), Pandosia (Head, *Guide*, Pl. 15, 11 = our Plate VI. 8), Metapontum (where a beautiful Bacchic head with this hair also occurs.   Friedländer v. Sallet, *Berl. Münzkab.* No. 731), and Terina (Berlin) example of the severe style (*loc. cit.* No. 688) ; then the earlier type of the Athena head of Thurii (Head, *Guide*, 25, 17 = our Plate VI. 5), and its numerous repetitions in other towns of lower Italy (Herakleia, Velia, Neapolis, Cumae, Hyria, Nola, and others).   All these types of coins originate in the middle decade of the fifth century (cf. *infra*, p. 104).

[4] The somewhat earlier relief of the flower-girl from Pharsalos (Friederichs-Wolters, *Gipsabg.* 41) may also be quoted.

[5] Notably also the female heads upon coins, which follow immediately on the types enumerated above in note 3.

[6] Especially the numerous repetitions of the earlier type of Athena from Thurii in the towns mentioned above (cf. *infra*, p. 106).

[7] Helbig, *Museums*, No. 607.

[8] In the *Amalthea*, quoted *supra*, p. 6.   Feuerbach and Hettner agree with him.

Lemnia did not, like many of the statues in the Akropolis, stand on a low pedestal, but upon a higher base in the form of a column or pillar, such as was customary in earlier times both on the Akropolis and elsewhere. Excavations on the Akropolis have brought to light numerous bases of this kind from pre-Persian times, the most celebrated being that supporting the statue by Antenor.[1] Later this mode became more rare, and if the Lemnia was really raised upon a pillar or column, Pheidias was in this again submitting to an earlier tradition.[2]

In the best copies of the Parthenos the leg is also rather short, though less so than in the Lemnia. It is probable that, in a colossal image made to be looked at relatively close, Pheidias kept the lower part a little short, because to a spectator standing near the upper part would naturally appear considerably reduced.[3]

Thus the extant works confirm the traditional reputation enjoyed by Pheidias for his delicate knowledge of optical laws. And the statues of Pheidias rank with the Parthenon, which as is known surpasses every other antique structure in its optical effects.

V. *Drapery and Pose of the Lemnia.*

We still have to discuss, in the dress and the position of the legs, the most important factors in the general effect produced by the statue.

Even the type of dress Pheidias found ready to his hand, and actually in use for Athena, as is clearly proved by a relief and a small statue, both from the Athenian Akropolis[4] (Figs. 4 and 5). These are at the same time the closest antecedents to the Lemnia of Pheidias that can be pointed out. The dress is the same on all three monuments; it consists of the Doric peplos, made of a simple piece of strong woollen stuff fastened upon the shoulders.[5] It falls over from the neck, so that the upper portion of the body is covered with a double piece of drapery. On the right side it is open, but is prevented from gaping by the girdle which is put on over the whole, so as to confine the *diploïs* also. A mass of pictorial material preserved on Attic vases enables us to specify with tolerable precision the date at which this dress was introduced into Athens.[6] It is absolutely unknown in the period of the severe style, which from the find of the Persian débris must be dated before 480; at this time the women wear exclusively the Ionic linen chiton. To help us to date the succeeding stages of Attic vase-painting, we have, in addition to the finely graduated development traceable in the paintings themselves, and to epigraphical criteria, certain definite points afforded by dated sculpture, such as the Tyrant-slayers, the metopes and the frieze of the Parthenon, and, finally, the reliefs of the Nike temple and its balustrades. Grouping the vases upon this basis, it results that even in the transitional vases of 'fine

---

[1] *Jahrb. d. Inst.* 1887, p. 139. Cf. *J.H.S.* 1890, 215; *Ath. Mitth.* 1890, 126.

[2] One is reminded of an anecdote told in Tzetzes, *Chil.* 8, 340 *seq.*, 353 *seq.* (Overbeck, *S. Q.* 772, 810), which, though a late invention, must contain a kernel of truth: it certainly implies the existence of a statue by Pheidias set upon a column and especially constructed for its high position. For the competition with Alkamenes which is the second element in the anecdote cf. p. 84 and note.

[3] Cf. Brunn, *K. G.* i. 195.

[4] Relief: Δελτίον ἀρχ. 1888, 103, 123; *Ath. Mitth.* 1890, 22, 9. Statue: *Sybel, Katal.* 5003; Roscher's *Lex.* i. 695, 35; Studniczka, *Zur Gesch. d. Altgr. Tracht.* p. 142; 'Εφ. ἀρχ. 1887, Pl. 8, p. 148 *seq.*; *Ath. Mitth.* 1890, 22, 8.

[5] Cf. Studniczka, *loc. cit.* 141 *seq.*

[6] For the change in dress at Athens in the fifth century cf. Böhlau, *De Re Vestiaria Graeca*, p. 56 *sqq.*; Studniczka, *Zur Gesch. d. Altgr. Tracht*, p. 26 *sqq.*; *Röm. Mitth.* ii. 54; Winter, *Die Jüng. Attischen Vasen*, p. 27 *sqq.*; Benndorf, *Jahrb. d. Oesterr. Kunstsamml.* xii. 1, p. 53.

Fig. 4.—Athena on a relief from the Akropolis.

severe' style, dating from 480 to approximately 465, the Doric peplos was still but little known in Athens. Only rare examples, on young girls and on Athena, occur at this time: in these the peplos is not girt over the *diploïs*, but it is either left loose or girt out of sight beneath it; in the latter case it is drawn over the girdle so as to form a *kolpos* that falls more or less low.[1] Now these are the two modes in which the Doric peplos makes its appearance in Peloponnesian art, where it occurs frequently in the severe style about the end of the sixth century. As a rule it is ungirt; yet it is frequently sewn together, instead of being open at the side. Some important artist of the period, *circ.* B.C. 500—Hagelaidas perhaps—must have adopted this dress for a statuary type of which we have the reiterated echo in numerous works.[2] One of its distinguishing marks is the severe symmetrical arrangement of the folds of the *diploïs*; the edge forms a level line in the middle both back and front, and then falls down to either side in corresponding folds. The attitude allows the one leg to be just a trifle relaxed.[3] This Peloponnesian type had an immense influence, extending far beyond the narrow Peloponnesian school;[4] figures reproducing it have been found even as far as Lykia,[5] in Pantikapaion,[6] and among the Phoenicians.[7] The artists of the Olympian temple sculptures were also under its influence: they make use both of the ungirt peplos and of the peplos with the *kolpos* under the *diploïs*.[8] Parian sculpture seems to have contributed especially to the propagation of the type.[9] It is also found in the west. A superb bronze statuette from Magna Graecia represents Athena clothed in this manner;[10] other bronzes of the same *provenance* show Athena striding, but clad as in the type where she is standing tranquilly.[11] The artists of the Hestia Giustiniani and of the

FIG. 5.—Statuette of Athena from the Akropolis. (From a drawing.)

---

[1] Ungirt: *Mon. d. Inst.* xi. 14, quite young girl.—Potsherd of the Akropolis, found by S.E. corner of the Parthenon, but certainly not among the Persian débris; Nike with Akrostolion.—With the kolpos: Gerhard, *Auserl. Vasenb.* 300, 301 girl; *Mon. d. Inst.* xi. 19, Athena.—The same two kinds, ungirt and with the kolpos, appear on two of the Charites in the well-known relief (Roscher's *Lexikon*, i. 881), the original of which is about contemporary with the Tyrant-slayers, and must therefore have been made about 470.

[2] Especially in the female supporting figures of the Corinthian mirrors and similar little Peloponnesian bronzes. Cf. *Olympia*, iv. *Die Bronzen*, p. 21, 56; 27; *Athen. Mitth.* iii. Pl. B. *Arch. Ztg.* 1881, Pl. 2, 2.

[3] For the corresponding male type in Argive art, cf. 50th *Berl. Winckelmannsprogr.* p. 124 *seq.*

[4] Cf. *e.g.* the Boeotian terra-cottas of the type Dumont-Chaplain, *Céram.* ii. Pl. 3.

[5] Three torsos in the Brit. Mus. in Parian marble, from Xanthos. A. H. Smith, *Catal. of Sculp.* i. 96—98.

[6] Gilt wooden figure from Kertsch, in the Louvre, about 50 cm. high, without head.

[7] Phoenician sarcophagus from Sicily, Perrot-Chipiez, *Hist. de l'Art*, iii. 189, Fig. 134.

[8] Standing women on the east pediment; Hesperides and standing Athena on the metopes. Cf. also Athena in the Terme Museum at Rome (mentioned above, p. 16, note 7).

[9] Cf. the close proof which I have endeavoured to give in *Arch. Studien, H. Brunn dargebracht* 1893, p. 69 *seq.*

[10] *Gazette Arch.* 1881, Pl. 7, an undoubted Greek original. On the other head, the Pozzuoli bronze, *Arch. Ztg.* 1881, Pl. 2, is only a late imitation, with the folds much weakened.

[11] In the Brit. Mus. from the Castellani Coll. Cf. above, p. 16, notes 1, 3. In Berlin, *Inv.* 6242. Both are originals of 470 —460; the striding Athena from the Akropolis, *Arch. Ztg.* 1873, Pl. 10, is probably pre-Persian.

originals[1] of the 'dancers' from Herculaneum take a more independent line : they give up the symmetrical folds, and aim at a more faithful reproduction of nature. The Herculaneum figures come at the end of the series ; in them the relaxation of the one leg begins to be emphasized. Possibly Kalamis and Pythagoras treated standing female figures in this manner.

Athens at first fought shy of this widely spread Peloponnesian type ; traces of its influence can certainly be detected,[2] but, as vases show, the Doric peplos was not popular in Athens until somewhere about B.C. 465. From that time, however, it became more and more frequent, though it is transformed in the independent Attic manner : it became customary to gird the peplos, open at the side, over the *diploïs*— a plain, homely fashion, which elsewhere was only employed occasionally for attendants,[3] but was at Athens exalted into a dress of distinction. At first the Ionic chiton was still worn underneath, as in the Athena of the Akropolis statuette, which is one of the earliest monuments that reproduce this new fashion, and in the Athena on some vases.[4] From the first the dress was by no means reserved to Athena : it was given indifferently to any young girls, divine or human. And by the side of this new mode the old ungirt Doric peplos now appears quite frequently. The dress, however, was evidently looked upon as a foreign innovation : wherever a company of young girls, Muses or Nereids, for instance, is represented, at first only one or the other wears it. Of the two Eleusinian divinities, Kore, the maiden, is the first to wear the Doric garment ; and only later was it given also to Demeter.[5] The dress only became really naturalized after 440, on the vases which correspond to the Parthenon frieze, and then upon the later vases, contemporary with the Nike temple and the Erechtheion. Alongside the special Attic fashion of girding over the *diploïs*, the old fashion with the under girding and the kolpos now came again into vogue.[6]

Returning now to the Lemnia, we see that the dress in which Pheidias repre-

[1] Comparetti de Petra, *Villa d'Ercol*, Pl. 14. These statues are certainly only late copies, and not, as has been supposed, Greek originals. This is convincingly shown by such external marks as the plinths, the technique, the buttons on the shoulders, etc.

[2] As in terra-cotta dolls, certainly Attic, of the type Dumont-Chaplain, *Céram*. ii. Pl. 4. The Attic origin is less sure in some bronzes from Athens (cf. *supra*, p. 23, note 11) ; it may probably be admitted however for the beautiful statuette, Fröhner, *Coll. Gréau, Bronzes Ant.* Pl. 27, which may be dated *circ*. 460.

[3] Cf. the two Olympian pediments, where it is worn by the attendants (these two figures, it is true, are only preserved copies), while the mistresses wear the established Doric types. Cf. also the maid behind Odysseus on the Polygnotan vase with the murder of the suitors.

[4] *Mon. d. Inst*. x. 54, and the Polygnotan Argonaut vase, *Mon*. xi. 39.

[5] Cf. *Arch. Anzeiger*, 1891, p. 118, 114.

[6] The following is a selection of characteristic examples : I. Peplos girt over the *diploïs* : vases of the time *circ*. 465—450 ; *Élite Céram*. i. 64 (Eileithyia), ii. 36, 41 (both Artemis) ; *Mon. d. Inst*. xi. 40 (Artemis) ; Berlin, 2381 (Nike, front view), 2521 (Maiden) ; Fröhner, *Burlington Fine Arts Exhibition*, No. 51 (Maidens playing musical instruments, the one in front view).—Rather later, from about 450 : Gerhard, *Auserl. Vas*. 243, 291, 305 ; *Mus. Greg*. ii. 19, 2. 21, 2 ; Dumont-Chaplain, *Céram*. ii. Pl. suppl. A. (Athena) ; *Sächs. Ber*. 1875, Pl. 3 c. (Athena) ; *J. H. S*. xi. 11 (Athena) ; *A. Z*. 1881, Pl. 15, 16 ; Millingen, *Div. Coll*. 57 ; *Mon. d. Inst*. x. 53 ; *Wiener Vorlegebl*. E, 12 ; Heydemann, *Vasenb*. i. 1 ; Overbeck, *Atl. d. Kunstmyth*. Pl. 12, 2 (Amymone) ; *Monum. d. Inst*. x. 39 (Aglauros, not Athena).—About 440 : *Élite Céram*. ii. 26, 62, 72, 86 A (one muse out of seven) ; i. 42, 47 ; *Coll. Sabouroff*, 55 ; Millin, *Vases Peints*, i. 54 ; Overbeck, *Atlas*, Pl. 15, 31 ; *Mus. Gregor*. ii. 82, 1 (Medea) ; *Mon. d. Inst*. ii. 15.—Towards 430 and later, on vases in the style of Aristophanes and Meidias, the dress has become the prevalent one.—II. Ungirt peplos. Earlier instances, from *circ*. 465 : *Mon. d. Inst*. viii. 5, 2 ; i. 6, 37, 38 ; Berlin, *Div. Coll*. 60 ; *Élite Cér*. ii. 57 (Artemis) ; *Mus. Greg*. ii. 24, 1.—About *circ*. 450— 440 : Berlin, 2388 (Muses), *Mon. d. Inst*. 5, 37 (Muse) ; *Mus. Greg*. ii. 13, 2 ; 15, 2. 19, 2. 20, 1. 63. 2 ; Gerhard, *Auserl. Vas*. 302, 5 ; Overbeck, *Atl. d. Kunstm*. Pl. 15, 13. 11. 23 ; 18, 15 ; *Élite Céram*. 1, 83. 91 ; *Coll. Sabouroff*, Pl. 63, 55 ; Millingen, *Div. Coll*. 55, 57. What Studniczka (*Z. Geschichte d. Tracht*, 27 *seq*.) has endeavoured to ascertain from literature with regard to the dress accords on the whole with the vases ; he is however mistaken in holding (*loc. cit*. 142 *seq*.) that the ancient image of the Polias already wore the peplos like the Parthenos. The prize amphorae, on which he relies, belong only to the fourth century, when the dress of the Parthenos was an established type ; the garment never appears on the old representation.

sented her had already been given to Athena in Attic art, though its invention was still quite recent, and by no means established and generally accepted. The individuality that lay in the thick simple Doric garment was still felt in all its freshness. The image of the pure and powerful maiden received thereby a material completion, while it was only with the girding over the *diploïs* that the dress became properly expressive of Attic sobriety and compactness. On vases of the time about 460—450 there are many figures that clearly reproduce this character. These are the vases that on other grounds may be brought into close connexion with the painting of Polygnotos.

The two marble works, of the Akropolis, named above, cannot belong to a very much earlier period. The relief must be dated at the earliest about 460, and the statuette somewhere *circ.* 465, the time when the first examples of the new dress appear also upon vases. It has been unnecessarily supposed that the statuette came from the Persian débris : this seems to be most unlikely. It is however probable, from the circumstances of their discovery, that both works came to be buried when the Periklean Parthenon was built.[1] A summary treatment of the past is customary in periods of great progress ; and the excavations on the Akropolis show how truly this applies to the time of Perikles. Style and workmanship as well as the Athenian fashion of wearing the girdle prove both works to be purely Attic.[2] The Doric garment of Peloponnesian art with its symmetrical folds, adopted also by the Parian sculptors, is completely given up, and replaced by independent fresh observation of nature.

The promise contained in these two works was more than fulfilled by Pheidias. The hard, constrained, and timid touches that may still be detected in statuette and relief disappear in the Lemnia. A freer, more majestic air pervades the whole. Even the *diploïs* is no longer so short and straight, but falls in greater fulness, and wherever on the relief the folds, with their round backs, lie side by side in uniform monotony, on the statue the intermediate spaces are made to vary in breadth, while the backs of the folds no longer present a round, almost padded appearance, but begin gently to sink and flatten in the middle.

Turning now to consider the way in which the Lemnia stands, the statue will be found to differ in this point from the type prevalent in the first half of the fifth century, according to which the leg in action is only slightly set free, and is brought either close to the other or in front of it, with the foot flat on the ground. In the Lemnia the leg is considerably more to the side, so that the foot, though not raised, yet rests solidly only on the ball. Even in this, however, Pheidias is not entirely without precedent ; the Apollo of Mantua, which has already been mentioned on account of the hair (p. 19), differs from the prevalent type, in having the same broad posture with the free leg very much to the side.[3] Some of the Herculaneum maidens also come near to the Lemnia in this respect. Pheidias has, however, known how to remove all constraint and hardness from the posture. In the Parthenos he ventures upon a stronger innovation ; the free leg is brought not merely to the side, but also drawn somewhat back, so that the heel is raised. The leg, released from the weight of the body, is not completely at ease, as in the case of a person standing still, but is slightly drawn up towards the other, as when a pause is

[1] The relief appears to have been built into a structure of the Periklean epoch, which has been taken to be the Ergasterion of Pheidias. The statue was discovered when the foundations of the Museum were laid.

[2] Studniczka, *loc. cit.* Ἐφ. ἀρχ. 1887, 153, unnecessarily explains the Athena to be the work of a Peloponnesian artist working for Athens.

[3] Cf. 50th *Berl. Winckelmannsprogr.* p. 140.

E

made in walking. The creation of later Argive art, with the leg still drawn back in the walking attitude, is exactly parallel to the pose introduced by Pheidias.[1] The Argive scheme was not adopted in Attic art till the period following upon the undoubted works of Pheidias. The pose adopted by Pheidias for the Parthenos is not found in earlier works, and grew out of the stage represented by the Lemnia; it was intended to give to the figure freedom of movement without detracting from its majesty, which, according to the Pheidian conception, would have been the case had the leg been quite drawn back in the ordinary walking attitude.

Our inquiry has shown the Lemnia to be closely connected with earlier fore-runners, and yet to be an absolutely independent work, pervaded with a powerful personal spirit. In none of the earlier statues do we find anything that can be even remotely compared with the broad energetic throw of the draperies, or with the eminently individual character of the superb head. Everything in the statue betokens a fresh and genial spirit, that enters upon its course with conscious strength. The Lemnia is its earliest manifestation that is known to us, and the Parthenos follows close upon it. Yet, according to the received view,[2] which places the birth of Pheidias at about B.C. 500, the artist must have been already fifty years of age when he created the Lemnia, so that not only his youth but the prime of his manhood, as well as the greater number of his works, must have fallen within the preceding period. Were we to judge only from the monuments, we should rather take the Lemnia to be a work of the artist's prime. This seems confirmed on the one hand by the bold freshness which even in the Parthenos had already somewhat faded, and on the other by that fidelity to earlier traditions which has been observed in sundry particulars.

VI. *Monuments related to Lemnia and to Parthenos.—The Athena Promachos.*

At this point it becomes important to note the existence of a number of monuments which may be grouped with the Lemnia and the Parthenos. Some are of the same date or only a very little earlier; others again are later, but they all bear more or less distinct traces of the personal style of Pheidias: thus it is about B.C. 450—though not earlier—that we come upon Pheidias everywhere.

A statue of Artemis[3] in the Villa Albani, of which the head is unfortunately missing, may serve as an example of a work closely akin to the Lemnia, though of slightly earlier date. The coarse woollen stuff is treated with the same vigour and naturalness, but the folds are still convex and show no depression. The majestic figure is clothed in the Doric peplos girt in the Attic manner. The peplos is closed at the side, and the part folded over is unusually long, falling below the knee. The right arm was raised, and the left hand carried a young roe, in archaic fashion. The leg in action is placed to one side, as in the Lemnia, though its movement is rather less energetic. Two heavy folds fall perpendicularly from the knee.

Another work very closely related to the Lemnia has been preserved in a torso

---

[1] For the apparently contemporary introduction of the 'walking' motive in Peloponnesian art, see below, at the end of the chapter on Myron. Cf. also Winter, *Die jüng. Att. Vasen.*

[2] Brunn, *K. G.* i. 164; after him Overbeck and others.

[3] No. 662. Gerhard, *Ant. Bildw.* Tf. 12; Roscher's *Lexikon*, i. 562; Clarac, 678 F, 1621 B.; Helbig, *Museums*, ii. 856. The head, right arm, and right foot are restored. The right arm was raised.

of the Louvre[1] and a replica in Madrid. It also represents a young girl wearing the peplos girt above the *diploïs*. The simple, firm, almost rough treatment of the drapery recalls the Lemnia, especially in the folds under the girdle. The attitude is even more vigorous than that of the Lemnia, owing to the feet being very much turned out; further, the left foot, although not drawn back, is placed more to the side. The girdle consists of a wide band of stuff tied in a bow in front. The whole figure is so unconventional, so full of fresh individuality and natural simplicity, and through these qualities so closely allied to the Lemnia without yet being in the smallest degree an imitation, that I imagine it to represent another creation of Pheidias.

A statue of the Capitol[2] akin to the work of Pheidias but not bearing the stamp of his individuality may be placed, owing to its pose and the treatment of the folds, somewhere between the Lemnia and the Parthenos.

A small statue in the Lateran[3] corresponds very closely to the Parthenos, and the same may be said of a beautiful statue in St. Petersburg,[4] in which, however, are to be seen some slight indications of a later style. This figure also represents a youthful goddess; she wears an Ionic chiton under the peplos.

Many more examples might be added,[5] such as a whole series of statues which reproduce the main features of the Parthenos combined with all sorts of later traits: in most of these one foot is drawn back in the walking position.[6] It is not however my intention to discuss these statues here. Mention need only be made of an Athena from Pergamon which is very closely related to the Lemnia. The statue has wrongly been taken for an original,[7] whereas it is merely a copy executed in the loose Pergamenian manner after an original by some artist of the fifth century, who utilized the Lemnia for the body of his Athena, but in the treatment of the head betrayed his affinities with the school of Kalamis, which we shall have to discuss in detail later on (p. 81).

We turn from this ugly Pergamenian Athena to a work which has every claim to be mentioned in the present connexion—namely, the Torso Medici in the École des Beaux-Arts in Paris (Fig. 6).[8] Its peculiarly Pheidian character has been generally recognized,[9] and it has been rightly placed in close relation to the Parthenos; its affinities to the Lemnia are no less marked. It may be said that a common character closely unites all three works. They represent the same conception of the maiden goddess, with the narrow hips of a boy, and the broad though undeveloped breast of a young girl. In all three the folds of the peplos, which is girt, are rendered with

---

[1] (a) Louvre, Gal. Denon. No. 2903, rather under life-size. Pentelic marble; head and right shoulder were put on separately, and are now lost. (b) Madrid No. 70, Hübner No. 43.

[2] Capitol, Salone No. 29, restored as Hygieia; the portrait head is foreign to the statue. Weight on the left leg, the right leg to the side and a little drawn back, the foot flat on the ground.

[3] Benndorf-Schöne, *Catal.* No. 6. (Phot. in the German Institute at Rome.)

[4] Stephani, *Compte Rendu*, 1881, Pl. VI. p. 130. Cast in Dresden. Cf. *Wochenschrift f. Klass. Philol.* 1885, p. 292; *Jahrb. d. Inst. Anzeiger*, 1889, p. 10. The head does not belong to the statue.

[5] Thus a statue in the Villa Mattei (Matz-Duhn 1375) is very similar to the Parthenos, though the weight is thrown on the left leg.

[6] Some instances are mentioned by K. Lange, *Arch. Ztg.* 1881, 197, n. 2.

[7] Conze, *Sitzungsberichte der Berl. Akademie*, 1893, xvi. p. 207. Puchstein, *Jahrb. d. Inst.* 1890, p. 95. Kalkmann's theory (*Prop. des Gesichts*, p. 66), that the head did not originally belong to the statue, is demonstrably false (see my remarks in the *Berl. Philol. Wochens.* 1894, p. 1142).

[8] Cf. Friederichs-Wolters, *Gipsabg.* 476; *Gazette des Beaux-Arts*, 1890, i. 281; Brunn-Bruckmann, *Denkm.* No. 171.

[9] Puchstein alone (*Jahrb. d. Inst.* 1890, p. 90), starting from his mistaken conception of the Parthenos, which he places in the period of the sculptures of Olympia, has disputed the Pheidian character of the torso.

*Plate III—Head in Bologna. (From the Cast.)

FIG. 6.—'Torso Medici.' (Ecole des Beaux-Arts, P

the same massive energy, and the coarse woollen stuff is indicated in the same way. The simple straight line at the lower edge of the *diploïs* and the converging folds at the girdle are points of special similarity. Any one who has an eye for essentials must admit that the three form a close group that stands out distinctly from other extant creations of the fifth century. There are of course many differences in detail. We have already characterized the Parthenos as a later work than the Lemnia. The Torso Medici will be found to be the latest of the three. It displays a greater richness of motive, more splendour, but less simplicity and restraint.

The folds of the peplos are crowded closer together. In the Lemnia the groove-like depressions on the backs of the folds practically only appear on the *diploïs* below the girdle, but in the Torso Medici they also appear on the large perpendicular folds over the leg which bears the weight of the body ; and they are more regularly and deeply hollowed. Further, in the drapery of the Lemnia a small round tube-shaped fold occurs sometimes in the furrow between two projecting ridges :[1] in the torso it is of much more frequent occurrence. We have already observed that, as compared with the Lemnia, the Parthenos produces a stronger effect through the greater definiteness in the scheme of its draperies. The Medici torso represents a still more advanced stage of the same tendency. The Lemnia charms more than either by the greater naturalness and truth with which the drapery is rendered. In the torso the regular perpendicular folds over the leg at rest, and the manner in which these folds rest on the foot (a motive not found in the Lemnia), mark an immediate connexion with the Parthenos.

In addition to the Doric peplos the Medici figure wears the Ionic under-garment. This in itself is no argument for a later date. On the contrary, this double garment seems to have found great favour in Athens as a transitional fashion [2] just at the time when the Doric peplos was introduced ; it appears frequently on Attic vases between 450—440, and particularly in representations of Athena.[3] But the artistic treatment of this garment on the torso, and the carefully thought out contrast between the fine clinging linen chiton on the right leg and the heavy woollen folds which cover the left leg, while leaving the right free, make it probable that the torso is a later work than the Parthenos. Already in the Parthenos there is, by comparison with the Lemnia, an attempt to emphasize the leg in action by means of the clinging drapery. By the arrangement of drapery adopted in the Medici torso the desired contrast between the two legs becomes still richer and more effective.

The artist's principal aim in the stylistic treatment of the linen garment was to express the nature of the material. This he did by means of fine parallel lines running downwards. Actual folds are few and broadly rendered. This treatment bears distinct traces of the archaic tradition. These small wavy stripes are only a freer form of the archaic method of representing linen. The archaic method, however, as is well known, did not combine with this technique any attempt at the rendering of real folds.[4] The linen chitons of the Charites on a relief which must be dated about B.C. 473 are still without folds, but completely covered with fine wave-lines. In the torso Medici we find this linen technique combined with a broad treatment of folds. The next step in development was to abandon the fine lines and to replace them by real folds. On a metope of the Parthenon (XXIX. S. side) the

---

[1] Cf. Puchstein's section, *loc. cit.* p. 94. This observation, which is emphasized by Puchstein himself, *loc. cit.*, ought to have sufficed to prevent him from separating the torso Medici from Pheidian work.

[2] As in the Athena from the Akropolis, Fig. 5.

[3] Cf. *Arch. Ztg.* 1876, Tf. ii. (Berlin 2354)?

[4] Cf. Studniczka's excellent remarks, *Röm. Mitth.* iii. 1888, p. 287 *seq.*

same method is employed as in the torso, but on the frieze and the pediments[1] the
linen of the Ionic chiton is scarcely even characterized by parallel wave-lines.   In
their place we have a multitude of small real folds, which though not strictly true to
nature produce a very rich effect.   The artist of the torso combined the wave-lines
with a few large folds, and thereby attained an infinitely more natural effect.
Hence it may be dated as contemporary with the metopes, and earlier than the frieze
and the pediments.   In the latter two the woollen garments are already less heavily
rendered, and the contrast between the wool and the linen is less emphasized.   On
the other hand, the famous Amazon statues belong to the same stage as the torso.[2]
True, the treatment of the linen stuff in each of the three Amazon types varies considerably in detail, but the principle is the same, and in the Mattei type not only the
principle but the whole manner is that of our torso.   The linen stuff is indicated by
the same closely drawn parallel wave-lines, and only the main folds are represented.
Although the wave-lines almost tend to become real folds, thus showing the
Amazon to be the later work, the stylistic affinities of the two statues make it
probable that they are nearly connected.   But we shall have to speak of the
Amazon again.

The rich drapery of our Athena is completed by a mantle thrown over the left
shoulder.   It is of the same strong woollen stuff as the peplos, and is treated in the
same manner.

The torso is a copy of Roman date,[3] as is evident to any expert from the style
of the work.[4]   Though good on the whole, it is, like most copies, not without dull and
lifeless parts.   Other but much inferior copies of the same original are in existence:
these are a small statuette, a torso three-quarters life-size, and a relief, all three in
Athens.[5]   The relief is specially important: on it an olive-tree with an owl appears
beside the goddess, whence it is probable that the original stood on the Akropolis;
the relief also shows that the statue carried the shield raised in the left
hand.   This agrees with certain indications on the colossal torso itself.   The left
upper arm is lowered and held somewhat away from the body; the forearm
was extended sideways and slightly raised; the hollow where it was let in is still to
be seen,[6] together with a broad contact-surface at the back of the shoulder, which
proves that some large object, which can only have been the shield,[7] was fastened on
at this spot.   Held in this way, a considerable portion of the inner side of the shield
would be visible from the front, as is also the case on the relief.   The mantle filled
the space between shield and body, while shield and mantle together formed a
magnificent background for the side of the figure represented at rest.

The other side was more animated.   The right arm was not close to the body, but,
as the torso and the relief show, it was placed somewhat to one side.   As the goddess
held the shield in her left hand as if in readiness for the fray, it is reasonable to suppose
that in the right hand, which is also missing on the relief, she held the spear, her
weapon of attack.   The statue stands like the Parthenos, the foot in action being
set back and the heel raised, not flat on the ground as in the Lemnia.   This foot

[1] Cf. the so-called 'Peitho' on the frieze, and the female figures in the right angle of the east pediment.
[2] For the three types see *Jahrb. d. Inst.* 1886, p. 14 ; cf. *infra*, chapter on Kresilas, p. 128 *sqq.*
[3] Puchstein, *loc. cit.*, is of the same opinion.
[4] Moreover the marble seems actually to be Italian, as Nibby first noticed.
[5] Von Sybel, *Ath. Mitth.* 1880, 102, Taf. 5.
[6] Both arms and the head were made of separate pieces.
[7] Just the contrary of what Wolters maintains in the note to Friederichs's *Bausteine*, 82 (Fried.-Wolters, 476).
It is impossible to suppose that there was nothing here but a nude forearm and a lance.

moreover is much more turned out than in either of the other statues, and in harmony with this movement the head is turned to the right. This point, not visible on the coarse and mutilated relief, is made quite clear by the small torso in Athens[1] and by the Torso Medici. In both the bunch of hair at the back of the neck is pushed towards the left shoulder, and in the large torso the hollow for the insertion of the upper part of the knot of hair (now lost with the head) plainly proves that the head was turned to the right.[2] On the head rested, as the relief shows, the helmet with its splendid triple plume, similar to the one worn by the Parthenos.

Thus restored, the statue, although standing so firmly and tranquilly, becomes instinct with life and almost with animation. An Athenian coin, struck in Imperial times,[3] shows that the right hand did not lean on the lance, but grasped it low down as if to raise it for the attack. The similar pose of the figure, the raised shield, and the turn of the head prove beyond a doubt that this coin reproduces the original of our torso.[4] This conception of the goddess is quite different from that of the pacific Lemnia who grasps the spear high up in order to lean on it, gently bending her head and carrying her helmet in her hand. It differs also from the stately festal Parthenos who has laid aside her lance and shield and grasps a figure of Nike. The Athena of the torso is the warlike maiden looking about her with courage and resolve, ready for defence or for battle.

Finally we have to remember that the original of the torso Medici must have been of colossal size. All the premises adduced point to the conclusion, bordering on certainty, that this original was the statue of the Akropolis known as the Promachos, an opinion which Konrad Lange expressed long ago.[5] The Pheidian style of the work, the warlike conception of the goddess, the presence of the traditional attributes of the Promachos such as lance and shield, the position of restrained activity testified to by the coins,[6] the colossal size, and the fact that the statue stood in Athens, seem to me, when taken altogether, absolutely convincing. Final confirmation is found in the turn of the figure, which, as Lange has pointed out,[7] is appropriate to the place occupied by the Promachos on the Citadel; the figure towered high above the Akropolis wall and looked towards the city, while its front was turned in the direction of the great gates. Like the Lemnia, this statue also was constructed with careful appreciation of the spot it was to occupy.[9]

According to Pausanias, the Promachos was a work of Pheidias. Neither Pliny,

---

[1] *Ath. Mitth.* 1880, Taf. 5, 2 ; p. 110.

[2] Curiously enough K. Lange did not observe this confirmation of his theory ; cf. *Arch. Ztg.* 1881, 203.

[3] Imhoof-Blumer and Gardner, *Num. Comm.* Pl. 2, I. II., p. 128 ; *Arch. Ztg.* 1881, 197 ; Collignon, *Pheidias,* p. 15.

[4] The omission of the under chiton and of the cloak and the simpler form of the helmet are mere simplifications introduced by the coin-engraver.

[5] *Arch. Ztg.* 1881, 197 *sqq.* ; Studniczka, *Verm. z. Gr. Kunstgesch.* p. 10.

[6] The tranquil attitude of the Promachos is plain from the coins which give the view of the whole Citadel, though, as K. Lange (*Arch. Ztg.* 1881, 198) and Imhoof-Blumer and Gardner (*Num. Comm.* p. 129) have already shown, these coins are no guide to the actual composition of the statue.

[7] *loc. cit.* 200.

[8] This remains true whether the statue stood upon the basis whose existing remains were formerly supposed to belong to it (Löscheke, *Tod d. Phidias,* p. 45, is of contrary opinion) or close beside it (Lolling, *Geogr. Griechenl.* 343, 352).

[9] The attempt lately made by W. Gurlitt (*Analecta Graeciensia, Festschrift z. Wiener Philologenversamml.* 1893, p. 101 *seq.*) to obtain certain knowledge of the 'Promachos' from Byzantine sources rests on absolutely untenable suppositions.—The zealous Byzantine scholar Arethas, writing in the ninth or tenth century A.D., made the following marginal note in his copy of Aristeides opposite the passage referring to the ivory and bronze Athena of the Akropolis—'This is probably the Athena which stands in the Forum of Constantine.' Niketas

however, nor any other ancient authority mentions it amongst the works of this artist.[1] A scholion to Aristeides (Overbeck, *Schrift. Quellen*, 640), on the other hand, ascribes it to one Praxiteles, expressly distinguishing it from the Parthenos of Pheidias. If we wish to criticize the question impartially, we must not, as is usually done, neglect this last testimony as worthless. The scholion doubtless goes back to some authoritative source which carefully distinguished the three most important statues of Athena on the Akropolis—viz. the old Polias, the Parthenos, and the Promachos, giving in each instance the material, the size, and the artist's name.[2] Now there are three other known instances in which Pausanias assigns to Pheidias himself statues ascribed by Pliny and others to pupils or assistants of Pheidias. Such is the case with the Nemesis at Rhamnus, the Mother of the Gods at Athens, and the Athena at Elis: in all these instances Pausanias gives, as every one acknowledges, the less trustworthy tradition. We must therefore allow for the possibility that the information of Pausanias, in the case of the Promachos also, may have been incorrect, and that one of the pupils or colleagues of Pheidias may have been called Praxiteles; further, that common tradition wrongly assigned the statue to Pheidias, while it was in reality by another artist, perhaps even that the name of this artist was inscribed on the statue, as in the case of the Nemesis of Rhamnus. At any rate it seems evident that the Promachos was not signed by Pheidias, from the passage of Lucian[3] in which it is related as something remarkable that Pheidias thought the Athena Lemnia worthy of being inscribed with his name. This statement would be quite meaningless if the name of Pheidias could have been read close at hand on the Promachos.

The copies of the Promachos do not help us to a decided answer to this question. They, however, make it absolutely clear that the statue bore a very close relation to the authentic works of Pheidias. If a Praxiteles made it, it is evident that he worked in the manner of Pheidias. The differences which mark off the Promachos from the Parthenos and the Lemnia are of such a kind as may

---

(thirteenth century) states that this Athena was represented drawing up her drapery with her left hand. Gurlitt concludes therefore that the figure which Niketas saw was an archaic one in the Ionic costume of the well-known 'pre-Persian' maidens of the Akropolis, and that, like these, the left hand held the drapery. More than this, he gives unlimited credence to the suggestion of Arethas, and identifies this figure with the so-called 'Promachos' of Pheidias. He bases this opinion on the presupposition, which we have already shown to be false, that Pheidias was a semi-archaic artist, who soon after 480 B.C. was in a position to be intrusted with the most important commission the Athenians had in their gift. Now the hypothesis of Arethas appears entirely groundless and without authority. But even supposing him to be right, it is still doubtful, first, whether Niketas understood correctly the motive of the left arm, and, secondly, whether Gurlitt was right in identifying this motive with that of the archaic statues. The motive, which is very rare for Athena (it occurs only in quite archaic art, and apparently never in statues), contradicts the traditional type and character of Athena in the periods preceding and following the Persian wars. Therefore we must assume either that the statue seen by Niketas was an archaic work, and that Arethas was mistaken, or else that the Byzantine scribe of the thirteenth century misunderstood, not only the movement of the right arm (as Gurlitt admits), but also that of the left. Nor is it necessary to suppose that the dainty archaic motive gave rise to the description of Niketas. Just as the right hand had lost the lance it once grasped, so too the left hand may have lost a shield. If there was any drapery hanging over the left arm, Niketas might easily mistake the outstretched left hand, robbed of its shield, for a hand holding drapery.—But we need neither the confused account of Niketas nor the hypothesis of Arethas; the evidence for the Promachos derived from the monuments themselves is infinitely more reliable than any conclusions based on these Byzantine writers. Petersen (*Röm. Mitth.* 1893, 350) also opposes Gurlitt's hypothesis; he supposes that the statue seen by Niketas may have been an Alexandrine work in the style of the archaistic Athena published by him *ibid*.

[1] It is not likely that the *Cliduchus* (Plin. xxxiv. 54) is identical with this statue.

[2] The Scholion to Demosthenes *c. Androt.* 13, p. 597 (Ov. *S. Q.* 642, 646), goes back to the same source: the artists' names only are omitted.

[3] *Imagines*, 4.

be regarded as necessary developments of the style of Pheidias. Only the tendency to greater restlessness and animation and the lack of severe simplicity could outweigh these considerations and make it possible to assign the figure to any other than to the creator of the Parthenos.

Before discussing this question further, the date of the Promachos must be fixed more exactly. The work, as we have seen, is probably later and certainly not earlier than the Parthenos. If this be so, then the usual assumption that the Promachos was a monument of the Kimonian period must be false. The assumption is indeed a pure conjecture which must be abandoned in face of more exact knowledge. If the torso Medici is a copy of the Promachos, the Promachos cannot belong to the Kimonian epoch. K. Lange rightly drew the same conclusion. From the earliest testimony concerning the Promachos, that of Demosthenes (*Fals. Leg.* § 272), it follows with certainty, as I believe, that the statue, which he only calls the large bronze Athena, was a votive gift for the Persian war. He describes it as ἀριστεῖον τοῦ πρὸς τοὺς βαρβάρους πολέμου, and the stele with the curse upon Arthmios, who had brought the money of the great king, was set up beside the Athena, according to Demosthenes, precisely because the Athena was the monument of the Persian war. The further assertion that the statue was erected out of the money contributed by the Hellenes is obviously mere rhetorical exaggeration and inaccuracy.[1] Now supposing that the Promachos was a votive gift for the Persian war, there is still a large margin within which to date it. It has long been acknowledged that the assertion made by the late authors, such as Pausanias, Aristeides, and the Scholiast to Demosthenes, to the effect that the statue was a votive gift from Marathon, cannot be relied on.[2] Probably the dedicatory inscription described the statue merely as a votive gift ἀπὸ Περσῶν or ἀπὸ Μήδων. A shortened inscription of this kind would be quite in the fifth-century manner,[3] and would best explain the comprehensive wording of Demosthenes.

The extant copies show the Promachos to be later than the Lemnia and the Parthenos. The design for the latter must have been executed about 447 B.C.;[4] and as we need allow only a short interval before the making of the Promachos (which is earlier than the frieze and the pediments of the Parthenon), we thus obtain the years 445—440 B.C. as the approximate date of this work. Now it seems to me far more likely that the statue was erected about this time than during the administration of Kimon.

The career of Kimon was one long conflict with the Persian power; any monument therefore celebrating the close of the national struggle would have been unsuitable to the spirit of his time, for it was his aim rather to keep animosity alive. Memorials of isolated exploits, such as the gilt Athena and the bronze palm-tree dedicated at Delphi after the battle on the Eurymedon,[5] were appropriate, but

---

[1] Otfried Müller (*De Phidiae Vita*, i. § 10) suggests that there is also an allusion to the tribute of the allies. Preller, *Phidias*, p. 165 (*Hall. Encycl.* iii. vol. 22), suggests the distribution of the booty after Plataia. But if Demosthenes, as Wachsmuth (*Stadt. Athen*, i. 542) assumes, really means the money which was brought by Arthmios, his statement is a purely rhetorical invention; the general connexion of the statue with the Persian wars was a well-known fact which Demosthenes takes for granted and works up into a rhetorical period.

[2] So already by Otfried Müller, *De Phid. Vita*, i. par. 9.—For the inscribed fragment *C. I. A.* i. 333 which Kirchhoff referred to the Promachos, cf. Michaelis, *Ath. Mitth.* ii. 92, and Wachsmuth, *Stadt. Athen*, i. 542. It probably comes from a smaller anathema erected in the lower city soon after the battle of Marathon.

[3] Cf. especially the inscription of the golden shield in the temple of Delphi, Ἀθηναῖοι ἀπὸ Μήδων καὶ Θηβαίων (Aeschin. *in Ctesiph.* 116), also the existing inscriptions, Ἀθηναῖοι ἀπὸ Πελοποννησίων (Röhl, *Inscr. Ant.* 5), Θούριοι ἀπὸ Ταραντίνων (*ib.* 548 seq.), Μεθάνιοι ἀπὸ Λακεδαιμονίων (*ib.* 46), etc.

[4] Cf. U. Köhler, *Sitzungsber. d. Berl. Akad.* 1889, p. 225.

[5] Paus. x. 15, 4.

F

if we are to trust Demosthenes the Promachos was not an offering of this kind, and the indirect testimony of the later witnesses confirms the account of Demosthenes, for they would never have given Marathon as the occasion of the offering had the inscription mentioned any other victory.

It was not until the death of Kimon that the foreign policy of Perikles completely asserted itself. Its first aim was to bring the Persian war to a close so as to concentrate every effort on the attainment of Athenian supremacy in Greece. Negotiations for peace were accordingly begun. Kallias brought the Athenian proposals (a record of which was probably set up on the Akropolis) to Susa. This occurred about 445 B.C. Although it is unlikely that the peace so triumphantly celebrated by the orators of the fourth century ever took the shape of a formal treaty, yet the practical result of the negotiations was a complete cessation of hostilities between Persians and Greeks for a long period.[1] It would naturally be to the interest of the Periklean policy not to let the close of the Persian war pass unrecorded, and no better means of commemorating it could be imagined than a colossal votive gift to the patron goddess of Athens bearing some such inscription as Ἀθηναῖοι ἀπὸ Μήδων.[2] This votive gift was, I believe, the Athena Promachos.

The period (445—440) to which, for stylistic reasons, we have assigned the statue thus becomes probable on historic grounds also. Just such a gift is what we should expect from Perikles, and certainly Pheidias from his relation to Perikles would have some share in the work. Perhaps he made the first sketch, and handed over the execution of the large model and the casting in bronze to one of his assistants—in a word, to the Praxiteles named as the artist by a tradition which was probably derived from the actual inscription on the statue. According to Pausanias, the reliefs on the shield were made by Mys from drawings by Parrhasios. At least one ancient inscription must have testified to the fact that these two artists worked together. This inscription, which may actually have been on the shield of the Promachos, gave rise at a later date to the epigram preserved in Athenaeus (p. 782 B).[3] From what we know of Parrhasios independently (the date of Mys depends on his) it is by no means impossible that he was working as early as 440 B.C., and if so the reliefs on the shield would be, as is most natural to suppose, contemporary with the erection of the statue.[4] The statement of Pausanias as to the reliefs not being by Pheidias affords further proof that the statue was by another artist, for Pheidias appears to have always executed the reliefs on his large works with his own hand, and, having himself been a painter, to have dispensed with the aid of painters or engravers.

The main reason for the widespread belief that the Promachos belonged to the period of Kimon lies in the assumption of a 'Kimonian Pheidias.'[5] The only evidence however for the assumption is that of Pausanias, who says that the group dedicated

[1] For the so-called 'Kimonian treaty' cf. Busolt, *Gr. Gesch.* ii. 512 *sqq.*; Holm, *Gr. Gesch.* ii. 201 *sqq.*; Curtius, *Gr. Gesch.* 6th ed. ii. 183, 832 ; *Stadtgesch. v. Athen*, 205 ; Köpp, in *Rheinisches Museum f. Philol.* vol. 48 (1893), p. 485. The date of the embassy of Kallias is to be found in Suidas, *sub voc.* Καλλίας (in the year of the invasion of Pleistoanax). Krateros incorporated the decree in his collection. The theory of Curtius, *Stadtgesch.* 205, that at the beginning of the fourth century a fictitious inscription was cut in stone and set up on the Akropolis, is scarcely tenable ; Isokrates at least in 380 B.C. considered the record genuine. [Cf. Grote, v. 195.]

[2] Cf. *supra*, p. 33, note 3.

[3] Preger, *Inscr. Gr. Metr.* No. 185, dates the epigram either in the first century B.C. or in the first century A.D.

[4] Cf. Brunn, *K. G.* ii. 97 *seq.* He supposes that they are contemporary, although he places the Promachos in the period of Kimon (i. 165).

[5] See especially Löschcke, *Tod des Phidias*, p. 45, n. 1.

make the temple statue itself, especially when we remember that the Lakedaimonians had just been allowed to celebrate their victory over the Athenians by erecting an akroterion over the completed temple. The only direct ancient tradition we have about the date of the Olympian Zeus places it, as is well known, after the Parthenos. Yet the theory that the Zeus is older than the Parthenos, and that the date of Pheidias as given by Pliny (Ol. 83 = 448 B.C.) refers to the unveiling of the Zeus, is one of long standing. It was held by Winckelmann,[1] though he afterwards abandoned it,[2] and Chr. G. Heyne attempted to prove it in detail.[3] Lately Löschcke revived the theory with great acuteness;[4] and in spite of the lively opposition of other scholars he has again quite recently defended his point of view.[5]

We shall take Löschcke's thesis for a point of departure: he maintains that there were two ancient and contradictory traditions concerning the date of the Olympian Zeus between which we have to choose. This view is, however, inexact: we have only the one tradition mentioned above, for Plutarch's narrative, which, according to Löschcke, affords 'convincing' although 'indirect' proof that the Zeus was made before the Parthenos, is no evidence for this at all, either direct or indirect. There is not a word in Plutarch to indicate that the trial of Pheidias, which he relates in detail, took place immediately after the dedication of the Parthenos, so that Pheidias would have no time to execute any other commission. On the contrary, the whole context, combined with the express statement that the trial of Aspasia took place about the same time, distinctly shows that Plutarch thought of the trial as taking place just before the outbreak of the Peloponnesian war. Thus Plutarch's narrative does not contradict the tradition that the Zeus was made immediately after the completion of the Parthenos. It is not about the date of the Zeus that we have two traditions; evidence is only divided as to the date of the trial and death of Pheidias. The narrative of Plutarch places the prosecution of Pheidias, as we have seen, just before the war, and makes Pheidias die in prison at Athens after his condemnation. On the other hand, the account preserved in the Scholia to Aristophanes is based on the presumption that the trial with all its consequences occurred directly after the dedication of the Parthenos, these consequences being that Pheidias escaped from prison, made the Zeus in Olympia, was accused a second time by the Eleians, and finally was put to death. It is between these two traditions that we have to choose.

Philochoros, quoted by the Scholiast to Aristophanes,[6] after giving the date of the dedication of the Parthenos, adds some information about the fate of the artist, but by using the expression λέγεται seems to decline being responsible for its veracity.[7] The Scholiast accordingly takes it for granted that the events which Philochoros relates concerning Pheidias, τὰ περὶ Φειδίαν γενόμενα, i.e. from the trial

---

[1] In the first edition of the *Geschichte d. Kunst*, 1764, p. 332.

[2] *Geschichte d. Kunst*, book 9, cap. 2, § 11 (Werke, ed. Meyer and Schulze, vi. 1, 39; ed. Eiselein, v. 358).

[3] *Antiquarische Aufsätze*, i. (1778), p. 203; he dates the making of the Zeus Ol. 81, 1—83.

[4] *Phidias Tod und die Chronologie des olympischen Zeus*, in *Hist. Untersuch. A. Schaefer, gewidmet*.

[5] *Festschrift z. 50 Jähr. Jubil. d. Vereins v. Alterthumsfr. im Rheinland*, 1891, p. 16 *sqq.*, where the latest literature on the subject is referred to. Curtius, *Griech. Gesch.* 6th ed. ii. 884, should be added to the list.

[6] After the investigations of Schöll and von Wilamowitz it may be considered certain that the long and trustworthy scholion from Φιλόχορος to λέγουσι δέ τινες is taken from Philochoros, and that nothing ought to be subtracted from it. Cf. also Löschcke, *loc. cit.* 20 *seq.*

[7] This may be concluded from the word λέγεται, although it does not directly prove the uncertainty of the tradition.

to the execution of the artist in Elis, took place in the same year as the dedication of the Parthenos, to which they form the sequel in the narrative of Philochoros. From this passage the Scholiast concludes that the misfortune of Pheidias happened seven years before the Megarian *Psephisma* and the outbreak of the war, and consequently could have had nothing to do with either. Now the Scholiast is evidently in error. Philochoros assigns a date to the dedication of the Parthenos only: what he adds about Pheidias, including the first prosecution, is undated, for, as he certainly does not place the completion of the Zeus and the second prosecution in the year of the dedication of the Parthenos, we need not assume that he wished to assign that date to the first prosecution either. The fact is that he dates neither prosecution, but merely makes the ultimate results of an event follow immediately upon it, probably because he had nothing else to date them by.[1] Plutarch's chronology of the prosecution is confirmed by testimony from other quarters, and notably by Aristophanes himself. In the *Peace* (605), Hermes, with that cunning of the townsman which can trace below each event the personal motive hidden from the stupid peasants, Trygaios and the chorus, alludes to the calamity of Pheidias, and to the fear felt by Perikles lest he should be involved in it, as being the causes of the Megarian *Psephisma* and of the Peloponnesian war. The point of the witticism would be lost had Pheidias died six years before the *Psephisma*, at a time when Perikles stood at the zenith of his power without the slightest cause for fear of any sort.[2]

On the other hand, as regards the death of Pheidias, we have the version reported with reservations by Philochoros, and the version of Plutarch. It is now almost universally acknowledged that the trial in Elis, ending with the execution, is only a 'reflection' of the first trial.[3] It is due to rhetorical inventiveness, working upon the favourite theme of the world's ingratitude towards its great men and the ill luck which befalls them. In order that the story of the second trial might be coherent it was necessary to make Pheidias escape from the prison in Athens and flee to Elis. Plutarch, who gained his information, as is generally admitted, from the best sources, and from sources substantially older than Philochoros, ignores that version. His statement that Pheidias died in prison in Athens is incomparably more credible than the other story, and admirably fits in with the allusion in Aristophanes to the misfortune of Pheidias, an allusion which would certainly not be consistent with the escape from Athens and honourable reception at Elis. Besides, no one would have dared to invent the story of the second trial, which must be at least as old as the third century B.C., if the Olympian Zeus had not been confessedly a more recent work than the Parthenos. Thus the only direct testimony to the date of the Zeus remains uncontroverted.

We assume, then, relying solely on the best-accredited tradition, that Pheidias began the Zeus immediately after the Parthenos in 438, and finished it for the eighty-seventh Olympic festival; thereupon followed the trial and death in prison. There is nothing improbable in this assumption. If Pheidias could complete the Zeus in six years, though he required nine for the Parthenos, it was probably because, in making the Zeus, he had two assistants, Kolotes and Panainos. Nor is it necessary to suppose that Pheidias was at Olympia all the time: when once the design and the models were made, the master's presence was not always

---

[1] This is a common proceeding of Philochoros; cf. Böckh, *Plan d. Atthis d. Philochoros* (*Abh. Berl. Akad.* 1832), p. **7**.

[2] Cf. Nissen, *Histor. Ztschr.* N.F. xxvii. 1889, 406.   [3] Cf. Löschcke, *loc. cit.* 21.

indispensable ; in the great workshop or *ergasterion*[1] numberless workmen would be put in charge of the several parts ; and the assistants of Pheidias would suffice to superintend the work. The master himself must have had ample time for visiting his home in Athens, and for setting other tasks on foot. Thus I consider it not only possible but probable that, even after the year 438, he continued to superintend the Periklean works, and more particularly the completion of the Parthenon.[2] Not till this temple was quite finished and the position of Perikles began to be insecure did the accusation of embezzlement, the particulars of which we do not know,[3] take definite shape against Pheidias. His death in prison followed upon the trial. It was a most natural resolve on the part of the surviving members of his family to abandon their home and settle in Elis. There the memory of the great artist was held in reverence, and we have evidence, at least in later times, that his descendants were invested with the honourable office of φαιδρυνταί[4] of the image of Zeus.

This chronology of the Zeus fits in with everything else we know about the statue, and first with the legend of Pantarkes, which, when its tangled threads are once unravelled, yields the following facts. The story must of course have arisen from some definite circumstance. This was the inscription on the finger of Zeus,[5] in real fifth-century Attic fashion, of the 'love-name' Παντάρκης καλός. We cannot be sure whether the inscription was from the hand of Pheidias, as was believed in antiquity, or from one of his colleagues or assistants, but it seems at least likely that the Pantarkes of the inscription was identical, as the ancients also believed, with the Eleian boy Pantarkes who was victorious at Olympia in 436 B.C., and whose statue stood in the Altis (Paus. vi. 10, 6). We know absolutely nothing about the artist or the motive of this statue. On the other hand, the *ciceroni* of Olympia were merely inventing when they told Pausanias that a likeness to Pantarkes, the favourite of Pheidias, was to be seen in the face of a youth binding a fillet[6] about his head which adorned the throne of Zeus. It is only in modern times that the statue of an *Anadumenos*, unnamed, which Pheidias made and set

[1] In the time of Pausanias this was still shown ; it may probably be identified with the long narrow building immediately south of the Byzantine church. At Epidauros too, as the inscription Ἐφημ. ἀρχ. 1886, 145 *sqq.*, shows, was a carefully built ἐργαστήριον for the temple, provided with κονίασις. The building on the Akropolis south of the Parthenon may have been the workshop of Pheidias. There is no reason to doubt the Ergasterion in Olympia as Robert does (*Hermes*, xxiii. 453).

[2] In the year 433—432 the works on the Parthenon were still going on ; in 434 begins the inventory of the contents of the interior, which must then have been complete. Cf. Foucart, *B.C.H.* xiii. 174 *sqq.* It will be remembered that Plutarch reckons the Propylaia, which were erected between 437 and 432, among the buildings under the superintendence of Pheidias.

[3] The reasons given by different authorities are at variance. Schöll has shown that Plutarch's stories about the gold used for the Parthenos and the portraits on the shield are mere inventions ; what Philochoros says about the ivory, although it sounds more probable, is assuredly another invention ; Diodoros, who relies on Ephoros, only says πολλὰ τῶν ἱερῶν χρημάτων ; it is quite evident that the ancients had not mastered the numerous and complicated details of the accusation ; Ephoros gives the general drift, and his account is probably correct.

[4] Paus. v. 14, 5.

[5] Cf. Robert in *Hermes*, xxiii. 447 ; von Wilamowitz, *Comment. Gramm.* iv. 16, 1. The evidence is reliable and in itself quite credible ; the cathedrals of the middle ages afford examples of far greater licence. Clement of Alexandria, who usually derives his information from the best sources, has the story, and it is quoted as a well-known fact in the passage in Photios (which is probably derived from Polemon) about the Nemesis of Agorakritos. Pantarkes is here called Ἀργεῖος, but that is probably only a mistake of the person who made the extract, or perhaps of the copyist. The correct word is probably Ἠλεῖος. There is no trace here of any ancient controversy about the native place of Pantarkes, such as has been imagined. The testimony of Gregorius Nazianzenus and of Libanius, who connect the inscription with other statues, is naturally valueless.

[6] Paus. v. 11, 3 : ἐοικέναι τὸ εἶδος Παντάρκει λέγουσιν.

up in the Altis, has been wrongly brought into connexion with this question. It is a separate work, and has nothing to do with Pantarkes.[1] The presence of the 'love-name' is best explained by assuming that the Zeus was still unfinished in 436, for it is extremely unlikely that such an inscription was added when the statue was once complete and dedicated for worship.

More important than the Pantarkes question are the observations made by Dörpfeld on the temple of Zeus and on the Parthenon.[2] A piece of very decisive evidence is afforded by the fact that the basis of the Zeus, as well as the pavement immediately in front of it, were made of black Eleusinian stone. This was well calculated to set off the surrounding pavement of white Pentelic marble and the golden reliefs of the basis itself. Dörpfeld lays stress on the circumstance that Eleusinian stone was employed in a similar way in the construction of the Propylaia and of the Erechtheion, but not in any older buildings, and notably not in the Parthenon. He is no doubt right in considering the square space in front of the Zeus to be a conscious imitation of the similar larger space in front of the Parthenos. The further observations that the Zeus and the Parthenos stood at the same distance from the cella door, that the cella at Olympia had to be altered before the image could be set up, and that the Zeus was too large in proportion to the cella in which it stood, while the Athena completely harmonized with its surroundings, in themselves neither prove nor disprove the priority of one or the other image. But it seems most natural to suppose that Pheidias imposed upon Olympia the conception which had belonged by right to the Parthenon, and that the Eleians submitted to such an alteration in their building at the hands of the celebrated artist of the Parthenos, because they were anxious to possess a statue as magnificent as the one in Athens. In the year 456, immediately after the completion of the temple, the date to which Löschcke assigns the beginning of the Zeus, all this would be quite unintelligible.

Löschcke, however, thinks it strange that the temple should have been left eighteen years without an image. True, if temple and image were planned at the same time, as in the case of the Parthenos, they would naturally have been begun together, but if this was not so there is nothing to fix one date for the image rather than another. We cannot tell whether it was originally intended to set up a new cultus image, or an image at all, in the temple. In the temple at Delphi, for instance, which was built about the same time, no cultus image was erected so far as we know.

Löschcke further lays stress on the circumstance that Pliny, in the very passage where he mentions a joint work of Panainos and Kolotes in Elis (xxxv. 54), assigns Panainos to the same Olympiad as Pheidias (Ol. 83). This date Löschcke concludes to be that of the completion of the Zeus. To my mind it is evident that Pliny, owing to the paucity of chronological material at his disposal, is dating Panainos not independently but merely from his brother Pheidias. He was only in possession of the dates of a few leading artists, about whom he grouped lesser artists, according to the traditions of their connexion with one another. The whole passage containing the date of Panainos is one of Pliny's most characteristic and arbitrary pieces of

---

[1] Paus. vi. 4, 5. The usual identification of the ἀναδούμενος of Pheidias with the victor statue of Pantarkes, of which we know neither the artist nor the motive, must be rejected. Pausanias says— and we have no reason to doubt his word—that the statues stood in different parts of the Altis. The ἀναδούμενος was a votive gift which only bore the name of the artist (cf. Gurlitt, *Pausanias*, p. 378 *sqq.*); the name of the person represented was unknown, as Pausanias expressly says (cf. Schubart's translation). I shall attempt later to point to a copy of this Anadumenos. Cf. *infra*, p. 244. The three monuments— viz. the victorious athlete, the Anadumenos, and the figure on the throne—are all quite correctly distinguished by Dörpfeld, *Olympia, Baudenkmäler, Textbd.* ii. 21.

[2] *Olympia, Baudenkm. Textbd.* ii. 16, 20.

chronology-making.[1] It seems evident from a later passage[2] that he found the date of Pheidias ready to hand, and invented that of Panainos.

Löschcke finds confirmation for the early date to which he assigns Panainos and the Zeus in Robert's hypothesis that the paintings of the Stoa Poikile were finished about 460, and that the battle of Oinoë, there represented, happened about the same time.[3] But valid objections to this theory have been brought forward by Judeich,[4] and the earlier view, the evidence for which has been carefully collected by Wachsmuth[5]—viz. that the picture of the battle of Oinoë did not belong to the original cycle of the Polygnotan paintings—is still the prevailing one. This picture was not painted, as the others were, on the large central wall, the name of its artist is not mentioned, nor did it enjoy the same celebrity as the other three. The group by Hypatodoros and Aristogeiton (Paus. x. 4) in Delphi must assuredly, as Robert assumes, have been an older work, and the battle of Oinoë, with which Pausanias connects it, is certainly the same that formed the subject of the picture in the Stoa Poikile. Whether, however, Pausanias is right in connecting the battle with the Delphic group is another question.[6] Again, according to Robert's hypothesis, the Stoa was erected about the time of Kimon's exile, and was intended to celebrate the victory over the Lakedaimonians, who favoured the Kimonian faction. This seems highly improbable, seeing that Peisianax, Kimon's brother-in-law, dedicated the porch. It is more likely that the building was undertaken after Kimon's return, i.e. after 457, and that in true Kimonian spirit it was designed to celebrate the great exploits of Attic heroes against the barbarian Amazons, Trojans, and Persians. We are not even sure that Panainos was employed on the Stoa at all. It is true that Pliny and Pausanias call him the painter of the battle of Marathon, but in other authorities the same picture is ascribed not only to Polygnotos (which would mean little, considering the fame of Polygnotos), but also to Mikon.[7] Even if Panainos was engaged upon the Stoa that is no reason why he should not have worked about 456—450 in Athens, and about 438—432 in Olympia and Elis.

Finally, Löschcke calls attention to some purely aesthetic reasons for dating the Zeus in the older period. Of the 'archaic elements in the form and arrangement of the beard' which he sees in the copies on coins I can discover no trace. The coins seem to me to show that the beard was similar to that of the seated Poseidon on the Parthenon frieze. The line of the profile is decidedly against Löschcke's theory. In all the copies it is very straight, corresponding to the profiles seen on the Parthenon frieze, so that the Zeus must be later than the Lemnia, whose nose, as we have seen, forms an angle with the forehead.

---

[1] Cf. my Essay in ix. Suppl. Bd. of *Fleckeisen's Jahrb.*, ' *Plinius und seine Quellen*,' p. 16 *sqq.*; and Robert, *Arch. Märchen*, p. 25.

[2] Plin. 36, 15 . . . *picturam aut statuariam, quarum utraque cum Phidia coepit octogensima tertia olympiade*; as regards painting, this refers to the passage on Panainos in 35, 54. Cf. Robert, *loc. cit.*

[3] Robert, *Hermes*, xxv. 1890, 412.

[4] *Fleckeisen's Jahrb.* 1890, 757.

[5] *Stadt. Athen*, ii. 502 *sqq.* Cf. also Benndorf, *Jahrb. d. Samml. d. Kaiserh.* xi. 1, 22.

[6] Probably the inscription, as usually in the fifth century, gave no more exact information. The words ὡς αὐτοὶ Ἀργεῖοι λέγουσιν, which Robert would refer to an inscription in contradistinction to the following ἐμοὶ δοκεῖν, recall the exactly analogous ἐμοὶ δοκεῖν and Μεσσήνιοι αὐτοὶ λέγουσι in the passage which discusses the occasion of the dedication of the Nike of Paionios, where the inscription on the statue says nothing about it. In the case of the Argive votive gift we have also a mere hypothesis, and a very improbable one, on the part of Pausanias, possibly suggested to him perhaps by the picture in the Stoa Poikile.

[7] Probably as early as by Lykurgus in the speech περὶ τῆς ἱερείας (cf. Brunn, *K. G.* ii. 19), then by Aelian, Arrian, and Sopatros.

G

In a head of the Louvre, the so-called Zeus Talleyrand,[1] Löschcke sees a copy of a work belonging to the middle of the fifth century B.C., and evidently influenced by the Pheidian Zeus. This is a daring assertion, depending on premises which will not bear examination. It is true that many works which were formerly called 'eclectic' have now been proved to be genuine copies of originals of the severe transitional period of the fifth century, but it would be a strange perversion of logic to proceed to deny *in toto* the existence of an archaic art containing mixed elements of style, and to insist on calling every production which shows a touch of the archaic manner a faithful copy of an earlier original. The mixed style of the archaic period is an historical fact demonstrable in hundreds of monuments. The Zeus Talleyrand is a good instance. On the one hand the archaic pointed beard which follows the convention of the sixth century, and on the other the straight profile and the modelling of the eyes, form a mixture of heterogeneous elements quite inconceivable at a period when art was developing in a natural and healthy manner.[2] The hair is drawn up above the ears into a kind of loop, and then falls again in a broad band,[3] according to a fashion much affected by archaic artists.[4]

The work, which is imperfectly reproduced in the Talleyrand head, with the admixture of later elements, certainly does not belong to the middle of the fifth century, but is about half a century earlier. This is proved by a small statue in the Museo Torlonia, a poor but faithful copy of an ancient work of art[5] representing Dionysos wearing a short cloak, which falls in purely archaic folds, and a panther-skin over it. The head is remarkably like the Talleyrand Zeus, except that the affected modernizing element is wanting. The whole character of the statue and some details, such as the roll of hair and the position of the body, which rests on the left leg, while the right is only slightly bent,[6] make it reasonable to suppose that this figure is an early work from the cycle of Hagelaidas.[7] So too the Zeus, as far as it contains real archaic elements, must be referred to an Argive work of about 500 B.C. It has nothing whatever to do with Pheidias.

The aesthetic reasons which Löschcke gives for his date of the Zeus are thus demonstrably false. In addition to the straight profile, the mode of dressing the hair also affords strong evidence for the later date. Numerous vase-paintings help us to an exact knowledge of the development of the fifth-century Attic type of Zeus. In the older style, up to about 450 B.C., Zeus has long hair, either hanging down over his back or taken up behind. The Zeus of Olympia, according to the coins, had shorter hair, falling in curls only as far as the shoulders. This mode of wearing the hair is not found in the Zeus of vase-paintings till after 450 B.C., when the free style had been perfected;[8] in vases of the ornate style about 430 B.C.,[9] the short curly hair,

---

[1] The doubts which have recently been expressed concerning the genuineness of this head are completely without foundation ; the head is assuredly ancient. [The head has lately been removed from the public galleries to the *Magasin.*—E. S.]

[2] Cf. Friederichs, *Bausteine*, 60 (ed. Wolters, 449) ; Kekulé in *Arch. Ztg.* 1874, p. 98.

[3] This is so stiffly worked that it might easily be mistaken for part of a diadem. This is also the case with the hair in front of the diadem.

[4] Numerous instances may be found on the so-called Campana terra-cotta reliefs (cf. the *Gorgoneia* and the archaic Perseus, which exist in several variants, good examples in *Bull. Nap.* N. S. 1, 5).

[5] *Mus. Torl.* Taf. 124, No. 484. Cast in the Museum at Carlsruhe.

[6] The right foot is wrongly restored as if drawn back.

[7] Cf. 50th *Berl. Winckelmannsprogr.* p. 125 *sqq.* Studniczka refers to the statuette, and suggests Kalamis (*Röm. Mitth.* 1888, 299, note 74).

[8] One of the earliest examples is a kylix to be dated about 440 B.C. *Mon. d. Inst.* v. 48.

[9] Style of Meidias and Aristophanes ; for the Io-vase see Overbeck, *Atlas z. K. M.* 7, 16, etc.

falling only to the nape, soon becomes typical of Zeus. These facts alone show the Zeus to have been made after and not before 450 B.C.

The Pheidian Parthenos still wears the long curls, falling on the breast, of archaic art: now, if the Zeus were earlier than the Parthenos, we should expect to find him represented with the same long thick hair. It may be urged, on the other hand, that the curly hair, lying close to the neck, as shown on the coin, begins to appear in works of art just about the year 450.[1] This is quite true, but it does not hold for Zeus, in whose case the adoption of this fashion is of later date.

Except the coins there are no direct copies of the Zeus in existence. But it would be very strange if no copies had ever been made at least of separate parts of a work which comprised, besides the principal figure, so many reliefs and statuettes. For instance, it is highly probable that the silver-gilt relief from Galaxidi, the design of which corresponds exactly with the central group of the gold relief on the basis of the Zeus, as described by Pausanias, is really a copy of this group.[2] It has recently been pointed out[3] that the main features in the design of the silver relief (features which doubtless were to be seen in the work of Pheidias), such as the goddess half emerging from the waves, the attendant divinity who raises her, the lifted head of the goddess, her flowing hair, and the drapery held in front of her, are all borrowed from an older work. But the composition has been remodelled in the spirit of the freest style, with a tendency to vigorous, almost passionate movement and to picturesque detail. It is the very manner—even to the rendering of the waves—which we admire in the pediments of the Parthenon.

Another of the designs on the throne of Zeus—Apollo and Artemis slaying the Niobids—can, I think, be traced with tolerable certainty. Several reliefs of Roman date have preserved to us in varying arrangement extracts from a once famous and surpassingly beautiful representation of this subject,[4] which must be based upon an Attic original of the Pheidian epoch. That this is so is plain from the dress of the women,[5] from the schemes of the drapery,[6] from the style of head and body in one well-copied figure,[7] and finally from the character of the motives.[8] It further seems probable that the original was by Pheidias himself, for the bold and individual design of one of the

---

[1] Cf. the two Apollo heads, *Röm. Mitth.* 1891, Taf. 11, 12 ; Petersen, p. 379 ; cf. *infra*, p. 49 *sqq.*

[2] *Gazette Arch.* 1879, Pl. 19, 2 ; p. 171 *sqq.* Roscher's *Lexikon*, i. 1356.

[3] By Petersen in *Röm. Mitth.* 1892, p. 49 *sqq.*

[4] They have lately been collected by Hauser (*Die Neuattischen Reliefs*, p. 73 *sqq.* No. 104—107 b). Strangely enough, even in this new discussion of the subject the most random and unfounded doubts are expressed about the genuineness of the reliefs. I examined the St. Petersburg relief in the original not long ago ; it is proved to be genuine by the remains of real incrustation on the marble. The relief is not complete ; it consists of two pieces, while the connecting piece between the group of the two girls and the figure hastening to the right is a modern restoration. The work is hard, and late in style. The disc in the British Museum is likewise absolutely genuine, and is also partly covered with incrustation ; an ocular examination of it is sufficient to disprove the extraordinary arguments against its genuineness lately adduced by Overbeck, *Sächsische Berichte*, 1893, p. 58 *seq.*   [5] The peplos girt low down with or without kolpos is characteristic.

[6] The rendering of the folds of the drapery in the less agitated maidens is specially characteristic. With the cloaks of the youths and of the Apollo (the best replica of the Apollo is the fragment Hauser 107 b) cf. the mantles on the later Parthenon metopes, and those of the 'Kephissos' and of the Kekrops in the west pediment.

[7] The Apollo on the above fragment, which though certainly not finely worked is stylistically faithful. The nearest parallels to the head are found in the frieze of the Parthenon (*e.g.* north frieze, figs. 114, 115, Mich.) Cf. also the Theseus head recently brought into this connexion by Helbig (*Mon. Ant. dei Lincei*, i. 4, 1892).

[8] Hauser has already pointed out that the nearest analogies are afforded by the monuments in the style of Polygnotos. The group of the dying boy, whom his elder sister has caught in her arms, is of peculiar beauty : he clings round her neck and greets her for the last time in death. The group belongs to a series of Polygnotan creations (cf. 50th *Berl. Winckelmannsprogr.* p. 160 *seq.*), and is one of the most marvellous inventions of antiquity in existence. It was frequently copied in ancient times, especially on gems, and was

figures corresponds to a figure on the shield of the Parthenos.   It is that of a Niobid
who has fallen backwards over a rock.   The head is down, the hands clasped behind
it, while the legs, bent at the knees, still seem clinging to the rock above (Fig. 7).   Just
the same motive is introduced on the shield, but here the figure is that of an Amazon

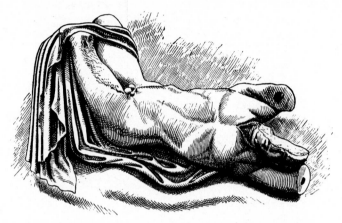

FIG. 7.—Niobid from the disc in the British Museum. (From a drawing.)

dressed in a short chiton.   Now we know that on the throne of Zeus, presumably
along the sides of the seat, were represented Artemis and Apollo slaying the Niobids ;
we may therefore venture to recognize in the reliefs, whose conception we have seen
to be Pheidian, echoes of those compositions. As we only possess fragmentary portions
of the original design, the arrangement of the separate parts remains uncertain.   We
may be sure, however, that the composition was a frieze, as the divinities are aiming
straight in front of them.[1] If our conclusions be correct, they afford a fresh proof that
the Zeus was not a work of the severe style, for the Niobid composition has a markedly
pictorial character, and its motives are full of consummate freedom and beauty.

  The authentic copies of the reliefs on the shield of the Parthenos show the
same pictorial character, and the motives are equally free and daring.   This relief of
the *Amazonomachia* is a priceless document for our knowledge of Pheidias ; it proves
beyond a doubt that it is not, as some have supposed,[2] vase-paintings of the severe
style which will help us to recover the style of Pheidias.   The designs of the shield
recall a distinct class of vases, distinguished by a free and animated style, and an
essentially pictorial quality, which Polygnotos was apparently the first to introduce.[3]
On these vases as on the shield the figures stand on undulating ground either above
one another or side by side.   The same vigorous action characterizes the figures on
both—the long strides, the raising of the foot on an elevation, the fall, the headlong
plunge, the brandishing of weapons, the interchange of back and front view—all these
are to be found on the vases as on the shield.   We have here a fixed standpoint

adapted for other figures in different designs. Cf. the Attic vase (Millin, v. p. ii. 49), which may be dated as early
as 430 B.C., and the famous Semele mirror (Friederichs, *Kleine Kunst*, 36).

  [1] Heydemann rightly emphasized this point.   The arrangement on the disc cannot possibly be the right one,
for the divinities are shooting into the air.   Note also that the female figure which was intended to be running to
the right has been placed as if lying on the ground.   [2] Puchstein, *Jahrb. d. Inst.* 1890, 112—116.

  [3] Cf. *Sammlung Sabouroff*, i. *Vasen, Einleit.* p. 5; also Robert, *Die Nekyia des Polygnot*, p. 42 *sqq.*   Winter
(*D. Jüngeren Attischen Vasen*, p. 36) rightly saw in the Aryballos Fiorelli from Cuma (*Not. dei Vasi Cumani*, 8) the
direct influence of the Parthenos shield.   To the same series belong the 'Giant' vase of Melos (*Wiener
Vorlegebl.* Ser. viii. 7), the Aristophanes kylix in Berlin ('Εφημ. ἀρχ. 1883, 7), and the Xenophantos vase (*Compte
Rendu*, 1866, 4) ; also Millin, *Vases Peints*, i. 56, 61 ; Naples, 3251 (Heydemann). All these are purely Attic vases
of about 430 B.C.

whence to meet all attempts to push back the art of Pheidias to an antiquated stage which it had long left behind. True, Pheidias could represent calm and religious repose in a masterly manner when it was fitting to do so. The assembled gods who assist at the birth of Pandora on the basis of the Parthenos were naturally conceived of in repose, as is shown by the copies.[1] The reason lies partly in the nature of the subject, partly in that of the place which the design was to occupy; the ornamentation on the basis of a religious image must have a certain solemnity. Even on the bases of the Parthenos and of the Zeus, however, Pheidias did not limit himself to the representation of divinities calmly looking on, but he bounded his composition on the one side with the animated figure of the rising Helios, on the other with that of the sinking Selene. The movement of the Helios on the Parthenos basis was, as the existing copy shows,[2] of the fiercest, and the rearing horses were led by a figure whose impetuous stride recalls the attitude of the warriors on the shield.

The cosmical frame thus formed by the sun and moon is a purely pictorial invention,[3] which, if it be due to Pheidias, is due to Pheidias the painter. *Phidian ipsum initio pictorem fuisse traditur clipeumque Athenis ab eo pictum*, says Pliny. Pheidias began life as a painter; the shield to which Pliny alludes was presumably that of the Parthenos, on the inner side of which the Gigantomachia was probably not in relief, but painted.[4] One vase-picture would seem to afford a conception of this painting,[5] which in its main lines apparently resembled the Amazonomachia. On the vase, however, the vault of heaven over-arches the whole, while the rising Helios and the setting Selene again frame the composition. There are a few more Attic vase-paintings in which this same idea has been made use of.[6] To judge from their style they all belong to the period about 430, and are composed in the Polygnoto-Pheidian manner.

At this point it becomes possible to answer more definitely the question of what was the share of Pheidias in the execution of the sculptures of the Parthenon.

The metopes of the temple have been admitted to differ greatly in style,[7] and

---

[1] Cf. Puchstein, *Jahrb. d. Inst.* 1890, 114; also Hub. Schmidt, *Diss. Philol. Hal.* xii. 131 *sqq.* In the Lenormant statuette, the three figures in the centre are intended to give an indication of the peaceful assembly of the gods, to which Helios and Selene form a kind of setting (cf. Schreiber, *Parthenos*, p. 57). This interpretation should never have been doubted, and is now confirmed by the Pergamene basis, which also only gives an extract from the original.

[2] On the basis of the Lenormant statuette.   [3] Cf. *Samml. Sabouroff*, Text to Plate 63, p. 2.

[4] It is true that Pliny reckons (36, 18) the Gigantomachia among the other ornaments in relief of the Parthenos, but this is a rhetorical passage (cf. Robert, *Arch. Märchen*, p. 24); on the inside of the shield ornament in relief would be unsuitable, and finally the analogy of the Athena by Kolotes in Elis seems to point to painting. The shield at Athens which Phidias painted can hardly be other than that of the Parthenos (as Urlichs, *Chrestom. Plin.*, already pointed out; Robert, *loc. cit.*, agrees with him). It is worthy of note that shields with painted ornamentation inside only occur on those vase-paintings which are nearly analogous to the pictorial ornamentation of the Parthenos shield and to its style; cf. for example the 'Giant' vase of Melos, also Ἐφημ. ἀρχ. 1883, 7, and Overbeck, *Gall. Her. Bildw.* Taf. 11, 1 (where the Athena seems to be influenced by the Promachos).

[5] *Monum. d. Inst.* ix. 6; Overbeck, *Atlas z. K. Myth.* Taf. 5, 8; cf. Robert, *Arch. Ztg.* 1884, 47; Kuhnerdt in Roscher's *Lexikon*, i. 1659; M. Mayer, *Giganten und Titanen*, p. 268, 353; Petersen, *Röm. Mitth.* 1893, p. 231.

[6] The Judgment of Paris is framed in by Helios setting and Selene riding away and looking back: *Wiener Vorlegebl.* Ser. E. 11; by Helios alone, on the hydria, Overbeck, *Gall.* 11, 1. The setting Helios on the Delphic pediment and on the vase (*Compte Rendu*, 1860, 3) is probably influenced by Pheidias.

[7] The supposition that the metopes of older style had been made for the 'Kimonian' Parthenon (Kekulé, *Weibliche Gewandstatue aus dem Werkstatt der Parthenongiebelfiguren*, p. 22) is inadmissible, because the general uniformity of the metopes, in spite of isolated variations, forbids referring any of them back to so remote a period. Between the older Parthenon and the Parthenon of Perikles a long interval must have elapsed (see below). The discovery of the treasury of the Athenians in Delphi can teach us what metopes were like at the date of the first Parthenon. Besides, it is most improbable that there were ever any finished metopes belonging to a temple which never rose beyond the lowest drums of the columns.

clearly show the influence of various persons, while frieze and pediments are homo-
geneous throughout, expressing the spirit and manifesting the methods of a single
artist. If we except a few instances of a transitional and less individual style, all the
metopes exhibit two conflicting tendencies. The one, represented only by a small
number of examples, is to harshness and angularity, both in bodily form and in movement, only a very feeble and clumsy use being made of drapery. This style resembles
that of the metopes on the so-called Theseion [1] and of the frieze on the temple at
Sunium.[2] It is the direct successor of the style known to us from the 'Tyrant-
slayers' by Kritios and Nesiotes,[3] and shows little essential advance on those masters.
The other tendency is to greater softness, roundness, and flow in the forms of the body
(the abdomen more particularly is quite different); with it motion becomes incomparably more vigorous and fiery, and the treatment of drapery richer, with a certain
leaning to the pictorial. The rendering of the woollen stuff is at the same stage as
in the Lemnia and Parthenos, *i.e.* it is heavier and more solid than in the frieze and
pediments; where linen occurs it is sharply differentiated from wool, and is treated as
in the Promachos, not as in the frieze and pediments. Hence the metopes, as seems
natural from the history of the building, must have been made at the same time as
the Parthenos. Now the relief on the shield of the Parthenos proves that of the two
manners noted on the metopes, only the later and more pictorial (where the swing
and rhythm of the attitudes correspond to the reliefs of the shield) can belong to
Pheidias; compare for example the figure rushing forward on the metope South VII.
or the fallen man South XXVIII. with the analogous figures on the shield. We may
conjecture that a small number of the earlier metopes were intrusted to pupils of
Kritios, and that afterwards Pheidias, who had at first been more exclusively occupied
with the Parthenos, turned his attention to this department of the work also, when the
other artists employed on the metopes tried to suit their style to his.

The frieze and the pediments, which, except for some trifling inequalities in
execution, may be considered uniform, must from stylistic reasons be later than the
metopes, while the pediments are somewhat later than the frieze. The frieze
must certainly have been finished before the last roofing was put on, and this
was probably done before the image was set up in 438 B.C.[4] The figures of the
pediments, which were completed in the round below, and fixed in their places
afterwards, must have been made after 438 B.C.[5] We have seen that Pheidias may

[1] I cannot consider the Theseion to be later than the Parthenon : I hold it to be just a little earlier. The
arguments of Julius, *Ann. d. Inst.* 1878, 205 *sqq.*, have not been refuted. The counter argument brought forward
by Dörpfeld, *Athen. Mitth.* 1884, 336, is not convincing. If the frieze on the cella of the Parthenon owes its
existence to an alteration in the plan of construction, as Dörpfeld plausibly argues, it cannot be placed at the
beginning of a new development. Dörpfeld could only urge this if the frieze with its regulae were part of the
original design (as was formerly held), for only in that case would the Doric regula be a sign of earlier date.
The frieze on the Theseion corresponds in style to the Parthenon metopes of the second manner. The fact that
the two styles occur together on the Parthenos shows that it is not necessary to suppose that the metopes of the
Theseion were taken from an older building.

[2] *Athen. Mitth.* 1881, 233 (Lange); 1882, 396 (Furtw.); 1884, 338 (Fabricius); cf. 1884, 336 (Dörpfeld). It
is quite certain that the style corresponds as closely to the metopes of the Theseion as it differs essentially from
the frieze of the same building. If the architectural forms of the marble temple at Sunium do not admit of being
dated at about 450 B.C., the frieze must be assigned to the older structure of poros stone.

[3] In addition to the head, abdomen and breast are specially characteristic. I can detect nothing peculiarly
Myronian in these works; rather do they recall Kritios.

[4] Dörpfeld has communicated to me his opinion that the frieze was finished about the same time as the cultus-
image, though he believes that the question cannot be decisively settled.

[5] Two fragments most probably belonging to the building records of the Parthenon contain the accounts
which refer to the purchase of marble blocks for the pedimental figures (*C.I.A.* iv. 297 a.b.) Löschcke (*Tod des
Phidias*, p. 46) pointed out that, as in one fragment mention is also made of a purchase of wood, the account is
probably to be dated after the making of the roof, *i.e.* after 438 B.C.

have retained the superintendence of the building after 438. There is not the smallest reason for disputing the tradition which makes him overseer of all the works or for denying his authorship of its principal sculptural decorations, *i.e.* of the frieze and the pediments. The aesthetic quality of the work is all in favour of the tradition : the fiery attitudes of some of the pedimental figures, such as the striding Poseidon and the Hermes, can only be matched on the shield and basis of the Parthenos ; the pictorial touches, which in the pediments find expression in the rocky seats and the waves of Okeanos, are paralleled by the wavy ground lines on the shield relief, while the rising Helios and the sinking Night of the east pediment have been shown to be genuine Pheidian conceptions, which could be introduced in a shortened form because the artist had expressed them fully elsewhere.[1] In the rendering of form, and especially of drapery, the frieze and the pediments are the immediate outgrowth and development of the metopes of freer style. Compare for example the mantle of the recumbent Greek on metope South XXVIII. with that of the 'Theseus' or the 'Kephissos' of the pediments. The style is absolutely the same, though equally characteristic in both, the only difference being that the folds in front of the pedimental figures—not at the back, where the correspondence with the metopes is absolute—are cut more deeply in order to make the drapery look lighter. To ascribe the metopes to the artist and deny him the frieze and the pediments means a refusal to acknowledge that he was capable of development at all. Now the existence of the Parthenos and its relation to the Lemnia afford irrefragable proof that Pheidias was by no means an artist who remained wedded to a fixed manner, but one who developed decidedly and rapidly. The Parthenos differs from the Lemnia, as we saw, in the treatment of drapery, the artist showing a tendency to abandon simple characterization of woollen stuff and to give more attention to the effective arrangement of folds. Besides this, the stuff appears lighter and thinner, and clings more closely to some parts of the body, which thus become more prominent in the design. The difference in drapery between the frieze and the pediments on the one hand, and the Parthenos and the metopes on the other, only represents a further stage in the same perfectly normal progress. To make his development close with the Parthenos and the metopes would be most unjustifiable. On the contrary, as the frieze and pediments were made in the lifetime of Pheidias, and as tradition tells us that he superintended the works on the Parthenon, we have every reason for ascribing the growth of style—not to the school—but to the master himself. Only in certain details of slight importance the assistants may quite possibly have gone beyond the master's orders, but in all essentials the design is emphatically his very own. That powerful and dominant personality which undoubtedly governed the frieze and the pediments can, on the evidence of style and of tradition,[2] be none other than that of Pheidias himself. His name is and remains closely associated with that flower of Attic art which continued unrivalled for all time.

The decorative sculptures on the colossal images of Athena Parthenos and of

---

[1] The pediment, owing to lack of space, gives a shortened form of the composition on the relief: it contains no new elements, except that the rider Selene is replaced by Nyx in a chariot as filling more suitably the angle of the pediment.

[2] Kekulé (*Weibliche Gewandstatue*) has recently attempted to assign the pediments to Alkamenes and Agorakritos. As the basis on which his arguments rest is false, his whole theory falls to the ground. The supposed differences between the pediments do not exist ; Kekulé mistakes differences in the characterization of stuff for differences of style (*e.g.* in the case of the 'Iris'); the supposed statues of Alkamenes which Winter believed he could point to, and which Kekulé uses as the basis of his contention, have no connexion whatsoever with Alkamenes (see *infra*, p. 84, note 8), and, even if they had, the pediments would none the more be by Alkamenes.

Zeus—the Amazonomachia, the boundary motive of Helios and Selene, the Niobids, the Anadyomene, and the Gigantomachia—show how intimate was the artist's connexion with painting, and thus confirm the testimony of Pliny, who says that Pheidias began life as a painter, and only turned to sculpture later on. His brother Panainos remained a painter. Pheidias himself carried out the painting on the inner surface of the shield of the Parthenos, while the corresponding decoration of the Zeus was handed over to his brother.

So far our conclusion is that the ascertained works of Pheidias are all comprised within a period of about twenty years. Pheidias, it is true, may have worked before this period, but the analysis of the Lemnia and its forerunners has shown, and will show us further still, that it is improbable his artistic career began further back than some ten years before the Lemnia, so that either he did not live to be old, or he was no longer young when he turned from painting to sculpture. Of the two hypotheses, the former seems to me the more likely ; in that case Pheidias would scarcely have lived to the age of sixty. This theory seems, however, to be contradicted by the tradition reported by Plutarch, according to which Pheidias introduced on the shield of the Parthenos his own portrait as a bald-headed old man. On the copy of the shield in the British Museum this figure is clearly to be seen. It represents an elderly man with hollow cheeks, short full beard, and bald head, save for some scanty locks at the back.[1] The man is brandishing a weapon with full force against an Amazon.[2] A man of about forty (the age of Pheidias at the time of the Parthenos, according to our calculation) could very well, at least in our modern life, look like this figure, but in the art of the fifth century such a figure would be meant to represent a more advanced age. The short-cut beard and hollow cheeks especially are part of the conventional type of the 'old man.'

To the question, then, whether Pheidias was an old man when he created the Parthenos I should incline to answer distinctly in the negative, for this so-called portrait is probably as apocryphal as are the numerous portraits of artists, their friends and relations, which ciceroni identify in famous pictures of Christian art. The legend given by Plutarch, that the portraits of the artist and of Perikles were the occasion of the prosecution of Pheidias, is a foolish and meaningless invention, as Schöll[3] and A. S. Murray[4] have already shown. The information given by Plutarch about the portrait of Perikles, and confirmed by the copy, shows what sort of likenesses we have to expect ; the arm of the figure was, it seems, raised and held in front of the face, so as to cover it. This is said to have shown the cunning of the artist, who wished to conceal the likeness. But it simply means that there was no likeness at all. The whole story probably arose from the rather individual characterization of the old man : he was supposed to be Pheidias, hence the warrior beside him must be Perikles, even if his face was almost covered. There is much evidence for believing that the 'old man type' was a general favourite in the cycle of Polygnotos. In combination with youthful figures he served to vary the design, and in the representation of the Amazonomachia this active greybeard was appropriate as showing how all Athenians young and old united in patriotic resistance to the invading enemy.

[1] For the whole shield see Collignon, *Hist. de la Sculpture Grecque*, p. 545.

[2] A stone according to Plutarch ; the same in the Lenormant statuette (Michaëlis, Taf. 15, 1 b.) ; a battle-axe on the shield in the British Museum ; the figure of the Capitoline fragment on which Schreiber (*Parthenos*, p. 600 (58) *sqq.*) recognizes the 'Pheidias' is a copy of some other figure of the original.

[3] *Sitz. Ber. d. Münchener Akad. Phil. Hist. Cl.* 1881, 1.

[4] *Encycl. Brit.*, 'Phidias.' [Mr. Murray, however, supposes the Strangford shield to be wholly a later work, 'produced subsequently to illustrate some current story on which that description (*i.e.* of the portraits) was founded.' The same view, only very slightly modified, in *Hist. of Gr. Sc.* vol. ii. p. 121.—E. S.]

PLATE A

PLATE B

Fig. B3 - Head of Zeus, Boston, Museum of Fine Arts

Fig. B1 - Bronze coin of Elis. Enlarged reverse side and actual size.

Fig. B2 - Coin of King Philip of Macedon (ca.,356 BC) showing head of Zeus Olympios. Possible an adaptation of the work of Pheidias.

Fig. C1 - Young warrior found in the harbor of Salamis. Possibly one of the figures from the pedestal of Zeus Olympios, Chicago, Private Collection

Fig. C2 - Wounded warrior, a late Hellenistic copy. Possibly one of the figures from the pedestal of Zeus Olympios, Chicago, Art Institute

PLATE C

Fig. D1 - Line drawing of the Strangford Shield (cf. Fig. D2)

Fig. D2 - Marble copy of the shield of Athena Parthenos depicting a battle between the Greeks and the Amazons (the
Strangford Shield), London, British Museum

PLATE D

Fig. E1 - Athena Parthenos, profile of the
Varvakeion statuette, Athens,
National Museum (cf. p.1)

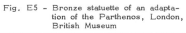

Fig. E2 - Golden medal with the
head of Athena Parthenos,
Leningrad.
Gem with profile of Athena
Parthenos signed by Aspasios.
Rough sketch of bronze Athen-
ian coin showing the statue of
the Parthenos.

Fig. E3 - The Lenorman Athena, unfinished
marble statuette of Athena Parthenos,
Athens, National Museum

Fig. E4 - Athena Parthenos, the Varvakeion statuette (best known copy)
Athens, National Museum

Fig. E5 - Bronze statuette of an adaptation of the Parthenos, London,
British Museum

PLATE E

Fig. E6 - Parthenos Borghese, late Hellenistic adaptation of Athena Parthenos, Paris, Louvre

Fig. F1 – Head of a bearded warrior, Pheidian style, Chicago Art Institute (cf. Plate C, Fig. C2)

Fig. F2 – Head of Anacreon Borghese, Copenhagen, Ny Carlsberg Glyptotek

Fig. F4 – Hermes Propylaios, Attic copy (ca. end of 2nd century B.C.) Found in Piraeus, Piraeus, City Museum (see figure p. 87 for copy of Hermes Propylaios from Pergamon)

Fig. F3 – Hermes Propylaios by Alkamenes, late Roman copy, New York, Metropolitan Museum of Art

PLATE F

Fig. G1 - Apollo, Pheidian style, Florence, Bargello Museum

Fig. G2 - The deLaborde head (East pediment of the Parthenon), Paris, Louvre

Figs. G3 & G4 - Sculptures from the pedestal of the Statue of Nemesis at Rhamnus, work of Agoracritos of Paros, pupil of Pheidias, Athens, National Museum

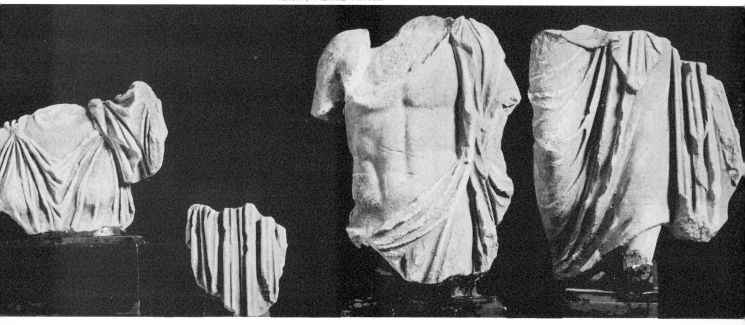

PLATE G

Fig. H1 - Athena, Jacobsen head (cf.fig. 43, p.98) Copenhagen, Ny Carlsberg Glyptotek

Fig. H2 - Roman copy of a Caryatid from the Erectheion, Rome, Hadrian's Villa

Fig. H3 - Terra cotta head from a stat ..uette of Athena, Athens, Stoa of A talos Museum

Fig. H4 - Elgin's Caryatid removed from the Erectheion, London, British Museum

Fig. H5 - Torso from a copy of Athena Parthenos with cast of the Copenhagen head, Baltimore, Walters Art Gallery (once in Massarenti Collection, Italy)

Fig. H7 - Roman Caryatid, free adaptation of the Erectheion original, Rome, Vatican Museum

Fig. H6 - Replica of the Parthenos on a coin of Aphrodisias (ca. 375 BC)

PLATE H

VIII. *Other Works related to the Lemnia.—The Master of Pheidias.—Early Pheidian Works.—The Anakreon.—Pheidian Eros and Aphrodite.*

Hitherto we have discussed only those works which are in close relation to the Lemnia, either through the forms of the body or the treatment of the drapery. We must now take the head as starting-point for a further inquiry.

There exist a whole series of heads really related, though in varying degree, to that of the Lemnian Athena. A complete list of these is not given, as it would be useless without illustrations. It must suffice to select a few of the more important. These fall into two groups, according as they are earlier or later than the Lemnia.

Foremost in the first group must be placed the Apollo recently found in the Tiber, and now in the Museo delle Terme in Rome (Fig. 8 ; head alone, Fig. 9).[1] It is only a mediocre copy, of poor workmanship, yet it preserves enough of the original to produce a great effect ; magnificence combined with gentle beauty is its pervading quality.[2] This general characteristic, as well as the unusual pose of the head, which is energetically turned to the side, recalls the Lemnian Athena. The head, however, exhibits a somewhat older style, the hair coming from the crown of the head and lying flatter than in the Lemnia. A still closer relation between the two works makes itself felt in the spiritual expression of the refined face and in the peculiar beauty of the closed mouth. By way of contrast we may compare the head of the Capitoline Apollo, which has been grouped with the Apollo of the *Terme.*[3] There is a superficial similarity between the two, and they belong to the same period, but those finer elements of form on which the spiritual expression depends differ totally.[4] Very different also is the Cassel Apollo (*infra,* Fig. 80), which reproduces another type of the same period. The only points it has in common with the *Terme* Apollo are the forehead broadening at the base, and the large open eyes ; but these are features individual to the god represented. We shall have to return to this point later on.

Thus there is every probability that the Apollo is an earlier work by the artist of the Lemnia.[5] The attribution is of special weight, as the Apollo, in spite of the individual character which distinguishes it from contemporary works, is still clearly limited by certain traditions of the older school, while the Lemnia at once takes its place as the creation of a finished and independent artist.

Now the school traditions alluded to are those of the Argive Hagelaidas.[6] In the first place the position is typical of that school, *i.e.* the body is supported on the left leg,

---

[1] *Röm. Mitth.* 1891, p. 302 ; 377 *sqq.* (Petersen), Taf. x.—xii.

[2] Petersen is right in speaking of the ' indescrivibile espressione di dolcezza' in the head.

[3] *loc. cit.* Taf. xi., xii., on the left ; Overbeck, *Atlas Kunstmyth.* Taf. 20, 22.

[4] I cannot agree with Petersen in ascribing both statues to the same artist. The Capitoline head is much more nearly related to the charioteer in the Pal. Conservatori. It would be nearer the truth to say that the Capitoline Apollo must be by the same artist as the Cassel Apollo. In reality the original of the Capitoline figure was probably by an artist of the second rank, who was influenced by the artist of the Cassel type in the body of his statue and in the head by the artist of the *Terme* Apollo (*infra,* p. 197). It is impossible to identify all the Apollo types of the period with the few which are handed down by tradition, for the simple reason that the existing number is far larger than the number reported in literature.

[5] The first suggestion is due to Petersen, *loc. cit.* After what has been said on p. 35 it is of course impossible to identify this statue, as Petersen does, with the Apollo of the Delphic group ; nor is it likely that the *Terme* statue reproduces the Parnopios. We must always remember that only a very small fraction of the actual works, even by the greatest artists, is recorded by tradition.

[6] See 50th *Berl. Winckelmannsprogr.* 1890, p. 134 *sqq.* The theories recently propounded by Kalkmann, 53rd *Berl. Winckelmannsprogr.* (1893), according to which the figure by Stephanos goes back to an original by Pythagoras, seem to me completely to miss the mark.

H

Fig. II—Apollo, Mantua Museum. (See p. 52, note 6.)

Fig. 8—Statue of Apollo in Museo delle Terme (Rome

the right leg is slightly bent at ease, but the foot is flat on the ground, the right arm hangs somewhat quietly down, the left is in action, the head is turned to the left and inclined. The figure has a broad firm pose, owing to the leg at ease being set well to the side.

FIG. 9.—Head of Apollo in Museo delle Terme.

This trait recalls the Apollo of Mantua,[1] a work which I have already named as one of the forerunners of the Lemnia (p. 25). The *Terme* Apollo forms the link between them. Other marks of the school are the excessive breadth of the shoulders in proportion to the hips, the hard contour of the right shoulder, which as usual is

[1] *loc. cit.* p. 139 *sqq.*

slightly raised, and the closeness of the right upper arm to the body. The motive of the left arm too (which was raised very high, and no doubt originally rested on a laurel stem[1]) already occurred in works from the school of Hagelaidas. Such are an Apollo, preserved in two small marble copies, unfortunately only torsos;[2] a statue turned into an Antinous by a copyist of the time of Hadrian;[3] and finally an admirable bronze statuette of Apollo in the Louvre.[4] All these works, which are connected more or less closely with the school of Hagelaidas, show the same motive as our Apollo. The latter, however, differs from them all in the more decided and energetic bend of the head to the left, by which it gains in power and majesty;[5] and in the markedly individual modelling of the spare but powerful body.

Fig. 10.—Bronze Apollo of the Mantuan type from Pompeii, Naples.

In spite of these differences the connexion of this work with the school of Hagelaidas is evident even in the formation of the head. The Mantua Apollo is clearly its immediate forerunner, as may be seen more especially from the peculiar mouth.[6] Thus the surpassing beauty of the mouth of the Lemnia is not an isolated phenomenon, but the artist derived it from that older master to whom we owe the Mantua Apollo. The resemblance must impress any one who compares the two statues.

In a former essay I tried to prove that the artist of the Mantua Apollo, while belonging to the school of Hagelaidas, held his own definite position within that school.[7] His type of head is not the conventional type of the school, the mouth especially being formed in a manner entirely his own. Now this artist, as the facts we have just investigated reveal, must have been the teacher of the artist who made the *Terme* Apollo—in a word, of the young Pheidias.

[1] A very favourite motive on vases of the fifth century ; similarly on coins and a gem, cf. Roscher's *Lexikon*, i. 457.

[2] (*a*) Louvre, Gal. Mollien (No. 2955) ; (*b*) torso in the Museo Chiaramonti, 199.

[3] 50th *Winckelmannsprogr.* p. 147 ; *Bull. Commun. di Roma*, 1886, 7.

[4] Longpérier, *Notice des Bronzes Antiques*, No. 439, ' Achille.' This is not a Greek original bronze, probably not even an exact copy, but a free modification of the Augustan period. The head recalls the Zeus Talleyrand, the hair being dressed in the same affected archaistic manner ; the side curls are rendered as in the Munich Artemis of Gabii (cf. *infra*, Appendix) ; the body however is an example of the type under discussion.

[5] Another difference consists in the strong growth of curled hair on the pubes, a detail traditionally absent from the other works of the Hagelaidas school. The front of the figure is much injured by the action of the water, but the back is in good preservation.

[6] The different copies, the bronze of Pompeii, the marble statues of Mantua and Paris agree in their rendering of this mouth, which means that they correspond to the original. On the relation of the copies to one another, see my article *Berl. Phil. Wochenschrift*, 1894, p. 81 *sqq.* Fig. 10 gives the upper part of the bronze Pompeian statue from a photograph of the original.

[7] 50th *Berl. Winckelmannsprogr.* p. 140 *sqq.*

A bronze from the Akropolis [1] proves that this artist worked in Athens, or at least for Athens. The head appears to be earlier than the Apollo; it is rather harder, and it should probably be dated in the period immediately preceding the year 480 B.C.[2] By the help of tradition we can proceed a step further, and name this artist. It is Hegias whom we know as the teacher of Pheidias. An inscription on the Akropolis shows that he was working there shortly before the Persian sack.[3] And from the monuments we have learned that, though a pupil of Hagelaidas, he followed out his own artistic instincts, and gave to the head of his statues a new spiritual expression. The beauty he strove to embody was softer, fuller, and more sensuous than the ideal of the Peloponnesians, but it was left to his pupil to develop and idealize it.

Of the two ancient traditions concerning the masters of Pheidias, the one, giving the name of Hegias, comes down to us on the excellent authority of the learned Dion Chrysostom,[4] who was specially interested in Pheidias. In the same passage he shows himself to be well informed about the master of Polygnotos and his brother. It is certain, then, in the opinion of the best ancient scholars, that Pheidias was the pupil of Hegias. The other account, in which the better known and more famous Hagelaidas was named,[5] was however not entirely false, for the art of Hegias was derived from that of Hagelaidas, and the youthful works of Pheidias showed on the face of them their close connexion with the types of the school of Hagelaidas. The monuments have taught us that the two traditions are really in accordance.

Hitherto we had not been able to form an exact notion of the style of Hegias, because the ancients only characterize him in the most general way along with Kallon, Kritios, and Nesiotes as a representative of the older and harder manner. We now perceive that there are essential though subtle differences between the work of Hegias and that of Kritios. How radically Kritios differs from the school of Hagelaidas I have attempted to show elsewhere.[6] I may here cite a work which on account of the subject—it represents Apollo—is appropriate for comparison, and which is in my view an excellent sample of the work of Kritios. The statue stands in the Pitti Palace, and though scarcely known is of capital interest for the history of art.[7] The slender form of the god is supported on the right leg, the left being somewhat advanced; the small head (which is unbroken) is turned slightly to the left, but not bent; the eyes look straight out, as in the statue of a boy from the Akropolis, which I consider to be likewise an early work by Kritios.[8] The formation of head is the same as in the boy, the hair too is similarly arranged in a roll subdivided into different masses; but the Apollo wears in addition long curls falling over the neck, after the fashion of the *Terme* Apollo. The lifelike and slightly rounded modelling of the body marks an advance on the Hagelaidas school, but seems severe and restrained in

---

[1] *Musées d'Athènes*, Pl. 16; for the discovery cf. *Ath. Mitth.* xii. 372.

[2] Cf. 50th *Berl. Winckelmannsprogr.* 140 *seq.*, 148.

[3] Δελτίον ἀρχ. 1889, p. 37; *C. I. A.* iv. 373, 259. The stone is blackened by fire, and therefore Lolling dates it before the year 480.

[4] *De Hom. et Socr.* i. O. Müller's emendation of the ΗΠΟΥ of the MSS. into ΗΓΙΟΥ is scarcely an emendation at all, whereas E. Gardner's suggested reading Ἡγελάδου (*Classical Review*, 1894, p. 70) strays far from the traditional reading.

[5] Only in the Scholia to Aristophanes (*Frogs*, 504), whence Tzetzes and Suidas derive their information. The statement in the same passage about the date of Hagelaidas had of course no connexion originally with the assertion that Pheidias was his pupil; for whoever placed Hagelaidas in the period of the Peloponnesian War could not possibly suppose him to be the teacher of Pheidias.

[6] 50th *Berl. Winckelmannsprogr.* p. 150 *seq.*

[7] Dütschke, ii. 4; Overbeck, *Apollon*, p. 170, 5.

[8] 50th *Berl. Winckelmannsprogr.* p. 150; cf. pp. 7, 19.

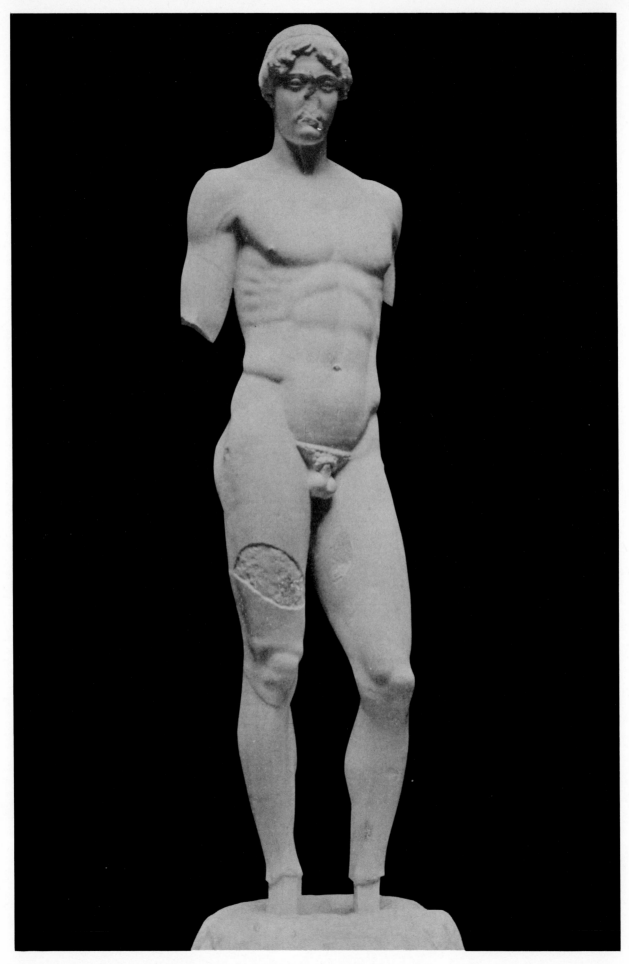

Fig. III—The So-Called Apollo on the Omphalos, Athens,
National Museum. (See pp. 3, 10 sqq. 33 seq.,
182, 190, 298.)

comparison with the so-called Omphalos Apollo, and corresponds to what we know of the manner of Kritios. The left arm is raised high,[1] just as it is in that Argive work which inspired the statue attributed to the young Pheidias, who must also have known the Apollo assigned to Kritios, since their statues are connected by the arrangement of locks on the nape of the neck.

The Apollo of the *Terme* must be dated about 460—455 B.C., some five or ten years earlier than the Lemnia. We possess a whole series of works belonging to the same period, and showing in all essentials the same tendency, but only a very few of these can be said to have a connexion with the Lemnia direct and personal enough to warrant us in ascribing them to Pheidias himself.

The strongly plastic treatment of the hair in long lifelike curly waves, as we find it in the Apollo of the *Terme* and, still more developed, in the Lemnia, is common to several heads of the time between 460 and 450, whose type of face however makes it impossible to attribute them to Pheidias. Such are a head in the Braccio Nuovo,[2] probably representing a horned river god, and a terminal bust of similar style in the Capitoline Museum (Fig. 11).[3] In these examples curls fall on the back of the neck as they do in the Apollo of the *Terme*, but the whole expression, and especially the harder rendering of the lower part of the face, shows more analogy to the Capitoline Apollo[4] than to the *Terme* Apollo or to the Lemnian Athena, and lead us to suppose that we have here two works by another artist. This was probably that contemporary of the young Pheidias whom we shall shortly learn to recognize as the creator of the Athena Albani: the two heads just mentioned certainly appear more closely related to this Athena than to any other work. The forehead, the way in which the front hair is parted over it, the eyes, the mouth, and the furrow between nose and mouth correspond in a remarkable manner.

A bearded head in the Palazzo Barberini (Fig. 12)[5] seems to answer more nearly to what we should expect of the young Pheidias. The hair, in short curly rings, is treated in a thoroughly plastic and individual fashion. It is parted along the top of the head as in the Lemnia. The line of profile and the shape of the skull also correspond approximately to the Lemnia, but the head is somewhat earlier. In many particulars it represents a preparatory stage to an Asklepios in Dresden,[6] which belongs to the circle of Pheidias, and is some twenty years later, and, like it, may have been intended for an Asklepios or some hero of kindred nature. The expression of the face is calm and dignified, the forehead—still very low—is smooth and unruffled.

The head of a youth from the Jacobsen collection (No. 1095a) is of great interest because of its relation to the Lemnia. It is a small head, turned energetically to the right, with short full locks, into which a fillet presses. Its connexion with the old Argive type, as we know it from the athlete by Stephanos, is still marked.

---

[1] The cloak falling from the upper arm and the lyre below are additions of the copyist. In the original the left hand probably grasped a laurel staff, and the lowered right hand held a bow.

[2] *Bonner Studien*, Taf. 8, 9 ; Winter, *loc. cit.*, interprets the head as Iacchos ; *Röm. Mitth.* 1891, p. 153 ; (Sauer, according to whom the head represents Aktaion) ; Helbig, 9. The head is wrongly set ; it was intended to be upright as in the cast in the École des Beaux-Arts at Paris.

[3] *Mus. Capit.* i. 83. In the room of the Philosophers, No. 85.

[4] *Röm. Mitth.* 1891, Taf. 11, 12, to the left.

[5] Matz-Duhn, *Zerstr. Bildw.* No. 1741. Cf. Gräf, *Aus der Anomia*, p. 63, note ; phot. in German Inst. at Rome.

[6] Treu has lately identified a replica of this work in Olympia (cf. *Arch. Anz.* 1890, 107 ; 1892, 66). His interpretation and restoration of it as a Zeus seem to me at present quite unproved.

a

a.—From the original.

FIG. 11.—Terminal bust in the Capitoline Museum.

b

b.—From the cast.

FIG. 12.—Head in Palazzo Barberini, Rome.

Attempts have lately been made to refer the Hermes Ludovisi[1] to the earlier period of Pheidias. It is certainly the work of a very great artist of the period in question, but its relation to the Lemnia is not close enough to warrant us in assigning it to Pheidias. The difference is plain, even in the fashion of the fillet, which lies flat on the hair, without pressing into it as in the Lemnia. The formation of the lower part of the face, the rather thin lips, and the picturesque boldness in the rendering of the cloak which is slipping off,[2] and even the bodily forms, are not in harmony with the style of Pheidias. There is an admirable replica of this head in the collection at Broadlands[3] (Fig. 13). The style is here rather freer than in the Ludovisi example, the copyist having made plentiful use of the drill, and put more modelling into the cheeks, but the winsome grace and the sweet roguish expression of the head must be due to the original. Ionic art is the only possible source of such a work.[4] On a Phokaean electrum coin,[5] an ἔκτη Φωκαΐς (Pl. VI. 19), occurs a head of Hermes very similar to that of the statue, wearing the same petasos and short curls, with the same profile, and evidently belonging to the same period. It seems admissible to bring this Hermes type into connexion with Telephanes of Phokis, who apparently lived about this time.[6] The further analogy between our Hermes and the head of a youth on a Thessalian relief[7] strengthens this theory, since Telephanes is known to have worked for Thessaly.

There is a female type which may very well have belonged to Pheidias's early period, and be regarded as a forerunner to the Lemnia. Its best replica is the beautiful head in the Hermitage (profile in Fig. 15).[8] The hair is dressed with the simplicity so much affected by the wider circle of Hagelaidas, and which the Lemnia retains, though in a richer form, i.e. it is waved back from the front and rolled up behind. The parting has not yet appeared ; the lines of hair come straight from the crown of the head. The way the hair frames the forehead, the line of the profile, the mouth with its full lips—all seem to me so many analogies to the Lemnia, and indications that Pheidias is the artist. There is a variant of this head with less severe expression and more open mouth in the Coll. Barracco (Fig. 14).[9] Like the one in St. Petersburg, this head is distinguished by unusual dignity and beauty, and may also be referred to Pheidias. A small and slightly worked head of the same type is to be seen in the Braccio Nuovo, on an Artemis of more recent style, to which it does not

[1] Cf. B. Gräf in *Aus der Anomia*, p. 69. In the Museo Boncompagni (Helbig, *Museums*, 871).

[2] In the replica by Kleomenes, the so-called ' Germanicus' of the Louvre, the folds of the mantle are modified in Praxitelean style.

[3] Michaelis, *Anc. Sculpt. in Gr. Brit.* p. 219, Broadlands 9. The edge of the petasos is wrongly restored. The nose is uninjured and antique. The head is placed incorrectly in an upright position on a modern term. The length of the face m. 0·163 (the Ludovisi copy 0·165). To the list of replicas of the head should be added Uffizi Dütschcke 13 = Arndt-Brunckmann, *Einzelverkauf*, 83, 84.

[4] 50th *Berl. Winckelmannsprogr.* p. 152, where I suggested Pythagoras of Samos as the artist.

[5] The replica in the British Museum is illustrated in the *Catal. Ionia*, Pl. IV. 23. The Berlin example (Pl. VI. 19) is more severe in style and more like the statue.

[6] The author who makes him work for Xerxes and Darius (*apud* Plin. xxxiv. 68) is of course thinking of Darius II., but forgets that this monarch was separated from Xerxes by an interval of forty-two years ; he probably only meant that Telephanes worked for the Persian kings of the fifth century B.C. The fact that Telephanes is grouped with Polykleitos, Myron, and Pythagoras shows that he must have flourished about the middle of the century. Cf. Julius Lange, *Fremstilling af Menneskeskikkelsen*, p. 133 *seq.*

[7] *Bull. de Corr. Hell.* 1888, Pl. VI.

[8] Guédéonow, *Sculp. Ant.* No. 32, 'athlète.' Length of face 0·156 ; length of head c. 0·22. The proportions correspond to those of the Lemnia. Mouth to inner angle of the eye (64 mm.)=the length of the nose up to the arch of the eyebrows=the lower part of the face=twice the length of one eye ; width of the mouth (42 mm.) =height of the forehead.

[9] *Coll. Barracco*, Pl. 36, 'tête d'éphèbe,' and in the text 'tête d'athlète'! The eyes are hollow. A small replica of the Barracco head in terra-cotta from a high relief is now in Dresden (Coll. Dressel).

I

Fig. 13.—Terminal bust in the collection at Broadlands. (From a photograph.)

Fig. 14.—Head in the Collection Barracco (Rome). (By permission of Messrs. Bruckmann in Munich.)

Fig. 15.—Head in the Hermitage.

Fig. 16—Terminal bust of Athena from Herculaneum (Naples)

Fig. IIIa—Head of Hermes Ludovisi, Rome, National Museum (See p. 57)

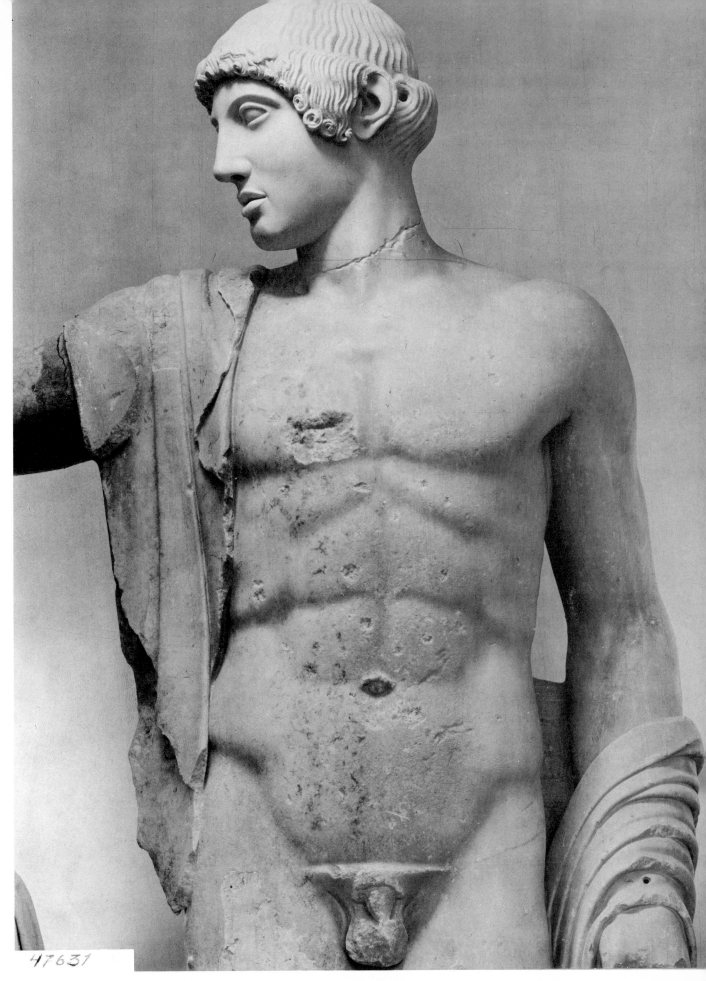

47631

Fig. IV—Apollo, West Pediment of the Temple of Zeus
at Olympia, Olympia Museum

belong.[1] True, there is something of the nature of Artemis in the pure, straightforward, maidenly, Amazon-like expression of the heads, so the mistake is not surprising.[2]

A beautiful female head in the Villa Albani (No. 63) is also possibly a replica of an older Pheidian work.[3] It may be placed about midway between the well-known Madrid head,[4] which is so closely allied to the Olympia metopes, and the Lemnia. The hair is arranged as in the Madrid head. It is parted down the middle as in the Lemnia, but is treated in a much simpler manner. The low forehead with its delicate modelling, the mouth, and even the shape of the ears recall the Lemnia.

We can judge with greater certainty when we come to works contemporary with or only slightly later than the Lemnia.

In connexion with the Albani head just mentioned, it is fitting to discuss an Athena type which is certainly of Pheidian origin. It survives in three terms, two of which are from Herculaneum—the first of these is given in Fig. 16—the third is in the Capitol.[5] This beautiful head shows analogies to the Albani female head mentioned above and to the Lemnia. The style is that of the Lemnia, but the expression, less serious and solemn than kindly, as well as the carriage of the head, brings it nearer to the Albani type. The goddess wears her helmet pressed low down on the forehead, as does the Parthenos at a later date. A gorgoneion on an aegis-like background of scales forms the symbolic ornament of the helmet. Curls fall down at the side as in the Parthenos. Although this conception of the goddess differs not only in external particulars but in expression from the Lemnia, yet the inner analogy between them is in my view undeniable; the mouth and the lower part of the face are peculiarly characteristic. On the other hand, an Athena head in the Munich Glyptothek[6] shows how style can differ in spite of striking external similarity. It is a replica of a work belonging to the same period, but not by the same artist.

To the period of the Parthenos itself belongs a superb work of Pheidias which survives, as I believe, in one complete copy and in various reproductions of the head. I mean the Anakreon standing in an attitude of rapt enthusiasm and declaiming his poems to his own accompaniment on the lyre (Fig. 17).[7] This work is now universally

---

[1] Helbig, *Museums*, No. 20; Clarac, 571, 1220. Arndt informs me that the head is put on with a straight junction surface, that it does not belong to the statue, and that the whole back from the girdle upwards is new. The type of this torso, a fourth-century modification of the Parthenos, was also used to represent Isis (cf. *Beschr. d. Antiken Skulpt. in Berlin*, p. 529, No. 60 a). The quiver band shows that the statue was originally intended to represent Artemis. The quiver itself is omitted.

[2] It is interesting to note that the St. Petersburg and Barracco heads, like that of the Lemnia, were formerly supposed to be male.

[3] Length of face 0·175. I find no mention of this admirable work in literature. (Cf. *Berl. Winckelmanns-progr.* p. 130.)   [4] *J. H. S.* 1884, Taf. 45.

[5] (1) Naples, *Inv.* 6322, Comparetti de Petra, *Villa Ercol.* Tav. xx. 1; *Jahrb. d. Inst.* 1893, Taf. 3, pp. 174, 177; (2) Naples, *Inv.* 6282, *Jahrb. d. Inst.* 1893, p. 176; (3) in the Philosophers' Room of the Capitol, No. 54: *Mus. Capitol.* i. 56, *Jahrb., loc. cit.* p. 176. In all three instances the term is antique. In (2) and (3) the breast is covered with drapery which can hardly be copied from the original. The turn of the head varies, as is often the case in term copies (see *term* in Index). Wolters (*Jahrb., loc. cit.*) attempts to trace back this type to Kephisodotos, the artist of the Eirene; but the forms of brow, hair, eyes, and mouth show by their style that the head belongs to the fifth century and to the Pheidian epoch.

[6] Placed on a statue (No. 86) which does not belong to it.

[7] The statue, formerly in Villa Borghese, and now in Copenhagen (Ny Carlsberg), is published *Arch. Ztg.* 1884, Taf. 11; cf. Friederichs-Wolters, *Gipsabg.* 1305. I know three replicas of the head: (a) in Rome, Helbig, 599; (b) in the Palazzo Riccardi in Florence, to the left of the entrance upstairs (Dütschke, ii. 200)— the head is wrongly set; (c) in Berlin, *Jahrb. d. Inst.* 1892, Taf. 3. Kekulé's notion, *ibid.* p. 119 *seq.*, that the Berlin head is a fifth-century original, is absolutely false: it is an ordinary Roman copy, in a bad state of preservation, and much restored. The head in the Louvre, 1946, seems to be a fourth, very poor replica. A fifth, badly preserved, in Glienecke, is mentioned by Kekulé, p. 120.

Fig. V—Centaur and Lapith Woman, West Pediment of
the Temple of Zeus at Olympia, Olympia Museum

admitted to be of fifth-century date.[1] Any one who comes fresh from the study of
the Lemnia cannot fail to be struck by a wonderful likeness between the two heads
which can only be explained by identity of authorship. Although rather short, the
hair is parted as in the Lemnia, and the fillet presses deep into it, while the refined
forehead with its flat and restrained modelling, the eyebrows, and the thin eyelids are
so many points of definite resemblance ; even the ear has the shape characteristic of
the ear of the Lemnia. The head, although conceived in an attitude of vigorous movement, yet produces as a whole that wonderful effect of combined dignity, beauty, and
repose which was peculiar to Pheidias. Moreover, the only complete parallel to the
drapery occurs on the Parthenon metopes of free style, which are to be referred to
Pheidias. Nowhere else do we find the peculiar clinging of the mantle to the nude
forms, the broken folds, or the same true characterization of the soft yet heavy
material.[2] This fixes the date of the statue at about 445–440. The frieze and the
pediments show a definite advance in style. The way the short cloak hangs round
the shoulders echoes archaic tradition and recalls the Oinomaos of Olympia. But
the influence of the circle of Hagelaidas has long ceased to dominate the artist.
The bodily forms are nervous and fresh as in the metopes of free style. The feet
are placed on the ground in the old scheme, but the upper part of the body is
turned, giving to the whole composition novelty, vigour, and exquisite freedom of
rhythm.[3]

The Pheidian statue of Anakreon was doubtless identical with the one which
stood on the Akropolis, and whose attitude, according to Pausanias, was 'suggestive
of a man singing in his cups.'[4] In ascribing the animated and inspired turn of the
head to a liberal use of wine, Pausanias was making no unnatural supposition in the
case of a man who was the poet *par excellence* of wine and intoxication, and who
himself appears intoxicated in a work of art which, whether real or fictitious, is alluded
to in epigrams.[5] Beside the statue of Anakreon, Pausanias saw that of Xanthippos,
the father of Perikles and friend of Anakreon. It has long been rightly supposed that
both statues were set up by Perikles.[6] Of course they were not public monuments,
but purely private dedicatory gifts, meant to express the filial affection of Perikles
for his father and his reverence for his father's distinguished friend. If the name of
Perikles came first in the dedicatory inscription, it is easy to understand why
Pausanias begins to speak of Perikles just in the very passage where he names these
works, although the statue of Perikles himself, as he says, stood at some distance.

The artist was probably not named. If we remember Lucian's statement about
the inscription of the Lemnia, we can hardly suppose that the name of Pheidias was
to be seen on *another* statue of the Akropolis outside the Parthenon. Considering
the artist's close relation to Perikles, his authorship would at that time appear
so much a matter of course that his signature could be left out.   The statue

---

[1] Cf. Winter, *Jahrb. d. Inst.* 1890, 159 ; Helbig, *loc. cit.* ; and especially Kekulé, *loc. cit.*

[2] Cf. the metopes Michaelis, South ii., viii., xxviii. Cf. Kekulé, p. 121.

[3] The pubes with its thickly curled hair resembles that of the *Terme* Apollo.

[4] [Tr. Harrison and Verrall, *Myth. and Mon. of Anc. Athens*, p. 471.]

[5] Wolters (*Arch. Ztg.* 1884, 150) rightly doubts the existence of the work ; in any case there are no
grounds for identifying it with the statue of the Akropolis. Cf. also Kekulé, p. 119, note 4.

[6] Brunn in *Ann. d. Inst.* 1859, 183. Brunn is wrong, however, in connecting the portrait of Perikles,
which according to Pausanias stood in quite a different spot, with these two statues, and in ascribing them to
Kresilas. The Perikles was a private *anathema* of Kresilas. Kekulé, p. 125, follows Brunn, and, arguing from a
supposed stylistic connexion between the Anakreon and the Perikles, suggests the Anakreon was also by Kresilas.
There is, however, no stylistic connexion, except in so far as both works belong to the same epoch. Sal. Reinach,
Chron. d'Orient, No. xxvi. p. 11, comes nearer the truth in suggesting that the Anakreon might be by Kolotes.

was set up, as is proved by the style, during the period when Perikles was most powerful, and could without opposition place upon the Akropolis, ἐν ἐπιφανεστάτῳ τόπῳ, images of his father and of Anakreon, the friend of tyrants.

The influence exercised on more recent art by this work of Phedias is shown

FIG. 17.—The 'Anakreon Borghese' (Ny Carlsberg Glyptothek, Copenhagen).

in a beautiful head in the Vatican,[1] a copy of a work of the fourth century B.C.: it represents a poet with inspired upturned look, and is visibly a development, even to the form of the beard, of the Anakreon of Pheidias.

A magnificent bearded head in the Museo Torlonia (Fig. 18) is closely analogous to the Anakreon, and must likewise be by Pheidias. The strikingly noble and elevated beauty of this head must dwell in the memory of all who have seen it.

[1] Helbig, *Museums*, No. 287. The old interpretation of the head as Zeno, and Helbig's suggestion of Aratos, are equally unproved and inappropriate.

For my own part, since I first beheld it in 1877, it has kept its place in my remembrance as the gem of the collection.[1]　The delicate forehead swells almost imperceptibly in the middle, and is low, just like that of the Lemnia, to which the eyebrows and thin eyelids also correspond closely.　The hair is again bound by a diadem, broader in front, narrower behind, with short curls escaping from it.　The general similarity to the Anakreon in hair and beard is striking, although many of the details are quite different.　In turning to identify the head, we note that two small wings are attached—not to the head itself—but to the diadem.　Analogies are found in contemporary vases of the period ranging from 460—450, where daemonic attributes appear fastened to the diadem.　Athena, for example, wears a diadem on which Pegasoi are seated,[2] and Thetis a diadem adorned with small wings, to indicate her transformations.[3]　More important still is the painting on a white lekythos of the British Museum; the black outline drawing shows a bearded man with wings on his head rising from a wide fillet; he rushes forward to meet an advancing warrior, and strikes him on the arm.　Without attempting to interpret this vase-painting, I wish to point out that the art of the time apparently had not the courage to effect an organic connexion between the wings and the head.　Further, in the Torlonia head the wings are purposely kept small, in order not to break the fine outline of the skull.

FIG. 18.—Head with winged fillet, Museo Torlonia, Rome.　(From a drawing.)

The winged diadem apparently has much the same signification as the wings attached actually to the head in later times: one might imagine the head to be that of a bearded Hermes, were it not that the type of features is absolutely foreign to that god.　The similarity to the Anakreon brings us seemingly nearer the truth: may we not have here a head of Mousaios, the old god-inspired poet, who, according to Attic legend, had received the gift of flight—and therefore, we may suppose, the gift of wings—from Boreas?[4]

　　To the same group belongs a beautiful bearded head in the Museo Chiaramonti (Fig. 19),[5] which expresses marvellous elevation and distinction.　It is nearly related to the last-mentioned heads, and also to the Lemnia, and must be referred, if not to Pheidias himself, as I believe, at least to a master of his school and of the period about 450—440.　The treatment of the wavy hair on the upper part of the head, the roll of hair on the neck, and the small curls escaping from it recall the Lemnia.　Entirely Pheidian, too, are the finely modelled forehead, the thin eyelids, the spring of the nose, the arrangement of the beard, and the shape of the ear.[6]　It is difficult to form any conjecture as to whom the head represents.　The tuft of short hair rising in front above the twisted fillet is quite unique, and the tangled hair

[1] No. 48 in the Catalogue of 1876; now No. 50.　Benndorf, *Röm. Mitth.* i. 113, notices the analogy to the Anakreon.

[2] *Élite Céramogr.* i. 29, and Millingen, *Div. Coll.* 49.

[3] *Mon. d. Inst.* i. 37.

[4] Onomakritos, *apud* Paus. i. 22, 7.

[5] *Mus. Chiaram.* Tav. 33; Helbig, 71.　The tip of the nose is restored.

[6] The end of the nose has been distorted by the restorer, and too much curved.

Fig. 19.—Head in the Museo Chiaramonti (Vatican).

a   *b*

Fig. 20.—Double terminal bust in Madrid.

about the chin is also probably a characteristic mark. The current interpretation as Dionysos is absolutely groundless. It very probably represents a hero, but, until we know which hero, the finer intentions of the artist must remain a mystery.

Two female types still have to be mentioned in the present connexion: one is the head of a young goddess,[1] with a wide fillet wound three times round it and a bunch of hair behind tied up in a σάκκος. The type is of the same period as the Lemnia, and probably owes its existence to Pheidias.

Closely allied to this head, although stylistically somewhat later, is the 'Sappho,' of which so many copies have survived (Figs. 20 b, 21 b).[2] Here too we have the wide fillet wound several times round the head, although arranged in a slightly different manner. The forehead is freer and higher, the curls only escape freely above the ears. This is quite in the manner of the Parthenos,[3] of which the head appears to be contemporary. The rich plastic waving locks on the upper part of the head are genuinely Pheidian. In front of and behind the ears (which again are shaped like those of the Lemnia) a few wisps stray from the mass of hair. The mouth is a little open, giving a glimpse of the teeth.[4] The head is slightly turned to the side, the expression fresh and gracious.[5] The long narrow form of the eyes is characteristic. There can be no question of a portrait,[6] but the rich fillet, the expression of the face, and the form of the eyes are more appropriate to Aphrodite than to any other goddess. This interpretation, already suggested by Helbig,[7] is strongly confirmed by a wonderful statuette from Syria, now in Paris in the Collection de Clerq. This work represents a nude Aphrodite binding a wide fillet round her head. Except for some few omissions and unimportant alterations, the head of the Aphrodite is of the type under discussion. Although the body imitates forms of the fifth century B.C., the whole conception is merely an invention of Hellenistic times, uniting the head-type of Pheidias with the motive of the Diadumenos of Polykleitos.[8]

---

[1] Four replicas of the head are known to me: (a) with inserted glass eyes in the Museum of the Capitol, 'Philosophers' Room,' No. 55, *Mus. Capit.* i. 57; (b and c) in the Museo Torlonia, Nos. 54 and 58 (formerly 52 and 56); (d) in the Ny Carlsberg Glypt. in Copenhagen.

[2] I have examined and compared the following instances in the original: (a) in Berlin, *Skulpt.* 330; *Arch. Ztg.* 1871, Taf. 50—poor; (b) in Brunswick—mediocre copy, the face much polished over; (c) in the Brit. Mus.— much damaged; (d) in the Hermitage, No. 188—face worked over, hair good; (e) in the Palazzo Riccardi (Dütschke, ii. 162)—a very good copy, clear and careful work, the nose antique; (f) in Rome, Mus. Chiaramonti, 50; (g and h) in the Villa Borghese, Helbig, 926, 930—the first specially good; (i) in the Villa Albani, 109; (k) in the Coll. Barracco; (l and m) two very good copies in the Museum at Corneto; (n) a very good copy in Naples— turreted crown restored, but draped term genuine; (o) in the Louvre—a very good copy, but placed on a torso to which it does not belong, No. 1739; Fröhner, No. 413; Bouillon, i. 50; (p) the double term in Madrid, *Arch. Ztg.* 1871, Taf. 50; Friederichs-Wolters, 1609. I only know this from the cast: it is one of the best (Figs. 11, 12). All these instances are real copies, and correspond in size. There are besides: (q) a free adaptation in colossal size from Smyrna in Constantinople. This is a Hellenistic, not a Roman work; the severity has disappeared, the manner is grandiose but somewhat coarse. The existence of this copy shows that the original must have been famous in the Pergamene period; (r) a free replica on a small scale, a head, which has been placed on the Ludovisi group (Schreiber, 50). There is a beautiful antique variant in Oxford of the same style and with the same narrow eyes (casts in the Ecole des Beaux-Arts, in the South Kensington Museum, at Bonn, etc.) This head must be referred to another work from the inner circle of the master.

[3] K. Lange, *Ath. Mitth.* 1881, 93, has already classified this type with that of the Parthenos. Compare especially the *Minerve au collier* in the Louvre, where the hair on the left side is evidently a faithful copy.

[4] Especially in (e), (g), (o).

[5] The attitude varies slightly in the different examples; the heads (e), (f), (g) are turned to the left, while (h), (i), (n), (o) are turned to the right. This is explained by the fact that all these heads belonged to terms; the copyists turned the head now one way, now another, for decorative reasons. The same was the case with the Skopasian Herakles.

[6] The colossal replica (p) is evidence to the contrary.   [7] Helbig, *Museums*, 926.

[8] This charming figure, about 30 cm. high, is intact, with the exception of the left arm. Beside the left leg is a vase with the discarded drapery over it. The head is much inclined. The same motive, with reversed sides,

Fig. Va—Oenomaos, East Pediment of the Temple of
Zeus at Olympia, Olympia Museum.

If the head had not been originally meant to represent an Aphrodite, it could hardly have been adopted for the goddess in this instance.

Unless the Pheidian original was itself a term,[1] it must, from the indication of a chiton on one of the busts, have represented the goddess draped.[2]

Thus, we may claim to have recovered an Aphrodite of Pheidias : it was perhaps the one in Rome in *Octaviæ operibus*, distinguished by Pliny as *eximiæ pulchritudinis*. These words of praise, as well as the statement that the statue was in Rome, fit in admirably with the existing copies. The *eximia pulchritudo* of the work must

a   *b*

Fig. 21.—Profiles of the double terminal bust.

at once be acknowledged. It has the majestic and elevated beauty which distinguishes all that Pheidias did, combined with a winning sweetness of expression. This is the goddess who, as the Attic vases show, dwells in fresh gardens where golden fruits

is to be seen on a carnelian, apparently a purely Hellenistic work (Caylus, *Rec. d'Ant.* vi. 38, 4). For the signature *Skopas* cf. my article, *Jahrb. d. Inst.* (1893) viii. 185.

[1] Terminal Aphrodite in Athens, Paus. i. 19, 2.

[2] See the Naples copy (*n*). Some notion of the statue that belonged to this head-type may be formed from the so-called 'Sappho Albani,' now generally interpreted as a Kore or Demeter (Helbig, 841); it is a work of the Pheidian period, though manifestly not by Pheidias. Cf. R. v. Schneider, *Jahrb. d. Oesterr. Hofmuseen*, xii. 72. A good illustration in Brunn-Bruckmann, *Denkm.* No. 255. Besides the replicas mentioned by Schneider there are : (1) a torso in the Louvre, No. 2001 ; Fröhner, *Not.* No. 574 ; (2) a poor torso half life-size, also in the Louvre, No. 2912 ; and (3) a half life-size figure with head restored in Naples. The type, as Sauer (*Festschrift für Overbeck*, p. 73) shows, already occurs on one of the metopes of the Parthenon.

grow, where nymphs and Erotes serve her, where reign harmony and bliss ;[1] but she is a goddess still, not a mortal woman with human feelings and desires, such as Praxiteles was to conceive her.

One of the copies of this Aphrodite head appears on a double term associated with the head of a youth (Figs. 20 *a*, 21 *a*),[2] which must also have been famous, since it occurs separately in various replicas.[3] The delicate young face is framed in full curls which cover the ears ; a circlet presses deeply into the mass of hair. In some at least of the examples a fillet is wound round the circlet. The artistic kinship of this head to the Aphrodite is evident. They are both works of Pheidias, and nearly contemporary. The stylistic treatment of the hair and of the face (especially of the full, slightly open mouth) represents the same stage of development as the Aphrodite.

FIG. 22.—Cameo in Berlin.

The youth who appears united with Aphrodite on a double term should, according to all analogy, be nearly related to her in significance. He can be none other than Eros, who in the time of Pheidias[4] was represented—not as an effeminate youth, but—as an ephebe. A good instance of the Pheidian Eros type, nearly akin to the head we are studying, is to be seen on a cameo of the Berlin collection (Fig. 22), presumably of the Augustan period. It represents just such a terminal bust of Eros as the one in question, whose original may actually have been executed in this form. If our interpretation is exact, it is plain that Pheidias did not give to his Love-god, any more than to his Aphrodite, the expression of human longing which distinguishes him in the period of Praxiteles.[5]

There is another 'Sappho' type which should be noted here, as it belongs originally to the circle of Pheidias. On a statue formerly in the Palazzo Cepparelli in Florence (Fig. 23)[6] has been placed a head evidently of later Pheidian style, and an immediate forerunner of the well-known Albani head which has lately been again interpreted as Sappho.[7] The close connexion of the two heads, evidenced by the coif, by the twisted curls in front of the ear, and by the general type of face, is unmistakable. Equally plain is the fact that the Florentine head, as shown by the style, especially by the treatment of the regularly undulating hair, belongs to the later Pheidian period. The body of the statue is of the same date as the head, but

---

[1] Cf. the vase belonging to the period about 430, Stackelberg, *Gräber*, 29 ; Müller-Wieseler, *Denkm.* 3rd ed. ii. 296 d.

[2] The Madrid term p.

[3] *e.g.* Museo Chiaramonti, 695 (nose and lips restored) ; in the Museo Torlonia, 44 (nose and lips restored) ; in Dresden, 32 (much defaced). Published in Becker's *Augusteum*, ii. 85 ; the Madrid copy is the best ; mouth and nose are antique ; the fillet hanging down is merely a decorative addition ; it is missing in the Chiaramonti head.

[4] The witticism of Phryne, recorded in Athenaeus, xiii. p. 585, would seem to prove the existence of an Eros by Pheidias ; it at any rate implies a play on the name Φειδίας (cf. Brunn, *K.G.* i. p. 187) ; and though this in itself is insufficient to prove the existence of an Eros statue by this master, there is no doubt that the *jeu de mot* would have been more pointed and appropriate had there been a well-known Eros by him.

[5] The Eros of the period, about 420 B.C., with which I identify a small head from Brauron (*Arch. Studien H. Brunn. dargebr.* Taf. 3, p. 89) is less serious and more youthful.

[6] Dütschke, *Zerstr. Bildw. in Florenz*, 413 ; now in the Museo Archeologico.

[7] *Jahrb. d. Inst.* 1890, Taf. 3 ; p. 151 *sqq.* (Winter). Two poor replicas in the Bigliardo of the Villa, Nos. 332, 333. The Pitti head published *Ann. d. Inst.* 1879, Tav. o, in which Gamurrini and Wolters (*Gipsabg.* 1609) recognize Sappho, is not a replica of the Albani head, as Winter (*loc. cit.* p. 152) affirms, but a different though related type.

it is not certain that they belong together.[1] The narrow eyes are characteristic of
Aphrodite. In order to interpret the Albani head, which, to judge by the formation

Fig. 23.—Statue formerly in Pal. Cepparelli (Florence).

of the eyes, was derived from this older type, we must go to the group of figures
representing Aphrodite, or divinities akin to her. For there is no evidence whatever

---

[1] According to a communication from Milani the head is of the same Parian marble as the torso. But as
the lower part of the neck is restored, and as the original head was probably inserted, the present head can
scarcely belong to the statue.

that the head is a portrait, and nothing in the work itself to warrant us in calling it Sappho. The apparent coincidences found on coins are deceptive.[1]

Another Pheidian Aphrodite—the Ourania in Athens (Paus. i. 14, 7) I incline to

FIG. 24.—Statuette of Aphrodite (Berlin).

think—has survived in a statuette from Corneto (Tarquinii), now in Berlin (Fig. 24),[2] which is evidently an original free adaptation made in the actual school of Pheidias.

[1] Pollux (*Onom.* ix. 84) says that the Mytileneans represented Sappho on their coins. This is the oldest testimony on the subject, for to see an allusion to it in Aristot. *Rhet.* 2, 23 is purely arbitrary. None of the extant coins of Mytilene with ascertained representations of Sappho (*i.e.* which give her name in the coin legend) are earlier than Imperial date, any more than the coins of Chios with the portrait of Homer, which are mentioned immediately after by Pollux. Now of these undoubted representations of Sappho, *not one* shows the least resemblance to the Albani type; they differ from it and from each other. They are as follows: (*a*) the Paris coin with ψαπ(φ)ω, Jahn, *Darst. Gr. Dichter*, Taf. 8, 1; (*b*) Sappho seated, with and without the name; (*c*) the head inscribed Σαπφω on coins of Eresos. The coin inscribed Σαφους, Jahn, Taf. 8, 2, is very possibly a forgery. There is no reason to suppose that the hooded head of the autonomous bronze coins and of an electrum coin of Mytilene (Sallet's *Zeitschr.* ix. Taf. 4, 4—6; *Jahrb. d. Inst.* 1890, Taf. 3 below) represents Sappho. In the period before Alexander, to which some at least of these coins belong, there is no instance of a portrait of a distinguished person on a Greek coin. Hence the head must be a divinity, perhaps Aphrodite. The coif was a favourite headdress in Asia Minor. Thus Winter's hypothesis, that Seilanion was the artist of the Albani head, is untenable. The Sappho of Seilanion is still to seek.

[2] Berlin. *Skulpt.* 586, h. o. 83. Hands, feet, and some trifling details are restored together with the face of the idol.

A

A—From a lost original.

Fig. 25.—Two heads of Athena from casts in Dresden.

B

B—Head of Athena Farnese (Naples).

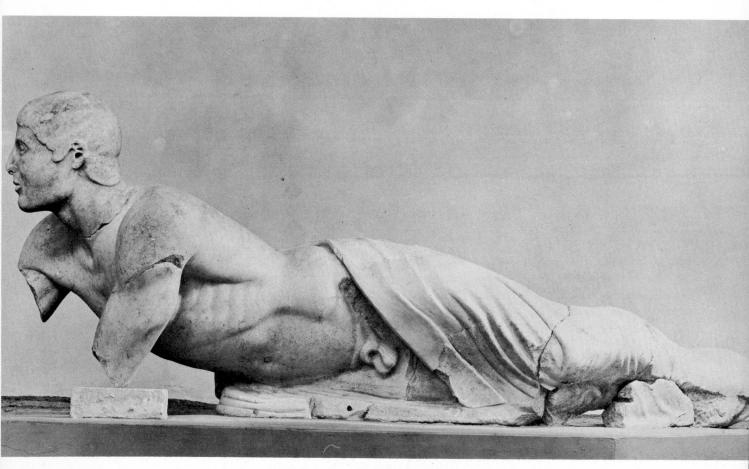

Fig. VI—River God Kladeos, East Pediment of the
Temple of Zeus at Olympia, Olympia Museum

Aphrodite, leaning upon her own ancient image and drawing her veil aside with her right hand, is represented in solemn repose—in a sort of subdued majesty. The left foot rests on the ground with full sole, and is placed somewhat to the front. The drapery —more especially the folded-over portion of the himation in front—is quite in the style of the Parthenon frieze.[1] The head is of the usual genuine Attic type of the Pheidian epoch: its finer details, however, have been left out in this small reproduction.[2]

IX. *Pheidias and his Pupils—Alkamenes and Agorakritos.*

We must now try to trace the career of Pheidias beyond the period of the Parthenos. Among the many works which are more or less related to our subject we select a significant statue, again representing Athena, which throws light on the relations between the master and his pupils.

Fig. 25 reproduces side by side two heads of Athena, both from casts in Dresden. The head on the right hand (B) is evidently taken from the well-known Athena Farnese in Naples (Fig. 26).[3] The original of the other cast (Fig. 25, A ; profile, Fig. 28)[4] has disappeared, but even from the cast it is absolutely clear that the bust, with the ends of the curls and of the bunch of hair behind, is modern, while the neck, with the portion of the curls adjoining it and the upper part of the bunch of hair behind, is antique. The restorer copied the bust of the Cassel Athena, or of one of the two Lemnia statues in Dresden, but he misunderstood the drapery on the shoulder.

The two heads go back to two different Greek originals, and yet they are so similar in certain external particulars that we cannot suppose them to be entirely independent of each other. The hair in front corresponds even in the form and number of separate strands. The principal proportions (length of face and of eyes) are the same in both. The helmets differ only in so far that while on A there are griffins beside the Sphinx, on B (the upper part of the helmet has been left out in the cast; cf. Fig. 26) there are Pegasoi; further, A has a volute at the side instead of the turned-up cheek-piece of B. The curls on the neck are different. In B there are two short artificially twisted spiral curls, while A shows a curl slightly waved and falling naturally, apparently divided in the middle, and in the continuation, now lost, probably parting into two separate strands. Great differences are noticeable in the finer modelling of the face; A is on the whole narrower and more delicate, the forehead is lower than in B, the nose somewhat longer and narrower, and the mouth narrower. Finally, the eyelids of A are thin, those of B very thick, while the

---

[1] *i.e.* in short grooves rounded at the ends. Cf. Pallat, *Jahrb. d. Inst.* 1894, p. 17. For the chiton cf. the 'Peitho' of the E. frieze.

[2] A later echo of this Pheidian creation occurs in the statue recently published by Kekulé, *Weibliche Gewandstatue aus d. Werkstatt d. Parthenon Giebel.* 1894.

[3] Gerhard u. Panofka, *Neapels Ant. Bildw.* (1828), p. 41, No. 118 ; Clarac, Pl. 458, 851 A.

[4] Hettner says it is in the Hope collection (*Verz. d. Abg.* p. 109, No. 172); but in that collection there is only the well-known statue (Michaelis, *Anc. Sculpt.* p. 290, No. 39), and the cast cannot possibly be of this statue, because of the difference in the bust. Even if we leave the restored bust out of account the curls on the neck do not exactly correspond ; in the Hope statue each is separated more distinctly into two parts, so that it could not easily be mistaken for a single curl as the restorer has done. The Dresden cast is not from the Mengs collection ; its original is unknown. There is a second example of it in Bonn ; Welcker (*Bonner Kunstmus.* 155 = Kekulé, 306) says vaguely that the original is in England. A third copy of the cast is in the Humboldt collection in Schloss Tegel ; the Waagen catalogue says nothing of the original. In the New Museum of Berlin, built by Stüler, this cast has been adapted for a decorative head.

L

FIG. 26.—Athena Farnese (Naples).

FIG. 27.—Hope Athena in the collection at Deepdene, Surrey. (From *Spec. of Anc. Sculpture.*)

modelling of the forehead, the curve of the eyebrows, and the formation between eyebrow and upper lid are completely different in the two examples.

The head B is still unbroken on its statue, the Athena Farnese in Naples. Head A, too, has a body belonging to it; for it is a replica of the famous Hope Athena (Fig. 27) at Deepdene (Surrey), from whose priceless collection, unfortunately, students and public alike are now jealously excluded.[1] This and the Athena Farnese were formerly looked upon as copies of the same original;[2] but more exact comparison will show that this is not the case. Head A, in all those particulars in which it differs from head B, corresponds exactly to the Hope Athena. In this statue the curls disfigured by restoration on head A are seen in their proper form. They split naturally into two wavy ringlets falling down over the aegis. In spite of the remarkable external similarity between the two statues, they differ not only in the type of head, helmet, and side-curls, but also in other respects. To begin at the top, the opening in the middle of the aegis is wider in the Hope statue, and shows more of the chiton; the gorgoneion is of a distinct type with hair not raised on end but smoothly waved close to the head, as on the aegis of the Parthenos. The snakes on the aegis correspond on the whole, but they are arranged in less conventional circles, and although not so effective are more various and natural (note especially the second snake from the top on the left shoulder, which is so much more simply rendered in the Hope statue, and thus affords a better motive for the bend in the edge of the aegis). The folds of the chiton under the left arm and of the edge of the mantle next it are more broken, less schematic and more natural. The upper part of the sleeve on the left arm is shorter and simpler, the folds of the mantle itself are heavier and better defined at the edges, the abdomen is not so visible under the folds as in the Farnese Athena. In all these peculiarities of the drapery the Hope statue more nearly resembles the Albani Athena, which we shall study immediately. Further, the position of the feet is slightly different in the two statues. In the Hope statue the left foot is not drawn back quite so far as in the Farnese, which is really in the walking attitude.

The assumption that these variations are all due to different copyists, and that there is only one original in the background, is not difficult to refute. For these alterations are not arbitrary caprices intended to suit a later taste; they are systematic, thoroughgoing distinctions, which manifest themselves most clearly just where the finest artistic feeling comes to light—that is, in the forms of the face.[3]

We next have to consider which of the two types is the older and more original,

---

[1] I have not seen the statue, but the engravings (*Spec. of Anc. Sc.* i. 25 and ii. 9) seem accurate and reliable. Cf. Michaelis, *Anc. Sculpt.* p. 290. The head is inserted, not broken: only the nose is restored. On the head A the nose seems to be ancient.

[2] I did the same in Roscher's *Lexikon*, i. 700.

[3] Of the Hope type I only know the one replica, now lost, of which we possess a cast. The Farnese type exists in five replicas: (*a*) fragment of head in Dresden, formerly placed on one of the Lemnia statues, Becker, *Augusteum*, i. 15; cf. *supra*, p. 5; (*b*) statue in the Louvre, wrong head, Bouillon, iii. stat. Pl. 2, 4; Clarac, 320, 852; Fröhner, 115; now No. 1650; (*c*) Demidoff statue, wrong head, Clarac, 470, 895; (*d*) Albani statue, now lost, Cavaceppi, *Raccolta*, i. 1; Clarac, 458, 901; a sketch of it in Quatremère de Quincy, *Jup. Olymp.* (1815), Pl. 9, 4. The statue is exactly like the Farnese one, except that the eyes are hollow. Winckelmann expresses great admiration for this statue, and distinguishes it clearly from the Albani statue with the skin helmet. When he speaks of the *Pallas in hohem Stil* of the Villa Albani, *e.g.* (*Hist. of Anc. Art.* Bk. viii. 2, § 4; tr. Lodge, ii. 133), he invariably means the Cavaceppi statue, not the one with the skin-helmet, as Friederichs, *Bausteine*, 86 (=Wolters, 524), maintained. Cf. the Meyer-Schulze ed. vol. iv. p. 339, n. 331 =tr. Lodge, i. 476, and for the profile Pl. XVIII. A of the latter work. According to the *Specimens of Ancient Sculpture* (on i. 25), this Albani statue was brought to Paris: it is, however, not to be found in the Louvre.—A head in Palazzo Torlonia is very similar to, but not quite identical with, the Farnese type.

and which is the derivative. After our enumeration of the separate distinctions the answer can scarcely be doubtful: the Hope type is the earlier. The position of the feet and the treatment of the drapery are evidences of an earlier stage of development; the long curls on the breast and the lower forehead are equally certain marks of the same; and in general the greater naturalness and simplicity which we have observed in this work imply a greater degree of originality.

Pheidias himself must be the author of the Hope type. The head is another example not only of marvellous and peculiar beauty, but of a style purely Pheidian. In essential and personal characteristics its kinship to the Lemnia is so close as

FIG 28.—Profile of the head of Athena (A, Fig. 25).   **Fig. VII—Athena Farnese Head, Naples Museum**

to carry conviction. Quality of this sort is not easy to define in words; all we can do is to lay stress on certain details. The forehead, slightly raised in the middle, is very delicately modelled; the eyebrows are curved as in the Lemnia,[1] the line being more nearly horizontal than in the Athena Farnese. Thus the part between eyebrow and upper lid is sparely modelled and slightly concave, a peculiarity which the Lemnia and the Hope types have in common, and which distinguishes them from the Farnese type. Again, the thin eyelids, the gentle transition between the under lid

[1] It was when I observed the analogy between the Dresden cast A and the Bologna head that it first occurred to me that the latter was a copy of the Lemnia.

and the cheek, the narrow, finely cut nose forming a decided angle with the forehead, are as many points that resemble the Lemnia and differ from the Farnese head. Lastly, the mysterious beauty of the mouth may be compared to the Lemnia. The general contour of the face, too, with its slender and refined proportions, is similar. The hair recalls the style of the Lemnia; it springs out in soft full masses, on which the separate lines are vigorously but not deeply cut. Although the hair of the Farnese head is dressed in the same way, the rendering is harder and more schematic.

Compared with the Hope type the Farnese head seems rough, even coarse; it is also beautiful, but its beauty is as the beauty of a head by Giulio Romani beside one by Raphael. The master who made it was on less intimate terms with nature than the creator of the Hope type: he aims at more powerful effects, and, in doing so, becomes more conventional and formal. The deeper mysteries of Pheidian beauty were unrevealed to him; his coarser sensibilities expressed themselves in ruder forms which possibly seemed to him more appropriate to the powerful personality of Athena.

Wherever in modern art we have opportunity for comparison, we find that between the works of the really great masters and those of their most immediate and favoured pupils a great gulf is fixed. However remarkable the external similarity of their works, in the finer inner elements they are wide apart, for the 'inimitable never lies in externals.'[1] No wonder, then, if we recognize a decided difference between the work of Pheidias and that of the pupil to whom we owe the Farnese type.

The work of Pheidias should be assigned to the period shortly after the Parthenos. The wreath of snakes round the aegis follows the new system of which the Parthenos affords the earliest example.[2] There is more animation and freedom in the attitude, the left foot being turned more outwards and drawn farther back than in the Parthenos. The goddess thus conceived manifests neither the serious severity of the Lemnia nor the solemnity of the Parthenos in her hall of state. She is gentler and softer. With an animated gesture of kindly greeting she bends her head and steps forward to receive her worshippers. In her right hand she bore, not the Nike of processions, but more probably only a kylix. Her drapery is softer and richer than in the other statues; she wears not the peplos of the severe maiden, but the old Ionic costume, which at that time, as we see from vases, was still in great vogue in Athens.

It is extremely likely that the original was of bronze; perhaps it was the very statue mentioned by Pliny (xxxiv. 54) which Paulus Aemilius dedicated in Rome.

In the Villa Albani is a bronze head barely half life-size, broken off a statue, and fixed on an alabaster figure to which it does not belong.[3] It is a noble head of admirable workmanship, a free rendering of the Hope Athena. The side-curls are missing, and the hair leaves the ears freer. Otherwise not only in externals but in expression the head corresponds with the Hope—not the Farnese type. This is a very valuable monument, which deserves to be better known.[4]

In the same Villa is the well-known Athena wearing the skin helmet (Fig. 29).[5] The great similarity of the body with that of the Hope statue compels us to

---

[1] Justi, *Velasquez*, ii. 283.   [2] Compare *supra*, p. 10.

[3] Clarac, Pl. 462 C, 902; Villa Albani, No. 945. Sphinx and griffins on the helmet are restored. The alabaster figure is antique, but does not belong to the head.

[4] Winckelmann, *Hist. of Anc. Art.* vii. 1, § 21 (Vol. v. 89, note 2, ed. Eiselein), calls it 'a glorious head of a lofty character' (tr. Lodge, ii. 385); later critics seem to have overlooked it. (Cf. Roscher's *Lex.* i. 700, 23.)

[5] Friederichs-Wolters, *Gipsabg.* 524; Helbig, *Museums*, 781; Brunn-Bruckmann, *Denkm.* No. 226.

FIG. 29.—Athena in the Villa Albani, Rome.

Fig. VIII—Lapith Woman, West Pediment of the Temple
of Zeus at Olympia, Olympia Museum

FIG. 30.—Head of Athena Albani. (From the cast.

draw a close analogy between the two. The drapery is essentially the same, except that here the *diploïs* is longer, while the position of the legs differs only in so far that the left foot is rather less drawn back in the Albani statue than in the Hope. Indeed, all the earlier features which the Hope statue shows in contradistinction to the Farnese type appear in rather more pronounced form in the Albani statue. Another mark of older origin is the thick stiff edge of the aegis and the arrangement of the snakes.

This work must be connected in some way with Pheidias. The idea that it may have been one of the prototypes from which he worked may be dismissed, for how should Pheidias at the highest point of his creative power have clung so closely to a type by another artist? The head-type is another proof to the contrary (profile, Fig. 30); for it is remarkably severe in style, so that there is a certain incongruity between head and body. This is a mark, not of an independent creative artist of the first rank, but of an inferior worker who failed in unity of conception.[1]

[1] The curious hide (clearly that of a wolf or dog, and *not* of a lion) drawn over the head deserves elucidation. Winckelmann rightly observed that the muzzle was pointed, and called it a dog-skin, *Hist. of Anc. Art.* ii. 2, § 21 (=tr. Lodge, p. 184, and note, p. 428). A similar head-covering in ancient art occurs, so far as I know, only in the following instances : (*a*) on a youthful male winged figure on an Attic statuette-vase belonging to the end of the fifth century (*Ath. Mitth.* 1882, Taf. 12, p. 381 *sqq.* Mylonas)—the cap corresponds exactly to our statue ; (*b*) on two images of Hades in Etruscan tombs of the fourth century (Conestabile, *Pitt.* xi. ; *Mon. d. Inst.* ix. 15) ; (*c*) on a head on a coin of Amisos of the first century B.C. (Brit. Mus. *Catal. Pontus*, etc., Pl. 4, 3, p. xvi., Head, *Hist. Num.* 425) ; (*d*) it is worn by Athena on two Roman monuments from the neighbourhood of Trèves (Hettner, *Röm. Steindenkmäler*, No. 27, d. ; 55) : the pointed ears show quite clearly that the head is that of a dog, and not of a lion. In (*b*) it is certainly the cap of Hades, the Ἄϊδος κυνέη of the Epos, which, by a play on words, is represented as the skin of a dog (cf. Helbig, *Annali*, 1870, 27) ; the type must be of Greek invention. The same interpretation is very likely correct for (*a*), and the daemon carrying off the girl may be Thanatos ; in a replica in Berlin (Vases, 2906) the figure wears an ordinary Phrygian cap, and the artist probably had some other intention. In the case of (*c*) also this interpretation seems the most likely, for the head, which I think is male, probably represents Perseus, so often celebrated on the coins of Amisos : he is wearing the cap of Hades. The corresponding head-covering for Athena can hardly have a different meaning. The passage in the Iliad where Athena in the conflict with Ares puts on the cap of Hades (v. 845) seems to prove that in some cultus known to the poet Athena possessed the Ἄϊδος κυνέη as an attribute. Such, for instance, might be the cultus of Athena Itonia, who was worshipped together with Hades in her old sanctuary near Koroneia (*Strabo*, p. 411) ; Foucart's proposal (*Bull. d. Corr. Hell.* 1885, 427 *sqq.*) to read Ἄρης for Ἅϊδης is made impossible by Pausanias, ix. 34, 1, who calls the companion god Zeus ; Hades might be confused with Zeus, but not so Ares. It is instructive to note that the same Homeric singer who thinks of Athena as wearing the cap of Hades also gives her the surname Ἀλαλκομενηΐς (Il. iv. 8 ; v. 908) ; the ancient sanctuary at Alalkomenai was the nearest neighbour of the Itonian sanctuary (for locality see *Bull. de Corr. Hell.* 1894, 475) ; the group of Hades and Athena by Agorakritos, in the Itonian temple, probably survives on a gem (Gori, *Mus. Flor.* ii. Pl. 72, i. ; Müller-Wieseler, ii. 226 ; Overbeck, *Zeus*, 46 *sqq.*; *Gesch. d. Plastik*, 3rd ed. i. 278) ; the two divinities are here enthroned. Now Athena Itonia was also worshipped in Athens, and in the fifth century she

The other hypothesis, that the work is by a pupil of Pheidias, is disproved by the evidence of the head, which is of an earlier type, and has features which entirely differ in style from the work of Pheidias. A third possibility remains, that the work is by a contemporary of Pheidias, who belonged to a school more dependent on early tradition, but who made use of the creation of Pheidias as a prototype for the body and drapery of his statue.

What this school was we shall be able to define more exactly if we look at the head of the statue; for the head is in style the immediate successor of a closely connected group of monuments, of which the Hestia Giustiniani, the 'Aspasia,'[1] the so-called Omphalos Apollo, and the 'Charioteer' of the Capitol are among the most pronounced examples.[2] The Albani Athena represents a later stage of the same style. We have already assigned (p. 55) two heads of Pheidian period, the river god of the Braccio Nuovo and the Capitol head (Fig. 11), to the artist who made the original of the Albani statue. To these we may add, as nearly related, the so-called Lysias of the Villa Albani (No. 62), and a beautiful head of a youth

FIG. 31.—Head in Munich.

in Munich (Fig. 31),[3] of somewhat freer style. These works form a close group sharply differentiated from other contemporary productions by the arrangement of the hair over the forehead, the formation of the lower part of the face, and the peculiar expression of the mouth.

Now this school, whose earlier stage falls about 480—460, and whose later stage coincided with the career of Pheidias, about 460—440, may in my view be identified with the school of Kalamis, for this master of *quadrigae* and *bigae* was very probably the author of the charioteer.[4] A work like the Albani statue would certainly be very appropriate to Praxias, the pupil of Kalamis and contemporary of Pheidias.

There are many other traces of this Kalamidian influence which kept its own

had her own treasury there, and therefore perhaps also her own image (*C. I. A.* i. 210), of which the Albani statue may be a replica. On the vase-painting of the severe R. F. style (*Mon. d. Inst.* vi. 58, 2) there is a hint of Hades being associated to Athena in Athens; Athena is placed—not beside Zeus, Hera, and Apollo, but—beside Poseidon and Hades, towards whom she turns her head. For a cult of Athena Itonia in Thessaly, cf. Paus. x. 1, 10. (*d*) would seem to prove that the cult of Athena Itonia made its way as far as the Roman provinces of Trèves.

[1] There are two good copies: (*a*) Berlin, *Skulpt.* 605; *Arch. Ztg.* 1877, Taf. 8. (*b*) Louvre, No. 558 (phot. Giraudon, 1219). [2] *Bull. d. Comiss. Commun. di Roma*, 1888, Tav. 15, 16; Helbig, *Museums*, 597.

[3] Glyptothek, 49. A very similar head in Palazzo Torlonia.

[4] For the Omphalos Apollo as presumably a work of Kalamis cf. 50th *Berl. Winckelmannsprogr.* p. 150.

M

side by side with that of Pheidias. For example, in the interesting 'Demeter' with the veil[1] of the Berlin gallery pose and drapery has been influenced by Pheidias, and seems to be more recent than the Parthenos, while the head is a direct successor of the 'Aspasia' type.

The Herakles head of severe style, also in Berlin[2] (Fig. 32), while belonging to this group, has a character and individuality of its own. I believe that the body corresponding to this type of head survives in a Herakles torso of the Louvre[3] (Fig. 33) which may be regarded as a direct development of the Omphalos Apollo. The position and attitude are the same, the bodily forms also are similar, though rounder and freer. Herakles has tied the lion-skin round his neck, the end of it falls over his outstretched left forearm, the right hand rests on the club ; the hind at the left has certainly been added by the copyist.

We must now return to Pheidias, and try to gain some more exact knowledge about the pupil who created the Farnese Athena type. The great number of existing copies justifies the conclusion that the artist was famous and distinguished.

Here too we must be guided by the type of head, always the part of a statue on which personal style is most clearly impressed. The nearest parallels to the Farnese type are three closely related heads, each of them preserved with its statue. These are the Capitoline 'Hera' or 'Demeter,'[4] the 'Venus Genetrix,'[5] and the Barberini 'Hera' of the Vatican.[6] The three are remarkably alike in arrangement and rendering of hair, and in the essential characteristics of the facial forms—such as the outline of the rather broad face, the form of the forehead, the attachment of the nose, the mouth, and the somewhat heavy eyelids—except that the Aphrodite has been distinctly modified through stress being laid on the qualities of grace and charm. To these three sisters we may now add the Farnese Athena as a fourth.

Many have agreed with me in identifying the 'Genetrix' with the famous Aphrodite of Alkamenes ; this point may now, I think, be considered fairly settled.[7] In the Capitoline statue Petersen conjectures we have the Hera of Alkamenes.[8] I cannot feel quite sure that the work is a Hera,[9] but it is certainly by the artist of the Aphrodite. Lastly, the Barberini 'Hera,' usually but incorrectly supposed to be of much later

[1] *Skulpt.* 83 ; Overbeck, *Atlas d. Kuntsmyth.* Taf. xv. 25. In a painting by Michelangelo Cerquozzi (1600—1660) in the Cassel gallery, No. 516, this statue is represented standing on a pedestal in a garden ; the arms are still unrestored.

[2] *Skulpt.* 188. The bust seems to be identical with the one published in the *Gall. Giustin.* 2, 26. The head is antique only as far as the neck, which is of Parian marble, while the restored bust is of coarse inferior bluish marble. The head was originally turned to the right, as may be seen by the fact that the right ear is carelessly worked, and the left ear well rendered.

[3] No. 1404, Salle des Caryatides.

[4] Overbeck, *Atlas d. Kuntsmyth.* xiv. 13, 20 ; *Antike Denkm.* i. 55, 1 ; Helbig, 507.

[5] *Antike Denkm.* i. 55, 2 ; *Gaz. Arch.* 1887, Pl. 30.

[6] Helbig, *Museums,* 301 ; Overbeck, *Atlas,* ix. 10, x. 33.

[7] Cp. *supra,* p. 9, note 3. The doubts expressed by E. Reisch (*Eranos Vindobonensis,* p. 18 *sqq.*) are easily refuted. He asks why, out of the great number of Aphrodites of the Pheidian epoch known from literature, only the Aphrodite of Alkamenes should be taken into account in estimating the *Genetrix* figures. But that 'great number' consists solely of the two Aphrodites by Pheidias in Athens, and in Elis, and of the Aphrodite ἐν κήποις, by Alkamenes. R. argues further that this garden Aphrodite was an Aphrodite Ourania, and as the impersonation of 'heavenly' love must have looked more matronly than the *Genetrix*; but, first, we do not know that the Aphrodite ἐν κήποις was surnamed Ourania ; and, secondly, even if she were, that ethical meaning of the surname is a philosophic notion dating not earlier than Plato (cf. Plato, *Symp.* viii. D ; Preller-Robert, *Gr. Myth.* i. 355), and can therefore have had no influence upon Alkamenes.

[8] *Röm. Mitth.* 1889, 65 *sqq.*

[9] The figure on the relief mentioned by Petersen cannot be a copy of the statue. It only shows that Hera was represented in the same costume, and we know from the monuments that the same type was used for different goddesses.

FIG. 32.—Head of Herakles (Berlin).

Fig. IX—Centaur and Lapith Boy, West Pediment of
the Temple of Zeus at Olympia, Olympia Museum

date, shows clearly by the type of head [1] that it is a work of the same artist, nor is there anything in the style of the body to contradict this view.[2] The transparent chiton is treated as in the Aphrodite, and the piece slipping down over the left breast betrays the same taste. Whether the statue was originally intended for a Hera is a question we must set aside for the present.[3]

The Farnese Athena, then, is probably also a work of Alkamenes, doubly valuable to us because it shows in what relation the artist stood to his master Pheidias. We have seen that in the head-type he followed out his own ideal—an ideal inferior, it would seem, to that of Pheidias. The Aphrodite and the Athena show that within its limits he could individualize strongly. He introduces the complete walking motive—(in this respect the Athena and the 'Hera' Barberini are closely allied)—and everywhere strives after stronger effects than the master— a tendency which removes him proportionately far from the simple observation of nature.[4]

According to an anecdote which has only reached us in a late and evidently exaggerated form,[5] but which undoubtedly contains a kernel of truth, Pheidias and Alkamenes made rival statues of Athena for a competition in which Pheidias obtained the prize. The story cannot be a mere late invention; it evidently underlies the statement made by Pliny, and more in detail by Pausanias,[6] to the effect that Alkamenes was a contemporary and rival of Pheidias, but obtained in competition with him only the second prize in respect of knowledge in the making of statues. Now the story of such a competition might easily be invented by a later generation, if two Athena statues very similar to each other were in existence, one by Pheidias and one by Alkamenes. We have now sufficient evidence from the Hope and Farnese statues for the assumption that this really was the case.

Alkamenes seems to have been a very productive artist,[7] whose works were much prized and extensively copied in antiquity. He must be largely represented among existing antiques.[8] A beautiful head over life-size, an admirable copy,

---

[1] The head of the Vatican statue is not broken, but inserted with a piece of the chest, very well preserved. A good replica of the head is in Museo Chiaramonti, No. 511 A ; Overbeck, *Atlas*, ix. 11. The head of the replica formerly in the Villa Borghese, and now in Copenhagen, is the bust ; it has never been separated from the statue ; no diadem.

[2] The Palatine torso, now in the *Terme*, is not an exact copy, but adds Hellenistic details.

[3] The sarcophagus (*Mon. d. Inst.* iv. 9) quoted in support of the theory gives Hera an entirely different type.

[4] On the ground of the statues just discussed some few more works may be ascribed to Alkamenes : *e.g.* the type of the so-called Hera of Ephesos known unfortunately only in a torso (Friederichs-Wolters, 1273), which exists in several replicas (cf. Lanckoronski, *Pamphylien u. Pisidien*, i. p. 94) ; it was also used in Imperial times for portraits.—The much-restored Stockholm head, *J. H. S.* ix. 4 (p. 35, Farnell), belongs also to this series.

[5] Tzetzes, *Chil.* 8, 340 *seq.*, 353 *seq.* ; Overbeck, *S. Q.* 772, 810. Cf. *supra*, p. 21, where it was suggested that the first part of the anecdote may have arisen from the existence of a statue by Pheidias set upon a column.

[6] Plin. xxxiv. 49 : Pheidias flourished Ol. 83, *quo eodem tempore aemuli eius fuere Alcamenes* (the following names are arbitrarily added by Pliny ; cf. my essay, *Plinius u. Seine Quellen*, p. 22 *seq.*) Paus. v. 10, 8 : Ἀλκαμένους ἀνδρὸς ἡλικίαν τε κατὰ Φειδίαν καὶ δευτερεῖα ἐνεγκαμένου σοφίας ἐς ποίησιν ἀγαλμάτων. This passage has been much misunderstood (also by me, *Preuss. Jahrb.* vol. li. 380 ; the later literature is quoted *Jahrb. d. Inst.* 1890, p. 97, note 37), owing to the connexion with that anecdote not being recognized.—Plin. xxxvi. 16, where Pliny expressly names Alkamenes as pupil of Pheidias, and only as such, goes back to another source.

[7] *Opera complura* in the temples of Athens, Pliny, xxxvi. 16.

[8] Lately Winter thought he had discovered two *originals* by Alkamenes (*Jahrb. d. Inst. Anz.* 1894, p. 44, 46) ; but the statue of the Akropolis cannot represent Prokne and Itys. It is an insignificant coarse piece of work ; it is quite impossible that Alkamenes should have dedicated such a monstrosity to the goddess (Paus. i. 24, 3), or exposed it to the ridicule of his fellow-artists. The other statue from Pergamon is obviously not a fifth-century original, but only the copy of one ; its workmanship is quite similar to that of the Athena of Pergamon (*supra*, p. 27). The treatment of the drapery differs totally from that of the originals of the Pheidian school.

certainly after Alkamenes, is reproduced in Fig. 34.[1] The body is unknown. The hair is gathered into a coif like that of the Aphrodite and of the 'Hera' statues; the stylistic treatment of the waves of hair, the thick eyelids, and the shape of the ear are the same. It is difficult to decide whom the head represents. The form of cheeks and chin and the full mouth resemble the Farnese Athena, so that the head very probably represents a bareheaded Athena.[2]

The works of Agorakritos, Pheidias's second pupil of distinction, must have been

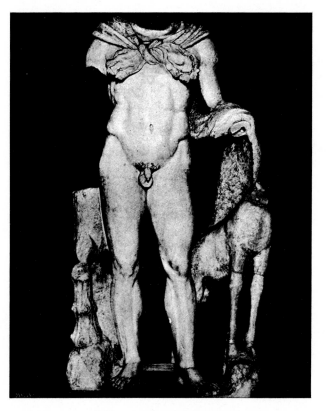

Fig. 33.—Torso of Herakles, Louvre. (From a photograph by A. Giraudon.)

Fig. X—Hercules Mastai, Vatican Museum

closely allied to those of Alkamenes. This is clear from the remaining figures of the basis of the Nemesis of Rhamnus: their type of face and the rendering of the thin transparent chiton[3] recall the works we assigned to Alkamenes. Among the statues

[1] Berlin, *Skulpt.* 608. Length of face 32 cm. The end of the nose is restored. Compare L. Mitchell, *Hist. of Sc.* p. 321, and Roscher's *Lexikon*, i. 413, Z. 1. A head on a statue in the *cortile* of the Pal. Borghese (Matz-Duhn, 1374) appears to be a replica.

[2] In Roscher's *Lexikon, loc. cit.*, I was misled by the stylistic resemblance of the head to the *Genetrix* into thinking it an Aphrodite, but the forms are too massive and powerful, the carriage too vigorous and erect, for the φιλομμειδής.

[3] Ἐφημ. ἀρχ. 1891, Taf. 8, 9; *Jahrb. d. Inst.* 1894, Pl. 1—7. Cf. especially Ἐφ. 9, 1 = *Jahrb.* i. 6, with the Hera Barberini and the Ephesian torso. In the *Jahrb., loc. cit.* p. 16, Pallat makes some correct observation

FIG. 34.—Head of a goddess (Berlin).

Fig. XI—Detail of Lapith Woman, West Pediment of
the Temple of Zeus at Olympia, Olympia Museum

Fig. XII—Head of Girl from Chios, Boston, Museum of
Fine Arts

FIG. 36.—Apollo Barberini (Munich).

FIG. 35.—'Ceres' in the Rotonda of the Vatican.

FIG. 37.—Athena in Capitoline Museum.

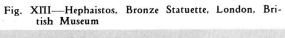

Fig. XIII—Hephaistos, Bronze Statuette, London, British Museum

-MARBLE HEAD FOUND IN ROME, AND NOW IN THE VATICAN MUSEUM (larger than life size).

-Hermes of Alca-
enes. (Constantinople.)

represented by existing copies there are three which, although they resemble the work
of Alkamenes and are certainly to be referred to a pupil of Pheidias, yet point to

a different personality. They form a closely
compact group. The heads have been preserved with the bodies. I mean the colossal
' Ceres ' in the Vatican (Fig. 35),[1] the Barberini
Apollo in Munich (Fig. 36),[2] and an Athena
in the Capitol (Fig. 37).[3] Even external
details, such as the peculiar wide girdle, the
folds in the hem of the *diploïs*, besides the
rendering of other parts of the drapery and the
attitude, prove that the three works are all by
one man. I am inclined to name the artist
Agorakritos, and to see in the 'Ceres' his
famous Nemesis.[4] This artist conceives divinities otherwise than Alkamenes : his gods walk
with solemn processional gait, looking straight
out, with head erect. The artist aims at giving
a general effect of majestic dignity rather than
at individualizing like his fellow-pupil.

Statues of male divinities by Alkamenes
must certainly exist. I believe that the Hephaistos admired by Cicero survives in a beautiful statue at Cassel. Unfortunately it is only
a torso, but the workmanship is unusually
good (Fig. 38).[5] That it is a Hephaistos and
a work of the Pheidian school seems to me
self-evident. The torso wears the *exomis* of
the craftsman, girt with a leather strap. On
the left shoulder lies a small cloak which fell
down over the outstretched forearm.[6] The
chiton is treated in the style of the Parthenon
frieze.[7] The torso stands in a specially close
relation to the Orpheus relief, another monument of this epoch. Here the clinging drapery,
the fall of the folds between the legs,[8] and
the delicate folded hem on the thighs and

FIG. 38.—Conjectural restoration, showing the torso in
Cassel combined with the head of the Hephaistos
Chiaramonti.

on the difference between the treatment of drapery still observed on the Parthenon frieze and that of the
Agorakritos basis and other later works.

   [1] Helbig, *Museums*, 297 ; Brunn-Bruckmann, *Denkm.* No. 172.
   [2] Munich, Glypt. 90.   Replica, *Bull. Commun.* 1887, Tav. 20, 21.
   [3] In the lower hall, No. 3 ; Clarac, 461, 858.   An important work with a genuine head spoiled by the
modern curls on the shoulders ; behind the ears are remains of the original curls.   The head is very like the
Barberini Apollo.
   [4] The head seems to correspond with the original fragment (Brit. Mus. *Cat.* 460 ; cf. Rossbach, *Ath. Mitth.*
xv. 46) ; a large diadem formerly rested on it.   The hair is simply taken up behind, the left arm is wrongly
restored as raised.
   [5] Cassel, ii. 9.   The statue was a short time in Paris, and is engraved by Bouillon, ii. stat. *Thésée.*   The right
interpretation as Hephaistos is hinted at in his text.   The beautiful youthful head does not belong to the statue.
Our sketch, Fig. 38, gives the antique parts without the restorations ; marble Pentelic, workmanship fresh and good.
   [6] The beginning of the elbow is still in existence.   [7] Cf. north frieze, 133 ; west frieze, 23.
   [8] Best example Villa Albani, 1031 = Helbig, *Museums*, 790 ; other replicas in Louvre, Naples, etc.

upper arm[1] are so surprisingly like the torso that one is inclined to assign both works to one artist. The peculiar formation of the body proves that the torso represents Hephaistos. The chest is broad and robust, and what is left of the arms (especially the right) shows a powerful muscular development. On the other hand, it is noteworthy that the remains of the legs—*i.e.* the knees and parts immediately around them—are unusually small and slender. Now the combination of a strong body with weak legs is a characteristic of Hephaistos already established in the Homeric poems.[2]

An Hephaistos from the school of Pheidias, as we have seen the Cassel torso to be, could hardly be any other than a copy of the famous statue of Alkamenes formerly in Athens. We know from Cicero[3] that the figure stood with both feet planted on the ground. So did the torso; the weight of the body is on the left leg, and the right foot is placed at ease a little to one side, but with the sole full on the ground. Cicero says the figure was draped, and in this point also the torso corresponds. The attitude of repose notwithstanding, Cicero professes to see the lameness of the god plainly indicated in the statue; but he remarks that this is done without detracting from the beauty of the figure. It seems clear from this that the figure must have resembled our torso. Like other authors who wish to say something witty and epigrammatic about a work of art, Cicero perhaps read rather more into the statue than the unbiassed observer will find there. Strictly speaking, a limp in the gait could not be expressed in a figure standing on both feet; we may be sure that Alkamenes did not wish, any more than the Attic vase-painters, to make the god limp, but he suggested the characteristic peculiarity in a sufficiently true and natural manner by the contrast between the slender legs and the powerful body. The head, now lost, no doubt gave more effect to this contrast by its broad, strong forms. I believe that the head-type survives in the well-known term of the Vatican, so eloquently analyzed by Brunn.[4] In order to show how well this head would suit the torso, I have combined them in the drawing.[5] The term is only a poor, shallow, and sketchy copy, worked with a plentiful use of the drill. Yet in the rendering of the curls of hair, in the massy arrangement of the beard, and in the large eyes it is easy to recognize the style of the later Pheidian epoch. The form of the hair rising on the forehead is very like the Asklepios head of the same school.[6] We need hardly lay stress on the masterly way in which Alkamenes has individualized the head.[7]

The artist shows himself no less great in the creation of his Ares. The statue by Alkamenes in the temple at Athens is preserved to us, as I think we may now assume, in the famous Ares Borghese and its replicas.[8] The head is stylistically

[1] Cf. the striking agreement between the right upper arm of the Hermes on the Albani replica and the left upper arm of the torso.   [2] Cf. Roscher's *Lexikon*, i. 2039.

[3] Cicero's words are : *Volcanum . . . in quo stante in utroque vestigio atque vestito leviter apparet claudicatio non deformis.* Reisch, *loc. cit.* p. 21, suggests that this Hephaistos was identical with the temple-image mentioned Paus. i. 14, 6, as standing together with Athena ; he further identifies these two statues with the two images named in *C. I. A.* i. 318, 319, which must have been completed in 421—420. His further attempt to recognize the Athena in the distinctly Praxitelean Borghese statue (Helbig, *Museums*, 935) is not so happy.

[4] *Mon. d. Inst.* vii. 81 ; Brunn, *Götterideale*, Taf. ii. ; Profile, p. 23 ; Helbig, *Museums*, 89. Löschcke refers the head to Alkamenes.

[5] The head of the torso was evidently turned as it is in the term. It is true that the neck of the term is thicker than the neck of the torso, to judge from what remains. But the copyist may easily have increased the size of the neck in order to adapt it to the terminal bust. The head is not broken, and the greater part of the term is antique.

[6] Cf. especially the Palatine head, now in the Terme ; and the head of the Naples statue, Roscher's *Lexikon*, i. 634.

[7] The inequality of the two sides of the face (Brunn. *loc. cit.* p. 25) is due to careless execution.

[8] Conze (*Beiträge*, p. 9, note 2) already inclined to ascribe this work to Alkamenes. The ring above the

analogous to the Hephaistos, the body and the attitude are both purely Attic.
The Diskobolos 'taking up position,'[1] long ago ascribed to Alkamenes, is its nearest
parallel. It is also instructive to compare this Ares with a helmeted and bearded
head,[2] of which the best replica is the so-called 'Miltiades' in the Louvre, a work
belonging to the period of the Parthenos, and so pronouncedly Pheidian in character
that it may with some reason be ascribed to the master himself (Plate IV.)

Alkamenes thus becomes a personality we can grasp.[3] We have seen what his
relations to Pheidias were, and how his creative instinct asserted itself independently.
None of the works referred to him are earlier than the late period of Pheidias—*i.e.*
than the epoch of the Parthenon frieze. What we otherwise know about his life
shows that his activity must have extended to the close of the century, when he
executed the commission for Thrasybulos (Paus. ix. 11, 61), about 403 B.C., and made
the Dionysos for the new temple beside the theatre at Athens. According to
Dörpfeld's observations of the material used in the foundations, this temple must
be later than the Periklean buildings.[4]

To return to the master himself—for we have not yet enumerated all the works
which may be brought into direct relation with him.

Even among the Athena heads there is one more which is not, like so many others,
a derivative from the Pheidian types, but apparently a new creation of the master's,
belonging to the period when he was working on the Parthenos. The magnificent
head, intended to be inserted into a life-size statue, is at present in the museum
at Brescia (Fig. 39).[5] A helmet, presumably of metal, was placed on the head,
the back of which was only roughly hewn out; only the edge of the helmet is
indicated just on the forehead. The curls escaping from under the edge of the
helmet, and spreading as far back as the ears, are remarkably like those of the
Parthenos, and are purely Pheidian in style.[6] The wavy hair which falls closely round
the neck, although a new feature for Athena, is most appropriate to the maiden
goddess, and occurs besides in two works of Pheidias—the *Terme* Apollo, and the
Zeus of Olympia. The profile of the forehead which slightly swells out below, the

---

right ankle, which occurs only in the Borghese, not in the other replicas, must have been added by the copyist to
illustrate the favourite story of Ares bound by Hephaistos. Immediately above the ring on the inner side of the
leg is a hole (antique) filled with lead. This probably served to fasten some part of the fetter. The copyist
wished to represent Ares in love, a favourite conception of later times. He did not understand that the
melancholy earnestness in the face was appropriate to the god of war, and had nothing to do with love-
stories.   [1] Helbig, *Museums*, 331.

[2] Cf. p. 36, note 1. Replicas of less importance in the Capitoline Museum (Helbig, 488) and in
Pal. Colonna. The helmet resembles that of the Parthenos; the beard, that of the Poseidon on the Parthenon
frieze.

[3] The belief in the existence of an older Alkamenes is based on an old suggestion of mine (*Ath. Mitth.*
1878, p. 194; cf. Löschcke, *Westl. Giebelgr.*, Dorpater Progr. 1887, p. 7). But the only testimony which could
make this assumption necessary—that of Pausanias concerning the artist of the west pediment at Olympia—seems,
like the corresponding information about the east pediment, to be a random statement. What Pausanias remarks
in the same passage on the relations of Alkamenes to Pheidias is, as we saw above (p. 84), nothing but a
jumbled reproduction of the anecdote respecting the rivalry of the two artists. Further, Köpp (*Jahrb. d.
Inst.* 1890, p. 277) has shown that the story of the destruction of the temple of Hera (Paus. i. 1, 5) by the
Persians is a mere invention: the Hera therefore is of no use as a date, any more than the Hekate, as
we shall see later on (Appendix).

[4] Kindly communicated to me by Dörpfeld; cf. *Jahrb. d. Inst.* 1890, 276, note. A full exposition will be
given in Dörpfeld's forthcoming work on the theatre. Cf. E. Reisch in *Eranos Vindob.* 1893, p. 1. He dates
the Dionysos on historic grounds, B.C. 420—413.

[5] Dütschke, *Oberitalien*, vol. iv. No. 335; Labus, *Museo Bresciano*, i. 44, 2. Length of face, 0·17. A
good copy.

[6] Dütschke, *loc. cit.*, compares this to the Bologna head (*i.e.* the Lemnia).

Fig. 39.—Head in Brescia. (By permission of Messrs. Bruckmann, Munich.)

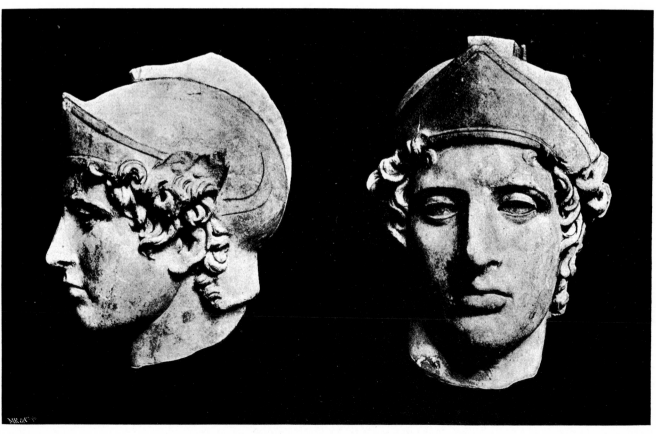

Fig. 40.—Head of Ares, Louvre. (From a photograph by A Giraudon.)

obtuse angle formed by nose and forehead, the slightly receding lower part of the face, the formation and expression of the full mouth and even the elongated ear— are, as is evident from a comparison with facts so far established, purely Pheidian in character. The head is decidedly later than the Lemnia, and perhaps even than the Hope Athena ; the characteristic part between upper lid and eyebrow is, especially towards the temple, much softer and more naturally modelled than the same part in the Hope Athena : if the copies are trustworthy in this point, it follows that the Brescia head is the more recent of the two. The whole expression bears out this view. The quiet repose and restraint to be observed in the Lemnia and the Hope Athena are lacking here. The carriage of the head is freer and bolder, the face shows the power and full proportions which apparently were characteristics of the Parthenos.

In this series may be further placed a beautiful head of a youth with a helmet, known from two copies in the Louvre (Fig. 40)[1] and the Museo Torlonia respectively.[2] In the latter replica the frontlet is adorned with a design in relief of a little Eros surrounded by sprays. This, although of course an addition of the copyist, enables us to determine the original meaning of the head. It must represent Ares, for Ares in love was a favourite theme of later artists ; the copyist's addition here is to be explained much in the same way as the fetters on the Ares Borghese (p. 89, note 8). The ears, swollen as from the boxing-contest (especially clear in the Torlonia copy), are quite appropriate to the war god. I know no other copies of the head, and no torso which could belong to it. A helmeted head in the Lateran,[3] placed on a statue that does not belong to it,[4] is closely analogous to the Louvre head ; but it is only a variant, and not a replica.[5]

A colossal Ares statue in the second *cortile* of the Palazzo Borghese is another interesting work (Fig. 41).[6] The head, which has never been broken, shows many points of similarity with our Paris type, though it is not a replica. It is turned more decidedly to the left, the edge of the helmet on the forehead is different, and the hair, notwithstanding a general resemblance, varies in detail ; finally, slight whiskers have been added similar to those worn by the Ares Borghese of the Louvre. The motive of the statue is much the same as that of the Munich Diomede, a work to be assigned, as we shall try to show later, to Kresilas. The right hand is lowered, and doubtless held the sword, while the empty scabbard is suspended on the left side ; the left hand probably held a spear. The chlamys falls from the shoulder in perfectly simple folds.

[1] Louvre, No. 2986, in the same room as the Ares Borghese. Thasian marble. First discussed by Treu, *Arch. Anz.* 1889, 57. He referred it to Polykleitos. I subsequently thought of Kresilas (*Arch. Anz.* 1891, 36). Restored in plaster : nose, left upper lip, most of left eyebrow, and left upper eyelid.

[2] *Museo Torlonia*, Tav. 26, No. 104. *Galleria Giustiniani*, ii. 45 (here the Eros in front is wrongly drawn as a sphinx ; on the helmet appear the antique remains of an animal couchant to serve as plume-bearer ; in the Museo Torlonia the figure has been restored). The nose and chin are restored. The points of hair over the forehead are broken away.

[3] Helbig, *Museums*, 638.

[4] Also observed by Overbeck, *Ber. d. Sächs. Ges.* 1861, p. 80. A replica of this torso in Lansdowne House (Michaelis, p. 453, n. 63) preserves the original head, which is that of Marcus Aurelius. From the workmanship, which belongs approximately to the period of this Emperor, it is probable that the Lateran statue also represented Marcus Aurelius.

[5] As Treu had pronounced it to be, *loc. cit.*

[6] Matz-Duhn, *Zerstr. Bildw.* No. 1338. The figure is much defaced, owing to exposure ; the head was never broken. Restored : nose and chin (lips formerly), right arm, the left hand, and the lower part of the body. The latter was probably made to replace a still existing but battered original. This seems evident from the complete correspondence in style, and from the fact that a piece of unbroken drapery belonging to the antique upper part of the torso hangs down below the join, which would hardly be possible if the whole of the lower part of the body had not been originally preserved.

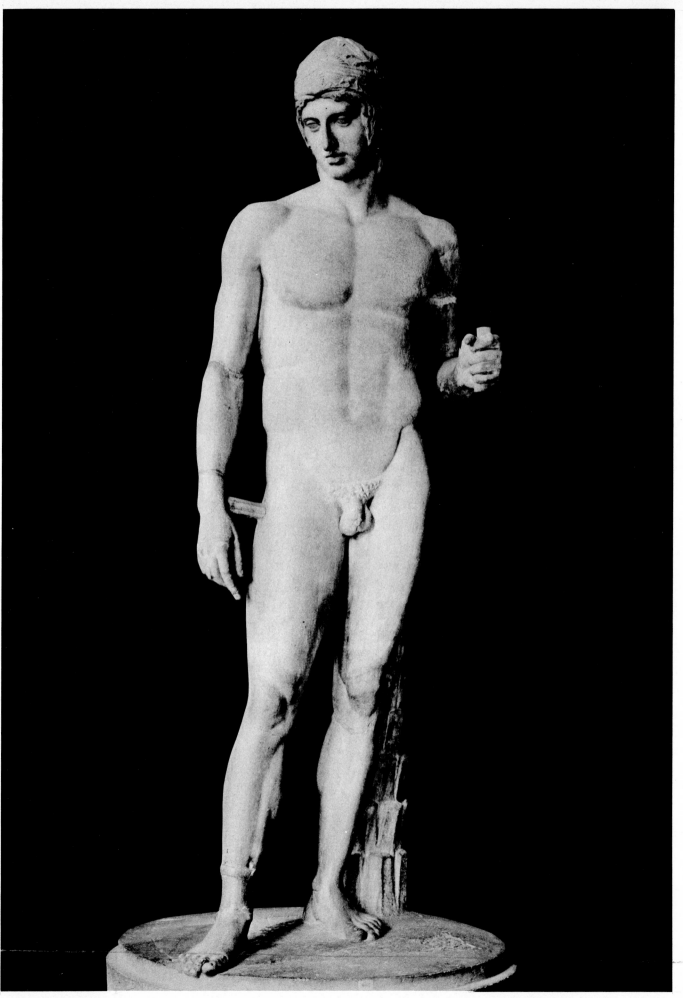

Fig. XIIIa—Ares Borghese, Louvre. (See p. 89 seq., 148)

We possess, then, three variants of the same type: (*a*) the variant represented by the Paris and Torlonia heads, body unknown; (*b*) the Lateran variant, body unknown; (*c*) the variant in the cortile Borghese, of which both head and torso are preserved.[1] I do not think that these variants are merely due to the copyists. The Borghese statue and the Paris head give the impression of being essentially faithful copies from fifth-century originals. Of these originals we may suppose that one was a new creation by a distinguished artist, and the others more or less dependent conceptions

Fig. 41.—Ares in the Pal. Borghese (Rome).

by inferior artists of the same period. Now there can be no doubt that of the three variants the Paris head has the best claim to represent the original creation. It is analogous to the Parthenos, and must be a product of the circle of Pheidias. The curls are bunched out in front of the ears and partly cover the edge of the helmet, in a manner marvellously similar to that shown in the Parthenos and in the Brescia head

[1] The head of the so-called 'Theseus' at Ince Blundell Hall (Michaelis, p. 351, No. 43; *Arch. Ztg.* 1874, Taf. 1) may be a fourth variant. I have not seen the original, but Michaelis doubts whether the head belongs to the body; or the latter, cf. *infra*, p. 359, n. 3.

discussed above. The ' Aphrodite ' (p. 68) and the Anakreon should also be compared. The treatment of detail is somewhat freer than in the other works ; the Ares must at any rate be later than the Parthenos. The helmet is another point of likeness : like that of the Parthenos, it has three plumes, the middle one supported by a sphinx,[1] and turned up cheek-pieces decorated with griffins rampant.[2] I can see nothing to prevent our attributing the original to Pheidias himself. Individuality manifests itself specially in the lower part of the face ; the distance between nose and mouth is rather longer than usual, and the lower lip recedes ; the mouth is close, the chin firm, the forehead broad and powerful. The head is held upright with an easy turn to the right. It conveys an impression of youthful defiance and brave resolution, of passion latent in sensuous beauty. And these are traits eminently characteristic of Ares.

The Ares Borghese of the Louvre, which we have attributed to Alkamenes and compared to a bearded and helmeted Pheidian head (Plate IV.), should now be compared with this Pheidian Ares : it is clear that the system of form common to the Parthenos and to the Pheidian Ares is very different from that affected by the younger artist. Starting from the same principles, the later work has developed and emphasized the older conception, and brought in new elements. The Ares of Alkamenes seems restless and excited beside the other, and more stress is laid on the gloomy wildness of the god's personality : instead of the carefully dressed curls which belong to the style of the Parthenos, the hair hangs straitly, giving an effect of neglect and carelessness intended perhaps to indicate the Thracian origin of the god.

X. *The Dioscuri of Monte Cavallo, and the Elder Praxiteles.*

We have kept for the end a magnificent creation of Pheidias belonging to the last period of his activity. Not only is this work easily recognizable from the style, but it has the additional advantage of being authenticated by an inscription. I refer to one of the two colossal figures on the Monte Cavallo in Rome—to the one holding the horse with the right hand, whose basis bore till 1589 the antique inscription[3] *opus Fidiae.*

Strangely enough, this work has been so misunderstood that even at the present day people are astonished if it is ascribed to the artist whose name is attested by the inscription.

This inscription is of a kind of which there are many examples in Rome. They are preserved on the bases of statues, but the statues themselves are lost. These works, designated as *opus Polycliti, opus Bryaxidis, opus Praxitelis, opus Tisicratis, opus Timarchi,*[4] were, as no one disputes, either originals by the artists named, set up again in Rome, or copies from these originals. The similar inscription Λυσίππου ἔργον on a copy is definite evidence for the last case,[5] sometimes the formula ὁ δεῖνα

---

[1] Cf. p. 92, note 2.

[2] The legs of the griffin are still to be seen on the Louvre head. The cheek-pieces of the Borghese head are ornamented in the same way.

[3] It is well known that when the Colossi were set up again in the year 1589 the two artists' inscriptions were not only renewed but reversed. The antique inscriptions designated the figure holding the horse with his right hand as the work of Pheidias, the one holding the horse with his left hand as the work of Praxiteles. We keep exclusively to the antique designations.

[4] Cf. Löwy, *I. G. B.* 489 *seq.*

[5] Löwy, 506 ; for the genuineness cf. *Hermes,* vol. xxii. 153.

ἐποίει is used on the copy to designate the artist of the original.[1]   The fact that the
Colossus of Monte Cavallo can as a matter of course not be an original by Pheidias
is no evidence against the correctness of the inscription, since copies were marked in
the same way.   Nor should the date of the inscription (late Imperial epoch)[2] arouse
any suspicion as to its exactness.   The two Colossi originally formed the decoration
at the entrance of a large building:[3] to judge by their workmanship, they cannot
be later than the earliest period of the Empire.   In more recent times they were
placed as nearly as possible in their original positions on a massive pedestal of
masonry into which were built older architectural fragments,[4] probably belonging
to the building at whose entrance the Colossi at first stood.   The pedestal was
faced ·with marble slabs, and on these stood the inscriptions in fine large letters.[5]
It is of course possible, though very unlikely, that the inscriptions were invented
at that time.   The fact that so much trouble was taken to re-erect the statues
on large and handsome pedestals proves that they were works of some note, and
that the inscriptions were merely renewals of older ones.   Such renewals must
have been frequently necessary in ancient Rome, where works of art were constantly
changing locality.   The ascription of these two statues to their respective artists
probably took place in the same early Imperial period to which the precisely similar
inscriptions quoted above belong.   There is no reason to suppose that any one of
these was arbitrarily invented: on the contrary, all the facts seem to point to the
conclusion that such inscriptions formed a storehouse of authentic material on which
were based many of the literary notices of works of art in Imperial Rome.

Only in one case could we be justified in rejecting the testimony of the inscription
—i.e. if the style of the statue were absolutely at variance with the style of the artist
whose name it bears.   Now it will not be difficult to show that exactly the reverse is
the case.

It has, it is true, been maintained that the style has nothing to do with Pheidias.
Martin Wagner the sculptor, the first who made a close study of the style,[6] confines
himself to combating the opinion that the statue was an original by Pheidias: he
misses the 'geistreiche Auffassung der Natur' to be seen in originals, and finds here
only a 'mehr systematischen, auf Regeln gegründeten Vortrag'; according to him the
works are Roman.   Otfried Müller[7] was more definite, and maintained the style to
be not Pheidian but Lysippian—a theory which has found many adherents.   It is
strange that the eye can be so deceived!   For in the whole range of ancient art of
the free style no stronger contrast exists than that between these statues and the
works of Lysippos.   Any one who will take the trouble to examine the matter for
himself, even only through the medium of photographs, will I am sure be convinced
that this is so.

The two Colossi of Monte Cavallo (quite irrespective of the inscriptions) can be
accounted for historically and artistically in no other way than by referring them to
the circle of Pheidias, within which they more especially belong, to the epoch of the
Parthenon friezes and pediments.   Placed side by· side with these originals, the
Colossi at first naturally suffer by the comparison.   They lack the spontaneity and
refined execution which form the peculiar charm of first-hand work.   While in the
Parthenon figures the muscles seem to show naturally under the skin, in the Colossi

---

[1] Cf. e.g. Löwy, 488 ; Röm. Mitth. 1891, 323, etc.   [2] Cf. Löwy, p. 326.
[3] Fogelberg, Ann. d. Inst. 1842, 202.   [4] From the testimony of Flaminio Vacca.
[5] Cf. the engravings of Lafrérie.   [6] Kunstblatt, 1824, p. 373 sqq., 381 sqq.
[7] De Phidiae Vita et Op. i. § 8, note (Kunstarch. Werke, ii. 13).

they are more drily rendered, 'mehr schulgerecht,' as Wagner expressed it. But
the same laws of style are obeyed. The different parts of the body are marked
off in large distinct planes—in direct contrast to the rounded modelling and fine
transitions of fourth-century technique, which reached their highest development
under the influence of Lysippos. The structure of the mighty chest is specially
characteristic. In the metopes of the Parthenon, even in those of freer style, the
chest is less developed than in the figures of the frieze and pediments, to which
the Colossi correspond. Further, the manner in which the edge of the ribs projects,
and the modulation of the abdominal muscles (cf. especially the deep depression
between the straight and oblique muscles, and the *inscriptiones* of the former),
are precisely the same on the Colossi and the torsos M and H of the west and
H of the east pediment of the Parthenon.[1] The evidence of the heads is equally
plain (Fig. 42). In this respect also the youths of the Parthenon frieze afford the
nearest analogy—the heads turned to the front and wearing a slightly excited
expression, such as No. 2 of the west frieze (Pl. V.), are surprisingly like the Colossi.
For the profile, No. 118 of the north frieze should be compared. The shape and
modulation of the forehead, the sharp edge of the eyebrows, the wide-open eyes, the
complete absence of all those natural forms which art after Praxiteles and Lysippos gave
to the parts around the lower eyelid both in the region of the nose and of the temples,[2]
the formation of the mouth and chin, the characteristic wavy lines of the hair which
frames the face as with a crown of rays, even the way the fillet cuts in and the
hair rises on either side of it—all this is as genuinely Pheidian, and of the Parthenon
period, as it is diametrically opposed to the style of Lysippos. Each one of the
forms analyzed would be strong proof by itself; taken all together, they remove all
possibility of doubt. Only the difference in size, and the fact that the Parthenon
frieze is original work while the Colossi are copies from bronze, make some variations
inevitable; in artistic essence and individual style they are the same.

Again, it is striking how nearly the horses of the Colossi correspond with those of
the Parthenon frieze, and how widely they differ from those of later art—compare,
for instance, the sculptures of the Mausoleum and the basis of Bryaxis,[3] or, as a stronger
contrast still, the horses on the Pergamene reliefs. In the proportions of the bodies,
in the relation in size to the human figures, in the details of form—especially in the
head—in the shape of the eyes, the jaw, the nostrils, and particularly of the lower half
of the mouth—these horses of the Colossi resemble those of the Parthenon frieze and
pediments, except that they lack the fire and spirit of the originals. I say nothing
of the armour and drapery. It has long been acknowledged that the coat of mail is
an addition of the copyist, who wanted a marble support for the outstretched leg
of the figure. The piece of drapery hanging from the arms, which is evidently meant
to serve the same purpose, is most likely another addition of the copyist.[4] It is not
worked as clearly and definitely as the other parts of the figure.

[1] Even the *pubes* is characteristic, and quite different from the Lysippian.

[2] Precisely those peculiarities which Hugo Magnus (*Die Darstellung des Auges in der Antiken Plastik*, 1892)
dwells on are quite decisive in favour of assigning the works to the Pheidian epoch. They consist in the
extremely sharp arch of the eyebrow and of the upper rim of the eye-socket, in the modelling of the space
between that upper rim and the upper eyelid, and in the absence of any indication of the lower rim of the eye-
socket. It is strange after this accurate analysis that Magnus (p. 76) should separate the figures of Monte
Cavallo from the Pheidian epoch : he was misled by the deep hollowing out of the iris and the pupil; but this is a
most unessential detail; the copyist added it because in such a colossal work he could not rely on the effect of a
merely painted eye-pupil (cf. Conze, *Sitzungsber. Berl. Akademie*, 1892, Febr., p. 49 *seq.*); the bronze originals
had of course inserted eyes.

[3] *Bull. de Corr. Hell.* 1892, Pl. 3, 7.   [4] Cf. p. 56, note I.

O

FIG. 42.—The Dioscuri of Monte Cavallo. (From the cast.)

FIG. 43.—Head in the Jacobsen collection at Copenhagen. (By permission of Messrs. Bruckmann, Munich.)

FIG. 44.—Head in the Louvre.

Finally, the motive of the youths with their horses and the rhythm of their movement are special to the Parthenon and its artistic circle. It has long been noticed that one group, the youth leading the horse with his right hand, reappears in very similar form on the west frieze of the Parthenon (No. 27).[1] And the same figure—the one designated by the old inscription as the work of Pheidias—occurs again in all its essential features on another authenticated work of Pheidias, the relief on the basis of the Athena Parthenos.[2] The only distinction is that the youth on the basis leads with his right hand not one horse but a team of four. The horses are rearing in both instances. If then it be admitted that Pheidias used the 'horse-taming' motive, the question next arises whether it was his own invention or borrowed from another artist. All the evidence seems to be in favour of the former view. The motive in its principal features—a broad swinging stride to the right, the head thrown well to the left, one arm (usually) raised, the other bent at an angle—enters Greek art as a complete idea, and from the time of its entrance becomes a common property to be employed over and over again. It is quite unknown before the time of the Parthenos. It first appears in that free and animated style which we have learned to recognize as the style of Pheidias in his Parthenos epoch (cf. p. 44 *seq.*) Among the metopes of the Parthenon this 'horse-taming' motive is met with only in a few of the freest examples;[3] on the 'Theseion' it appears only in the frieze[4] (which is similar in style to the more advanced metopes of the Parthenon), and not in the metopes at all; it is represented on the shield of the Parthenos as well as on the basis, it is quite familiar on Parthenon frieze and pediments, and in all works nearly related to the style of these sculptures, such as the reliefs of Phigaleia, a certain series of Attic vases, etc.[5] We may, then, assume that Pheidias, if not actually the inventor of the motive, is principally responsible for its adoption into Attic art.

Formal analysis has taught us that the Colossi of Monte Cavallo, irrespective of their inscriptions, must be referred to originals from the epoch of the Parthenon frieze and from the circle of Pheidias. This being so, we have no grounds for doubting the correctness of the traditional inscriptions, which give us the artists' names: Pheidias and Praxiteles.

This Praxiteles is no longer unknown. He is of course identical with the artist of the Promachos (p. 32). This statue, we saw, was a work closely connected with Pheidias, perhaps partly invented by him, and we drew thence the conclusion that Praxiteles was an intimate colleague of Pheidias. This accords admirably with the facts gathered from a study of the Colossi of Monte Cavallo and the inscriptions. The two figures are conceived in the same spirit, and there must have been a strong bond between the two artists. Such collaboration and division of labour were common enough in antiquity in the case of larger commissions involving several figures.[6] It was a great mistake to imagine that the two different artists' names inscribed on the Colossi could not possibly both be correct. Yet if a work of this kind is to have any general uniformity of character, the root-idea must be the invention of one mind. In the present case we surely cannot be wrong in ascribing this root-idea to Pheidias, though in the working out of it and in the execution of the details each of the artists concerned would become alone responsible.

[1] Cf. also north frieze No. 58, and the Hermes on the Echelos relief, Ἐφημ. ἀρχ. 1893, Πιν. 9.

[2] In the portion given by the Lenormant statuette. Cf. *supra*, p. 45.

[3] South xiv. xvi., East ix.

[4] Cf. Overbeck, *Plastik*, 3rd ed. i. 348, Fig. 5.

[5] Those named on pp. 44, 45.

[6] For instances corroborated by inscriptions see Löwy, *I. G. B.* p. xv. In addition to these we have the examples handed down by literature.

In spite of the great similarity between the two figures and the disappearance in the copies of many an individual and distinctive trait which no doubt existed in the originals, we can still detect differences in the artists. The work of Praxiteles—the youth holding the horse with his right hand and turning his head to the left—shows more stress and fire in the attitude. This difference comes out most clearly in the heads (Fig. 42, 1, Praxiteles ; 2 and 2 a, Pheidias). The head by Praxiteles has a more passionate, free, and enthusiastic expression, and on this account has been generally preferred to the other.[1] This is just the distinction which we found to subsist between the Promachos and the works of Pheidias : in the Promachos, too, we found a mood of greater excitement expressed by a more restless and animated exterior. We could however assert this only of the body, for the head of the Medici torso is lost.

Yet the head of the Promachos, the work of Praxiteles, seems to have been preserved in one copy. This is a colossal head of the Jacobsen collection in Copenhagen (Fig. 43). We saw that the Promachos held her head turned to the right, and showed in her whole attitude defiant warlike excitement. The Copenhagen head corresponds admirably to such a conception, and I think every one must be struck by the similarity in style to the heads of the Dioscuri, especially to the one by Praxiteles. The vigorous movement, the expression, the forms of the individual features, more particularly of the open mouth and the chin, are wonderfully like. The angle formed by forehead and nose is rather more marked in the Athena, thus pointing to a slightly earlier date. The hair springs out in full masses in front of the ears, and recalls the Lemnia rather than the Parthenos.[2]

If we imagine the Medici torso completed by this head [3] or one of its replicas, and the arms restored with lifted shield and lance held ready for the fray, we have a majestic and moving image of the war goddess gazing in joy of conflict and assurance of victory from her citadel away across city and country towards the quarter whence her worst enemies threaten—whence a few decades later was to come the power which crushed and overthrew her proud supremacy.

The originals of the Monte Cavallo Colossi can hardly have stood in Athens. They represented, there is little doubt, the Dioscuri.[4] Hence it seems probable that the Colossi were set up in some city specially devoted to the cultus of the Dioscuri, where

---

[1] Cf. Friederichs, *Bausteine*, p. 128 (= Wolters, p. 456), where the names have changed places according to the modern mistake.

[2] The copyist has used the borer freely, and apparently not understood his original. The work recalls the Parthenos copy in Berlin, *Ant. Denkm.* i. 3. On lips and nostrils and on the frontlet of the helmet are traces of red colour. The back and the upper part of the head are made of separate pieces. Holes in the ears for earrings. The teeth are indicated, the lower edge of the frontlet is broken, it originally ran downwards in a point, as in the Parthenos.

[3] The face of the Jacobsen head is 31 cm. long. This would agree approximately with the dimensions required by the proportions of the Medici torso. There is a curious similarity between the shape and size of the hollow intended to receive the head on the torso Medici and the portion of bust which is prepared for insertion in the Jacobsen head. Both form an ellipse narrowing into a point in front ; on the torso the length is 40—41 cm., its breadth 32 cm. ; on the head length and breadth are 43 cm. and 24 cm. respectively. It is certain, however, that the head does not belong to the torso Medici, but to a replica of it with a similar hollow for the head.

[4] The coin of Maxentius quoted by Donati shows, it is true, the Dioscuri standing quietly and the horses rearing. But the Dioscuri are represented in the motive of the Monte Cavallo group—on a sarcophagus now in the Museo delle Terme (in the centre a married couple, on each side a Dioscurus with his horse in the Monte Cavallo motive, but with the addition of pileus, chlamys, and sword ; workmanship of the third or fourth century A.D.) The fact that the Colossi do not wear the pointed cap does not tell against the interpretation, as in the fifth and fourth century B.C. this attribute was not yet given to them. (Cf. Roscher's *Lex.* i. 1172.)

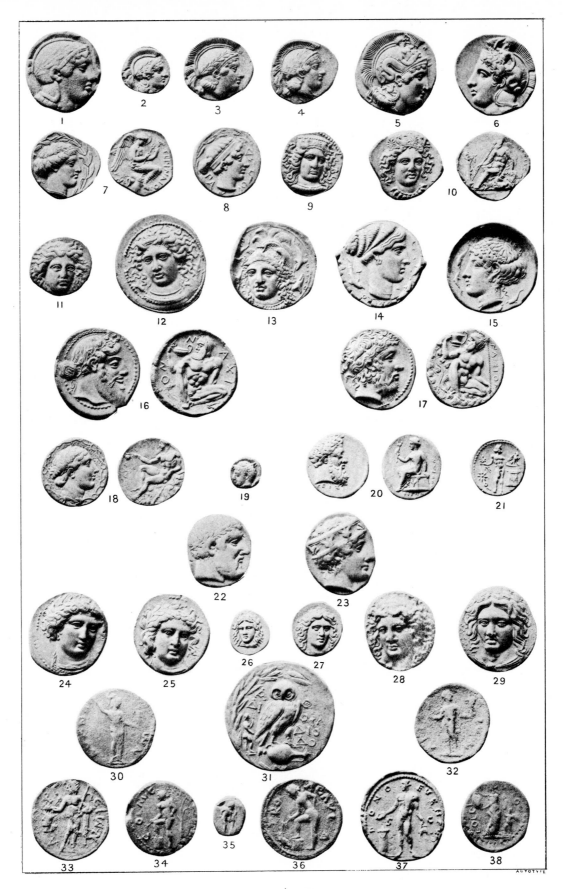

*Plate VI

Greek Coins.

1, 3, 5, 6. Thurii.—2. Sybaris.—4. Neapolis.—7. Terina.—8, 10. Pandosia.—9. Hyria.—11. Neapolis.—12-15.
Syracuse.—16, 17. Naxos.—18. Herakleia.—19. Phokaia.—20. Lokri Epizephyrii.—21. *Roman denarius.*—
22, 23. Elis.—24, 25. Amphipolis.—26. Miletos.—27-29. Klazomenai.—30, 31. Athens.—32, 33. Argos.—
34, 36. Alexandria Troas.—35. Heraia.—37. *Coin of Antoninus Pius.*—38. Corinth.

a huge votive gift of the kind would be appropriate. Such a city was Tarentum,[1] where bronze Colossi were in great favour, and whence the originals could easily have been removed to Rome. The copies are adapted as decoration for a gate, but it does not follow that the originals served the same purpose. Nor is the symmetry of the composition a proof of decorative intention. In ancient art, from the earliest to the latest times, symmetry was a necessary factor in the typology of the Divine Twins. The one is always the exact counterpart of the other. Originally the horses would be placed not at a right but at an obtuse angle to the figures, according to the more natural arrangement. Since the publication of Wagner's penetrating remarks on the subject it is generally and rightly assumed that the originals were of bronze, and if so they were probably not decorative, but intended to stand free.

The Dioscuri belong to the time of the Parthenon frieze. The Promachos, which we assigned to the years between 445 and 440, is therefore a somewhat older work of Praxiteles than the Dioscuri—a conclusion which we reached independently from a study of the style.

It remains to find out whether anything more is known about this Praxiteles. He is of course the elder Praxiteles, long acknowledged as a person distinct from his younger namesake.[2] However, since all conjectures concerning this artist have hitherto been of extreme vagueness, it will be best to sum up what is really known, rejecting what is false or untenable. First of all we have the notice in Pausanias (i. 2, 4) about the γράμματα ἀττικά on the group of Demeter, Kore, and Iakchos, but this only gives us a general date before the time of Eukleides. More definite information is supplied by the statement that the temple image of Hera at Plataia was by Praxiteles, for the splendid large temple to which this ἄγαλμα μέγα belonged was built in 427—426 (Thuc. iii. 68). This would roughly give us the period from B.C. 445 to 425 for the activity of the elder Praxiteles, who accordingly would be a somewhat younger contemporary of Pheidias, and would be still at work in the time of the Peloponnesian War.[3] His works themselves have shown us that his connexion with Pheidias was a close one; Pheidias must have held him in high esteem, and probably obtained for him the commission to make the Promachos. Very soon afterwards the two artists in collaboration made the group of the Dioscuri. No doubt the commission was intrusted to Pheidias, and he is responsible for the original design, but Praxiteles brings his individuality strongly to light in the figure which bears his name. Although standing in the shadow of one greater than himself, his own significance and importance cannot be concealed.

The idea we have formed of the work produced by the elder Praxiteles is well illustrated by an interesting head (Fig. 44), of which there are two replicas,[4] representing

[1] The cultus of the Dioscuri at Tarentum is proved by numerous coins and terra-cottas; it was derived from Laconia.

[2] Cf. Klein, *Oesterr. Mitth.* 1879, 8; Brunn, *Bayr. Sitzber.* 1880, 443; Kroker, *Gleichnamige Künstler*, 44; U. Köhler, *Ath. Mitth.* ix. 78; Robert, *Arch. Märchen*, 62, 156.

[3] The Artemis on a kylix of about 480 cannot, as Robert, *Arch. März.* p. 156, assumes, be referred to the Brauronia. I consider Studniczka's hypothesis about the latter very probable (cf. *infra* on Praxiteles, p. 323). The head called 'Iakchos' by Winter (*Bonner Studien*; cf. *supra*, p. 55) is too severe for our Praxiteles. If Praxiteles worked with Kalamis (Pliny, xxxiv. 71), it could only have been at the end of the period of Kalamis, and this does not justify the supposition that the style of Praxiteles was severe.

[4] (*a*) Fig. 44; in the Louvre, No. 2547, from the Coll. Campana; d'Escamps, *Marbres Campana*, Pl. 63. The whole neck with the term, the lower part of the curls, the nose, the upper lip, and the back of the head are restored. (*b*) Vatican, *Mus. Chiar.* 145; Visconti, *Mus. Chiar.* i. 10; Müller-Wieseler, *Denkm.* ii. 119; Overbeck, *Apollo*, p. 118; Helbig, *Museums*, No. 72. Poor late work. Brows and pupils plastic. Fillet in the hair (not in *a*).

a delicate youth with rich curls falling over his forehead and down over his neck. The Pheidian manner is evident in the stylistic treatment of hair and face, particularly in the eyes and mouth. But a slight hint of inward excitement, the mouth open as if to ask an impatient question, and the intentional *asymmetria* of the hair over the forehead, are signs of the artistic tendency we have already traced in Praxiteles. Moveover, the type of head is remarkably like the Eubouleus of the younger Praxiteles (Plate XVI.)[1]— so like that there must be a bond of some kind between the two productions. The essential features are the same, but they are worked out in the one instance according to Pheidian tradition, in the other after the manner of later Praxitelean art. It is very instructive to notice how the same idea is expressed in the

*Plate XVI
Head of Eubouleus.
ATHENS.

forms of two widely different epochs. The hair lies in the same general scheme of arrangement, but the style of rendering is not the same. Forehead and eyes differ; only in one detail the older head—if we may trust the Louvre copy—oversteps the Pheidian circle and touches on the newer formation—*i.e.* the lower eyelid is more definitely set off from the cheek, through the indication of the lower rim of the eye-socket, a nicety of modelling not customary in the fifth century.

As the 'Eubouleus' of the great Praxiteles certainly represents an Eleusinian divinity, the interpretation of the earlier head must be sought for within the same

[1] The head in the Louvre is therefore also called Virgil, like the replicas of the Eubouleus in Rome and Mantua. Both the Louvre head and a head in the Villa Albani (No. 48, 'Alessandro'), which I also attribute to the elder Praxiteles, have already been touched upon in connexion with the 'Eubouleus' by Benndorf in the *Anzeiger d. Wiener Akad.* 1887, 16th Nov.

mythological circle. It is probably a copy of the Iakchos of the elder Praxiteles.
The delicate face framed in curls would answer admirably to the ὡραῖος θεός

FIG. 45.—'Jupiter de Versailles' (Louvre).

(Aristoph. *Frogs*, 395) who stood as torch-bearer beside Demeter and Kore.[1] The elevated beauty of this head accounts for its great popularity in Athens (Cic. *in Verr.* iv. 60, 135).

First among other surviving works belonging to the same series of Pheidian works as the Monte Cavallo horsemen may be placed the fragment of a colossal statue, the 'Jupiter de Versailles' in the Louvre (Fig. 45).[2] The head is near akin to the Dioscuri, the strong undulating hair, the form of the forehead, the large eyes, and the open mouth being unmistakable evidences ; even the hair on the upper part of the head and on the neck behind shows correspondence. The short curled beard, on the other hand, recalls the earlier Pheidian manner as exemplified in the Barberini head (Fig. 12). The majesty and energy of the whole conception have no parallel except in the Dioscuri. Unfortunately only the upper part of the body survives. A mantle passes behind from the right hip to the left shoulder, the right arm was stretched forward. The short hair and the excited expression seem to me less appropriate to Zeus than to Poseidon. It is possible that this statue also may have its source in a work of the elder Praxiteles.[3] At any rate it must have proceded from the school of Pheidias. I may mention in conclusion a female type with waving, fluttering hair and open mouth, known in different variants, and representing a goddess of animated nature.[4]

XI. *Pheidian Influences in Sicily and Magna Graecia.—Coins and Vases.*

It is not, however, my intention to write an exhaustive treatise on the works of the Pheidian school ; I only aim at tracing a ground-plan for future investigation. I believe we have found in the Lemnia on the one hand, and in the Dioscuri on the other, two fixed points which represent the opposite poles of Pheidian art : here calm repose, there impetuous motion ; here manifold threads of connexion with old forms, there the full freedom of the new style.

---

[1] This Iakchos was certainly not represented with horns. The βουκέρως Ἴακχος (Sophokles, frag. 871, Nauck) is not the Iacchos of Attic cultus, but only a poetic name for Dionysos : it is expressly stated that he dwells on Nysa, which is true of the bull-Dionysos, but not of the Attic Iacchos. The poetic blending of Iakchos with Dionysos, which occurs from Sophokles downwards (cf. especially *Antig.* 1115 *seq.*), does not prove that the mingling had taken place in Attic cultus and art of the fifth century.

[2] Bouillon, i. 1 ; Müller-Wieseler, *Denkm.* ii. 4 ; Overbeck, *Kunstmyth. Atlas*, Taf. 2, 15, 16 ; *Zeus*, p. 83, No. 14 ; Fröhner, *Not.* No. 31.—Our illustration omits the restorations.

[3] There was a Neptune by Praxiteles, possibly the elder, *in Pollionis Asinii Monumentis*, Plin. xxxvi. 23.

[4] Head on a statue in St. Petersburg (*Compte Rendu*, 1881, Pl. VI. 1, 2). Similar, but not identical, is the head of the Vatican Artemis (Helbig, *Museums*, 37).

But in order to make our notion of these two consecutive developments of Pheidian art still more complete and definite, we must see how they were reflected and reproduced in coins. And first we must emancipate ourselves from the current dating adopted for the coins in question. When coins can only be dated from their style, this should only be done by reference to the fixed points gained by a study of the aggregate of other monuments, and especially of sculpture. It is true that in this way only the date when any given type arose can be discovered, and not the period of its duration, which, as Athenian coins show, is sometimes disproportionately long. From the point of view of art, however, it is just the period of the rise of the coin-type that is the most significant.

In B.C. 445 ten ships sailed westwards from Athens to found Thurii, which in B.C. 443 was strengthened by immigrations from all parts of Greece. The new colony naturally had the same patron goddess as Athens, and on its coins was stamped a head (Pl. VI. 1, 3) whose typical features—form of helmet, wreath of olive, arrangement of hair—were taken straight over from the Athenian coins of the period.[1] The severe style however, which had been retained in Athens from external reasons, was abandoned on the coins of Thurii; they follow the style of the time. Only in the rendering of the hair on the forehead with regularly waved contour and parallel inner lines is there an echo of the older prototype. The establishment of this type with the wavy front hair may certainly be assigned to the earliest period of the colony.[2] From the existence of numerous dies with slight variants it seems clear that the type held its own for a considerable time, but its place in the history of art is fixed by the fact that it is an Attic creation of the period when Pheidias was working at the Parthenos. Its close relation to the art of Pheidias is quite evident. This earlier type of Thurii most definitely recalls the Lemnia. The undulating front hair of the Lemnia (cf. p. 19), the line of her profile, with the low forehead and the nose at a slight angle to it, the restful beauty of the full closed mouth, and the finely wrought transitions in modelling—all this has no such close parallel on coins as the earlier type of Thurii. Somewhat later there appears in the same city a type corresponding to the later style of Pheidias and his circle; the hair above the forehead flows back over the edge of the helmet nearly as it does in the Parthenos, and the expression is more animated and restless than in the other coins (Plate VI. 6).[3]

Among the dies of the older type those signed Φ are specially fine. Among these are found both staters (the helmet with simple olive-wreath)[4] and distaters with Skylla on the helmet (Pl. VI. 5).[5] These dies are most probably the work of the artist who signs with a Φ in Terina, and whose personality makes itself so distinctly felt on its

---

[1] Cf. Head, *Guide*, Pl. 13, 21, 23, 30, and the imitations of this type in Lykia, *ibid.* Pl. 11, 38, 20, 39. On the Phokaian electrum *hektai* the type is very similar (Berlin Coll.), but without olive-wreath.

[2] This is most clearly proved by the small coins of New Sybaris, which was founded immediately after Thurii; the Athena head is exactly the same as on the older Thurii type (Garrucci, *Le Monete*, Tav. 108, 23, 25; Gardner, *Types*, Pl. I. 31, 16, 18 = our Pl. VI. 2). Further imitations of that Thurii type, which are to be traced in Kyme, must be dated before 420 B.C., in which year Kyme was destroyed. Head (*Hist. Num.* p. 71) follows the majority of numismaticians in dating the coins of Thurii after 420 B.C.; and the type with Skylla on the helmet he places after 390, although, as the style of face and hair proves, it must have arisen very soon after the type with the olive-wreath. Gardner (*Types*, p. 103) estimates the dates more correctly. [A beautiful early coin of Thurii (Brit. Mus. *Cat. Thur.* i.), belonging to the series referred to by Prof. Furtwängler, but still earlier than any of the examples he cites, has been pointed out to me by Mr. G. F. Hill. It is now published for the first time, Pl. VI. 1.—E. S.]

[3] *E.g.* Gardner, *Types*, Pl. V. 18; Garrucci, *Le Monete*, Tav. 106, 9, 10, 14; Friedländer u. Sallet, *D. Kgl. Münzcabinet*, Nos. 739 (pub. *ibid.* on Pl. VIII. but marked by mistake 736), 743.

[4] Head, *Guide*, Pl. 15, 7.

[5] Friedländer u. Sallet, *Das Münzcab.* No. 741; the head as in Head, *Guide*, 25, 17.

P

coinage.[1] His style, in the design of the seated Nike of the reverse (Pl. VI. 7), for instance, bears so surprising and unmistakable a resemblance to that of the Parthenon frieze [2] that he must have stood in the closest relations to the artist of the frieze—in other words, to Pheidias. His activity in Terina is evidently somewhat later than his Thurii period, for the Thurii work recalls the style of the Lemnia, while the head of the nymph on the coins of Terina is, like the reverse, in the manner of the Parthenon frieze. These coins of Terina, following, as they do, closely on coins of the period in which the trammels of archaic convention are still felt, must from evidence of style be dated in the same time as the Parthenon frieze—*i.e.* between 440 and 430 B.C.

It is highly probable that the same artist's hand is to be traced in the reverse of a coin of Pandosia,[3] also signed Φ. The young huntsman seated is quite in the manner of the Parthenon frieze (Pl. VI. 10). The obverse (*ibid.*) is even more striking, for it bears a head of Hera facing, with wavy hair fluttering out to the sides—another instance of the more recent Pheidian tendency, which we saw brought to expression in certain figures of the Parthenon frieze (Pl. V.) and in the Dioscuri of Monte Cavallo. The whole scale of gradation from the Lemnia to the Dioscuri, which we traced in the large monuments, is exactly reproduced, step by step—and this is a confirmation of the results attained so far—in the works of a die-cutter.

The remarkable fact that the Pheidian style in its different phases was carried straight from Athens to Lower Italy comes to light nowhere more clearly than on the coins just discussed. But the influence which transplanted art exercised on native work, principally through the agency of the colonists of Thurii, is to be traced in a number of other circumstances.

The types of the Athena heads of Thurii, especially the one with the regularly waved hair, were rapidly and widely adopted in Lower Italy. More particularly in the Greek towns of the Campanian coast, Kyme,[4] and Neapolis (Pl. VI. 4),[5] we find exact copies of the oldest type of the staters of Thurii. About the time when Thurii was founded, Athenians seem to have settled in Neapolis:[6] at all events it became a second centre from which Attic art spread to other places. The neighbouring Italians—not only the Campanians, but the inhabitants of Hyria, Nola, and Phistelia [7]—stamped on their coins the head of the Attic Athena. Other Greek

[1] Compare Stuart Poole, *Num. Chr.* 1883, 269 *sqq.* Pl. 11, 12. Poole was the first to emphasize the purely Attic style of these coins. In Terina the artist Φ distinguishes himself very clearly from his much less important contemporary and imitator, the artist who signs Γ.—Poole's attempt (p. 273) to identify the artist Φ with the artist who signs Φι, Φιλις, Φιλιστι, Φιλιστίων has been refuted by Evans, *Tarentine Horsemen,* p. 110, note. The Terina coin with Φιλις is quite different in style from those with Φ, and considerably later : it is by the same Philistion who worked for Velia, Tarentum, probably also for Metapontum and Herakleia, at the end of the fourth century (cf. Evans, *loc. cit.* 106 *sqq.*) Gardner's hypothesis (*Types,* p. 121), that the artist Φ might be Phrygillos, who made the bull for the reverse of the coin of Thurii, cannot be entertained, as this artist's style is quite different.

[2] The correspondence between *Num. Chron.* 1883, Pl. 11, 4, and the Athena of the Parthenon frieze is specially striking.

[3] Cf. Poole, *loc. cit.* p. 276, Pl. 11, 14 ; Head, *Guide,* Pl. 25, 22.—In the series of coins of Pandosia the type follows immediately on a head of severe style ; Head, *Guide,* Pl. 15, 11 ; *Hist. Num.* p. 92, fig. 60. The coin of Velia with Φ, which Poole, Pl. 11, 13, ascribes to the same artist, must, I think, be later.

[4] Poor example, Brit. Mus. *Cat. Italy,* p. 86, No. 6 ; a better one Berlin, exact imitation of the oldest staters of Thurii. Garrucci, *Le Monete,* Tav. 83, 27—29. Cf. *supra,* p. 105, note 2.

[5] Head, *Guide,* Pl. 15, 3 ; Garrucci, Tav. 84, 19, 85, 14.   [6] Cf. Busolt, *Gr. Gesch.* ii. 591.

[7] Imhoof-Blumer (*Wiener Numism. Ztschr.* 1886, p. 226) has shown that these coins of Campania were struck in Neapolis : the Athena head is identical on both. Among the coins of Hyria (cf. Imhoof Blumer, *loc. cit.* p. 206 *sqq.*) there occur exact imitations and freer modifications of the older Thurii type. The same Thurii die appears in Hyria and in Nola. As the nymph's head of free style on the coinage of Neapolis and Nola appears to be from the same die, it is probable that the Athena heads of Hyria and Nola were also stamped in Neapolis.—Small silver pieces of Phistelia with the older Thurii type in Berlin (not mentioned by Head, *Hist. Num.*)—Allifa : Garrucci, Tav. 88, 20.

cities, like Poseidonia[1] and Velia,[2] imitated the Thurii type; even proud Syracuse used it for small gold coins,[3] in the period about 430 B.C. Herakleia, too, which was founded in 403—402, stamped coins first with the earlier, then with the later, types of Thurii,[4] and the bareheaded Athena peculiar to Herakleia (Pl. VI. 18) is, as we saw above, a thoroughly Attic conception (p. 15), its nearest parallel in style being the older type of Thurii. Tarentum borrowed from her daughter-city for her small silver coin, the diobol, not only this bareheaded Athena (cf. p. 15), but notably also the helmeted goddess of the Thurii type.[5]

Next to the Athena type of Thurii, which recalls the Lemnia, that other and later Pheidian type, showing a head facing, with fluttering hair, exercised a powerful influence in Lower Italy. We found it in Pandosia adopted for Hera; it appears in Kroton and Poseidonia,[6] and again in Campania—i.e. in Hyria-Vesernia (Pl. VI. 9),[7] in a fairly exact copy of the Attic original belonging to Pandosia. Essentially the same type, except that the high headdress is replaced by a broad fillet, is seen on a series of beautiful coins from Neapolis (Plate VI. 11) and Phistelia.[8] This is the same head which we know in sculpture from the two variants in St. Petersburg and the Vatican (p. 104). On coins its noblest and most beautiful form is due to Kimon, the die-cutter of Syracuse, who made the famous head of Arethusa facing (Plate VI. 12). Arthur Evans has lately shown in a convincing manner that Kimon originally entered the circle of Syracusan die-cutters as a foreigner, and introduced into Syracusan coin-types certain elements belonging to Neapolis, such as the form of the earrings, and above all the type of head with the fluttering hair.[9] Now this type, like the Attic Athena, had come to Neapolis from Pheidias and his circle. Another design, to which we may ascribe Attic-Pheidian origin, is the beautiful Athena head with curly hair, wearing a triple helmet, which appears on the Syracusan tetradrachms by Eukleidas (Plate VI. 13),[10] and which seems, like the head on the St. Petersburg gold medallion,[11] to have been suggested by the Parthenos.

If we now pass from these minute details to the whole development of style in the coinage of Lower Italy and Sicily, we shall see that a sudden and almost universal revolution took place about 440 B.C. At the same time the coin-engravers begin to sign their works. Eumenes in Syracuse is the first to do so (Plate VI. 15).[12] The magnificent but hard features of the transitional Arethusa head

[1] Garrucci, Tav. 121, 36—38.

[2] The older Thurii type is rare (Garrucci, Tav. 119, 17); the later is more common (ibid. 119, 11).

[3] Head, Num. Chron. N. S. XIV. Pl. 3, 10. A better copy in Berlin; Head's date, 412, is certainly too late; the inscription also is older.

[4] Exact imitation of the old type on a coin in Berlin stamped over an incuse of Metapontum or Kroton; hippocamp on the helmet. Cf. Garrucci, Tav. 101, 19, 20, 36. Those with the griffin are late poor imitations of the type (ibid. 101, 31); those with Skylla (ibid. 101, 32) follow the later Thurii type.

[5] The earlier Thurii type, with a hippocamp on the helmet, as in Herakleia, Garrucci, Tav. 100, 5; the later in many variants, ib. Tav. 99, 51, 52; 100, 1—4. The reverse, Herakles with the lion, also corresponds with Herakleia.

[6] Kroton: Garrucci, Tav. 109, 37, 38. A later modification ib. 36, 39. Head, Guide, Pl. 25, 20. Poseidonia: Head, Hist. Num. p. 68; Garrucci, Tav. 121, 4.

[7] Imhoof-Blumer in Wiener Numism. Ztschr. 1886, Taf. v. 6—13.

[8] Fine illustrations in A. J. Evans, Syracusan Medallions, Pl. III. 1—3.

[9] A. J. Evans, Syracusan Medallions, p. 77 sqq.; Pl. III. (Num. Chron. 1891), where the imitations of Kimon's head of Arethusa facing are discussed; it was copied with special exactness at Larisa in Thessaly.

[10] Weil, Künstlerinschr. Taf. 3, 7; Head, Guide, Pl. 26, 31. Cf. Evans, loc. cit. p. 70 seq.

[11] Ath. Mitth. 1883, Taf. 15.

[12] For the date of this artist see the remarkable researches of A. J. Evans, Syracusan Medallions, London 1892. This book makes it unnecessary for me to controvert the usual date given to the Syracusan coins, and which I have always held to be false. Evans has proved finally that the tetradrachms all belong to the fifth century, and that even the dekadrachm types of Euainetos and Kimon were created towards the close of this century (after 413 B.C.)

(Plate VI. 14) now give place to softer and fuller forms ; the hair is disposed in thick undulating locks ; the sharp lines are given up, and the whole treatment becomes more pictorial. Just as the older style was presumably developed under the influence of Pythagoras, so this later style may be referred to the Attic influence of Pheidias. So too in Naxos, the superb Dionysos head of the severe style, probably suggested by some famous plastic work of Pythagoras (Plate VI. 16),[1] is immediately succeeded by the dignified head with diadem and short hair, which looks as if it had been cut out of the Parthenon frieze (Plate VI. 17).[2]

The great streams of artistic tendency due to the separate influence of men of genius and their schools may everywhere be traced on coins. The theory which refuses to see in the smaller art of the die-cutter anything but local style and auto-chthonous development is entirely mistaken.[3]

In the time of Perikles, Athens, as is well known, was in constant communication with Lower Italy and Sicily. Traces of peace negotiations with Egesta about 454—453 have been accidentally preserved on the fragment of a record.[4] Coin-types prove that Attic art of the Periklean-Pheidian epoch spread from Thurii and Neapolis to other places. This stream was too strong to be checked either by the political vicissitudes or even by the final defeat of the Athenians before Syracuse. The splendid dekadrachms of Kimon and Euanietos, struck immediately after the victory over the Athenians, are a product of that Attic style[5] which was brought to Syracuse chiefly by Kimon's agency. In the fourth century, in Syracuse as in the whole of Magna Graecia, artists drew at first only from the great storehouse of types provided by Attic-Pheidian art, and new conceptions grew but slowly.

There is still a second class of monuments which shows clearly how strong was the influx of Attic art into Magna Graecia in the Pheidian period, and how powerful was the stimulus it gave to fresh production. I refer to the vases. The style and composition which we have proved to belong to the reliefs on the shield of the Parthenos, and to correspond with one series of Attic vases, reappear all at once in a class of vases made in Southern Italy. These vases must be considered as the first products of new potteries, since there is no early red-figured painting proper to this district. They are not the superficial half-misunderstood imitations of imported vases which the non-Hellenic craftsmen of South Etruria and Campania were in the habit of making about the same time or earlier ; they are a purely Greek product. Their relation first to the Attic vases of about 440 B.C. and then to those of the following decades is a very close one. At first they correspond exactly to the Attic vases in form and decoration[6] as well as in the composition and general style of the paintings. And yet there is an individual touch in the style and typology of the figures from the very beginning ;[7] although they cannot compete with their Attic prototypes in beauty and

---

[1] Cf. the analogous type of the bronze head from Herculaneum (the so-called ' Plato '), which on account of its similarity to the Dionysos of the Naxian coins I am inclined to refer to Pythagoras (cf. 50th *Berl. Winckelmannsprogr.* p. 130, note 18).

[2] Good illustrations of both types in Head, *Guide*, Pl. 17, 29, 30 ; Gardner, *Types*, ii. 22, vi. 14.

[3] In this respect P. Gardner estimates more correctly ; he feels the necessity of connecting the coins with great artists ; he is however mistaken in ascribing (*Types*, p. 118) to Polykleitos a greater influence on coins than to Pheidias.   [4] Cf. Lolling in the Δελτίον, 1891, p. 105.   [5] Cf. Arthur Evans, *loc. cit.*

[6] The technical marks are very different. The clay is much paler and duller than that of Athens, and is usually covered with a thin coat of red colour intended to imitate the colour of the Athenian vases, but which is rarely well preserved. Superimposed colours, red and white, are only sparingly used, and many details, which in Attic vases are wont to be painted, are constantly merely blocked out.

[7] *E.g.* the type of the bearded Seilenos differs from the Athenian type.

refinement of drawing and technique, they have a rough incisive force all their own.

To make clear which are the vases I mean, I will cite a few of the principal types. We possess a series of bell-shaped kraters which only the most exact and careful observation of technical and stylistic points can distinguish from the corresponding Attic kraters of the period between 440 and 430.[1] An excellent example, though not one of the earliest, is the krater with the Expiation of Orestes in the Louvre ;[2] it may be dated about 420 B.C. Among the hydriae, the one with the frieze of Argonauts in the Cabinet des Médailles[3] should be named first. It is exactly akin to the Attic hydriae of about 440 B.C. The Berlin hydria (No. 3164) with Zeus and Io is somewhat later, and may be grouped with Attic hydriae of 430 B.C. and after, such as the one with Paris and Kadmos (Berlin, 2633, 2634). The hydria with the death of Kanake, a subject derived from the *Aiolos* of Euripides,[4] also belongs to the fifth century. Further, there are a few amphoras with volute-handles to be named in this connexion ; more especially one in the Jatta Coll. in Ruvo,[5] which displays on one side an Amazonomachia closely analogous in composition and motives to the shield relief of the Parthenos, and on the other the Rape of the Leukippidai conceived just as on Attic vases of about 440 derived from Polygnotan prototypes. Equally Polygnotan in design is the episode of Phineus and the Argonaut on another volute-amphora of the same collection.[6] A specially conspicuous instance from the period about or soon after 430 is a krater in the Cabinet des Médailles : on one side is Odysseus conjuring the shade of Teiresias, on the other the Judgment of Paris.[7] To the same class belong a krater of somewhat more recent style in the collection of Sir Francis Cook, in Richmond, representing the Blinding of Polyphemos[8] (from the *Kyklops* of Euripides), and the charming krater with the humorous and forcible rendering of the Pursuit of Dolon.[9] The very shape of the 'Vasi a colonnette' was taken over by Lower Italy straight from Athens, in the middle of the fifth century B.C.

Vases of the kinds just mentioned are found in Lucania (*e.g.* Pomarico, Anzi, etc.) and also in Apulia (especially Ruvo). Technically and stylistically they form a preparatory stage to the later Lucanian vases, which rapidly assume a strongly local stamp and are hardly ever found in Apulia, which has a special vase-manufacture of its own (*i.e.* the Tarentine). It cannot be doubted that these earlier Lower Italy vases belong to the fifth century, for their existence can only be understood on the supposition that they are nearly contemporary with the parallel productions of Attic art. The real 'Apulian,' *i.e.* Tarentine, class develops rather later, but it still belongs to the fifth century ; its nearest analogies are the Attic vases of the period

[1] Many in Naples and in the Museo Jatta at Ruvo ; good examples in Berlin, Nos. 3179, 3180, 3182.

[2] *Mon. d. Inst.* iv. 48.

[3] Gerhard, *Auserl. Vas.* 153, 154.

[4] Now at Bari. Shoulder decoration pub. *Arch. Ztg*, 1883, Pl. 7, 1 (p. 51, Kalkmann). Another hydria of the series, Millingen, *Vases de Div. Coll.* Pl. 4, 5.

[5] Jatta, 1096 ; *Bull. Nap.* n. s. ii. (1854), Tav. 4 ; *Mon. d. Inst.* xii. 16.—Another volute-amphora with a Pheidian Amazonomachia is in Geneva (Giraudon, *Vases Ant. des Coll. de la Ville de Genève*, Pl. 31, 32) ; even the details of the drapery exactly imitate Attic vases of 430 B.C.

[6] *Mon. d. Inst.* iii. 49. Ornamentation precisely like the Attic. The line indicating the ground is incised A third volute-amphora with Herakles and Kyknos in Jatta (*Bull. Nap.* n. s. i. 6 ; cf. Roscher's *Lexikon*, i. 2231) stands very near Attic prototypes of 430 B.C.

[7] *Mon. d. Inst.* iv. 18, 19.

[8] *Jahrb. d. Inst.* 1891, Taf. 6 ; the original (which I examined in 1888) shows burning fire on the logs of wood ; the youth clearly wears a pilos. Winter's suggestion that the vase is Attic is untenable, alike from technique and style ; with the head of Polyphemos cf. for example the Phineus, *Mon.* iii. 49.

[9] *Bull. Nap.* i. (1843), Tav. 7 ; Overbeck, *Gall.* Taf. 17, 4.

after 430. A conspicuous instance occurs on the volute-amphora (St. Petersburg, No. 523), where the Gigantomachia [1] is treated as on the shield of the Parthenos, and the drawing of the wavy hair, the ornaments on the drapery, etc., are plain echoes of those Attic prototypes. In this connexion it is instructive to study the fragments of an unusually large and splendid Attic krater (unpublished) from Kertsch in St. Petersburg,[2] which show in a striking manner how closely Tarentine work clings to Attic tradition of the end of the fifth century. Both groups of vases, the early Lower Italian and the Tarentine (Apulian), are merely offshoots of Attic art transplanted into new soil. The subjects of the earlier group, such as the various Argonaut pictures and the Rape of the Leukippidai,[3] are at first derived from the circle of Polygnotan painting, but subjects from the Attic drama soon make their appearance and afford the strongest confirmation of the essentially Attic character of these vases ; this dramatic material is brought straight over from Athens fresh and undiluted. In the Tarentine group, which was still developing in the last decades of the fifth century and continued to flourish through the first half of the fourth, the tragedies of Euripides, as is well known, hold the chief place. They dominate vase-painting, not as 'classical' literature, but as the new, sensational, and fashionable poetry of the day. Even the Sicilians, we know from reliable tradition,[4] were enthusiastic admirers of Euripides as early as 412 B.C., and eagerly learned by heart fragments of his dramas brought to them by Athenian deserters.

The facts touched upon so far seem to me to be capable of the following explanation. With the founding of Thurii, Attic ceramic art was transplanted into the district. Its exotic development began about 440 B.C. The products of the new workshops were distributed not only in the inland district of Thurii and the Siritis, but also in a north-easterly direction towards Apulia. Then came the contest with Tarentum, and the treaty which found outward expression in the establishment of a common colony, Herakleia. I think it probable that the manufacture of vases was continued in the latter city and spread thence to Tarentum, where it would flourish greatly owing to the wealth and power of the city, and thus gradually come to supplant the import trade from Herakleia, at least so far as Apulia was concerned. The Herakleian potteries thus lost their importance, their wares (the later Lucanian vases) became poorer, and assumed a more and more exclusively local character.[5]

The export trade of Athens itself was naturally materially injured by the existence of this new centre of vase-painting in Southern Italy. After 400 B.C. no Attic vases of later style seem to have come to Apulia, although the export to Campania continued to flourish for some time. Thus the attempt of Athens to found an independent colony, Thurii, was prejudicial, in this particular as in others, to the Mother City. Athens gave of her strength, and received nothing in return.

---

[1] *Bull. Nap.* ii. (1844), Tav. 6.

[2] On one side, above, a great assembly of the gods with Zeus enthroned, below the Dioskouroi riding (?) and Herakles as victor : presumably the picture represented the institution of the Olympic games and the first victors. White and yellow are laid on freely, many of the heads are drawn facing, all this as in the Tarentine vases.

[3] Since the appearance of Köpp's admirable essay (*Arch. Anz.* 1892, p. 124 *sqq.*) the paintings on vases of Tarentine manufacture relating to the Persian war may be reckoned among those representations inspired by the Polygnotan circle.

[4] Plut. *Nikias*, 29.

[5] During this whole epoch Sicily had no potteries of her own. Her market was supplied, after the fall of the Attic power, by different potteries of Lower Italy. This is the result of my observations in Sicilian collections.

Nevertheless, for a right appreciation of the power and significance of Attic art as it was when Pheidias had impressed upon it the mark of his genius, the history of its triumphal entrance into Magna Graecia will always be of the highest importance. We have only touched upon some of the chief features of this history; much remains unsaid. I will close with one more example. The famous Ficoroni Cista in Rome by a master of Praeneste is the genuine offspring of Polygnoto-Pheidian art. Its types are derived from the same source as those of the Argonaut pictures on early Lower Italy vases—viz. from the paintings of the Polygnotan circle. This is evident from the separate motives and their details, although there are many concessions to Latin taste. The Cista must be of nearly the same date as the vases.[1]

We have travelled far from our original starting-point, the Lemnia of Pheidias. The great creations of the brilliant Attic period are like suns, each the centre of a multitude of smaller stars on which they pour light and life. The art of Athens in the fifth century was as far-reaching and widespread as her empire; and the style which, as we have tried to show, was individual to Pheidias accomplished the vast success and gave the strong stimulus which we have studied in some of their manifestations.

[1] The inscription, as is well known, only gives a *terminus ante quem*. The ornamentation and the picture on the lid point to an older period; no less the feet of the cista, which, like the relief of Theseus, Peirithoos, and Herakles (Helbig, *Museums*, 826), are derived from a relief of Pheidian style. It is as certain that the cista, the feet, and the handle were all made at the same time, as it is that the whole was made in Rome.

Fig. XIV—Attic Kylix Showing Sculptor's Workshop,
Berlin, National Museum

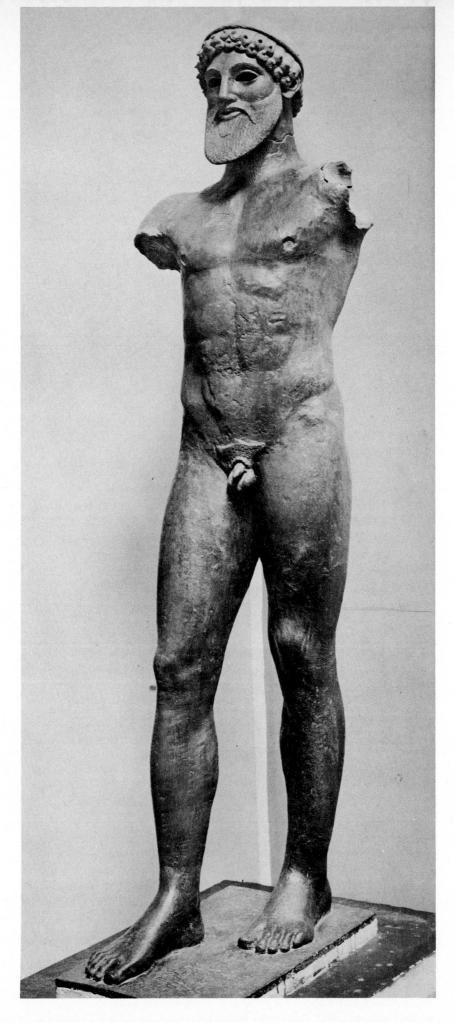

Fig. XV—Poseidon or Zeus, Bronze Statue from Boeotia,
Athens. National Meseum

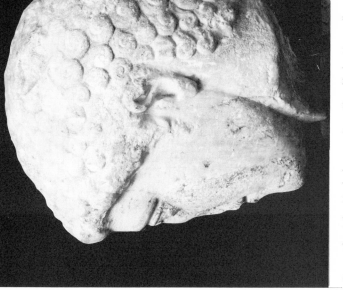

Figs. I 2 & I 3 – Head of Harmodios, New York, Metropolitan Museum of Art

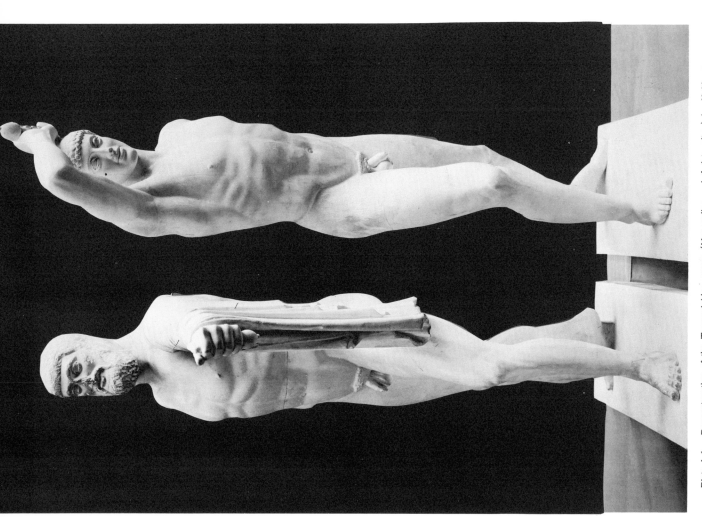

Plate I 1 – Reconstruction of the Tyrannicides group (Harmodios and Aristogeiton) by Kritios and Nesiotes (477-476 BC), New York, Metropolitan Museum of Art

PLATE I

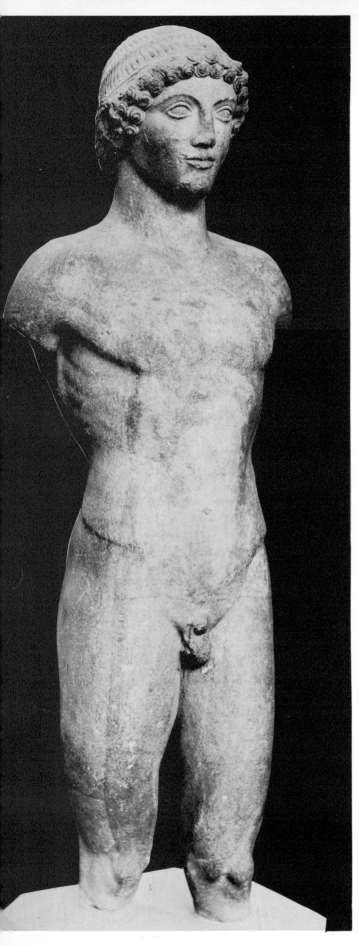

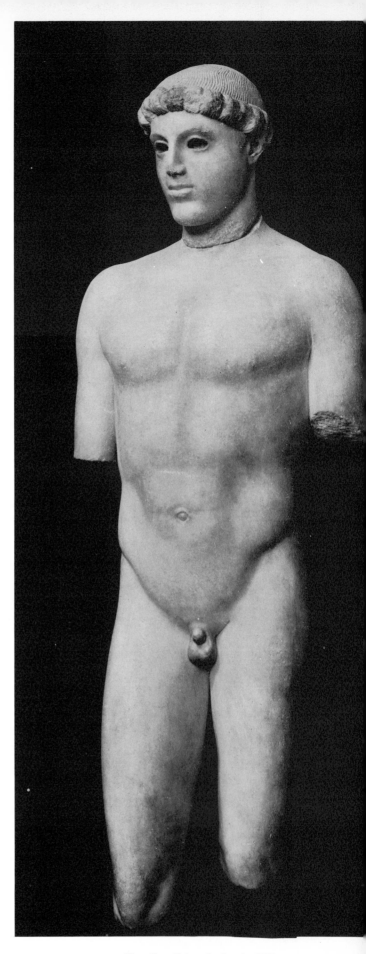

Fig. J1 - The Strangford Apollo, London,
British Museum

Fig. J2 - Statue of a boy by Kritios
according to the dedicatory inscription, Athens, Acropolis Museum

PLATE J

PLATE K

Fig. K2 - Grave stele of a helmeted warrior, Athens, National Museum

Fig. K1 - Zeus and Ganymede, terra cotta akroterion from a building at Olympia (470 BC) Olympia, Olympia Museum

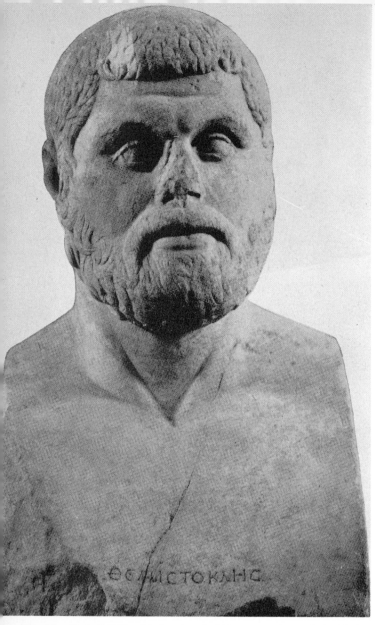

Fig. L1 – Portrait of Themistocles, Inscribed Roman copy from a lost original, Ostia, Ostia Museum

Fig. L2 – Head of an old man, east pediment, Temple of Zeus at Olympia Olympia Museum

Fig. L3 – Maidens from the Parthenon frieze, Paris, Louvre

PLATE L

Fig. M1 – Deities from the Parthenon frieze, Athens, Acropolis Museum

Fig. M2 – Battle of Greeks and Amazons from the frieze of the Temple of
Apollo at Phigaleia, London, British Museum

PLATE M

Fig. N1 – Horseman from the Parthenon frieze, London, British Museum

PLATE N

Fig. O1 - Nike binding her sandal, relief from the parapet of·the Temple
of Athena Nike on the Acropolis, Athens, Acropolis Museum

PLATE O

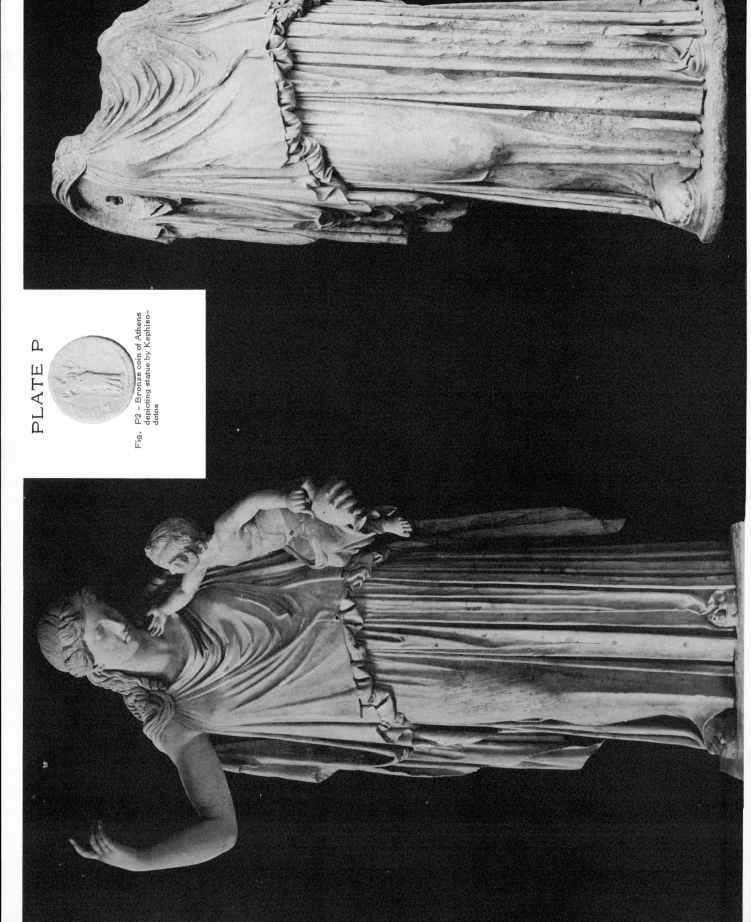

Fig. P2 – Bronze coin of Athens depicting statue by Kephiso-dotos

Fig. XVI—Perikles Bust, Rome, Vatican Museum. (See
p. 117 sqq.)

MVNIFICENTIA·PII·IX·PONT·MAX

Fig. XVII—Marsyas, Rome, Lateran Museum. (Restored Arms Removed)

KRESILAS AND MYRON

I. *Literary and Epigraphical Evidence for the Life of Kresilas.*

SIDE by side with Pheidias and his immediate circle there were other artists who followed an independent line. Among these Kresilas has long been recognized as one of the most important. Pliny, in his history of bronze statuary, mentions him no less than three times: first, in the larger alphabetical list of the *insignes* (xxxiv. 74), where he names him as the artist of a statue representing a wounded man, 'in which might be seen how much of life remained,' and of a portrait of Perikles, worthy of the epithet 'Olympian'—adding that it is marvellous how the art of portraiture can make a celebrated man still more celebrated. The second mention occurs as an appendix to the list of artists given under *C*. It states that Cresilas also made a 'doryphoros' and a 'wounded amazon' (xxxiv. 76). The MS. reading of the name is, it is true, corrupt, but there is little doubt that Brunn's reading, *Cresilas*,[1] is correct. Finally, Pliny names him among the *laudatissimi* who made statues of Amazons for a competition; Kresilas being placed third in the order of merit, after Polykleitos and Pheidias (xxxiv. 53).

Neither Pausanias nor any other writer mentions the artist by name, if we except a corrupt passage in the *Auctor ad Herennium* where Brunn[2] restores with strong probability . . . . *caput Myronium, brachia Praxitelia, pectus Polyclitium, ventrem et crura Cresilaea.* We can however scarcely conclude from these words that Kresilas really excelled in the rendering of the abdomen and the legs, for the rhetor is obviously connecting at random particular parts of the body with the names of celebrated artists;[3] so that, even were Brunn's reading absolutely certain, we could only gather from it that the rhetors reckoned Kresilas among the most famous artists.

Fortunately, several inscriptions from works of the artist himself have been preserved, no less than three of which are from the Akropolis. The first of these belongs to the portrait of Perikles;[4] from the character of the epigraphy, Lolling has dated it *circa* 440–430. The second inscription, belonging to the base of a votive statue put up by a certain Hermolykos,[5] can be dated as far back as the middle of the fifth century. The third[6] seems to be rather later; it is metrical, and found its way into the *Anthology*. In it the artist mentions Kydonia in Krete as his birthplace. The work

---

[1] *Gesch. d. Künstler*, i. p. 261. [2] *Sitzungsber. d. Bayr. Akad., Philos.-philol. Classe*, 1880, p. 481.
[3] See Kekulé, *Kopf des Praxit. Hermes*, p. 23 seq. [4] Δελτίον ἀρχαιολ. 1889, p. 36.
[5] Lowy, *I. G. B.* No. 46. [6] Löwy No. 47.

was the gift of a certain Pyres; and the wording of the inscription, τόνδε Πυρῆς ἀνέθηκε Πολυμνήστου φίλος υἱός, εὐξάμενος δεκάτην Πάλλαδι τριτογενεῖ, shows that it was probably the portrait of the donor.[1] All these inscriptions are in pure Attic characters, thus proving that the artist must have resided at least some time in Athens.

A fourth inscription shows him, on the other hand, at work in the Peloponnesos, in the province of Argolis; it comes from the basis of an offering to Demeter Chthonia at Hermione,[2] dedicated by a certain Alexias. In it Kresilas again calls himself a Kydoniate, but this time he uses the characters of the place where he is at work, and in so doing is moreover guilty of a blunder.[3] An inscription from what is evidently the companion work to this gift of Alexias,[4] an offering on the part of his son, gives the name of an artist from Argos. Kresilas is thus shown engaged on work for a family of Hermione in company with an Argive artist; and the probability is that he was living at Argos at the time, and received the commission conjointly with the native artist. As these inscriptions have nothing archaic about them, it seems probable that the artist came to Argos after—and not before—his sojourn in Athens. An inscribed basis of blackish limestone which has lately been discovered at Delphi during the French excavations[5] must be of still later date, as on it the name of the artist and his nationality appear inscribed in pure Ionic characters.

Even from these few dates we can gather a good deal of information concerning the artist's life. Born at Kydonia in Krete, he must have left home early, in order to cultivate his talents—for we know of no school of artists in Krete at that time. To judge from coins, the dominating note of Kretan art in the fifth and fourth centuries was purely barbaric. Yet side by side with an astonishing lack of artistic skill we can detect here and there proofs of a special aptitude for pictorial and realistic representation. The celebrated coins of Gortyna with Europa or with Zeus Velchanos seated in a tree, the pieces representing oxen, much foreshortened, licking themselves, the coins of Phaistos with the seated figure of Herakles resting—all seek to reproduce nature in a bold and direct manner.[6] These coins are later, it is true, than the youth of Kresilas, but they show in what lay the special artistic quality of the islanders, and we shall not be surprised if we meet in him with the like characteristics.

It was, of course, only natural that the young artist should turn his steps to the brilliant and artistic Athens. Here he seems to have succeeded in working his way up among the first artists, and in obtaining a great reputation, especially as a portraitist. Otherwise he would certainly not have been intrusted with the bust of Perikles, the most distinguished and powerful man in the city. The commission was, it is true, only a private one, as we learn from the inscription; but this makes no difference, for Perikles and his friends could certainly command the best artistic skill of the day just as well as the state. And supposing the portrait to have been, as has been suggested, a gift on the part of the artist (see infra), this would at once prove him to have stood in close personal relations to Perikles. As to the migration of Kresilas to Argos, it was doubtless occasioned by the outbreak of the Peloponnesian War, which must have rendered residence in Athens unpleasant for an

---

[1] Cf. Ath. Mitth. 1880, p. 28, note 1, and more especially the inscription of a votive portrait-statue from about the close of the fifth century, Ἐφημερὶς ἀρχ. 1891, p. 56, Plate 6: Λυσικλείδης . . . ἀνέθηκεν τόνδε θεᾷ τῇδε . . .   [2] Löwy, No. 45.

[3] Writing in the second line X instead of Ψ. See Kirchhoff, Studien, 4th ed. p. 160 seq.

[4] Unfortunately only known from a transcript taken by Fourmont, Löwy, No. 51. Cf. Kirchhoff, loc. cit.

[5] Shortly to be published by the French.

[6] Cf. St. Poole, Num. Chron. 1864, 240; P. Gardner, Types, p. 161.

artist, especially if he were a foreigner. The cessation of artistic activity, the uncertain turn of the war, the breaking out of the plague, and above all the death of Perikles, whom we may look upon as his patron, would be sufficient reasons for leaving Athens. Argos on the other hand had, at this time, undoubted attractions for an artist : being a neutral state, it enjoyed absolute peace, and its famous school was gradually becoming the leading artistic centre in Greece, now that numerous calamities were forcing Athens into the background.

A study of the marble copies executed in Roman times after the works of Kresilas will help materially to fill up this outline of the artist's career.

II. *The Portrait of Perikles.*

The existence of copies of the portrait of Perikles by Kresilas may be taken as proved.[1] Two terminal busts, one in the British Museum and one in the Vatican, bear the ancient inscriptions of the name of Perikles ; they go back to the same original, and from the style this original must have belonged to the time of Perikles. Their identification as copies after the celebrated work by Kresilas has lately been further confirmed by the discovery on the Akropolis of the inscribed basis that supported the original. It is only a fragment, but it bears the inscription, restored indubitably correctly, by Lolling :—

$$\Pi\epsilon\rho]\iota\kappa\lambda\acute{\epsilon}o\varsigma$$
$$K\rho\epsilon\sigma]\acute{\iota}\lambda\alpha\varsigma \ \acute{\epsilon}\pi o\acute{\iota}\epsilon$$

If, as is probable, the inscription occupied the middle of the block, the basis cannot have been more than some 40 cm. broad, a size to which the smallness of the lettering[2] would be well adapted. Now so narrow a basis could not carry a statue, but only a term, so that it seems proved that the terms with the inscription 'Perikles'[3] are reproductions of the actual work by Kresilas. The original inscription shows that the work was only a private offering ; as the donor is not mentioned, Lolling supposes it to have been put up by the artist himself. Pausanias also mentions this portrait of Perikles on the Akropolis, without however naming the artist.[4]

Of the two replicas, the one in London undoubtedly gives the best idea of the original (Plate VII. ; profile in Fig. 46).[5] The head has never been separated from the bust and the neck is unbroken, so that the exact carriage and turn are preserved. In the Vatican replica,[6] the head had been broken off and a piece of the neck is restored ; the neck has become shortened in the operation, and the characteristic pose of the head—and with it one of the chief charms of the work—is thus lost. Both these copies are well and carefully executed ; their substantial agreement testifies to their

---

[1] First asserted by Bergk and Brunn (*K. G.* i. 262).

[2] Lolling in the Δελτίον ἀρχαιολ. 1889, p. 36 *seq.* I have examined the basis myself. Its original breadth was probably 0·44. The depth is now only 8—9 cm. In the upper surface on the right a mortise hole is distinctly visible (also in Lolling's illustration), but it need not be original. The fragment affords no decisive evidence for or against the assumption of a terminal bust.

[3] The breadth of the shaft of the London term is 28 cm., which would suit a basis of about 40 cm. very well.

[4] Paus. i. 28, 2 ; 25, 1 ; ἀνδριάς need not necessarily mean a whole statue. For the site cf. *supra*, p. 10 *seq.* It has been remarked (p. 62, note 6) that the Xanthippos and the Anakreon stood elsewhere, and had nothing to do with the Perikles portrait or with Kresilas.

[5] The older publications are cited in Friederichs-Wolters, *Gipsabg.* No. 481.

[6] Brunn-Bruckmann, *Denkmäler ;* Helbig, *Museums,* 281.

fidelity. The Vatican replica, however, reproduces the separate curls of the beard with greater precision and severity, and shows the hair on the top of the head immediately below the eyeholes of the helmet, a detail which must have been in the original, since it emphasizes the high shape of head peculiar to Perikles. There is a third very mediocre replica (without inscription) in the Barracco collection at Rome.[1]

This portrait of Perikles is a vivid commentary on what Thucydides wrote concerning the temper and manner of the great statesman. Artist and historian alike show us a man raised far above his fellow-citizens by the superiority of his mind and the distinction of his character. Although we possess numerous contemporary portraits, it would be difficult to match the tranquil dignity of this bust of Perikles. The pose of the head, which is inclined a little to one side and slightly thrown back, is so personal that it must have been studied from the life. In this pose lies the secret of that gentleness which is a distinguishing characteristic of the head—a gentleness arising not from weakness, but from an innate nobility of soul. The artist, though confined to a bust, has yet contrived to suggest the whole personage. We can almost fancy that we see Perikles before us raising his head in dignified unconcern, however loud the voices of his accusers and slanderers might rise about him. This outer security well expressed the inner purity of that incorruptible nature to which Kresilas and Thucydides bear equal witness.

The mouth, which almost borders on ugliness, is specially distinctive.[2] Broader than is customary, with voluptuous lips—the under lip is especially full—it is not the mouth of a man accustomed to impose his will on others with an arbitrary and iron determination, but its mobile and sensuous curves accord admirably with the eloquent manner and persuasive grace of Perikles, and are not without a suggestion of the tender and faithful lover of Aspasia and of the patron and protector of artists.

The external mien of Perikles was conspicuous not only for mildness and tranquillity, but for the seriousness of its expression : he had ' a gravity of countenance which relaxed not into laughter' (Plutarch, *Per.* 5). Should any one interpret this to mean starched and formal dignity—a quality for the rest quite foreign to the Greek genius—the portrait would promptly undeceive him. A profound seriousness pervades the features, but there is no trace of self-importance. Rather do we seem to be looking upon the ideal portrait of the ruler of a democracy, on whom it is incumbent to be the first in intrinsic merit as in mental distinction.

The other peculiarities are more superficial : as, for example, the mode of wearing the hair and beard, which are cut somewhat short, the beard allowing the full round chin to be clearly seen underneath. The short curly hair is very thick, and the back of the helmet seems to rest on it, as on a pillow. The close, well-ordered hair and beard are not without significance in the portrait of the man who surpassed his fellow-citizens even in εὐκοσμία and εὐσχημοσύνη. We must also remember that in the days of Perikles artists left off representing the gods with long abundant locks, and gave short close hair even to the most august of the Olympian gods.

The helmet, as noted long ago, marks the office of *strategos*, which Perikles filled without a break from about 445 B.C. It would be absurd to suppose—with later classical authors—that the artist represented Perikles wearing the helmet in

---

[1] *Coll. Barracco*, Pl. 39, 39 a. The head in Munich, called Perikles (Brunn, *Glypt.* 5th ed. 157), evidently represents quite a different person, as Friederichs (*Baust.* p. 125) had already observed.

[2] In the Vatican head the characteristic form is somewhat weakened, but the London head reproduces it with evident fidelity.

order to hide the long shape of his head, for, as we see from the Vatican replica, he evidently tried to make this characteristic obvious even through the open eyeholes.

The inscription from the Akropolis, as noted above, is approximately dated at 440—430 B.C. Within this period there is no event so likely to have occasioned the dedication of the portrait in the sanctuary of Athena Polias as the return of the

*Plate VII—Perikles, London, British Museum. (See p. 117 sqq.)

FIG. 46.—Terminal bust of Perikles in the British Museum.   (From the original.)

victorious general from the most difficult and glorious of his campaigns—the one undertaken against Samos in B.C. 439. Gratitude for his successful return would afford a specially suitable occasion for his friends to dedicate his portrait to the goddess who had lent him her aid. The work would thus have been executed at a time when Perikles had roused immense popular enthusiasm by his funeral oration over those who had fallen in the war—an occasion on which the women adorned him with crowns and chaplets (Plut. *Per.* 28). Maybe that the image of Perikles as he stood there before the people on that day inspired the artist at his work.

In turning to consider the formal peculiarities of the work, we note first that the eye is very long and narrow, and, although the glance is inclined upwards, it yet seems scarcely opened, while the lid has a heavy droop. The lids are very strong and full, and the lachrymal glands are prominent. The distance between the inner corners of the eyes is not great, and the root of the nose is narrow.[1]

The face is, in the manner of the time, represented with the smooth skin tightly drawn over and without any lines, except that on either side of the root of the nose, at the birth of the eyebrows, the artist has introduced a little vertical wrinkle, and below it, to mark off the nose, two little horizontal cuts. These lines are of course appropriate to the serious thoughtful man, no longer in his first youth, but the way in which they are introduced and executed must certainly be peculiar to the artist.

The distinguishing quality of the hair is its plastic fulness, indicated in spite of its shortness. It is not arranged symmetrically, but is composed of a maze of little curling locks. Similar locks occur here and there in the beard,[2] though the hair of the beard is on the whole still shorter, and instead of curling merely turns up at the ends.

It is scarcely likely that this portrait of Perikles was the only work of the kind undertaken by Kresilas,—and, among the many similar helmeted heads preserved, it is not unreasonable to hope for some trace of his hand. The Berlin collection, for instance, possesses a marble head,[3] which—allowance being made for the differences of copyists—resembles in the highest degree the peculiar style of the Perikles (Fig. 47). It has been placed on a term that does not belong to it; the neck below the beard and the hair at the back are modern. Nothing else is restored except the lower half of the nose, the top of the helmet, and the point of the visor. The head is turned a little to the right. The copyist has made great use of the drill both in hair and beard.

In the general conception of the individual, a quality more easily felt than described, there is singular coincidence between the two portraits, as may be seen by comparing them to other contemporary works. The separate features, however, are in some respects completely different. The Berlin head has long hair, parted in front and smoothed away behind the ears, at the back falling loose upon the neck, thus affording no opportunity for the little close curls of the Perikles. But for all that the treatment is closely allied; as in the one the little curls, so in the other the larger strands, cross and intertwine—perhaps just a trifle mechanically. The beard, too, in the Berlin head is longer than in the Perikles, but has the same round outline, and is composed of similar little meshes of hair with curling ends. As the beard is thicker, these meshes do not lie close to the chin and cheeks in the same way, yet the resemblance would be materially greater had not the copyist, by using the drill freely, introduced an element quite foreign to the original. The likeness to the Perikles is enhanced by the manner in which the beard grows from the cheek and by the cut of the moustache, which leaves the line of the lip quite free. The hair is kept well away from the under lip, another point in which the head resembles

---

[1] The proportions, measured on the London head, are as follows: clear length of eye = 36 mm.; without lachrymal gland = 32 mm.; height = 12 mm.; distance between inner corners only 28—29 mm. instead of a whole eye-length as elsewhere. The length of mouth, according to a very usual proportion = 1½ times the length of the eyes (54 mm.); it seems that the length of the mouth (a feature peculiar to the man pourtrayed) brought the unusually long eye in its train.

[2] At any rate in the Vatican head, which in this respect is the more faithful; cf. p. 117.

[3] *Skulpt.* No. 311.

FIG. 47.—Head of a *strategos* (Berlin).

Fig. XVIII—River God, Alpheios, East Pediment Temple of Zeus at Olympia, Olympia Museum

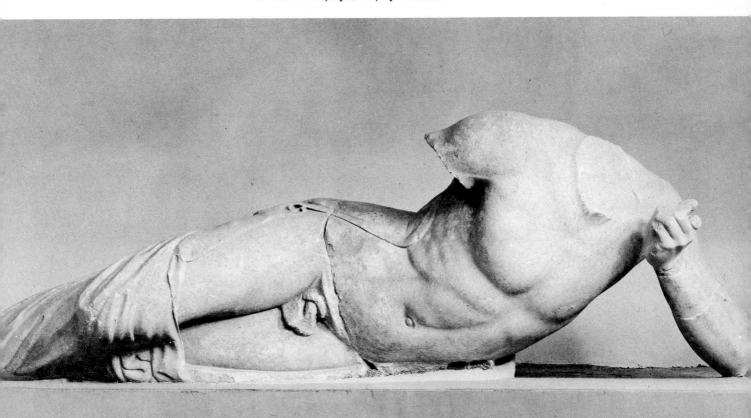

the Perikles. Then in the eyes we have again the heavy eyelids and pronounced lachrymal glands — just a little altered by the hand of the copyist — together with the relatively narrow nose.[1] It is especially instructive to find that the Berlin head displays, upon an otherwise smooth skin, precisely those same stylistic little lines at the root of the nose which in the Perikles were seen to be treated in a manner quite personal to the artist. The helmet differs slightly from that of the Perikles in having just above the ears what seems to be the turned-up end of a broad leather strap.

The Berlin head, then, may be accepted as a copy of another portrait of a Greek general from the hand of Kresilas, rather later than the Perikles, for in spite of substantial agreement the treatment of hair and beard gives an impression of greater freedom and of technical advance.[2] We may think of it, therefore, as executed somewhere about the beginning of the Peloponnesian War.

III. *The Diitrephes.*

Another celebrated work of Kresilas mentioned by Pliny (xxxvi. 74) represented a wounded man on the point of death. An ingenious theory connects this work with the bronze statue of a certain Diitrephes pierced with arrows, noted by Pausanias[3] in his description of the Akropolis as standing close to the Athena Hygieia the basis of which may still be seen on the eastern side of the Propylaia. In the year 1839 a square basis inscribed Ἑρμόλυκος Διειτρέφος ἀπαρχέν· Κρεσίλας ἐπόεσεν[4] was found built between the Propylaia and the Parthenon; and, since this basis might easily have got shifted farther eastwards from its original position for later building purposes, L. Ross at once suggested that it had belonged to the statue of Diitrephes mentioned

---

[1] The head is life-size, like the Perikles; the nose and lower part of the face have the same proportions; the eyes are shorter (33 mm.), but the mouth is also of normal width. The distance between the inner corners of the eyes is a full eye-length.

[2] There also exist copies of two beautiful heads of *strategoi* by a master closely related to Kresilas, though he is quite distinct from him both in general conception and in the treatment of details. The first is the so-called 'Themistokles' in the Vatican (Helbig, 482); the second is the Pastoret head (Fr.-Wolters, 484), of which the Munich head in the Glyptothek, 157 (F.-W. 483), is only a mutilated replica, though valuable on account of the careful execution of what remains; a third replica of the same portrait is in the Villa Albani, 40. It is especially in the peculiar treatment of the beard that the same hand becomes apparent for both heads. The 'Themistokles' is probably the earlier work; the Pastoret *strategos* has very disordered hair, and sundry realistic details, especially in the neck. An immediate development of this tendency in portraiture is the Archidamos (*Röm. Mitth.* iii. Pl. 4), in whom I recognize the Archidamos of the Peloponnesian War (cf. *infra*, p. 321). It is not impossible that the personality at the back of these works (with which many others may be grouped) is that of Demetrios, the famous ἀνθρωποποιός, who worked at the time of the Peloponnesian War and at the beginning of the fourth century. In later antiquity it was a commonplace of the rhetors (as appears from Quinctilian and from Lucian, *Philops.* 18) to find fault with Demetrios as a realist. Probably this merely goes back to some exaggerated statement in an Attic comedy (it is only necessary to remember the sentence passed by the older comedy on the realist Euripides); for no artist can go beyond the limitations of his time, and actually realistic portraits, as understood in later days, would be out of the question at that epoch. The caricatured description in Lucian is moreover put into the mouth of the lying philosopher Eukrates, and cannot in the least imply what the moderns have taken it to mean.

[3] From the wording it might be only the statue that was struck by arrows, but both internal and external evidence are against that supposition. Moreover, arrows shot at the statue could not stick in the bronze but would glance off, and the marks that they would leave would not be of a kind to show what they came from.

[4] Löwy, *Inschr. Gr. Bildh.* No. 46, where see all the older literature. For the latest discussion of the question, *Jahrb. d. Inst.* 1892, p. 185 *sqq.* (J. Six), cf. *infra*, p. 123, n. 2. My earlier opinion (*Ath. Mitth.* v. p. 28), that—as Bergk first supposed—the inscription referred to the statue of Hermolykos (Paus. i. 23, 10), and that Pausanias was mistaken in identifying him with the Pankratiast of Herodotos, I now withdraw as improbable; for Pausanias could scarcely have overlooked the difference of the father's name. Cf. still more recently Weizsäcker in *Fleckeisen's Jahrb.* 1886, p. 16 *seq.*

by Pausanias. Certainly the son of Diitrephes would be the most likely person to have set up the statue, since Diitrephes, who was represented as dying, could not well have done so himself. Further, Ross also identified this Diitrephes pierced with arrows, which the inscribed basis showed to have been a work of Kresilas, with the wounded man by Kresilas mentioned in Pliny. The one serious objection to the theory is that the information given by Pausanias about Diitrephes is impossible to reconcile with the date of the inscription. According to Pausanias, he was a general in 414 B.C., while the characters of the inscription belong to a considerably earlier date. Kirchhoff accordingly (C. I. A. i. 402) rejected the whole identification. There is, however, no definite proof that the information of Pausanias really applies to the Diitrephes of the Akropolis statue. Pausanias has evidently no personal knowledge of the matter, and is merely drawing from Thucydides (vii. 29, 30), where it is narrated how Diitrephes led back the Thracian troops in the year 414 and took Mykalessos by the way. This same general is again mentioned by Thucydides (viii. 64) in connexion with the events of the year 411 : we know nothing about the manner of his death. Clearly this man cannot be the Diitrephes of the Kresilas basis. Thucydides, however, also mentions another and earlier Diitrephes as being the father of a certain Nikostratos (iii. 75 ; iv. 119, 129), who was an Athenian general at the beginning of the Peloponnesian War ; and it is not impossible that this father of Nikostratos was also father of Hermolykos, and therefore identical with the Diitrephes pourtrayed by Kresilas. Like his son Nikostratos, and like his later namesake, he may have been an Attic *strategos*, and have been slain by arrows in some engagement of which the record is lost to us. Considering the scantiness of tradition concerning the *Pentekontaetia*, it is not surprising that so little should be known of him ; but we at any rate do know that just about the time when this elder Diitrephes would be active there took place the last bloody campaigns against the Persian hosts and those great expeditions to Cyprus (459—449 B.C.), in all of which the Attic troops would be brought face to face with Oriental bowmen. It is certainly not difficult to believe that Pausanias only remembered the Diitrephes whose exploits were recounted at greater length by Thucydides, and knew nothing of his earlier namesake.[1] The death of Diitrephes, whose statue was dedicated to Athena by his son, probably in fulfilment of a vow, must have been an episode well known at the time. The general, holding out to the very last, may have secured privileges to his family by his heroic death, and would thus well deserve the honour of a statue at their hands. Pliny's description shows that the man was actually represented as dying—besides, any less serious situation would have cheated the sympathies of the spectators.[2]

Pausanias could not gather from the extant inscription that Diitrephes was the name of the wounded man : he either learnt it from older literary sources, or, as seems more probable, the name of the person pourtrayed was inscribed on the actual statue.[3] The statue of the older Hermolykos, the hero of Mykale (Herod. ix. 105), was on a different spot of the Akropolis, nearer to the Parthenon and next to the hoplitodrome Epicharinos (Paus. i. 23, 10). He was probably represented as a victorious athlete, and his prowess in the pankration was probably known to Herodotos from his statue on the Akropolis.

[1] Löwy, *loc. cit.* p. 37, has already hinted at this possibility.

[2] The purely arbitrary theories propounded by J. Six, *Jahrb. d. Inst.* 1892, p. 185 *seq.*, have been successfully refuted by A. Gercke, *Jahrb. d. Inst.* 1893, p. 113 *seq.*

[3] So Myron inscribed his name on the thigh of his Apollo (Overbeck, *S. Q.* 537). Since the Diitrephes dates about the middle of the fifth century, it would still come within the limits of the period in which it was usual to set inscriptions upon the statues themselves. Cf. R. v. Schneider, *Erzstatue vom Helenenberge*, p. 20.

From the actual basis of the Diitrephes we learn [1] that the figure was not lying but standing,[2] and further that the main weight rested probably upon the ball of the right foot, which was drawn back and fastened with a strong peg, while the left, with the sole on the ground, must have been advanced. A vase-painting from a white-faced Attic lekythos (Fig. 48) [3] shows that the attitude was not an impossible one for a wounded man. This single figure can well be conceived of as a statue. The warrior, pierced by two arrows, is falling backwards; he is naked, as beseems the idealizing treatment of sculpture; he only wears a helmet, and carries shield and lance. The latter he holds still raised, although it is evident that he can never drive home another shaft.

As it is precisely among the class of vases to which this lekythos belongs that reproductions of statues have been found,[4] it is reasonable to suspect one here. The lekythos, to judge from its shape, is almost contemporary [5] with the red-figured vases of the fine period, and cannot therefore be much earlier than about 450 B.C. Therefore it perhaps really gives us a free rendering of the actual statue of Kresilas directly after it was set up.[6] The sculpturesque nudity of the figure and the uniqueness of the representation [7] both favour this supposition. I know of one similar figure only (Fig. 49);[8] it occurs on a gem. Here the warrior is pierced in the breast by an arrow, the knees give way, the left hand holds the shield, the right not a lance but a sword. The gem belongs to a special kind of later Italian product, closely connected with the severe scarab style (about the fourth to the third

FIG. 48.—White-faced Lekythos.
(Bibl. Nat., Paris.)

FIG. 49.—Gem in Berlin (slightly enlarged).

---

[1] Michaelis, *Ath. Mitth.* i. 289; Six, *loc. cit.* 187.   [2] Weizsäcker, *loc. cit.*

[3] Original in Paris, Cabinet d. Méd. ; Luynes, *Vases Peints*, Pl. 16 ; photograph in *Vases Peints du Cab. d. Médailles*, Pl. 111 A. Poor illustration (with the lightly incised inner lines left out), *Jahrb. d. Inst.* 1892, p. 185. Gercke's objections (*Jahrb. d. Inst.* 1893, 113 *sqq.*) against using the vase-painting for the recovery of the statue are not valid, still less so is Kekulé's remark (*Arch. Ztg.* 1893, 76) that the vase was too archaic to be compared.

[4] Cf. Löschcke in the *Ath. Mitth.* v. p. 381 ; Pl. 13 *ibid.* gives the statue of a hoplitodrome on its basis, which Löschcke supposes may be that of Epicharinos on the Akropolis.

[5] Shape and decoration are those of the red-figured lekythoi of the style mentioned. The eye is approximately oval. Helmet and shield are only indicated in outline. Just at this time purely outline designs first make their appearance on lekythoi. The incision of the muscles is thin and light. Cf. *Ath. Mitth.* 1891, Taf. ix. (Mayer), p. 307 *seq.*

[6] Benndorf made this suggestion some time ago, but without publishing it. In the meantime Six expressed the same hypothesis.

[7] The wounded warrior falling backwards, a favourite figure of Duris and his school (cf. Robert, *Scenen d. Ilias u. Aethiopis*, p. 6 *sqq.*), is similar and yet very different : it shows what Kresilas had to work upon.

[8] Tölken, *Verz. der Geschn. Steine*, iv. 257 ; Winckelmann, *Descr.* iii. 230.

century B.C.), and it also may give an indirect echo of the statue by Kresilas. The position of the legs on gem and vase corresponds roughly with the requirements of the basis of the Diitrephes.

We may further expect to find traces of the statue among the marble copies of

Fig. 50.—'Gladiatore Farnese' in Naples. (The restorations are omitted.)

later times, since it is mentioned by Pliny among celebrated works, and since it stood in so accessible a spot. It has been shown (p. 115) that the statue must be the earliest of the works of Kresilas known to us, and must be dated about 450, so that it doubtless retained a certain severity of treatment. All the required conditions are met with in à torso at Naples, there restored as the so-called Farnese Gladiator

(Fig. 50).[1] It represents a man wounded to death, still standing upright on both feet; the left is advanced and flat on the ground, the right is drawn back, and rested probably only on the ball. In order to preserve his equilibrium, the man places his legs as far apart as possible, yet it is apparent from the bending knees and the backward inclination of the trunk that he is already losing his strength : he will soon grow faint, and in another moment he must fall, for the principal wound is near the heart. Thus the breath is already leaving him ; the heaving breast and contracted abdomen show that he pants for air. In effect, here is a *volneratus deficiens, in quo possit intellegi quantum restet animae,* and the muscular man, almost exaggerated in his strength—there is a fine heightening of effect in so representing him—is the sure prey of death.

The small but fast-bleeding wounds on two corresponding places in the right and left breast favour the supposition that they are inflicted by arrows. In the bronze original actual arrows were doubtless inserted. The equipment of the warrior may be pictured approximately from the vase and gem : he would wear the shield on his left arm, and carry either the lance or, more probably, the sword, as on the gem, in his right hand ;[2] on his head he would wear a helmet. The supporting tree-trunk was, of course, absent in the original, and the position of the legs would in consequence produce a much more direct effect.

A certain hardness and severity of style at once strikes the eye.[3] The prominence of the lower edge of the ribs and the straining of the whole trunk are true and correspond to the situation, though the divisions effected by the straight abdominal muscles are rather harshly indicated ; the transition from the deltoid to that portion of the large pectoral muscle that adjoins the clavicle is also characteristic, and not less hard are the nipples with their sharp rim (in the original they were doubtless inserted). Other noticeable features are the stream of blood, which is represented plastically and truthfully, the swollen veins at the birth of the arm, and the rendering of the navel with the little skin round it. In all these things, as also in the working of the flesh, we recognize an artist striving, within certain limitations of style, regardlessly after realism, and expressing himself with force and energy ; the feeling for measure and repose is still quite foreign to him.

The statue gives a hint of the master to whom the youthful artist must have attached himself in Athens. Not only does it recall the descriptions of the Ladas who lost his breath,[4] but also the Marsyas of Myron, which, in the instantaneous attitude with legs wide apart and trunk thrown back, offers a close parallel to this wounded man. We shall enlarge upon these resemblances in a wider connexion.

A work of decidedly later date presents so much affinity to the one just described that it must be mentioned here. It is a statue in the Vatican (Fig. 51)[5]

---

[1] *Museo Borbon.* vii. Tav. 25 ; Clarac, 870, 2210 ; 872, 2210. Cf. Gerhard and Panofka, *Neapels Antike Bildw.* i. 14, No. 30.

[2] The gem is also more faithful than the vase in indicating the situation of the wound ; on the vase the arrows are sticking only in the leg, because they could not well introduce them into the crowded upper half of the picture without coming into collision with arm, shield, or lance.

[3] It is especially marked in the working of the little tight curls of the pubes ; they recall the hair of the Perikles, but have a still more archaic quality.

[4] Brunn, *K.G.* i. 264, relying on Pliny's description, laid stress on the resemblance between the wounded man and the Ladas. Cf. J. Six, *loc. cit.* 188.

[5] Sala della Biga, from the Villa Mattei ; Helbig, 329 ; first published in Venuti, *Mon. Matth.* i. 101 (here with an older restoration ; right forearm stretched forward, right foot placed on a flat rocky elevation, the support draped ; the left arm unrestored) ; then in Visconti, *Mus. Pio-Clem.* 2, 42 ; Pistolesi, *Vatic.* 6, 10, 1 ; Clarac, 837, 2099 (the present restorations indicated) ; Brunn-Bruckmann, *Denkmäler*, No. 129. Cf. Brunn, *Bayr. Sitzungsberichte*, 1892, p. 660.

which passes as Alkibiades. It resembles the wounded man in a number of characteristic points, such as the contracted abdomen, the powerful chest that expands in the act of fetching a deep breath, the position of the upper arm, and the sharp marking off of the deltoid from the large pectoral muscle. Also, so far as the indifferent copy permits us to judge, the indication of the veins on the upper arm and the treatment of the flesh are similar, though more harmonious and less hard.[1]

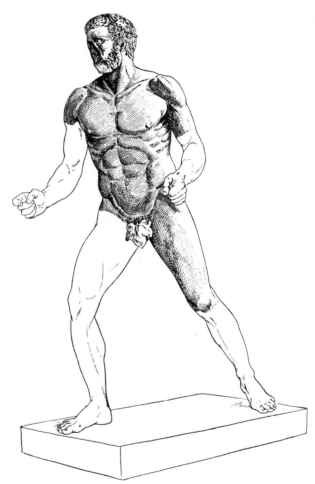

Fig. 51.—Alkibiades in the Vatican. (Attempt at a reconstruction; old restorations omitted.)

The head is fortunately unbroken, but the greater part of the face (almost the whole right side, the nose, mouth, chin, and the front part of the left jaw) is restored. What remains shows unmistakable indications of being a portrait. The beard on the left cheek is very similar to that of the Perikles, the stylistic treatment of the little locks being the same. The hair has a very individual character; it is not crisp and curling as in the Perikles, but smooth and straight, and in life was apparently worn cut short, not parted but combed down over the forehead. These peculiarities the artist has rendered clearly, without however sacrificing any plastic quality: on the forehead, for instance, the hair lies full and massive, while all over the head the separate locks tangle in and out in lifelike confusion.[2] The forehead, which is prominent above the eyes (with a flat depression in the middle), the eyes (the lids unfortunately are much damaged),[3] and the rather thin cheeks are somewhat less stylistic than in the Perikles, and bear accordingly a more individual stamp, though the difference is not vital. The short strong neck, too, must be a feature characteristic of the person pourtrayed.

The restorer has certainly not been happy in placing a helmet under the right foot. A warrior actually fighting may be expected to have his helmet on his head.

[1] The realistic detail of the navel is likewise modified, and the pubes is less strong: there are, however, the same little curls, but lying somewhat smoother and formed more freely.

[2] The hair at the back of the head is peculiarly fine and sharp, consisting of flat meshes, curved now upwards, now downwards.

[3] The left eyelid wholly ancient, the right partly so; the eyelids were rather heavily formed.

From the strongly inflated chest, however, it seems more probable that a *runner* is represented,[1] and that the body was originally bent more forwards so that the right foot would rest on the ground. The glance is directed towards the goal. The turn of the head is amazingly fresh and lifelike. The arms from the elbows were probably both extended ; the right certainly so, as is proved by a puntello above the hip. The original was of course of bronze, and did not require the hideous support between the legs.

To find a statue of an athletic victor which is purely a portrait is very note-worthy. We know from Pliny that, in Olympia at any rate, those only who had won three times were allowed the privilege of a portrait-statue.[2] Now at the time to which the original of this statue must be referred occurred the three Olympian victories of the celebrated runner—known to Plato, and through him to later writers —Krison of Himera, who won in the three successive Olympiads 83, 84, and 85 (B.C. 440). It is quite possible that his portrait has survived in this statue, which must in any case have been made soon after the date of Krison's third victory, or only a trifle later, since its style is nearly allied to that of the Perikles.

In the whole range of fifth-century art there are no works with which this Vatican statue is more closely and narrowly connected than with those referred to Kresilas. We must therefore be bold to rank it among them, and to recognize in it, as compared with the wounded man, an advance on the part of the artist in the direction of harmony, repose, and a softer technique.

IV. *The Amazon.*

Besides the Perikles and the wounded man, the wounded Amazon, the third of the celebrated works by Kresilas mentioned in Pliny, also survives in copies.

Among the several Amazon types preserved in statues, there are two which represent the heroine as wounded. One of these has been generally attributed to Polykleitos, for reasons so sound that they need not be even discussed ; the second type however needs to be studied all the more closely, inasmuch as the wound in this case is in a far higher sense the fundamental motive of the statue, and accounts for the title *volnerata*. O. Jahn had claimed this—the so-called Capitol type—for Kresilas, and it is an error of later times to have diverged from his view. The external probability that in the numerous copies of this type we have the *volnerata* of Kresilas is increased almost to certainty—to such certainty as is possible in these matters—by comparisons of style.

First, however, a few words must be said concerning the much-debated question of the 'Ephesian Amazon statues.' Polykleitos, Pheidias, Kresilas, and Phradmon were the four sculptors who, according to the well-known passage in Pliny, simul-taneously and in competition made each an Amazon for the temple of Artemis at Ephesos. This statement has met with undeserved contempt, though it should rather be considered as confirmed from the fact that copies of precisely four statues of standing Amazons still exist, which on the one hand are clearly to be referred to four different artists, and, on the other, are evidently closely connected by identical

---

[1] Cf. the statues of the *Pal. Conservat. Bull. Munic.* 1876, Tav. 9, 10 (Helbig, *Museums*, 573—575), which seem to me to represent runners, not wrestlers. The prominent edge of the chest shows the hard breathing.

[2] *Statuae iconicae*, rightly referred by Scherer to portrait features of the face, *De Olympionic. Statuis*, diss. *Gott.* 1885, p. 9 *seq.*

measurements,[1] by a general similarity of conception and of dress, and by their belonging to the same period of art.

This important fact is in my opinion beyond all doubt. In the first place, four types are preserved, and not three only, as is generally supposed. True, the fourth type

FIG. 52.—Amazon in Villa Doria-Pamfili. (Wrongly restored as an Artemis; the right arm, the left from the middle of the upper arm, the legs from the knee downwards, the dog, are modern.)

exists only in one copy, and that a mere torso (Fig. 52); it stands in the Villa Pamfili, and has been commonly and erroneously ranked among the replicas of the Polykleitan type,[2] from which, however, it is absolutely distinct. It certainly comes nearer to that

[1] Length of foot in the three types = 30 cm.   [2] Michaelis, *Jahrb. d. Inst.* i. 16, H.

S

type than to any of the others, but it is somewhat severer, and designed with more uniform symmetry.[1] This would be in favour of an attribution to Phradmon, who, being an Argive, must naturally have had points of contact with Polykleitos. The fact that only one copy of Phradmon's Amazon has survived, and that this shows his statue to have been the weakest and least original of the four, not only bears out the judgment recorded by Pliny—according to which his name figures last in the list of competitors—but also explains the exiguity of his fame.

It has further been denied that these four types could have arisen in one and the same period, but so far as I can see without a shadow of proof. The Mattei type is said to be distinctly later than the others, yet the treatment of the dress with its girding, as well as of the body, brings it on the whole within the same stylistic period, while it bears every mark of fifth-century art. In fact, we have already noted (p. 30) that the stylistic treatment of the dress is very closely related to that of the torso of the Medici Athena, i.e. of the Promachos. Unfortunately, none of the copies of this type preserves the original head ; for the head of the Petworth replica, which Michaelis took to belong to the statue, is undoubtedly foreign to it,[2] and may not impossibly belong to the Phradmonian Amazon.

It has also been denied[3] that Pheidias and Polykleitos could have been working at the same period, although we have the classic testimony of Plato to the fact.[4] In the *Protagoras* (p. 311 C), as is well known, he brings in Polykleitos and Pheidias as contemporaries, and in another passage in the same dialogue (p. 328 C) he speaks of the sons of Polykleitos, and says expressly that they are of the same age (ἡλικιῶται) as the sons of Perikles, who, as appears from p. 319 E, is thought of as still living. There is no doubt therefore that, in the eyes of Plato, Polykleitos belonged to the age of Perikles, and that his life and activity coincided with that of Perikles and Pheidias. Now Plato, it is true, was not unfrequently guilty of anachronisms in matters of detail ; he seems to have confused the first and the second stay of Protagoras in Athens, and not to have known the exact time when a certain comedy was performed. But it is impossible that he should have placed a celebrity of the first order like Polykleitos in quite the wrong period. The supposition of Robert,[5] that Polykleitos worked about 435—390, and that Plato in this dialogue, written probably before and certainly not much later than 390,[6] referred the sons of a still living man back to a remote age, is still less conceivable. No stronger witness than that of Plato could be required to prove that Polykleitos was a contemporary of Pheidias, even though he doubtless survived him.

Therefore, far from there being any grounds for doubting Pliny's story concerning the Amazons, the copies preserved of the four types show that there is every reason to believe it. The only improbable part of the anecdote is the statement that the artists worked competitively, and, as self-constituted judges, determined the respective merits of their work. It is however easy to see how such a story may have arisen :

---

[1] This is especially clear in the folds between the legs and the compact kolpos with its straight lines. The motive was so far similar to that of the Polykleitan Amazon that the right upper arm was raised, the left lowered. But she certainly is not wounded, and the left hand does not seem to have rested on anything. The chest, which is quite covered by the chiton, corresponds in its broad outlines to the Polykleitan.

[2] As Löschcke and I ascertained at Petworth in 1888. Cf. *Arch. Anz.* 1890, p. 164. The fillet corresponds to the remains of the head of the Pamfili statue. The character of the head (Michaelis, *Jahrb. d. Inst.* i. p. 27, 'Typus III.') would well suit the Argive Phradmon and the Pamfili statue. Michaelis lays stress on the severe but not melancholy expression of the face.

[3] Robert, *Arch. Märchen*, p. 100 seq.

[4] Cf. Schöll, *Sitzungsberichte d. Bayr. Akad.* 1888, i. 42, note 1.   [5] *Arch. Märchen*, p. 98 seq.

[6] Bergk, *Griech. Litteraturg.* iv. 440, dates the dialogue as early as 407 B.C. Christ, *Platon. Stud.* p. 46, as late as 387 B.C.

the four statues probably formed together one single offering, and, like similar groups of the fifth century and even later times,[1] they presumably stood side by side upon one large plinth, although each was a work complete in itself. In addition to the general inscription referring to the whole set, the artist's inscriptions would be placed under their respective statues. The names being celebrated, there was only a step to the invention of the anecdote of the *certamen*, which was possibly based on some earlier verdict, current in the Argive school, ascribing artistic pre-eminence to Polykleitos.

This offering would scarcely be made by the Ephesians themselves, but by some rich man who tried to get the most prominent artists of the day. The subject, single figures of Amazons, is fully explained by the great importance of these heroines in the legends of the Ephesian temple. According to the earlier tradition, it was they who founded the sanctuary,[2] who set up the miraculous image of the goddess, and celebrated her in the dance.[3] Later a particular Amazon, Otrera the wife of Ares, was named as founder of the temple.[4]

Since two of the Amazons are represented as wounded, it was thought that the commission must have stipulated for the heroines to be represented as fugitives and seeking refuge in the sanctuary, thereby recalling the tradition that the Amazons pursued by Dionysos, and later by Herakles, fled as suppliants to the temple and there obtained quarter. Not only however are two of the Amazons represented unwounded,[5] which would alone suffice to disprove the proposed theory, but even the statues of the two wounded Amazons can scarcely be reconciled with the supposed situation, for they have not in the least the character of suppliants; whereas it is the seeking refuge with the goddess that is the kernel of the tradition: the Amazons were imagined as actually seated upon the altar in the manner customary with suppliants.[6] Finally, that legend seems to be quite late; it is only found in historians of Imperial times,[7] and the story of the pursuit of the warlike Dionysos, on which especial stress has been laid, was probably merely elaborated from the story, originating after the campaign of Alexander, of the exploits of Dionysos among the Indians; by analogy the god was made to fight with other wild races also, such as the Tyrrhenians, Lydians, and Iberians.

The commission seems only to have stipulated for single figures of Amazons, not on horseback, but standing; they were to be an offering to the goddess, whose cult and sanctuary the Amazons had founded. With regard to such externals as size and dress, the artists probably came to an agreement among themselves, in order to avoid any great want of harmony.

The question was how to make an Amazon, composed as a single figure, characteristic. Legend invariably represents the Amazons as courageous combatants; but—after a brave resistance—they are always the vanquished. To give effect to these two essential features, nothing could seem better adapted than to represent an Amazon with a wound in the breast, as becomes a brave fighter. Another main characteristic, in the conception of the fifth century at any rate, is that

---

[1] Cf. the monuments commemorative of battles set up by Attalos I. in Pergamon.

[2] Pindar makes the Amazons who fought against Athens found the sanctuary of the Artemis of Ephesos (Paus. vii. 2, 7).

[3] Kallim. *Hym. in Dian.* 237; the Amazons set up the *bretas*.

[4] Hygin. *Fab.* 223, 224.

[5] The figure referred above to Phradmon is certainly not wounded.   [6] Tacitus, *Ann.* 3, 61.

[7] The Ephesians themselves refer to it before the senate in the reign of Tiberius (Tacitus, *Ann.* 3, 61). Pausanias cites the same legend in order to refute Pindar, who had ascribed the founding of the sanctuary to the Amazons (Paus. vii. 2, 7). In Plutarch's account (*Quæst. Gr.* 56) the Amazons, pursued by Dionysos, flee from Ephesos, where they had settled, and betake themselves to Samos.

they are daring horsewomen. Though the terms of the commission evidently excluded representation on horseback, this characteristic could still be suggested : hence the 'Mattei type'—the Amazon preparing to leap. The artist remembered doubtless the epithet πολύσκαρθμος, the strong leaper, applied in the Iliad (ii. 814) to the Amazon Myrine.

Kresilas, as Pliny informs us, represented his Amazon as wounded. Let us now examine more closely the 'Capitol type,' which must be his[1] (Fig. 53).

The restoration of the statue proposed by Michaelis may, it seems to me, be improved upon in one important respect. Michaelis restores the figure as grasping the spear high up with the right hand, the elbow being only slightly bent.[2] He is guided in this by the Louvre copy, in which the right arm seems to be for the most part antique. On looking at the original, however, it seems more than doubtful whether the pieces out of which this supposed antique arm is made up really belong to the statue ; while, on the other hand, the familiar gem which is the basis for the restoration of this type gives a different position of the arm, bringing the right hand quite close to the head instead of far above it. It becomes evident, on experimenting with a model, that the attitude reproduced on the gem is not a caprice of the engraver, but must have been the original motive. It is infinitely more natural, and affords a real support, at the same time producing a much finer and more self-contained rhythm than the restoration proposed by Michaelis. In the gem however, for want of space, the right hand is placed rather too low ; to correspond with the traces of the upper arm left on the Wörlitz torso, the hand must have had hold of the spear a little above the head (Fig. 53). There is thus presented a wounded combatant, leaning heavily upon her spear, for the left leg on which she stands does not suffice to support the body ; with her disengaged hand she draws away her dress from the smarting wound, and her head is inclined wearily to that side.

FIG. 53.—Amazon of the Capitoline type. (Restored.)

---

[1] The replicas have been carefully collected by Michaelis (*Jahrb.* i. p. 17) ; to his list should be added a head, which he excludes, in St. Petersburg (*ibid.* p. 18, note 3) ; it has little interest, except as showing the extent to which a fine Greek original can be disfigured at the hand of a wretched copyist. There is at Dresden also an old cast of a head of this type, the original of which I am not acquainted with (perhaps = Michaelis m.; cf. c). It is a fair replica. Finally the head of the term in the Villa Albani (No. 76) deserves notice ; it is nothing but an adaptation of this type of Amazon to a decorative purpose ; in these terms long hair on the shoulders was popular, and is accordingly added, little as it suits the head ; the turn of the head is also completely changed (cf. *supra*, p. 66, note 5). A similar transformation is seen in a head of the Barracco collection, also probably from a term. One of the best of the copies, Michaelis 'l,' is given in Fig. 54 from the cast ; the head is wrongly set upon a statue of the Mattei type. It is unfortunately not perfect, the nose, part of the under lip, the chin, and the neck being restored, but even so it is decidedly better than the head of the torso in Wörlitz, which hitherto is the only one well published. The best copy I know is n (Michaelis), in the Conserv. Pal. ; Helbig, *Museums*, 579.

[2] See the drawing in *Jahrb. d. Inst.* i. p. 28 ; Helbig, *Museums*, 503.

[3] Remains of a support on head o (Michaelis, *loc. cit.* p. 18, 33) show that head and hand were connected. I have not examined the original.

FIG. 54.—Amazon head of the Capitoline type, wrongly placed on the Mattei statue in the Vatican. (From the cast.)

Fig. XIX—Amazon of the Capitoline, Rome, Capitoline Museum. (See p. 132 sqq.)

Fig. XX—Amazon, Mattei Type, Rome, Vatican Museum. (See pp. 132, 137 sqq.)

The stylistic qualities most emphatically confirm the attribution to Kresilas. They readily catch the eye on a comparison of the head with the Perikles. Above all, the eye has the same characteristic shape, elongated and narrow, with thick heavy lids and strongly marked lachrymal glands, met with neither in Pheidias nor in Polykleitos. The only difference is that the distance between the two eyes is greater [1] and the root of the nose rather broader. The replica given in Fig. 54 has preserved in the little folds, which run along the rims of both lids,[2] an interesting detail, which is slurred over in most of the copies. In the hair is seen the same principle of plastic fulness as in the Perikles.

If the attribution of this 'Capitol type' to Kresilas be accepted, its special qualities may be next applied to the further characterization of that artist. They are most clearly seen by a comparison with the Polykleitan statue. The contrast, the profound gulf that separates them, is well emphasized by Michaelis.[3] Kresilas has selected the attitude and posture of his Amazon, not with an eye to mere beauty, but primarily because he felt them to be true and appropriate to a wounded person, while Polykleitos is entirely concerned with the beauty of the motive.[4] Kresilas enters into the feelings of the wounded woman, and works from the spirit to the form. Polykleitos aims primarily at a beautiful pose and pleasing drapery. That this contrast exists is undoubted ; at the same time, we must not go too far, and regard Polykleitos as giving his Amazon a wound on the right breast (Fig. 55)[5] absolutely without thought. Certainly the wound would be fretted by the raised arm, and the pain only increased ; yet the artist may have had in his mind the true Doric ideal, an heroic maiden heedless of pain ; he may have intended to give expression to the constant καρτερεῖν united with the fullest κοσμιότης in bearing and dress.

It would thus be his special conception of the subject which induced Polykleitos to give a beautiful position to his wounded Amazon, making her support herself as if merely tired,[6] with one arm on her head regardless of her wound. Besides, in the position adopted, resting on the right leg and with the head turned to the right, the artist has scarcely left himself an option except to place the wound on the right side, leaving the left completely secondary in importance.

Polykleitos represents the self-controlled masculine woman, retaining her brave bearing even when wounded. Kresilas represents only the wounded woman, natural and human, giving way to her pain and trying to lessen it. In the details of the statues the contrast is strongest in the dress. The Polykleitan Amazon wears only a short tunic, which leaves the powerful breast as free as possible ; but this tunic is disposed in the most elegant pleats, and the portion below the hips is treated quite decoratively. In contrast to this elegance, the simplicity of Kresilas is conspicuous.

---

[1] The distance is 34 mm., a full eye-length.

[2] These small folds have nothing to do with the 'bronze technique' of the original, but are a mark of style. On the other hand, the fine groove round the lip represents the edge which in the bronze separated the inserted lips from the rest of the face.

[3] *Jahrb. d. Inst.* i. p. 41 *seq.*   [4] Cf. Kekulé, *Idolino*, p. 12.

[5] The existence of the wound, as Michaelis correctly infers from the material at his disposal, can no longer be doubted. For the agreement of the copies makes it impossible to regard the wound, identically introduced in all, as a capricious addition of the copyists. That some of the copies omit the drops of blood is assuredly only because these were indicated by painting. In the bronze original they must have been rendered plastically. The bronze statue of the Chimaira at Florence, whose antique Greek origin can now scarcely be doubted, has a wound-cut plastically indicated with drops of blood, precisely like the two wounded Amazons (on the lion-body a drop of blood was even especially let in ; it has now fallen out). Cf. also Fig. 50 and p. 126.

[6] Michaelis is right in supposing the supporting pillar to be part of the original. The copies bear him out. The whole attitude of the figure requires a support ; without one it would fall.

Here again his first aim is to be natural. The folds show no artistic arrangement, no attempt at decorative effect, but only a conscientious endeavour to indicate the character of the material. Although the copies differ considerably in the dress, all

Fig. 55—Lansdowne Amazon, now in New York Metropolitan Museum

reproducing it carelessly,[1] the general character is unmistakable. Note, for instance, the simple straight folds falling from the left breast, the kolpos below the belt, the lower edge of the tunic cut off in a straight line, and broken only in the middle where

[1] The two Capitoline statues correspond fairly well, but Michaelis c is the better copy. In the Colonna copy the folds of stuff are altered, and made more like those of the Polykleitan statue. The Torlonia copy has less severe drapery than the Capitoline.

the stuff is a shade drawn up in dainty folds,[1] and lastly the neat pleats proper to fine linen (cf. *supra*, pp. 29 and 46), which play a large part, especially in the lower portion of the tunic.   The artist did not, like the creator of the Mattei type, understand how to combine with these pleats the livelier motive of actual folds, and his Amazon appears in consequence the more archaic;[2] he sought to make his drapery not rich and pleasing, but only simple and true.

Another token of the feeling of Kresilas for sincere characterization is the rider's cloak which he gives to his Amazon, to the complete disfigurement of the back view, so pleasing in the other statues.   For it is as the cloak, appropriate to horsemen in the fifth century, that we must interpret the piece of drapery which is fastened round the neck in front, and falls down behind in heavy folds.   As we learn from vases,[3] this cloak—which was introduced from the north—was of heavy material; and the hard, straight, almost ungainly folds about the neck in front must be taken therefore as true to life.   The Parthenon frieze, it must be owned, represents the rider's cloak much more pleasingly.   It is, finally, a delicate trait to make the wounded Amazon press a corner of the cloak to her side with her left elbow, as though she were cold.[4]

On the Polykleitan statue the waving of the hair has nothing individual or characteristic; it was simply the mode of the time, and we find it given, especially in the Peloponnesos, to the most different women.   The waving hair of this Amazon of Kresilas is, on the contrary, something original and eminently characteristic, that we find nowhere repeated; at once warrior and horsewoman, she has cut off the long locks of her thick hair and simply gathered up the shortened ends into a knot—a mode evidently adopted without regard to appearance, but for freedom of movement and to save time and trouble.[5]

The mouth with Kresilas is more in the plane of the face and blended in a way true to nature with the adjoining parts, while with Polykleitos the lips protrude and are more strongly formed in order to retain a clear plastic shape.   Again, with Kresilas the cheeks, and still more the nostrils with the adjoining parts, are more fleshy and living, and the forehead has more modelling than with Polykleitos, who makes everything flat and abstract.   In like manner, Kresilas makes the breast more fleshy and breathing, while Polykleitos lays special stress on the strong bony structure.   Finally, both heads, in accordance with the general style of the century, show nothing of that contraction of certain muscles caused by pain; they try rather to express the suffering only through the general bearing.   Yet here again there is a difference.   The Polykleitan head, apart from the statue, has absolutely no indication of suffering; in the Kresilaian head the observer, even looking at it alone, would at once detect a certain nameless sadness, which is tangibly expressed only in the slight droop at the corners of the mouth.[6]

The head of the third Amazon ('Mattei type') is unfortunately unknown.   It would be of the greatest possible interest to bring it into comparison, for from all that has been said it follows that, as O. K. Müller maintained, we have in this statue

---

[1] This detail, which occurs in the Polykleitan statue, may be seen in Michaelis c; in b, f, and h this part is restored.

[2] If the Amazons were not all made in the same year, this one, and not the Polykleitan, should be the earliest.

[3] Cf. *e.g.* the interior of the Geryones Kylix by Euphronios.

[4] The Wörlitz figure seems not to have reproduced this motive.

[5] Cf. the cameo in *Comm. in hon. Th. Mommseni*, p. 479; the intaglio Cades, iv. A, 118; further, a beautiful carnelian in Berlin, *Gemmen, Inv.* 1933 b (head to the right; fairly exact copy; indication of the mantle under the neck).   [6] Cf. Michaelis, *loc. cit.* p. 26 *seq.*

the Amazon of Pheidias. The little that, in addition to its mention by Pliny, we know from Lucian of this work goes to confirm this conclusion. Lucian describes it, evidently to distinguish it from other Amazon statues, as the one leaning upon a short spear, τὴν ἐπερειδομένην τῷ δορατίῳ. Now, as a fact, the Mattei Amazon leans upon a lance,[1] preparatory to swinging herself upon her horse. It is true that the 'Capitol type' also leans on a spear, but in this statue the wound is so evidently the leading motive that it would naturally give the descriptive title, while in the Mattei type, on the contrary, it is precisely the strong anticipatory leaning of both arms upon the lance that first strikes the eye and is the most noticeable feature. It has indeed been said[2] that the lance of the Mattei type could not be described as a δοράτιον; but is that term any more applicable to the spear of the 'Capitol type'? And could a spear on which an upright figure would lean be anything materially smaller than that required by our Mattei Amazon? By δοράτιον, then, Lucian must have meant a lance of this kind; and this is not very surprising, for he was probably mentally contrasting it with the Macedonian lances 5½ metres long. Nor can any exception be taken to the expression ἐπερειδομένη; for the Mattei Amazon is *leaning* just as much as the wounded Amazon, and is on the point of leaning yet more heavily for the spring, employing moreover both hands in the action.

The Amazon of Pheidias differs from all the others in its distinctive motive; even the Amazon of Kresilas, resting as she does on one leg with the other drawn back, has less affinity with the Pheidian than with the Polykleitan type. The Pheidian Amazon is preparing to leap, and holds the spear almost as required for the actual spring, but the left hand has not yet tightened its grasp, and will have to take a little higher hold of the spear. The right arm is restored by Michaelis at rather too high an angle; it would be more natural for it to come more forward; the spear, as the Mattei gem indicates, was held obliquely, so that the point came farther to the front. The left foot rests lightly on the ground, as if feeling for a firm footing. On this foot the run would be started, and from it the spring be made on to the horse—whose head must be thought of as facing—the right leg being passed over the horse's back as she swings herself into the seat.[3] In a similar way the 'Diskobolos taking up position'[4] stands on the left leg and feels tentatively with the right before transferring to it his whole weight. And as in the Diskobolos a whole series of movements must intervene before the throw, so in the Amazon before the leap. She must first raise the spear, tighten the grasp of the left hand, and take the run; then set the spear on the ground again and make the spring. Her attention is naturally

---

[1] Michaelis should have emphasized what he says only dubiously (*loc. cit.* p. 45); a lance is proper to the warlike Amazon, and not a leaping-pole, such as the boys used in the gymnasium and palaestra when learning to ride (as on the Attic Kylix, *Arch. Zg.* 1885, Taf. 11, p. 183; cf. also Holwerda, *Jahrb. d. Inst.* iv. p. 39). On the Natter gem the rim cuts off the design immediately above the hand, so that the point of the lance does not appear. The reproduction in Overbeck, *Plastik*, 3rd ed. i. 393, is wrong, for it gives the staff as ending off at the top; in the Natter design it is cut through by the rim, and thus incomplete. This gem, a convex root-emerald (*plasma di smeraldo*), seems moreover, according to Natter's statement, to belong to a certain class of stones especially in favour at the time of Caesar and Augustus, affording far and away the most numerous and faithful reproductions of statues. This class of stone was, so far as I know, never counterfeited in the last century. On these grounds, though I know the gem only from Natter, I feel able to answer quite positively for its genuineness. It is and remains the solid basis for the reconstruction of the statue. A recently unearthed *bronze statuette* in the Museum at Verona is known to me only through a photograph (Arndt-Bruckmann's *E. V.* No. 8); this suffices to show that it is an unmistakable forgery; it is one of a whole series of forgeries known to me, which display just such defects in the casting as the statuette; the head belongs to no definite style, and is quite without the character of the antique: in the right hand the forger has copied the restored remains of a bow from the Mattei type. [2] Cf. Michaelis, *loc. cit.* p. 47.

[3] Cf. the Kylix, *Arch. Ztg.* 1885, Taf. 11. [4] Helbig, *Museums*, 330; cf. *supra*, p. 90.

T

wholly directed to the left. With this accords the carriage of the head, which is not to the right, as Michaelis was deceived into thinking by the head wrongly placed on the Petworth statue, but a little to the left. This is fully proved by the antique piece of the neck remaining on the Petworth statue,[1] and also by the half-neck preserved in the Turin replica.[2] Directly it is restored with the correct carriage of the head, the statue gains extraordinarily in life and animation (Fig. 56).

FIG. 56.—Amazon type. (Attempt at a restoration.)

As regards the lost head, I cannot refrain from a conjecture which has been gaining upon me, although sundry external circumstances are against it. May not this type be preserved in that well-known bronze term which at one time stood in the Villa at Herculaneum as companion to the Doryphoros term (Fig. 57)? The carriage and turn of the head are not, it is true, those required, for the head turns a little to the right and is set too straight on the neck: we know however that the copyists were not over particular about preserving the carriage of the original, when they adapted heads of statues to the term-form. The Herculaneum head passes indeed as a replica of the Polykleitan Amazon,[3] though it is sufficiently extraordinary that it should; in reality the heads have scarcely a superficial likeness, and are fundamentally distinct, both in the facial forms and in the arrangement and treatment of the hair. On the bronze head the hair does not, as in the Polykleitan Amazon, lie smooth upon the skull, but forms a thick, heavy, waving mass. The hair about the forehead, too, is not rolled back, but simply combed to either side. The arrangement at the back is like that of the Polykleitan head, but the execution is quite different. On the other hand, we find that nowhere can the hair be better paralleled than in the works which we have referred to Pheidias: the way it grows from the parting is similar to the Lemnia. We may also recall in this connexion the girl's head (Figs. 14, 15, p. 59) in which we recognized a youthful work of Pheidias; both the hair and facial forms make it clear that this is only an earlier stage of the type given in the bronze term. In the latter the facial forms, though imperfectly and coarsely rendered by the copyist,[4] have a distinct Pheidian character; the full mouth, with the strongly arched lips, is especially noteworthy. Such a mouth explains why Lucian went to the Amazon of Pheidias for the στόματος ἁρμογή of his ideal beauty. In this particular the term may be compared with the

[1] Cf. *Arch. Anzeiger*, 1890, p. 164.

[2] In the Turin statue (Michaelis, ε) the lower half of the neck is antique, and shows a slight turn to the left. The statue—only the torso is antique—was a careful copy executed on a reduced scale, about three-quarters, because of the costly material (green basalt). This is exceptional, for most copies of statues, other than colossal works, are either of the same size as the original or quite small statuettes. In the other copies the neck is missing. The supporting figure from Luku in Athens (*Exp. de la Morée*, iii. 88; v. Sybel, *Catalogue*, 442; Durm, *Gr. Baukunst*, 2nd ed. p. 259), which adapts the type to a decorative purpose but copies it badly, makes the head look almost straight out, but keeps a slight turn to the left.

[3] Michaelis, *loc. cit.* p. 16, I. Cf. P. Wolters, *Gipsabg.* p. 233.

[4] The term is probably by an artist inferior to the one who signed his name on the shaft of the corresponding term. The hair is good, but seems to have been cast and put on separately. The face is poorer. The eyeballs are restored, as is the case in most heads from Herculaneum.

FIG. 57.—Bronze terminal bust of an Amazon from Herculaneum (Naples). (By permission of Messrs. Bruckmann, Munich.)

Fig. XXI—Wounded Amazon of Capitoline Type, Rome, Vatican Museum

Fig. XXIa.— Amazon of Lansdowne Type, Ny Carlsberg Glyptotek, Copenhagen

two heads in which we conjectured an Aphrodite and an Eros by Pheidias (Figs. 20, 21, p. 67 *seq.*)   The facial forms are entirely different from the Polykleitan type: there are, for example, none of the retreating planes so characteristic of both the Amazon and the Doryphoros of Polykleitos.   Now, if the stylistic qualities of this bronze term point to Pheidias, it is probable that it reproduces his Amazon, to whom the powerful structure of the face (the Lemnia looks quite soft and delicate by contrast) is eminently suitable.

The Mattei type may then be conjecturally restored with a head of the type of the Herculaneum bronze, and in it may be recognized a work of Pheidias (Fig. 56).

The dress of the Mattei type has certain definite features that mark its period. As was seen above (p. 30), it is especially closely related to the Promachos (B.C. 445—440), a work of the Pheidian school.   The attribution to Pheidias is thus confirmed.   But now the possibility of more exactly dating the Amazons is brought within our reach.   Taking the Parthenon as standard of comparison, we find that they coincide, not with the figures of the pediments, but with the later metopes. The Amazons all display a manner of indicating fine linen by parallel folds which is not seen either in or after the Parthenon pediments.   Kresilas adheres most to the bare defining of the material; Polykleitos lets this fall into the background, and aims rather at beautiful though over symmetrical folds.   The Mattei type, on the other hand, contrives to unite the folds indicative of the stuff with genuine folds, in a rich but natural manner which recalls the linen chiton of the woman on the Parthenon metope, South XXIX (Michaelis).

The Ephesian Amazon statues would thus date roughly about 440, that of Kresilas coming close to his Perikles.   For Polykleitos the date is especially significant, for it gives us a work by him twenty years earlier than his gold-ivory Hera.   The Amazon of Pheidias was a brilliant achievement of the most brilliant period of the master's career.   The wealth of motive in the dress, which finds a parallel only in the Parthenon, and seems to anticipate the pediments; the original arrangement of the garment—the more lifelike and natural because quite unsymmetrical—so well adapted to the situation; the framework of the body, so free from stumpiness or heaviness; finally, the clear and freshly conceived motive—all tend to give to the work the bold and untrammelled note which has erroneously been taken as sign of a later origin.

Finally, as to the way in which the four statues stood in the temple at Ephesos, no more satisfactory arrangement can be devised than to place the Amazon of Pheidias next to that of Kresilas, and on its left; the supporting legs of each statue would thus be on the outside, the two spears on the inside, and both heads would be turned inwards.   The Amazons of Polykleitos and Phradmon, too similar to look well side by side, would then come at either end.   Assuming this arrangement to be correct, it might almost be suspected that the anecdote of the evaluation of the statues by the artists merely grew out of the order in which they were placed: first, to the left, would come Polykleitos, then Pheidias and Kresilas, and last of all Phradmon.

We know of only one other figure of an Amazon famous in antiquity—the statuette of Strongylion, so dear to Nero.   It too appears to be preserved in a copy; for the attribution [1] of a bronze statuette of an Amazon on horseback to Strongylion is extremely probable, since that artist was celebrated for his horses, while the style of the bronze points clearly to a late fifth-century original.[2]

---

[1] Apparently first expressed by M. Hoffmann, *Philol.* 1865, 402; cf. also Overbeck, *Plastik*, 3rd ed. i. 476, note 114.   [2] Especially in head, hair, and drapery.

The fact that there are more replicas of the Amazon of Kresilas than of any of the others speaks highly for the appreciation in antiquity of the qualities peculiar to this work. It has, in effect, a directness of sentiment and force of conception lacking in the others. Kresilas, living at a time when Pheidias dominated the artistic life of Athens, was yet able to preserve a perfect independence and individuality.

V. *The Athena from Velletri.*

In presence of the head of the Amazon attributed to Kresilas, Michaelis [1] felt reminded of that famous type of Athena preserved in the Albani bust in Munich, and in the statue from Velletri in Paris. He is right; for this work also may be brought within the range of Kresilas.

The admirably preserved colossal statue found in a Roman villa at Velletri, and now in the Museum of the Louvre (Figs. 58, 59),[2] is the one complete copy remaining of a magnificent composition which is generally taken as the most perfect expression of the character of Athena.[3] The goddess stands in a majestic attitude; she rests upon the left foot and draws up the right, which she has moved rather to the side. This sideways position of the free leg constitutes a difference between her attitude and the simple walking motive of the Polykleitan Doryphoros. The same pose, designed apparently to give greater breadth to the lower portion of the body, and to lend a certain repose in the movement, was seen in the Farnese Athena in Naples (Fig. 26), referable to Alkamenes. The garment, as in the Lemnia and the Parthenos, is the Doric peplos, and it is similarily girt with a snake: it is not however open at one side, but sewn up; the gorgoneion on the aegis is almost exactly similar to that in the best copies of the Parthenos, though the actual aegis is much narrower in front, and resembles rather that of the Athena on the west pediment of the Parthenon. The border of snakes has of course that richer form introduced with

[1] *Jahrb. d. Inst.* 1886, i. 27.

[2] Fröhner, *Notice de la Sculpture*, No. 114. The two hands and the lower half of the right forearm are restored; the rest of the right arm is antique, but has been twice broken; at the right elbow there seems to be a bad join, the forearm was certainly more bent. The arm with the nude part under the armpit is antique, made in a separate piece. The nose is intact. The statue is made of coarse-grained 'Thasian' marble. There are two copies of the torso in the form of statuettes: (*a*) Broadlands (Michaelis, p. 225, No. 31); (*b*) in the Pal. Conservat. Rome. The head by itself is preserved in several replicas: (*a*) the famous Albani bust at Munich (Glypt. 92), the head of which is thought to be better than that of the Paris statue; certainly the work is rather more animated and less dry, but for fidelity in detail the statue may claim the advantage. This appears from a comparison even of the accessories; such as the aegis, which in the statue displays a much richer trimming of snakes, and the gorgoneion, which in the statue is more severely and evidently more faithfully modelled. In the form of the eyes and of the mouth too the Velletri replica is the more reliable; the mouth is more austere and less soft and fleshy than in the Albani bust; (*b*) in the Berlin collection (*Skulpt.* 79); it is of inferior workmanship, yet it agrees in the main with the statue in the formation of eyes and mouth, and in this respect is better than the Albani bust; (*c*) poor and hastily worked replica in St. Petersburg (Guédéonow, *Mus. de. Sc.* 176; (*d*) in Lansdowne House (Michaelis, p. 469, No. 93); (*e*) Brit. Mus. (*Anc. Marbles*, i. 1); (*f*) in Madrid (Hübner, No. 92). Finally there is a seventh reproduction, without value for the knowledge of the original, but interesting in another respect—*i.e.* (*g*) it is the head from the monument of Eubulides in Athens (*Ath. Mitth.* 1882, Taf. 5), originating therefore somewhere about the middle of the second century B.C. It is not a copy in the same sense as the others, for the artist intended the work to pass as his own, and only fell back upon an older original from want of inventive faculty. Incapable however of entering into its special character, he brought in contributions from his own style, and his reproduction is thus only a travesty of the original. At that period real copying, as understood in Roman times, was unknown, as is proved by the Pergamene imitations of older statues (cf. p. 27): these are never close copies. For the monument of Eubulides cf. the researches of Milchhöfer, which settle the question (*Arch. Stud. H. Brunn dargeb.* 1893, p. 44 *seq.*)

[3] Ottfr. Müller (*Handb.* § 369) describes the ideal of Athena from this work.

Fig. 58.—'Pallas de Velletri' (Paris).

the Parthenos (cf. p. 11). The snakes along the upper border of the aegis are an innovation.[1]   A cloak of the same heavy woollen material as the peplos lies over the left
shoulder and is wound round the body below the waist, falling in a great three-
cornered drapery.   The artist has, it seems, borrowed this mode of wearing a cloak
from male figures like Zeus ;[2] and to it is due a good deal of the majestic impression
produced.   The head is nearly erect, and has a scarcely perceptible turn to the side
of the supporting leg—a turn which enhances the repose and grandeur of the figure.
With a lance in her right hand, held obliquely and grasped high up, not in the least as

FIG. 59.—Head of Athena from Velletri.

if she required support, she displays the serene dignity of her godhead without any
touch of pathos.   In strong contrast to the right arm, the left lies close to the side
with the hand held out, as if to carry an object of a certain weight.   It has been
conjectured that this must have been a Nike which Athena, goddess of victory,
would here, like the Parthenos, carry as her co-ordinate daemon ; and, in effect,
this conjecture has been confirmed by an Athenian bronze coin (Pl. VI. 30),[3] which
evidently reproduces the type of our statue.   This coin is significant, too, as teaching

[1] Cf. Puchstein, *Jahrb. d. Inst.* 1890, v. 85, note 20.
[2] For the rare instances in early times of Athena wearing a mantle, cf. Roscher's *Lexikon d. Myth.* i. 696.
[3] Imhoof-Blumer and Gardner, *Num. Comm. on Pausanias*, Pl. Z. 22, p. 133.

that the original of the statue stood in all probability at one time in Athens; for it is known that the types of the gods on these later Athenian bronze coins were as a rule taken from famous works of art in the city. The fact that later the Athenian Eubulides took this statue as model is also in favour of this supposition.

The general qualities both of dress and head prove beyond doubt that, as is almost universally admitted, the statue must belong to the great second half of the fifth century. Pheidias himself has been thought of,[1] but our present knowledge of that master quite excludes this notion. The Velletri type is quite foreign to all the representations of Athena with which we are familiar in Pheidias and his school, and, on the other hand, there is absolutely no ground to take it, as some have wished, as Polykleitan.[2] Nor can so thoroughly individual a work be brought under the rubric of a school.

The original, as already noted, stood probably in Athens. The snake girdle and the arrangement of the folds about the girdle show further that the artist must have been acquainted with the Parthenos, while the narrowness of the aegis suggests that the figure can scarcely be earlier than the Parthenon pediments. On the other hand, the treatment of the lower folds of the chiton, between the cloak and the feet, shows that we may scarcely venture to exceed that date;[3] indeed, from the folds alone the statue would have to be dated much earlier. They are in reality treated in a pre-Pheidian manner: they are very uniform and not deep, and the ridges are for the most part simply rounded; the style of Pheidias, even in the Lemnia, was more advanced. On the right side, the seam which holds together the peplos is indicated in the same realistic manner as in an extant original statue (probably Parian) of the severe style (about 460—450).[4] The dress, finally, is not allowed to fall over the foot of the supporting leg, as in later Pheidian works. The head contrasts strongly in shape of helmet and type of countenance with that ideal of Athena which the influence of Pheidias and his circle impressed upon the Athens of the second half of the fifth century, and which, as we learn from many minor works of art, had a wide-spread popularity up to the times of Alexander.[5] The Pheidian Parthenos and her derivatives have full, well-rounded features, surmounted by the round Attic helmet, which like the hair is treated decoratively. Our statue, on the contrary, wears the Corinthian helmet, and displays a complete neglect of the decorative element in helmet as in hair; the bony structure of the face is clearly apparent, the expression is full of mature gravity, as beseems the thoughtful goddess.[6] The artist found the elements which he thus embodied ready to hand in the Peloponnesian art of the severe style;[7] by deepening and expanding them, he created a type which has never been surpassed. The forehead is high in the middle (the only statue that comes near to it in this respect is the Farnese Athena), and broad above the eyes. The cheek-bones are not very prominent, but the chin is strong and bony, and, in profile, the

---

[1] Thus Wieseler, *Denkm. d. Kunst*, ii. 144 ; Bötticher, *Verz. d. Abgüsse*, No. 672.

[2] So Wolters, *Gibsabg.* p. 552, 225 ; also Kekulé, *Ann. d. Inst.* 1868, p. 318, by false analogy with the 'Hera Farnese ;' for the latter work cf. *infra*, p. 223, n. 1.

[3] Cf. Puchstein, *Jahrb.* 1890, p. 85, who calls it a 'little later than the Parthenos.'

[4] In the Villa Ludovisi, Schreiber, 29 ; Helbig, 889 ; Brunn-Bruckmann, *Denkm.* No. 357. Braun (*Ruine und Museen*, p. 594) noticed the same. Cf. *Arch. Studien H. Brunn dargeb.* 1893, p. 81, note 62.

[5] Cf. Roscher's *Lexikon*, i. 697, 700 *seq.*

[6] Cf. Feuerbach, *Griech. Plastik*, ii. 23 ; describes the Albani bust as 'pure abstract thought in embodied marble.'

[7] Cf. Roscher's *Lex., loc. cit.* The relief of the Akropolis (*supra*, Fig. 4) shows Peloponnesian influence in the head.

under jaw is very marked. The hair is smoothed back in the plainest and most unpretentious way.

It again follows from all this that the artist, living in Athens during the thirty years of Pheidian supremacy, must have preserved a perfectly independent line, which left him free to give a characteristic colour, derived from Peloponnesian influences, to his conception of Athena.

Sundry details lead yet further. If a cast of the head of the Velletri statue be compared with the Perikles bust, the similarity is quite striking in many particulars, but especially in the formation of the eyes;[1] both have the long narrow slit and the singularly thick, substantial lids. To this must be added that the helmet of the Athena resembles that of the Perikles down to the smallest detail; and since the Corinthian helmet admits of great diversity of treatment in the detail—as is proved by examination of other heads of Athena and of *strategoi*, in all of which the helmet differs somewhat from that on the two heads under discussion—this resemblance may serve as clue to guide us to Kresilas.

The relation of the head to the Amazon has been already justly observed by Michaelis. It appears quite clearly in the eyes, in the mouth, and in the profile; the delicate modelling of the brow, too, is similar; parallel with the clear-cut eyebrows there is a flat depression which disappears in the centre where the forehead becomes a trifle prominent. The simple compact folds of the woollen riding-cloak worn by the Amazon admit of direct comparison with the cloak of Athena; further, the severe pleats in the linen chiton of the Amazon—the uniformity of the folds and the level termination of the lower edge, the fundamental sacrifice of all mere decorative effect to the true rendering of the stuff—are characteristics that reappear in the woollen garments of the Athena. A certain greater freedom and boldness in the execution of the Athena may be explained by its being later than the Amazon: it cannot however have been much later, and must have been executed while the artist still lived in Athens, previous to B.C. 430.

We may reasonably expect to find some trace of so signal a work in literary tradition, and I believe, in effect, that it is actually mentioned by Pliny among the works of Kresilas. Directly after naming the wounded man and the Perikles of Kresilas, Pliny makes an additional statement and, drawing apparently from a Roman source,[2] mentions in terms of the highest admiration a Minerva and an altar in the harbour of Athena, in the great and splendid sanctuary of Zeus Soter—naming as the artist a certain wholly unknown Cephisodorus.[3] That sanctuary, the Disoterion, has been reasonably assumed to be contemporary with the superb laying out of the Peiraieus by Hippodamos in the days of Perikles,[4] and it is only natural to suppose that the great cultus-statue and the altar were set up at the same time, presumably by an artist from the *entourage* of Perikles. Now the original of the Velletri statue would be admirably adapted to Athena Soteira, the powerful and wise protectress, who would certainly be represented in a colossal statue and would very probably carry a Nike, to whom sacrifices were offered in conjunction with Zeus and Athena;[5]

[1] The other copies of the Athena have lost the characteristic formation of the eyes. This is especially the case in the Albani bust; the Berlin copy is better.

[2] Cf. Oehmichen, *Plinianische Studien*, p. 151, who suggests Varro or Mucian.

[3] Thus the MSS. The modern reading *Cephisodotus* is a mere conjecture. Pliny treats of the two Cephisodoti in quite another connexion under the heading of those artists who *ejusdem generis opera fecerunt*.

[4] Wachsmuth, *Stadt Athen*, ii. 141 *seq.*; cf. i. 560.

[5] Cf. Wachsmuth, *loc. cit.* ii. 144. Pausanias (i. 1, 3) mentions a sceptre and a Nike for Zeus, only a lance for Athena, but this does not exclude a Nike. Milchhöfer, too, in *Arch. Studien H. Brunn. dargebr.* 1893, p. 48, note 2, interprets the Velletri statue as Soteira, but I think he is quite wrong in detecting in it the style of Kephisodotos.

U

while it would be excellently appropriate for Eubulides to have derived his Paionia, the goddess of healing, from the Soteira, the saving goddess. It seems not impossible that Pliny intended this addition for Kresilas—from the list of whose works it is divided off only by the word *Cephisodorus*. It has perhaps taken the place of some work by *Cephisodorus* which stood originally under his name.[1] With Pliny's method of writing, this is only too possible; and it may at least be surmised that the Athena of Kresilas, which we have been describing, is no other than the Soteira of the Peiraieus.

What is however certain is that this noble creation of Athena affords a new proof of the capacity of Kresilas—by independent absorption in his task—to work from the spirit to the form, and so to create the permanent and the enduring.

VI. *The Diomede.*

The series of works that may be linked on to the Perikles and the Amazon can be considerably enlarged. A chief addition—a work of extraordinary force of invention—is the Diomede of Munich. Flasch and Brunn have recently emphasized the close connexion of this work with the 'Alkibiades' of the Vatican (*supra*, p. 127, Fig. 51), and point out the 'absolutely identical artistic spirit.'[2] And I know, on the other hand, from personal communication, that Löschcke and Studniczka have anticipated me in the conjecture that we have here a work of Kresilas.[3] The confidence with which I include it in my list is increased by this community of opinion with other scholars.

The reproductions of the statue in Figs. 60, 61 are taken from the latest casts, from which the restorations have been removed;[4] only the lower end of the garment in front remains to be discounted. There is a replica in the Louvre,[5] but it is very inferior to the Munich statue, and displays the carelessness of the copyist, especially in the head, where the variations from the Munich replica are of no import to the knowledge of the original, being purely due to neglect of detail—the hair in particular is flatly and dully rendered. The head has been broken off and unskilfully replaced with the help of plaster, but it belongs indubitably to the statue—which has the further advantage of being preserved to below the knees. It can be seen that the left leg was drawn back in the walking attitude; by the side of the

---

[1] A few paragraphs further (xxxiv. § 79) Urlichs has noticed that the Autolykos of Lykios seems to have got among the works of Leochares. The Tyrant-slayers are introduced by Pliny in the same book under Praxiteles (34, 70) and under Antignotus (34, 86). It is probable that both notices are wrong, and that the 'Tyrant-slayers' belong to Antenor and Kritios (cf. Benndorf, *Annali*, 1867, 306).

[2] Flasch, *Vorträge in der* 41 *Philologenversammlung*, 1891, p. 9; Brunn, *Bayr. Sitzungsber.* 1892, p. 660, 673.

[3] This was communicated to me by Löschcke in the summer of 1890 at Bonn, where on seeing the cast of the figure I became convinced that it belonged to the circle of Kresilas.

[4] Cf. Brunn, *Glypt.* 162; *Bayr. Sitzungsber.* 1892, p. 651 *seq.*; Brunn-Bruckmann, *Denkmäler*, No. 128. The statue first appears in Lafrérie, *Spec.* 77 'Romae,' placed in a niche. It shows here an older restoration, which is to be seen also in Bracci, *Memorie d. Incisori*, i. Tav. 23. The left foot is wrongly restored as if placed flat on the ground, and a cuirass is used as support for the right leg. The Nike on the left hand proves the identity. Bracci calls it 'gladiator victor' in the possession of Verospi. The present restoration was probably made for the Albani collection. An older cast of the bust, probably made when the statue was in the Musée Napoléon, is now in the Ecole des Beaux-Arts, Paris (No. 2739); another copy of the same is in Bonn (wrongly designated by Welcker as 'Büste im Vatikan').

[5] In the Salon du Mars Borghese (No. 2138); Fröhner, *Notice*, No. 128; Bouillon, iii. *Statues*, Pl. 2, 3; Clarac, Pl. 314, 1438. Photograph *édit. Giraudon*, No. 1402. Kalkmann is wrong in supposing (*Gesichtsprop.* p. 34) that the body is not genuine: there is no doubt whatever that the head and body belong together.

supporting leg the copyist has used a tree-stem as a prop.[1] The naked body corresponds closely with the Munich statue, but sheath and sword-belt are omitted. Since the belt in the Munich statue is treated in a manner quite at variance with the general style, and is thoroughly Graeco-Roman in character (it is shaped

FIG. 60.—Diomede in Munich. (From a cast with the modern restorations omitted.)

like a scarf, fastened with effective loops, and finishes off in a fringe), the assumption that it is an addition of the copyist is on the face of it probable ; it is yet further assured by the Paris replica. In this replica the two little flat cross folds which in the Munich statue appear on the garment, above the remains of a support, are also

[1] The upper part is antique.

omitted ; folds of this kind are also peculiar to Graeco-Roman style. The whole treatment of the drapery on the shoulder is somewhat simpler in the Paris replica, with less striving after effective depth and with more severity of treatment. In this it is evidently the more faithful of the two. From the absence of the sword, however, it need only be concluded that the sword of the original was not fashioned like that of the Munich replica, and not necessarily that there was no sword at all, for it is known positively that in the earlier Greek works objects of this kind were always put on separately. A real belt and sheath, put on to the original bronze, presented the copyist with no art-form that could be imitated : if he wished to introduce that addition into his copy at all, he had to invent one for himself, as did the Munich copyist. It is impossible to know whether the Paris replica may not have had a sword-belt of some other material put on, for the falling portion of the drapery, which might have shown traces of the fastening, is not antique.[1] The copyist of the Harmodios (Naples) hit upon a middle course, replacing the real sword-belt of the bronze original by a painted one, and adding a sheath of other material. An instance, corresponding to the Munich Diomede, of the plastic fashioning of the sword-belt in a form selected by the copyist is met with in a replica of the Borghese Ares at Dresden,[2] which has a sword-band adorned with sprays, omitted in the other copies ; it is to be assumed that here also the original wore a real sword-belt.

The Munich copyist has thus sought to heighten the effect of the original, and to suit it to later taste, by the execution in marble of the sword-belt and by the slight change in the dress. Other details fit in very well with this. The hair is very carefully worked, and, far from its being smoothed over through carelessness, as in the Paris copy, there is an attempt, just as in the folds, to give by deeper cutting an effect of light and shade stronger than in the original. This is proved by a third copy, known only from an old cast of the Mengs Coll. in the Dresden Museum (Fig. 62). This cast, though in the form of a bust, is obviously taken from a statue. The head, as can still be recognized, has been broken off and replaced. I have at last, after a long search, found a trace of the lost original : the cast is evidently from the statue which Cavaceppi (*Racc.* i. 9) describes as being in London in the possession of 'Enrico Jennings' ; and it was doubtless taken when the figure was still in Rome.[3] According to Michaelis,[4] the Jennings collection was sold later by auction, and the statue in question —described by Cavaceppi as an 'Atleta'—came into the possession of Lord Cadogan. Doubtless it is still in England. Now this third replica seems to be the best preserved and the most faithful in style. The legs appear to be in the main antique ; they have at any rate the correct walking attitude and the right proportions ; beside the right leg a tree-stem again appears as support. The garment seems to be perfectly preserved in this replica only ; it hangs to the knees in simple broad folds. Both arms are apparently restored from the elbows. The sword-belt is again absent, which strengthens the supposition that in the Munich replica it is an addition. The head can be closely compared with help of the cast. At first sight the hair looks very different from that of the Munich replica, but on a closer examination it is seen that—with very slight variations—it corresponds lock for lock, and that a difference exists only in the

---

[1] In front only the upper part lying on the shoulder and breast is antique ; at the back the falling end.

[2] Becker, *Augusteum*, Taf. 35.

[3] Winckelmann knew the figure, and mentions it with the Albani statue (now in Munich) in *Hist. of Anc. Art.* Bk. v. chap. 5, § 35 (=tr. Lodge, ii. 399) on account of the crushed ears. His statement that the Jennings statue was formerly in the Palazzo Verospi is wrong. The Jennings statue came from Cavaceppi. According to Bracci, it was the Albani statue that was formerly in the Palazzo Verospi.

[4] *Anc. Sculpt. in Gr. Brit.* p. 93, note 242.

working; in the Munich head the marble is deeply dug out round each lock, while the numerous flatly chiselled inner lines of the cast are replaced by fewer and more deeply cut lines. The difference is naturally far more obvious in the thick hair of the head than in the little flat curls of the beard. There can be no doubt that in the rendering of the hair the Dresden cast is more faithful to the original than the Munich statue; the latter is evidently a further development of some original in which the hair must have looked very like that of the Dresden head. The piece of drapery, which in its main outlines corresponds to the Munich copy while exhibiting the simpler treatment of the Paris one, and the absence of the plastic sword-belt, witness further to the greater fidelity of this Dresden replica.

Moreover, it is highly probable that on the Munich head the furrows on brow and cheeks are cut deeper than they were in the original; every feature seems more strongly and sharply marked, the opened lips are more compact, and the expression of strained energy is thereby enhanced. It is however most improbable that this expression should have been entirely introduced by the copyist, or that it could have been so completely foreign to the original as it is to the Dresden head. The latter seems rather to be the work of an inferior artist, who, while faithfully copying the forms of the locks of hair, failed—like the majority of copyists—in the more delicate forms of the countenance, and contented himself with a general dull rendering of the main points. Thus the modelling of the forehead accords perfectly as to essentials in the two heads, but in the Munich head it is far more delicately and sharply executed. The more subtle modulation at the root of the nose[1] and in the cheeks must be regarded, it is true, as exaggerated, but not as foreign to the original. On the other hand, in the Dresden head the eyes, although rendered superficially, are archaic in shape, and so doubtless more faithful to the original; the Munich copyist had tried to modernize them by rounding the eyeballs, by curving the upper eyelid, and by the general clear-cut formation of the lids. In the Dresden cast the formation of the eye is similar to that of the Athena from Velletri and to the Perikles: on the lower lid may be seen a fine incision, on the upper a more strongly marked fold.[2]

The chief result of this critical examination of the replicas[3] is to show that Brunn's arguments[4] against the reference of the composition to the fifth century are unsubstantial; for the shoulder-belt and its tassels, the working of the chlamys and the hair in the Munich copy, on which he bases his objections, have been shown to be later introductions of the copyist.

We now turn to the examination and explanation of the composition.

Brunn's interpretation of the Munich statue is, in my opinion, indisputable: it represents Diomede carrying off the Palladium from Troy.[5] The left hand bore the idol, which, hewn from the same block of marble, was joined to the body below the

---

[1] On the original of the Dresden cast the nose was probably restored.

[2] The Munich copy of the Diomede bears the same relation to the Dresden copy as the Borghese copy of the Anakreon does to the other copies, which are more exact in details (cf. *supra*, p. 60).

[3] Besides the three mentioned I know of no other full-size reproduction of the statue. Two other replicas in statuette size: (*a*) Terme Museum, only a torso; (*b*) Berlin, *Skulpt.* 515, torso restored. Of the head there is a possible replica in Madrid (Hübner, No. 189). [In the spring of 1893 I saw a full-size torso in the *Terme*, with sword-belt and sheath; phot. in German Inst. at Rome.—E. S.]

[4] *Bayr. Sitzungsber.* 1892, p. 656 *seq.*

[5] The objections adduced by Flasch (*loc. cit.* p. 9 *seq.*) against Brunn's interpretation carry little weight. F. interpreted the statue as a 'boxer' on account of the swollen ears, and almost in the same breath as a warrior, because of the sword, and on account of the lance with which he proposes to restore the statue as a Doryphoros.' In the end he leaves it quite uncertain which of all these interpretations he himself adopts, nor does he give any explanation of the naked sword.

Fig. 61.—Head of the Munich Diomede. (From the cast.)

Fig. 62.—Cast at Dresden of a replica of the Diomede. (Original presumably in England.)

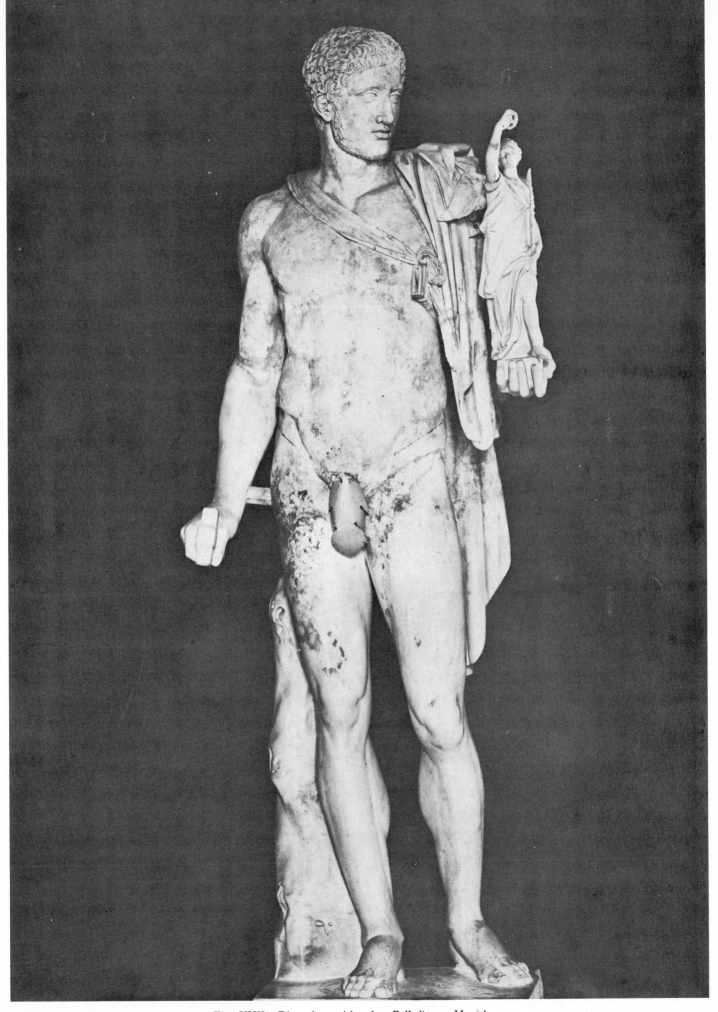

Fig. XXII—Diomedes with the Palladium, Munich, Glyptothek

left shoulder by the great support on the drapery.[1]   The lower portion of the right arm, which hangs down and was presumably turned a little outwards, was joined by a support to the thigh, and the hand grasped the naked sword ; the empty sheath hangs at the left side.

This interpretation[2] is decisively confirmed by the fact that the motive of the statue, as numerous monuments prove,[3] became typical of Diomede the stealer of the Palladium, and this not merely in later times, for one of the monuments dates back, as will appear, to the epoch in which the statue itself originated.   The motive in all its details can be fully and wholly explained by this interpretation alone ; and when other figures are found represented with the same motive, a transference from the Diomede to them, and not the reverse, must be supposed.

The hero has accomplished the bold deed, has torn away the miraculous image from the sanctuary, and is in the act of retreating.   It is now a question of keeping his booty and repelling assaults from others.   To this end, pausing in his stride, he turns his head to the side with a quick energetic movement ; he scents danger, and is on the look out with strained attention, ready with his drawn sword to defend himself at any moment.   The entire motive of the statue—the stride, the head turned to the side away from the supporting leg, the sword held lowered and ready in the right hand, the precious booty carried in the left hand—all take their rise necessarily out of the situation represented.   The beauty of the motive, the effective contrast of the two sides, have not been invented for their own sakes ; they are not formal but purely practical in nature, and have an entirely objective purpose.

This purpose can be yet more closely defined ; for the statue has reference evidently to the tradition that Diomede was threatened as he retreated by the envious Odysseus, who came upon him in pursuit from behind.   Diomede, with his back still to him, is warned by the gleam or the shadow of the sword in the moonlight, draws his own sword, and Odysseus, discovered, relinquishes his design.   This tradition, treated in the little Iliad, is of Argive origin ;[4] it celebrates the heroic king of Argos, who alone carried off the true Palladium and conveyed it to his birthplace, where he was afterwards worshipped in a common cult with Athena ; on feast days, his cultus-symbol, the shield, was carried in procession together with the Palladium.   From this alone it would be probable that the original of our statue stood at one time in Argos ; the supposition is made certain from the reproduction of this very statue on an Argive coin of the time of the empire, when celebrated works of art were so readily copied.[5]   It was therefore undoubtedly made for Argos, and for the cult of Diomede there established.[6]

Another work of art derived from the statue is scarcely less interesting to us. It is an Attic vase-painting of the last decade of the fifth century,[7] representing

---

[1] Brunn's idea of a small Palladium of bronze fastened to the marble support (*Bayr. Sitzungsber.* 1892, 653 *seq.*) is, I think, untenable, as being contrary to all known procedure on the part of copyists.

[2] Kalkmann agrees with Brunn (*Gesichtsprop.* p. 34).   His theory, however, that the Diomede formed part of a group is quite untenable (cf. my remarks in *Berl. Phil. Wochenschr.* 1894, p. 1142).

[3] Cf. Chavannes, *De Palladii Raptu, Berliner Dissert.* 1891, pp. 4, 6, 15, 23, 24, 25.

[4] For the tradition of the legend and its origin cf. Chavannes, *loc. cit.* pp. 42 *seq.*, 78 *seq.*

[5] Coin of Antoninus Pius, Imhoof-Blumer and Gardner, *Numism. Comm.* Pl. K, 44, p. 39 ; cf. Chavannes, *loc. cit.* p. 5.   The right forearm is a little more raised.   [Pl. VI. 32 is reproduced from a still more distinct example of this coin ; it belongs to M. Imhoof-Blumer, to whose courtesy I am indebted for the impression.—E. S.]

[6] This removes Flasch's objection that 'a statuary representation of Diomedes in the period to which the original belongs is problematic.'

[7] Naples, No. 3235 A. (Heydemann) ; *Mon. d. Inst.* ii. 36 ; Overbeck, *Gallerie*, Taf. 24, 19.   Cf. Chavannes, *loc. cit.* p. 6 *seq.*   The numerous restorations have never been noted ; these are—all of the Odysseus

Diomede with the Palladium almost exactly according to the scheme of the statue; the sole differences are immaterial, and lie in the arrangement of the chlamys, in the introduction of the petasos about the neck, and the wreath on the hair. The painter has however utilized the motive in a form of the tradition first introduced to the Athenian stage by Sophokles,[1] according to which Helen assists in the theft. The picture represents the two heroes, Diomede who carries the Palladium, and Odysseus, both with drawn swords and engaged in a dispute, which Helen appears to be soothing. This vase-painting, which is for the rest a fresh testimony to the direct influence of the Attic stage on contemporary vase-painting,[2] must either be derived together with the statue from a common source, such as a wall-painting, or else the figure on the vase is derived from the statue. The last appears the more probable, partly because the design is so entirely statuesque in character, and partly because the figure does not fit in very well with the whole scene, but is conceived rather as a single figure. This view can only be reconciled with our previous conclusion that the statue was destined for Argos, on the supposition that the artist worked in Athens, where the design could easily have passed into the workshops of the vase-painters.

In later antiquity again this statue was utilized in representations of the theft of the Palladium—as on the beautiful Spada relief[3]—precisely because in it had been found the most pregnant expression for the deed and character[4] of the hero.

Now, though the original must have belonged to the free style of the fifth century, it is equally clear that it comes under none of the chief tendencies familiar in this epoch. It does not belong to the narrow Polykleitan circle; for the contour of the face and the hair, as also the general bearing and conception, are quite different. As little does it conform either in head or body to the Attic style of the Parthenon frieze and pediments and similar works—except in so far as the energetic turn of the head recalls the Promachos and the Dioscuri of Monte Cavallo—or to that Attic manner chiefly known from the Munich and Florence athletes.[5]

On the contrary, it brings us again to Kresilas. The similarity of the beard to that of the Perikles (especially in the Vatican replica) is startling. We recognize (in the Dresden cast) those long-slit, heavy-lidded eyes, familiar from the Perikles and the Amazon; and again (Munich replica) the marking off of the brow from the nose by two vertical depressions as in the Perikles. And the likeness of the mouth to that of the Amazon at once catches the eye, in spite of the difference in the expression. The hair also—in this respect only the Dresden cast can come into question—is similar to that of the Amazon and the Perikles; it consists of heavy, plastically full

(except the upper half of the body and the hands), the shaft of the lance and the handle of the sword painted above the sheath. Originally the sheath was empty, and Odysseus held the drawn sword in his right hand. He was of course bearded. In the Helen a piece of the middle of the body, the left arm, the back of the head, the nose, and the forehead are new. The cloth hung up is quite out of harmony with the style of the vase, and is also modern. The Diomede is all antique. The inscriptions are given correctly in Heydemann's facsimile, wrongly in the text and illustrations. The style of the vase is that of Aristophanes and Erginos, which begins about 430 B.C.

[1] In the Λάκαιναι; cf. Chavannes, *loc. cit.* p. 51 *seq.*   [2] Cf. *supra*, p. 110, and *Arch. Anz.* 1890, p. 89.

[3] Schreiber, *Hellenist. Reliefbilder*, Taf. 7; cf. gems (Chavannes, *loc. cit.* p. 15), *Mon. d. Inst.* vi. 51 D; *Arch. Epigr. Mitth. aus Oester.* iii. p. 40.

[4] The characterization is carried to the verge of portraiture; hence Fröhner, *Not.* 128, explained the Louvre replica as a Roman portrait; cf. Brunn, *Glypt.* 5th ed. p. 217. Lately Winter, *Jahrb.* v. 1890, p. 167, went so far as to try to trace the original back to Seilanion, on the ground that the Munich Diomede offered points of resemblance to portraits (*e.g.* the Plato) by that artist. Brunn in his latest essay on the statue, *Bayr. Sitz. Ber.* 1892, p. 663 *sqq.*, merely tries to show that the art of Seilanion, like the Diomede, marks a transition from the style of the fifth century to that of Praxiteles and Lysippos. Previously however (1891) Flasch had thoroughly vindicated the fifth-century character of the body, and his results are confirmed by the analysis given above.

[5] Cf. *Mon. d. Inst.* xi. 7; *Röm. Mitth.* 1892, p. 81, Taf. 3. Cf. *infra*, pp 259-262.

masses, with shallow inner lines carved upon them ; the crown is deeply embedded. The hair of the so-called Alkibiades (Fig. 51) is very similar ; but there it is evidently copied from the person pourtrayed, while in the present instance the artist (as will presently appear) submitted, in the whole arrangement of the close-cropped hair, to the influence of an older heroic type.

On the ground of the treatment of the hair, the Diomede should be placed in the same period as the Perikles, the ' Alkibiades,' and the Amazon, *i.e. circa* 440. Yet other considerations—the dress, the structure, and the modelling of the various facial forms—would suggest it to be perhaps somewhat earlier. The dress—abstraction always made of the modernized details in the Munich replica—is closely related, in its simple true defining of the thick woollen material and in the singular force with which the folds are rendered, to the Velletri Athena.

The body seems at first sight to resemble the Polykleitan canon ; and it does so, both in the broad outline and in the details ;[1] yet a close inspection brings marked differences to light. The whole body is more compact and more strained ; all the forms display more tension, more readiness for the energetic manifestation of force. In Polykleitos, for instance, the lower line of the chest is graduated more gently and harmoniously—one might say, more schematically—than is the case in the Diomede, where its projections and depressions produce far richer modulations. In the Diomede also, as in the other works attributed to Kresilas, is to be found the harsh passage of the deltoid into the shoulder. The straight and oblique abdominal muscles, too, are rather more hardly marked off than with Polykleitos, and even the navel, notwithstanding its general similarity, is less flat and more substantial. All these differences bear witness, however, to the indisputable connexion with the characteristics observed in the earlier of the works attributed to Kresilas. The Diomede continues their tradition, tending in the direction towards Polykleitan forms.

The modelling in the face of the Diomede is singularly rich, even allowing for the fact that in the Munich copy it is probably exaggerated. The bony eminences of the brow are strongly emphasized. Their junction with the nose has already been cited as especially Kresilaian. The interciliary region also is perceptible though faint, since the whole lower half of the forehead projects strongly. The root of the nose, *i.e.* the point where the frontal bone and the nasal bone meet, is treated with especial delicacy and richness, and is carefully marked off from the adjoining parts. The treatment is similar in the Perikles, though not so advanced. The bridge of the nose is narrow.[2] The delicate, natural shape of the nose affords a good contrast to the schematic shape affected by Polykleitos. The nostrils are of singular energy in their swollen cartilaginous formation. Finally, the spare cheeks and the parts about the mouth are richly modelled. On the other hand, in the strong emphasizing of the oblong, angular shape of skull may be recognized a tendency towards the Polykleitan canon.

All these observations tend to prove that the Diomede most probably originated in the period *circa* 440—430. This is the epoch to which we referred the Velletri Athena, a work with which the Diomede corresponds in every respect. It will be remembered that in the Athena the Polykleitan influence was apparent in the walking attitude.

This result admirably fits in with the required condition, that the artist of the

---

[1] *E.g.* the formation of navel, abdomen, and pubes.

[2] In the Munich copy the nose is antique. A characteristic point is that the distance between the inner corners of the eyes corresponds not to the full eye-slit length, but only to the length without the tear-gland.

Diomede made in Athens a statue destined for Argos. The later removal of Kresilas to Argos, which we dated after 430, would thus be prepared for by earlier relations with that town, attested both by the fact of the commission and by the influence of the Argive school.

Finally, it is sufficient to indicate in what a pre-eminent degree the Diomede exhibits that Kresilaian power of individualization which characterized the Amazon. Of the facial forms, the thinness of the cheeks is especially to be noted, as well as the unusually broad and powerful chin, the strong structure of the lower jaw, and the hard prominence of its corners, which it had been customary to conceal under a fatty stratum of skin. All these details express the rough obstinate force of the son of Tydeus. The cropped hair and the sprouting whiskers [1] serve to define the powerful youth, so do the ears swollen from the boxing-match (this detail undoubtedly belonged to the original: the Munich and Dresden replicas exhibit it, and only the indifferent Paris copy omits it. This allusion to skill in the roughest and most dangerous of sports is as appropriate to our hero as it is to Herakles).[2] The ear is for the rest very carefully modelled: it has a long thin lobe, clearly separated from the rest of the ear.

It was natural that so forcible a creation as the Diomede should make a strong impression on its own and on later times. The earliest monument derived from it, the Attic vase, has already come under our notice. A statue of Ares, referred to in an earlier connexion (p. 94, Fig. 41), would appear, from the whole attitude and bearing, the arrangement of the garment and the sword, to be also derived from the Diomede. The reverse is certainly not the case; for in the Diomede every detail has its reason in the situation represented, while in the Ares we only get a beautiful motive used without special significance—whence also the less emphatic turn of the head. The dull and meaningless drapery of the Ares likewise denotes an artist of the second order.

It will be seen presently that the Diomede seems to have stirred up emulation even in the circle of Polykleitos.

To later, perhaps only to Roman, times pertains the transformation (preserved in a charming bronze statuette found at Zürich) of the Diomede into a Hermes.[3] The winged cap and shoes denote Hermes; but the entire motive, down to the garment on the left shoulder, is borrowed from the Diomede; even the close-cropped hair, the shape of skull, and the expression retain something of the prototype.

On the other hand, a larger, much mutilated bronze statuette in Berlin appears to be an original of the good Hellenistic period.[4] The Diomede forms the basis for a portrait conceived heroically. The garment is omitted; but the prototype can be traced not only in the motive but also in the forms of the body, and—notwithstanding the portrait-character and the different hair—even in the countenance, which has the same angular jaw and slight whiskers.

Finally, the Diomede, like so many celebrated Greek statues, had to serve as model for portraits of the Roman emperors. A good instance is a statue of Augustus

[1] Cf. Brunn, *Bayr. Sitzungsber.* 1892, 654 *seq.*

[2] As far as I know, the first dated representation of Herakles with swollen ears appears on the coins of Euagoras I. (410—374)—cf. Roscher's *Lexikon*, i. 2163, 5; yet there are many instances which may be earlier.

[3] *Mitth. d. Antiqu. Gesellsch. in Zürich*, Bd. xv. Taf. 5, 23, and xvii. 7, p. 133, No. 57 (Benndorf).

[4] Antiquarium, *Inv.* 7419, height 0·20, from Asia Minor. The figure is cast hollow with thin walls; square patches are let in, as often occurs on larger Greek bronzes. Arms and legs were cast separately, and are now missing. The surface is much rubbed.

in the Vatican ;[1] the garment is there altered to suit the Roman fashion.   Lastly, it seems to have been present to the mind of the artist of the superb bust of Caracalla in Berlin,[2] which recalls it in bearing and expression, in chlamys and sword-belt, and even wears the same whiskers.

VII. *The Medusa Rondanini.*

To the surprise doubtless of many, the Medusa Rondanini—that noble and unique creation which once so inspired Goethe in Rome—does not belong, as has been supposed, to later Greek art, but is inseparably linked to the series of works now under discussion and associated with the name of Kresilas.

The Rondanini mask, now in Munich [3] (reproduced from the cast in Fig. 63), is admirably preserved ; save for some insignificant bits of the snakes and of the hair, only the extreme point of the nose and the edge of the left nostril are modern. The mask is cut straight off at the back, and has been fastened in modern times upon a square plaque.   The existence of two replicas preserved in Rome, now in the Museo Torlonia,[4] witnesses to the celebrity of the work in antiquity.   They have no background ; in modern times they have merely been placed upon busts.   Two Medusa masks in the Vatican [5] and a colossal one in Cologne [6] are similarly cut off at the back and unprovided with a background : they have however at the most only a very distant dependence on the Rondanini mask, imitating it in externals but trans- lating it into the late half-effeminate and half-pathetic manner.

The circumstance that these masks were worked without a background suggests that they were intended to be fastened by the purchaser against a wall—that is to say, to hang simply against the wall of a house.   They certainly could not, as has been suggested,[7] have stood in any definite relation to the architecture, for in that case they would have been worked into the architectural member they were intended to adorn, and it would be difficult to explain the existence of exact replicas. The latter suggest rather a famous Greek original, copied for its own sake and absolutely independent of varying architectural surroundings.   This original must have been cast in bronze, to judge from the network of snakes, so little suitable to marble, and from the smoothness of the surface of the face.   It will be felt, too, how much more effective the work would be in bronze than in marble.   The best (No. 294) of the two Torlonia replicas is significant, because it renders the hair generally without the deep undercutting of the Rondanini replica, and is rather more severe and evidently more faithful in the details.   Thus the little curling lock at the side near the left eye is formed quite in the archaic manner with a tightly rolled end. In other respects the faces show that the Torlonia replicas are both inferior works.

The general place of the Medusa in the history of art, notwithstanding the gross error of judgment in which I had myself concurred,[8] is unmistakable on a close

---

[1] Gall. delle Statue, No. 262 ; Bernouilli, *Röm. Ikonographie*, ii. 1, Taf. 3, p. 58.   The head unbroken.
[2] *Skulpt.* 384 ; Mitchell, *Select. from Anc. Sculpt.* Pl. 20.
[3] *Glypt.* No. 128 ; Brunn-Bruckmann, *Denkm.* No. 239 ; Brunn, *Götterideale*, p. 60.
[4] *Museo Torlonia*, Taf. 74, Nos. 294, 296.
[5] Pistolesi, *Vatic. Descr.* iv. 13 ; Helbig, *Museums*, 10.   [6] Friederichs-Wolters, *Gipsabg.* 1598.
[7] Brunn, *loc. cit.*, and *Verhandl. d. Philologenversammlung in Dessau*, p. 76 ; *Götterideale*, p. 60 ; Dilthey, *Annali d. Inst.* 1871, p. 228 ; K. Bötticher, *Erkl. Verz. d. Abgüsse*, No. 793.
[8] In Roscher's *Lexikon d. Myth.* i. 1724.   The coin of Seleukos (Gardner, *Types*, Pl. 14, 6) compared by J. Six, *De Gorgone*, p. 73, is quite different, and is probably at the most a distant Hellenistic derivative of the Rondanini type.   The hair is Lysippian.

FIG. 63.—The Medusa Rondanini (Munich).

Fig. XXIII—Medusa Rondanini (Photo of the Original.)
Munich, Glyptothek

inspection of the replicas. The stylistic treatment of the eyes and their adjoining parts (such as the sharp edges of the eyebrows), of the hair, and of the mouth is never met with at all so late as the fourth century. The work is of the free style of the fifth century—a result to which the development of the art type of Medusa does not in the least run counter.

The Medusa head with beautiful, undistorted features appears on an Attic vase as early as about the middle of the fifth century,[1] not it is true in the form of a mask or of a gorgoneion, but as a severed head with the neck, in the hand of Perseus. A great artist must be at the back of this conception (cf. *infra*, p. 200). Following on this come several gorgoneia with the severed neck; they exhibit the same type of pure beauty, and from their style they must be dated in the second half of the fifth century.[2] The endeavour was to dispense with all external tokens and to define the Medusa by the expression alone, mostly by wide-opened eyes and bristling hair.

But now our artist invested the old traditional gorgoneion with beauty of feature. In doing so he did not entirely give up the severe character of the mask: he also retained the two snakes which encircle the head and twine into a knot under the chin, and which had been a familiar feature in the distorted gorgoneia of the type immediately preceding;[3] and he adds to the head the further attribute of two wings, similarly borrowed from more archaic art, though it was not common there,[4] and had still a certain air of innovation. For the rest he is in substantial agreement with the other works of the epoch that represent the new 'beautiful' type of Medusa.[5] He too gives her big wide-opened eyes and short bristling hair. Only, to give full effect to the wings and snakes, he had to let the motive of the hair fall more into the background, whereas other artists of the time lay chief stress upon it. He too, like most of the others, lets the hair lie smooth and well arranged in the centre over the forehead; but he makes it stand out at the sides and frame the countenance as far as the region of the ears; the ears themselves he omits, as is usual in the 'beautiful' type. On the other hand, the character he strives to give to the mouth seems to be peculiar to himself. He throws into it the chief expression. While the others either make the mouth beautiful though quite ordinary,[6] or else recall the older type in a mechanical and discordant way by introducing into the face the projecting tip of the tongue,[7] our artist has contrived, without impairing the beauty, to retain something of the older conception, by making the mouth unwontedly broad and with parted lips, showing the upper teeth. The discovery of the place occupied by our Medusa in the development of the type affords a key to the right understanding of the intention of the artist.

Above all, it exposes as false the ordinary notion that the Medusa is conceived as dying. Goethe it was who first discovered in the mask 'the agonized stare of

---

[1] *Annali d. Inst.* 1881, Tav. F. Style of the Orpheus vase (50th *Berliner Winckelmannsprogr.* 1890, Taf. ii.) For the date see *ibid.* p. 162.

[2] Thus the terra-cotta relief, *Arch. Anz.* 1891, p. 122, Fig. 17 a; the Panofka tile, *Terrak. v. Berlin*, Taf. 62, 1; bronze masks in Berlin Antiquarium, No. 7484.

[3] Frequent on the gorgoneia of the 'middle' type; so on the shield of the Parthenos (British Museum copy) and on the shield of the Athena of the Nike balustrade; on the aegis of the Albani Athena (Fig. 29, p. 79) and of the Munich Athena (Brunn, *Glypt.* No. 86).

[4] Cf. Roscher's *Lexikon*, i. 1722 *seq.*, where several certain examples of the older fifth-century type are given.

[5] See Roscher's *Lexikon*, i. 1721 seq. For the gem with Solon's name cf. *Arch. Jahrb.* 1888, p. 310; the monuments which in Roscher I placed in the beginning of the fourth century should probably be dated in the fifth. For important new evidence cf. the terra-cotta in *Arch. Anz.* 1891, p. 122, Fig. 17 a.

[6] *E.g.* the bronze attachments for the handles of pails, Berlin Antiquarium, *Inv.* 7484, and Roscher, 1722.

[7] Cf. the terra-cotta mask, *Arch. Anz.* 1891, p. 122, Fig. 17 a.

death.'[1] He was followed by many others—*e.g.* Friederichs,[2] O. Jahn,[3] Dilthey,[4] and Kekulé,[5] who expanded on this theme. The representation of a dying, defeated woman stiffening in death is, however, far removed from the intention of the whole series of works with which the Rondanini mask must historically be ranked. What these works really do is to substitute for the wild brutality of the older type[6] a tranquil human conception ; for the grim look of fury, a fixed wide-opened eye that fascinates the beholder by its daemoniac power—and this effect is heightened by the bristling hair. By the powerful chin and the broad open mouth our artist has depicted yet more intimately the wild force and constraining strength of the daemon,[7] and at the same time has suggested the powerful voice which tradition attributes to the gorgons. Above all, he alone has known how to invest the whole expression with a freezing horror.

It was not till a much later date—till the epoch after Alexander—that the type was created of the agonizing gorgon, looking out with blank despairing gaze.[8] Yet not even at this time is she ever represented as exhausted or dying, and those gorgoneia still preponderate which depict the force, the wrath, and the wild anger of the grim daemon, though in the pathetic and realistic fashion of the time.

This historical survey exposes what was incorrect in Brunn's[9] interpretation of the Rondanini mask. Brunn did not, certainly, fall into the error of seeing in it a dying creature : he describes the general expression admirably as a 'cold stare,' but he attributes this fixity to an 'architectonic petrefaction of the form,' the mask having, according to him, served an architectonic purpose. The objections to this view have already been raised. But the so-called tectonic character of the mask, its severely symmetrical composition within an outline of almost geometrical simplicity—an inverted triangle—is nothing more than one of the proofs for the relatively early date of the work. For this character is common to all earlier gorgoneia without exception. It is most strongly marked in the earliest period, and is afterwards gradually modified,[10] till it completely disappears in the Hellenistic epoch, when the severe full view is also commonly given up.

It is true that our mask is distinguished from among works of the same time and epoch by its severe lineal structure : this structure is however not selected for any external purpose, but only as lending itself to the mental expression. The mask has only to be compared with others to appreciate how considerably the severe structure contributes to the daemoniacal expression : even as the serried ranks of an army produce more effect than the same troops in loose array—so it is with art-forms.

---

[1] *Schriften der Göthegesellsch.* Bd. ii. *Tageb. über Briefe Göthe's aus Italien*, p. 240 = *Ital. Reise*, Rome, 25 Dec. 1786. Cf. April 1788, where he notes 'the discord between death and life, pain and delight ('Zwiespalt zwischen Tod und Leben, zwischen Schmerz und Wollust').

[2] *Bausteine*, No. 672 (= Fried.-Wolters, *Gipsabg.* 1597). 'At the moment of turning to stone ' ('im Moment des Erstarrens').

[3] *Aus der Alterthumswissenschaft.* p. 278 ('im Tode erstarrend'; 'eine lähmende Kälte . . . lösch den letzten Lebensfunken aus '). [4] *Annali d. Inst.* 1871, p. 220 *seq.*

[5] *Entstehung der Götterideale*, p. 25 *seq.*: 'unterliegt in Trotz und Schmerz.'

[6] Dilthey, *Annali*, 1871, 220, takes for granted that the archaic gorgon was represented as dying. It is however easy to prove that the old type came into existence without any thought of death. On the contrary, the type was, although inappropriate, adopted for the scene in which Perseus kills the gorgon. Cf. Roscher's *Lexikon*, i. 1701 *seq.*

[7] Meyer noticed (on Winckelman's *Geschichte d. Kunst*, v. 2, § 20) that the forms incline to the wild and terrible ('zum Wilden und Schreckenden'). [8] Cf. Roscher, *loc. cit.* 1724.

[9] *Glypt.* 5th ed. p. 164 *seq.* ; *Verhandlungen d. Philologenvers. in Dessau*, p. 76 ; *Götterideale*, p. 59 *seq.*

[10] Cf. Roscher's *Lexikon*, i. 1719, 15 *seq.* In the older period the circle is the fundamental form.

The mask terminates above in a broad horizontal, which exerts a gloomy massive effect upon the whole.   Thence the lines converge downwards in the manner of an equilateral triangle; at their point of intersection the terrible expression of the whole culminates in the half-opened mouth with the snake-knot beneath.   But above the wings broaden levelly out—surely and inevitably, as when a bird takes its quiet flight through the air,[1] does the spectator feel the ghostly head approach, while beneath the shadow of the wings hiss the snakes.[2]

We have endeavoured to explain the Rondanini mask by the period and the subject; but complete comprehension is only possible with the recognition of the personal note, of that quality in the work which belongs, not to the nature of Medusa, but to the personality of the artist who created her.

After all that has been said, no detailed proof is needed to show that this personality is the one with which we have been occupied.   The broad likeness— the likeness of a child to its parents—strikes the eye at once.   Among the single features, the eyes again first claim attention.   Although the Medusa type required the eyes to be wide open, the artist has given them the heavy thick lids noted in all his heads, nor is the little fold on the lower lid omitted, while the strongly marked lachrymal gland also belongs to his system of forms.   In the centre of the forehead the smooth interciliary region is again indicated; to the sides the lower part of the forehead is markedly prominent, but without being separated off by depressions, as in the Diomede, from the sharp edge of brow—a difference based on the character of the heads: in the one everything is concentrated towards the centre, and in the other a massive breadth dominates the whole design.   A further point of agreement is the way in which the nose is formed, with a narrow rounded bridge rising gently in the middle and very lifelike nostrils, although its lower part is essentially different, being made broader to lead on to the unusually broad mouth, while the nostrils of the gruesome creature are strongly inflated.   And again it is indisputable that the drawing of the mouth accords with the works already examined, and in particular with the Diomede.   Finally, the hair about the forehead closely resembles that of the Athena in arrangement and treatment.

We find, then, in the Medusa all the characteristic details of the work of Kresilas, and, more than this, we find that general type so difficult to define in words.   It is, finally, a fresh witness of the artist's power of entering into the heart of his subject, and of making the outer form expressive of the inner qualities.   It must, of course, be reckoned among his later works.

Being a work of the fifth century, the mask could not have served a mere decorative purpose; it must have been set up in some public building and have had a religious significance; something like the 'golden' (probably brazen) gorgoneion on the outer side of the south wall of the Akropolis (Paus. i. 21, 3); or like that older stone one at Argos, ascribed to the Kyklopes (Paus. ii. 20, 7). Precisely Argos, the home of the legend of Perseus and Medusa, might well have given this commission, and our Medusa may be thought of as a possible offering in the sanctuary of Demeter Chthonia at Hermione, for which an inscription

---

[1] The wings are not sunk as Brunn (*Glypt.*) and Kekulé (*Entst. d. Götterideale*, p. 26) assert.   In the *Verh. d. Philologenvers. zu Dessau*, p. 76 (*Götterideale*, p. 59), Brunn himself says that the wings are raised in a threatening manner.   I only know one instance of a wearily sunk pair of wings, *i.e.* a Medusa head on a gem of doubtful authenticity (from Coll. Blacas, now in Brit. Mus. *Catal.* 1253; King, *Anc. Gems*, ii. Pl. 20, 6; cast in Cades, Cl. ii. F, 56).

[2] The snake-heads are restored, but evidently right on the whole.

shows Kresilas to have worked. Since the Γοργείη κεφαλή, according to ancient conception,[1] had a ghostly existence in the underworld and was subject to Persephone, the Medusa mask might well be set up in a sanctuary of the goddess of the lower world. It has been seen that the mask was intended to be fastened to any wall. Pausanias (i. 2, 5), in the description of a Temenos of Dionysos at Athens, reports that the mask of the Dionysiac daemon Akratos was attached to the wall of the sanctuary; and, according to Pliny (xxxvi. § 13), there was a mask of Artemis, an archaic work of Boupalos and Athenis, on the wall of her temple in Chios.

The creation of Medusa also influenced succeeding art, were it only by its external scheme, which was repeated with more or less similarity in so many later gorgoneia; as to its spiritual character, that could only be copied, never imitated.

VIII. *Statue of an Athlete at Petworth.*

As last and latest link in the personal growth we have been studying, there remains to be added the head of a youth adorned with the victor's chaplet, which is preserved in four copies. The finest is at Petworth, in the collection of Lord Leconfield;[2] it is reproduced in Fig. 65 from a photograph taken from the original by permission of the owner; Fig. 64, from an old cast in Dresden belonging to the Mengs collection, shows the profile. Nothing is restored in the head except the tip of the nose. The neck is almost entirely preserved, but it is cut sharply off and set on to a coarse modern nude bust. The head is probably identical with one published by Count Caylus in 1736.[3] This youth with the curling hair has wound about his head the victor's chaplet, taenia or mitra.[4] The ears, which are not swollen, and a certain refinement and gentleness in the whole form, would indicate that he is no hero of the glove and the pankration, but has conquered in a different way— either in a running match or in the combats of the Pentathlon, where skill rather than brute force was required. The chaplet is not twisted in a knot at the back, but wound round the head, with the ends tucked in and pushed through the fillet on either side above the temples. This method of fastening, though very practical and doubtless often employed in real life, is yet nowhere else represented in plastic art. The artist

---

[1] Nekyia of the *Odyssey*, xi. 634; Aristoph. *Frogs*, 475. Cf. Roscher's *Lexikon*, i. 1703; Max. Mayer in *Jahrb. d. Inst.* 1892, p. 201.

[2] No. 24, Michaelis, *Anc. Marb. in Gr. Brit.* p. 609; *Specim. of Anc. Sculpt.* i. 30. The marble is fine in grain, the nude parts polished.

[3] Caylus, *Rec. d'Ant.* ii. Pl. 48, 2; p. 142. The engraving (reversed) certainly gives a head of this type. According to Caylus, the neck was cut off below and fitted on to a Roman draped bust which he severely criticizes. He says further: 'Ce buste *était* dans le cabinet de M. le chancelier de Pontchartrain.' Probably it had been recently sold and sent to England. The Petworth collection was being formed at the time Caylus wrote (1750—1760; cf. Michaelis, *loc. cit.*) For the new possessor the Roman bust may have been replaced by a nude Greek one. The other replicas are: (*a*) a poor copy, lately at the art dealer Abbati in Rome—see *Bull. d. Inst.* 1867, 33 (Helbig); *Mon. d. Inst.* ix. 36; *Annali*, 1871, 279 (Conze); Brunn-Bruckmann, *Denkm.* No. 84 (from the cast). (*b*) A fragment of the right half of the head, found at Trèves—see Hettner, *Die Röm. Steindenkmäler des Provinz. Mus. zu Trier*, No. 695. According to Löschcke, *apud* Hettner, *loc. cit.*, the head comes rom a relief. Löschcke informs me that the relief belonged to the incrustation of the Thermae, where famous athlete statues had been copied in relief on the scale of the originals. (*c*) In the Palazzo Riccardi in Florence, left of the doorway leading to the staircase—Dütschke, ii. 182.

[4] The woollen fillet which was given to the victor in addition to the wreath was called μίτρα in the earlier period (cf. Pind. *Ol.* 9, 84; *Isth.* 4, 62; Böckh, *Expl.* p. 193); as was also the similar fillet used in symposia and worn by Dionysos (cf. *Samm. Sabouroff*, Taf. 23).

Y

here evidently desired to vary for once the ordinary arrangement. The locks of hair fall so freely over the chaplet that at the back they almost conceal it. On the crown

of the head and also on the left side above the chaplet is a rectangular broken surface, which proves the right arm to have rested on the head with the hand hanging over on the left side.[1] The head is slightly inclined to the left. The expression is one of complete repose, to which the motive of the arm on the head, as in the famous statues of Apollo and of Dionysos, would further contribute.

In an athlete, it is true, this attitude is open to another interpretation. It occurs in representations of athletes cleaning themselves with the strigil : the youth places one hand above his head in order to scrape himself under the arm with the other, as for example in a statuesque figure from a fifteenth-century Attic grave-relief.[2] But the tranquillity of this head, and above all the festive wreath of the victor, exclude the notion of a youth scraping or anointing himself, and still more of course the idea of a youth exercising. The

Fig. 64.—Profile of athlete. (Petworth Coll.)

victor must therefore have been represented in repose, in which case the left arm would also require a certain support. The leaning attitude, adopted for the gentler divinities, would of course be quite out of keeping for an athlete. It might therefore be suggested that, resting firmly on the right leg, he supported himself lightly with the left hand upon an athletic weapon, the *akontion* or short spear, something in the manner of the young athlete on a Spartan relief.[3] This would denote him a pentathlete or conqueror in the five combats, as already hinted. In the relief the athlete is further characterized as a pentathlete by the

---

[1] This broken surface occurs both on the Petworth and Abbati copies. Conze was the first to interpret it correctly.

[2] Friederichs-Wolters, *Gibsabg.* 1017 ; for the date cf. *Samm. Sabouroff,* i. Introd. p. 41, note 9. Here the left hand is laid on the head ; cf. *Annali,* 1862, Tav. M. Note also the copy of a statue on a wall in Pompeii, *Röm. Mitth.* 1888, p. 200, fig. 2, where the right arm lies on the head ; the action is Lysippian in character. The motive of the Skopasian head of an athlete in Athens (*Annali d. Inst.* 1876, Tav. G ; Friederichs-Wolters, *Gipsabg.* 1300) is not quite clear ; the right hand rests on the head, and the left, which probably held the strigil, is close to the head. In the head we are now discussing this cannot be the motive, as in that case the rough surface on the top of the head would have to be much larger. Cf. a relief on a marble seat in Turin (Dütschke, iv. 311) ; between Ionic pillars is a figure (evidently in imitation of a statue) of a youth holding his right arm over his head and slinging round his neck a sword, the belt of which he holds in his right hand. (Dütschke took the sword for a bow.)

[3] *Arch. Zeitg.* 1883, Taf. 13, 2 ; p. 228 (Milchhöfer).

addition of the springing weights in the right hand, as the spear alone might in this case be open to misinterpretation. Of this there would be no danger in a statue with the victor's chaplet, and bearing besides its appropriate inscription. An athlete statue thus reconstructed would be briefly described in the late Greek art jargon

FIG. 65 – Head of an athlete. (In the collection of Lord Leconfield, at Petworth.)

as a 'doryphoros,' like the famous athlete of Polykleitos, who also carried the short spear, the *akontion* and not the *doru*, in his left hand.[1]

---

[1] This is evident from the careful copy on the Berlin gem, Tölken, *Kl.* iv. 249. It belongs to the same class of stones as the Natter Amazon gem. In *Ath. Mitth.* iii. p. 292, note 2, I laid stress on the incorrectness of calling an athlete a Doryphoros, but I now think that the interpretation of the *Doryphori* of Pliny as statues of victors is too probable on other grounds to be invalidated by these considerations. Cf. *infra* on Polykleitos, p. 228. —The length of the athlete's casting spear was, as we know from the Spartan relief and many vase-paintings, about the height of a youth.

Now, although Pliny[1] mentions a Doryphoros among the celebrated works of Kresilas, it would be presumptuous to ascribe this work to Kresilas solely on this ground; it is the style which definitely points to his authorship. This style has been generally described as fourth-century Attic.[2] But the head is certainly not of the usual Attic type—its fellow would be looked for in vain on the numerous Attic reliefs—and, more than that, it has all the marks not of fourth- but of fifth-century work. This may be recognized in the treatment of the hair alone, with its separate tight curls and the arrangement over the ears, and is seen still more decisively in the eyes and adjoining parts. Comparison with the fourth-century Attic type of youth, so admirably shown on grave-reliefs, or with the Skopasian athlete-head in Athens, who also rests his hand upon his head, brings home the complete contrast of epoch more forcibly than words can describe it. Everything is different, but the most readily appreciable difference lies in the stylistic treatment of hair and eyes.

The familiar indications are easy to recognize: the eyes are long and heavy-lidded,[3] with strongly marked lachrymal glands; the two vertical depressions[4] start upwards from the angle formed by eyebrows and nose; the root of the nose has the formation more especially pointed out in the Diomede and the Medusa, but its modulations are more delicate; the nose has the narrow rounded bridge with the rise in the centre like the Diomede; the modelling of the forehead is almost identical with that of the Diomede, but somewhat flatter and daintier. We recognize Kresilas again in the lower part of the face with its rich modelling, though he makes it softer and more refined, and also a little shorter in proportion to the nose, than he had done hitherto. All these forms are but the direct continuation of what was observed in the Amazon. Since however in the Riccardi replica (*supra*, p. 161, note 3 (*c*)) the cheeks and the parts about the mouth present a much simpler, harder, and severer appearance, owing to the absence of the detailed modelling of the flesh given in the Petworth head, and the bony structure is more prominent, it is just possible that the Petworth head, like the Munich copy of the Diomede, represents a slight intensification of the original. The ear with the long narrow lobe is similar to that of the Diomede. Finally, the hair again envelops the skull in plastic abundance;[5] its main motive consists in the little tight curls with twisted ends already studied in the Perikles. In some places, as for example in the chaplet above the left temple, may be recognized the old severe primitive form; but the hair as a whole has become more mobile, freer and more elegant, and its tangled irregularity is yet more natural. In the centre above the forehead the hair is slightly parted; but this only serves to accentuate its capricious character, for it falls quite unsymmetrically over the chaplet, and the

[1] Cf. p. 115. Only one other Doryphoros is named, that of Aristodemos, probably a Peloponnesian artist who stood in close relation to Lysippos, and who seems to have enjoyed a general reputation for his statues of athletes (Overbeck, *S. Q.* 1605).

[2] Michaelis, *loc. cit.*: 'Attic . . . no doubt of the fourth century.' He recalls the Diadumenos which Kalli-stratos describes and assigns to Praxiteles; but, apart from the fact that this ἔκφρασις only shows a general acquaintance with the usual Diadumenos motive, and is therefore worthless (cf. *Jahrb. d. Ver. d. Alt.-Fr. im Rheinl.* vol. xc. p. 65 *seq.*), the motive of the youth has nothing to do with the Diadumenos.—Conze, *loc. cit.*, fixed the time more exactly about 400—350 B.C., and Helbig (*Bull.* 1867, 33) recognized a stage preparatory to the later Attic school. Only Brunn, *apud* Julius, *Annali*, 1875, p. 31, dates the head correctly in the fifth century, since he compares it with the sculptures of the Parthenon.

[3] The length of eye-slit is the same as in the Perikles head (36 mm. with tear-gland, *circa* 31 without, height 11 mm.) The mouth is only 1½ eye-length without tear-gland (46 mm.)

[4] These are distinct in all the replicas.

[5] Although the Riccardi copy only indicates the hair, it well reproduces this plastic character.

chaplet itself diverges from strict symmetry in allowing the two strips to overlap and the ends to show on the one side above, on the other below the band. Evidently the artist, like his contemporary the older Praxiteles, had fallen under the spell of *asymmetria*.

IX. *Relation of Kresilas to Myron.—The Riccardi Head.—The Diskobolos and kindred Heads.—Pythagoras of Rhegium.—Myronian Portrait-heads.*

Among contemporary works, those which have just been associated with the name of Kresilas form a conspicuous group ; and this would be yet more obvious had we the bronze originals instead of marble copies, which are all more or less indifferent and inaccurate. For all the works that have been quoted seem to be without exception copied from bronzes, and it is only among the bronze workers that Pliny names Kresilas.

The development of the formal elements in our artist corresponds in general to that observed everywhere in the second half of the fifth century. Yet the style of Kresilas has met with no proper continuation, only with an occasional imitation in late antiquity of certain details.[1] While the personal style of Pheidias carried all before it to the farthest corners of the Greek world, the art of Kresilas remained an individual art, confined within narrow limits. It does however point backwards ; the style of those works attributed to Kresilas hangs on by a thousand threads to earlier manifestations, and it is at once an attractive and fruitful task to examine the soil in which the individuality of the Kresilaian works had its rise.

The inquiry must start from a work that is unmistakably to be recognized as the forerunner of the Diomede. Only head and breast are preserved, in a copy in the Riccardi Palace at Florence, which is of bust-form (Fig. 66).[2] Like the Diomede, this youthful hero wears a garment on the left shoulder, falling in perfectly simple folds. He also has the close-cropped curling hair and the swollen ears, though, as the garment proves, he is no athlete, but, again like the Diomede, a hero noted for his

[1] A signal instance of this kind of imitation is afforded by the famous Pourtalès Apollo and the Apollo from the Baths of Caracalla, now both in the Brit. Mus. (Overb. *Apollo*, p. 141, Nos. 5, 6 ; cf. Brunn, *Götterideale*, p. 84 *seq.*) From the similarity in their proportions and main features, there can be no doubt that the two heads are merely different versions of one and the same original, while from the qualities common to both it is evident that this original was not materially earlier than Alexander. Now the copy from the Baths of Caracalla displays exclusively the forms proper to that period : the eye is deeply recessed and exceedingly pathetic (the god is supposed to be sunk in musical inspiration), the hair aims dexterously at the most realistic treatment. In a word, there reigns complete harmony between the conception and the stylistic forms. The fidelity of this copy to the lost original is attested by the existence of an exact replica in the Palazzo Giustiniani (Ov. *Apollo*, p. 142, No. 7 ; until the statue on which this head is, is properly cleaned, it is impossible to tell whether they belong together or not). In the Pourtalès head, on the contrary, we note an irreconcilable contradiction between style and conception : an artist enamoured with the style of Kresilas has evidently attempted to introduce the formal qualities of that master into a head of totally different style. Accordingly, the deeply recessed and pathetic eyes have been transformed into Kresilaian eyes with strong prominent lids and overshadowed by sharp angular brows ; in the hair conventional little curls with twisted ends replace the naturalistic fall of the loop of hair over the forehead, and the loop itself hangs more over to the front , further, the mouth is sharply outlined, and the brow has touches that recall the Amazon.

[2] Dütschke, *Zerstr. Bildw. in Florenz;* Heydemann, *Mitth. aus Ober- u. Mittelitaliens*, Taf. 6, p. 101 ; Friederichs-Wolters, *Gipsabg.* 458 ; Brunn-Bruckmann, *Denkm.* 361. The adaptation as bust is ancient ; right side of the breast with the sword-belt is new. The original is now in one of the rooms of the palace ; its place in the *cortile* has been taken by a cast. There are two replicas of the *head:* (*a*) in the Pal. Conserv. (No. 5) in Rome—poor, restored, and worked over ; (*b*) in Berlin, *Skulpt.* 472 (Fig. 67 on p. 167)—better, though superficial copy ; modelling of the forehead good ; the whole of the back of the head is restored. In addition to these two, Arndt thinks that a bust in the Loggia Scoperta of the Vatican which has been turned into a Hermes is a further third replica.

FIG. 66.—Head of a hero (Palazzo Riccardi, Florence)

FIG. 72.—Head in Brescia. (By permission of Messrs. Bruckmann, Munich.)

strength. There is a further resemblance in the broad, forcible chin, in the slightly opened mouth, the heavily lidded eyes, in the modelling of the forehead and the manner in which it is framed by the hair. Yet all these forms are essentially harder and more archaic: the hair, for instance, still lies upon the skull like a heavy cap,

FIG. 67. – Replica of the Riccardi head (Berlin).

instead of growing from it; no depression as yet indicates the actual crown, and the separate masses, unnatural in their extreme smallness, are only as it were carved on the surface, almost without relief; it is only in the mass that the hair has any plastic effect. Moreover, the skull is higher at the crown, and its outline is rounder—not so angular as in the Diomede. Finally, the hero's attitude and bearing was simple and constrained, as compared with that of the Diomede, which vibrates with energy. He stood quietly, with his upper arm lowered, and his head turned slightly to the right; the conception lacks that expression of conscious energy and mental strain which animates the Diomede. Kresilas must have known the original of this work, certainly twenty to thirty years older than his, and must have stood in close relation to a master whose creation he was further to develop. Now by the help of the extant copies of the Myronian Diskobolos it becomes possible to determine with comparative certainty who this older master was : it was Myron.[1]

The head of the Diskobolos of Myron is known to us, not only from the Massimi statue,[2] in which it is attached to the body, but from at least three separate copies. The first of these three heads is the one that has passed from Steinhäuser's possession to the Museum of Bâle ;[3] it has been considerably restored ; the second head, in the collection at Catajo, is intact save for the front part of the nose, which is modern (Fig. 68) ;[4] the third head, which is at Berlin (Fig. 69),[5] though much worked over and restored, is yet of considerable value. A comparison of these four replicas of the head shows that the copyists allowed themselves great freedom in the execution of detail, and especially so in the case of the hair. It is evident that in this respect the Berlin head presents by far the closest and most faithful copy of the original : the elaborate detail of the hair is obviously intended to imitate the chiselled bronze locks of the severe period, and cannot possibly be explained as an invention of the copyist. On the other hand, the greater freedom and lightness of treatment in the case of the other heads is doubtless to be ascribed to carelessness or neglect on the part of the copyist. The case is identical with that of the two replicas of the Riccardi type mentioned above. The copyist of the Catajo head has treated the original of Myron with the greatest freedom, keeping only to the general character of the close-cropped hair, and indicating the detail boldly and openly according to his own ideas. He has even chosen to modify the characteristic wavy dent, made by the outline of the hair over the forehead. The Massimi copyist was more careful, though he too has for the most part dispensed with the delicate little fringed curls which encircle the head, or has at any rate simplified them to a great extent. It is only about the forehead that he has represented them at all elaborately ; and even here he is content to suggest them without working them out. Behind the ear and on the neck he has omitted them altogether, and substituted simpler motives. In this one respect the Steinhäuser head, which reproduces the little tight curls behind the ear and in the neck, is almost as faithful a copy as the Berlin head. With the help of the latter it becomes possible to realize what care Myron must have bestowed on the hair of his Diskobolos. On the upper part of the head the individual locks only slightly turn up at the ends, while on neck and brow they form a fringe of tightly twisted curls. In the Riccardi bust the hair is treated in precisely the same manner, and produces the same singular effect of a cap fitting close to the head—similarities that lead one to infer that Myron was the artist of both works. In the case of the

[1] Wolters (*Gipsabg.* 458) was the first to recognize this, though he certainly went too far in speaking of 'vollständiger Uebereinstimmung,' and in considering the Riccardi head to be almost a replica of the Diskobolos.

[2] Reproduced from the old well-known photograph, Collignon, *Hist. de la Sculp. Gr.* i. Pl. xi. ; Brunn-Bruckmann, *Denkmäler.* An excellent small plaster reduction of the original can be purchased in Rome. The Munich Bronze (F.-W. 453) is late Roman ; only the motive—not the head—derives from Myron's statue.

[3] The head was first recognized by Helbig, *Bull. d. Inst.* 1870, 12. Cf. Kalkmann, *Prop. des Gesichts*, p. 74.

[4] Dütschke, No. 699 ; Arndt-Bruckmann, *Einzelverkauf*, Nos. 54, 55.   [5] *Beschr. d. Ant. Skulpt.* 474.

Riccardi head, however, the hair is richer and more plastic in its effect; the curls of the fringe are somewhat larger; and the line of hair upon the forehead falls quite simply and naturally without forming the dent noted in the Diskobolos.

In the shape of the face there is considerable agreement among the different replicas of the Diskobolos, and if we compare them further with the Riccardi head the general resemblance of the two types is very striking. It lies especially in the formation and modelling of the forehead, in the straight, sharply defined, and projecting eyebrows,

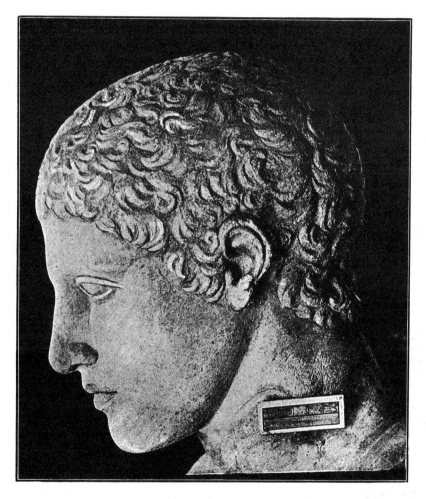

Fig. 68.—Head of Diskobolos (Catajo).

in the spring of the nose and its naturalistic formation, and in the full lines of the lips. Such points of difference as are worth noticing rest chiefly on the obvious endeavour to give a different character to the two personages represented. The pentathlete who is hurling the discus is of comparatively slight build, and consequently the lower part of his face is less powerful and more rounded than that of the confident hero, with the swollen ears, pourtrayed in the Riccardi bust. Other differences show, as do those noted in the treatment of the hair, that the hero is a somewhat later work by the artist of the Diskobolos; for instance, whereas the lips of the Diskobolos, though not tightly set, are closed, in the Riccardi head the lips are parted; further, the expression

Z

of the Diskobolos is still constrained, while that of the boxer is more open.   Again,
the ears in the Riccardi head are placed somewhat lower ; the skull is somewhat less
high, its upper line inclining more to the horizontal, and the head when looked at
from above appears a trifle longer and narrower than that of the Diskobolos.   These
differences are after all insignificant, and in the main the two heads are very similar.
Finally, we must notice the eyes.   Even the Diskobolos has somewhat heavy thick lids,
that lie in a natural manner on the eyeball ; still, the Riccardi head shows considerable
advance in the attempt to give substance and a natural look to the upper lid.

If the Riccardi head is a copy of an original by Myron, executed at a somewhat
later date than the Diskobolos, it follows that Myron must have been the master who
influenced Kresilas in his Diomede.   And it further becomes evident that Kresilas,

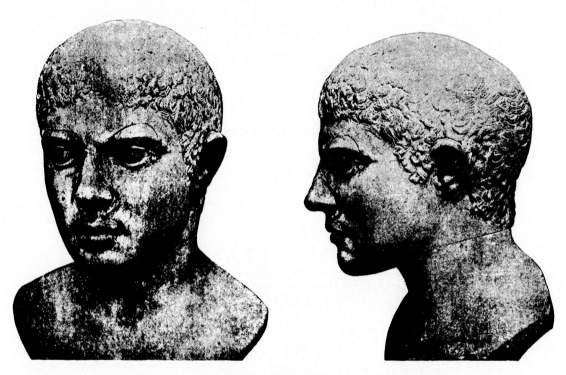

FIG. 69.—Head of Diskobolos (Berlin).

both in the representation of detail, such as the eye and hair, and in his attempts at
expressing individuality, merely developed what Myron had begun.

It has, however, been lately urged by P. Herrmann that the Riccardi head
differs from the Myronian type, and is to be classed with the head of a youth from
Perinthos, now at Dresden (Fig. 70).[1]   The only point I can admit in this contention
is that the Perinthos head can have nothing to do with Myron.   P. Herrmann quite
correctly points out that it differs from that of the Diskobolos in having a shorter
crown, which when seen from above appears rounder, but he should have also noticed
that the Riccardi head has a still longer crown than the Diskobolos, and, further,
that the two last works are linked together, as we saw, by a thoroughly
characteristic treatment of the hair, while in the Dresden head the locks of

[1] *Ath. Mitth.* 1891, p. 313 *seq.* Pl. IV. V.

hair are curled all over the head with considerable uniformity, in a manner differing totally from the Myronian, and recalling on the whole the hair of the Lapith, who is being bitten by a Centaur, from the west pediment of Olympia (a comparison made by Herrmann himself).

Another still more essential difference between the Riccardi and Dresden heads consists in the formation of the eyes. Herrmann rightly criticizes the prominent angular lids of the Dresden head, which produce a wholly unnatural effect, ' as though they possessed no power of move-ment.' This is precisely the manner characteristic of the art of Kritios and Nesiotes, and of the sculptors of the Olympia pediments ; and one of the most precious results obtained from studying the extant copies of the Diskobolos is the knowledge that Myron treated the eyes in quite a different way. The lids of the Myronian statues lie naturally on the eyeball, and their edges are neither prominent nor broad nor angular, as in the Dresden head. In this respect the Riccardi head marks a further advance upon the Disko-bolos. We find a similar treatment of the eyes to the Myronian in the works ascribed above (p. 54) to Hegias, the master of Pheidias, and to Kalamis (p. 81). Finally, the lifeless ' perfectly horizontal line' of the mouth of the Dresden head offers a complete contrast to the life-like modelling of the mouth of the Riccardi bust, which in this point too is so clearly in Myron's style as we know it from the Diskobolos.

Fig. 70.—Head from Perinthos (Dresden).

The Perinthos head belonged to the statue of a victorious pankratiast, and there are a few heads of athletes which are really allied to it : first among these is the boxer in the Louvre ;[1] next, and in a somewhat later manner, an athlete of the Giardino Boboli, formerly erroneously taken for Harmodios ;[2] and, lastly, a statue of an athlete in Lansdowne House.[3] The expression, as well as the round, rather short crown, the hair, the flat eyes, and the wide horizontal opening of the mouth common to all these heads, seem to me to link them together indissolubly, and to mark them

[1] *Mon. d. Inst.* x. 2 ; *Annali*, 1874, Tav. I ; phot. Giraudon, 1207. Cast of the head in the Ecole des Beaux-Arts and in Bonn.

[2] *Mon. d. Inst.* viii. 46 ; Arndt-Bruckmann, *Einzelverk.* 96—98 ; Dütschke, *Zerstr. Bildw. in Florenz*, No. 77. Cf. *Berlin. Philol. Wochenschrift*, 1888, 1448. Separate casts of the head and of the torso in the Ecole des Beaux-Arts, at Paris, No. 2844.

[3] Michaelis, p. 446, 36. The head belongs to the statue, and resembles that of the Louvre boxer, especially in the eyes and forehead, though the statue itself is later in style.

off sharply from the type created by Myron. The statues in the Louvre and the Giardino Boboli[1] apparently belong to the heads set upon them: they represent the athletes in violent movement. The artist, who evidently was a man of note, since his statues were afterwards copied, must have been a contemporary of Myron, inasmuch as he vied with him in representing athletes in violent exertion; but his system of forms has more in common with Kritios and the sculptures of Olympia than with Hegias and Myron. There is no artist to whom all the characteristics noted would apply so well as to Pythagoras; the Perinthos head possibly gives us a

FIG. 71.—Head in the collection at Ince Blundell Hall (Lancashire).

copy of one of his earlier athletes, produced about B.C. 480.[2] Thus we should at last have obtained approximately reliable material for recovering the style of this remarkable master, of whose celebrated athletes some copies must have survived. In the whole range of Greek sculpture, however, the series of statues just discussed seem to me the only ones that can be brought into connexion with him.[3]

It follows that the well-known head from the Ince Blundell collection (Fig. 71) must be classed, not with the Perinthos head as Herrmann had it, but with the Riccardi head, and is therefore also Myronian.[4] The hair agrees minutely with that of the Riccardi bust, even the little tapering locks about the forehead being practically identical in both. The eyelids are also thoroughly Myronian, and differ totally from those of the Dresden head; indeed, they already have something of the manner of Kresilas. Further, the formation of the part between upper lid and brow deserves close attention, as it marks an advance upon the

[1] The neck in both is a modern restoration; yet the marble and the workmanship of head and body seemed to me, after repeated examination, to correspond exactly in character and movement. Moreover, on the left-hand side of the upper part of the head of the Louvre athlete is a great square puntello which indicates that the left arm was raised above the head; this same motive is displayed by the torso. The Boboli statue too is naturally that of an athlete in active movement; the left arm is parrying, the right striking out.

[2] Herrmann and Arndt also thought of Pythagoras in connexion with the Perinthos head (*Ath. Mitth.* 1891, 333). Concerning the athletes of Pythagoras and the probability of their attitude being one of movement, cf. Reisch, *Weihgeschenke*, p. 44.

[3] Further, a much-mutilated statue of a youth in Olympia (*Arch. Zeit.* 1880, 51, erroneously described as Apollo—solely because of the headdress) may, I think, be regarded as a Roman copy after Pythagoras. It belongs to the close of the severe style; the upper part of the body is slightly twisted, the head inclined towards the side of the free leg; the drapery is falling from the left arm. In close relation to it comes a torso of a youth in the Lateran (No. 52).

[4] *Arch. Ztg.* 1874, Plate 3. Kekulé was the first to pronounce the head Myronian. Cf. Friederichs-Wolters, *Gipsabg.* 459.

Diskobolos, and is far more realistic than in the Dresden head. Quite different from the latter also is the full sensuous mouth. Yet just as the Riccardi head, although it recalls the manner of Myron, differs totally from the Diskobolos in expression and character, so does the Ince Blundell head differ in certain particulars from both. The features are more closely packed, the modelling throughout is rounder, and the cheeks fuller.[1] The shape of the head resembles the Riccardi head, though when seen from above it presents a longer, narrower ellipse. On the forehead the transitions between the different planes are effected with peculiar softness and delicacy. The full mouth indicates a powerful and sensuous nature, but the expression of the face is sombre and gloomy. This is accounted for by the swollen ears: the man is a boxer, and, as I have shown elsewhere, it was a favourite device to represent this class of athletes with a sombre look.[2] The head has doubtless retained much of a real model.

The Ince Blundell and Riccardi heads belong together to the same period, but are later than the Diskobolos. The strikingly different individuality of the three heads need not perplex us ; for from what artist should we expect such variety sooner than from Myron, who *multiplicasse veritatem videtur ?* It is specially interesting to learn from the Ince Blundell head that, side by side with the usual broad type of face, Myron also had a narrower type with a more delicate root to the nose, inasmuch as we discovered that the works of Kresilas also exhibit both types.

We are now in a position to understand an adverse criticism which Pliny passed upon Myron : *capillum quoque et pubem non emendatius fecisse quam rudis antiquitas instituisset.* The Berlin copy of the Diskobolos bears witness to the archaic character of the hair in this famous masterpiece, and we cannot wonder that the critic, judging from his Lysippian standpoint,[3] should have viewed with contempt this manner of treating the hair, and merely seen in it a sign of *rudis antiquitas.* The criticism recorded by Pliny has, however, generally been taken to mean that Myron bestowed no care or pains upon the hair—an interpretation which is entirely contradicted by the Berlin head. As a fact, in comparison with the artists of his time, Myron treats the hair with exceptional richness and naturalness. How keenly he appreciated its varying effects is evident from the trouble he has taken to distinguish between the little curling fringe of hair and the masses on the top of the head.[4]

Closely bound up with this ancient criticism upon Myron's treatment of hair is another that accused him of neglecting to express the ' sensations of the mind ': *corporum tenus curiosus animi sensus non expressit.* This is perfectly intelligible in the case of the Diskobolos : the quiet impassive expression of the head clashes with the violent movement of the body. The critic was quite justified in his remark, judging, as he did in the case of the hair, from the standpoint of the fully developed art of Lysippos. But he would not have been justified had he wished to criticize from the historical standpoint ; for the absence of emotional expression was merely a characteristic of all

---

[1] This difference comes out clearly in the measurements : in both heads (the Ince and the Riccardi) the length of the lids (34—35 mm.) and of the lower part of the face, and the distance from nose to brow (70 mm. in each case), are identical ; but the distance between the inner corners of the eye differs markedly (Ricc. 34, Ince 29 mm.), as also the width of the mouth (Ricc. 51—52, Ince 44½ mm.)

[2] Cf. *Olympia*, vol. iv. *Die Bronzen*, text p. 10 *seq.*

[3] Cf. my treatise *Plinius u. seine Quellen*, p. 69 *seq.* (ix. Suppl. vol. of *Fleckeisen's Jahrbuch*).

[4] The pubes of the Diskobolos is treated with just the same care : it is arranged in four rows of small, flat curls, elaborately worked in a manner suggestive of the most careful chiselling ; those of the upper rows are comparatively larger and less curled than those of the lower ones. The pubes seems most accurately rendered in the torso of the Capitol (Helbig, *Museums*, 446). The affinity to the hair of the Berlin head is striking in this case. Next in accuracy comes the London copy ; the Vatican statue is less exact.

FIG. 73.—Portrait-head in the Villa Albani. (From the cast.)

FIG. 74.—Portrait-head in the Hermitage. (From the original.)

work of the earlier part of the fifth century, though it was less striking in the case of figures in repose than in those represented like the Diskobolos in violent movement. Yet if we compare the head of the Diskobolos to other works of about the same date, such as those athletes we saw reason for attributing to Pythagoras, or to the so-called Apollo on the Omphalos, or to the sculptures of Olympia, we shall indubitably find that a more refined and spiritual life pervades it than is the case in any of those other works. But it is precisely because this head transcends by its spiritual refinement that we realize the limitations that separate it from works of the free style—that we realize all the more keenly a certain fixedness and dulness in its expression. And this anomaly may have influenced in some measure that unjust ancient criticism. We shall see, however, that Myron himself at a later stage rose beyond his own earlier limitations (see p. 181).

Before passing to works which lead us gradually away from the Diskobolos to a somewhat later period in the artist's career, we must consider one head which exhibits the stage of art that immediately preceded the Diskobolos. It is the head of a youth in Brescia (Fig. 72),[1] whose affinities with the head of the Diskobolos seem to me unmistakable, although everything about the head points to a cruder and an earlier artistic phase. The origin of the characteristic dent formed by the hair on the forehead of the Diskobolos is explained in the Brescia head, where it forms an angle instead of a curve, and practically amounts to a parting over the forehead. The treatment of the hair itself is very similar in both heads: on the raised, modelled masses the individual masses are delicately carved; they represent short, tangled hair, with a tendency to curl thickly at the ends; a narrow circlet presses into this soft mass. Moreover, the head in its general outline, especially in the powerful development of the skull at the back and in the line from the circlet to the neck, resembles the head of the Diskobolos, except that it is not quite so high. On the other hand, the head is inferior to that of the Diskobolos in the modelling of the forehead (which is also lower), in the rendering of the eyelids (especially of the part between the upper lid and the eyebrow), of the mouth, and of the whole lower part of the face. The form of face so vividly recalls the type of Hagelaidas as it appears in the figure copied by Stephanos,[2] that in spite of the difference of expression it appears to derive from it. The points of affinity with the Diskobolos would lead one to suppose that the Brescia head is a copy of an *early work* belonging to Myron, in which he combined the type current in the Hagelaidas schools with the treatment of hair, the shape of head, and the expression individual to himself. This result is specially interesting, because it seems to confirm the tradition that Myron was a pupil of Hagelaidas—a question to which we shall have to return.

Fig. 73 reproduces a head in the Villa Albani.[3] It is obviously a portrait, the unusually wide mouth and thin parted lips[4] being distinct traits of individuality. Hair and beard are short. All these characteristics, joined to the erect

---

[1] Dütschke, *Oberital.* vol. iv. No. 336. Length of face 0·14. Earlier notices: Conze, *Arch. Anz.* 1867, 108 (who calls the beautiful head 'a wretched copy'); Kekulé, *Annali*, 1865, 62; *Gruppe des Künstlers Menelaos*, p. 40, 4 (Benndorf); Heydemann, *Mitth. aus Oberital.* p. 29, No. 44, 3.

[2] This resemblance had also struck Conze, *loc. cit.*

[3] *La Villa Albani descritta*, No. 744, 'Pericle,' evidently so called on account of the similarity of beard and hair to the Perikles of Kresilas. Brunn, *Bull. d. Inst.* 1851, 88, proposed to recognize Peisistratos, but cf. Helbig, *Museums*, 834.

[4] The width of the mouth (51—52 mm.) measures $1\frac{3}{4}$ the full length of the eye (29—30 mm. from corner to corner). Nose to arch of brows 60 mm.

Fig. XXIV—Diskobolos, The Massimi Copy, Rome (See
p. 168 sqq.)

Fig. XXV—Diskobolos of the Regina Elena, Rome,
National Museum

carriage of the head and its straightforward glance, produce an impression of great energy. The hair frames the forehead in a manner that recalls the Riccardi head and the head at Ince; on the top it is left blocked out in masses which only slightly curl at the end, while over brow and neck it spreads into a profusion of ringlets in the true Myronian manner. Quite in Myron's style too are the form of the eyelids and the tear-glands, the forehead that bulges out towards the root of the nose, the round cranium, and the slight depression in the neck. It is evident however that the work is somewhat later than the Diskobolos, and equally evident that in it we have the immediate forerunner of the Perikles and of the Vatican 'Alkibiades.' The form of the moustache, which leaves the upper lip uncovered, and the shape of the beard recall in particular analogous traits in the Perikles. Since there were plenty of occasions for the private dedication of portraits in the days of Myron, and since we have absolutely no nearer data to go upon, it is naturally impossible to name the personage pourtrayed.

A head in the Hermitage (reproduced from the original, Fig. 74)[1] has a still more marked individuality, though in point of style it is closely akin to the preceding. The treatment of hair and beard, the heavy eyelids with the strongly defined tear-glands, the rounded though elongated shape of the head, with the slight depression in the neck, are all obviously the same in both heads. The outline of the profile of the Hermitage head is further surprisingly like that of the Massimi Diskobolos. This head appears to stand in much the same relation to the Albani portrait that the Ince Blundell boxer does to the Riccardi. It belongs to the small-faced type,[2] in which the corners of the eyes are nearer together, the root of the nose and bridge more delicate, the mouth smaller. These common characteristics receive a singularly animated and individual expression by the addition of a number of interesting details. First we note the mouth, with full, parted lips, very different to the thin lips of the Albani portrait; then the moustache with its curling ends, the rich beard, elegantly parted in the middle, thus leaving the line of the lower lip uncovered. The forehead is modelled[3] like that cf the Ince Blundell boxer. The eyes do not look straight out, but the gaze inclines a little to the left. The whole expression is indicative not so much of prowess, as in the Albani portrait, but rather of cleverness, of worldliness, and of a certain refined sensuousness. We can scarcely doubt that we possess in this head a copy of a work by Myron, belonging to the same period as the Ince Blundell boxer, and affording fresh proof of the artist's remarkable power of reproducing individuality.

We can associate with this portrait a work whose subject is taken from the circle of the heroes—a head of Herakles over life-size, which was found in the Villa of Hadrian, near Tivoli, and is now in the British Museum (Fig. 75).[4] The individuality of the hero is thoroughly accentuated, yet the characteristics of style are essentially those which we observed in the head from the Hermitage. The eyes are unusually big and round, rather than long—a trait which especially distinguishes Herakles in archaic art;

---

[1] Guédéonow, Musée de Sculp. Ant. No. 68.

[2] Clear length of eye 36—37 mm., without the gland 32 mm.; this last measurement is also that of the distance between the inner corners of the eyes. The width of the mouth amounts to $1\frac{1}{2}$ the length of the eye without the gland (48 mm.) Nose to the arch of the brows 71 mm. (= twice the length of the eye). Length of ear 62 mm.

[3] Unfortunately not clearly enough indicated in our reproduction.

[4] Well produced in Specimens of Anc. Sculp. i. 9, 10. Less well in Anc. Marbles of the Brit. Mus. i. 12. My notice of the head in Roscher's Lexikon, 2163, 10, was influenced by this untrustworthy reproduction. Only the front part of the nose and the edges of the ears have been restored.

on Attic vases of the severe style, for instance, dating about the time of the Persian wars, he is represented with large, wide-open eyes.[1]   Lids and glands are rendered as on the Albani and Hermitage heads.   The edges, too, of the sharply moulded lids terminate in a little wrinkle, as in the Riccardi head.   On the sharp edge of the brow the hair of the eyebrows is slightly indicated—a singularity which is not, I think, to be

Fig. 75.—Herakles in the British Museum.

ascribed to the copyist, but to the artist's search after realism, or after some touch that should emphasize the powerful nature of the hero.   Hair and beard are quite short, and arranged in small tight curls.   The vases teach us, again, that these short ringlets belong to the typical conception of Herakles in archaic Attic art.   The moustache alone is smooth, and is treated similarly to that of the Albani head.   The framing of the forehead by the hair resembles the heads already mentioned, with this

[1] Cf. Roscher's *Lexikon*, i. 2161 *seq.*

difference, that the forehead in this case is lower and wider, and that just over the centre the little locks are brushed up, obviously in order to heighten the impression of strength. At the sides and over the temples, however, the hair of the Herakles is treated similarly to that of the other Myronian heads we have been discussing. The modelling of the forehead is also the same, except that the forms are more pronounced. We should also notice two furrows in the forehead, which start upwards from the point where the line of the eyebrows meets the root of the nose; this is another detail in which the art of Myron appears as the immediate predecessor of that of Kresilas. The nose, too, is interesting in this respect. Enough of it is preserved to show how realistically the ridge, which in this case is naturally made wide, broadens out in the middle. The lips are full and slightly parted, as in the previous heads; the line of the under lip is left uncovered by the beard, as in the Hermitage portrait. The lower part of the cheek-bones is strongly defined under the beard. The ear, however, is not represented as swollen. The copyist has made the curls of hair stand out in very realistic fashion by means of under-cutting—doubtless imitating in this particular the sharply chiselled bronze of the original. The shape of the cranium is round, and the depression that usually marks the transition to the occiput is omitted, owing to the unusual prominence of the muscles of the neck that begin at this point. Thus at every point in this head we note the attempt to emphasize the character of the hero, and the conception of him that was thus established inspired all subsequent representations of Herakles, even down to the age of Lysippos. The unnatural size of the eyes was, however, abandoned at a later date. The relation of this head to the heads previously discussed is so close, in spite of certain deviations necessitated by the different nature of the subject, that I incline to attribute it also to Myron. We know of as many as three statues of Herakles from his hand : of these, one made a short sojourn in Rome,[1] and another remained there.[2] It is probable therefore that in our store of copies more than one Herakles after Myron may be preserved.[3]

X. *Statues by Myron.—Diskobolos and Marsyas compared.—Kindred Works.*

So far we have dealt solely with heads which can be traced to Myron : we now turn to whole statues. It would be strange indeed if among the numerous copies which have been preserved there were not found a considerable number after statues of an artist who, precisely in the age in which the copies were made, was always named among the most eminent of sculptors, along with Pheidias, Polykleitos, Praxiteles, and Lysippos.

The two statues of which we have undoubted copies, the Diskobolos and the Marsyas, afford a firm basis for further investigation. In both the body is represented in violent exertion, in both the energies of body and of mind are concentrated in one dominating movement. The prevailing note of Myron's artistic temperament was doubtless love of movement, though he cannot have always had an opportunity for indulging it.[4] His statues of the gods must have been represented in tranquil attitudes, according to the fashion of his time. Coins show us the Athena in the Marsyas group

---

[1] Strabo, xiv. p. 637, 6 = Overbeck, *S. Q.* 536.   [2] Plin. xxxiv. 57.
[3] See *infra*, p. 202, with regard to a probable second Herakles after Myron.
[4] Cf. Kekulé, *Kopf des Praxit. Hermes*, p. 15 *seq.*

standing calmly,[1] while the Riccardi bust proves that Myron had represented one hero at least in an attitude of repose. The same marked powers of individualization that we noted in the treatment of the heads make themselves felt in the bodies of the Diskobolos and of the Marsyas. The first shows us a well-bred youth, carefully trained and developed in the palaestra, executing a studied movement with graceful precision. The second statue shows us a wild, sinewy creature of the woods, accustomed to move by bounds and springs, ignorant of any training, tormented by unbridled passions, and at this moment a prey to curiosity and fear alike. The contrast to which we allude runs through the whole of each figure, and may be observed from head to foot.[2] Both hair and beard are in the case of Marsyas treated in an exceptionally characteristic manner ; the great moustache is rough and bristly ; it is not connected with the rest of the beard, which is itself divided into two distinct parts, consisting of the hair flowing from the chin and of the whiskers. The hair of the head not only bristles up in front, but grows also on the neck in short, flame-like wisps that go up instead of down. This arrangement of hair is affected by our modern clowns, and suits the excitable nature of the droll Seilenos much better than those heavy masses of hair flowing downwards from the back of the head that were generally given to Satyrs in Myron's time.[3] With the exception, however, of the front wisps, the hair lies close to the small head, the round outline of which passes into the neck without the break noted in other Myronian heads. Thus Myron, who had given to the Diskobolos the long crown of the aristocrat, gave to the Seilenos the small round head of the plebeian.[4]

The Marsyas undoubtedly bears the stamp of a later date, and we can see that the character of Myron's works varies considerably according to the time of their production. Further, while in the Diskobolos the expression of countenance is quite unaffected by the violent movement of the body, in the Marsyas expression and movement are in perfect harmony. Astonishment and fear combined are admirably expressed in the head. That ancient criticism about the want of continual expression in Myron applies, like that about his archaic treatment of the hair, properly only to the Diskobolos and kindred heads, and not to the Marsyas ; and it would be unfair to allow it to influence us in our judgment of Myron's artistic capabilities.

The more marked the differences between the Marsyas and the Diskobolos, the more must we insist on their common elements. To these belong above all the severity and the spareness of the forms in both statues. Even in the Diskobolos, who has, it is true, a somewhat fuller body, there is nothing of the nature of soft flesh ; indeed the forms, in their severe sobriety, may almost be accused of hardness and meagreness, though the spirited action of the statue helps us to overlook this defect.

---

[1] L. von Sybel, *Athena u. Marsyas, Bronzemünze des Berl. Museums*, Marburg 1879.

[2] Even the pubes is treated characteristically. In the case of the Diskobolos the hair is cut straight off above and arranged in the same little curls as in the hair of the head (cf. *supra*, p. 173) ; in the case of the Seilenos it takes the form of larger, coarser curls, and spreads in a triangular shape high up the belly.

[3] The nearest analogy to the head of Marsyas and its flat short hair is presented in the Argive bronze, reproduced (very inadequately) *Rom. Mitt.* 1889, p. 170, which is undoubtedly later than Myron. This bronze justifies the supposition that in his Marsyas Myron possibly allowed himself to be influenced by Argive models.

[4] It is only the head of the Lateran statue that can be considered as an approximately faithful copy of the original. The replica *Coll. Barracco*, Pl. 37 and 37 a, which is usually taken as better (see Friederichs-Wolters, *Gipsabg.* 455, and more recently Collignon in *Mélanges d'Archéol. et d'Hist.* 1890, p. 118 *sqq.* Pl. 2 ; *Hist. de la Sculpture Grecque*, i. p. 468), proves on closer examination to be decidedly inferior. The copyist of the Barracco head has obviously taken exception to the simplicity and hardness of the original, and tried to improve upon it ; he has introduced richer and more flowing but more conventional lines ; the typical characteristics dwelt on above, such as the treatment of the moustache, its separation from the rest of the hair of the face, the peculiar treatment of the hair of the head—all this is abandoned and made commoner.

If one imagines the Diskobolos standing upright in repose, and then compares it with the so-called Apollo on the Omphalos, this peculiarity comes out very strongly. The Apollo has full, soft flesh ; the Diskobolos, flat, spare forms. In this point Myron comes into intimate connexion with the group of works which I have felt obliged to ascribe to the school of the Argive Hagelaidas.[1]

In the Diskobolos, further, the obvious difficulties caused by the violent bend of the body are by no means quite overcome : this is especially striking in the representation of the lower part of the trunk.[2] Moreover, the treatment of the planes, which remind one of work in relief, may be taken as a sign of confusion of ideas, due probably to the fact that just about this time figures in motion were being transferred from relief to the round. The Marsyas, on the other hand, is already conceived throughout for execution in the round.

We accordingly find that the ancient orators name him among the last masters of the severe style.[3] The culminating point of his career would be reached about 465—450, a view which has lately been confirmed by the discovery that his son Lykios was already an artist of independent position in 446 B.C., or at any rate at a period previous to the building of the Propylaia.[4] Thus Myron flourished before the mighty artistic revolution which found expression shortly after the middle of the century in the sculptures of the Parthenon, where only a few metopes preserve that severer style which we have noted as a characteristic of his works.[5] Our next task is to find out whether some conception can be arrived at, through extant copies, of the statues of Myron that stood in repose.

Among extant statues there is only one which I could at once bring into immediate relation to the Diskobolos. It is a Mercury in the Vatican, which, though fully deserving the epithet 'bad' given it by Brunn[6] (for it is an extremely poor copy), is yet of considerable significance (Fig. 76).[7] The family likeness of the head to that of the Massimi Diskobolos is self-evident : it is particularly striking in the expression and the shape of the lower part of the face, with its full mouth and round chin. The framing of the forehead by the hair resembles the Riccardi and kindred heads, and the forehead itself, in spite of the poorness of the copy, preserves the modelling characteristic of Myron.[8] The profile shows substantial agreement with that of the Diskobolos ; even the ears have the characteristic wide shape, with the small lobes. The hair is arranged in little curls, which in the original would doubtless appear fuller than in the copy. The upper eyelids are somewhat heavy. The turn of the head, and the quiet upright pose of the figure with hanging arms, correspond exactly to what we should imagine was the pose of the statue from which the Riccardi bust was copied. The weight of the statue is thrown on the right leg, leaving the left leg comparatively free, though it is not drawn back, but is planted with full sole on the ground. The somewhat severe, spare, and wiry forms correspond on the whole with those of the Diskobolos. The feet, for instance—in the rendering of which the copyist

---

[1] Cf. 50th *Berl. Winckelmannsprogramm*, p. 134 *seq.*; *supra*, p. 52 *seq.*

[2] Cf. Jul. Lange, *Fremstilling af Menneskeskikkelsen* (*Abh. d. Kopenhag. Akad.* 1892), pp. 394, 397, 462.

[3] Cicero and Quinctilian in the oft-quoted passages (Overbeck, *S. Q.* 600—602).

[4] Lolling, Δελτίον, 1889, 181 *seq.*

[5] I should not like however to bring either these or the metopes of the Theseion into direct relation with Myron himself. Cf. *supra*, p. 46.   [6] Brunn, *K. G.* i. p. 613.

[7] Vat. *Gall. delle Statue* (Not. 417) ; *Mus. Pio-Cl.* iii. 41. The head had been severed from the body, but certainly belongs. Nose, both forearms, and the piece of hanging drapery are restored.

[8] Unfortunately not visible on the photograph from which our illustration is taken.

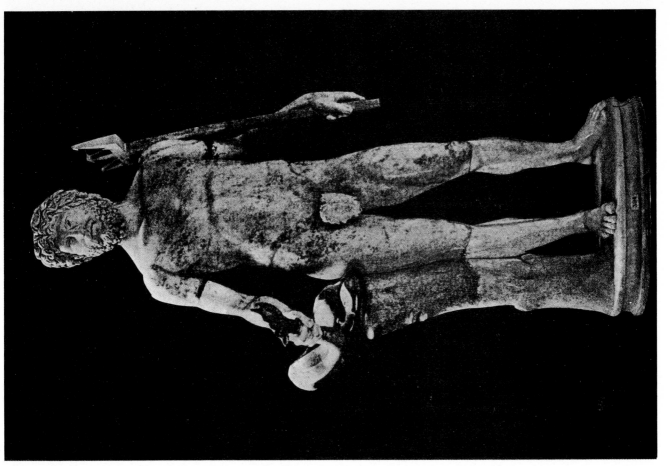

FIG. 77.—Statue restored as **Neptune** (Vatican).

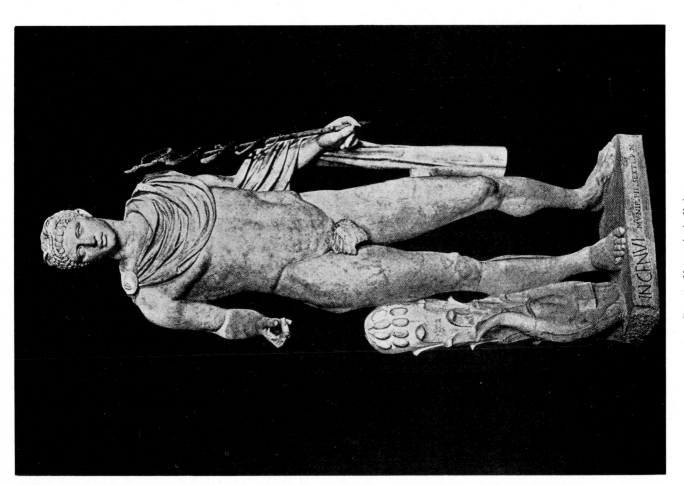

FIG. 76.—Mercury in the Vatican.

has succeeded best—show in their vigorous shapeliness, and the realism with which even the veins are indicated, a special affinity to the feet of the Diskobolos.[1] On the other hand, the chlamys, which is fastened on the right shoulder with a great round button, cannot have been part of the original statue, and was evidently added by the copyist; for the character of the folds is purely Roman—indeed, it may be definitely stated that the addition of the chlamys is a favourite device of a certain group of copyists of the later Empire. For instance, it was given to the later replicas of the famous 'Meleager' after Skopas; the earlier copies are without it.[2] Some copyists also gave a chlamys to a statue of Apollo of which the original must have been very like the bronze Apollo Sabouroff in Berlin.[3] These instances could easily be multiplied; the last one is particularly interesting, because the chlamys of this Apollo agrees so closely with that of our Hermes that one might almost assume both statues to have been executed in the same workshop at the end of the second or the beginning of the third century A.D.[4]

Further, the wings on the head,[5] which are attached in a manner both thoroughly inorganic and thoroughly non-Greek, are certainly an addition of the copyist, just like the wings that appear from time to time on heads imitated from Polykleitos. In Roman times it was not uncommon to turn Greek figures of youths into statues of Mercury.

It is now impossible to determine whether the original by Myron represented a hero, a mortal, or Hermes (without the wings on the head). Pose and attitude have the merit of being natural and unstudied. The youth stands at ease, though not at rest; ready at any moment for energetic action. This is quite a contrast to those attitudes of rest that seem to have been the ideal of the art of the Peloponnesos.

A few other statues may be grouped about the Vatican Mercury. In the very same room of the Vatican—unfortunately, in a very unfavourable light—is a statue of a bearded man (Fig. 77)[6] restored as a Poseidon; in pose and in attitude, as also in the spare, attenuated forms of the body, it agrees very closely with the Mercury. Both arms hang in the same way, and the head has the same turn. Although the copyist, who belonged at the earliest to the age of the Antonines, has, like the artists of the sarcophagi executed at that time, worked the hair elaborately by means of the drill, it is still clear that the type of head is of the fifth century, and on close examination traits may be detected which recall the technique of Myron. Hair and beard, in spite of the modernized appearance due to the drill, still bear witness to the

---

[1] The pubes is also identical.

[2] List of replicas, *Röm. Mitth.* 1889, p. 219 (Gräf). The copies with the chlamys (which moreover varies in each) all belong, so far as I can tell, at the earliest to the later Empire; the Vatican and the Borghese statue in particular are characteristic works of the age of the Antonines. The beautiful Berlin torso without the chlamys is undoubtedly older.

[3] *Skulpt.* No. 51; Overbeck, *Apollon*, p. 226, 5. For the Sabouroff bronze see *Sabouroff Coll.* Pl. 8—11; Overbeck, *loc. cit.* p. 227.

[4] Cf. also the very similar chlamys of the statue of the youthful Marc. Aurelius mentioned above, p. 92, note 4, and other portrait-statues of the same period. Visconti also (*Mus. Pio-Clem.* iii. Pl. 41) says that the Mercury is certainly not older than the age of the Antonines, possibly much later: he quotes in support the inscription on the plinth, which however need not necessarily be of the same date as the statue.

[5] The right wing is ancient.

[6] *Gall. delle Statue*, No. 394; *Mus. Pio-Clem.* i. 32; Clarac, Pl. 743, 1796; Overbeck, *Kunstmyth.* Part ii. *Poseidon*, p. 287, No. 14, p. 289 *seq.*; for the head, cf. p. 267, No. 10; *Atlas*, Pl. XI. 9, head in profile; XII. 35, the whole statue. Both arms from the middle of the upper arm are restored, as also the lower parts of the legs and the attributes, fish and trident. The portion of the shaft of the trident against the upper part of the arm is ancient; its squareness led Visconti to recognize in it the remains of a trident. However, as the fragment of shaft had been separately attached, we cannot feel certain that it belonged to the original.

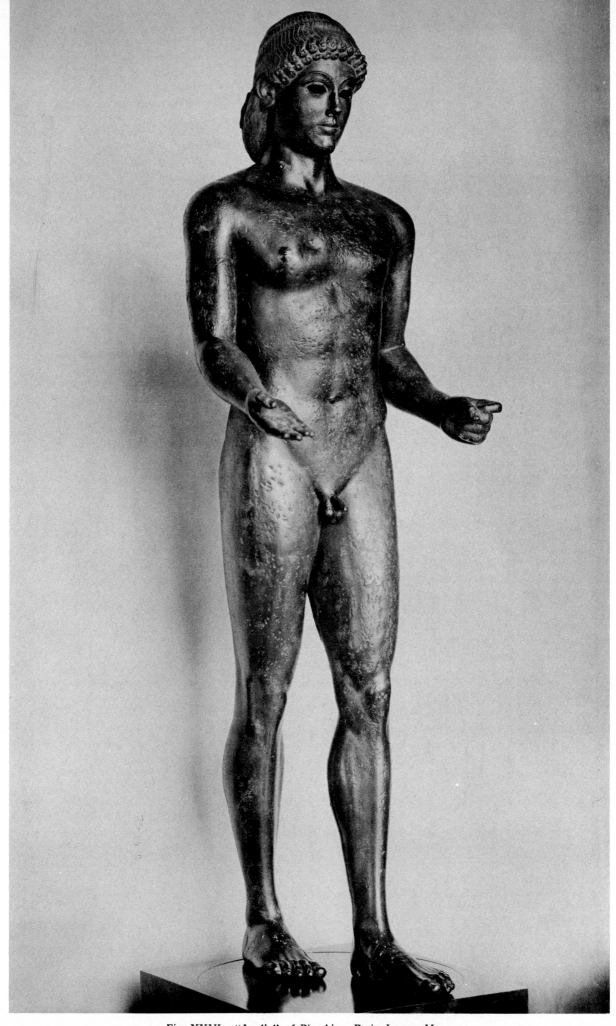

Fig. XXVI—"Apollo" of Piombino, Paris, Louvre Museum

severer style of the original, in the simple, heavy strands that curl up at the ends. The semicircular framing of the forehead by the hair, the vigorous modelling of the forehead which projects towards the eyebrows, and the slightly open mouth are all familiar to us. The hair is brushed up from the forehead. Certainly this statue is no portrait, but an ideal type, in which power and majesty are united. The statue may well represent a god, perhaps Poseidon, as Visconti conjectured.[1]

Even if the head has lost by the hand of the copyist something of its original severity, the statue, whose connexion with the Vatican Mercury is obvious, yet serves to give us a notion of the dignified manner in which Myron represented the gods. The conception is really godlike and quite distinct from human types ; the same power of individualization makes itself felt here that was noticed in the other works attributed to Myron. The attempt to individualize the gods must have been quite novel in those days ; for instance, the hair that rises up from the brow of the ' Poseidon' had not yet become a fixed characteristic of the sons of Kronos, and was apparently now introduced for the first time.

There is another statue very closely related to our Vatican Neptune ; I mean the statue to which a beautiful head in the Berlin collection,[2] reproduced in Fig. 78, belonged. If we disregard superficial mannerisms due to the copyists, the general likeness of the head to that of the Neptune is very striking. The hair of the massive beard, without being deeply carved, produces a rich and varied effect, vividly recalling the beard of the Marsyas ; the moustache, with the simple, straight lines and its clear line of demarcation against the upper lip, is akin to the moustache of the Albani ' Peisistratos' and to that of the Perikles. The hair—exactly like that of the Vatican Neptune —is treated after a method which disappears in the second half of the fifth century (cf. *supra*, p. 19) : it radiates from the crown of the head towards a circlet that confines it ; below this circlet it falls loosely forward, forming a rich crown of locks ; on the neck it is just left long enough to cover the nape. The hair rises up on the centre of the forehead to show the growth, and then falls away gently to either side ; in the Neptune, however, the side locks are, so to speak, forced to the sides instead of flowing of their own accord. Possibly the first arrangement was intended to suggest a mild and the second a vigorous nature. At the point where the root of the nose meets the forehead there occurs the same depression which we noticed in heads by Kresilas. In order to emphasize the nature of the god, the forehead, as compared with heads of athletes, assumes a more powerful and pronounced form, though the main lines remain the same. The cranium is less developed at the back, but this is a point which I incline to charge the copyist with ; it is not impossible that he was limited, as was not unfrequently the case, by the size of his block of marble. The well-defined eyelids with the delicate little wrinkle, the lachrymal glands, the slightly open mouth—all recall the manner of Myron. The body to which this type of head belonged forms, as we shall see, an inseparable group with the Vatican Mercury and Neptune.

We recognize a replica of the same head in a statue at St. Petersburg from the Campana collection (Fig. 79).[3] Though this statue is poor enough in itself, it is

---

[1] Undoubted Poseidon statues, like those in Scherschell (Overbeck, *Kunstm. Atlas*, Pl. XII. 34), may be conceived as later developments of the type under discussion. Cf. also coins, Müller-Wieseler, *D. A. K.* 3rd ed. ii. 72 d.   [2] *Beschr. d. Ant. Skulpt.* No. 158.

[3] Guédéonow, *Mus. de Sculpt. Ant.* 314 ; d'Escamps, *Marbres de la Coll. Campana*, Pl. 14. The head had been severed from the body, but my examination of the statue has convinced me that it belongs. There are only trifling restorations at the point where it joins on : the left side of the head, the right arm, together with the staff of Asklepios, the left forearm with the flat cup, are restored.

FIG. 78.—Head of a god (Berlin).

Fig. XXVII—"Apollo", Choiseul-Gouffier, London, British Museum

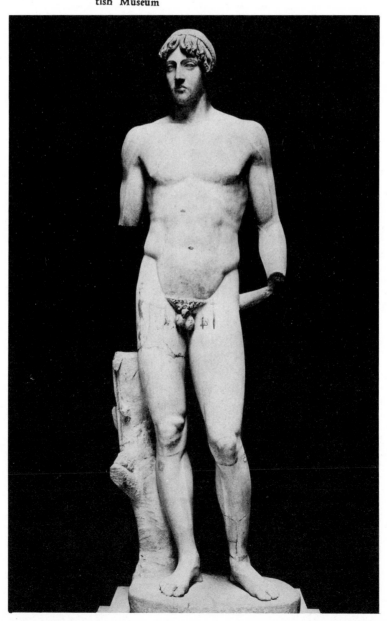

invaluable for our purpose, inasmuch as body and head belong together. The general pose is much the same as that of the Mercury, and the same spareness is conspicuous in the body, though the copyist has evidently tried to modify it. The god—for there can be no doubt that it is a god we have before us—wears sandals, and a mantle, which is flung over the left shoulder and covers the whole lower part of the body, but in such a way as to leave the origin of the thighs free. This whole arrangement of the mantle, and especially the portion of it that falls from the shoulder, bears witness to the severity of the original. The simple straightforward lines recall the drapery of the Riccardi bust. The depth of the folds between the thighs may be due to the copyist, who altered the shallower forms of the original, to suit the taste of his time. In the arrangement of the drapery about the lower part of the body we recognize the hand of the artist on whom Kresilas modelled himself, when he executed the mantle of the Athena of Velletri. On the other hand, drapery like that of the Zeus from the eastern pediment of Olympia (a statue which in other respects is intimately related to the one under discussion) leads to the pictorial draperies of the Parthenon. So we may recognize two contemporary tendencies, and we now understand that Kresilas's treatment of drapery was historically a development of the Myronian manner.

The most probable interpretation of the statue is that it represents Zeus—a view brought home to us by comparison with the afore-named Zeus from the eastern pediment of Olympia. Both statues agree so well in their main features that one is tempted to conjecture that our type, with its quiet, simple lines, was known to the artist of the Olympia pediment. The line formed by the mantle on the right hip is just the same in both, the principal difference being that in the Olympian Zeus the mantle has slipped off from the left shoulder and has been wound round the arm. The interpretation as Zeus is further confirmed by the great likeness to a statue in the Louvre,[1] which is known to represent Zeus by reason of the eagle sitting below and of the recurrence of a similar type on coins.[2] In conclusion, the attitude of the statue is favourable to the view that the left hand which hangs down grasped the sceptre, while on the right, which is extended, was held the thunderbolt or the eagle.

It must be owned, however, that an examination of the other replicas does not at first favour the Zeus theory. Of the eleven replicas of the Hermitage statue that are known to me, four certainly, and a fifth probably—to judge from the remaining attributes—represented Asklepios; while the others, though without the attributes of Asklepios, are equally without those of Zeus.[3] Still, in my opinion, it is not probable that the original represented Asklepios: statues of this god were relatively still

[1] Fröhner, *Notice*, p. 65, No. 34; phot. edit. Giraudon, 1224.

[2] Cf. the coin of Laodikea, Overbeck, Zeus, *Münztaf.* 2, 29; p. 138.

[3] The replicas consist partly of statues of the same proportions as the Hermitage statue, partly of statuettes of varying dimensions. The statues are: 1. Berlin, *Beschr. d. Ant. Skulp.* 290 (probably intended for an Asklepios rather than a Zeus). 2. Capitol, lower hall, 41 : feet, arms, whole of the right breast new ; the head of Zeus does not belong: the flatness and rigidity of the body, especially about the navel, is characteristic. 3. Louvre, Gall. Mollien, No. 2936: lower part of the legs new, head does not belong ; the left arm as far as the middle of the forearm preserved. 4. Rome, Palazzo Altemps : Clarac, 560 A, 1160 D : Matz-Duhn, 58 : head does not belong: the lower part of the serpent staff is old : on the feet Roman shoes in place of sandals: the copyist regarded the stouter covering for the feet as more appropriate to Asklepios: in the body the severity of the forms is well preserved. 5. Pacetti: Clarac, 545, 1146 : not known to me in the original : the serpent staff is stated to be restored. The statuettes are : 6. Mus. Chiaramonti, 113 : Clarac, 549, 1157. Undoubtedly Asklepios from the votive inscription, serpent staff restored : head does not belong. 7. Mus. Kircheriano : feet and arms new : head does not belong : poor. 8. Cassel, ii. 15 : head does not belong, forearms new : the severity of the style is well preserved. 9. Mus. Torlonia : Visconti, Tav. x. 39: serpent staff old, head modern. 10. Giustiniani : Clarac, 552, 1167 A : the serpent below reported to be ancient. 11. Rome, in the market, noted by me 1892 : head foreign.

FIG. 79.— Statue restored as Asklepios (Hermitage).

Fig. XXVIII—Asklepios from Melos, London, British Museum, (See p. 210)

rare towards the middle of the fifth century, though in the period of the copyists representations of him were in great demand. Considering that at this late period there was a rage for old types, it is conceivable that the copyists, for want of old originals of Asklepios, should sometimes have seized upon originals pourtraying Zeus, and by a change of attributes have turned them into statues of Asklepios. The restful conception that marks the older type of Zeus exactly suited the mild character of Asklepios. Anyhow, the erect, kingly pose of our statue; its gesture, better suited to grasp the royal sceptre than to hold the healing staff; its analogies to other statues of the god; and, finally, the type of head, to which we shall have to return, make it clear, in my opinion, that a statue of Zeus was the original from which the Hermitage statue was derived.

The number of replicas found in Rome [1] shows not only that the original was famous, but that it was probably to be seen in Rome; our analysis of the statue has led us to Myron as the artist; and a Zeus by Myron actually was in Rome in an *aedicula*, erected by Augustus on the Capitol.[2]

Another point of special interest about our statue, and one which further confirms its interpretation as Zeus, lies in the fact that the head exhibits in the arrangement of the hair and the modulation of the brow all the fundamental characteristics which were to develop into the famous type of Zeus known from the Otricoli bust. An historical study of the system of forms of this celebrated head shows it to belong not to the circle of Lysippos, as was formerly maintained, but to that of Praxiteles.[3] Thus, even as the Hermes of Praxiteles marks the culminating point of a line of development that begins with the heads of Myron's athletes,[4] so it would seem that the bust from Otricoli is the Praxitelean development of a type of Zeus created in the days of Myron.

XI. *The ' Cassel Apollo.'—Argive Influences traceable in Myron.*

The three statues which we have considered so far and have referred to Myron have the same position and attitude. In all probability the statue from which the Riccardi bust (*supra*, Fig. 66) is copied formed a fourth in the series. The common characteristics of this attitude are found in the main in all statues in repose of the first half of the fifth century. Still, among these works, all of which have the free leg placed slightly forwards, and the head turned a little to one side, there are several sharply defined groups.[5] Those ascribed to Myron are most closely allied as regards the pose to the so-called Apollo on the Omphalos, which I refer to

---

[1] To the twelve statues and statuettes mentioned above, of which only the Petersburg example preserves the original head, must be added the Berlin head (our Fig. 78) and two replicas of the same: (*a*) in the Palazzo Riccardi: Dütschke, *Zerstr. Bildw. in Flor.* 161: the head is set up as a pendant to the Riccardi head; (*b*) a freer copy in the Palazzo Colonna, No. 12.

[2] Strabo, 14, p. 637; the statue belonged originally to a group with Athena and Herakles in Samos. Collignon (*Hist. de la Sculpt. Gr.* i. p. 465) thinks that the Zeus of Myron may be recognized on the coins of Augustus which were struck after the dedication of the temple of Jupiter Tonans (Cohen, *Méd. Imper.* 2nd ed. i. 88; cf. Roscher's *Lex. d. Myth.* ii. 748). This is a mistake. The ναΐσκος that Strabo mentions is certainly not the famous temple of Jupiter Tonans; further, the statue of Jupiter Tonans on the Capitol was by Leochares according to Pliny (xxxiv. 79); the motive of the statue as shown on coins confirms this statement, and excludes Myron, since it is not till the second half of the fifth century that statues are represented resting their arm high against the sceptre.   [3] Cf. *infra* under Praxiteles.

[4] Cf. Kekulé, *Kopf des Praxit. Hermes.*   [5] Cf. 50th *Berl. Winckelmannsprogr.* 1890, p. 149 *sqq.*

Kalamis (cf. *supra*, p. 81 *seq.*) Together they stand in vivid contrast to the type which I ascribe to the school of the Argive Hagelaidas, where the advanced free foot is more markedly unincumbered, the shoulder droops a little, and the head is inclined. With Myron as with Kalamis the upper part of the body and the head are more upright, the whole presentment expressing power and energy. As regards the rendering of the bodily form, however, we have already seen that Myron differs essentially from Kalamis, inasmuch as he—to compare especially breast and abdomen—exhibits a flatter, sparer style, which seems to betray his connexion with the Argive school.

In the Apollo—generally known as the 'Apollo of Cassel,' from its principal replica [1]—we possess a statue which is unmistakably connected with the Myronian works we have just been studying, and which at the same time shows us the artist under the influence of the Argive type as regards the position of the body.[2] The figure rests on the left leg; the left forearm is stretched forward in a horizontal position to hold an attribute (in this case a bow), the right hangs idly down, and perhaps held some slight object, such as a twig. The head is inclined to the left. The flat smooth forms also recall the Argive tendency. On the other hand, the statue differs from the Argive type in certain deep-seated differences, and its close relation to the statues ascribed to Myron is no less evident. The head is not inclined forward; one shoulder does not droop; the god looks straight before him, with a look not of concentrated repose but of a strong and active will. The free foot is placed more to the front, and is more turned out than is customary in those Argive statues: this helps to give energy to the pose. The same was the case in the Zeus and the 'Mercury' of Myron.[3] The treatment of the bodily forms also comes nearest to that of the Myronian statues. We have noted their connexion with the Argive works; it remains to point out the differences. Above all, the contrast, so characteristic of Hagelaidas, between the narrow hips and the over-broad angular shoulders can no longer be detected; it is only by comparison with the Myronian Zeus and 'Neptune' that the Apollo still appears somewhat hard. Further, just as the turn and pose of the head correspond to that of the Myronian statues of gods, so also does the relation of the head to the rest of the body; in this respect it seems also to agree with the Diskobolos; the head is somewhat larger than is usual in the other works from the circle of Hagelaidas.[4] Further, the muscles are more

---

[1] Known to me are : Entire statues—1. In Cassel, Overbeck, *Apollon*, Pl. 20, 24 ; p. 166, 1 ; 108, 1 ; where also see the older literature. The work is hard, but careful in all parts : it gives the impression of great exactness. Through a mistake in putting the fragments of the statue together a wrong turn has been given to the upper part of the body ; the mistake lies in the middle of the left thigh and under the right knee ; it can be checked by the aid of the Paris statue. 2. Louvre, Overbeck, *loc. cit.* 2 = our Figs. 80, 81. 3. Torso, Athens, Central Museum. Finally the following heads : 4. In Athens, found to the east of the Olympeion, Sybel, 747 ; Overbeck, *loc. cit.* 108, 3. Careless and feeble work of Roman time, much damaged. 5. From Greece, now in the Louvre, No. 2032 (phot. Giraudon) ; very probably identical with that noted by Benndorf, *Ann.* 1880, 198, 5, at a dealer's in Athens. Poor Roman work. 6. From the Esquiline, Rome, Barracco Coll. : Overbeck, p. 108, 4 (see our Fig. 80). 7. From Rome, formerly in Barracco Coll., now belonging to Brunn in Munich. 8. In Naples, set on the term of the so-called Polyhymnia. Mus. Naz. *Inv.* No. 6393. I have not seen the following heads noted by others as copies: Overbeck, p. 108, 6, belonging to Herr v. Keudell ; Schreiber, *Villa Ludovisi*, 315 ; Dütschke, *Zerstr. Bildw. in Florenz*, 520 : acc. to Benndorf, *Annali*, 1880, 199, probably belongs to the series ; *Arch. Anzeiger*, 1891, p. 181, 3, in Vienna, University Collection.

[2] Cf. 50th *Berl. Winckelmannsprogr.* p. 135 *seq.* ; *supra*, p. 49.

[3] The middle part of the feet of the Cassel statue as well as a piece of the plinth is old; the feet are close together. The restoration of the legs in the Paris statue should be corrected accordingly.

[4] The Argive bronze, published by me in the 50th *Winckelmannsprogr.*, shows that at a later date, *circa* B.C. 460, the old Argive canon was improved in Argos also : the head was made larger, and the hips broader.

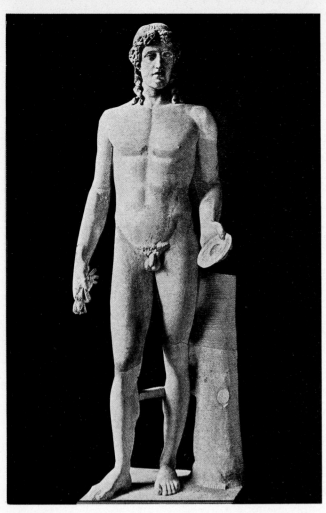

FIG. 80.—Apollo of the 'Cassel type (Louvre).

Fig. XXIX—"Apollo", Rome, Capitoline Museum

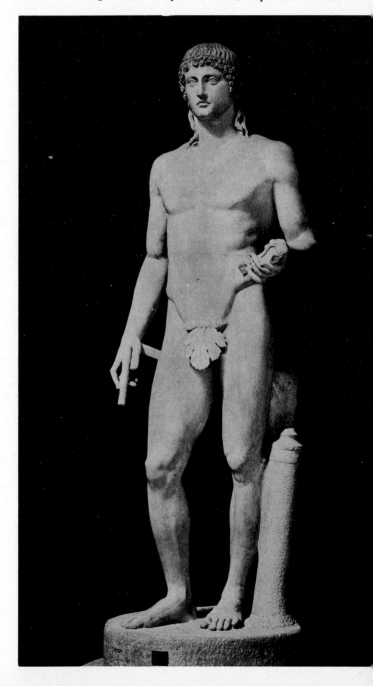

energetic than in this latter school ; the prominence of the collar-bone just under the
neck dimple recurs on our Myronian statues and in the Diskobolos, though it is
not usual in the flat quiet treatment of the early Argive statues.[1]

The head seems to afford definite proof of the Myronian authorship. We
recognize in it the characteristic lower part of the face with the slightly open mouth
and the form of the mouth [2] itself, not to speak of the chin, which accords very closely
with that of the Riccardi bust. Then the modelling of the forehead and the well-
defined arch of the eyebrows are very like the Diskobolos, while the peculiar parting

FIG. 81.—Head of Apollo.

*Plate IX—Head of Perseus, London, British
Museum. (See p. 197 sqq.)

of the locks in the middle of the forehead is the same as in the ' Neptune ' after
Myron. Further, the heavy tresses curling at the ends in the Apollo are identical
with those of the ' Peisistratos ' (Fig. 73), while the plastic treatment of the beard
must be compared to that of the Marsyas.

[1] It is further characteristic that the pubes is fully and powerfully formed, as in the Diskobolos and the
Myronian ' Mercury ' ; in the circle of Hagelaidas it was invariably left out in the case of youthful beardless
figures. The pubes of the Apollo is interesting in itself : it consists of two parts—an upper row of smooth,
scarcely turned up, and very regularly disposed hair, and a lower row immediately about the *membrum*,
consisting of the same full plastic locks that appear on the brow. I know of no exact parallel to this method
of representing the pubes, though the nearest analogy occurs on Myronian statues : the upper smooth row of hair
is found on the best copies of the Diskobolos, and the lower curled part of the pubes resembles that of the
Marsyas.

[2] Next to the Cassel head the mouth should be studied in the Louvre head (*supra*, p. 191, note 1, No. 2),
which is very careful in this point : the lips are defined here too by incised lines in imitation of bronze technique.

C C

The points in the Apollo that deviate from the usual Myronian head are only such as may well have been chosen to suit the character of the god (Fig. 81). The most striking of these is the great length of the lower part of the face, which is not otherwise found in Myron, though it is found in Kritios and Nesiotes[1] (with whose work, however, the Apollo has in other respects absolutely nothing in common). Now, as the length of the lower part of the face together with the slightly open mouth, in which the teeth are visible, contributes materially to produce the impression of an exalted and unapproachable divinity, I incline to think that the artist chose it solely on that account. Indeed, the head betrays in every point a studied adaptation of the facial forms to the production of a definite expression. The shape of the brow is especially notable in this connexion: it is high in the middle, and broadens out very considerably at the base towards the temples, where it attains its greatest width in the strongly projecting eyebrows above the outer corners of the eyes. This formation is continued by the wide cheek-bones and the broad round skull, which Myron, as we have already seen, was wont to make characteristic, and not after a conventional pattern. The eye is correspondingly large, with a long narrow slit. As the brow is given a overhanging shape, the slant of the eyeball from top to bottom is very considerable. The art of later days kept to the leading traits of this creation: the broad scheme of the upper part of the face becomes henceforth characteristic of Apollo, just as we noted that the later ideal of Zeus was based upon the type created by Myron.

The treatment of the hair is also turned to account to express divine majesty and power. We have already noticed the ample crown of hair in the Neptune and the Zeus of Myron. In the Apollo it has a somewhat stiffer character, owing to the work being on the whole somewhat earlier. This rich crown, consisting of individual locks treated in a very natural manner, was something new, and our Apollo seems to afford the earliest example of it. It took the place of the sober roll of hair worn by the earlier Apollo of the school of Hagelaidas, which has been ascribed to Hegias (p. 52). Doubtless this Argive Apollo was known to our artist, for he reproduces the main features of the hair: in the Myronian statue, as in its predecessor, we get the two twisted locks at the side falling to the upper edge of the breast, together with the trim coiffure at the back and the part above the forehead. But the favourite[2] roll of hair of the Peloponnesian artists, with its stiff, smooth regularity, is here dispensed with, and replaced in front by a wealth of natural curls, at the back by the plait that was in vogue in the Attico-Ionian school.[3]

One may indeed pretty confidently suppose that an Apollo by Myron exists among the marble copies that are preserved to us of older originals. For the inscription Ἀπόλλων Μύρωνος on a headless term in Rome[4] shows us that an Apollo of Myron was known in Roman times, and that its head was highly enough valued to be copied alone apart from the body. Pliny (xxxiv. 58) also mentions an Apollo by Myron, which remained for a long time at Rome, until Augustus restored it to the Ephesians. Moreover, as Verres had despoiled Agrigentum of another Apollo of Myron, there was evidently more than one statue of this god by this artist, and those that are known to us in copies need not necessarily be identical with either of the two which happen to be mentioned in literary tradition.

The *provenance* of the copies affords no clue whatever to the place where the

---

[1] Cf. the Harmodios and the Boy from the Akropolis.
[2] Cf. 50th *Berl. Winckelmannsprogr.* p. 128 *seq.*
[3] Cf. *Ath. Mitth.* 1883, 246 *seq.* (Schreiber).   [4] Kaibel, *Inscr. Gr. Ital.* p. 698, 1256 a.

FIG. 82.—Apollo head of 'Cassel type' in Barracco Collection (Rome).

FIG. 84.—Female head in Giardino Boboli (Florence). (By permission of Messrs. Bruckmann, Munich.)

original stood. These copies all belong to Roman times, and as usual with copies doubtless served to decorate private houses, baths, and the like. The same holds good for the head and torso from Athens; both came in all probability from the Roman ruins of the city of Hadrian around the Olympieion;[1] and we should not be justified in concluding from this circumstance that the original was in Athens.[2] All that we can say positively about this Apollo, which is avowedly one of the grandest ideal creations of Greek art, is that it must have been highly prized in antiquity, seeing the many copies of it which have survived.

On the other hand, it becomes possible to throw light on Pliny's statement (xxxiv, 57) that Myron was a pupil of Hagelaidas, now that we have clearly detected in the Apollo the influence of the old Argive canon. We have seen that the artist of the Apollo was thoroughly acquainted with the epoch-making creations of the old Argive school, even though his work is at the same time widely different from them; in addition to this, we have detected a certain Peloponnesian influence in Myron's whole treatment of the bodily forms, and, in the case of the Marsyas, even in his treatment of the head. It is, however, no longer possible to ascertain whether Myron was really a pupil of Hagelaidas or whether the tradition arose, as in the case of Pheidias (cf. p. 54), owing to some ancient art critic's observing in Myron traces of the master's influence. The latter seems to me the more probable. The tradition, for which Pliny is responsible, is derived from the same good old source (probably Xenokrates) as that which says that Polykleitos also was a pupil of Hagelaidas[3]— an impossible relationship in its literal sense, since Polykleitos, even dating him as far back as possible (cf. *supra*, p. 130), is still too widely separated from Hagelaidas to admit of it: his master must have belonged to the intermediate generation—a generation that was however soon forgotten, inasmuch as it achieved no renown; in time therefore the head of the later school was made to follow close on the famous head of the old. All the same, it is true that the canon of Polykleitos was developed from the old canon of Hagelaidas, as we too may still recognize,[4] but the actual teacher of Polykleitos must have been some artist like that Argeiadas (Löwy, *I. G. B.* 30) who was proud to be known in Olympia as the pupil of Hagelaidas. If the story of the pupilship of Polykleitos is not literally true, it is unlikely that the similar story about Myron should be any the more true, though in his case chronological considerations do not stand in the way. The traditions must have had their source in those works which reveal a point of contact between Myron and Hagelaidas; who it was that transmitted this influence remains unknown to later ages. It is however quite certain from monuments such as the Apollo that the story is no mere capricious invention.

The Apollo enables us to look not only backwards but forwards. It again proves how entirely Myron was the forerunner of Kresilas. In order to be once more convinced of this it suffices to consider the stylistic treatment of the hair of the Apollo

---

[1] The statue of a boy, *Jahrb. d. Inst.* 1893, Pl. 4, in which Mayer (*ibid.*) sees a copy of the *Splanchnoptes* of Styppax, was also found in the same region.

[2] Nor do the coins of Athens afford any certain clue. The type of Apollo on coins—Imhoof-Gardner, *Num. Comm.* Pl. CC., XV., XVII.; Overbeck, Apollo, *Münztaf.* iv. 33—shows close agreement in the general scheme with our type (left leg bearing weight, left forearm extended with bow, right hanging); another Athenian coin (Imhoof, etc., *loc. cit.* Pl. CC., XVI.; Overbeck, iv. 29) shows much the same Apollo, only seen more from the front, and for this reason with the supporting leg reversed. I formerly tried to identify this with the Omphalos Apollo (Roscher's *Lexikon*, i. 456); it could also be referred to our Cassel type (cf. also Winter in the *Jahrb. d. Inst.* 1887, 235, note). But this too is quite uncertain, and there is yet another possibility open to us, which I shall discuss in connexion with Euphranor (*infra*, p. 356).

[3] Plin. 55, 9. Cf. Robert, *Arch. Märchen*, p. 92.   [4] Cf. 50th *Berl. Winckelmannsprogr.* p. 149.

(compare the form of the little curls with those of the Perikles), the shape of the eyes (in the better copies, such as the one in Cassel), and of the mouth with the teeth, which reminds us at once of the Medusa.

In conclusion, the Apollo invites comparison with the other statues of Apollo of the same period—*i.e.* of the years ranging from about 475 to 460. First and in notable contrast come the two statues, in which we recognized the style of Kritios (p. 54 *seq.*) and of Hegias respectively (p. 52 *seq.*) The one referred to Hegias is under the immediate influence of Hagelaidas : it is a beautiful work, though somewhat heavy and dull in tone ; the other is quite independent of that master, and in many respects—especially in the pose—less perfect, though fresher in conception. Somewhat later follows the so-called Omphalos Apollo, attributed to Kalamis,[1] also independent of Argos ; the body is a magnificent creation, teeming with force, while the head scarcely rises as yet above a human type ; it even relinquishes the attempt made in the two preceding statues to mark the god at any rate by the headdress. It is very different with the two approximately contemporary works that follow—an earlier work of Pheidias (*supra*, p. 49), still somewhat constrained and recalling his master Hegias, and the work executed by Myron at the highest point of his development. Both try to go deeper than their predecessors, both try to mark more clearly the character of the god and to raise it above the human type, yet both works are absolutely different. Myron's assuredly deserves the prize. The genius of Pheidias is still under the constraint of youth, and his attempt to express the spiritual element in the god proceeds rather on the lines of a gentle beauty, while Myron creates with sure hand true Apolline grandeur and majesty.

In close proximity to these two works we must note finally another Apollo that proceeds from some second-rate artist[2] who copied the body of Myron's statue, and for the head modelled himself superficially at least upon Pheidias, though he either could not or would not adopt the special forms that lend the face its expression. The form he employs seems to indicate that this otherwise insignificant artist belonged to the school of Kalamis.

XII. *The Perseus.*

A head of Perseus, which is preserved in two replicas, will be found to afford the final external proof that the original of the Cassel Apollo and its replicas was a work by Myron. The general characteristics of the Perseus show that its original must have been an older work of the fifth century. Now we are acquainted through literature with one famous statue of Perseus belonging to this period, and with one alone,[3] that of Myron. It stood on the Akropolis of Athens, and is mentioned by Pausanias (i. 23, 7), and also by Pliny (xxxiv. 57) in his short list of the most famous works of Myron. Since this statue was undoubtedly copied, there is every probability that, if we can point among extant copies to a Perseus of the fifth century, it will be to the statue of Myron.

The two extant copies are a head in the British Museum (Plate IX.), which A. S.

---

[1] Cf. *supra*, p. 81 *seq.* ; the attributes preserved in the replicas establish this statue as undoubtedly an Apollo.

[2] The statue of the Capitol mentioned above, p. 49; Overbeck, *Apollon*, p. 275, 4; 112, 1; *Atlas*, Pl. 20, 22.

[3] It is true that an anonymous writer—probably Favorinus—in a passage quoted in the *Corinthiaca* of Dion Chrys. (p. 106, k. ii.) speaks also of a Perseus by Pythagoras ; but it seems more than probable that this rhetorician of the later Empire substituted for the name of Myron that of his rival Pythagoras, who is so often named in conjunction with him. Cf. W. Klein, *Arch. Epigr. Mitth. aus Oesterreich*, 1883, p. 68. L. Urlichs (*Ueber Griech. Kunstschriftsteller*, p. 48) attributes to the same rhetorician yet another confusion, between Alkamenes and Euphranor.

Murray identified and published as a Perseus,[1] and its recently discovered replica in
Rome (Fig. 83).[2]   The interpretation as Perseus may be accepted as certain, since
Hermes, who alone could also come into question, might perhaps have worn a petasos
or a winged pilos, but not the distinctive cap covered with scales or little feathers, and
doubtless intended for the wonderful tarn cap of Hades.[3]   The head of Perseus on an
electrum coin of Cyzicus of the early fifth century[4] also wears a similar close-fitting round
cap, passing at the back into great wings.   On the coin the hair, though treated more
severely, escapes in short curls from under the close edge of the cap, just as in the
marble heads.   One might say that the artist of the head of the statue had modelled
himself on a type of beardless Perseus wearing a round winged cap, already current in
the art of Ionia.

FIG. 83.—Head of Perseus (Rome).

The original can be recovered from a study of the two copies of the head.   The
London replica is rather harder, though at the same time it is in some points more
accurate; the Roman one is a hasty yet intelligent piece of work.   The London
copy gives the cap more accurately, but the hair, which is much injured, seems less good ;
the Roman head represents the forms of the face with more delicacy and roundness,
and the lips are closed, while in the other they are slightly open ; the last is likely
to be more correct.

The connexion between the Perseus and the Cassel Apollo is striking and quite

[1] *J. H. S.* 1881, Pl. IX. p. 55.

[2] *Bull. della Comm. Arch. Comm. di Roma*, xviii. (1890), Tav. 13, with Klein's text.   [An interesting view
of the Brit. Mus. Perseus, both facing and profile, is given by Kalkmann, *Proport. des Gesichts*, p. 77.—E. S.]

[3] On the top of both the Roman and Brit. Mus. heads some further object, not of marble, was attached ; cf.
Murray and Klein (*loc. cit.*)   Unfortunately the objects visible on the cap of the kneeling Perseus on a Cyzicene
coin of the free style (*Num. Chron.* 1887, Pl. III. 26, p. 89), which comes next in point of time, are not clear.

[4] *Num. Chron.* 1887, Pl. III. 24, 25 (p. 88).

undeniable. Since in the case of the Perseus tradition is in favour of Myron,[1] we gain at the same time a piece of external support for referring the Apollo to this master. This connexion is all the more weighty and convincing in view of the difference of the characters represented—in the one case a calm divinity, in the other a strong hero. The two works cannot have been far apart from each other in point of time. There is a special affinity between them in the treatment of the arch of the eyebrows, with their powerful development towards the sides, and in that of the eyes themselves; the forehead presses heavily above the eyes, the upper lid comes prominently in front of the lower, and the eyeball slants back.

The longer side locks of the Perseus have the same wavy form with curled ends noticed in the Apollo. The shorter locks over the forehead and in the neck present the unsymmetrical tangle so often noted as genuinely Myronian, except that they seem handled with greater freedom than in those older heads after Myron that have already been dealt with. The receding lower part of the face, with the full, slightly opened mouth and the strongly curved lines of the lips, are all equally characteristic. The points of difference between the Perseus and the head of Apollo serve simply to express character. To begin with, the Perseus lacks that unusual length of the lower part of the face; in the Perseus this part is of normal Myronian proportions, inasmuch as its length is the same as the distance between the nose and the arch of the brows.[2] The close stylistic resemblance between the Perseus and the Apollo confirms the view that the length in the lower part of the Apollo's face was merely a means of expressing character. The forehead is especially interesting. The modelling, which in the head of Apollo is so slight that most of the copies have ignored it, is here exceptionally marked.[3] From either side of the root of the nose strongly marked swellings rise upward in an oblique line in the direction of the points where the wings are attached, reaching their highest point in the middle. The wings in this way are, as it were, counterpoised by the powerful forehead, and the expression of extreme energy is secured. This same end is served also by the broad, bony chin, and the powerful muscles of the cheeks.

A long train of stylistic development undoubtedly lies between the Diskobolos with his impassive countenance, his severe, flat hair, and the marked angle of brow and nose, and the Perseus with his full, flowing locks, straight profile, and rounder, freer modelling. Yet the Diskobolos contains all the essential forms of the Perseus. It must also be remembered that the close-cropped hair of the athletes and kindred figures by Myron must necessarily appear different from the clustering curls—not long, it is true, but very thick—that Myron gave to the Perseus.

This Perseus must have been a work full of grandeur and energy, as can be best realized in the London head, in which the whole neck and a piece of the breast have been preserved. A. S. Murray, with fine insight, inferred a powerful original, and appositely said of this head that the sculptor had in view 'a first impression not of form but of action.' The total effect however must have been greatly enhanced by the wings, now

---

[1] Klein now rejects the Myronian authorship, and takes refuge in the theory of a Perseus by Pythagoras—a work which he had himself proved to be apocryphal (*supra*, p. 197, n. 3); evidently the only statue he thinks of in connexion with Myron is the Diskobolos, and he forgets the distance that separates its head from that of the Marsyas. Not only does tradition afford no adequate grounds for assigning a Perseus to Pythagoras, but the statues of athletes which we have felt obliged to assign to him bear a totally different character to the heads under discussion.

[2] Namely 72—73 mm., twice the length of the lids from corner to corner, 36—37 mm. Width of mouth 55—56 mm.

[3] The Perseus head on the coins from Amisos of the time of Mithradates Eupator also exhibits a remarkably prominent forehead and large eyes (Brit. Mus. *Catal. Pontus*, Pl. 3, 12).

missing, which to judge from the attachments must have been of considerable size, and have given a supernatural expression to the head.

According to Pausanias, Myron's Perseus on the Akropolis was represented as τὸ εἰς Μέδουσαν ἔργον εἰργασμένος. The deed was accomplished. The view formerly entertained was that he was represented as in flight, running, with the wallet (κίβισις) slung about him. The head teaches us now that he was standing quietly, probably holding in his hand the severed head of the Medusa. Even without the help of monumental evidence we must have known that these would be the main lines of the Myronian conception ; a Perseus running through the air with his winged shoes might prove an attractive subject for archaic sculpture, which liked to pourtray Nike in a similar manner, but could never have been so for Myron. The running Perseus is an archaic type, and moreover one not easily presented without the pursuing Gorgons. On the other hand, the Perseus at rest is admirably attested as a type in statuary of the free style. For instance, a similar statue has been reproduced on a series of Imperial coins from Argos, which explain the violent turn of the head to the left.[1] Perseus held in his right hand the newly severed head of the Medusa, and turned his head in horror and alarm towards the other side, to protect himself from the petrifying glance. The kneeling Perseus too, on a vase of Cyzicus of the free style of the fifth century,[2] and on an Attic vase of the time about 450,[3] displays this same motive, though with a change of sides, so that the weapon is in the right, the head of Medusa in the left, and the head of the hero consequently turned towards the right.

Since the turn of the head on the Argive coin coincides with the head after Myron, we may imagine the whole statue restored in its leading features on the lines of this coin. The hero would be represented standing on the right foot, holding the weapon in the left hand, and the head of Medusa in his right hand stretched to the side. On his feet were naturally the winged shoes.

Possibly the statue of the Argive hero was not erected at Athens without reference to Argos : it might almost be surmised that it bore some allusion to the close relations between Athens and Argos, which began with the treaty of 461 B.C.[4] In any case the statue on the Akropolis of this Argive hero, to whom the goddess of Athens owed her Gorgon's head,[5] and in whom accordingly the tie between Argos and Athens found mythical expression, would have been a very fitting offering at a time when politics were emphasizing this tie. To judge by the style, we must imagine the Perseus to have been created about 450 rather than 460. The statue in Argos, which is attested by the coins, must have been a replica of the Myronian statue, which may have been already set up at that date, or perhaps only later.

---

[1] Imhoof-Blumer and P. Gardner, *Num. Comm.* Pl. I. xvii., xviii. p. 35. The type appears unchanged from Hadrian to Septimius Severus ; a variant, which practically only reverses the sides, appears in a single instance at Argos on a coin of Sept. Severus (*ibid.* Pl. FF, xxii. p. 159) and at Asine on a coin of Julia Domna (*ibid.* Pl. GG, xxiii. p. 163). Similar type on the autonomous bronze coins of Ikonium. Another ruder type, also based on some statue, occurs on the coins of the Pontic towns of Amisos, Amastris, Sinope (Brit. Mus. *Catal. Pontus*, Pl. 3, 13 ; 19, 8 ; p. 99). [The type appears without variation from Hadrian to Lucius Verus, and also under Valerian (Brit. Mus. *Cat. Pelopon.* p. 153) ; the variation on another coin of Septimius Severus, in which the head of Perseus is not turned away, is probably due to the caprice of the copyist (*supra*, Pl. VI. 33). I regret that, owing to an oversight which I only noticed after Pl. VI. had been photographed, this coin was reproduced instead of one belonging to the series mentioned by Furtwängler.—E. S.]

[2] *Num. Chron.* 1887, Pl. 3, 26 : cf. *supra*, p. 198, n. 1.

[3] Millin, *Vases Peints*, ii. 3. For a second vase illustrative in this connexion, cf. *infra*, p. 201 *seq.*

[4] Concerning the significance of this treaty cf. latterly Robert, *Hermes*, 1890, 412.

[5] In Athens quite old vases already attest the connexion between Athena and Perseus as the slayer of the Medusa. The saying in Euripides, *Ion.* 987, which has found no expression in art, can never have been popular in Athens.

The motive of the Perseus, so far as we have proved it, was certainly the pattern for the Diomede of Kresilas; in this case also it was Myron on whom Kresilas modelled himself. The essential character of the effective attitude and pose of the Diomede had already been invented by Myron for his Perseus, though Kresilas no doubt treated this motive with still greater effect.

What can have been the appearance of the head of the Medusa which Perseus held in his hand? This was no gorgoneion, no mask, but in all probability a solid head worked in the round with severed neck, as it is represented also on the Argive and Cyzicene coins of the latter half of the fifth century.[1] Myron was accordingly free from the severe mask type. On an Attic vase of the middle of the fifth century[2] the head of Medusa in the hand of Perseus is represented as that of a beautiful woman free from any distortion. This led us to conclude (*supra*, p. 158) that Medusa must have been so represented at Athens in the greater arts even previous to this vase, for the vase-painters never invent such bold novelties for themselves. Since the vase-painting which represents Perseus with the severed head of the Medusa in his hand agrees with Myron's statue, and since the motive of the Perseus on the vase is the same as that which we have recovered for the statue (*i.e.* Perseus standing on his right foot with the Medusa head in his extended right hand and turning his head in the opposite direction), we can have no doubt that the vase-painter was conditioned, not only in the whole figure but especially also in the Medusa, by Myron's work; that Myron's Medusa represented, not a hideous mask, but a beautiful head worked in the round.

A. S. Murray, in commenting on the remarkable similarity between the profile of the Perseus and a type of Medusa that appears on Roman gems, is apparently referring to that type best preserved in the gem of Sosos,[3] and less well in the cameo of Diodotos,[4] and other unsigned replicas. The similarity to the Perseus is striking throughout, not only in the way in which the head and neck are rendered, but also in the whole line of the profile, and especially in the forehead and eye. Courage, power, and beauty are expressed here in the same forms as in the Perseus. It is the severed lifeless head of the Medusa, and no mask; it has undistorted, beautiful traits; it is just such a head as we have conjectured for Myron. On the one hand, the type has nothing to do with the pathetic representation of the Medusa, common in a later age; on the other hand, it is an individual, powerful creation, which cannot be referred to the gem-cutters, but must be traced to some older original. Therefore it seems to me probable on all grounds that the original was the Medusa of Myron, held in the hand of the Perseus on the Akropolis. And so again Myron appears as the forerunner of Kresilas in his representation of the lifeless head of the Medusa. Myron had the courage to cut himself entirely adrift from the traditional type of the wild-eyed Gorgon. Kresilas also has bestowed on the actual gorgoneion mask a delicate beauty of feature.

Our inquiry into Myronian statues has enabled us to form a very different view of the artist from that generally in vogue. He is no longer the one-sided sculptor of athletes, interested only in violent momentary exertion, and caring nothing for the spiritual elements of his figures. Myron has created gods and heroes too, which

---

[1] *Num. Chron.* 1887, Pl. 3, 26.

[2] *Ann. d. Inst.* 1881, Tav. F.—The early Lower Italy vase, Millingen, *Vases de Div. Coll.* 3, which belongs to the class characterized above, p. 108 *seq.*, must be mentioned here, since it undoubtedly reproduces an Attic model: it again shows the severed head and neck of beautiful type.

[3] *Jahrb. d. Inst.* 1888, Pl. 8, 18; p. 214. For the inscription cf. *Arch. Anz.* 1891, 136.

[4] *Jahrb. d. Inst.* 1889, Pl. 2, 6; p. 63 *seq.*

D D

for depth of conception and power in the presentation of character surpass all contemporary work. The ancients, however, were so lost in admiration of his two figures representing athletes in violent movement, the Discos-thrower and the Ladas, and of the cow with its fidelity to nature, that, by the side of these, other aspects of his work became obscured.

If we compare Myron with Pheidias, leaving out of account such points of difference as are due to the different times at which the artists lived, we find that the bent of Pheidias is towards the peaceful, the mild, the reflective, the beautiful ; while Myron's is to energy, power, character, and truth. In Pheidias, too, we find a certain pictorial instinct, which found expression in the decorative modelling which he cultivated to so great an extent. Myron has nothing of this, and, further, we know him only as a maker of bronze statues in the round. In this respect also he was followed by Kresilas, who likewise worked only in bronze, and held quite aloof from decorative modelling in other materials.

XIII. *Myronian Female Head.—The Herakles Altemps and Kindred Works.—Asklepios in the Uffizi.*

The foregoing sketch of Myron's artistic personality can be made still more definite by means of a few other monuments.

Among the ten figures of gods of which mention is made in our scanty literary tradition of him, no less than three represented female deities. It would be interesting to know what a goddess by Myron looked like, for so strong an individuality as his cannot have failed to impress itself upon his female types also. Now the head of the Perseus makes it possible to trace back to Myron, conjecturally at least, a beautiful woman's head, preserved to us in a copy, placed upon a statue that does not belong to it, in the Giardino Boboli at Florence (Fig. 84).[1] The peculiarly energetic expression, the wide mouth and chin, and the slightly drooping corners of the mouth present a decided affinity to the Perseus, to whom this head forms the female counterpart—a goddess of earnest and grave character, certainly no amiable beauty A diadem encircles her head ; her hair flows simply back ; it is dressed low over the forehead and is parted, though it consists of short tangled locks tolerably freely treated and characteristic of the now familiar Myronian manner. The same is true, too, of the eyes and their strongly marked lids. The head must, however, be somewhat older than the Perseus, and belong to about the year 460. In particular the part towards the temples between the eyebrows and the upper lids is somewhat harder and less developed than in the copies of the Perseus, and betrays the same stage of development as the Riccardi head.

Next come a few more works which appear to follow on those that have been already described as after Myron, and to belong to the second period of the artist's work.

In the court of the Palazzo Altemps at Rome is an excellently preserved colossal seated statue of Herakles.[2] In opposition to the bearded Myronian Herakles belonging to the artist's earlier days, the Altemps statue appears to belong to his

---

[1] Dütschke, No. 79 ; much knocked about, and weather-beaten, nose abominably restored. Arndt-Bruckmann, *Einzelverk.* Nos. 101, 102 ; cast in the Ecole des Beaux-Arts.

[2] Matz-Duhn, 123 ; Clarac, 802 F, 1988 A ; *Röm. Mitth.* 1889, p. 333, fig. 2 ; Kalkmann, *Gesichtsprop.* p. 74, Pl. I. II. K. also suggests Myron. Even the left arm with the club is antique. Only a little piece at the top is new. The upper part of the head is broken, the nose new.

Fig. XXX——Asklepios, Florence, Uffizi Gallery. (See
p. 205 sqq.)

later years. The head and hair are closely akin to those of the Perseus. The body
is spare ; the pose is majestic, with a fine, energetic swing, but still somewhat hard
and angular. The hero sits upright, the left arm is raised and supports the club,
the right is stretched straight out. The original probably stood in Rome, for it was
turned to account in the time of Trajan for the representation of a Herakles seated
amid trophies of weapons and holding an *akrostolion* in his hand.[1] It is quite
possible that this original was the very Herakles by Myron that was set up near the
Circus Maximus *in aede Pompei Magni* (Pliny, xxxiv. § 57).

The second statue which we must name here is the so-called Diomede of the
Palazzo Valentini at Rome,[2] in which the stooping posture, as has often been
remarked, recalls the Diskobolos.[3] Probably it represents a hoplitodrome, not only
on account of the likeness in the attitude to the Tübinger bronze,[4] but also on
account of the helmeted head, which has usually been taken to be foreign to the
statue, but which seems to me to belong to it. This head, which is much restored
and wrongly set,[5] shows kinship to the Perseus.

Among heads belonging to the period of the Perseus may be named an athlete
in the Capitol :[6] the youth was apparently winding round his head a curious
contrivance of thongs.

On the other hand, the statue in Munich of an athlete dropping oil into his
hands,[7] the beautiful Florentine athlete,[8] and the types akin to these, must be kept
quite distinct from Myron, for they have no immediate connexion with any of his
works. They must belong to other Attic artists of the generation after Myron—*i.e.*
of the second half of the fifth century.[9]

Among bearded types of Myron's later period may be mentioned a beautiful
head of the Museo Chiaramonti (Fig. 85).[10] The braid of hair at the back, reaching
only from ear to ear, resembles that of the Apollo. The longish hair, coming from the
crown of the head, is brought without a break towards the front, where it rolls up
into little curls and mingles with the short ringlets that surround the forehead. This
rich tangle is repeated in the beard, where the moustache alone flows in smooth
lines, as in the older heads of Myron. The eyelids are strong and marked with
a little crease in the manner so often observed in the Myronian heads. The root
of the nose is narrow. The mouth is slightly open, the expression is exceedingly
distinguished—yet it is not quietly indifferent, but full of vivacity. The head is
rather the representation of a noble hero than a portrait. I can imagine the

---

[1] Cf. Petersen, *Rom. Mitth.* 1889, 331 *sqq.* The Altemps statue represents the Greek prototype, and is not, as
P. thinks, a replica of what he calls the Trajan type. The weapons of the latter are wanting, the arms are
different, and head and body alike betray a considerably older style. The replicas of the statuette of the Trajan
type display the usual Hellenistic-Roman character.

[2] Matz-Duhn, 1097 ; Clarac, 830, 2085. A cast of the torso alone in the Ecole des Beaux-Arts (No. 3836).

[3] Also interpreted as a 'Diskobolos' by Matz-Duhn.

[4] Hauser rightly points this out, *Jahrb. d. Inst.* 1887, p. 101, note 24, but on account of the tree-stem he
dissents from the restoration as a hoplitodrome ; this stem however could scarcely constitute an impediment to
the attachment of a bronze shield.

[5] Restored : whole neck, back, upper, and front part of helmet, nose, and a part of the lips. The serpent on
the helmet is ancient. The head is set on with far too violent a turn ; still it was slightly inclined to the left :
the relation of the marble of the head to that of the body could only be decided after a thorough cleaning.

[6] Helbig, *Führer*, No. 415 : curiously interpreted as 'Juba,' and by Helbig as 'Barbarian chief' with
'negro blood.' The so-called Juba head at Athens has not the faintest likeness to this.

[7] *Mon. d. Inst.* xi. 7. Cf. Kekulé, *Kopf des Praxit. Hermes*, pp. 13, 18.

[8] Dütschke, *Uffizi*, 72 ; *Röm. Mitth.* 1892, p. 81 *seq.*   [9] Cf. *infra*, under Polykleitos.

[10] *Museo Chiaram.* No. 287 A. The terminal bust and the nose are modern. Mentioned as a portrait by
Schreiber, *Ath. Mitth.* 1883, p. 255.

Erechtheus of Myron, so much admired by Pausanias (ix. 30, 1), and which no doubt lurks somewhere among our copies, conceived somewhat after this fashion.[1]

Akin is a head in the British Museum (Fig. 86),[2] evidently by an artist of the second rank, who, working about 450, comes between the earlier manner of Pheidias and the later one of Myron.

FIG. 85.—Head in Museo Chiaramonti.

Another bearded type that we come to last takes us back again to the earlier time of Myron. The beautiful Asklepios of severe style in the Uffizi at Florence (Fig. 87)[3] was always in my opinion one of the most attractive statues of that

[1] As the Erechtheus of Myron was highly esteemed by connoisseurs, to judge from the words of Pausanias, it seems to me more probable that it was a single figure, identical with the statue of the eponymous hero in the Agora (Paus. i. 5, 2), and not a member of the fighting group on the Akropolis (Paus. i. 27, 4), in which Eumolpos must have looked very like his opponent. The eponymous hero, however, was certainly conceived as a quiet and exalted figure: cf. the Erechtheus on the vase contemporary with Myron, *Mon. d. Inst.* x. 39. Statues of eponymous heroes probably came into existence in the time of Kimon; cf. Wachsmuth, *Stadt Athen*, i. 509; Curtius, *Stadtgesch.* 117.—For the question of Erechtheus see latterly Kalkmann, *Pausanias*, p. 192, 2; Sauer, *Anfänge d. Gruppe*, p. 60.

[2] Acquired with the Castellani collection 1873; place of discovery unknown. The term restored. At the back of the head a piece that had been separately attached is missing. Fully life-size. A head known to me only through the engraving in Cavaceppi (*Raccolta*, iii. 23) seems very like, especially in the arrangement of the hair on the forehead.

[3] Dütschke, *Uffizi*, No. 198; Clarac, 547, 1152; Müller-Wieseler, *Denkm. a. K.* ii. 771. Cast in the Ecole des Beaux-Arts.

collection.   I formerly thought to discern in it a creation of the early Argive school,[1] on grounds which will immediately be made clear ; but the Myronian character of the head seems to me now beyond doubt.   The head is unbroken, and only the nose restored ; on the other hand, the whole of the right arm with the shoulder is modern, as well as the left hand with the serpent staff, both legs including the whole of the right knee and the portion of the drapery that flows freely out behind.   The restorer committed the great mistake of letting the right leg appear drawn back as in the act of walking.   The ancient portions show that the disengaged

Fig. 86.—Head in the British Museum.

right foot was far more probably planted lightly on the flat of the sole next to the supporting left.

On the drapery of the left shoulder are seen the remains of a hand ;[2] the drapery too on the left side is less finished than elsewhere : evidently a second figure, now lost, stood on this side.   A small replica in the Palazzo Barberini (Fig. 88),[3] of careless workmanship but well preserved, puts us in perfect possession of the group.   It is Hygieia who thus lays her right hand on the left shoulder of Asklepios.

[1] Sabouroff Coll. i. Pl. 24. Text, p. 2.
[2] Erroneously taken by Dütschke for the remains of a sculptor's point, although the mark had long been recognized as that of a hand—viz. by the editors of the Galleria di Firenze, ser. iv. vol. i. p. 72 ; after them by Clarac in the text to No. 1152 ; further by Wieseler in the Denkm. a. Kunst to ii. 771, and in the official Catal. della R. Gall. d. Uffizi, No. 209.
[3] Matz-Duhn, 51 ; cf. Matz, Bull. d. Inst. 1870, 36.   Phot. in the German Inst. at Rome.

Fig. 87.—Asklepios in the Uffizi (Florence).

The head of the Florentine statue shows that the original of the Asklepios was an early work of the fifth century. The question now arises whether this original also formed a group with Hygieia. This must, I think, be negatived. It is clear, in spite of the poor workmanship, that the Hygieia of the group[1] is based on a type that hardly came into existence before the fourth century, and is in any case much later than the original of the Asklepios. Certainly the composer of the little group has lost all traces of the severe style in his Asklepios, so that one might assume that the same thing has happened in the case of the Hygieia; but the characteristic style of the dress of the latter and the position of the feet are so decisive that, in spite of the poor execution, we can safely say that her original cannot possibly have been contemporary with the Asklepios. We gather then that the Asklepios

FIG. 88.—Asklepios and Hygieia in Palazzo Barberini (Rome).

was composed as a single figure, and needed no Hygieia: indeed, this figure, who likewise stands on the left leg and likewise holds a serpent staff in her left hand, forms but a sorry complement to the Asklepios. We have here a fresh instance of the device common in the time of the Empire, of making up into groups figures that were originally unconnected. The little group, to judge from the workmanship and the shape of the plinth, was composed in the second or third century A.D.; the statue in the Uffizi, to judge from the manner in which the hair is treated, must be ascribed to the age of the Antonines.

The Asklepios, then, must have been originally intended as an isolated figure. Its motive, however, remained unaltered by adaptation to a group; just as the old Argive athletes were left unchanged when they were grouped together as Orestes with Elektra or Pylades,[2] or as the Borghese Mars when he was united with Venus.[3] The motive of the hands in the Asklepios of the Barberini group is so entirely in harmony with the whole pose of the figure, that we must assume it for the original. The god is in the act of feeding his snake. In the left hand he holds a cake or something of the kind,[4] and is on the point of breaking off a morsel, as it seems, with his right to give it to the snake, which is raising its coils on his left side. In the little group the creature is coiling itself round the traditional knotted stick of Asklepios, which is leaning up against the figure in a most improbable manner, and evidently only serves to hold up the snake. Had the stick been part of the original composition, it must have been supported under the left shoulder, or the left hand must have rested on it.[5] Neither is however the

---

[1] The head is modern.   [2] Cf. 50th *Berl. Winckelmannsprogr.* p. 136.   [3] Cf. *infra*, on Venus of Milo, p. 384.
[4] Zoega conjectured—probably correctly—a honey-cake; Matz, a liver.
[5] This is the case in the Berlin bronze, which is reproduced in Müller-Wieseler, *Denkm. a. K.* ii. 772; in

case. The staff was naturally indispensable in the eyes of the copyist in marble
as a support for the serpent. We can leave it out of account in the bronze original—
(the treatment of the hair of the Florentine head clearly points to bronze). There
is nothing in the attitude of the god to lead us to expect the existence of the staff:
he does not support himself upon one, but stands firm on the left leg, leaving the
right free, but with the whole sole down—(the Barberini group shows that the
Florentine statue should have been thus restored); he holds the cake for the snake
in the left hand, which is extended horizontally, and moves the right in the same
direction. Snakes lifting themselves up without any support were, as is well known,
a favourite theme of quite early Greek art, both in decorative[1] work and in the
round, as for instance on the old Spartan reliefs, notably on one where a
snake is raising itself up in front of a youth who is offering[2] a fruit to it. On
a Thessalian coin of the fifth century Asklepios is feeding a serpent that appears
upright in front of him.[3] In a statuette from Epidauros[4] which goes back to some
fifth-century original the snake is likewise not wreathed about a stick. The bronze
original of our statue must accordingly have had at its side a great snake which,
resting on its coils (compare the snake at the side of the Parthenos), lifted its
head to the level of the god's hand.

Our marble copies obviously represent Asklepios. The addition of Hygieia
makes this plain. It does not however follow as a matter of course that the original
belonging to the first half of the fifth century also pourtrayed Asklepios. A
bearded divinity, feeding a snake, is a figure appropriate to more than one
cult, and to whom different names might be assigned. In the Graeco-Roman
period this type became confined to Asklepios, while the other kindred deities of
health, from whose midst he sprang, retained only a local significance. Our statue
might very well have represented originally some Athenian divinity, akin to Asklepios,
associated with the serpent, a divinity significant only in some local cult. Such were,
for example, at Athens the popular Hero Iatros and the Hero Alkon,[5] at Oropos
Amphiaraus, and at Lebadeia Trophonios; the two last were, we know, represented in exactly the same way as Asklepios.[6] The reason for this likeness lies, not
in an extension of the Asklepios type to the others, but in the fact that this type
had originally a wider signification. It might even be that our statue represents Zeus
Meilichios, who was intimately associated with the snake, and was a genuine Chthonian
divinity of benign character.[7]

In this statue the personality of such a god is very effectively embodied. The
hair combed down from the crown of the head on the forehead and framing the face,
together with the long beard, give to the face an expression of solemn melancholy. In
the turn and inclination of the head, however, and in the kindly mouth, we read

---

Roscher's *Lexikon*, i. 636. (Friederichs, *Kl. Kunst. u. Industrie*, No. 1846.) This bronze, like its replica in Berlin
(Friederichs, 1846 *a*), belongs in design and technique to the 16—17th century: the design seems to have been
suggested by the Florentine statue: the artist skilfully allows both hands to rest on the staff.

[1] Cf. *Olympia*, vol. iv. *Die Bronzen*, No. 906 *seq.* Text, p. 145 *seq.*

[2] *Ath. Mitth.* 1877, Pl. 25; *Skulpt. in Berlin*, No. 732. Cf. also the great Meilichios snake, *ibid.*
No. 723, and various other reliefs, *e.g.* Le Bas, *Voy. Arch., Mon. fig.* 39: also the vase Ἐφημ. ἀρχ. 1890, Pl. 7.

[3] Brit. Mus. *Catal. Thessaly*, Pl. 5, 9.   [4] Kabbadias, γλυπτὰ ἔργα 270.

[5] Cf. Deneken in Roscher's *Lexikon*, i. 2483; *Sabouroff Coll.* i. *Introd.* p. 20.

[6] For Trophonios see *Paus.* ix. 39, 3, 4; for Amphiaraos, Deneken, *loc. cit.* 2588, and Δελτίον ἀρχ. 1891,
p. 89, No. 23. It is far more likely that one of these two and not Asklepios is represented on the Boeotian
vase, Ἐφημ. ἀρχ. 1890, Pl. 7.

[7] Cf. *Sabouroff Coll.* i. *Introd.* p. 22. A votive relief of the fourth century in the Peiraieus represents Zeus
Meilichios (name inscribed) enthroned with a horn of plenty and a bowl; the sacrificial victim which is being
offered to him is a pig.

E E

gentleness and goodness. The action is above all characteristic, in that the god pays
no heed to himself, but feeds his snake, seemingly wholly absorbed in the occupation.
In this we see the tenderness and care he bestows on all that trust in him ; the
nature of the healing god is thus accentuated, and at the same time the snake, which
is his attribute, is brought into close and actual union with him.   Only an artist of
exceptional originality can have created this characteristic figure, which differs from
most of the statues of gods of the time in the fact that the god is represented as
engaged in some action.   We believe that Myron may have been this artist.

Let us examine the figure more closely.   The pose is evidently borrowed from
the canon of Hagelaidas ; the left supporting leg with the right leg placed close to it,
the drooping left shoulder, and the inclination of the head to the same side, the left
forearm horizontally extended and holding some object, the upper part of the arm
lying close to the body, and the broad shoulders, are all traits that recall this canon.
At the same time we can also observe great differences ; quiet and dull repose are
replaced by action and concentrated attention.   The head and the upper part of the
body are not simply inclined to the left side, but turned that way ; and the right arm
does not hang down but is in active movement—in a word, everything combines to
represent a definite action.

The fidelity to the canon of Hagelaidas, together with the bold departure from it in
certain respects, alike point to Myron.   The head decides the question.   The forehead,
the eyes with their rather pronounced lids, the full mouth with the slightly parted
lips, the tangled profusion of curls, and the shape of the head, are all distinctly
Myronian.

For criticism of detail, two heads in the British Museum (Fig. 89)[1] and in the
Louvre[2] respectively are of weight: the original which they reproduce[3] must have
resembled our Asklepios so closely that it almost seems as if the two heads were
merely variants, due to the hand of the copyist.[4]   Both are quite erect ; the one is
furnished with a terminal bust, and the other probably terminated in the same way.
It is conceivable that both reproduce our 'Asklepios' head, but altered and posed
erect in order to suit the exigencies of a terminal bust.   Still, if a different original
did actually underlie them, it certainly proceeded from the same artist and had
substantially the same significance as our 'Asklepios.'

In both heads the stylistic treatment of the hair and of the moustache produces
an impression of far greater fidelity to the original than in the Florentine statue, where
the finicking character of the work reveals the mannerism of the age of the Antonines.
Both the heads also display to perfection Myron's modelling of the forehead : the
eyelids are pronounced, and the full mobile mouth allows the teeth to show as in the
Cassel Apollo.[5]   The delicate root of the nose and the line of the bridge of the nose—
preserved in the London copy—are all quite in Myron's manner. Further, in the last-
named head the hair of the eyebrows is indicated ; this detail, which we also noted in the
bearded Herakles (p. 179), may possibly be referred to the original.   The treatment

---

[1] *Spec. of Anc. Sculpt.* i. 16 ; *Anc. Marbles*, ii. 29 ; Brunn-Bruckmann, *Denkm.* No. 229. Term with
head, preserved without any restoration.

[2] Louvre, No. 2055, belong to the Campana Collection, unfortunately very unfavourably placed at present in
the *Salle du Mars Borghese*.   The head is broken at the point where it joins the neck ; term restored :
otherwise only the nose is modern.   The beard and the locks of hair about the middle of the forehead are much
damaged ; workmanship good and careful.

[3] The heads are replicas, the hair agreeing lock for lock.   There is a third very poor replica in the Pal.
Orlandini in Florence.   Dütschke, ii. 503 ; Arndt-Bruckmann, *Einzelv.* 240, 241.

[4] The chief difference is in the hair at the sides falling over the ears.

[5] The teeth are plain in the Paris head.

FIG. 89.—Terminal bust in the British Museum.

FIG. 91.—Head of statue in Munich.

of the moustache with its long flowing lines that pass into the beard, and the way in which the locks of hair are detached from the ground, recall the same bearded Herakles the two works probably belonging to the same period of the artist's career.

The hair falls over the middle of the forehead in a rich unstudied mass, which contributes in no slight degree to the sombre expression. A simple fillet cutting deep into the locks is the sole adornment. In spite of the severe style the head is perfect in its expression of character. The custom that prevailed in later days of emphasizing the under-world divinities[1] by hair falling low over the forehead is merely a development of what was begun in these heads.

The drapery of the ' Asklepios ' is arranged in a simple and appropriate manner, without regard to beautiful or effective motives. The piece brought down over the shoulder may be compared with the corresponding arrangement in the Riccardi bust. We cannot enter into details, for the copyist of the statue was in all probability as inexact in the drapery as in the hair ; he doubtless tried to add richness to the broad, severe traits of the original by the introduction of lesser intermediate folds ; we must probably subtract considerably from the number of folds, and conceive the main features of the drapery to have been treated more simply and severely.[2]

Thus this statue of a god or hero of healing appears to be a copy after an earlier work by Myron, in which however he had already unfolded to the full the powers of characterization which we have learnt to admire in his later figures of gods and heroes ; among these the Florence Asklepios, in which a definite action is combined with the turn of the upper torso, deserves a special place.

XIV. *The Munich Zeus and the first Argive School.*

Another statue of extreme interest must be considered next, as much for its points of difference as of resemblance. We have seen that Myron, like Pheidias in his younger days, often employed the canon of Hagelaidas. It is therefore well to become acquainted at this point with a statue almost contemporary with the Myronian works, and which not only exhibits this old canon but seems to have been created in Argos itself.

I refer to the familiar statue in Munich (Figs. 90, 91)[3] which Brunn and Kekulé refer to Polykleitos, but which differs widely from the undoubted Polykleitan works, and is plainly considerably earlier. It is quite clear that the type of Hagelaidas underlies this conception, and has only been so far modified that the right leg is drawn back in the walking motive. For the rest there is the same characteristic hardness so familiar in works of the old type, the same disproportionate width of the breast in comparison with the hips, and the same angular shoulders well drawn back.[4] The attitude of repose with the weight on the left foot,

---

[1] The type afterwards so frequently used for Sarapis must have come into existence by the end of the fifth century. A very well preserved and significant statue of the Louvre (Fröhner, 33 ; Bouillon, iii. *stat.* 1, 3 ; Clarac, 311, 681) represents Zeus (eagle and thunderbolt are in part ancient) quite in the style of the fifth century : the head has the wisps of hair falling over the forehead. It is probably a Zeus Meilichios, and its artist should perhaps be looked for in the school of Alkamenes.

[2] The Cassel copy of the Lemnia is a clear example (*supra*, p. 5 *seq.*) of the extent to which copyists remodelled the simple draperies of more ancient statues at times.

[3] Brunn, *Glypt.* 5, No. 160 ; Friederichs-Wolters, *Gipsabg.* 480 ; Kekulé, *Jahrb. d. Inst.* iii. 1888, p. 37, Pl. 1 ; L. v. Urlichs, *Beitr. z. Gesch. d. Glypt.* p. 16 ; Brunn-Bruckmann, *Denkm.* No. 122. No replicas are known to me.

[4] Cf. 50th *Berl. Winckelmannsprogr.* pp. 138, 140, 143, 146.

FIG. 90.—Statue in Munich.

the droop of the left shoulder, the inclination of the head to the same side, the hanging right arm, and the left forearm extended horizontally—all these are familiar and unmistakable traits of the old scheme. The head shows also that the artist was completely under the influence of Hagelaidas. This is especially evident in the profile: the whole outline of the head, the line of the neck, the fillet that lies flat on the hair, its shape, and the very way in which the hair meets it; further, the form of the short thick curls themselves—all these accord so remarkably with the best copies of the head of the figure by Stephanos (Fig. 92),[1] and on the other hand present such marked contrasts to the other works of the same period, such as those of Myron, that there can be no doubt about the tendency of the artist. He must stand in direct relation to the artist of the Stephanos figure, whom we conjecture to have been Hagelaidas. As compared however with the style which we must assume for Hagelaidas, the artist of the Munich statue is considerably less hard; he gives fuller, softer flesh to the body; he indicates the veins and sets the eyes more deeply; he opens the mouth and makes the lower part of the forehead project; in a word, his system of forms shows a development equal to Myron's. Yet one has only to compare the modelling of the forehead or the treatment of hair and beard to find that he lacks all that character of individuality, that charm of real life, which stamps the Myronian works.

The inclination to recognize in the Munich statue the manner of Polykleitos originates in a perception, which I fully share, that all the Argive works of the fifth century bear an inner relation to one another. In the head of the Munich statue, for instance, the first aim, as with Polykleitos, is to secure pure bright beauty of form, not, as with Myron, the expression of individual character. I myself some years ago conjectured this statue to be an early work of Polykleitos as pupil of Hagelaidas, and found a support for my theory in the oldest extant basis of Polykleitos, that of Kyniskos in Olympia, on which the traces of the feet point to a figure standing much like the Munich statue.[2] But the stylistic divergences from Polykleitos are too pronounced, and the whole system of forms so strongly contradicts this artist's personal style,[3] that I now consider my former theory quite untenable. On the contrary, the statue must belong to the generation of Argive artists who intervened between Hagelaidas and Polykleitos.

It is often assumed—on the ground of the familiar passage in Pliny—that it was Polykleitos who introduced the walking motive. This opinion is however erroneous. Polykleitos borrowed this motive for his canon, and thereby won for it widespread favour and popularity; but he did not invent it. The merit of the invention belongs to the Argive artists of the generation that preceded him, about the 80th Olympiad. Any doubts as to this point owing to the Munich statue being the work of a Roman copyist can be disposed of with the help of an original monument. This is a block of marble from the dedicatory offering of Smikythos in Olympia; to judge from the perfectly plain footmarks, it once supported a statue which stood in just the same attitude as the Munich statue.[4] The period of the offering is the same as that which

---

[1] Specially with the head in the Lateran, No. 356 (Fig. 92), and with the Orestes in the Louvre group: the last may be studied to advantage in the cast of the Ecole des Beaux-Arts, No. 6757; 50th *Berl. Winckelmannsprogr.* pp. 136, 138. The Capranesi head in the British Museum (*ibid.* p. 148, note 82) may also be compared. The face measurements of the Munich figure come close to those of the Stephanos figure. Cf. Kalkmann, *Gesichtsproport.* p. 60.

[2] Cf. *infra*, under Polykleitos, p. 249 *seq.*   [3] For instance, in the treatment of abdomen and pubes.

[4] It is the block with the largest fragment of the dedicatory inscription. Löwy, *I. G. B.* No. 31 *a*; deep depression for the back part of the left foot, which stood firm. Close by, on the same level as the heel of the left foot, is the hollow for the ball of the right foot. On the Munich statue too the ball of the

must be ascribed to our statue, about the 80th Olympiad (soon after B.C. 466); and its artist, Dionysios of Argos, belongs to the school of art to which the Munich statue must be ascribed.

The first introduction of the walking motive was clearly a significant departure on the part of some individual artist. In the period preceding the basis of the work of Dionysios and the Munich statue there is no trace of it, and after them, even in the Argive school, the older attitude of repose remained long in favour. In the works of Myron, and above all in the older Attic works, the walking motive is wholly unknown. We may, then, conjecture that it was Dionysios of Argos or his contemporary Glaukos, the artists of the offering of Smikythos, who first introduced this innovation. And to them or to an artist of the same standing must also be ascribed the original of the Munich statue. This statue, while still keeping in everything else to the old type of Hagelaidas, shows what a powerful new impetus was derived from the introduction of the walking motive; not but what the hard angular forms, in which this motive first appears, are separated by a long distance from the perfect rounded harmonies which Polykleitos imparted to it.

We have still to consider an interesting find from Olympia, which shows that the statuary type of the master of the Munich figure was employed in this centre of Peloponnesian art activity, as we can prove to have been the case with the canon of Hagelaidas.[1] A colossal torso from the Olympia excavations[2] displays so close a resemblance to the Munich statue that it must be referred to the same artist. Unfortunately it is not an original, but evidently only a late copy, executed in Pentelic marble, possibly to replace a stolen bronze original, or possibly it was a new dedication, copied from an older work. The torso accords with the Munich statue in all but trifling points;[3] in it too the shoulders are disproportionately wide,[4] yet here again, as compared with the canon of Hagelaidas, the forms display the same full, round, fleshy character; here too the veins on the arms are indicated.

The torso of Olympia by reason of its size is in all probability to be referred to a statue of Zeus; indeed, from the place where it was found, one might hazard the conjecture that it was a Zeus named by Pausanias without mention of the material, which had no inscription, but which was described as a dedication of Mummius;[5] a statue of this kind might very well be copied from an earlier work. The Munich statue

right foot is on a level with the heel of the left foot. The block belonged to the offering of Smikythos erected on the north side of the temple, assigned by Pausanias (v. 26, 2) to Dionysios. There are ancient footmarks on two other blocks of this offering; in this case however both feet were resting with full sole. From these it is apparent that the figures were considerably less than life-size (length of the footmark 16 cm.) The Roman footmarks on the under side of two of these blocks are quite different.

[1] Cf. in 50th *Berl. Winckelmannsprogr.* p. 146 *seq.*

[2] Perfectly nude torso in the museum at Olympia: the neck is altogether wanting, as also the legs from a little above the middle of the thigh; a considerable part of the left upper arm is preserved; smaller portion of right upper arm. From the hollow of the neck to the upper edge of the pubes 0·75, to the navel 0·555. Distance between the nipples 0·40. Greatest breadth in the hips 0·49, in the shoulders 0·75. The statue was therefore considerably larger than the Munich one (where the distance between the nipples measures 0·32).

[3] The left upper arm of the torso is somewhat drawn back instead of forward, as in the Munich statue. Further, the left shoulder of the torso droops less: the forms are altogether somewhat less meagre. The Munich statue is considerably better in technique, and seems a more careful copy than the Olympian torso.

[4] The pubes is sharply defined as in archaic work: the locks of hair are treated in the stiff style, but they are only lightly indicated, and not worked out.

[5] The torso was found on the 12th of March 1880, between the western terrace walls and the western Altis walls, a little south of the southern line of the *palaistra*, lying free (*i.e.* not built into any construction) below the green deposit that came down from the Heraion, and according to all appearances in its original site. Treu, to whom I am indebted for the above information, is reminded of the Zeus of Mummius, which stood here near the west wall of the Altis facing towards the west (Paus. v. 24, 8): this identification seems to me very probable.

Fig. XXXI—Zeus of Artemision, Athens, National Museum

is interpreted by Kekulé as Zeus, bearing in his left hand the eagle, in his right the lightning. This interpretation satisfactorily explains the position of the arms, and also the whole majestic, kingly personality of the figure, and is now further cor-roborated by the kindred Olympian torso.[1] Yet how comes Zeus to have quite close-cropped hair? We certainly can only then interpret this figure as Zeus, when this strange and wholly unwonted mode of treatment is attested for the epoch and school to which our statue belongs. And this actually appears to be the case. It is true that among the numerous representations of Zeus on monuments of every kind I can only point to two examples with the same close-cropped hair, but these are sufficient. Shortish hair is quite common in representations of Zeus: on Attic vases the type

Fig. 92.—Replica of the head of the statue by Stephanos.

appears first in the period about 403 B.C. (cf. *supra*, p. 42), and at a later date becomes very popular; quite in accordance with these Attic vases is the type on the familiar Eleian coins of the fourth century.[2] But this type of hair, in which the locks though short are yet flowing, does not help us where the question is of hair close-cropped like an athlete's; besides, it belongs to a considerably later period than that of our statue. On the other hand, an isolated example of the type in question occurs in archaic vase-painting in the Zeus engaged in combat with the Giants.[3] On this follows a famous coin-type of Elis[4] (Pl. VI. 22), which however was only struck

[1] It must however be mentioned that a coin of Nicaea (Brit. Mus. *Catal. Pontus*, Pl. 32, 13; p. 158) struck under Commodus represents Hephaistos with a hammer in the right hand and a bar of metal in the left, in a scheme closely resembling that of the Munich statue; the original must have been a work of the same school.

[2] Head, *Hist. Num.* p. 355, fig. 234; *Guide*, Pl. 23, 33.   [3] Overbeck, *Kunstmyth. Atlas*, Pl. 4, 6.

[4] Only two specimens of the coin are at present known: (a) London (Head, *Hist. Num.* p. 354, fig. 230; *Guide*, Pl. 14, 29; P. Gardner, *Types*, Pl. 8, 6; Stephani, *Compte Rendu* for 1876, p. 224, Pl. No. 5). (b) Berlin

F F

during quite a short period, and may probably be dated *circa* B.C. 420 ; for it is the counterpart to the beautiful type of Hera, which according to a plausible conjecture of Percy Gardner's is to be referred to the League contracted in that year between Elis and Argos (Pl. VI. 23).[1]   In the head of Hera it is thought, and probably correctly, that we have the Polykleitan Hera of Argos ; the head of Zeus too must have been based on some famous work of art, but not on one of the period of 420, for the whole type—with the slanting profile, the massive beard, and the ear set rather high up—seems to me to point pretty clearly to the fact that we have on the coin a work of the severer style rendered with the freedom natural to the fifth century ; the obvious suggestion is that this was an Argive work, dedicated by the newly formed League, and highly prized by them.

The next and last instance of a short-haired head of Zeus occurs on the coins of Syracuse[2] and of the Italian Lokri (Pl. VI. 20).[3]   It is merely a type which was stamped after B.C. 345[4] on a portion of the coinage of these two cities (which were intimately connected both politically and commercially), after the expulsion of the tyrant Dionysios from both, on the occasion of the restoration of the Democracy. This type is, however, evidently the free reproduction of an older work of the fifth century,[5] for it has nothing in common with the types that reproduce the spirit and taste of the epoch *circa* B.C. 345.   The inscription on the Syracusan specimens, which characterizes Zeus as Ἐλευθέριος, leaves no room for doubting what this older work was : it was the colossal figure of Zeus Eleutherios—of Zeus the Deliverer—which the Syracusans had set up as an enduring memorial of that earlier expulsion of a tyrant and democratic revolution in 466.[6]   To this pledge of freedom the people had recourse on the similar occasion in the fourth century, when the festival and the great sacrifices in front of the statue were once more revived.   Now it is an old conjecture of Haverkamp, approved by Eckhel,[7] that a reproduction of this Syracusan Zeus Eleutherios has been preserved in a coin-type of the two consuls of the stormy year 49 B.C.—L. Cornelius Lentulus and C. Claudius Marcellus.[8]   On these coins the type is associated with a design that is purely Sicilian—namely, with the *triquetra*, which appears on the reverse in its essentially Sicilian form.[9]   This must evidently have been selected with reference to the Consul Marcellus and his glorious ancestor the Conqueror of Sicily.[10]   The conjecture has therefore everything in its favour.   The figure of Zeus in

---

(still unpublished) : from a different die to the London specimen, yet agreeing with it almost exactly ; the hair is somewhat better preserved.   The little curls are very like the hair on the Munich statue ; it clearly imitates a work of this style.   The moustache streams on either side over the beard.

[1] P. Gardner in the Brit. Mus. *Catal. Peloponn.* p. 36 *sqq.* Pl. 12, 11.

[2] In Syracuse only in bronze : Head, *Hist. Num.* p. 157 ; *Numism. Chron.* 1874, Pl. 7, 10, 11 ; 1876, Pl. 2, 6 ; 3, 17 ; cf. Overbeck, *Zeus*, p. 213.   On the electrum and silver coins of the same period is represented an ordinary free type of Zeus, corresponding to the taste of the time.

[3] In Lokri in both silver and bronze : Head, *Hist. Num.* p. 86 *seq.* ; *Guide*, Pl. 25, 21 ; Gardner, *Types*, Pl. 5, 14 ; Sallet's *Numism. Ztsch.* xvii. Pl. 1, 7 ; Overbeck, *Zeus*, p. 101.   The finest silver specimen appears to be that in the Gotha collection.   [4] For the date cf. Head (*loc. cit.*)

[5] This is also Von Sallet's view, whom I was able to consult on the point.

[6] Diodor. xi. 72, 2.   Cf. Kekulé in *Jahrb. d. Inst.* 1888, p. 43 ; Busolt, *Griech. Gesch.* ii. 292.

[7] *Doctrina Num.* v. 182.

[8] Good reproduction in Head, *Guide*, Pl. 66, 16.   Cf. Babelon, *Monn. de la Républ. Rom.* i. 424 ; *Jahrb. d. Inst.* 1888, p. 43.

[9] We find too as reverse the curly head of a youth, closely related to the Zeus Hellanios of the Syracusan coins (Overbeck, *Zeus*, Münzt. 3, 1, 2 ; p. 196), and therefore possibly connected with it : this is rendered however less probable by reason of the fact that a similar type—though at the same time less akin to the Syracusan—appears elsewhere on the coins of Roman families, where it is explained as Vejovis.

[10] So Eckhel (*loc. cit.*), who also remarks—and rightly—that these coins need not on this account have been struck in Sicily, which would be unlikely after the events of the year 49 ; this supposition has been made into a fact by many of the more recent authorities.

question—and this is what is of special interest to us—displays a decided likeness to the Munich statue. The design on the coin, in spite of the careless execution, reproduces as though intentionally just the same pose, particularly in the drooping left shoulder and the disproportionate width of breast. The lower part of the right leg seems to have been conceived as drawn back, though this is not very obvious, by reason of the front view which has been adopted. The sole divergence in the pose— the right hand stretched out sideways—may be explained from the impossibility of representing the thunderbolt from the front. The head is so slightly and carelessly indicated that we must not lay too much stress on the fact that it seems to wear the usual crown of hair. Thus it seems permissible to conjecture that the Munich statue is actually a copy of the Zeus Eleutherios erected in Syracuse in 466. This date would exactly accord with the style of the statue, and would not conflict with what we have ascertained about its school, for the Argive artists, Hagelaidas among the first, seem to have been employed on many occasions for the West, and the artists who worked for Smikythos might well have received commissions from Syracuse as well.

It is quite in keeping with the spirit of the Argive artists that they should have wholly divested the king of the gods of his characteristic adornment of hair, and formed him after the same pattern of manly beauty as the victorious athletes; for, in their search after pure beauty of form, they got further away from the power of characterization.

Still this type could only have a transitory duration. The characteristic creations which Attic art was producing about this time soon became the prevailing types in the representation of the gods. We have on several occasions tried to show that in this Myron played a leading part; we may recall by way of contrast the Zeus that we ascribed conjecturally to him; there we found a deep understanding of the nature of the god represented; it was the veritable Zeus, while in the statue we have just been studying we seem merely to behold a beautiful man.

With this contrast we close for the time our inquiry concerning Myron, and in the following chapter turn to Polykleitos himself, who follows immediately upon the stage of art with which we have just become acquainted.

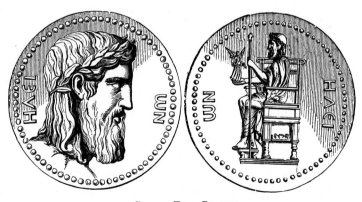

COIN OF ELIS—ZEUS OF
PHEIDIAS.

Fig. XXXII—Diadumenos Farnese, London, British Museum. (See p. 238 sqq.)

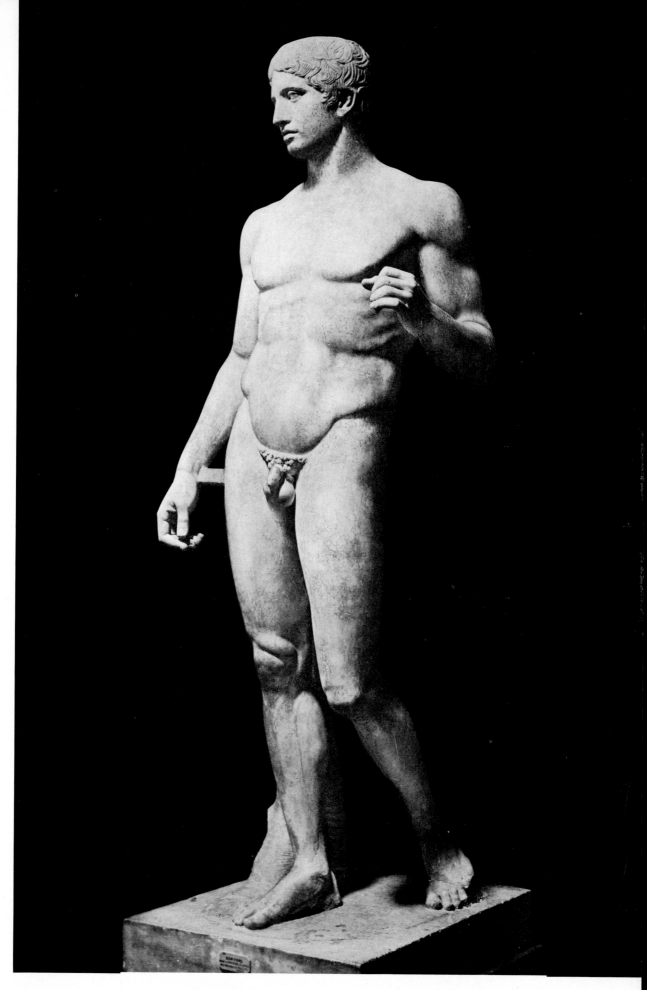

Fig. XXXIII—Doryphoros (or Canon), Copy after Po-
kleitos, Naples, National Museum

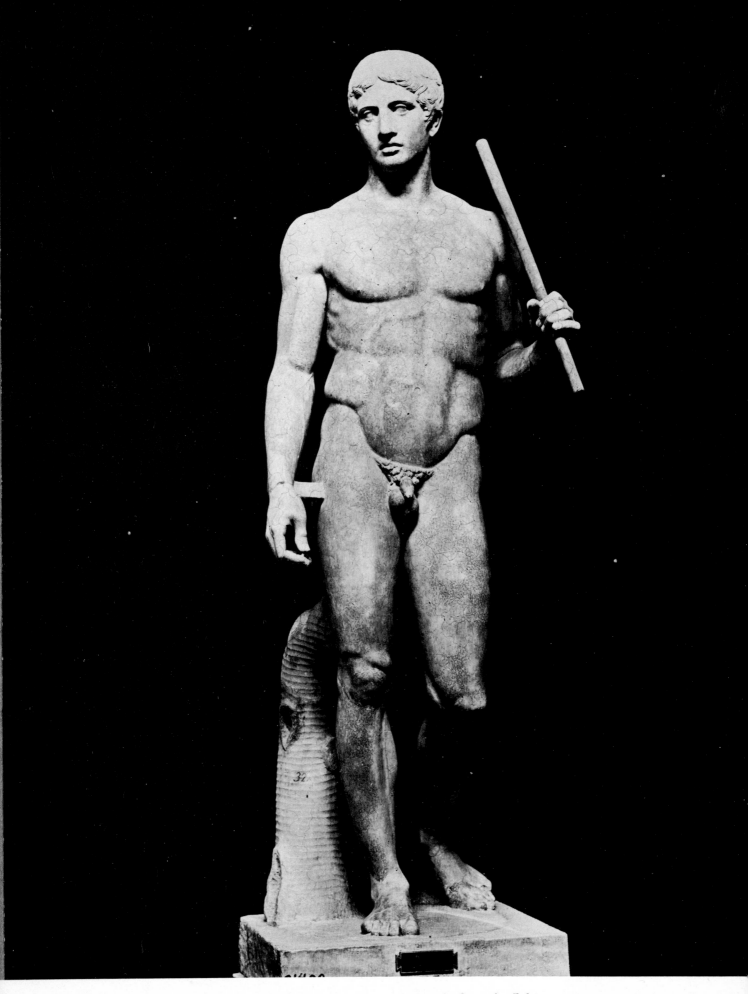

Fig. XXXIV—Doryphoros (or Canon), Copy after Polykleitos, Naples, National Museum

POLYKLEITOS

I. *Historical and Epigraphical Evidence.*

THE preceding chapters have already taught us something about Polykleitos, which it is well to begin by recapitulating. As regards his date, we saw (p. 130) that there was no reason for doubting the evidence of Plato, who makes Polykleitos a contemporary of Pheidias. We next obtained B.C. 440 as the approximate date of his Amazon, a work which must naturally have been executed at a time when he was already an artist of acknowledged position. The famous Doryphoros must belong to a still earlier period, partly because it anticipates the Amazon in many points, and partly because of the flat treatment of the hair. These considerations show that the artistic activity of Polykleitos began at least as early as B.C. 450, a date at which the walking motive must have been current in Argive art, since, as we noted before, the Argive artist Dionysios employed it as early as about B.C. 460. We saw too (p. 196) that Polykleitos cannot have been, as ancient tradition had it, actually the pupil of Hagelaidas, for a whole generation of artists intervenes between him and the founder of the school.

The next certain date in the life of Polykleitos is B.C. 420 (Ol. 90), when he made the gold and ivory Hera for the new temple at Argos, an event by which his whole career was dated in classical times (Plin. xxxiv. § 49). We can obtain a fair notion of the artist's style at this period; for it seems certain that his Hera was the model for the majestic head of the goddess which makes its appearance on the coinage of both Argos and of Elis at the very time when the statue of Polykleitos was set up (Plate VI. 23).[1]

---

[1] See *supra*, p. 218. It is scarcely necessary to remind the reader that there is no connexion whatsoever between the Hera of Polykleitos and either the Farnese 'Hera' (Conze, *Beiträge z. Gesch. d. Grie. Plastik*, p. 1, and others) or the girl's head recently discovered during the American excavations at the Heraion of Argos (see *Arch. Stud. H. Brunn dargebr.* 1893). As to the Farnese head, the affinities it presents to the Artemis of the Aktaion metope from the Heraion at Selinos, and the further affinities between these Selinuntian metopes and the school of Kritios and Nesiotes, make me refer this 'Hera'—or more correctly this Artemis—to the latter school.

Nothing is known as to the date of the death of Polykleitos; he may have lived to extreme old age, and for all we know he may have been working up to the end of the fifth century. None of the works, however, known to be undoubtedly by him can be dated later than B.C. 420. The Zeus Meilichios, which, according to an anecdote in Pausanias (ii. 20, 1), should be dated after 418, is really not a dated work at all, for the anecdote is only an explanation of the name Meilichios, and therefore has no chronological value.[1] It is not altogether impossible that the tripod with the figure of Aphrodite consecrated at Amyklai after the battle of Aigospotamoi (B.C. 405) was a work of the elder Polykleitos, though it is highly improbable; for as Polykleitos passed on to his pupils the work on the more splendid votive offerings, put up in Delphi after the same battle, he would hardly have undertaken a comparatively unimportant commission for obscure Amyklai. It is more likely that the tripod was by the younger Polykleitos.[2]

A number of bases inscribed with the name Polykleitos and belonging to statues of athletes have been found in Olympia; but it is by no means always easy to decide to which of the two artists each basis should be ascribed. The basis of the Kyniskos has undoubtedly been correctly assigned to the elder artist (Löwy, *I. G. B.* 50). It is not so much the archaic character of the writing that proves this, for Arkadia was singularly conservative in this respect,[3] as the way in which the words are distributed around the upper surface of the base. Next comes the basis of the Pythokles (Löwy, *I. G. B.* 91) on which the Argive *Lambda* occurs. Now on the well-known Polystrata relief from Argos—a piece of sculpture which from its style should be dated before rather than after the Peloponnesian War[4]—this same Argive *Lambda* appears together with the Ionic H. Thus it is safe to date the Pythokles as early as 430, since the Argive alphabet was falling into disuse at a still earlier period. The basis of the Xenokles (Löwy, *I. G. B.* 90) follows closely upon those just mentioned, for, though the inscription is entirely Ionic, there are still all sorts of archaic elements about it. It should probably be dated about 420; for, as Ionic letters were already being introduced into Argos even before the Peloponnesian War, it is quite likely that by 420 the Ionic alphabet was fully established. Both the Pythokles and the Xenokles may therefore be ascribed to the elder Polykleitos. On the other hand, the Aristion inscription (*I. G. B.* 92) has a totally different character;[5]

---

[1] Cf. Robert, *Arch. Märchen*, p. 102.

[2] The fact that the signatures of Polykleitos and of Lysippos (Löwy, *I. G. B.* No. 93. See also Robert, *Arch. Märchen*, p. 103 *seq.*, and E. Preuner in *Bonner Studien*, p. 217 *seq.*) appear side by side cut in identical characters on one block of stone (found at Thebes) which supported two statues by these two artists, has given rise to the theory that this younger Polykleitos was a contemporary of Lysippos. But the character of the epigraphy shows that the Theban basis belongs to the period succeeding 316, when the city was rebuilt after its destruction by Alexander. It is evident that, as Preuner (*loc. cit.* p. 220) has already hinted, two statues which were originally unconnected were now set up anew side by side and inscribed afresh. There are many examples of such renewals of artists' signatures. The basis is therefore no guide for recovering the date of the younger Polykleitos, and all the theories lately advanced by Robert (*loc. cit.*) become untenable. Rather must we admit that works handed down with the name Polykleitos and belonging to the end of the fifth century may just as well be by the elder as by the younger artist. The view propounded above accounts for the Boeotian form ἐπόεισεν that occurs on the basis. I note that in the latest publication of the inscriptions in *C. I. Gr. Septentr.* i. 2532, 2533, Dittenberger dates them on epigraphical grounds after 316. His further improbable conclusion, that the Polykleitos named here is an unknown artist, the third of the name, need not be discussed after what has been said above.

[3] See Kirchhoff, *Studien*, 4th ed. p. 159.

[4] This is also the opinion given in the *Beschr. d. ant. Skulpt. in Berlin*, No. 682, where however the illustration reproduces the inscription incorrectly with an E instead of the H which is clearly visible on the stone in the ἀνέθηκε. Kirchhoff (*Studien*, 4th ed. p. 100) assumed that the relief belonged to the period after the war, on the ground of the style, but it is just this that points to an earlier date.

[5] It is also carelessly executed and not deeply graven.

it belongs evidently to the fourth century, and must be assigned to the younger artist.

Polykleitos was an Argive. Plato, our earliest authority in the matter, calls him Ἀργεῖος in a dialogue (the *Protagoras*) written in any case shortly after the death of the artist. To Plato, Argos was the home of Polykleitos in the same sense that Athens was that of Pheidias, to whom he applies the adjective Ἀθηναῖος immediately after calling Polykleitos an Argive. He is evidently citing the two most celebrated artists and leaders of the two schools[1] most in renown at the time in which the dialogue is supposed to have taken place.

In the Pythokles inscription, which, as we saw, there is good reason for assigning to the elder artist, Polykleitos expressly calls himself Ἀργεῖος. It is true, however, that this epithet only occurs in the restored inscription of the first century B.C., and it is not quite certain if it was part of the original. The other Polykleitan inscriptions mention no nationality, probably because the artist was so famous and well known at Olympia. The younger Polykleitos, to whom the Aristion base must belong, signs simply Πολύκλειτος ἐποίησε, without any epithet. He does this probably with intention, for it was not to his interest to be distinguished from his famous elder namesake, who, as the Xenokles basis shows, signed his later works in this simple manner. Pausanias in various passages calls both elder and younger Polykleitos simply Ἀργεῖος. Moreover, Naukydes, whom Pausanias calls the brother of Polykleitos, meaning of course the younger, is also Ἀργεῖος, as is proved by Pausanias (vi. 1, 3)[2] and by his own signature on a basis at Athens. It is only the third brother, Daidalos, who in an inscription calls himself a Sikyonian (Löwy, *I. G. B.* 89), as he is also styled by Pausanias (vi. 2, 8, etc.) He evidently migrated to Sikyon. From Sikyon also came two of the artists employed on the great Delphic votive offering—Kanachos, a pupil of Polykleitos, and Alypos, a pupil of Naukydes. Among other later members of the Polykleitan school we must also reckon Kleon of Sikyon, who belongs to the fourth century. These facts seem to show that a branch of the Polykleitan school in Argos was established in Sikyon,[3] probably by Daidalos, about the end of the fifth century. In the fourth century this Sikyonian offshoot gradually overshadowed the parent school, and Lysippos, its greatest outcome, eventually cast Argos and her artists completely into the shade. Its school of painting in the fourth century would in itself have made Sikyon a leading art-centre ; but in the fifth matters had been very different, for sculpture was then in the hands of Aristokles and his pupils, who were absolutely insignificant as compared to the Argive school founded by Hagelaidas and developed by Polykleitos. The assertion, found only in Pliny (xxxiv. 55), that Polykleitos was a native of Sikyon, must in all probability be due to that same historian of art whose Lysippian and Sikyonian bias can be so clearly detected at various points of Pliny's borrowed narrative (cf. *supra*, p. 171 *seq.*) He was guilty of a sort of anachronism in transferring Polykleitos to Sikyon. There is however some excuse for his error in the later migration of the Polykleitan school to Sikyon, and in the eventual exclusive leadership exerted by the Sikyonian school in the Peloponnesos.[4]

---

[1] This passage does not necessarily imply (as Robert assumes, *Arch. Märchen*, p. 101) that Polykleitos was resident in Athens.

[2] The corrupt Μόθωνος (Paus. ii. 22, 7) must for the present remain a mystery. Robert's last suggestion, νεώτερος (*Hermes*, 1888, 429), is based on his untenable hypothesis concerning the family of Patrokles (*Arch. Märchen*, p. 107).

[3] Cf. also Brunn, *Bayr. Sitzungsber.* 1880, p. 473. Löwy, *I. G. B.* p. 67, No. 86.

[4] It seems to me better to set aside the information of Pliny than to try to combine it with the ascertained fact

Polykleitos was the head of a large school, and in his actual family were many artists, though his sons, according to Plato,[1] cannot have attained to any great distinction. It is likely, though not actually proved, that the younger Polykleitos was related to the elder. As he was brother to Naukydes and Daidalos, he must have been a son of Patrokles. Now the facts, we know, fit together best if we regard Patrokles as a somewhat younger brother of Polykleitos, so that the younger Polykleitos, together with Naukydes and Daidalos, would be nephews of the elder.

However much Polykleitos may have been—as he indubitably was—the dominating personality in his circle, we must yet allow for the possibility that Patrokles may have kept at his side a certain independent style of his own, which he bequeathed to his sons. At any rate Naukydes and Daidalos, who mention their father in their inscriptions, very probably do so because he had been an artist of merit. The monuments will throw further light on this point.

II. *The Doryphoros.*

The Doryphoros of Polykleitos has been longer and better known than any other statue by this artist. It has, however, not yet been subjected to an exhaustive analysis based on a careful comparison of all its numerous replicas, nor has its great significance in the history of art been determined by reference to all other monuments. Though I am not in a position to undertake this task, a few modest contributions may yet be offered here.

We have already assigned this work to the period *circa* 450—440—the very time when Pheidias produced his Parthenos. Now the rise of Polykleitos in Argos marked no less an epoch than that of Pheidias in Athens; the Doryphoros is as decided an advance on its predecessors as the Lemnia and the Parthenos are on theirs.

The Doryphoros may be compared with two works dating *circa* B.C. 460, which belong to the generation of Argive art immediately preceding Polykleitos. The one is the Munich Zeus already described; the other, the little bronze athlete from the Argolis now in the Berlin Museum.[2] In the Zeus, the walking motive is already introduced, so that Polykleitos found it ready to hand; some attempt is also made to represent the muscles and to indicate the veins. There is still, however, a wide gulf between this statue and the Doryphoros. The attitude is stiff and angular, and there are evidences throughout to show that the old canon of Hagelaidas has not been superseded: the shoulders are too wide, the hips too narrow, and the stomach flat and wooden. No attempt is made to show the effect produced on the muscles

that Polykleitos was an Argive, by means of such conjectures as—that Polykleitos was made a citizen of Argos after his gold and ivory Hera had been set up (Löschcke, *Arch. Ztg.* 1878, p. 11), a theory on which Robert (*Arch. Märchen*, p. 101) builds further improbable conjectures.

[1] οὐδὲν πρὸς τὸν πατέρα εἰσί. Plato would certainly not have said this, if at that time any sons of Polykleitos had been distinguished artists. The son of Polykleitos whom Löwy conjectures in the inscription *I.G.B.* 89 is quite problematic. So too is the conjecture of Robert (*Arch. Märchen*, p. 107) that a Patrokles who was employed B.C. 404 on the Delphic votive offerings was the son of Polykleitos, and to be distinguished accordingly from the elder Patrokles. This is quite unnecessary, for even were Patrokles the father of Naukydes and Daidalos he could quite well have been working after B.C. 404.

[2] 50th *Berl. Winckelmannsprogr.* 1890, '*Eine argivische Bronze*,' Taf. i. The provenance of this bronze, Ligurio in the neighbourhood of Epidauros, has been certified to me in the most reliable manner. Fröhner's statement (*Coll. Tyskiewicz*, text to Pl. 13) that it was found at Olympia is quite unwarranted (cf. *Berl. Phil. Woch.* 1894, p. 1140).

between breast and hip by the position of the left leg, and the lowering of the left shoulder ; a treatment that practically makes no sort of distinction between the two sides of the trunk when the body is in motion cannot be true to nature. In various other points we see signs of archaic treatment ; the hair, for instance, lacks variety and delicacy, and the fillet encircles the head in an archaic, lifeless manner. The bronze athlete, on the other hand, is much less stiff and angular ; the shoulders are no longer too broad, and the hips, like those of the Doryphoros, are fuller ;[1] the abdomen is rounder and more natural, and the back is really excellently modelled. The old canon is, however, closely adhered to in the pose of the figure and in the archaic treatment of the hair.[2]

These works form the foundation on which arose the harmonious conception of the Doryphoros. In this marvel of proportion all stiffness disappears, and every detail of attitude and movement produced by the momentary pause on one leg while walking is rendered with truth and accuracy. The artist has overcome that crux of former times, the rendering of the muscles between breast and hip on the side of the leg that carries the weight of the statue. The powerful muscles are developed equally all over the body without any undue exaggeration of particular parts, and all the principal veins are indicated. The formation of the abdomen is not inferior to that of any other part ; it is in its way quite as true as that of the breast ; the fondness for large plane surfaces with clearly defined edges—in a word, the very quality which, by comparison with nature, produces a highly conventional effect in the breast and abdomen of the Doryphoros—was universal in Greek art up to the time of Praxiteles and Skopas, when a rounder and more natural method was introduced. The carefully balanced proportions of the Doryphoros show at a glance how far it surpasses its predecessors ; and this superiority can be more accurately estimated by the help of measurements.[3] The head too, with its flat, almost angular contour, is noticeable as a characteristic innovation of Polykleitos. The hair is no longer in any way archaic, though it lies close to the skull and is only faintly modelled ; the attempt at realism in its superimposed layers is particularly noteworthy and original. The symmetrical parting over the brow is quite in keeping with the harmony and measured proportion that governs the whole figure ; it may almost be said that the desire for regularity is excessive. Apart from the walking motive, the actual pose differs from the old Argive canon in two points. The one is purely external, and consists in making the figure rest on the right leg, instead of on the left, as was the case with all the earlier artists, including the immediate predecessors of Polykleitos. The other difference is more essential, for it involves a complete reversion of an old arrangement whereby the arm on the side of the supporting leg was bent at the elbow and stretched out, while the other arm hung loosely down on the side of the free leg. Thus the body fell into two separate halves, the one absorbing all the tension and movement, the other being left in complete relaxation. Now in such cases the introduction of the walking motive only tended, as we noted in the Munich Zeus, to emphasize disagreeably this lack of balance. Polykleitos, by simply reversing the position of the arms prescribed by the old canon, restored the necessary balance between the two halves of the body, and produced moreover a great effect by means of the crossing lines of the upper and lower extremities. In his statues therefore the inactive arm hangs down on the side

---

[1] Cf. 50th *Berl. Winckelmannsprogr.* p. 142 *seq.*

[2] The omission of the pubes is also a sign of the old canon.

[3] Cf. 50th *Berl. Winckelmannsprogr.* p. 142 *seq.*

of the supporting leg which is in full muscular action, where it harmonizes with the curving outline infinitely better than it did with the free leg, while the other arm, which is stretched out and holds some attribute [1]—in this case a spear—is of agreeable effect on the same side as the leg which is carelessly drawn back. In this manner activity and relaxation are equally distributed between the two sides of the body.

The harmony of the whole is further heightened by the position of the head, which, following the old canon, is turned to the side on which the weight is thrown ; it is not bent forward, but is set fairly straight.[2] The expression of the face is resolute and determined, but not very animated : it has however none of the heaviness and dulness that is so universal in the heads of the old type.

The word 'Doryphoros,' as we saw before when discussing the statue of that name by Kresilas,[3] is merely a vague term borrowed from the art jargon of a late period. Literally the name was given to 'an attendant bearing a lance,' and was not at all applicable to our statue, which not only does not represent a servant, but in its original form, as we learn from a copy on a Berlin gem, carried a short spear or javelin.[4] The original Doryphoros is much more likely to have been the statue of an Olympic victor, probably of a pentathlete with his javelin. It must have been first set up in Argos, as we find it adopted there for a figure on a heroic relief.[5]

One proof that it is the statue of an athlete lies in the fact that a marble copy of the Doryphoros has been discovered in the Altis of Olympia,[6] for a statue of this kind found on this site must also necessarily be that of an Olympic victor. The material, like that of all later statues at Olympia, is Pentelic marble. It was no doubt dedicated by an athlete of some later period, who preferred a copy of the famous figure of the Doryphoros to an original statue. Unfortunately only the torso survives, and that in a damaged condition. The execution, though rather mechanical, is on the whole less hard than in most of the Italian replicas. The copy probably belongs to the first century B.C. or A.D.

There are many other replicas of the torso of the Doryphoros in different museums.[7] Two of these are so superior to the others in execution that they have a real aesthetic significance. The first, which is in the Uffizi at Florence, is executed in green basalt, and produces the effect of a bronze covered with an exquisite patina.[8] It is a fine bit of careful workmanship.[9] The other torso, of equally good workmanship, is the Pourtalès torso at Berlin.[10] It is interesting to notice in it the veins on the abdomen. As they do not occur in other replicas, I cannot feel certain that they

---

[1] In the excellent Florence copy (*Mon. d. Inst.* x. 50, 2) the right arm is (correctly) stretched horizontally forward.

[2] Michaelis points out (*Annali*, 1878, p. 9) that in the Naples copy the head is rather too upright, and that the other replicas are more correct in this respect.

[3] Cf. p. 163 *seq.*

[4] On the relief (*Ath. Mitth.* 1878, Taf. 13) a short javelin appears, not a long δόρυ.

[5] *Ath. Mitth.* 1878, Taf. 13. Collignon's view (*Hist. de la Sculpt.* i. 490), that the Doryphoros was a decorative statue from one of the gymnasia at Argos, involves an anachronism, for such purely decorative statues were not in vogue till much later.

[6] Still unpublished, and apparently unnoticed.

[7] Thus in Mus. Chiaramonti, No. 293 ; *ibid.* in reduced scale, No. 484 ; both unrestored. Two with wrong restorations in Pal. Giustiniani, two in Pal. Massimi alle colonne, and others. One in Vienna was lately published by R. von Schneider, *Die Erzstatue vom Helenenberge,* 1893, pp. 16, 17 (*Jahrb. d. Kunsth. Samml. d. Kaiserh.* Bd. xv.)

[8] No. 307. Dütschke, *Uffiz.* 535 ; Arndt-Bruckmann, *Einzelverkauf,* Nos. 94, 95. The back is admirably worked.

[9] This is the only replica in which the pubes is really well executed. It shows that Polykleitos also arranged the curls on the pubes quite symmetrically from the middle outwards towards the two sides.

[10] Friederichs-Wolters, *Gipsabg.* 507.

existed in the original. Quite different is it with the veins on the extremities, which appear on all the replicas, and which were already usual even in the severe style. We shall see, however, that late Polykleitan art certainly represented the veins of the abdomen, and perhaps the copyist got the idea in this way and transferred it to the Doryphoros.

There are a considerable number of heads which are copies of the Doryphoros.[1] The one which gives the best idea of the original is evidently the bronze bust by Apollonios at Naples;[2] the carefulness of the workmanship, into which no incongruous elements have been introduced, produces a singular impression of fidelity; the hair especially seems to be very faithfully copied. In comparison to this bronze most other copies appear superficial, and allow themselves every sort of simplification in the hair; the proceeding is the same as that noted in the case of the Myronian Diskobolos. In the main features, however, such as the division of the hair over the brow, all the copies are unanimous. In addition to the marble heads, there is a good copy made of the same green basalt as the Florentine torso; it is unfortunately much restored.[3]

The Doryphoros and the 'canon' of Polykleitos were, according to the exact wording of our tradition, two distinct works, yet it is probable that the same statue has been handed down under two names;[4] both appellations are moreover equally inappropriate, and belong to a much later period. When Lysippos, as Cicero (*Brutus*, 86, 296) tells us, called the Doryphoros his teacher, he must have referred to the canonical figure of Polykleitos. The monuments are quite in favour of this interpretation, for they prove how very frequently the Doryphoros was used as a model.

I shall only discuss here those works that are intimately connected with the Doryphoros, although to confine oneself to these is to gain only a very partial idea of the influence exerted by the statue. It is quite certain that a very considerable influence must have been exercised upon subsequent art by the combination exhibited in the Doryphoros of perfect dignity and calm with the walking attitude, yet this influence is mostly matter of conjecture, and can only be definitely pointed to in a very few cases.

The most notable figure directly derived from the Doryphoros is a bronze statuette in Paris[5] representing the young Pan. Though lacking the finishing touches of the chisel, it is an exquisite original from the immediate circle of Polykleitos. I pointed out some years ago the strong affinities which this bronze offered to the Doryphoros, not only in the motive but in the system of bodily forms. The only difference is that the arms, the left one particularly, are not so close to the body,[6] and that the left arm is more bent owing to the substitution of a short pedum for the lance; yet the fingers of this hand correspond exactly with those of the Doryphoros. The head is

---

[1] So in Mus. Chiaramonti, on a statue to which it does not belong.—A good copy in the Vatican, also on a wrong statue.—In the Pal. Valentini (staircase) on a wrong statue.—Inferior copies in Museo Torlonia, 469, in the *Coll. Barracco*, Pl. 43, 43 a, good; Pl. 44, indifferent; in the Palazzo Pitti (Dütschke, ii. 12), in the Uffizi (downstairs), in the Villa Mattei (Arndt-Bruckmann, *Einzelverkauf*, Nos. 116, 117), and others. Also, *Notizie degli Scavi*, 1879, i. 1; Cavaceppi, *Raccolta*, ii. 2.

[2] Friederichs-Wolters, 505. The clumsy eyeballs are a modern restoration. (Cf. p. 138, note 4.)

[3] Guédéonow, *Ermitage, Sculpt. Ant.* No. 75, called 'Drusus l'ancien.'

[4] There is no need to alter Pliny xxxiv. 55. It is undoubtedly correct to put a comma between *puerum* und *fecit*, as Detlefsen does. The comment on the Doryphoros (which belongs to that on the Diadumenos) and the comment on the canon probably come from quite different sources, which would account for the use of different names.

[5] *Ath. Mitth.* iii. 1878, Taf. 12 (Furtwängler); Babelon, *Cabinet des ant. de la Biblioth. Nat.*

[6] The illustration in the *Ath. Mitth.* is from a cast in which the right arm is closer to the body than it is in the original.

also entirely Polykleitan in character, although the fuller, more plastic treatment of the hair and the greater softness of mouth and chin point to its being a later work. The interval between them however need not have been very great, and there is no reason for dating this bronze later than the fifth century. Though no one is likely to regard it as an actual work of Polykleitos, it can be assigned almost certainly to one of his pupils, and it proves that within the school the Doryphoros was treated as a model, and adapted with the slightest possible alterations to youthful figures of a quite different order.

No other monument equals this in importance and originality, but the relief from Argos[1] may be taken as the next in merit. From this free adaptation of the Doryphoros to an heroic subject we learn how highly that statue must have been esteemed in Argos about the middle of the fourth century.[2] Passing now to marble statues of the Roman period, we can recognize in a statue of the Villa Albani[3] the Doryphoros transformed into a youthful hero, perhaps an Ares, armed with a sword. In design and bodily structure alike it follows the model exactly, only the lance being here replaced by the sword. The head is unfortunately lost. The original probably belonged to the Polykleitan circle. Two bronze statuettes, the one in the British Museum,[4] the other at Geneva,[5] are based on the Doryphoros, and carry a spear in the left hand; but the head with its Corinthian helmet and the structure of the body differ from the model in their rounder, softer treatment.

A statue of Hermes in the Boboli Gardens[6] at Florence follows the Doryphoros in the structure of the head and body, and, but for the right arm, also in motive; the head, however, is rather more inclined. The right arm supports a small boy, probably the infant Dionysos, of whom only one tiny foot is antique. The addition of an ordinary Roman chlamys thrown over the breast,[7] and of wings on the head, considerably disfigures the original Polykleitan type. The workmanship (the pupils of the eyes are carved on the ball) is that of the second or third century A.D. As it is only owing to the Roman additions of chlamys and of wings that the Polykleitan athlete has become a Hermes, and as the child on the arm does not fit the figure, it may be that the whole statue is merely a Roman composition or pasticcio. However, it is also possible that the original was a Polykleitan Hermes, who, of course, would carry the kerykeion as his sole distinguishing attribute.[8] There is no doubt that the group of Hermes and the infant Dionysos was not first introduced into statuary by Praxiteles, for we know the composition from a Roman bronze found in France, copied from a work that was not only pre-Praxitelean in style but probably actually Peloponnesian.[9]

[1] *Ath. Mitth.* iii. 1878, Taf. 13, p. 287 *seq.*

[2] This date (*ibid.* 289) has recently been confirmed by the basis-relief of Bryaxis (*B. C. H.* 1892, Pl. 3, 7), on which the horses are modelled in a strikingly similar manner.

[3] No. 604. Clarac, 833 C, 2074 A. Cf. Flasch in *Bull. dell' Inst.* 1873, 10; Michaelis, *Annali*, 1878, 9, K.; Helbig, *Führer*, 824; Brunn, *Bayr. Sitzungsber.* 1892, p. 674; Kalkmann, *Gesichtsprop.* p. 53, note 6. The middle of the sword is antique. On the right thigh a puntello has been planed away, which, as in the Doryphoros, was for the support of the forearm. A piece of the neck is restored, and the head is probably foreign.

[4] The so-called 'Bunsen Mars.' The right arm is missing. Workmanship latish.

[5] Geneva, Musée Fol. 1275. The head with the hair parted in front is nearer to the Polykleitan type than the London bronze.

[6] Dütschke, *Zerstr. Antiken in Florenz*, 84; Arndt-Bruckmann, *Einzelverk.* Nos. 103—105. Cast in the Ecole des Beaux-Arts. The head is certainly genuine. The lower part of the left wing is ancient.

[7] As in the Myronian Hermes (see p. 182 *seq.*)

[8] The suggestion of Overbeck (*Gesch. d. Plastik.* 2nd ed. ii. 7), that the group is derived from Kephisodotos, seems to be quite unwarranted.

[9] *Revue Archéol.* 1884, vol. iv. Pl. 4. The original was probably a work of about 400 B.C. This is shown

A statue of Hermes of Roman date recently discovered at Troezene resembles the Doryphoros,[1] both in motive and in the bodily forms. The god, who in this case wears a chlamys of good Greek style, leads a ram by the horn with his right hand, and in the left he holds the herald's staff. Although the head with its winged petasos is not purely Polykleitan, the statue must be referred to an original of the school. This motive, the leading of a ram by the horn, recalls Pliny's mention of the *immolans arietem* of Naukydes,[2] which was perhaps similarly composed.

A series of Polykleitan heads representing Hermes with the petasos or with wings will be considered later in connexion with another type of Polykleitan Hermes which differs in pose.

A list of torsos must however be given here which follow the Doryphoros more or less exactly in forms and attitude, but which are shown by the chlamys, or by the end of a cloak thrown over the left shoulder, to be either representations of Hermes, or perhaps mere portrait-statues.[3] As the drapery is by no means the same in all, and is for the most part decidedly late in its treatment, these torsos are interesting only as showing that even up to quite late times the Doryphoros did duty as a model. A well-preserved and interesting statue from Carthage has recently been acquired by the Louvre; it repeats the figure and pose of the Doryphoros with the additions of a chlamys over the left shoulder; the right hand hung down, holding an attribute. The head however is totally different, being slightly turned to the left, and of the ordinary Dioscurus type with the pilos; a horse's head below serves as attribute. This association of heterogeneous elements in head and body is essentially Roman.[4] Lastly, in a statue at Carlsruhe a later type of head has been combined with the body of the Doryphoros, though the action of the arms has been reversed.[5]

Passing now to bronze statuettes of later date, we find that the largest and most important of all is in the closest possible connexion with the series we have just considered. This is the well-known Hermes from Fins d'Annecy,[6] at present to my knowledge in the possession of M. Dutuit at Rouen. For all the delicacy of the workmanship, this charming bronze, which was once gilt all over, must be considered as a Roman work of the Augustan age. The finely modelled body is evidently inspired by the Doryphoros; the arms, however, are too short, and, just as in the Carlsruhe statue, their action has been reversed.[7] Other variations from the model betray a late and imperfect style. The head is very similar to that of the Dory-

by the unnatural rendering of the child, the simple flat modelling of the principal figure, the attitude, recalling a Peloponnesian Hermes type which rests on the left leg (to be discussed later), and finally the head with the parted hair.

[1] *B. C. H.* 1892, Pl. 2, 17; p. 165 *seq.* (Legrand). Poor Roman work: not an exact copy, but a free adaptation of a Polykleitan type.

[2] The current identification with the 'Phrixos' on the Akropolis is quite uncertain.

[3] (a) Naples, Mus. Naz. No. 6102; measurements = those of the Doryphoros: portrait-head foreign.—(b) Villa Albani, 596: the head is foreign, and appears to be a replica of the Ludovisi Hermes; the bodily forms are somewhat softer.—(c) Mus. Torlonia, 343: head, left forearm, with sword and right arm, are modern.—Palazzo Valentini: restored as Pertinax.—(d) Lateran, No. 836 (Benndorf-Schöne, 445): puntello for the right arm in the usual place, yet the left seems to have been raised.—(e) Lower torso in the Vatican, Belvedere, No. 8: puntello or the right arm in the usual place; a cloak hangs down behind; a horn of plenty on the tree-stem; probably a portrait in the character of *Genius*.

[4] Louvre, No. 2735. Colossal statue of coarse marble much weathered; good Roman work.

[5] Sketched without the restorations in *Arch. Anz.* 1890, p. 4, No. 6. The position of the arms is fixed by the puntelli.

[6] *Mon. d. Inst.* x. 50, 4; *Annali*, 1878, 25 *seq.* (Michaelis); *Gazette Archéol.* 1876, Pl. 18. Cf. *B. C. H.* 1892, 169. I saw the original in 1881.

[7] They are cast separately, as is so frequently the case in larger bronzes.

FIG. 93.—Bronze statuette in British Museum.

phoros, but here and there, especially at the back of the head, the Roman artist has introduced later elements into the hair. The statuette probably represented a Roman deity, but it is hard to determine which, as the remains of the attribute are doubtful.[1] The current view of its being a copy from an original composition of Polykleitos (Michaelis ranks it as third along with the Doryphoros and the Diadumenos) is absolutely untenable. This figure can only be correctly appreciated in connexion with later adaptations from the Doryphoros, and it certainly cannot help us to recover the Hermes of Polykleitos.

A much-rubbed Roman bronze in the Louvre shows the Doryphoros type without any addition of drapery, but marked as Mercury by the winged feet.[2] Other Roman bronzes unite in a most disturbing manner the Polykleitan torso with a head of the ordinary later Hermes type.[3]

Very common are the Mercury bronzes in which the chlamys is added to the Polykleitan body: in the best examples it is arranged after the older fashion, so as to cover the entire left arm. The finest specimen comes from Gaul, and is in the British Museum (Fig. 93).[4] Both head and body are excellent, though not wholly Polykleitan.[5] Still better in style, but not in such good preservation, is a figure at Copenhagen found at Pompeii.[6] A similar but

[1] It might possibly be the end of a bow.

[2] Louvre, Bronzes, 1031 : the left arm is missing, the right is lowered ; the head still shows the Polykleitan type.

[3] Paris, Cab. d. Médailles, Coll. Janzé, 81 : the body reproduces with fair accuracy the forms of the Doryphoros ; veins on the abdomen. The right arm is missing.—Similar but inferior is a bronze in Brunswick, No. 289, with prominent muscles.—British Museum, R.P.K. xlvi. ; others from the Thames *Archæologia*, vol. xxviii. Pl. 5.—Fröhner, *Coll. Gréau, Bronzes Ant.* 933.

[4] *Specimens of Ancient Sculpture*, i. 33, 34 ; Müller-Wieseler, *Denkm. a. K.* ii. 314. Cf. my remarks in *Iahrb. d. Ver. v. Alterth. fr. im Rheinl.* vol. xc. p. 58.

[5] The pubes less good than the hair. Veins on the abdomen as in the Pourtalès Doryphoros torso. The left foot less drawn back than in the Doryphoros.

[6] Bronzes, No. 14. Pub. by Jul. Lange, *Fremstilling af Menneskeskikkelsen* (*Abh. d. Kopenh. Akad.* 1892), p. 407, fig. 62. The lowered right hand is empty ; the left evidently held the kerykeion.

inferior one belongs to Sir Francis Cook at Richmond,[1] a fourth is in Paris.[2] None of these statuettes can claim to be an actual copy of a Hermes by Poly-kleitos.[3] They all vary in detail, and must be regarded as Roman creations, founded on the Doryphoros, and borrow-ing the chlamys from some other fifth-century model.

Among these figures also are some in which the Polykleitan head is replaced by that of a later type of Hermes,[4] while others again show the body of the Doryphoros draped in a chlamys hang-ing from the shoulders in a point in front.[5] We have an interesting work of this class in a bronze Mercury of the Oppermann collection in Paris (Fig. 94).[6] Here a fine chlamys executed in the style of the fifth century covers the whole body to the knee. The parted hair points to a Polykleitan inspiration, but the Doryphoros attitude is consider-ably modified by the increased inclina-tion of the head and right shoulder, and by the extension of the right arm. These changes give a softer, sweeter effect to the whole figure. It need not surprise us to find the Doryphoros so often adapted to representations of Hermes in Roman times, for copies of this statue were placed ·in the various palaestrae and gymnasia,[7] which were all conse-crated to Hermes.

FIG. 94.—Mercury, Coll. Oppermann (Bibl. Nat., Paris).

All this is interesting, as showing the vast influence exercised by one creation of Polykleitos ; but it has added nothing to our knowledge of the artist himself, since not one of the works described can be definitely referred to any actual work of his. The

[1] Height, 0·15. The left forearm raised, the left hand held the kerykeion ; remains of a purse in the lowered right hand. The left foot was slightly drawn back. Polykleitan characteristics in the head much weakened. Rich sandals ; eyes and nipples of silver.

[2] Cab. d. Médailles, 3351. Head much defaced, with traces of Polykleitan type. The lowered right hand empty, the extended left hand probably held the kerykeion.

[3] Cf. Treu, *Arch. Anz.* 1889, p. 57.

[4] Paris, Cab. d. Médailles, 3350.—Clarac, 666 D, 1512 F.

[5] Sacken, *Bronzen in Wien*, Taf. 10, 4.

[6] Paris, Cab. d. Médailles, Coll. Oppermann. Height, about 0·20. The left hand evidently held the kery-keion ; the right has a hole, possibly for the purse. To judge by the colour of the metal, the figure seems to be from Gaul.

[7] The Naples copy comes from the Palaestra of Pompeii. Cf. Nissen, *Pompej. Studien*, p. 166. As the figure carried a lance, it cannot possibly be a Hermes. But the Ephebe statues with the lance, which according to Pliny (xxxiv. 18) were called *Achilleae*, and were set up in the gymnasia, were very likely for the most part copies of the popular Doryphoros by Polykleitos.

H H

assumption that Polykleitos often repeated himself by adapting the Doryphoros type to other statues is certainly not supported by the monuments themselves.

On the other hand, our study of the Doryphoros will enable us to point among our copies to other original creations by Polykleitos. There is, for instance, a type of head (Fig. 95) so like the Doryphoros that it is often confused with it, though it differs

FIG. 95.—Head of Herakles. From Herculaneum (Naples).

in a distinct detail, *i.e.* in the rolled fillet round the head, and also in size, being only life-size, while the Doryphoros is rather above. The rolled fillet is a well-known attribute of Herakles, and as at any rate one replica of the head in question shows an evident attempt to give the characteristics of that hero [1] (though it must be admitted

[1] The head from Herculaneum in Naples, Comparetti de Petra, *Villa Ercol.* Tav. 21, 3 (our Fig. 95). B. Gräf (*Röm. Mitth.* 1889, pp. 215, 202 *sqq.*) had already conjectured a Polykleitan Herakles. He also mentions

that in so doing the artist abandoned the original and introduced traits belonging to a later type), it is quite possible that the head actually represents Herakles. In favour of this interpretation is the fact that almost all the replicas known to me originally belonged to terminal busts, which explains why so many heads and no statues belonging to them have been found ; for it was precisely terms of Herakles that were in great demand for palaestrae and gymnasia. The Skopasian Herakles likewise is found almost exclusively in the term-shape. Both types appear to have

FIG. 96.—Head of Herakles. From the collection at Broadlands (Hampshire).

been very popular for this purpose, and in both the inclination of the head varies from right to left,[1] though the former is more common ; it is very slight either way, and in the original the head was probably set straight.

two replicas—viz. Lateran, 896 = Bennd.-Schöne, 491, and Museo Chiaramonti, No. 139 (Helbig, *Museums*, 69). In the second the neck is antique, the bust modern. The head might have belonged to a statue ; the ends of the fillet are missing. The work is sketchy and poor. Other replicas are : A term at Broadlands (Fig. 96 ; Michaelis, *Anc. Sc.* p. 220, No. 10). The hair is worked in much more detail than in the other copies named above.—In Berlin, No. 478, mediocre copy ; probably intended for insertion into a term.—The janiform term, Berlin, No. 477, may be counted among the good copies. Slight turn to the left. Hair very carefully rendered, as in the Broadlands example, much better than the Chiaramonti copy.—A replica in Dresden, for insertion in a term (*Zug. Verz.* 1106) from Rome. The length of face in five copies is 0·182—0·185 (in the Doryphoros, 0·200—0·204), width of face at the cheek-bones 0·113 (in the Doryphoros, 0·156).

[1] So Chiaramonti, 139 ; Berlin, 477.

This Polykleitan Herakles may perhaps be copied from the statue in Rome mentioned by Pliny (xxxiv. 56)[1]; unfortunately all the replicas are very mediocre. The term in Naples is undoubtedly the most characteristic of Herakles, and has least in common with the Doryphoros. The chin and lips are unusually full and powerful, and the nostrils are distended. The widely opened eyes appear to project a little, the hair of the eyebrows is indicated, and two deep furrows rise from the root of the nose. In the other replicas all these details are lost; their features assimilate to those of the Doryphoros to the extent of appearing even calmer and more impassive. The careless treatment of the hair in the Naples replica shows, however, that it is not accurate in matters of detail; the intention of satisfying the common ideal of Herakles by just giving a look of concentrated strength to the face is so evident that we must be cautious how far we trust this head in those points where it contradicts the other replicas, in which the hair at any rate is much more accurately modelled.

The resemblance between the Polykleitan Herakles head and the Doryphoros is, as remarked before, very great. The stylistic treatment of the hair is the same; yet a close examination brings differences also to light. There is less anxious symmetry in the Herakles; the hair on the top of the head is treated in broader, looser masses, and the locks towards the ends are accordingly all the richer. The little wisps on either side over the middle of the forehead are not symmetrical as in the Doryphoros.[2] It is not till we come to the next two larger meshes of hair with their points turned inwards (these meshes are a chief sign by which our head can be distinguished from the Doryphoros) that we find approximate symmetry. The little curls in front of and behind the ears[3] are more varied in form and movement than they are in the Doryphoros. Further, the modelling of the forehead is somewhat more accentuated, while the lower part of the face produces a more delicate effect. From all these remarks it may be inferred that the Herakles is later than the Doryphoros.

The rolled fillet in the hair, shown in all the replicas, and which is sometimes decorated with flowers, must have belonged to the original, but without the long ends falling on the breast; these are absent from some copies, and vary in the others, and seem to have been introduced by the copyists who made the terminal busts. There are other instances of Herakles wearing the rolled fillet, e.g. in the beautiful statue of the Museo Chiaramonti (infra, Figs. 146, 147), where he is represented carrying the infant Telephos on his arm. It may therefore be regarded as an external means of characterizing the hero. It is no simple victor's fillet; it seems borrowed from the symposion, and distinguishes the glorified hero, rejoicing in the heavenly banquet. Of inner characterization by means of an individual form of head there is scarcely a trace, if we leave out of account the additions made by the Naples copyist. The head is of pure youthful beauty, but it might just as well represent any other hero.

How different are those other two Herakles types, which we ascribed to Myron— the bearded head from the artist's earlier period (p. 179), the beardless from the later (p. 202), in both of which we can trace something of wild heroic force. The gentle beauty of the Polykleitan head is most closely paralleled by the Herakles head on some

[1] Pliny, xxxiv. 56, *Herculem qui Romae.* By Detlefsen's punctuation, which is certainly correct, the following *hagetera arma sumentem* is a different work. Cf. Benndorf in *Festschr. für Springer,* 1885, *Eine Statue Polyklets,* p. 1, note i. ; Roscher's *Lexikon,* i. 2157.

[2] In the Naples copy these are omitted. The Broadlands head (Fig. 96) and the Berlin janiform term (477) give them exactly. In the Dresden copy they are broken away.

[3] These are carelessly copied on the Naples and Berlin (478) heads. The Broadlands (Fig. 96) and the Berlin (477) copies (which agree exactly), and still more the Dresden head, give a more exact version,

coins of Kleonai and Stymphalos,[1] *i.e.* from the neighbourhood of Argos, a district where Polykleitan art must have been a dominant influence.

The Herakles of Polykleitos is by no means a mechanical repetition of his Doryphoros, and yet the work shows a striving rather towards harmonious repose

FIG. 97.—Polykleitan statue in Coll. Barracco, Rome. (By permission of Messrs. Bruckmann.

and pure abstract beauty than towards characterization. We can understand the judgment of antiquity as given by Quinctilian, according to which Polykleitos *non explevisse deorum auctoritatem videtur . . . nil ausus ultra leves genas.*

[1] Cf. Roscher's *Lexikon,* i. 2163, *l.* 53 *seq.*

Another creation, which must be assigned to Polykleitos himself, and which has in common with the Doryphoros the walking motive (the right leg being the supporting one), the turn of the head to the right, and, above all, the bodily forms, affords fresh proof of how little this artist simply repeated his 'canon,' and of how fresh and independent was each of his works. By merely altering the movement, in this case of the arms, he has created a totally new conception (Fig. 97).

The statue is known to us complete only on a much-reduced scale, but there are copies of the torso in the original size, which is the same as that of the Doryphoros.[1] The restrained repose of the Doryphoros is here abandoned. The left hand is laid on the back—it rests behind the left hip on the upper part of the gluteus —and the right arm, which hung down, appears, from a fragment above the right hip in one of the statuettes,[2] to have held an attribute shaped like a staff. The head is turned to the right with more animated freedom than in the Doryphoros. Finally, the left leg is not, as in the Doryphoros, simply drawn after the other in such a way that the front surfaces of both thighs lie in the same plane, but the left foot is more turned out so that the thigh too slants outwards. All these changes introduce more life and freedom ; in fact, the attitude might almost be called bold and unrestrained.

The analogy to the Doryphoros in the formation of head and body, although striking, does not amount to identity. In our statue all is rounder and less severe.[3] It is certainly a later work than the Doryphoros. Who is represented it is difficult to say, probably not an athlete. The bold presentment is not suited to a human victor, at least not according to the Doric notions of the time, which always lay stress in athlete statues on modesty and restraint. The remains of the attribute, too, would be difficult to explain. I therefore incline to interpret the figure as Hermes with the herald's staff in his right hand.[4] The motive of the left arm would make the figure a forerunner of the Belvedere Hermes.

III. *The Diadumenos.*

The Diadumenos is the second undoubted work of Polykleitos which survives to us in copies. Michaelis has shown, principally by comparison with the Doryphoros, that the statue from Vaison in the British Museum is a copy of this statue.[5] But the further questions as to the artistic value of this copy and the existence of other replicas have not yet been sufficiently investigated. Yet this inquiry is unavoidable in order to form an exact notion of the original.

[1] Statuettes : Gall. dei Candelabri, 269 B : head broken, but genuine ; right arm restored ; feet ancient ; workmanship poor. The Barracco statuette (*Coll. Barracco*, Pl. 45, 45 *a* = our Fig. 97) is better : clean, sharp workmanship ; no restorations.—Life-size torsos : (*a*) Palazzo Mattei (cf. Petersen in *Bull. della Commiss. Comm.* 1890, p. 191) ; (*b*) formerly in possession of Spiess the sculptor in Rome (photograph in the Berlin Museum), and is now in the Coll. Jacobsen, Copenhagen ; (*c*) in the Thermae of Caracalla (Matz-Duhn, 1013).

[2] In the Barracco copy. In the Jacobsen torso the arm hung down as in the Doryphoros (puntello at the same spot).

[3] The insipid Vatican statuette, in which all the forms have a marked roundness, is in this respect quite inexact : the mouth, for example, has lost all Polykleitan character. The Barracco statuette is much more severe, and more similar to the Doryphoros in head as in body. In the large torsos the body comes very near the Doryphoros.

[4] The Hermes of Polykleitos mentioned by Pliny was probably in Rome, as Pliny's words—*qui fuit Lysimacheae*—show, and must have been copied. For the motive cf. the coin of Chalkedon in the British Museum (*Catalogue Pontus*, Pl. 28, 3), where the left arm is set against the body, and the right hand holds the kerykeion, but the head has a different turn.

[5] *Ann. d. Inst.* 1878, p. 10 *seq.*; *Monum.* x. 49.

E. Petersen lately made an important contribution to this subject by discovering in a number of torsos copies of the body of the Diadumenos.[1] Most of these are better and more careful pieces of work than the Vaison statue. The following are worthy of special notice : a torso in Palazzo Giustiniani,[2] another in the Louvre,[3] to which I may add an excellent one in Turin[4] (not mentioned by Petersen). A small statuette torso worked as a cabinet piece should also be reckoned among the exact copies.[5]

For the study of the body of the original we have a reliable basis in these torsos. But what of the head ?

The head of the Vaison statue can give us but a very unsatisfactory notion of the original ; not so much because, like the body, it is a poor and careless piece of work, as because it is so much defaced and—worse than this—so much and so arbitrarily worked over. The forehead is completely damaged, the eyes are injured, the nose is entirely gone, the ears and all the prominent parts of the hair have been knocked off, and the edges of the fractures rubbed smooth, so that only the foundation or lowest stratum of the hair-modelling remains. On the top of this the modern restorer has engraved lines according to his own fancy.[6] This makes the hair look as if it lay close to the head and fell away from the crown in long wavy lines. In order therefore to form an accurate conception of the original we must begin by disregarding this head with all its misleading interpolations, and look for copies in better preservation.[7]

A terra-cotta statuette from Asia Minor is interesting in this connexion.[8] It belongs to a small class of terra-cottas which are real copies from statuary originals :[9] they are naturally somewhat less exact than the larger ones in marble, though they do not aim at being anything but copies ; further, they belong approximately to the same period—the first century B.C.—at which the exact copies in marble of older originals came into vogue. If we compare the body of the terra-cotta Diadumenos with that of the marble replicas, we find a very close correspondence,[10] so that the same is likely to be the case with the head. Now, from the treatment of the hair and the modelling of the forehead it is clear, in spite of the small scale, that the head reproduces a well-known Diadumenos type, known to us through separate heads, in Cassel and in Dresden, and usually supposed not to be Polykleitan.

[1] *Bull. della Comm. Arch. Comunale*, 1890, 185 *seq*.   [2] Petersen, No. 5.

[3] Petersen, p. 189, note 2. The statue is now numbered 2235 (photo. Giraudon).

[4] Museum, Turin. Torso without restorations ; no puntelli on the shoulders. Measurements the same as those of the other replicas.

[5] Berlin, *Skulpt*. No. 513.

[6] It was Löschcke who first called my attention to the fact that the Vaison head had been worked over. A. H. Smith kindly examined the original at my request, and confirms my suspicion. He writes : 'You are right : in those parts where the hair is especially sharp, the surface has been worked over by a restorer.'

[7] Michaelis (*Ann. d. Inst.* 1878, p. 11, A ; tav. d'agg. B.) gives the first place among copies of the Polykleitan statue to a small bronze of the former Janzé Collection. He goes so far as to try to recover the proportions of the original from this bronze. This is a mistake, for the technique and style of the bronze prove it to be a Greek work of the best period, and as such it is excluded from the category of copies. The artist is of course influenced by the famous work of Polykleitos, but he gives a free imitation of it : no definite conclusions can be drawn from this bronze as regards the Polykleitan Diadumenos.

[8] *J. H. S.* 1885, Pl. 61 (A. S. Murray), now in the possession of Mr. C. Blacker in London. I have held the original in my hands, and can testify that it is genuine. The head of another terra-cotta belongs to M. Misthos in Smyrna.

[9] These figures survive mostly in fragments. They come from the neighbourhood of Smyrna ; there were numerous fragments of this kind in the former Gréau Collection.

[10] Opinions on this figure have hitherto been founded on wrong premises. E. Petersen, *Bull. d. Comm. Arch.* 1890, 186, 4, calls it an original. Von. Sybel (*Weltgesch. d. Kunst*, p. 194) assimilates it to the Farnese type, from which the motive alone would be enough to distinguish it. Sal. Reinach (*Gazette Arch.* 1887, 281) thought it might be a copy of a more recent work, perhaps by Praxiteles.

The most beautiful and best preserved of all the Diadumenos copies, the statue in Madrid (Fig. 98),[1] shows however, beyond a doubt, that this type is really Polykleitan. The head of the Madrid Diadumenos is still unbroken, and the body corresponds exactly to the torsos known to be after the Polykleitan Diadumenos. The head resembles, feature for feature, the Cassel and Dresden heads.

The head of the Vaison statue too was originally similar to these, although it could never have been a good copy. The strands of hair that have not been worked over correspond exactly to those heads. The measurements are throughout the same.

As there are so many torsos of the Polykleitan Diadumenos in existence, it would seem likely that there should be several copies of the head. And this is really the case. The heads which, from their agreement among themselves in measurement and in the forms of the hair and face, must be referred to one original, that original being, as the statues of Madrid and Vaison show, the Diadumenos of Polykleitos, are the following :—

1. The Dresden head (Plates X. and XI.),[2] a very exact and carefully executed work. The copyist evidently took some trouble to reproduce the original. He certainly interpolated nothing of his own : his work is dry, but the more reliable on that account. From the manner in which he indicates the eye-pupil and forms the upper eyelid, we can scarcely suppose that he worked before the latter half of the second century.

2. The Cassel head,[3] a somewhat earlier work, is less dry and expressionless, but also less exact in details. The hair is rendered in a looser and more general manner without the rich and luxuriant variety of No. 1, and yet the agreement of the two heads down to the most trifling details is so close that we must conclude they are derived from the same original.[4] The Cassel head is the better of the two as a work of art, but inferior as a copy.

3. Fragment of a head in the Louvre :[5] only the front part of the face—forehead, eyes, nose, and mouth—is preserved. This is a careful piece of work, but dry and lifeless. In the endeavour to render truthfully the sharp lines of the bronze original all refinement of expression has been lost. This fragment corresponds with the Dresden and Cassel heads even in the peculiar modelling of the brow.

4. Head in the Barracco collection in Rome. A poor copy, much defaced, especially in the hair. What is left, especially the hair on the top of the head and the forehead, corresponds exactly to the other replicas.

5. A head, formerly in the possession of Steinhäuser, in bad preservation, and much restored.[6]

6. A head which I noted in Rome in 1892 in the market : a very poor copy, the hair merely blocked out.[7]

---

[1] Michaelis, *Annali*, 1878, p. 11, c. Besides the legs, only the right arm is restored, and that wrongly. This is evident from the photograph. I have not seen the original.

[2] *Ann. d. Inst.* 1871, Tav. v. p. 281 (Conze). Friederichs-Wolters, 511. The nose down to the left nostril and the right half of the mouth are restored. Coarse-grained Parian marble.

[3] Conze, *Beiträge*, Taf. 2 ; Friederichs-Wolters, 510. Only the front half of the nose is restored. The mouth is in complete preservation. Parian marble. Clear traces of the drill in the hair.

[4] Michaelis was mistaken (*Ann.* 1878, p. 24) in referring the Dresden head to a different original.

[5] Bouillon, iii. *Bustes*, Pl. 3, 'Athlète' 2. Photographed as 'Diadumène de Polyclète' by Giraudon, No. 1283.

[6] Matz-Duhn, *Zerstr. Bildw. in Rom*, 1671. Known to me only through the cast in Strasburg (Michaelis, 592). Most of the face is restored, the hair much battered.

[7] Arndt-Bruckmann, *Einzelverkauf*, Nos. 190, 191 (incorrectly called a replica of the Farnese type).

FIG. 98.—Diadumenos in Madrid.

Fig. XXXVa–Diadumenos Statuette New York, Metropolitan Museum of Art

Fig. XXXV—Diadumenos Giustiniani, New York, Metropolitan Museum of Art (See p. 239)

7. A much-defaced head on a statue to which it does not belong, in the court-yard of the Palazzo Giustiniani.[1]

That these copies reproduce the famous work of Polykleitos seems probable from two considerations alone. First, they are all referable to the same original, which must have been a famous one. Second, all other 'Diadumenos' heads are entirely different and are certainly un-Polykleitan.[2] But this probability becomes a certainty when we add the evidence of the Vaison and Madrid statues.

Since, then, we possess reliable copies of the head of the Diadumenos of Poly-kleitos, as well as of the body, we have the material before us for a discussion of the whole work.

A correct appreciation of the great difference which undoubtedly subsists between the head of the Doryphoros and the Diadumenos heads enumerated above has given rise to the mistaken opinion that the latter were not the work of Polykleitos, but were specifically Attic in character. They were supposed to be better and larger replicas of the Farnese Diadumenos.[3] These hasty conclusions were the result of defective observation. The different arrangement of the fillet, which is tied in a bow behind, and the treatment of the hair are enough in themselves to exclude the Farnese type from all relation to these heads.

The softer execution of the Diadumenos shows it to be a later work than the Doryphoros. The contrast between the two works was summed up epigrammatically in the passage of Pliny, where the Doryphoros is ascribed as *viriliter puer*, and the Diadumenos as *molliter juvenis*.

The Diadumenos should probably be assigned to the same later period of the master's career as the Hera. I think I am not mistaken in finding a certain kinship between the head of Hera on coins of Elis (Pl. VI. 23) and the Diadumenos. The short yet full and plastic locks, the broad diadem sunk deep in the hair, the angular contour of the powerful skull, the large features and especially the lower part of the face, are strong points of resemblance made doubly remarkable by the difference of sex and of subject.

The body of the Diadumenos is scarcely to be distinguished from that of the Doryphoros. It is difficult to decide whether the small differences that do occur are due to the copyist or to the original, yet in the best copies of the Diadumenos the flesh-forms produce an impression of greater spareness and elasticity, and of softer transitions in modelling. With regard to details, it should be noted that on none of the Diadumenos copies do veins appear on the abdomen.

In movement and carriage the Diadumenos comes very near the Doryphoros. He also rests on the right foot, pauses in the act of walking, and inclines his head to the right. Here too, notwithstanding the different direction, the left arm is the one in more active motion; it is freer, and held more away from the body, while the right upper arm is kept as closely as possible to the body, till the forearm bends sharply back and upwards. The pose of head differs from that of the Doryphoros in being much more bent and inclined to the right, although the change is not required by the action represented. The intention evidently was to give to the figure a softer and more flowing rhythm. Another small point in which this figure differs from the Doryphoros is that—as we have already noticed in the figure of a youth laying his

---

[1] Clarac, 872, 2218; Matz-Duhn, 1091.

[2] The Farnese type and the Petworth type discussed above (p. 16 *seq.*)

[3] Cf. Bötticher, *Verzeichniss d. Abgüsse in Berlin*, 714, 715; then Conze, *Annali d. Inst.* 1871, 282; Michaelis, *Annali*, 1878, 23; Friederichs-Wolters, 510, 511.

hand on his back (Fig. 97)—the left foot is a little more turned out, so that the left thigh is no longer in the same plane as the right, but takes a slanting direction. This change adds animation to the pose.

The two statues differ to a far greater extent in the head than in either torso or attitude. It is from a study of the head that we first realize the rapid development of which Polykleitos was capable. He treats the hair of the Diadumenos in quite a new manner, gives up the flat clinging strands, and adopts the full raised plastic curls; the almost finicking trimness of the Doryphoros gives way to a living variety. Only at one spot in front does the hair really resemble that of the Doryphoros, just where the line which rises from the forehead makes, when seen in profile, a sharp turn almost at a right angle. The way in which the hair is here disposed in layers is essentially the same in both heads, and is thoroughly characteristic of the artist.

Again, the Diadumenos differs from the Doryphoros in the modelling of the forehead; what was begun in the head of the Herakles has now been carried further. While the forehead of the Doryphoros projects evenly below and falls away in simple planes to the sides, in the Diadumenos the forehead is slightly hollowed in the middle (i.e. at the intercilium), and the arches formed by the long framework of the eyebrows are distinctly emphasized above the inner ends of the eyebrows themselves.

Finally, the lower part of the face is in the Diadumenos decidedly softer and less prominent than the same part in the Doryphoros; the cheeks and mouth are modelled with a richer variety of planes; the same difference is to be observed in the nose,[1] which, instead of a hard angular formation, shows rounder and more lifelike modulations. The bend of the head enhances not a little the general effect of softness.

The innovations introduced by Polykleitos into the head of the Diadumenos—namely, the strongly plastic hair, the softer rendering of the lower part of the face, and the richer modelling—certainly approach the style which had obtained in Athens considerably before this time, probably as early as the middle of the century. We may assume a certain amount of Attic influence in the later period of Polykleitos, and for this Kresilas may well have been the medium, for we know that he was working at Argos just at this time. And we must bear in mind that, as I have previously shown,[2] the fragments of sculpture from the Heraion of Argos are worked in a style in which Attic elements preponderate, and are decidedly akin to the figures on the Nike balustrade at Athens; all of which seems to point to the probability that Attic artists were at work in Argos.

Withal, Polykleitos did not give up one jot of his individual manner in the Diadumenos; he only developed it further by bringing to greater perfection the ideal of abstract beauty which he had in his mind. Looking at the Diadumenos head we first rightly understand what Quinctilian means when he says that Polykleitos *humanae formae decorem addidit supra verum*.[3] The human form is indeed here represented with a degree of beauty which surpasses nature. It is not strange that this statue by Polykleitos should have fetched at an auction the price of one hundred talents (Plin. xxxiv. 55), an enormous sum in antiquity. Many a smaller, freer imitation,

---

[1] In the Paris copy the nose of the Diadumenos is almost intact. For the Doryphoros our most reliable evidence is the Naples bronze term.

[2] *Ath. Mitth.* iii. 1878, p. 296; *Archäol. Studien H. Brunn dargebr.* 1893, p. 90. The head lately found at the Heraion, which Waldstein considers to be Polykleitan, is more likely Attic. (Cf. p. 223, note 1.)

[3] Quinct. *Inst. Or.* xii. 10, 7. Brunn's translation of the word *decor* by 'würdevoller Anstand' (*Gesch. d. Künstler*, i. 225) is rather too one-sided. *Decor* means both 'decency' and 'beauty,' but in this passage stress should be laid on 'beauty.'

especially on engraved stones,[1] testifies to the admiration of the ancients for the head of the Diadumenos.   I may also mention a bronze head of magnificent workmanship applied to a decorative purpose (De Clerq Coll. in Paris) which is simply a free replica of the Diadumenos head.[2]

The one weak point about the statue is the motive.   The pause in the act of walking is not appropriate to the principal action represented.   No one walks along while tying a ribbon round his head.   Polykleitos, as we saw in his Amazon statues, cannot identify himself with his subject sufficiently to create the motive from the centre outwards.   The first consideration for him is the beauty of rhythmic movement: the meaning of the movement comes second.   The result of this is that the movement is beautiful indeed, but appears unnatural, nay, even affected.

In this respect the Farnese Diadumenos in the British Museum far surpasses the Diadumenos of Polykleitos by the very simplicity and naturalness of the conception.   The youth stands still and puts on the fillet just as he would have done in real life.   There is neither stride, nor bend of the head, nor forced attitude of the right elbow near the body.   Nor is there—we must at the same time confess—the charming effect produced in the other statue by rhythmic motion and beautiful closed curves.[3]

The ‘Farnese’ Diadumenos is almost universally designated as Attic,[4] and a closer comparison makes it possible to define still more exactly its claim to rank as such.   The head and the bodily forms, the whole appearance and bearing, are nowhere more closely paralleled than on the frieze of the Parthenon.   If we compare it, for instance, to the standing youth on the west frieze (No. 9), we shall see that the forms in the abdominal region, the waist, and the lower edge of the ribs have the same characteristics in both.

Now, since there is a tradition that a statue by Pheidias representing a boy, name unknown, winding the victor's fillet round his head,[5] stood in Olympia, and since the Farnese figure not only answers to this description but belongs to the very style which we must assume to have been that of Pheidias in the period when he was working for Olympia, we are justified in expressing the opinion (held already, though on insufficient grounds, by Gerhard and Bötticher) that the Farnese statue is a copy of the Pheidian Diadumenos in Olympia.

The statue fits admirably into the series of Pheidian productions with which we have become acquainted.   The attitude, with one foot set to the side and freed from the weight of the body, yet resting firmly on the ground (on the inner edge of the sole, at any rate), recalls the Lemnia and the Anakreon.[6]   The copyist has treated the

---

[1] *E.g.* Cades, iv. A, 112, 113 ; further, Berlin, Tölken, iv. 399 (= Cades, iv. A, 116 ; *Jahrb. d. Inst.* 1888, Taf. 3, 16) ; paste in Copenhagen (*Dänische Abdrucks. in Berlin*, No. 929) ; an inferior stone in St. Petersburg (*Abdrucks. in Berlin*, 23, 2).—For a good copy of the whole statue see Cades, cl. iv. F, 68 = *Impronte dell' Instituto*, 6, 73. It is an emerald-plasma of the same sort as those with representations of the Doryphoros (Berlin) and the Amazon (Natter).   (Cf. p. 137, note 1 ; p. 163, note 1.)   An inferior copy on another gem of the same kind is published, *J. H. S.* ii. 352.

[2] The neck of an oinchoë rises above the head, and the whole was used as a vase.   The eyes are of silver. The head (called Alexander in the collection) is of extraordinary beauty.   It comes from Syria.

[3] Cf. Kekulé, *Idolino*, p. 13.

[4] Only Brunn identifies it with the Polykleitan Diadumenos type (*Annali*, 1879, 218).   Cf. for a contrary view Michaelis, *Ann.* 1883, 154 *seq.*   Kekulé (*Idolino*, p. 12) reckons the Farnese statue among the Myronian series.

[5] Cf. p. 39.

[6] In common with the Anakreon, this statue has the closely curled pubes defined by a horizontal line at the top, a peculiarity also to be seen in the Dioscuri of Monte Cavallo.

hair very carelessly ; it seems to have resembled the hair of another Pheidian head which we conjectured to be an Eros (p. 69).[1]

It is usually taken for granted that the Farnese type is later than the Polykleitan : this opinion is founded on the presumption that Polykleitos, because his Diadumenos enjoyed the most fame, was the creator of the motive. Now it is clear from a consideration of form alone that the Farnese type is a pure product of the older style, as the attitude and the treatment of the hair show most clearly ; further, the natural simplicity of the motive as it appears in the Farnese statue proves that we have it here in its original form. Polykleitos borrowed the motive from Pheidias, and gave it an artistic elaboration which never could have formed part of the earliest conception. This order of succession is confirmed by the chronology of the two statues gained from other sources ; the work of Polykleitos was full fifteen years later than that of Pheidias.

For the invention of the motive, then, Pheidias is responsible. We can well believe that he was pleased with his subject, since he repeated it among the figures on the throne of Zeus.[2]

We may connect with the Diadumenos on account of the similar motive a statue of a youthful boxer, also a creation of Polykleitos (Fig. 99).

Unlike the Doryphoros and Diadumenos, which are above life-size, this figure is rather under life-size. It represents a youth just out of boyhood—that is, with more undeveloped and less powerful forms than the other two. The motive is again a pause in the act of walking, the weight being supported on the right leg. The head is turned to the right. As in the Diadumenos, the arms are both raised and bent, but there is a more marked difference between the attitude of the two arms: the right is lower, the left higher. The forearms are wound round with the boxing straps, the right fist ready for attack, the left for defence.

I know two copies of this work—one in Cassel, with the original head (Fig. 99), and one without a head in Lansdowne House.[3] The second gives the body better than the first. The bodily forms correspond with those of the Doryphoros and Diadumenos in all essentials (the abdomen and navel are very characteristic), except that they are more youthful and boyish.[4] The head, which survives only in the feeble sketchy Cassel copy, has hair arranged as in the Doryphoros.

The motive, in its fulness of dignity and balanced harmony, is incontestably fine, though for a real and energetic expression of this brutal sport we must turn to those

---

[1] The head, which is wrongly placed on the Penelope of the Vatican (*Ant. Denkm.*), is apparently, as far as the hair is concerned, a more accurate replica of the head of the Farnese statue. The principal proportions (fillet to chin 13½ cm.) correspond, although the eyes of the Penelope head are smaller and flatter, and the mouth is narrower. In these points the Farnese head is the more correct, but it gives only a sketchy rendering of the hair, which is more exact in the ' Eros ' head.

[2] Cf. p. 39. For a similar motive cf. a goddess on the frieze of the Athena Nike temple (No. 12, called Amphitrite by Sauer, *Aus der Anomia*, p. 94 *seq.*)

[3] The Cassel statue (ii. 17) is poorly illustrated in Bouillon, iii. *Statues*, Pl. 17, 1. Parian marble, the same in the head and body. The neck is restored, but the head seems genuine. The turn of the head is known from the one piece of the neck attached to the torso, and another piece attached to the head. The head was probably a little more bent. The left arm and the right shoulder are restored, the right arm and hand are ancient; the legs and basis are modern. In the Lansdowne statue (Michaelis, p. 438, 3 ; Clarac, 851, 2180 A), only the torso survives ; the head is foreign ; the left shoulder with the beginning of the raised arm is ancient ; the rest of the arms and the legs from the knees downwards are new. The proportions correspond with those of the Cassel statue ; distance between nipples 21 cm.; neck-pit to navel 31 ; neck-pit to line between nipples 13½ ; from the latter to navel 17½. The head of the Cassel copy is 19 cm. high ; face-length 13½, nose and lower face each 5½ cm.

[4] The pubes is accordingly but slightly developed.

violently agitated statues of severer style which we have ascribed to Pythagoras
(p. 172).

A bronze statuette found on the Akropolis[1] repeats the motive without attempting to be an exact copy. The right fist is clenched, but without the straps; the left

FIG. 99.—Statue of a boxer (Cassel).

is missing. The severe weathering the work has undergone has effaced most of the
detail, but the back and the glutei recall Polykleitos. The bronze should be dated
about 400 B.C.

[1] Akropolis Museum, among the older discoveries. Height 12 cm. Left hand broken. This bronze may
be said to bear the same relation to the Cassel boxer which the Janzé statuette does to the Diadumenos.

A marble torso in Florence, on the scale of the Doryphoros and analogous to it in modelling, is derived from a work the motive of which was very similar to that of the boxer. This was probably a more recent creation of the school of Polykleitos.[1]

Finally, the Roman artists made use of the Diadumenos, as they did of the Doryphoros, for portrait-statues.[2]

A bronze statuette in Carlsruhe, with an Etruscan inscription, evidently a derivative from the Diadumenos of Polykleitos, seems to me to be a forgery.[3]

In conclusion, and still in connexion with the Diadumenos of Polykleitos, we may mention a head which, although hitherto almost unknown, is one of the most beautiful antiques in existence. It is a head of a youth in the Turin Museum. The hair is full and curly ; a peculiar plaited fillet is imbedded deeply in the hair and tied behind.[4] The head is turned to the right and slightly bent ; the mouth is a little open. The hair is parted in the middle in Polykleitan fashion, but the locks are much fuller than even in the Diadumenos.[5] The ears are covered by a thick mass of curls, but the curls on the nape of the neck which appear under the fillet are remarkably like those on the Diadumenos, which the Turin head surpasses however in sweetness and serenity of expression. Whether it was Polykleitos himself who made this great advance on his own Diadumenos is a question impossible to decide. In any case, the original of the Turin head must have been the work of an artist of the first rank, who derived his inspiration from the Polykleitan statue.[6]

IV. *The Amazon.*

The Amazon is the third of those works of Polykleitos which are universally acknowledged to exist in copies. We have already discussed this figure in connexion with Kresilas and Pheidias (p. 128 *seq.*): it now remains to examine its relation to the other statues of Polykleitos.

In style the Amazon is nearer to the Doryphoros than to the Diadumenos : the head (*supra*, Fig. 55) shows this very clearly. The hard and prominent lower part of the face, the mouth projecting strongly in the middle and receding towards the sides, the simple flat-lying hair, connect the Amazon closely with the Doryphoros, and distinguish it from the Diadumenos. Even in attitude the Amazon is more like the former of the two, for the left forearm is bent and stretched forward horizontally, the thighs run parallel, the point of the left foot not being turned outwards. This conclusion is borne out by what we know from other sources as to the date

---

[1] Uffizi, 67 ; Dütschke, 76 ; Photo. Alinari, i. 1179. The head is foreign ; both arms new ; the left was raised, the right hung down. The palm-stem indicates a copy of a ' victor ' statue.

[2] The statue in Naples, *Inv.* 6271, evidently makes use of the Diadumenos, yet the turn of the head (now replaced by a restored one) is altered, and the round chlamys is added on the left shoulder. A dolphin and a polypus on the stem. Plainly a Roman portrait. The statuette, Museo Torlonia 72, is influenced by the Diadumenos ; the arms wrongly restored ; neck modern ; the head resembling Tiberius is antique, and probably belongs to the statue.

[3] Schumacher, *Beschr. d. Ant. Bronzen,* 932. From the style, especially of the head, and some external technical signs, I am inclined to suspect that the figure is not genuine.

[4] Dütschke (iv. 52), who describes it as a female head ! Marble Parian. The head is placed on an ugly nude bust. The nose, part of both lips, and the chin are restored. Face-length 19 cm. ; inner eye-corner to chin = hair to nostril 12½ cm.

[5] The full curl with rolled end is one of the chief motives. On the top of the head the hair is only loosely indicated.

[6] In presence of the original, Kresilas occurred to me, but I cannot prove the connexion by comparison, as I was unable to obtain a photograph.

of the Amazons, falling about 440 B.C. Our Amazon would thus come near to the Doryphoros, and be separated from the Diadumenos by a considerable period of time.

The Amazon of Polykleitos, as we have seen, expresses in one figure the Doric κοσμιότης and the Doric καρτερεῖν. The wounded heroine is not mastered by pain : her attitude shows weariness only,[1] her appearance and clothing are faultless in beauty and order. The lines of her form are rounded to a perfect harmony. Here too the motives are disposed in a crossing scheme : the raised arm is balanced by the pillar on the other side ; the right leg and the left arm are the carrying, supporting parts, the right arm and the left leg the parts at rest.

The motive which shows the left arm supported while the right is raised was a favourite in Praxitelean times. Polykleitos seems to have invented it for his Amazon,[2] though the left arm leans but lightly and the rest of the body is disposed as in the Doryphoros. We should expect to find other instances in the Polykleitan circle of this ' leaning ' motive, and there are, in fact, some other traces of it.

A Greek engraved stone of the fifth century, from the period of Polykleitos himself (Fig. 100),[3] represents the youthful Herakles, in an attitude corresponding in all

FIG. 100.—Greek gem.   FIG. 101.—Carnelian in St. Petersburg.

essentials to a Herakles torso of Polykleitan character at Dresden.[4] The hero is naked and without the lion-skin ; the weight is supported on the right leg, while the left is drawn back in the walking motive ; the club is shouldered and held by the right hand, but the left forearm is supported, as in the Amazon, on a low pillar. The lion stands beside the hero as an attribute. The whole design is clearly taken from a statuary composition of the period—perhaps of the school—of Polykleitos.

A second gem, this time of Roman date (Fig. 101),[5] represents Hippolytos in the walking motive of the Doryphoros, but with the left forearm, just as in the Amazon, supported—in this case against a tree ; the lowered right hand holds a hunting-spear ; below is a dog. The figure is evidently derived from a statue : the heavy forms of the body, the head with its large skull and close short hair, point to a work of the Polykleitan circle. The Eros standing on the tree behind and reading the love-letter on the *diptychon* is of course an addition of the gem-cutter, who wished to make clear

<hr>

[1] Wound and support are certainly genuine. Cf. *supra*, p. 134, notes 5, 6.

[2] Cf. Robert, *Arch. Märchen*, p. 109 ; but Polykleitos need not therefore be dated later.

[3] Cades, Cl. iii. A, 110. From the style, the above date is more likely to be too late than too early. Remnants of severe style ; a line round the edge. Species and owner unknown.

[4] Recent purchase ; till lately in Rome ; Arndt-Bruckmann, *Einzelverkauf*, No. 184. Preserved till below the navel. The connexion with the Doryphoros is striking. I had myself imagined it might represent the statue, to which the type of Herakles' head (Fig. 95, 96) belonged ; the measurements, which are practically the same as in the Doryphoros, are however too large. It is more probably to be restored on the analogy of the ' Theseus term (of course no Theseus, but a Herakles) in the Mus. Boncompagni-Ludovisi (Helbig, *Museums*, 861 ; *Mon. d. Inst.* x. 57, 2). The artist of the original had affinities to Kresilas, but was influenced by Polykleitos in the bodily forms. Breast and abdomen are quite Polykleitan, though the transitions are rounder, the edge of the ribs less accentuated, and the flesh softer. The right hand shoulders the club, the left hangs down, the head (differing in this from the Doryphoros) was turned to the side of the free leg, according to the Attic fifth-century scheme. Measurements : distance between nipples = 0·300 (Doryph. = 0·303) ; neck dimple to centre of navel = 0·455 (Doryph. = 0·450) ; breadth of hips, 0·389 (Doryph. 0·393).

[5] Carnelian in St. Petersburg (*Berl. Abdr.* 19, 24 = Cades, i. K, 91).

that the figure represented Hippolytos, and no common huntsman. The original statue probably stood in Troezene, for on coins of that city the same type, though roughly reproduced, occurs, the only difference being that the right arm is raised higher.[1]

The motive of the supported left forearm was used in the circle of Pheidias combined—not, of course, with the stepping motive, but with the left foot set slightly forward and full on the ground. On p. 71 we have tried to prove the existence of an Aphrodite by Pheidias represented in this motive.

V. *The Basis of the Statue of Kyniskos.—Statue of a Boy placing a Wreath on his Head, and Kindred Works.*

A sure foundation for the knowledge of Polykleitan statues is afforded by the discovery at Olympia of the inscribed bases that supported some of his works, inasmuch as the extant footmarks on these bases enable us to recover the attitude in which the statues stood. Three of them belong, as we saw, in all probability to the elder Polykleitos, one to the younger.[2] What first strikes us on examining the footmarks on the Polykleitos bases is that in not one of them does the scheme of the 'canon' occur—*i.e.* there is no single instance of a right foot bearing the weight of the figure combined with the left foot drawn back and resting only on the ball. Nor does this motive appear on the bases of works by Naukydes or by Daidalos; only the Zan of Kleon (Ol. 98)[3] and the following Zanes, so far as the footmarks can be made out, illustrate this scheme. The obvious conclusion is that Polykleitos himself as well as his school made use of other motives besides the one which we associate with the Doryphoros, the Diadumenos, the Amazon, and other analogous works.

The basis of Kyniskos, the earliest of them all, shows that the left leg bore the weight of the figure, while the right foot was set back and rested on the ball;[4] the statue represented a boy victorious in the boxing match.

Now we actually possess numerous copies of a statue of Polykleitan style representing a boy victor, in an attitude that corresponds closely with the footmarks on the Kyniskos basis (Fig. 102). To identify the statue with the 'Kyniskos' of Polykleitos would be no far-fetched theory, and I have long thought it worthy of adherence:

---

[1] Imhoof-Blumer and Gardner, *Num. Comm.* Pl. M. viii.

[2] We should have a fourth inscription of the older artist, could we see grounds for accepting Benndorf's conjecture (*Ges. Studien zu Kunstgeschichte, Festschrift f. Springer*, 1885) that the basis in the shape of an astragalos, found in Olympia, formerly supported the *nudum talo incessentem* of Polykleitos (Pliny, xxxiv. 55); there are, however, weighty reasons against this identification. Pliny's words mean literally 'a naked man advancing with a knuckle-bone.' Benndorf supposes that Pliny wrongly translated some Greek sentence such as γυμνὸς ἀστραγάλῳ ἐπικείμενος, and made nonsense of it. But even if a Greek sentence bearing the meaning supposed by B. ever existed (which seems doubtful), and if Pliny did understand ἐπικείμενος in the sense of 'advancing, pursuing,' he must have connected the word with ἀστραγάλῳ, and explained the whole phrase as 'advancing towards an astragalos.' There is no hint of this meaning in the Latin *talo incessens*; *talo* must be the instrument, the weapon, *with* which the nude man is advancing. As a knuckle-bone cannot be a weapon, there must be an error somewhere. If we read *telo* for *talo* (Benndorf's own former suggestion) all difficulty disappears (cf. Ovid, *Metam.* 14, 402, *saevisque parant incessere telis*, 13, 566; *telorum lapidumque incessere iactu coepit*). The corruption of the passage is then explained by the *talis ludentes* immediately following, from which *talo* was transferred to take the place of *telo*; the *item nudos* refers to the preceding *nudus*. The evidence, then, does not permit us to identify the bronze statue set up at Olympia on a marble astragal with a work of Polykleitos. The statue may, as Benndorf suggests, have represented Kairos; but it was very possibly only the portrait of a human being who, by the shape he adopted for the basis of his statue, recalled the particular stroke of good fortune which had moved him to bring a thank-offering to the divinity. As the attitude of the feet corresponds to the Kyniskos basis, the work belonged probably to the Polykleitan circle.

[3] Löwy, *Inscr. gr. Bildh.* 95.

[4] See drawing of upper surface of the basis, *Arch. Ztg.* 1882, 189; Löwy, *I. G. B.* p. 43, No. 50.

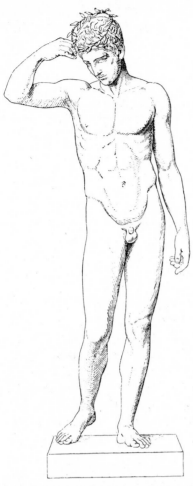

FIG. 102.—Statue of a victorious boy placing the wreath on his head. (Restored.)

lately both Petersen and Collignon have expressed the same opinion.[1] Unfortunately, however, absolute certainty can scarcely be attained,[2] as it is no longer possible to measure accurately the length of the foot of the Kyniskos figure ; in any case, it must have been more than 20 cm. ;[3] the length of the foot of the statue is 233 mm. ; the distance between the left heel and the ball of the right foot is, in the statue,[4] 16 cm. ; the two corresponding holes on the Kyniskos basis are about 175 mm. apart. These measurements are very nearly alike in the basis and the statue. The boy Kyniskos, like the statue, was of life-size, and his feet were exactly in the same position.

Two replicas of this statue have long been known. One is the so-called 'Westmacott' athlete in the British Museum, the other is in the Barracco collection.[5] The London copy is undoubtedly the better of the two. The Barracco figure is dull and slight in workmanship ; the London replica reproduces the body more sharply and finely, and the head especially with much more exactitude. The hair in the Barracco copy is carelessly rendered by mere indications of superficial effect ; in the London copy there is plainly a conscientious imitation of the bronze original.

To these two copies may be added a whole series of others. These are, it is true, mostly torsos and separate heads, but the very fact of their existence in such numbers proves that the original was famous and by a celebrated artist. The following are exact replicas : a statue in the garden of the Palazzo del Quirinale in Rome ; the head has never been broken.[6] It is not so good as the London copy, and

[1] Petersen, *Röm. Mitth.* 1893, p. 101 *seq.*; Collignon, *Hist. de la Sculpt.* i. p. 499.

[2] Petersen (*loc. cit*) thinks the identification more certain than I could venture to assert, as there must have been several Polykleitan statues of boys with the same position of the feet. Further, it is hardly likely that the original of our favourite and oft-copied statue was still in the *Altis* in the time of Pausanias, as the Kyniskos was, on whose basis there are no traces such as occur on the base of the Pythokles to show that the original had been taken away.

[3] Cf. Purgold, *Arch. Ztg.* 1882, 192. The distance between the two holes for the insertion of the left foot, probably meant for the toe and heel, is about 20 cm. ; the lower hollow may have been quite close to the point of the toe. Hence the foot need not have been more than 23 cm. long.

[4] In the London copy. Cf. following note.

[5] For discussion of these statues see Petersen, *Arch. Ztg.* 1863, 131 ; Helbig, *Bull. d. Inst.* 1885, 76 ; Winnefeld, *Hypnos*, p. 30 *seq.* ; Treu, *Arch. Anzeiger*, 1889, 57 ; Kekulé, *Idolino*, p. 13 ; Wolters in Lepsius, *Marmorstudien*, p. 83, No. 164 ; Philios, 'Εφημερὶsàρ χ. 1890, p. 207 *seq.*; Sauer, *ibid.* p. 211 ; Petersen, *Röm. Mitth.* 1891, p. 304 ; Collignon, *Hist. de la Sculpt.* i. 499 ; Helbig, *Rendiconti dell' Accad. dei Lincei*, 18 ; *Dic.* 1892, p. 790 *seq.*, '*sopra un tipo di Narcisso*' ; Milchhöfer, *Arch. Studien H. Brunn darg.* 1893, p. 63 ; Petersen, *Röm. Mitth.* 1893, p. 101.—Photograph of the London statue in Brunn-Bruckmann, *Denkmäler*, No. 46 ; of the Barracco statue in the *Collection Barr.* Pl. 38, 38 a. Sketches of both in Kekulé, *Idolino*, Taf. iv., and in the 'Εφημ. p. 207.—In the London statue the head is unbroken, and even the nose ancient. The left hand is broken but ancient. The execution is not slavish in detail, but gives the broad general characteristics ; the marble is Parian.

[6] Matz-Duhn, 210. On a fountain, drapery round the loins restored. The right arm may, I think, be antique.

comes nearer to the Barracco head. The right arm is joined, and perhaps antique. The hand makes a movement towards the head. There are two torsos in Berlin, one of them specially good,[1] another in Dresden,[2] of poor and exaggerated workmanship. The Museo Torlonia possesses a very good torso [3] restored as a Hermes ; the nipples imitate bronze technique. A poor copy in the Villa Albani is restored as a Brutus by the addition of a portrait-head representing a Roman of the end of the second century.[4]

Sir Edgar Vincent possesses a good copy of the head alone (Fig. 103),[5] preferable even to the London one. Mouth and cheeks, particularly, have kept a simplicity and a severity which can only be due to the original. The hair, though individual enough, is not worked with much detail. The style is distinctly Polykleitan. This is still more the case in a copy of the head in the Hermitage (Fig. 104),[6] by far the best that exists. Here the hair is carefully imitated from the bronze original: the way in which it is disposed in layers, the shape of the separate strands, especially behind and in front of the ear, are so entirely Polykleitan, and correspond so closely to the Doryphoros, that the work must be ascribed to Polykleitos, and dated not far from the Doryphoros. Entirely Polykleitan also are the angular build of skull, the large planes of the cheeks, the protruding mouth, the formation of the lower part of the face, and the regular forehead only slightly projecting at its base. It seems that a good replica of the head

FIG. 103.—Head of boy (in possession of Sir Edgar Vincent).

---

[1] Berlin, *Skulpt.* No. 514, is a very well executed, exact copy. A second copy in Berlin has restored head and limbs.

[2] Hettner's *Catalogue*, No. 254. Cf. Treu, *Arch. Anz.* 1889, 57.

[3] Mus. Torlonia, No. 59.

[4] Villa Albani, No. 46. Puntello for the left arm in the usual place.

[5] Formerly in the Van Branteghem Coll. ; from Italy. The right side of the head is less finished than the left.

[6] Guédéonow, No. 28. Bust and neck restored, otherwise in good preservation. Admirable workmanship. Cited by Conze, *Beiträge*, p. 7, as analogous to the Doryphoros. That it is a replica of the Westmacott athlete is proved by the correspondence in scale, the vigorous turn of the head, and the similarity in the hair. Even the bad copies, like the Barracco head, have the characteristic wisp of hair in front of the left ear. The rest of the hair matches the Westmacott copy strand for strand. The proportions of the St. Petersburg head are : length of head, 19 cm. ; length of face, 148 mm. ; length of eyeball, 26—27 mm. ; width of mouth, 39 ; inner corner of eye to hair, 58 mm. ; length of ear, 54 mm. The face-length is an important standard measurement for the torso ; from the ensiform process of the breast-bone to the navel, and from the navel to the insertion of the penis, are each one face-length. The chest, from the neck-pit to the ensiform process, is a little more.

stands in the Museo Torlonia.[1] I know a mediocre one from a cast in Strasburg,[2] and there is another in the Lateran.[3]

The Polykleitan origin of the statue, placed beyond a doubt by the good copies of the head, is confirmed by the modelling of the body. The points which distinguish it from the Doryphoros and the Diadumenos are only a consequence of the difference of age in the persons represented ; the style is absolutely the same. The large surface planes clearly marked off from each other are characteristic, and so are the details of form, such as the flat navel and its surrounding parts, the central groove or *linea alba* below the navel, and the well-marked hollow at the side of the gluteus,[4] a point on which Michaelis lays stress as being specially characteristic of the Doryphoros and the Diadumenos. In both cases it is striking that the hollow is equally pronounced on the side of the 'free' leg as on that of the 'supporting' leg. Michaelis was doubtless right in calling this a personal trait. Other peculiarities of bodily formation, cited by Michaelis as common to the Doryphoros and the Diadumenos, are here reproduced as nearly as they can be considering the more tender age of the subject : such are the modelling of the knee which bears the weight of the figure, and the strongly marked roll of muscle over it.

FIG. 104.—Head of a boy (Hermitage).

Again, the back of the figure (Fig. 105)[5] must be studied in order to understand that its distinguished beauty is in complete accord with the Doryphoros and Diadumenos.

The head proves that this statue must be dated much nearer to the Doryphoros and the Amazon than to the Diadumenos—that is to say, that it belongs to the period about 440 B.C. The hard, spare modelling and the flat rendering of the hair differ as much from the Diadumenos as they resemble the Doryphoros and the Amazon. It is also worthy of notice that the depression marking the crown of the head is as shallow as in those two works, and that, just as in the Doryphoros, the hair comes barely to the edge of the ear. Finally, the walking motive is expressed as simply as in the Doryphoros and the Amazon, both thighs being in the same plane.

The motive of the statue is allied in meaning to that of the Diadumenos. The one binds on the victor's fillet, the other presumably places the wreath, also a token of victory, on his head [6]—at least no more suitable restoration than this could

[1] No. 474. The head is placed leaning too far back.

[2] No. 597, Michaelis. I do not know where the original is.

[3] Lateran, No. 498. Neck new ; head wrongly set on. Petersen (*Röm. Mitth.* 1893, p. 101) mentions two further replicas : (1) a lower part of the face from the Palatine ; (2) a torso at Marinangeli's. I have seen neither. [4] Michaelis, *Ann. d. Inst.* 1878, p. 16.

[5] Cf. Michaelis, *loc. cit.* 17. Fig. 105 is from a photograph of the London statue.

[6] Winnefeld (*loc. cit.*) first suggested this, then Wolters, Treu, Petersen, Collignon (*loc. cit.*), and, hesitatingly, Kekulé. Philios, Sauer, Helbig, and Milchhöfer disputed it.

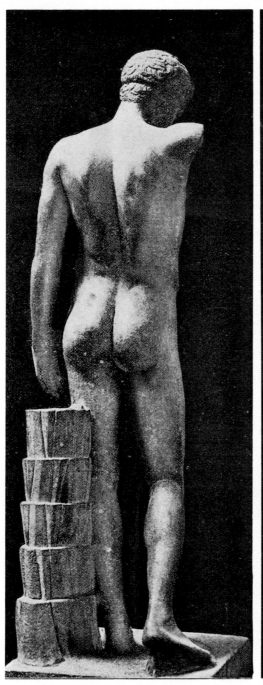

Fig. 105.—Back of Westmacott athlete (British Museum).

Fig. XXXVI—Westmacott Athlete, London, British Museum (See pp. 250 sqq.)

be found for the Barracco copy,[1] where the arm is preserved down to the wrist, and
the hand was not raised but slightly bent ; further, a whole series of monuments which,
as is evident by the correspondence in their attitudes, must be regarded as free
imitations of our statue,[2] show the boy in the act of placing a wreath on his head,
and the whole posture corresponds to this motive.[3] The bent carriage of the head is
no objection, for it is evidently meant to express the modesty which the artist, in the
true spirit of antiquity, conceived as the fairest ornament of victorious youth. That Polykleitos actually did think of the subject in this way seems certain from the evidence of
the Diadumenos, where the act is the same, and the head is bent. This is one of many
coincidences which intimately connect our statue with Polykleitos. The rest of the
body also is in a purely Polykleitan attitude ; besides the walking motive, we should
notice the arm hanging idle with open fingers by the side of the supporting leg.

A new feature, and one not found in any of the Polykleitan statues we have
hitherto examined, is that the head has a decided turn away from the side which
supports the weight of the body. This breaks the central line of the figure, and
makes the rhythm altogether more animated.

The Amazon of Kresilas shows such a striking resemblance in attitude to this
statue [4] that we might almost suppose that Polykleitos is here influenced by the Attic
master. The reverse is certainly not the case ; for the motive of the boy is slightly
artificial, and does not follow necessarily from the action as does the motive of the
Amazon. The boy might just as well look to the other side ; not so the Amazon, for
all her activity and emotion are centred on the wound. Again, the left arm of the
boy is not included in the activity of the body, but hangs carelessly down, following
the 'canon' of Polykleitos, while to the corresponding arm of the Amazon a necessary
share in the action is assigned. This is an instance of the contrast between the two
masters. The motive can only have been invented by the artist who makes it appear
a natural consequence of the situation. Polykleitos adapts part of it merely for the
love of beautiful form.

One figure of the Parthenon frieze [5] is very like the Polykleitan statue, only that
the movement is more animated, the sides are reversed, and the one arm does not
hang down, but leads a horse by the bridle ; the left hand was arranging the wreath ;
a direct connexion between this figure and the Polykleitan statue, which was the
earlier work, is not at all impossible.

---

[1] The bend of the hands is shown by the folds in the skin underneath the remaining portion ; the hand must
have held something over the head. The wreath was probably of bronze, even in the marble copies.

[2] I mean the monuments which correspond with our statue in having left supporting leg, the walking
motive, the hanging left arm, and boyish forms : *e.g.* the Berlin relief, 948 ; the Vatican relief, Mus. Pio Clem.
v. 36 ; the Zodiac relief, Le Bas, *Mon.* Fig. 21 ; Campana, *Opere in Plastica*, 94 ; an onyx gem in St. Petersburg
(cast in Berlin, 26, 56), motive well rendered ; another gem, where the motive is adapted for an Eros victorious, in
the Palestra (Cades, iv. F, 18). In all cases the boy is putting on a wreath with the right hand, the left occasionally holds a palm-branch. For modifications in the 'crowning' motive, cf. p. 255.

[3] The recent suggestion that the boy is holding a strigil in his raised right hand (Sauer and Philios, *loc. cit.*)
is certainly wrong : the strigil would come just over the forehead and in front of the hair ; looked at from below, it
would seem held even higher. Now a strigil was never used for cleansing the hair. The Pompeian painting (*Röm.
Mitth.* 1888, p. 199) on which the suggestion is based represents the athlete holding the strigil to his forehead ;
moreover, the weight is on the right leg, the forms are more adult ; the whole attitude different. Still less happy
is Helbig's most recent suggestion, that the hand is raised to shade the eyes from the sun. The lowered head
speaks against this view. The motive of shading the eyes with the hand is only natural, and as far as I know occurs
in ancient art only when the eyes are looking towards the light, *i.e.* towards the horizon or the sky, and never
when they are looking down to the ground as here. Nor is there any foundation for Helbig's interpretation of
the figure as Narkissos. The left hand is complete in the London statue : it was empty, and could never have
held a spear as Helbig suggests.

[4] Kekulé (*Idolino*, p. 14) noticed this.   [5] North frieze, 131 (Michaelis).

A statue found within the sanctuary of Eleusis[1] seems to be an approximately faithful rendering of the body of the original, although on a somewhat smaller scale; but the head, which seems less inclined, is rendered much more freely, in the Attic marble style of the good period.[2] The left arm may have been in a different position, as the puntello at the usual place is missing. The statue could hardly represent a victorious athlete; the provenance and the soft expression of the face suggest rather some divine boy, perhaps Triptolemos. A torso in the Museo Torlonia[3] would be an exact copy, except for a large round fracture-surface on the right gluteus, indicating that some object either touched the body or was connected with it by means of a support. A torso of the Villa Albani[4] is another ordinary copy; but an antique piece of a boar's head on the tree-trunk beside the left leg shows that the type was used for a youthful hunter—Adonis more probably than Meleager. The type was also adapted to Dionysos, as we learn from a torso of the Museo Torlonia; this is an exact copy, with the addition of a nebris reaching from the left hip to the right shoulder, the ends of which probably fell over the arms.[5] The statue has been made into a Hermes. A torso in the *Terme* resembles the usual copies in all respects, except that a chlamys of good Greek fashion is laid on the left shoulder and falls down over the arm, while the left hand holds the kerykeion.[6] Unfortunately in all these torsos only enough is left of the right arm to show that it was raised. We do not know how the motive was accounted for; the placing of a wreath would be appropriate only for a victor, and cannot be assumed for other subjects.

One variant of the 'crowning' motive is to be seen on a coin of Commodus[7] representing the youthful Herakles in the same position as our figure, but holding a club and a skin in the left hand. A coin of the Brettii[8] uses the motive for a young hero who carries lance and chlamys in his left hand.

The extant modifications in sculpture—for Triptolemos (?), Adonis (?), Dionysos, and Hermes—may be mostly referred to the good period of Greek art. Specially interesting is a coin of Troezene,[9] which evidently reproduces a statue of the city. It supplies a much-needed restoration for the Hermes torso in Rome mentioned above. The motive is that of the victorious boy, only that chlamys and kerykeion are held in the left hand; the right is brought close to the head, and is empty. The Eleusinian figure does not, then, stand alone as witness to the fact that the graceful motive of the victorious boy was adapted for representations of a religious character to be set up in Greek sanctuaries. Finally some gems show that the essential features of this beautiful motive reappear in other representations of the athletic circle.[10]

---

[1] Ἐφημ. ἀρχ. 1890, Taf. 10, 11. (Philios, p. 207 *seq.*) The body was found on the procession street between the Propylaia and the Telesterion, the head a little farther away.

[2] The statue is no Roman copy; judging from the workmanship, it appeared to me to belong to the fourth century B.C. It may come from the Praxitelean circle, from the period in which the master was an enthusiastic follower of Polykleitos (cf. *infra*, p. 317).

[3] Mus. Torlonia, 37. The torso unrestored: the puntello for the left arm is at the usual place.

[4] Villa Albani, 222, 'Meleagro.' Head foreign; arms and neck restored.

[5] Mus. Torlonia, 22. Only the torso (including the right thigh) is ancient: the nebris is only indicated in low relief on the back.

[6] Museo delle Terme, in the cloister garden. Proportions of torso correspond with the other copies. Torso unrestored, and the greater portion of the thighs remains. The attitude of the head and the right arm as usual.

[7] Fröhner, *Médaillons Rom.* p. 123.

[8] Garrucci, *Le Monete*, Tav. 124, 13, 14. The youth is crowning himself. Garrucci's explanation as Pan is wrong.

[9] Imhoof-Blumer and Gardner, *Num. Comm.* Pl. GG. xi. p. 162. Bronze coin of Septimius Severus.

[10] *Pasten in Berlin* (pp. 2377 and 2378): athlete holding discus in his lowered left hand, the right hand, empty, moved towards the head. Attitude of head and legs as in the statue.—Carnelian, Brit. Mus. (*Cat. of*

A famous painting by Eupompos,[1] of Sikyon, representing a *victor certamine gymnico palmam tenens*, seems to have been directly derived from the Polykleitan statue. The youth holds a palm-branch in his left hand, and the head is not bent, but in an upright attitude more appropriate to a painting. Eupompos seems to have followed the same tendency in painting as Polykleitos in plastic art. When Polykleitos was at the end of his career, and his disciples were beginning to migrate to Sikyon, Eupompos founded in that city a school of painting on much the same lines as the school of bronze statuary founded by Polykleitos. It is therefore not surprising that Eupompos should have followed Polykleitos very closely. Invention was in any case not his strong point.

This beautiful Polykleitan motive seems to have been adopted even by a modern painter: the Christ rising from the tomb by Fra Bartolomeo in the Pitti Palace[2] so strikingly recalls it that it is probable the artist had seen one of the copies of the statue.

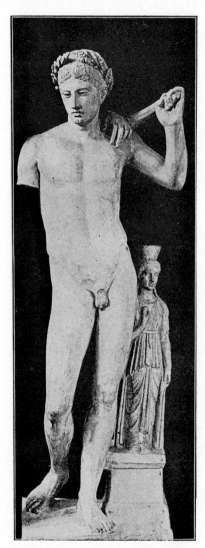

FIG. 106.—Figure from Ildefonso group (Madrid).

The same position of the feet visible on the **Kyniskos** basis, and which we found to be that of the 'boy crowning himself' preserved in the Westmacott statue and its replicas, occurs on two other bases at Olympia, which probably supported statues of the Polykleitan school. These are the basis in the form of an astragalos (p. 249, note 2), and the basis of Hellanikos of Lepreon,[3] who as a boy was victorious in the boxing contest (Ol. 89 = 424 B.C.) The footmarks are very similar to those of the Kyniskos; here also the boy was represented life-size: the left foot, firmly placed on the ground, was 22 cm. long;[4] the right was set back and rested on the ball; the stride was longer than the stride of the Kyniskos and of the 'boy crowning himself,' and the right foot was more to the side (the distance from

Gems, 1833); the youth holds the wreath in the lowered left hand, and with the right he leads a horse by the bridle; position of head and legs as in the statue; a victor with his horse.—Gem, Cades, Cl. iv. F, 46; the left hands holds a long palm-branch, the right is raised and placed on an urn over a fountain.

[1] Milchhöfer, in *Arch. Studien H. Brunn dargebr.* 1893, p. 62 *seq.*, maintained the opinion that the athlete putting a crown on his head with the right hand and holding a palm in the left, who is repeated frequently and with many variations in relief and painting, is to be referred to the work of Eupompos. This is no doubt correct. But the essential features of this composition as seen in their simplest form in some of the replicas (cf. p. 250, note 5) are those of this Polykleitan statue, which therefore must have afforded the model for the painter's work.

[2] Bruckmann, *Klassischer Bilderschatz*, No. 373.

[3] *Arch. Ztg.* 1878, p. 88, No. 138. Treu has rightly observed that the inscription only survives in its restored condition, *Arch. Ztg.* 1879, p. 208.

[4] The length of the foot can be exactly calculated, as beyond the depression for the main part of the foot the outline of the toes is still visible.

the left heel to the ball of the right foot being about 245 mm.)   In exterior the basis is very like those of Polykleitos and his circle ; the artist is not named.

Among surviving statues there is no doubt that one figure of the Ildefonso[1] group, that of a boy wearing a wreath (Fig. 106), should be reckoned as a work akin to the statue under discussion.   In the position of the legs it corresponds exactly, and in the attitude of the head approximately, to the Westmacott statue, but the arms are different ; the right hand hung down, the left was raised.   The head is of purely Polykleitan style, very like the Doryphoros in the hair and the modelling of the forehead, while in expression and formation of the lower part of the face it stands very near the best copies of the 'boy crowning himself.'   The eyes look modestly to the ground.   In the original, the raised left hand may have touched the wreath which it had just placed on the head, and the right may have held a fillet.   On the other hand, the body is much softer and feebler than we have any right to presuppose was ever the case in Polykleitan works.   We may conjecturally charge the copyist with the alteration, and assume that the original was by Polykleitos.   I know no other replica of this work.

We possess still another interesting Polykleitan statue of an athlete with the same pose of the feet as that shown by the Kyniskos basis, *i.e.* with the weight on the left leg and the right foot drawn back ; but the head is not turned, as in the other statues which fit the basis, to the side of the free leg, but according to the ordinary norm, to the side which supports the weight.   The work survives only in one copy, the 'Oil-pourer' at Petworth House in Sussex (Fig. 107, after a photograph from the original).[2] The statue is remarkable more for excellent preservation than for good workmanship. The head and both arms, even the right hand with the globular aryballos, are ancient ; the legs only are restored from below the knee.[3]   The tree-stem, with the two objects (probably boxing pads) hanging on it, is also ancient.   The right leg from below the knee, reckoning by the surviving knee-joint, was drawn farther back than the restorer has assumed, and was in the full 'walking' position.   The whole figure ought to be tilted a little more forward.   The athlete is past boyhood ; he is an ephebe, the forms of the body being distinctly more powerful than in the 'boy crowning himself.'[4]

Polykleitan style is unmistakable, especially in the head.[5]   Above the forehead there is the characteristic symmetrical parting of the hair just as in the Doryphoros. The forehead is divided horizontally, and modelled like the forehead of the Doryphoros ; the eyes are purely Polykleitan.   The lower part of the face, with the slightly open mouth, is most like the Dresden athlete which we are presently to discuss (Plate XII.) In bodily formation, too, our statue resembles this athlete, though the forms are more powerful to correspond to the advance in age.   On the other hand, a great interval separates it from the ripe adult forms of the Doryphoros and Diadumenos.

[1] For literature cf. Friederichs-Wolters, 1665 ; *Museo Espagnol*, ix. p. 217 *seq.* with plate ; Hauser, *Neuattische Reliefs*, 184 ; E. Bethe in *Arch. Anz.* 1893, p. 8.   The raised left arm with the torch is certainly a restoration— cf *Bull. d. Inst.* 1877, 154.

[2] Described by Michaelis, *Anc. Marb. in Gt. Brit.* p. 601, No. 9.   The statue had been published before in Bracci, *Memorie degli Incisori*, i. Pl. 26 to p. 293, 'Atleta in Londra.'

[3] The only other restorations are the end of the nose with right nostril and the projecting finger of the left hand.   The head has not been worked over.

[4] The pubes is beginning to grow : it is formed of two symmetrical pairs of curls on either side.   The undeveloped pubes here only characterizes the youthful time of life, and is totally different from the small pubes which appears on adult figures of the fourth century.

[5] Michaelis, *loc. cit.*

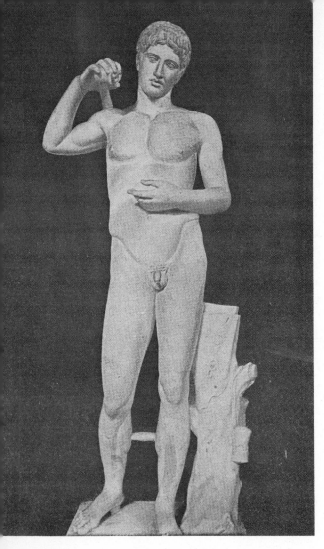

FIG. 107.—Athlete in the collection at Petworth House (Sussex).

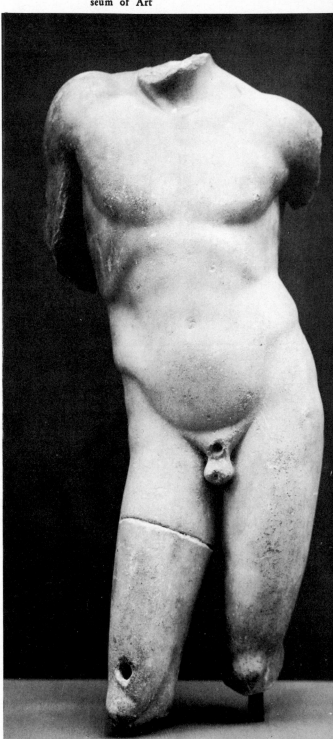

Fig. XXXVII—Torso of a Boy, a variant of the Poly kleitan "Narkissos," New York, Metropolitan Mu seum of Art

The abdomen with the flat navel, the chest modelled in large planes, the hollowed gluteus—all are true Polykleitan traits. In the bronze the nipples would be inlaid ; in imitation of this technique the copyist has surrounded them with a ring. The workmanship is poor on the whole, the hair is carelessly done, without detail. We may hope that a better copy will some day come to light.

In order to appreciate the intention of the motive we must first look at the other extant statues representing athletes pouring oil. Hitherto they have been all incorrectly classed together as 'replicas' or 'copies' of the same original,[1] although some of them have merely the essential features in common—features which are due more to the nature of the subject than to the invention of any one artist. Several red-figured vase-paintings of severe style,[2] earlier than any of the statues, show from their realistic representations of scenes in the palaestra that it was a well-established custom to hold the round aryballos high in the right hand and pour the anointing oil from it into the left hand, which was placed horizontally across the body. With regard to the attitude, accordingly, the statues, naturally enough, coincide. The action necessitates the weight of the figure being thrown on the left leg, for the left arm must be held as still as possible to catch the oil, and the head must be turned towards the left. Now all these common features simply grow out of the subject chosen. Given the subject, however, we may distinguish the following different renderings.

First the Munich statue,[3] of which there are three other replicas.[4] The conception, though full of life, is expressed by a somewhat hard and angular movement. The upper part of the body leans back too straightly and stiffly, the definite forward bend of the head produces a harsh effect. The bodily forms are simple, spare, and dry. Brunn noticed the analogy to the Marsyas of Myron,[5] and this analogy undoubtedly exists not only in the conception of the swift, momentary action but in the separate details of the attitude. As the head-type, too, may be considered to be a development from Myron, we are justified in suggesting that Lykios, the son and pupil of Myron, was the author of this work. We know that he was working about 440 B.C.,[6] and this is probably the date of the statue.

An entirely different creation, not at all, as has been asserted, a remodelled copy of the preceding,[7] has survived in the Dresden torso.[8] It has several replicas, some of them better and with the head preserved.[9] Only those features characteristic of the

[1] e.g. Wolters, Gipsabg. Nos. 462—464.

[2] Cf. those cited by Bloch, Röm. Mitth. 1892, p. 88, and especially Arch. Ztg. 1879, Taf. 4 ; Hartwig, Meisterschalen, p. 570.

[3] Friederichs-Wolters, Gipsabg. 462 ; Brunn-Bruckmann, Denkm. Nos. 132, 134, 135.

[4] A restored torso in the cortile of the Palazzo Mattei (Matz-Duhn, 1025 ; Clarac, 940 B, 2398 A). The spareness of the forms is well reproduced, but not so well as in the Munich copy. A torso has lately come from Rome to Dresden which, although in bad preservation, is certainly an exact copy of the Munich statue—Arch. Anz. 1894, p. 26, 6. A third very much restored replica in the Pal. Pitti (Dütschke, 25).

[5] Ann. d. Inst. 1879, 204.

[6] Klein's suggestion (Oesterr. Mitth. 1891, 6 seq.) that the encrinomenos of Alkamenes (Plin. xxxiv. § 72) was an enchriomenos (ἐγχριόμενος), and similar to the Munich Oil-pourer (it would have been better to say to the Dresden), is not tenable. Cf. Overbeck, Gesch. d. Plastik, 4th ed. i. 386. I cannot agree with Sauer (Festschrift für Overbeck, p. 28) in seeing a resemblance between the head of the Aphrodite of Alkamenes and that of the Munich Oil-pourer.

[7] Brunn's assumption (loc. cit. 217 seq.) rests on a false notion of the character of the surviving copies. (Cf. above, on the Diadumenoi.)

[8] Friederichs-Wolters, 463 ; Brunn-Bruckmann, Denkm. Nos. 133, 134.

[9] The Museo Torlonia contains a good torso (Plate 122, No. 476), with bad restorations ; the right leg is completely modern. There is a replica in the Palazzo Pitti (Dütschke, ii. 22), with unbroken head, although the whole figure is poor, and has been worked over. Both legs are preserved. In Rome, in front of the Villa

subject are the same as in the Munich type ; everything else is different.   The hard effect
has disappeared.   The attitude is quieter and more natural, but lacks the fire and
energy that distinguish the other composition.   The upper part of the body is
inclined slightly forward, the head is less bent than in the Munich statue ; the legs
are closer together and more in repose ; the weight of the body rests—as the subject
requires—on the left leg,[1] the right leg is placed to the side and slightly advanced,
the heel being somewhat raised.[2]   The attitude thus becomes lighter and more
graceful.   The bodily forms are powerful and of adult growth, a great contrast to
the spareness of the other work.   The modulations of the whole muscular system
are indicated by a number of finer details, altogether absent in the other statue.
The head is covered with short curls, the flesh of the face is full and firm, the
impression of power being heightened by the indication of whiskers and by the very
prominent forehead, from which the hair is brushed upwards.   Unfortunately there
is no good copy of the head ; its pure Attic character is however undoubted ; in spite
of the coarser workmanship, it is allied to the standing Diskobolos ascribed to
Alkamenes (p. 90).   The full plump forms of the body also recall this Diskobolos,
but the differences are such as to suggest another artist.   Certain details like the
formation of the chest and the navel, as well as the attitude, make me think that
this work is by the artist of the Florentine athlete which we are shortly to
discuss.   This artist must be sought for among Attic masters of the end of the fifth
or beginning of the fourth century.

There are some few statues under life-size which are akin in motive and,
generally, in style to the work last described,[3] without being copies of it.   They
are to be referred to different unimportant originals derived from the one prototype.

Other repetitions of the motive on a small scale are to be found in terra-cotta
statuettes from Myrina,[4] on Greek reliefs,[5] and on gems.[6]   These do not aim at
reproducing any particular statue ; they are simply instances of the general influence
exerted by a widely known and famous plastic motive.   As they are most nearly
related to the Dresden type, we may conclude that this was the most popular.

In contrast, then, to the Dresden and Munich statues, which are both derivatives
of Attic art, we have a third new and significant creation of the Polykleitan school in
the 'Oil-pourer' of Petworth.   Unlike the Attic statues, the Polykleitan conception

Borghese, on the right, is a replica with an unbroken antique head in very bad preservation.   The chin and the
upper part of the head with the pointed cap are new ; there is a breakage through the face.

[1] In the Dresden copy the back part of the left foot is ancient, but it is plain from the original that the left
heel ought to be not raised but on the ground.   (The remains of the old plinth are planed away under the sole of
the foot.)

[2] Thus in the Pal. Pitti copy, where the foot is old.   In the Borghese and Dresden copies it is wrongly
restored flat on the ground.

[3] Statue in Turin, Friederichs-Wolters, 464 ; the head broken but antique.   It differs from the Munich
statue and from the other types ; it is a poor, insignificant work.   Further, statue in Cassel (ii. 1) ; the head
belongs to a replica of the Polykleitan 'Narkissos' (cf. infra) ; no pubes ; rounded forms ; left hand ancient.
Finally, two of the small athletes in the Braccio Nuovo (Helbig, Museums, 41—45 ; Röm. Mitth. vii. 93).   The
head of No. 99 is ancient, but belongs to a reduced replica of the Florentine athlete ; No. 103 has a modern plaster
head.   These two statues might be reduced inexact copies of the Dresden type.

[4] B. C. H. 1886, Pl. 12 ; Pottier and Reinach, Nécrop. de Myrina, Pl. 41, 3 ; p. 450 seq.   A second copy
(with reversed sides) in the Coll. Misthos. in the National Museum at Athens.

[5] Sybel, Catalogue, 534 (Friederichs-Wolters, Gipsabg. 1798), grave-relief of the third to second century.   The
raised right hand is empty ; it was left to the spectator to supply an aryballos in imagination.   The same motive
occurs on a fragment of relief from the south slope of the Akropolis (only the upper part preserved ; the raised
right hand empty ; the left lies flat on the stomach).

[6] Stone of Cneius, Jahrb. d. Inst. 1888, Taf. 10, 12, p. 315.   Also Tölken, vi. 107, and Cades, iv. F, 73,
and a stone in Dr. Dressel's possession.   I no longer hold the opinion (Jahrb., loc. cit.) that the gems go back to
the Polykleitan Petworth type.   They correspond most nearly to the Dresden type.

begins with the walking motive, although this is as little appropriate to the chief motive of the figure as it is to the representation of an athlete binding a fillet about his head or putting on a wreath. For pouring oil a firm steady position is indispensable ; to do it while walking along is not natural—though it is just what we should expect from Polykleitos. The youth is not giving his mind to what he is doing ; he bends his head gracefully and modestly, thus forming a harmonious flow of line as in other statues of Polykleitan style ; but he looks out into the distance instead of fixing his eyes on the hand into which the oil is dropping. The right arm is only raised halfway, much less than in the two other statues. We have seen that when Polykleitos does raise the arm high, as in the Amazon and in the 'boy crowning himself,' he makes the bowed head fill the empty corner formed by the arm ; this could not be done here, because the head had to look to the left, hence the arm must not be raised so high. It is true that this change takes away from the animation of the figure, but it was the only way to obtain a graceful flow of line. From the right elbow the line rises nearly straight to the crown of the head. Again, the whole arm is so placed that it falls as nearly as possible in one plane with the body, thus avoiding entirely the projection towards the front which the arm must have formed in the other statues. We noticed a similar intention in the Diadumenos of Polykleitos.

Now pouring oil is an action far too energetic and requiring far too close attention to be appropriately rendered in the Polykleitan manner, and Polykleitos—if he and not one of his pupils is the author—seems to me to be less happy than usual in this figure. The material content of the motive is not satisfying, and the formal beauty is not, as in other statues, carried far enough to help us to forget the deficiency. Polykleitos is here entering a region familiar to Attic art, but completely strange to him. We may presume that he knew the older of the two Attic creations, and that he was perhaps attracted through it to the theme. The two statues we have assigned conjecturally to Lykios and Polykleitos must, however, have come close together in time ; the 'oil-pourer' of Polykleitos is at any rate older than his Diadumenos.

FIG. 108.—Apo-xyomenos on a gem.

In speaking of the second Attic, *i.e.* the so-called Dresden type of 'oil-pourer,' we had occasion to cite the Florence athlete as being akin in style. Before closing the present inquiry a few words must be said about this figure, as it has of late been interpreted as an athlete pouring oil from a lekythos held in his right hand into an aryballos held in his left.[1] Such an action is however unparalleled, unclassical, and, above all, absurd for an athlete to be engaged in. The left forearm lay close to the thigh, and the right crossed the abdomen diagonally in the direction of the left hand ;[2] now a gem reproduced in Fig. 108[3] explains this attitude, and corresponds to it so closely that we may conclude it is an imitation of the original of the statue. Moreover, the gem belongs to that class of convex stones which has already afforded us so many exact copies of statues.[4] The figure on the gem holds a strigil in both hands,

---

[1] *Röm. Mitth.* 1892 (vii.), p. 81 *seq.* (Bloch). The only possible evidence for calling the statue an 'oil-pourer' at all is the existence of a statue in Paris (*loc. cit.* p. 87 ; cf. *Arch. Anz.* 1891, p. 140) under life-size, in which the left hand, which is ancient, makes a gesture as if to catch oil dropping into it. But this small statue goes back to an original similar to, yet quite distinct from, the Florence athlete, so that even if it did represent an 'oil-pourer' this would prove nothing with regard to the Florence athlete.

[2] The right arm is restored with the shoulder, and perhaps had quite another movement.

[3] Impression, Cades, iv. F, 66 ; unquestionably genuine. Beside the athlete stands the usual hydria with a palm-branch and a wreath over it.   [4] Cf. *supra*, p. 137, note 1 ; p. 163, note 1.

and is in the act of removing the dust from his left thigh; the right hand holds the handle and the left the blade of the strigil, in order to scrape the skin with more energy. The tension in the muscles of the upper arm is appropriate to the action.   The youth is quite absorbed in what he is doing.   The leg released from the weight of the figure is placed well to the side with raised heel.   This attitude—a preparatory stage to the Lysippian scheme—is, as I have already pointed out, very near akin to the type of the Dresden 'oil-pourer,' and so is the full and muscular formation of

the body with all its characteristic details; we may therefore assume that both works are by the same artist.

The Florence statue, then, is not an 'oil-pourer,' but an *apoxyomenos*, a *destringens se*—a magnificent work, famous even in antiquity, as the remains of several copies prove.[1]

Polykleitos too was, according to Pliny, the author of a *destringens se*. I can trace no copy of this work in statuary, but I think there is an echo of it in a type very frequent on gems (Fig. 109).   If this be so, the original must have represented a youth leaning his weight on the left leg with the right drawn back in the 'walking' motive.   The right forearm is stretched forward, the left holds the strigil, and the intention is to cleanse

Fig. 109.—Apoxyomenos
on a gem (Hermitage).

the under side of the right arm.   The whole scheme is conceived in the Polykleitan manner; the act of scraping is subordinate and rules the composition only to a limited extent; the pleasant effect of the 'walking' attitude is evidently the principal thing in the artist's eyes, and the arms are very little removed from the plane of the body.   The number and remarkable similarity of the gem designs[2] prove that they are all derived from one definite and well-known original.

VI. *The Basis of the Statue of Pythokles.—Statue of a Boy in Dresden: its Adaptations and Derivatives.*

In the former section we took the Kyniskos basis as our starting-point. Another series of statues may be discussed in connexion with the Pythokles basis (*I. G. B.* 91).

This basis, whose upper surface is reproduced in Fig. 110,[3] is remarkable, not only in having in addition to the older first inscription a second inscription which is a

---

[1] A copy of the head in Museo Torlonia (Taf. 22, 86), worked over and much restored; neck new, bust not belonging. A better copy in the Hermitage, No. 65; the forehead modelled more fully and carefully than in the Florentine example. A reduced copy is No. 105 in Braccio Nuovo (cf. *supra*, p. 260, note 3; *Röm. Mitth.* vii. 92). The head is genuine but wrongly put on (the neck new); slight workmanship, but a real copy. Head, No. 99, Braccio Nuovo. Cf. *supra*, p. 260, note 3.

[2] The stone reproduced from a cast in Fig. 109 is specially good. It is an emerald-plasma in St. Petersburg. A modern paste from it is in the Stosch collection, wrongly described as ancient by Tölken, vi. 100. Several smaller ancient replicas in the Petersburg collection (Berlin impressions, 22, 37, emerald-plasma; 26, 34, 65; 29, 21; 34, 65; 44, 10, all of the so-called achatonyx or nicolo). Other replicas in Berlin, Tölken, vi. 99, 101, 102; in 103 the figure is seen more from the back; also p. 2404 (convex emerald-plasma). From other collections cf. *Impronte dell' Inst.* 7, 73; Cades, cl. iv. F, 65; in Paris (impressions in Berlin, 640), with the modern inscription Γναίου; another stone, also ancient, with the same modern inscription, Bracci, *Mem. d. Incis.* i. 52 (cf. *Jahrb. d. Inst.* iii. 317); stone of the Dressel collection; paste of the Bergau collection; and others. The motives of all these gem designs correspond. The figure also occurs in a few rare instances turned to the left, when the sides are also reversed (thus Tölken, vi. 106; Cades, cl. iv. F, 67; *Impr. dell' Inst.* 6, 72; *Paste Bergau*).

[3] Drawn by Lübke from my plan of the block.

restoration of the earlier one, and may be dated in the first century B.C., but in having supported two different statues in succession. The feet of the earlier statue were riveted into circular holes. Behind its right foot, on the upper surface of the basis, was inscribed the name of the artist, on the front surface the name of the victor. This statue must have been carefully detached and taken away. It was then replaced by another with a quite different standing motive, and the feet of which were fastened into hollows in the stone filled with molten lead. This second statue appears to have looked in an opposite direction to the first. The renewal of the inscriptions probably took place at the same time that the new figure was set up, for the new inscriptions recording the names of the artist and of the victor start in a line with its right foot. Subsequently this later statue was roughly broken away, probably at the destruction of Olympia. From these facts we gather that the genuine statue by Polykleitos was taken away from Olympia as early as the first century B.C., and that it was replaced—not by a copy—but by an entirely different figure, which was then inscribed as a work by the famous artist.

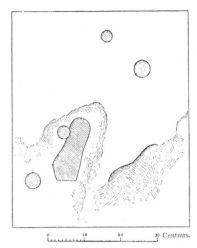

FIG. 110.—Basis of the statue of Pythokles in Olympia.

Now there has been lately found in Rome, and assigned to the period of Hadrian or the Antonines, a basis actually inscribed with the names of Pythokles the Olympian victor and of Polykleitos the artist.[1] It is true that the footmarks on this basis fit neither of the statues that once stood on the 'Pythokles' basis at Olympia, but Petersen has shown that these footmarks are due to some earlier use of the basis, and have nothing to do with Pythokles. This Pythokles statue in Rome may possibly have been identical with the original statue by Polykleitos which disappeared from Olympia in the first century B.C., and which was doubtless brought to Rome. It is, however, more likely that the existing basis with its statue was only a copy of the famous original by Polykleitos, and that this original was placed to more advantage in some other part of Rome; for the basis with its statue was set up by a club of athletes, whose ambition was to ornament their *curia* with figures of victors in gymnastic contests, but who probably could not afford to buy originals.

The genuine Pythokles of Polykleitos stood firmly on the right foot. The length of the foot, calculated from the circular holes, is about 24 cm.; the left foot was set back and—herein is the distinctive trait—well turned out; the left knee accordingly must also have been turned quite obliquely outwards.[2] This position is natural only when the whole attention of the figure is directed to the left side, *i.e.* when the head is turned to the left, and the left hand is occupied with something.

Among the works represented by copies which could come into question there is one, surviving in two replicas in Rome and Munich, which best reproduces all the

[1] *Bull. della Commiss. Comun. di Roma*, 1891, p. 280 *seq.*, Tav. x. 1; Petersen in *Röm. Mitth.* 1891, p. 304 *seq.*

[2] On renewed examination of the basis in the summer of 1894, it seemed to me that, since the left foot also had a hole for the ball, it was more probable the statue stood firm on both soles; in this case however the left must have been the supporting leg.

conditions of the Pythokles basis (Fig. 111).[1]   It is a youthful athlete, who stands in
the position required by the basis, and whose feet correspond in scale to the footmarks.[2]   The head is turned to the left, the left forearm is stretched forward, while

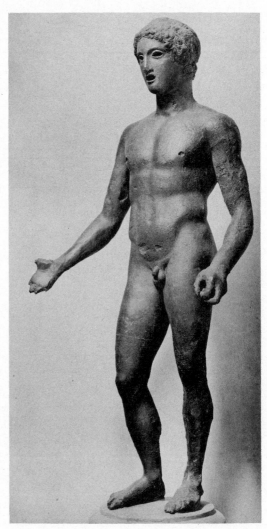

FIG. 111.—Athlete in the Braccio Nuovo (Vatican).

**Fig. XXXVIII—Bronze Statuette of an Athlete, School
of Polykleitos, Athens, National Museum**

the hand holds a globular aryballos.   The right arm hangs simply down, and blends
with the contour of the body ; the hand perhaps held a fillet.[3]

As regards the time of life represented, this youth is older than the ' boy crowning

[1] *A.* In Rome, Vatican, Braccio Nuovo, No. 101 (Fig. 111) ; cf. Helbig, *Museums*, on Nos. 41—45—' reveals
a close kinship with the Doryphoros of Polykleitos.'   Photograph in German Inst. at Rome.   Legs and basis
ancient ; arms and neck restored ; the head is ancient and belongs to the statue, only it is placed leaning a little
too far back.—*B.* In Munich Glypt. No. 303 ; Clarac, 858, 2175 ; black marble ; left leg restored, and the foot
is wrongly placed flat on the ground to the side, instead of being drawn back.   The head, both arms, and the left
hand with the oil-flask are ancient (*A* is restored from *B*).

[2] On *A* I measured 24 cm.

[3] The right hand which survives in *B* held some light object, probably a fillet ; in *A* the hand is wrongly
restored ; it simply hung straight down.

himself,' and younger than the Doryphoros ; he is very near in age to the 'oil-pourer.'[1] The comparison gives us some notion of how nicely the gradations from boyhood to adolescence were shaded off in the Polykleitan school.

This work stands very near the Doryphoros, not only in the stage of growth represented but in the style and mode of expression. The hair is treated in the same flat, spare, and restrained manner, divided into large strands which cling close to the head ; over the middle of the forehead is the same symmetric parting.[2] The hair leaves the ears free. The forehead too, with its horizontal division, and the whole expression of the head, which is not bent but freely turned to the side, show a special likeness to the Doryphoros. The same may be said of the body, except that the forms are less powerful. We must assign the work to a period not far removed from the time of the Doryphoros.

The motive of this statue, full of energy and character, reaches its most life-like development in the Diomede of Kresilas. The action of the Diomede is fully accounted for down to the smallest particulars by the nature of the subject. The like cannot be maintained of the athlete holding the aryballos. Hence we may suppose that Polykleitos, in this instance also, was under the influence of a creation of Kresilas. He saw an attractive motive (the Diomede, we have shown, was made for Argos), and adapted it to the figure of an athlete without troubling himself to account for the attitude on internal grounds. I have already suggested that he may have used the Kresilaian Amazon in like manner (p. 254). Nor were the motives of Diadumenos and 'oil-pourer' his own. It was certainly not in invention that lay the special strength of our artist.

A very close analogy to this Roman copy of a Polykleitan statue is afforded by an admirable small original work from Greece, a bronze statuette now in Athens.[3] It cannot be referred to the master himself, for it differs in too many respects from the works we know to be his, and is besides too insignificant in character, but it is an excellent specimen of school work from his earlier period. The hair is more uniform and restrained than in the statue we last discussed ; the head is peculiarly heavy ; the time of life represented is that of the Doryphoros, but the forms are drier. The motive is similar to the preceding, but shows more repose and simplicity. The head is not turned, but only bent to the side, and the left knee is not directed outwards. The left arm seems to have been raised, and was perhaps supported ; the right arm hung down. A small marble figure of very poor late workmanship from Athens, in the British Museum,[4] markedly resembles this bronze.

On the other hand, there is another admirable work which we may trace to Polykleitos himself, and which must have been one of his most beautiful creations. There is a well-preserved copy of it in Dresden (Plate XII. and Fig. 112).[5] A replica,

---

[1] The pubes is not indicated. This is plain in *A* in spite of the plaster covering ; in *B* the *membrum* is preserved intact.

[2] The head of *A* is much better and more carefully worked than that of *B*, but they are copies from the same original. *A* well reproduces the sharpness of the bronze.

[3] *Mon. d. Inst.* viii. 53; *Annali*, 1868, 316 *sqq.* (Kekulé) ; Brunn-Bruckmann, *Denkm.* No. 280 a ; presumably from Sikyon. The arms, now missing, were put on separately.—Lange (*Fremstilling af Menneskesk.* 419) is, I think, wrong in supposing the figure to be earlier than Polykleitos.

[4] A. H. Smith, *Catal. of Sculpt.* i. 502, 'Doryphoros.'

[5] Becker, *Augusteum*, Taf. 88 ; Clarac, 948, 2437 ; Hettner, *Catalogue*, 4th ed. No. 90, 'Doryphoros.' Mentioned by Michaelis, *Ann.* 1878, 8, among the 'variazioni' of the Doryphoros ; by Kekulé, *Ann.* 1868, 316, as a replica of the Athens bronze discussed above ; by Treu in *Arch. Anz.* 1889, p. 57.—The restored left arm is now taken away. Everything else is ancient except the left upper lip, the nose, and the *membrum*. The

formerly belonging to Cavaceppi, is probably somewhere in England.[1] Besides these there are two torsos in Rome,[2] and three replicas of the head alone (in Berlin, the Vatican, and the Coll. Barracco).[3]

Once more it represents a youthful victor with the feet placed as on the Pythokles basis, except that the left foot is not drawn so far back, and the toe is not so much turned out. In accordance with this modification the head is but gently turned to the left and inclined. The right arm again hung straight down beside the body ;[4] the left upper arm is directed somewhat to the side, the left shoulder is a little raised and advanced, so that the front of the upper trunk is not all in the same plane ; this produces an animated crossing rhythm. The right shoulder is not drawn back, but held in a comfortable natural position ; from the attitude of the left upper arm and from the absence of any puntello on the left side we conclude that the left forearm was advanced. The youth was holding some object on which he was looking down.[5] This was doubtless nothing but a victor's fillet or some simple instrument of the palaestra.[6] The modest reserve expressed by the attitude of the head seems to speak for the fillet. For just this modesty and reserve on the part of the victorious athlete were demanded by ancient custom, that the envy of gods and daemons might be appeased.

The time of life represented is a new variant between boy and ephebe. The ' Dresden athlete '—so we may call the type—is older than the ' boy crowning himself.' The formation of the body is stronger and the chest is fuller, bearing the same proportion to the lower part of the body as it does in the Doryphoros. On the other hand, the Dresden athlete is more youthful and delicately formed than the figure, presumably the Pythokles, which we discussed above, or than the ' oil-pourer.' It is a great mistake to imagine that the victor statues of Polykleitos were all made upon one pattern, and merely repeated the proportions and modelling of the Doryphoros ; the latter evidently gave the ' canon ' for the full-grown male figure only.

The ' Dresden boy ' bears such unmistakable marks of the personal style of Polykleitos that we may certainly ascribe it to the master himself, and it probably belongs to his later period.[7] It stands midway between the Herakles (discussed above, p. 234) and the Diadumenos, and is closely akin to both works. The hair resembles that of the Herakles, but is more developed in style ; the *asymmetria* of the

head was never broken. Height of head 198 mm., length of face 156, length of foot 253, distance between nipples 226.

[1] Cavaceppi, *Raccolta*, iii. 5 ; Clarac, 866, 2204. According to Cavaceppi, in the possession of ' Giuseppe ' Nollekens in England ; the arms and the armour as support are probably restorations ; in other respects the figure appears to be a replica.

[2] *a.* in Museo Torlonia, No. 18. Legs and arms wrongly restored, head antique but not belonging ; the torso is a good replica of the Dresden statue.—*b.* in the Vatican, Museo Lapidario, 124. Torso.

[3] *a.* in Berlin, *Skulpt.* 546. A very good copy. The hair corresponds exactly with the Dresden replica. The whole upper part of the head is restored. The sharpness of the bronze original is imitated ; the lips are slightly open, but do not show the teeth.—*b.* Vatican, Museo Chiaramonti, 507 (Helbig, *Führer*, i. No. 100). A good careful copy ; nose and neck restored ; edge of lips sharp. Mentioned by Flasch, *Verh. d. Philologenvers.* 1874, p. 163 ; by me in *Annali*, 1877, 203.—*c. Coll. Barracco* (Pl. 46). A good copy.

[4] Remains of puntello on the right thigh of the Dresden statue.

[5] Hettner assumed a spear, because formerly all Polykleitan figures were supposed to be variants of the ' Doryphoros.'

[6] On a Panathenaic prize amphora of the fourth century an athlete occurs very similar to the Dresden type. He carries a discus in his left hand (*Mon. d. Inst.* x. 48 g, 10).

[7] Kalkmann (*Proportionen d. Ges.* p. 55), in endeavouring to extract results from his rows of figures, places these and other statues to be subsequently discussed (such as the Pan, the ' Narkissos,' the ' Idolino ') in the pre-Polykleitan period ; this is only one of the many anachronisms into which Kalkmann has been induced by his figures.

FIG. 112.—Head of the boy's statue in Dresden. (From the cast.)

Fig. XXXIX—Head of a Young Athlete, New York, Metropolitan Museum of Art

short wisps over the forehead, which occurs first in the Herakles, is here more pronounced.   In the Herakles the hair already covered the upper edge of the ear; here
the motive is accentuated, and the ends of the small curls veil with their rich variety
the whole upper part of the ear.   The fashion, here so charmingly elaborated, of
separating the hair into numerous narrow strands with intertwining ends also made
its first appearance in the Herakles.[1]   There is no trace of it in the Doryphoros.

The 'Dresden boy' is associated with the Diadumenos by the fuller plastic treatment of the hair.   In both there is a depression on the crown of the head, while the
bunches of hair radiating from the crown—three in each case—are so similar as to
be almost identical; a sure confirmation of our theory that Polykleitos is the
master and that the 'Dresden boy' comes near the Diadumenos.   It is however
certainly the earlier of the two, for the hair still lies quite close to the skull, and
the step which divides the Diadumenos from all earlier Polykleitan works has not
yet been taken.

Further, the expression of the head, and especially the formation of the lower
half of the face (Fig. 112), indicate a stage preparatory to the Diadumenos.   The
modelling here is softer, rounder, and more developed than in the earlier works of
Polykleitos ; the full lips, the folds near the corner of the mouth and nostrils, the somewhat receding chin, and the expression of sweetness, satiety, almost of melancholy,
mark a decided approach to the head of the Diadumenos.   We can better understand
the place of the latter statue in the development of Polykleitos now that we have found
a connecting link leading up to it.

In studying the Diadumenos we recognized the influence of Attic style on
Polykleitos, and suggested Kresilas as its source (p. 243).   In the 'Dresden boy' this
influence is beginning to be felt, for it exactly explains the variations from the older
Polykleitan type.   Not only the formation and expression of the lower part of the
face, but the way in which the ends of hair tangle together, are clearly inspired by
works from the Myron-Kresilas circle, and more especially by the Diomede.   But
Polykleitos has not altered the fundamental characteristics of his hair technique ; he
entirely ignores the short, full crisp curls of Attic work ; in the 'Dresden boy' he has
arranged the hair on the upper part of the head practically in the same smooth
layers as in the Doryphoros ; only in the Diadumenos does he break away to some
degree from his old manner.

The body of the 'Dresden boy' is rendered in the style customary to Polykleitos :
e.g., it has the characteristic flat navel with the deep groove below it and the hollow
at the side of each gluteus.   Compared with an earlier work, such as the 'boy crowning
himself,' the transitions are softer and more rounded ; this is more than usually
noticeable in the divisions effected by the straight and oblique abdominal muscles
which are still so harsh in the former statue.

The 'Dresden boy' may be classed among the happiest efforts of Polykleitos.   The
attitude has more of nature and truth than his compositions usually manifest, without
being the less beautiful or harmonious.   The head has a charm of its own which makes
the earlier works of the artist seem cold and formal, and which is unsurpassed except
by the Diadumenos.

With this work two others are nearly connected.   One of these survives, as far
as I know, only in one copy, now in St. Petersburg (Fig. 113) ;[2] it is a figure very like

---

[1] Especially behind the left ear in the Dresden copy of Herakles.

[2] Guédéonow, No. 304, 'Mercure' ; also apparently cited as Hermes by Treu (*Arch. Anz.* 1889, 57).   Legs

the Dresden boy. The position of the feet and the turn of the head are the same, and here too the right arm hangs straight down, while the left forearm is extended. Yet the shoulders are well set back in the usual way; the body-forms are somewhat more youthful and delicate. The head—to which the restorer has arbitrarily added wings—is akin to the Dresden figure, but the hair is fuller and more curling; the personal style of Polykleitos is missing; the hair is not parted over the middle of the forehead, nor is it arranged in layers. The ears are not covered by the hair. The figure undoubtedly represents a boy victor; in his lowered right hand is a fragment of an attribute. The restoration as a purse is quite ridiculous; the fragment is a short straight piece not round in section but rectangular; it might very well be the handle of a strigil.

I am inclined to assign this work not to the master but to one of his pupils, who used the Dresden boy as his prototype; not only the head but the body shows a lack of the real personal manner of Polykleitos, and of all the finer shades of individualization which we have learned to look for in his authenticated works.

The second work survives in a great number of copies, and was clearly a favourite and widely known. Being only two thirds life-size, it was suited for the decoration of private houses. One copy shows distinct marks

Fig. 113.—Statue of a youth (Hermitage).

of having been used as a figure for a fountain in a Roman house. The statue represents a divine boy, Pan in almost human form, a subject we have already met with in an original of the Polykleitan circle (p. 229). I know four complete

and feet, with the moulded basis, are mostly ancient; left forearm is restored; right hand with the remains of an attribute (wrongly restored as a purse) is ancient. The neck is mostly restored, the head genuine and set on almost in the right position; the wings are a later addition placed on the hair, which is complete without them and carefully worked. The workmanship is not older than the time of Hadrian.

copies, and six replicas of the head.[1] The statue in best preservation is the one in Leyden (Fig. 114).

The feet are placed exactly as in the two works just discussed, and the head is inclined slightly to the left ; the left shoulder is rather more advanced than in the Dresden boy, and this produces a slight turn in the upper part of the body. The right hand again hangs simply down holding the short knotted stick (λαγωβόλον) which was commonly used in hunting the hare,[2] and which constantly appears as an attribute of Pan, the zealous huntsman. The left forearm, as we assumed in the case of the Dresden boy, is stretched forward, and holds the other chief attribute of Pan, the syrinx,[3] on which his lowered gaze seems to rest. The motive so suitable to the modest victor is here simply transferred to Pan, apparently without a thought whether it is appropriate to him or not.

The head shows the closest kinship to the Dresden boy,[4] as well in the form of the skull with the hollow in the nape of the neck, as in the face and its expression. The hair is rendered in the same narrow intertwining strands ; separate parts, such as the lock in front of the right ear, are strikingly similar. Yet the whole mass is fuller and looser than in the Dresden boy, and more like the Diadumenos. The body[5] also corresponds stylistically with the former, i.e. the transitions are softer than in the ' boy crowning himself,' while the forms throughout are Polykleitan.

Nevertheless, the artist has tried to characterize Pan ; the hair in front does not, as in its prototype, the boy victor of St. Petersburg, fall over the forehead, but grows upwards as in figures of Satyrs ; in order that it may not break the beautiful contour of the skull, it must of course lie close to the head ; the two horns lie equally close, their roots being skilfully hidden in the hair ; the long pointed ears, almost like those of a beast, are set flat against the sides of the head.

We have here most probably the production of a pupil who worked in immediate association with Polykleitos, and founded the conception of his own statue on that ' Dresden type ' created by the master himself for the representation of a boy victor. His work was certainly not far removed in time from this type and from the Diadumenos.

We can point to two more instances in which the beautiful Polykleitan creation of the Dresden athlete has been used for a mythological figure.

One of these works exists, so far as I know at present, in one copy only. It is a statue of a youth, resembling the Dresden boy in all particulars, even in the principal

[1] *Whole statues* with head. (*a*) in Leyden, Janssen, *Catalogue*, i. 62. Excellently preserved ; the legs, the basis, the right arm with the pedum, and the left arm are genuine ; the syrinx in the left hand is at least partly ancient. On the head only the end of the nose is new. In 1883 I examined the statues (*b*) and (*c*)—the two copies worked by Cossutius Cerdo, Brit. Mus. (*Guide Graeco-Rom. Sculpt.* Nos. 188, 190 ; *Anc. Marbles*, ii. 33, 43 ; Brunn-Bruckmann, *Denkm.* No. 47). The arms are wrongly restored ; in one the nose is complete and the hair carefully copied ; in (*a*) the body is better.—(*d*) Vatican, Gall. dei Candelabri, 246 ; Helbig, *Museums*, i. No. 389. The poorest of all. The left arm is new ; the right arm is ancient and hangs down holding an oinochoë, which is supported on a pillar and used as the spout of a fountain : hence the Pan must have been used as the decoration of a fountain. The head is very sketchy, the hair almost without detail.—*Separate heads :* (*e*) Good copy in the Conservatori Pal. (*Bull. Comunale*, 1887, Tav. iv. ; Helbig, *Museums*, i. No. 606). Here the polykleitan style is very exactly reproduced ; (*f*) a good but not well-preserved copy in the *Terme Mus.* (photographs in German Inst.) ; (*g*) less good, in Vienna, Hof. Museum ; the features are softened and inexact ; (*h*) in Palermo, in the second court of the Museum ; nose and chin new, hair fairly faithful ; (*i*) Hanover, Kestner Museum, poor copy ; (*k*) Lateran, 524 ; Helbig, *Museums*, i. No. 666, poor. Lateran, 288 (Helbig, *Führer*, No. 630), is a free modification of the type, not a copy.—Cf. *Annali*, 1877, 202 *seq.* ; *Satyr von Pergamon*, p. 29.

[2] For the straight form of the pedum cf. *Ann. d. Inst.* 1877, 212 *seq.*

[3] To be restored with pipes of equal length Cf. *Annali*, 1877, 214 *seq.*

[4] The head of the Leyden statue here published is not exact in the details of the head. *b, c, e,* and *f* are more true to the original.

[5] The body in the Leyden statue is more faithful to the style of the original than the copies by Cossutius Cerdo, which are too soft and plump.

proportions, except that a sword-belt crosses the body from the right shoulder to the left hip.[1]   Probably he held the sword or some other weapon in his outstretched left

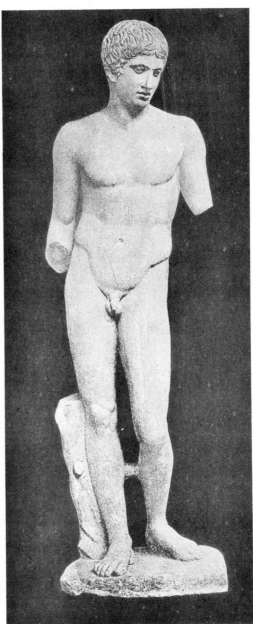

FIG. 114.—Youthful Pan (Leyden).   *Plate XII. *Statue of a Boy.*   DRESDEN.

hand, and we may call him Ares.   The copyist was one of that numerous class who reproduce Polykleitan originals in a soft and feeble manner.   Such copies are apt to

[1] Rome, Conserv. Pal. *Bull. Comunale*, 1886, Tav. i. ii. ; p. 54 *seq.* (Benndorf, who, mistaking the details of the statue, the technique, and the style, sees in it the Thespian Eros of Praxiteles) ; Helbig, *Museums*, No. 568 ; Robert, *Arch. Märchen*, 160 *seq.*   The upper part of the head and the back were pieced on.   The figure can never have had wings.

deceive an unpractised eye. Yet sufficient Polykleitan traits answering to the
Dresden type are left to make it apparent that the original was closely allied to
that type. The hair round the ears—covering in this figure also the upper part of
the ear—is treated in the same way; the modelling of the body, the characteristic
navel, the hollow at the side of each gluteus, even on the side of the leg at rest, and
other details, are all purely Polykleitan, though they are rendered in a weak manner
that lacks all energy. The original must have owed its existence to the immediate
circle of Polykleitos.

There are several replicas of a statue of Dionysos,[1] which, like the Pan, is two
thirds life-size. The motive is again essentially the same as that of the Dresden boy
victor; here too the right hand hung down, and the left was stretched forward.
The forms of the body most nearly resemble the Pan, and are quite in Polykleitan
style, without any mixture of the softness appropriate to Dionysos.[2] Unfortunately
there is only one authentic fragment of the head on one of the replicas.[3] The
god is characterized by long curls falling on the shoulders, by a bunch of hair on
the nape of the neck, and by a gracefully disposed nebris fastened on his right
shoulder. For the source of the work we must certainly look to the school of
Polykleitos.

Another statuary composition, also two thirds life-size, belongs to this same
series (Fig. 115).[4] Here the typical motive has become more pronounced, and
expresses quiet and pleasant repose. It is true that the essential features—the
attitude of the legs, the turn and inclination of the head, the boyish forms—are
unaltered; but in this instance the left hand rests on a pillar, and the weight of the
body is partly transferred from the right leg to the left arm. The right hand, in

[1] (a) in Dresden, Hettner (4th ed.), No. 163; Becker, *Augusteum*, ii. 74; Fried.-Wolters, *Gipsabg.* 1493. The
lower part of the r. leg and the l. leg from the middle of the thigh are new. Remains of a puntello in the right
thigh show that the right arm was lowered. The neck and parts of the head—viz. right ear, piece of cheek, and
hair above the ear—are ancient and unbroken. At the back, above the battered remains of a tail of hair of the
simple, severe style, the restorer has placed a knot of hair of the usual late fashion. Everything else about the
head is modern. (b) Berlin, *Sculpt.* 89. Torso, badly restored. (c) Clarac, 684, 1603 A, Ince Blundell Hall;
Michaelis, *Sculpt. in Gr. Brit.* p. 347, No. 32.

[2] Specially characteristic are the abdomen with the flat navel, the linea alba, and the sharply marked off
pudendum.

[3] In a. In c the whole head might from the style possibly be ancient. I have not seen the statue.

[4] The so-called Narkissos. Winnefeld (*Hypnos*, p. 30) has collected a list of replicas, among which some few
variants that really do not belong to the series have crept in. I described several replicas in *Bull. dell' Inst.* 1877,
158. I know the following in the original: *Statues with head:* (a) Berlin, *Beschr. d. Skulpt.* 223: stylistically faithful
copy, not very detailed in the hair; upper part given in Winnefeld, Taf. ii. = our Fig. 115. (b) Mus. Chiaramonti,
526: only the upper part preserved, very good. (c) Pal. Rospigliosi, Friederichs-Wolters, *Gipsabg.* 525: poor.
(d) Villa Borghese: upper part only. Cf. *Bull., loc. cit.* 159, 6. (e) Mantua, 65, Dütschke, iv. 650: holds an apple;
very poor, inexact, and rough copy. (f) Louvre, Coll. Campana, phot. éd. Giraudon, 1295. (g) Carlsruhe, Winnefeld, Taf. i.: style inexact, much softened down; small wings added to the head; workmanship of Hadrian's period.
Kalkmann (*Gesichtsprop.* p. 53) is wrong in thinking the head does not belong.—*Torsos:* (h) Mantua, 26: right hand
empty. (i) Genoa, Pal. Reale: an apple in the right hand, which is half antique. (k) Rome, Palazzo Colonna: head
does not belong. (l) Pal. Doria, Matz-Duhn, 223. (m) Pal. Barberini, Matz-Duhn, 975: apple in the right hand.
(n) Berlin, *Skulpt.* 224. (o) Naples, casually mentioned by Friederichs, *Arch. Anzeiger*, 1862, 309, and by others.
Height without basis 0·61, basis antique, lower part of legs restored to the ankles, head missing. Both hands
preserved: the right on the back holds an apple, the left is supported by a pillar on which lies drapery. In front
of the pillar a female term, draped above; the feet come out below; free style, long shoulder curls, full face.
—*Heads:* (p) Berlin, *Skulpt.* 263; much defaced, but gives the hair faithfully. (q) Cassel, ii. 1: a very good copy
placed on the torso of an oil-pourer. (r) Copenhagen, Coll. Jacobsen, No. 1094: poor, hair very sketchy;
wrongly called 'Doryphoros' in the catalogue. (s) *Ibid.* No. 1075: free copy, but unaltered in proportions; hair,
eyes, and mouth formed in later style, as in c and g. To see how copies *can* differ, cf. r and s. [To these eighteen
replicas may now be added (t) statue recently acquired by the Louvre; head and torso in exquisite preservation;
arms and legs broken but belonging; admirably published Pl. xvii. of *Monuments et Mémoires* (Fond. E. Piot),
vol i.; *ibid.* p. 115 *seq.* (E. Michon), where also further particulars on the Campana statue (f) are given.—E. S.]

order not to disturb the repose of the body, must have been laid on the back. The head was bent down close to the raised shoulder, and the whole composition was rounded off in a highly harmonious and pleasing manner. The bodily forms corre-

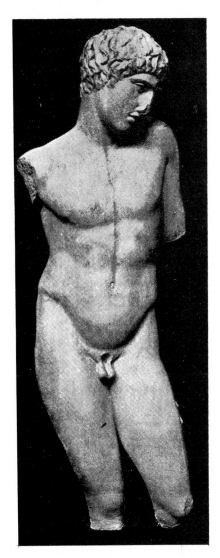

FIG. 115.—The 'Narkissos' (Berlin).

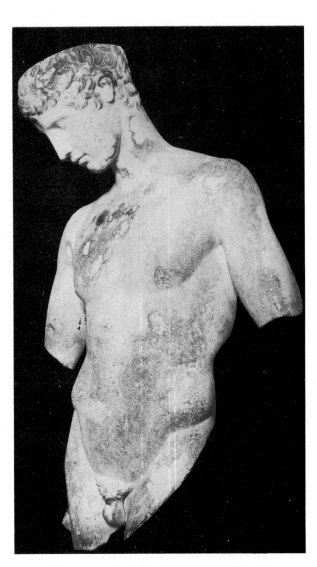

Fig. XL—Hermes, Boston, Museum of Fine Arts

spond to those of the Pan, and so does the stylistic treatment of the head and the magnificent Polykleitan build of skull. The hair, although full and plastic, clings for the most part closely to the head ; the upper part of the ear is covered ; there is no parting over the forehead. None of the copies show fine separate intertwining

N N

locks of hair as in the Pan ; this however may be accidental ; certainly the latter work affords the nearest stylistic parallel as regards the hair, and there is great resemblance in the facial forms.   Both works must be referred to the same circle of the master's pupils.

In the Amazon, Polykleitos had already created a figure at rest, leaning slightly against a support ; but it was a great step from this to a figure completely supported on one side like the statue we are now considering.   The motive strongly recalls the Herakles, leaning with weary bowed head on the club which props him under the left armpit, while his right hand is laid on his back or set against his side.   This Herakles type was developed as early as the fifth century,[1] and seems to have taken shape not only in drawings and reliefs, but in a work of statuary which must have come into being in the Attic artistic circle of about the end of the same century.[2] It is quite legitimate to ask whether one of these two creations, the boy or the Herakles, was not influenced by the other.   Since the motive as applied to Herakles has an eventful previous history extending back to the severe Attic style of vase-painting, and is closely bound up with the very nature of the hero of so many toils and troubles, and since the circle of Polykleitos is very deficient in inventive power, it seems reasonable to suppose that this is another instance of the transference of a magnificent statuary conception from Attic to Argive art.   In the present case the motive was adapted to the boyish type of figure resembling Pan.

We still have to consider the meaning of the figure, which copyists of Imperial times adapted to various interpretations.   One copyist made it into a Hermes (hardly a Hypnos) by adding small wings to the head.[3]   In some replicas there is an apple in the right hand ;[4] the intention of this addition is doubtful, but it may be the usual Aphrodisian attribute.[5] A figure in relief with an apple on the pillar support belonging to one copy (*o*) seems to corroborate this notion.   It is a veiled goddess ending in a term, and doubtless to be interpreted as Aphrodite, who as Ourania was represented in Athens in the form of a term.[6]   Our figure, then, must have some special relation to Aphrodite.   Another replica[7] has the arm supported on a wine-skin, hence it was probably intended to decorate a fountain.   The gems too, which show frequent reproductions of our statue, are of great importance.   On one fine piece a female figure almost nude, probably Aphrodite, is placed on the right of the boy.[8]   Another time he is characterized as a huntsman, and holds two spears in the left hand, which is propped on a rock ; dogs accompany him, and on the rock are a boar's head and stag's antlers supporting an image of Artemis.[9]   Both gems render the statue in a very exact and characteristic manner, and are certainly

[1] Cf. Roscher's *Lex.* i. 2173.

[2] Life-size copy in Dresden.   Style, end of fifth century.   The right hand is set against the side, not laid on the back.   According to Herrmann (*Arch. Anz.* 1894, p. 26), there is a replica in the Villa Borghese.

[3] *g* in the above list.   Winnefeld supposes Hypnos ; but the wings are like those given to Hermes, and Hermes often occurs in similar motives.

[4] *e, i, m, o.*   An apple, not a pomegranate.   Kalkmann (*Gesichtsproport.* p. 53) is wrong in supposing it to be an aryballos.

[5] The common supposition that the apple shows the figure to be a death daemon is untenable and quite unproven (*Satyr von Pergamon*, p. 30, note).

[6] *Paus.* i. 19, 2.   The manner of draping is specially common to terms, which render the body down to the hips.   Figures like Herakles and Pan, which are usually nude, are likewise draped when adapted to terms.

[7] I only know it through Laborde, *Voyage en Espagne*, Pl. 99 E.   Cf. *Bull. d. Inst.* 1877, 159.

[8] Cades, cl. i. K, 86 : probably a paste ; large, fine style ; drapery added on the left shoulder.   Evidently an imitation of the statue.

[9] Cades, cl. iii. B, 105 : drapery on the left shoulder, style of the statue well reproduced.   Admirable workmanship.

derived from it. Other gems give variants; the figure is turned to the left and the sides reversed. A stone of this kind makes the figure into a Ganymede by the addition of a Phrygian cap and of an eagle below.[1] Another makes it into Narkissos by an indication of water in the background and of a figure leaping into it.[2] A freer variation is one in which not the left hand but the forearm is supported on a pillar or pedestal: this type is once characterized as a huntsman and also as Hermes or *Bonus Eventus*;[3] with reversed sides and looking to the left he again appears as a huntsman.[4] An Attic grave-relief of the fourth century repeats the type, adding a small hare which rests on the boy's left hand.[5]

Nowhere do we find any indication that the type had a sepulchral signification.[6] On the other hand, it is important to note that the best gems represent the youth as a huntsman; those gems which make him into a Hermes, a Ganymede, or a Narkissos are few in number, of inferior workmanship, and evidently free modifications of the original design, like that statuary copy in which wings are added. Further, a near connexion with Aphrodite is assured, not only by one of the best gems, but also by one of the statues, and by the apple which occurs in several of the replicas.

The figure must have a mythological meaning; it is not the statue of a victorious athlete, but belongs to the same series as the Pan and the Dionysos of the Polykleitan school. Narkissos is not a familiar figure in this school, nor is there anything definite to suggest Hyakinthos, an interpretation I was formerly inclined to.[7] But if we call the boy Adonis, I think we shall find that everything fits admirably to the name. The cultus of Adonis is known to have been practised in Argos,[8] and it cannot have been more recent there than in Athens, where we find it established in the time of Alkibiades.[9] If there was an Adonis of the Polykleitan school at all, it would certainly be a figure without a trace of Oriental costume, and we could hardly think of it as a different type from our statue.

On an Attic aryballos from Kertsch, with reliefs of wonderful beauty carried out in a style akin to the Parthenon frieze, Adonis (inscribed) appears as a slender youth with no hint of the Oriental. He is closely grouped with Aphrodite and Eros, and is represented resting, with his arm over his head.[10]

---

[1] Formerly Coll. Schaaffhausen, *Catalogue*, 354 (impressions, 14): chlamys added; a lance leans on the rock. Poor workmanship.

[2] Carnelian; Coll. Thorwaldsen, Cades, iii. B, 93; *Impronte dell' Inst.* i. 73; Wieseler, *Narkissos*, Taf. No. 8; cf. p. 20. Late bad workmanship.

[3] The gem of Koinos, pub. *Jahrb. d. Inst.* 1888, Taf. 10, 20; discussed *ibid.* 1889, p. 51. Huntsman with spear and dog. Cades, cl. i. L, 26. Kerykeion in the supported left hand, therefore = Hermes. Poor workmanship. St. Petersburg (impression in Berlin, 1, 34): nicolo, from the ear of corn in the left hand, evidently a *Bonus Eventus*; very poor.

[4] St. Petersburg (impression in Berlin, 19, 31), carnelian; the r. hand holds a hare out towards an eagle; a dog beside it; two spears in l. hand on the back.

[5] Stele of Telesias, Friederichs-Wolters, *Gipsabg.* 1014; the left forearm is supported on the pillar; like the gems in note I.

[6] As I formerly maintained in *Bull.*, *loc. cit.*, this opinion was retracted in the *Satyr von Pergamon*, p. 29: it is still adhered to by Winnefeld, *loc. cit.*   [7] *Satyr von Pergamon*, p. 29.

[8] Paus. ii. 20, 6. The wailing of women was, here as at Athens, the principal feature of the cultus.

[9] Aristoph. *Lysistr.* 389 *seq.*; Plut. *Alkib.* 18; *Nik.* 13.

[10] Hermitage, newly acquired: the reliefs are of great beauty and interest. The scene is laid in Cyprus. To the left the hero Τευκρος (inscr.), the founder of the Kyprian Salamis; opposite him sits Tekmessa, who was given over to him by his dead brother (Soph. *Aias*, 563, 972 *sqq.*), and the boy Εὐρυσακης (inscr.); then Adonis ('Αδωνιος) seated, with Eros standing on his lap; he holds with his left hand Πειθω standing, who lays one hand on his lap; in her thin chiton she resembles the *Venus Genetrix* (of Alkamenes). Behind her, opposite to Adonis, sits 'Αφροδιτη, almost exactly like the Hegeso of the well-known grave-relief. The inscriptions are in Ionian characters; the style dates the vase in the time of the Parthenon frieze. Delicate painting and gilding.

It was no out-of-the-way idea to represent the beautiful huntsman who died young in the attitude of our statue, *i.e.* in a posture expressing weariness. If the work enjoyed such a measure of favour in later times, it was probably owing to the charm of the motive and the ease with which the figure, like the Pan, could be adapted for decoration.

The small scale (two thirds life-size) of the works we have just discussed is

a   b
FIG. 116.—Bronze statuette. (Bibl. Nationale, Paris.)

one of their characteristics; they were commissions of minor importance which fell to the share of the great master's pupils towards the end of his career or after his death.

A more recent school work, allied in motive to the 'Narkissos' discussed above, and to be classified in this series on account of the attitude of the legs and the droop of the head, can be studied in the admirable little bronze in Paris[1] (Fig. 116, *a* and *b*)

---

[1] *Cabinet des Médailles*, Coll. Janzé, No. 50. Height c. 0·25. Beautiful pale-green patina. The pupils were inserted. The left hand, now missing, was made separately. Both feet are restored in wax. I discussed statuette and gem in the *Archäol. Gesellschaft, Arch. Anz.* 1891, p. 141.

and a gem (Fig. 117) exactly corresponding to the statuette and evidently derived from the same original.[1] According to the evidence of the gem, the figure leaned with the now missing left hand on a staff round which a snake was twined.

Not only this attribute but the whole type is borrowed from Asklepios, for whom it had been already elaborated in Attic art at a period not much subsequent to the middle of the fifth century, as an interesting statue in Berlin shows.[2] Later, in the circle of Skopas and Praxiteles, the type was carefully fostered and intensified,[3] an effective upward turn being now given to the head. Our figure goes back to the old formula of the type, in which the head is only turned slightly to the left, and the right hip only curved slightly outwards. A variation is introduced in the snake-wound staff, which is not propped under the left armpit, but supported between the forearm and the body and held by the hand. This brings the position nearer the Polykleitan scheme.

Fig. 117.—Gem (Cades, ii. D, 16).

The modelling of chest and abdomen is clearly Polykleitan, while the head also offers conspicuously Polykleitan characteristics—in its large surface planes, in the formation of nose, eyes, and forehead, and in the symmetrical parting of the hair in front. The noble simplicity of the drapery corresponds to the style of the rest.

We may conclude, then, that the original is a work of the school of Polykleitos belonging—if we judge from the strongly plastic freedom of the hair—to the beginning of the fourth century, and based on an Attic Asklepios type of the fifth century.

But whom does the statue represent? An unbearded Asklepios would be nothing out of the way, especially in the Peloponnesos.[4] There is, for instance, a statuette from Epidauros representing an unbearded Asklepios whose forms indicate Polykleitan influence.[5] But the mural crown on our figure points to another interpretation; the person pourtrayed must be a protecting divinity, a hero allied in functions to Asklepios, and reverenced in a peculiar degree as guardian or founder of a city. The type of Asklepios was frequently transferred without alteration to heroes of the healing craft, witness the examples of Amphiaraos in Oropos and of Trophonios in Lebadeia; even the statue by Timotheos in the *temenos* of Hippolytos in Troezene represented the hero according to a scheme borrowed from Asklepios, but certainly unbearded.[6]

More definite evidence for naming our statue is supplied by two marble replicas of it found in Kyrene. One of them, in the British Museum,[7] is in excellent

[1] Cades, cl. ii. D, 16: without mention of owner or of species; probably an emerald-plasma. The gem belongs to the series which give exact copies of statues. The agreement with the bronze is striking.

[2] *Skulpt.* 68. Head Pheidian, like the Dresden Asklepios (p. 55, note 6). The original to be dated about 440 B.C., earlier than the Asklepios of the more recent Pheidian school (p. 89, note 6).

[3] Wolters, *Ath. Mitth.* xvii. p. 1 seq. Taf. ii.—iv. Among the fragments of reliefs from the Asklepieion in Athens I noticed in 1877 three examples of the type.

[4] Cf. Wieseler, *Göttinger Nachrichten*, 1888, p. 143 seq.

[5] Marble statuette, Central Mus., Kabbadias, *Cat.* No. 270; copy of an older work; weight on left leg, left arm supported, mantle leaving right breast free, beautiful youthful head with falling curls of moderate length; the head seems to belong to the statue, although the preservation of the surface differs in both; the rolled fillet shows at any rate that the head is that of a beardless Asklepios. The snake is at the side, as we assumed for the Florentine Asklepios (p. 208).

[6] Paus. ii. 32, 4, who calls it simply an Asklepios, but adds that the Troezenians called it Hippolytos. The statue of Hippolytos with spear and dog, which occurs on coins of Troezene (Imhoof-Blumer and Gardner, *Num. Comm.* Pl. M. viii.), is certainly not, as Wieseler (*loc. cit.* 146) thinks, the Asklepios of Pausanias, but another Hippolytos statue.

[7] Smith and Porcher, *Hist. of Disc. at Cyrene*, p. 103, No. 74; for the discovery, p. 77. Newton, *Guide Graeco-Rom. Sc.* ii. No. 114. *J. H. S.* iv. p. 46 seq. (Wroth) with illustration. The statue was found in the same

preservation, except that the upper part of the mural crown is missing, whence the existence of the crown has hitherto passed unnoticed. The other replica, in Edinburgh, is known to me from illustration and description ;[1] it is slightly modified in drapery and hair. Both figures are inferior productions of the later Roman period. The one in the British Museum certainly does not preserve much of that Polykleitan style which the bronze reproduces so well. Traces of this style are more visible in the body of the marble replica than in the head, for, though the hair is fairly exactly copied, the mouth and the expression appear to be softened down. The drapery answers, fold for fold, to the bronze. The discoverers suggested Aristaios as an interpretation, even without noticing the mural crown, and the existence of the crown only confirms their hypothesis. Aristaios, a divinity closely akin to Asklepios, guardian of Kyrene, institutor of the culture of the silphium, and by its means founder of the power and wealth of the city, son of the eponymous goddess Kyrene, satisfies all the conditions attached to the interpretation of our statue. Aristaios, son of Apollo in Kyrene, was also called son of Paion,[2] an epithet which designates him as a divinity of the healing craft like Asklepios. He was brought up by Cheiron the physician, and in Kyrene, as Pindar's allusion proves,[3] was considered to be a divinity allied in nature not only to Apollo but to Zeus. This may account for the head type of our statue ; the youthful age recalls Apollo, but the strong regal locks correspond to the type of Zeus, which was already fixed in the period to which we have assigned the statue.

We suppose, then, that the original was made for Kyrene by an Argive artist. Afterwards the motive was repeated elsewhere. A late echo of it is given by a bronze bust found in Gaul, a faithful enough though rough reproduction of the youth wearing a mural crown.[4]

Among other works belonging to the more extended circle of the Polykleitan school may be mentioned a beautiful bronze statuette of a youthful athlete in the Louvre ; it is in place here because its motive is allied to that of the Dresden 'boy victor.' The attitude of the feet, the turn and bend of the head, correspond ; the eyes, again, look down towards the outstretched left hand ; but the right arm is raised horizontally ; the youth appears to be holding the fillet in his right hand and letting it glide over the open palm of the left hand. The rendering of form is in its groundwork Polykleitan, though later realistic traits have also crept in. I think it probable that work like this was done by remote followers of Polykleitos in the fourth century, and among them by Kleon of Sikyon. The bronze is apparently a Greek original.[5]

small temple at Kyrene as the well-known 'Kyrene and Libya' relief. Cecil Smith confirms my opinion that remains of a mural crown are to be seen on the head.

[1] Michaelis, *J.H.S.* v. 157. Cecil Smith had the kindness to obtain for me more exact particulars from Dr. Anderson : it seems that the broken portion on the head ' might very well have been a mural crown.' Under the crown is added the rolled fillet which belongs to the Asklepios type. Good illustration in the *Archaeologia Scotica, Transactions of the Society of Antiquaries of Scotland,* vol. iv. Taf. 16, p. 337. The head is more softened down than in the British Museum copy, the curls are longer and fuller at the sides, but the symmetric parting over the forehead is the same. The drapery is stately ; a three-cornered piece falling over is indicated. The head is rather more raised. With these exceptions it agrees with the other replicas.

[2] Pherekydes, frag. 10 (Müller).

[3] Pind. *Pyth.* 9, 63 : θήσονταί τέ νιν ἀθάνατον Ζῆνα καὶ ἁγνὸν Ἀπόλλωνα.

[4] Fröhner, *Coll. Gréau, Bronzes Ant.* Pl. 43, No. 1108.

[5] Formerly in Coll. Pourtalès, then Gréau ; well illustrated by Fröhner, *Coll. Gréau, Bronzes Ant.* Pl. 32, No. 964. Fröhner's assumption that the figure is pouring oil is inconsistent with the position of the hands. For the above motive with the fillet cf. the Nike on a coin of Elis of severe style, Gardner, *Types,* Pl. 3, 42.

VII. *The Basis of the Statue of Xenokles.—The Idolino.*

The third Polykleitos basis at Olympia, which supported the statue of Xenokles, a boy victorious in the wrestling contest, is of great significance, for by its means we are able to connect with Polykleitos, in a more definite way than we could otherwise have done, a series of extant figures.

The basis (Fig. 118)[1] shows both footmarks in complete preservation; round the deep cavity for insertion the outline of the foot itself is distinctly visible. Each foot was 23 cm. long; hence the scale of the figure was the same as that of the 'boy crowning himself.' The attitude was one of repose; the weight of the body was on the right leg; the left leg was slightly advanced and set to one side, with the foot flat on the ground.

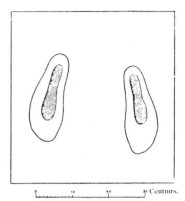

FIG. 118.—Basis of Xenokles in Olympia.

The same motive in which Xenokles was represented was also applied to another Polykleitan figure of a youth at a more advanced stage of adolescence. This is proved by an admirable bronze statuette of the Louvre, which, as is plainly to be seen from external marks,[2] is an undoubted genuine Greek original.[3] (Pl. XIII. and Fig. 119.) This work must belong to the immediate circle of the master's pupils, and have been directly inspired by the master himself, for it manifests his style in all its purity, and the execution is of marvellous perfection.[4] The forms correspond throughout to those of the Doryphoros and Diadumenos: they are strong and virile, and distinct from the forms that pertain to adolescent boyhood. We find here all the characteristics of the Polykleitan body: there is, in addition, an indication of veins on the lower part of the abdomen—a trait which we have frequently met with before, and which already occurs on some copies of the Doryphoros. The head is an excellent piece of work, the hair finely incised in the usual Polykleitan style.[5] The feet are placed flat on the ground side by side, the left foot, free from the weight of the body, being set slightly forward and to one side. One arm again follows the contour of the supporting leg, according to a favourite Polykleitan scheme. The position of the right hand, held with the thumb drawn in, corresponds to that of the Idolino, and is best explained if we imagine it to have held a kylix. The left hand, a little advanced, carried an attribute formed like a staff. The head is bent, and looks towards the supporting side. The bronze can hardly represent an athlete, as in that case the act of pouring libation which seems to be here represented would not be appropriate.[6] Some heroic or divine person whom we have no means of naming must be represented here. It is precisely in the Polykleitan circle that athletic types would be likely to influence even the types of divinities.

---

[1] Drawn by Lübke from my plan of the basis.

[2] Longpérier, *Notice des Bronzes Antiques*, 214, 'Mercure aptère.' The eyes of silver, inserted, the nipples of copper. Height 0·21. Cf. *Jahrb. d. Vereins d. Alterthumsfr. im Rheinl.* Heft 90, p. 53.

[3] For instance, each foot is pierced by a bronze nail which fastens it to the basis, a process only found in earlier Greek originals. The colour of the bronze, too, a splendid dark green, is peculiar to Greek, and more especially to Argive works (cf. 50th *Winckelmannsprogr.* p. 127).

[4] The back is specially fine.   [5] The pubes is less carefully rendered.

[6] I at least know no instance of an athlete pouring libation.

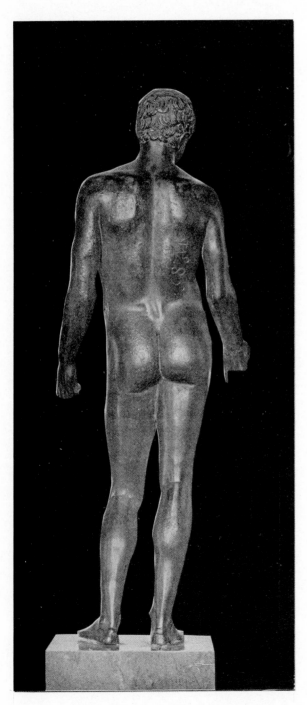

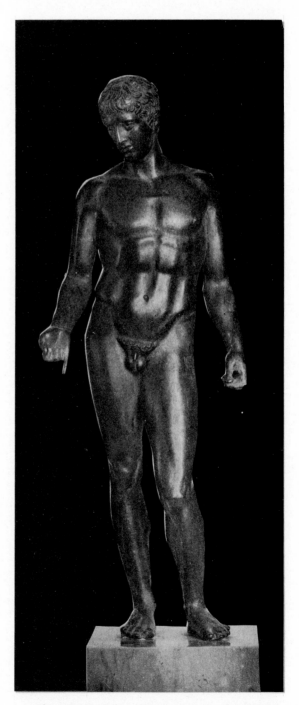

Fig. 119.—Bronze statuette in the Louvre.

*Plate XIII—Bronze Statuette in the Louvre

We must turn from this exquisite Greek bronze to some marble copies of the Roman period. These preserve to us a work of Polykleitos which in all essentials corresponded to the bronze and was probably its prototype. A youth is represented in the same simple attitude of repose seen in the bronze and witnessed to by the Xenokles basis. Both feet are flat on the ground; the left foot, relieved from the weight of the body, is almost parallel to the other, being placed scarcely perceptibly forward and outwards. Both arms are lowered: the right forearm was somewhat advanced, and certainly held an object, the left hung straight down; the head is turned to the side which bears the weight of the body, and is inclined. The forms of

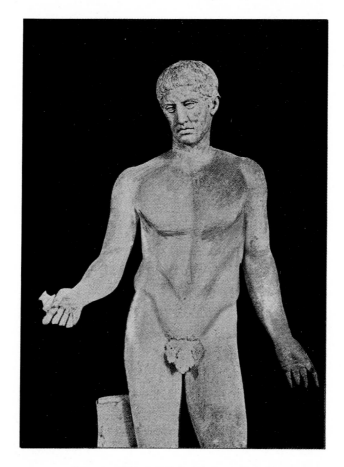

FIG. 120.—Athlete in Galleria delle Statue (Vatican).

the body are less full and powerful than in the Doryphoros and Diadumenos; the time of life chosen for representation lies between these two on the one hand, and the Dresden boy and the 'oil-pourer' on the other: the figure is an ephebe on the threshold of manhood.[1] In scale the statue is less than the Doryphoros and Diadumenos: it is just life-size.

The statue survives with the head in a copy of the Vatican (Fig. 120);[2] the head

[1] The pubes is indicated.
[2] Gall. delle Statue, 251; Clarac, 856, 2168. Mentioned by Michaelis (*Ann. d. Inst.* 1878, 8, G) as a 'variazione' of the Doryphoros; by Helbig (*Bull. d. Inst.* 1864, 30), as a replica of the Doryphoros; [modified view in *Museums*, 186—'betrays unmistakable kinship with the Doryphoros.'—E. S.]

belongs to the statue, but has been broken and put on again, and a small piece of the neck is restored. The head is in bad preservation, chin, nose, and almost all the mouth being new. The right arm is restored from the middle of the upper arm, the left from the middle of the forearm.[1] The left thigh has been incorrectly turned outwards (a piece between it and the trunk being new), and the shin has been wrongly restored. In another replica, without head, in the Vatican, both the feet are ancient.[2] Besides these two the Vatican possesses two replicas which are only torsos.[3] Two more torsos are in the Museo Torlonia and in the Palazzo Colonna respectively.[4] A replica in Naples corresponds perfectly, except that a chlamys is added on the left shoulder. In this case the original type was evidently used for a Roman portrait-statue.[5]

The head alone is preserved to us in good replicas in the Museo Torlonia[6] and in the Hermitage,[7] and in a much-defaced copy in Dresden.[8] With the help of this material we can form a judgment on the lost original. A work of Polykleitos which exists in so many copies must have been famous; probably it only represented an athlete.[9] The bodily forms manifest the manner of Polykleitos in its full purity, with new exquisite distinctions indicative of the period of life. The transitions, especially at the edge of the ribs, are less hard than in the Doryphoros, and the head seems to indicate that we have to do with a somewhat later work of the master. The figure is closely analogous to the Herakles. Small locks of hair fall round the forehead: these are parted in the middle, and are not symmetrical, but are arranged differently on each side.[10] The hair does not yet cover the ears, but just touches their edge, without falling over; it grows low down on the nape of the neck, ending in a curved, not in a straight line. The hair is altogether richer and more individual than in the Doryphoros, but is treated as a whole in the same flat, spare, and closely clinging manner.[11] The forehead projects decidedly at its base, and shows more variety of modelling than in the latter statue; the mouth is slightly open. The bend of the head alone gives it an expression different from that of the Doryphoros, an expression of mild and serious character, with a touch of melancholy, that harmonizes with the tranquil attitude. The old ideal of Argive sculpture, a resigned, self-sustained repose, has in this work become once again a living reality.

[1] Ancient puntelli in the thighs show the position of the arms.

[2] Gall. delle Statue, 392, 'Septimius Severus.' The emperor's head does not belong to the figure. Palm-tree stem as support. Both forearms new; one can still recognize that originally the right was slightly advanced and the left hung down. Both feet are ancient, the soles placed as on the Xenokles basis. Good workmanship.

[3] Sala a croce greca, 590. A wrong protrait-head has been placed on the torso, the whole neck restored, the left thigh incorrectly joined on (piece between restored). Pubes worked over. In the vestibule of the public entrance to the Museum, torso restored as Meleager; head does not belong.

[4] Museo Torlonia, 76. Restored as a Diskophoros; the head is a modern imitation of the Diskophoros of the Vatican. The right forearm to the wrist antique; the left arm with the diskos new. Palazzo Colonna, Matz-Duhn, 16. Head not genuine; torso good; right forearm extended forwards. The puntello is higher than in the first Vatican copy.

[5] Naples, Inv. 6055; Clarac, 925, 2351; Bernouilli, Röm. Ikonogr. ii. 1, p. 172, 15. The Roman portrait-head appears not to be genuine. The feet are restored, but the left leg is ancient nearly to the ankle, which gives the attitude. Bodily forms and pubes are of purely Polykleitan style; the round chlamys on the shoulder is evidently a Roman addition.

[6] Museo Torl. 469.

[7] Guédéonow, 83. Conze, Beiträge, p. 7, note 5. Good copy; only the point of the nose restored. Hair on the top of the head carelessly rendered except at the ends. The lips have incised edges in imitation of bronze. Length of face 182 mm., chin to nose = nose to eyebrow = two eye-lengths (65 mm.); width of mouth 48 mm.

[8] From Rome, lately presented by P. Arndt.

[9] The palm-tree as support on one copy is evidence for this.

[10] The copies match very exactly in the details of the hair.

[11] The pubes is rendered as in the Doryphoros, only the curls are still daintier and richer in detail.

A bronze head from the same villa at Herculaneum (Fig. 121, *a* and *b*)[1] which gave us the beautiful bronze copy of the Doryphoros head by Apollonios so strongly resembles the type we have just been discussing—which we shall call the 'Vatican athlete standing at rest'—and corresponds to it so closely in scale, that one would be tempted to regard it as a copy from the same original, did not small differences, which cannot be due merely to the copyist, bear witness that its original is to be sought for in a distinct though somewhat similar work. The locks falling over the forehead are fuller, and the arrangement is more symmetrical, while the treatment of the hair round the ears, as well as the full plastic rendering of the whole mass, show great similarity to the Dresden boy; on the nape of the neck the hair ends in a straight line. All these are points in which the Herculaneum head differs from the Vatican type. Owing to a lack of skill on the part of the copyist—for the face is slightly askew—the expression is one of intense melancholy, amounting almost to grief and distress. But the forms are essentially the same as in the Vatican type, the forehead again projecting strongly at its base. The original must have been later in date than the Doryphoros.

At this point we may mention two more Roman bronze statuettes. One, representing a Mercury, is in the Museum at Spires;[2] it follows the type of the 'Vatican athlete standing at rest,' except that the head is not bent, but turned straight round to the right. Face and hair are clearly derived from Polykleitan types; a purse is held in Roman fashion in the right hand, a kerykeion in the left. This is not a work based on a Hermes by Polykleitos, it is only another adaptation of a Polykleitan type to a Mercury. The same is true of a Hercules statuette,[3] the head of which, however, has already lost its Polykleitan character, and shows that type of youthful Herakles which sprang from an Attic source and became current at a later period; the body is a repetition of the Polykleitan figure standing at rest; the lowered right hand held the club, the left has the apple.

It is here that we must place the Idolino, the famous bronze statue of Florence,[4] for its motive connects it immediately with the series under consideration. The principal characteristics, the position of the feet, the attitude of the head and arms, are in essence the same, yet important differences are to be observed. The left leg, free from the weight of the figure, is placed much more to the side and outwards than in the Xenokles and kindred Polykleitan works. Again, the way in which the left hand hangs down, so that the arm forms an angle towards the leg, gives to the figure a special individual charm,[5] and is without parallel in any of the works we have assigned to the master himself. In this, as in the position of the legs, expression is given to a rhythmic feeling other than that which we found in the work of Polykleitos: a comparison with the Paris bronze, for instance (Plate XIII.), which is in other respects so similar, will make this clear.

In order to appreciate justly the bodily forms, we must decide the age of the boy. He is at a stage of growth midway between the 'boy crowning himself' and the Dresden boy. The chest is broader and more developed than in the first, sparer than

---

[1] *Inv.* 5610; *Bronzi d'Ercolano*, i. Tav. 53, 54, p. 187; Comparetti de Petra, *Villa Ercol.* 7, 4. The measurements correspond to the St. Petersburg head above. Technique and workmanship are as in the Doryphoros of Apollonios; the eyebrows are incised in the same manner; the two works may be dated about the same time.

[2] (Harster) *Katalog d. Histor. Abt. d. Museums in Speier*, 1888, p. 25.

[3] Known to me only from a cast in Dresden.

[4] Best illustrations in Brunn-Bruckmann, *Denkmäler*, Nos. 274—277. Cf. Kekulé, *Ueber die Bronzestatue des sog. Idolino.*

[5] Kekulé has remarked (p. 8) that this is a trait which, in the Renaissance, Donatello was the first to employ.

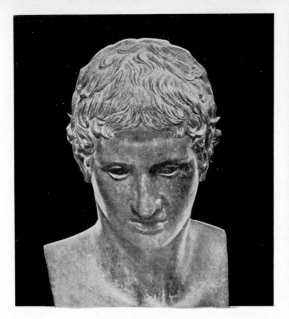

FIG. 121.—Bronze head from Herculaneum. (Naples).

Fig. XLI—The Idolino, Florence, National Museum (See
pp. 238 sqq., 290, 350 sqq.)

in the second. The same result is arrived at from the measurements : the figure is of life-size, like the two others ; the distance between the nipples and the length of the foot come exactly midway between the corresponding measurements of the other two figures of boys.[1] On the whole the forms harmonize with Polykleitan style ; the hips, the navel with the depression of the *linea alba* continued below it, the decided hollow at the side of the gluteus of the leg at rest—all are Polykleitan features. And yet in this instance too there are differences of no slight importance. Above all, the abdomen runs down to a much more acute angle than it ever does in the work of Polykleitos.[2]

Fig. 122.—Head of the Idolino (Mus. Naz., Florence).

The modelling of the Idolino is still under the influence of old Argive tradition, such as would be handed on by the bronze of Ligurio and the Stephanos figure.[3] Again, the Idolino lacks the lifelike and refined surface details such as we find them in Polykleitos ; the serrated muscle, for instance, is not indicated. The forms as a whole are

[1] Distance between the nipples, 215 (in the boy crowning himself, 205 ; in the Dresden boy, 225) ; length of foot, 243 (in other two statues, 233 and 253 respectively).

[2] It is drawn in towards the *membrum,* while in Polykleitan modelling the abdomen is always convex till it reaches the sudden division made by the line of the pudendum or the pubes.

[3] Cf. 50th *Berl. Winckelmannsprogr.* p. 137 *seq.* The Pompeian bronze Apollo has the same form of abdomen, which in other copies is remodelled after the later fashion.

wirier and less full than in the figures of boys by Polykleitos, and more intentional stress is laid on boyish spareness of flesh.

If these facts forbid us to derive the work from the master himself, yet we may look for its source at no great distance from him. This is made very plain by the head (Fig. 122), which bears the most unmistakable marks of the circle of Polykleitos—more particularly of the period just preceding the Diadumenos. We see the customary skull, elongated and angular, the characteristic hair, inclining to straightness, the various layers of short locks arranged one over another on the upper part of the head, the symmetric parting of the small pointed strands over the forehead, the drawing of the hair on the nape of the neck as in the Doryphoros and elsewhere in Polykleitos, the position and shape of the narrow ear with its long lobe attached to the cheek, the same shape of nose and flat nostrils—finally, the wonderful limpid purity and tranquillity, so proper to Polykleitos. The distinction which marks off this head from those assignable to the master consists chiefly, as it does in the body, in a more abstract treatment, in a still more restrained and flat rendering of form.

The Idolino is, from technique and execution, evidently a Greek original; only the round, moulded basis on which it stands must be of Roman date, since that sort of basis was not given to bronze statues at an earlier period. It is still plainly to be seen that the feet are hollow below, therefore they were formerly fastened with melted lead to a stone basis in the usual Greek fashion. Although the execution is of a kind characteristic of original work, yet we miss the degree of refinement which we have a right to expect in a master of the first rank. Our studies have shown that this statue cannot be by Polykleitos himself, but at most by an artist of his circle, who, however, seems to have followed a path of his own.[1] We may venture to remember in this connexion that side by side with Polykleitos the artist Patrokles, probably his younger brother, worked and taught (cf. p. 226); we conjectured that he had attained a certain independence of action within the general tendencies of style prescribed by Polykleitos. All that we can, however, positively assert about the Idolino is that it belongs approximately to the period of the Doryphoros, and is the later rather than the earlier of the two.

The inner surface of the outstretched right hand is left rough, evidently because some object lay upon it; the fingers are in the same position[2] as in the Paris bronze,[3] a position which can only be satisfactorily explained by restoring the statue with a kylix in this hand. The left hand is smooth inside, and was clearly empty. The boy was therefore represented pouring a libation. Now this does not fit in with the current interpretation of the statue as a victorious athlete, since, as we noticed above, the motive never, so far as we know, occurs in statues of athletes. If not an athlete, then what is the nature of the boy represented here? For although boys serve the libation—in fact, this is one of their special functions—yet I know of no single instance in all ancient art of a mortal boy performing the ritual act of pouring it.[4] In the same way they do not sacrifice, but only assist the celebrant. If then a boy be represented pouring a libation, he cannot be a mortal, he must be divine. Thus the youthful river god on coins of Selinos pours a libation over an altar. We have naturally no means of naming the god or daemon represented

---

[1] Cf. my remarks in *Jahrb. d. Ver. v. Alterthumsfr. im Rheinl.* Heft 90, p. 53.

[2] They are not in the slightest bent, as Kekulé (*loc. cit.*) wrongly assumes.

[3] Cf. the bronze published by me in *Bonner Jahrb.* Heft 90, Taf. ii. and *ibid.* p. 53.

[4] The material has been collected in Stephani's treatise on representations of libation in *Compte Rendu,* 1873. Cf. also Fritze, *de libatione veterum Graecorum, Berliner Dissert.* 1893.

in our statue.   That he should appear in the image of boy-victor is a genuine Argive trait.

An entirely different view to the one put forward here concerning the style and origin of the statue is held by Kekulé,[1] who classes it with the Munich Oil-pourer and the standing Diskobolos, and pretends to detect in it the same Myronian qualities which caused Brunn to bring the other two statues into connexion with Myron.   But there is no trace in the Idolino of just those very characteristics which Brunn found in the two Attic statues.   The concentration of the whole attention on one act which governs by its own inner necessity every movement of the body, while beautifully illustrated in the Oil-pourer and Diskos-bearer,[2] is entirely absent from the Idolino. His attitude is quite independent of his act—the libation ; he might hold any other object instead of a kylix in his right hand, and the effect of the whole would be unaltered.   The principal features of the Idolino motive were fixed creations long before they were used for a boy making libation.   We have seen that the motive was current in the cycle of Polykleitos ; we may now add that it was developed directly from the old Argive canon, and differs from it only in one important point—namely, in the reversal of the sides.   The motives of the two Attic statues, on the other hand, are new creations, invented for the actions they represent.   In the case of Argos the form is ready to hand, and significant content is given to it at the will of the artist ; in the case of Attica the significant content brings the form into being.[3]

A marble statue of the Palazzo Barberini in Rome (placed unfavourably high)[4] must be a copy of an original similar to the Idolino and belonging to the same artistic circle ; in fact, it might almost be a copy of the Idolino itself.   The left foot is here placed rather more back, so that the heel is raised ; the forms of the body are harder and more restrained ; the head is very similar.   The arms, so far as they are preserved, correspond.

VIII. *The Basis of the Statue of Aristion.—The later Polykleitan School.—The Beneventum Head.*

There is also evidence that the old canonical position of the feet employed by Hagelaidas and the Argive school[5] was used in the cycle of Polykleitos : this is proved by the basis in Olympia which once supported the Aristion, a work of the younger Polykleitos (cf. p. 224, and Fig. 123).[6]   The footmarks are here intact,[7] and show that the figure stood on the left foot, while the right was placed flat on the ground to

---

[1] *loc. cit.* p. 10.

[2] And also *e.g.* in the boy pulling out a thorn, which in an early essay I accordingly referred to Myron (*Der Dornauszieher und der Knabe mit der Gans*, 1875, p. 79). Kekulé (*Arch. Ztg.* 1883, p. 238, note 26) remarks on this point : 'It is quite impossible to refer to Myron all ancient works of art which represent a figure absorbed in a momentary occupation.'   Doubtless correct, but the boy pulling out a thorn is at least one of the works in which the absorption in one act makes the whole motive, while the Idolino is not.   Again, the boy pulling out a thorn belongs to Myron's period, the Idolino is later.

[3] It is still more difficult to follow Kekulé in his analysis of the forms of the Idolino.   From what has been said in a previous chapter on Myronian form, it will be seen that within the fifth century there could hardly be found a sharper contrast than between the Diskobolos and other Myronian works on the one hand, and the Idolino on the other.

[4] Matz-Duhn, 1111.   Right arm and left forearm restored ; palm-stem beside right leg.

[5] Cf. pp. 52 *sqq.*, 190 *sqq.*

[6] Drawing by Lübke from my plan.   The drawing in *Arch. Ztg.* 1879, 207, is inexact.

[7] Each foot was 29 cm. long.

288 POLYKLEITOS

the side.[1] This is the scheme of the old Argive school, already so fully discussed. To understand exactly how it was used by artists of the Polykleitan circle, we must study existing statues, and especially a Hermes type which is repeated frequently and in many variants.

The copy in Lansdowne House is at once the best preserved and reproduces most accurately the Polykleitan style (Fig. 124).[2] The god stands as did the Aristion by Polykleitos the younger : the right arm hangs simply down, as in the statues from

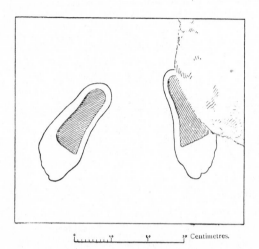

the school of Hagelaidas—even the hand corresponding exactly to that of the so-called Stephanos athlete ; the left forearm is stretched forward horizontally holding an object, doubtless a kerykeion ; the left shoulder is lowered, and the head turned to the left. On the left shoulder lies a chlamys arranged with great refinement in fine natural folds. There are no wings either on head or feet. We know from the figure of Pan how carefully the Polykleitan school when representing divinities suppresses all peculiarities not purely human. Chlamys and kerykeion were enough to characterize the god. The right hand was empty.

FIG. 123.—Basis of Aristion in Olympia.

The head repeats a Polykleitan type similar to the Dresden boy and the Petworth Oil-pourer. The hair is parted symmetrically in the middle ; the forehead projects decidedly at the base as in the 'Vatican athlete standing at rest,' to whom the bodily forms are also analogous.

This figure can certainly not be referred to the elder Polykleitos. The forms of the body are lacking in fulness and vigour ; they are spare and dry to a greater degree than is usual in the works of Polykleitos, and thus approach more nearly to the manner of the Idolino. We found in the modelling of the latter a survival of old Argive tradition. The same tradition has evidently influenced the attitude and carriage of this figure. The rhythm of the composition as a whole corresponds to the old Argive canon, and is foreign to the manner of Polykleitos, who always knows how to round off his work so as to produce a more harmonious and satisfying impression. But the figure was undoubtedly, as we see, especially from the head,[3] made under the immediate influence of Polykleitos, to whose later works it presents marked affinities, so that it is among the younger members of his circle that we must look for the artist. We suggested the name of Patrokles in connexion with the Idolino ; here we might think of the sons of Patrokles, one of whom, Polykleitos the younger, as the Aristion basis proves, actually employed the motive we are at present discussing. His brother and teacher, Naukydes, was the author of a *Mercurius*, according to Pliny. We may hazard the conjecture that this his most famous work was the original of our statue.

---

[1] The statue of the boxer Eukles by Naukydes (Löwy, *I. G. B.* 86) stood in a similar attitude. The foot was about 33 cm. long, hence the figure was rather over life-size.

[2] Drawn from a photograph ; badly reproduced in Clarac, 946, 2436 *A* ; described by Michaelis, *Anc. Sculpt.* p. 446, 35. Well preserved. No restorations, except possibly the left hand ; head unbroken. Distance between the nipples 0·23 ; neck-hollow to navel 0·365, to pubes 0·53 ; workmanship ordinary.

[3] Cf. the forehead, which is modelled throughout.

We thus obtain the interesting and not improbable result that Argive artists, most likely Patrokles and his sons, though working side by side with Polykleitos and dominated in many ways by his influence, did not cease for all that to foster old Argive traditions.

There is a replica (headless) of the Lansdowne Hermes in Berlin;[1] the wiry spareness of the forms is here characteristically reproduced. Wings are added to the feet. In a third replica in the Palazzo Pitti[2] the drapery has ceased to be an exact copy, while the head, which seems to belong to the statue although the neck is restored, has been entirely transformed in character; it is adorned with wings, and shows only feeble remains of Polykleitan modelling. The head is still more altered in a second Berlin statue,[3] which reproduces the drapery in a much simplified form without interest or beauty. The formation of the body in these two statues is somewhat softer and feebler, but otherwise not essentially different. Another replica from Aegion,[4] an inferior work of Roman period, retains the characteristic spare body, and has at least an echo of Polykleitan manner in the head; moreover, the wings are absent; but the drapery is completely altered, being wound round the forearm in the familiar later fashion. A statue in Naples,[5] with a head foreign to it, corresponds closely with the figure from Aegion; the forms of the body are characteristic notwithstanding the alteration in the drapery, and are faithfully copied from the original. The same is true of a copy in Palazzo Colonna, the head of which is also foreign.[6]

Finally, the figure was completely transformed to suit coarse Graeco-Roman taste; it appears with full realistic muscles,

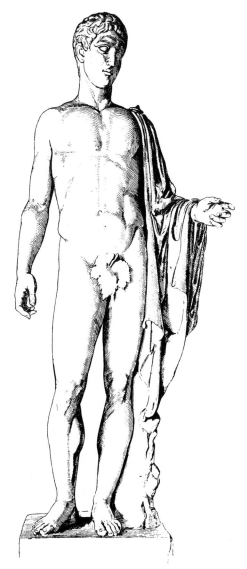

FIG. 124.—Hermes in Lansdowne House.

while the attitude became more animated and more nearly allied to the Lysippian, through the altered position of the right foot, which was now placed more to the side. The statue by Antiphanes of Paros in Berlin[7] and the 'Mercure Richelieu'

---

[1] *Skulpt.* 196. Part of the kerykeion lying on the arm is ancient.

[2] Dütschke, ii. p. 9, No. 16. Cast in Dresden. The right leg is wrongly restored as drawn back. The end of the kerykeion on the left arm seems to be old.   [3] *Skulpt.* 199. Wings on the feet.

[4] Central Mus., Athens, Kabbadias, *Cat.* No. 241; *Ath. Mitth.* iii. Taf. 5. The illustration is inexact, especially in the face and hair. Remains of kerykeion in the left hand.

[5] *Inv.* 6073; Clarac, 942, 2411 (wrongly given without pubes).

[6] Head of Trajan put on in a wrong attitude. Neck restored.

[7] *Skulpt.* 200. Found in Melos; head new.

in the Louvre[1] are instances of this transformation of an original whose principal features however are still evident through all the changes. The same hardly holds true of a Roman statue from Atalanti,[2] with the turn of the head reversed ; the statue has thus acquired quite a Lysippian air ; moreover, the head is modelled on Lysippian prototypes. Thus the original ended by becoming entirely transformed : instead of charmed repose, we now have impatient restless energy.

We have spoken of these variants in the order of their deviation from the original, but this is not the chronological order. The Atalanti statue was probably derived from an original of the circle of Lysippos himself—an original which really represented an attempt to modernize an old type. From this Lysippian original later and inferior artists borrowed separate details, such as the arrangement of the chlamys, and combined them with the bodily forms and attitude of the old original ; at any rate we may imagine the different variants to have arisen in some such way.

At this point may be cited some few Hermes heads which manifest Polykleitan character in a greater or less degree (cf. p. 231). The familiar Lansdowne head with the petasos[3] is a sketchy, flat, incorrect piece of work, behind which however seems to lurk the same original that is reproduced in the Lansdowne statue. A head in St. Petersburg,[4] showing holes for the insertion of wings, is a more faithful mirror of Polykleitan style ; there is no definite known original for this work ; the artist satisfied himself with a general adherence to Polykleitan types, and added the head-wings, which are quite inappropriate. Besides these, I know of two heads of less than life-size, Polykleitan in type and related to the Lansdowne statue.[5] They have small antique wings. There are two more, also less than life-size, wearing the round petasos, and in style not far removed from Polykleitos.[6]

We close here the series of works immediately connected with Polykleitos. Of more distantly related creations we may now discuss at least the most important.

And first the bronze figure of the 'Praying Youth' from Carinthia.[7] In my view this is not a Greek original dedicated by Romans of a later period, but, to judge by technical indications,[8] a Roman work of the same period as the inscription.[9] It seems to be a free imitation of an Argive statue of a victor. The style is not Polykleitan ; the hard and spare forms are more in the manner of the Idolino, i.e. they point to Patrokles as the artist.

On the other hand, a bronze head from Beneventum in the Louvre (Plate XIV.) is a splendid Greek original, and belongs to a statue of a victorious athlete which was

---

[1] Fröhner, *Notice*, 177 ; Clarac, 316, 1542 ; photo. édit. Giraudon, 1196. Neck new, head genuine.

[2] Central Mus., Athens, Kabbadias, No. 240 ; *Gazette Arch.* ii. Taf. 22, 23 ; Körte, *Ath. Mitth.* iii. p. 98, B. Photos of the bust at German Institute in Athens.

[3] Michaelis, *Anc. Sculp. in Gr. Brit.* p. 467, 88 ; Müller-Wieseler, *D. a. K.* ii. 304.

[4] Guédéonow, No. 179 ; Treu, *Arch. Anz.* 1889, p. 57, wrongly ascribed to Polykleitos.

[5] (*a*) In the Louvre, Salle des Caryatides, No. 1487 ; Fröhner, *Notice*, 197 ; photo. édit. Giraudon, 1273. Length of face 14 cm. Neck new. Turn to the left. Bad work. (*b*) Vatican, *Sala Geografica:* similar.

[6] (*a*) Set on an insignificant torso, Museo Chiaramonti, 589. Turned slightly to the right. Polykleitan manner evident in the hair. Round petasos as on the Lansdowne head. (*b*) Palermo. Placed on a torso to which it does not belong ; height 12 cm. ; sketchy work.

[7] R. v. Schneider, *Die Erzstatue vom Helenenberge*, Wien 1893 (*Jahrb. d. Samml. d. Oesterr. Kaiserh.* Bd. xv.)

[8] The metal has the yellowish colour of the good Gallo-Roman bronzes of the first century A.D. ; the casting very thick, no fine chiselling. The eyes are not inserted, as in all large Greek bronzes, but cast with the head ; all these are indications of non-Greek origin.

[9] Inscription was originally only lightly cut ; it was worked over in the sixteenth century.

taken from Greece.[1]   A wreath made of two sprays is worn in the hair: as these appear to be *kotinos* twigs, the statue probably once stood in Olympia.[2]   The essential elements in the structure of the face, which projects towards the middle and recedes in large surfaces to the sides, the mouth and nose with its oblique slope and flat nostrils, are characteristically Polykleitan; yet there is at the same time something alien to Polykleitos and akin to Pheidias and the Lemnia in the infinite charm of this head.   The hair is at the stage of the Diadumenos.   A peculiarity is the *asymmetria* of the locks of hair over the middle of the forehead; a similar treatment is to be seen in the Polykleitan Pan; only at the sides does the arrangement become symmetrical.   Clearly the artist, while deriving his inspiration from Polykleitos, was open to Attic influence.

The no less magnificent bronze head of a boy wearing the victor's fillet in Munich is a kindred work, also a Greek original.[3]   Here too the face, especially the nose and mouth, and the shape of the head, are closely analogous to the works of Polykleitos,[4] but at the same time we can trace, although less definitely, a certain foreign element probably due to Attic influence.   A marble head in the Vatican, the production of an inferior copyist, from its great similarity must, I think, be derived either from the Munich head or from an analogous work by the same artist.[5]   A basalt statue of a boy from the Palatine[6] shows the same analogy in the head; the body is still under the influence of the old Argive canon, but a slight turn of the head to the right (the side free from the weight of the figure), and a forward movement of the right shoulder, give a somewhat easier rhythm to the composition.   The master to whose hand these works are due is interesting as being nearly related to the Argive school, without however belonging to it.

In conclusion, we must mention a third bronze head, again an admirable original work—in Naples[7]—a boy wearing a wreath or a fillet in his curly hair, and therefore probably a victor.   Face, mouth, nose, forehead, and shape of head again show clear marks of Polykleitan influence; but the hair and the expression are different.   The same holds true of a marble head in Berlin.[8]

Thus the influence of Polykleitos spread to wider circles.   In his own immediate surroundings, however, he held almost absolute sway.   Although we have succeeded in separating to a certain extent the activity of master and pupils, we have found in this

[1] Cf. p. 18, note 1.   Fröhner obtained the head from Beneventum.   Casts are to be had.   The original shows that it was part of a statue.   The technique is Greek, but the chiselling not very detailed: well published in Brunn-Bruckmann, *Denkmäler*; cf. *Monum. et Mémoires*, fondation Piot. Pl. 10, 11, also good vignette in Kalkmann, *Prop. des Gesichts*, p. 27.   [2] Remains of small leaves in front.

[3] Glypt. 302; Friederichs-Wolters, 216.   Brunn supposes it a later casting, but the technique shows that the work is a Greek original.

[4] Polykleitan character has been recognized by Flasch (*Philologenvers*. Innsbruck, p. 162) and by Brunn (*Glypt.* 5th ed.; *Bayr. Sitzungsber.* 1892, p. 658).   Kekulé sees here a further development of the style of the Olympia sculptures and of the Spinario (*Arch. Ztg.* 1883, p. 246).   I cannot see any analogy to these works, which bear the impress of a totally different individuality.

[5] Museo Chiaramonti, 475.   The scale seems to be about the same.   The hair differs slightly, the ear being left freer.

[6] Now in the *Terme*.   Photo in German Institute at Rome.   Weight of the figure on left leg.   The right hand hung down, the left held something shaped like a staff, the mark of which is visible on the breast.   Twig in hair, hence a copy of a victor's statue.

[7] Naples, *Inv.* 5633; *Bronzi d'Ercol.* i. 73, 74; Rayet, *Monum. de l'Art Antique*, ii. 67; Comparetti de Petra, *Villa Ercol.* xi. 1.   The line of the wreath or fillet is quite visible.   The technique seems to show that the work is a Greek original.   The head has no connexion whatsoever with the 'Dancers' of Herculaneum, which are only copies.

[8] *Skulpt.* 479, where it is wrongly described as a replica of the Naples head discussed above.

inner group of workers comparatively little personal individuality.   Only Patrokles
and his kin seem to have shown some independence, although still in a very limited
degree.   In the circle of Pheidias we found much greater originality.   But the severity
of school tradition has ever been one of the essential conditions under which Argive art
developed ; as indeed there was more that was capable of being learned in the Argive
school than in the school of Pheidias.   Polykleitos did not excel in invention or wealth
of meaning ; in fact, he found his inspiration for a whole series of statues, as we have
seen, in foreign Attic creations, such as the Diadumenos of Pheidias, the Oil-pourer
of Lykios, the Amazon and the Diomede of Kresilas.

      We, like the ancients, know no creations of Polykleitos except youthful, beardless
figures.   This springtime of life is chosen for divinities as well as for human beings
whenever it is at all congruous—as in the case of Dionysos, Hermes, Ares, Herakles,
Pan ; the artist seems to have represented the Dioskouroi as boys playing with
knuckle-bones.[1]   But within these limits perhaps no artist has gone so far in representing the more delicate shades of distinction between boyhood and adolescence.
Nor is his choice of motives nearly so uniform as has hitherto been believed.

      Again, within the series of works of the artist himself we found a development
leading gradually from the Doryphoros to the Diadumenos.   It is true that the
harmony of reserve and repose characterizes all his creations.   Yet the Doryphoros,
the Amazon, and kindred statues have more freshness and energy, combined with
reasonable restraint, while the later works are penetrated by a softer spirit and a
greater degree of sentiment.   In this second period the master even sometimes
abandons the walking motive for the standing position of complete repose—a change
for which Attic influence is no doubt partly responsible.

      We have already had occasion to verify many instances of the influence of
Polykleitos on later art, and to trace many survivals of his style.   But the most
important researches in this part of the subject are still to come.

      [1] That the *pueri astragalizontes*, which would be inexplicable as a *genre* group by Polykleitos, represent
the Dioskouroi seems probable from the Greek gem published in Roscher's *Lexikon*, i. 1174, even if the gem is not
dependent on the work of Polykleitos.

Fig. XLII—Hera, Head Attributed to Polykleitos, Athens,

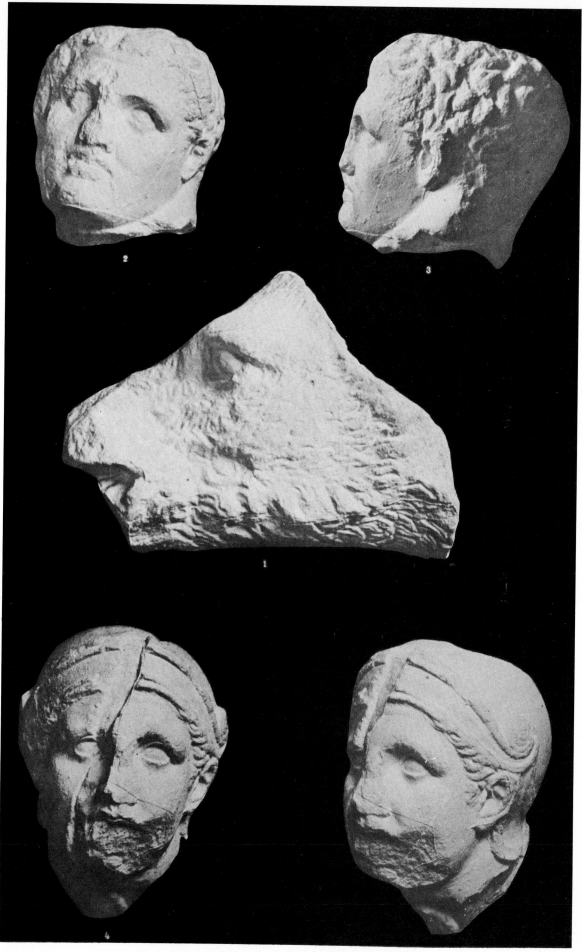

Fig. XLIII—Heads from the Pediment Sculptures of the
Temple of Athena Alea at Tegea, Attributed to
Skopas, Athens, National Museum (Photo of
casts)

Fig. XLIV—Meleager with Boar's Head and Dog, Copy
after Skopas, Rome, Vatican Museum (See p. 184)

SKOPAS PRAXITELES EUPHRANOR

THE succeeding ages of antiquity subsisted off the immense achievements of the art of the fifth century. Our increasing knowledge points with ever-growing certainty to the conclusion that the greater number of the most important types, both of men and of gods, had already been elaborated in the fifth century. In our previous inquiries we have been able to give some proofs of this, but it is in the fourth century more particularly that the influence of the preceding period may be traced for a long time more clearly than is generally supposed, even as we can trace the current and the colour of a mighty river long after it has mingled with other waters.

The Eirene of Kephisodotos affords a clear and well-known instance of this fact. This work by no means marks a normal transition between the style of two epochs; nor is Kephisodotos, as he is generally said to be, a 'forerunner' of the great fourth-century masters; he is one of them himself, and may very well have been the elder brother—though scarcely the father—of Praxiteles. The few extant dates relating to him belong to a period when Praxiteles must already have been at work,[1] and there is nothing to justify the assumption that these dates coincide with the close of the career of Kephisodotos; the contrary is far more likely.[2] A serious difficulty in the commonly received genealogy of the three successive generations—Praxiteles I., Kephisodotos, Praxiteles II.—is caused by the gap of half a century which inter-

---

[1] The Eirene of Kephisodotos should probably be dated after 375 to correspond with the institution of the annual offering to Eirene consequent on the victories of Timotheos (Isokr. xv. 109 ; Corn. Nepos, *Timoth.* 2 ; cf. Wachsmuth, *Stadt Athen,* i. 585, ii. 433 ; Curtius, *Stadtgesch. v. Athen,* p. 206 ; Wolters in *Jahrb. d. Inst.* 1893, p. 178). The statue was vowed in 374, and executed soon after, *i.e.* probably in 371—370, on the occasion of the festal Peace Congress in Athens (Von Stern, *Gesch. d. spartan. u. theban. Hegemonie,* p. 149). The date thus found would tally with that assigned by Pliny to Kephisodotos (Ol. 102). The large group in the *temenos* of Zeus Soter in Megalopolis seems from the late character of the architecture to have been a work of the younger Kephisodotos (Dörpfeld in *Ath. Mitth.* 1893, 218). On the other hand, the groups of Praxiteles in Mantineia fall soon after the rebuilding of the town (370). Pliny's date for Praxiteles (Ol. 104) is probably fixed by the battle of Mantineia (B.C. 362) (cf. Löwy, *Unters. z. Künstler Gesch.* p. 64).

[2] Kephisodotos's sister was the first wife of Phokion. Kephisodotos was therefore a contemporary of Phokion and of Praxiteles. He too made a 'Hermes with the child Dionysos.'

venes between the dates of the elder Praxiteles (cf. *supra*, p. 102) and those of the two younger artists. Probably an intermediate member of the family—father of the two younger artists—has been lost to tradition.

The Eirene of Kephisodotos,[1] though belonging to the years B.C. 375—370, follows in the treatment of the drapery the manner which was in fashion some sixty years earlier : it goes directly back to Pheidias, and forms a strong contrast to the whole intervening development, *i.e.* to the style of drapery that obtained in the time of the Peloponnesian War, such as we see it in the 'Caryatids' of the Erechtheion, the Nike temple, and the works of Alkamenes, Agorakritos, and Kallimachos ; it abandons the thin, clinging, semi-transparent tissues, and turns to the earlier forms ; once more the folds fall perpendicularly from the knee of the 'free' leg, and this leg is represented, not in the 'walking attitude,' but only, as in the Parthenos, set slightly to the side and very slightly drawn back. On the other hand, the infant Ploutos[2] is so like the little Dionysos by Praxiteles, and the whole motive and spirit of the group so akin to Praxitelean works, that we at once feel that we are no longer on the threshold of the new epoch, but completely within it, and that the artist is intentionally striving after an earlier style. In a monument of such political import as the Eirene this was probably not a mere accident. The statue was set up in the early years of the new maritime confederacy which (so the Athenians hoped) was to revive the ancient glories of their city. Thus the sculptor in his image of Eirene—of the Peace for which the naval alliance was to be the pledge—reverted to the style of the brilliant period of the old confederacy under Perikles.

I. *Skopas.—Lansdowne Herakles.—Hermes from the Palatine.—Statues with Foot raised.—Ares Ludovisi.—The Meleager.—Athena.*

The influence of the Argive artists of the fifth century upon the Attic artists of the fourth was especially strong. I shall first let the monuments tell their own tale.

The beautiful and excellently preserved Herakles in Lansdowne House (Fig. 125)[3] reproduces without a doubt an important original of the fourth century. The type of head is thoroughly Attic ; its predecessors are the Munich 'oil-pourer' (Lykios ? p. 289), the standing Diskobolos (Alkamenes ? pp. 90 and 260), and the Florence athlete (p. 26), while closely akin to it are the youth on the relief from the Ilissos,[4] two bronze heads from Herculaneum,[5] and other analogous works.[6] Now it is evident that these heads, and that of the Lansdowne statue more especially, form the basis for that type of Herakles which has been assigned to Skopas on good grounds,[7] and which in reality is only the earlier type slightly intensified by an admixture of pathos. The motive

[1] Friederichs-Wolters, 1210, 1211 ; Kabbadias, ἐθν. μουσ. 175. A replica of the Eirene, restored as Niobe, in the Mus. Torlonia, 290 ; a good replica of the child Ploutos in Dresden, head antique.

[2] On the Athens and Dresden copies the head survives, and strongly resembles the child Dionysos of Olympia, as do the body and the drapery. The little head from Ikaria is also very similar (*Americ. Journ. of Arch.* 1889, p. 474).

[3] *Spec. of Anc. Sc.* i. 40 ; Clarac, 788, 1973 ; Michaelis, *Anc. Sculpt.* p. 451, 61 ; Kalkmann, *Prop. d. Gesichts*, p. 61. From Hadrian's villa. Very well preserved. A replica of the torso among the restored statues of the Palazzo Massimi alle colonne. Palazzo Pitti, Dütschke, 35, is a later modification, and so is the bronze Colossus of the Vatican, Roscher's *Lex.* i. 2179.

[4] Kabbadias, ἐθν. μουσ. No. 869 ; Wolters in *Ath. Mitth.* xviii. p. 6 ; Von Sybel, *Weltgeschichte d. Kunst*, Fig. 204 ; *Zeitschr. für bild. Kunst*, N. F. ii. 293.

[5] (a) Comparetti de Petra, *Villa Ercol.* Tav. vii. 3 ; Friederichs-Wolters, 1302. (b) Comparetti de Petra, *loc. cit.* Tav. x. 2. Probably a youthful Herakles with twisted fillet, olive-leaves, and fruit ; looking to the left like the Lansdowne Herakles. (a) is somewhat more severe in the hair, and goes back to an older original.

[6] *e.g.* A good head of an athlete in the Museum of the Peiraieus ; one in the Terme Museum, Rome (*Röm. Mitth.* 1891, p. 304, 2, etc.)　　　　[7] By B. Gräf, *Röm. Mitth.* 1889, p. 199 *seq.*

of the Lansdowne statue is also genuinely Attic in the freedom and boldness of its attitude, with the left leg placed flat on the ground to one side, and the head turned in

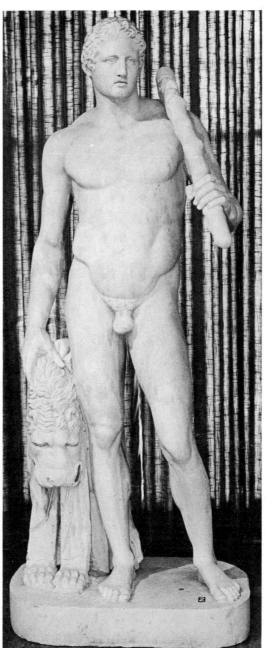

FIG. 125.—Herakles in Lansdowne House.[1]

Fig. XLIVa — Lansdowne Herakles, Malibu, California, J. Paul Getty Museum

the same direction as the free leg. The right arm hangs down, and the left forearm is extended, carrying some object. In this form the motive is purely Attic, and was

[1] [From the cast in Dresden. A good illustration from a photograph of the original is given by Kalkmann, *Prop. des Gesichts*, p. 61.—E. S.]

Q Q

elaborated in the fifth century. Kresilas altered it by the introduction of the walking motive, and by giving a more energetic turn to the head, and used it for his Diomede. Later, Polykleitos followed in his steps.

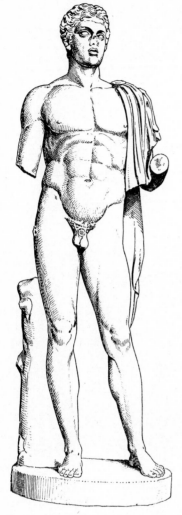

As an example of the original Attic composition I may cite the interesting statue of a young hero (Fig. 126),[1] which must belong approximately to 440 B.C. The motive is precisely that of the Lansdowne Herakles. A chlamys, falling in firm vigorous folds, is flung over the hero's left shoulder. The stylistic forms of the beautiful lifelike body are obviously derived from the Apollo of the Omphalos (Kalamis? p. 81), even to so small a detail as the little furrow above the navel. The head also is connected with the series, which I have already assigned (p. 81 *seq.*) to the school of Kalamis, but the treatment is somewhat freer: the hair has a strongly plastic quality, the eyes are heavy-lidded, the mouth full and open, resembling in expression and shape the mouth of the Herakles in Fig. 32. We therefore have here another work of that school of Kalamis which flourished alongside that of Pheidias. It was from statues of this type that the motive of the Lansdowne Herakles was developed.

Far simpler had been the conception of Herakles in the Pheidian circle, to judge from a copy of a Herakles which so closely resembles the Farnese Diadumenos (p. 244) in the bodily forms, in attitude, and in bearing that it can only be ascribed to Pheidias, or to an artist influenced by him.[2] The hero, with his lion-skin over his head, his left foot at ease and placed with full sole to one side, looks straight out to the right to the side of the supporting leg.

FIG. 126.—Heroic statue (British Museum).

Though the Lansdowne Herakles is closely connected in conception with all this Attic work, it differs from it in the bodily forms, which seem influenced much rather by Polykleitan models[3]

[1] Copy in Brit. Mus., Newton, *Guide Graeco-Rom. Sc.* i. No. 134, from the Pal. Farnese; Fig. 126 drawn from a photograph. Head broken but genuine, the lower part of legs modern, but the position is shown by what remains. Puntello for the lowered right arm. A still better copy of the torso in the Louvre (photo. Giraudon, 1289). A replica of the head in the Lateran, No. 891, broken under the chin, wrongly turned to the right. Both copies of the head have swollen ears; cf. the Riccardi bust, Fig. 66, and the Diomede, in which the chlamys may also be compared.

[2] Statue under life-size in cortile of Pal. Borghese (Matz-Duhn, 90; Winckelmann, *Mon. Ined.* 78). Head unbroken, upper half restored. Phot. in German Inst. at Rome.—Similar statue in Museo Lapidario of Vatican, No. 132. Attic-Pheidian of a rather severer type; except for the bent head, the motive is the same as in the Borghese statue.—A statue of Herakles in the Louvre corresponds so closely to the Ares Borghese that it must be either a later Roman copy or an adaptation from the workshop of Alkamenes of the Ares to the Herakles type. The head does not belong to the statue, which is identified as a Herakles by the lion-skin on the trunk, which is ancient (see D'Escamps, *Marbres Campana*, Pl. 40; *Zeitschr. f. bild. Kunst*, N.F. ii. p. 24, where Von Sybel wrongly considers the head to be authentic, and connects it with Skopas).

[3] Cf. also Kalkmann, *Prop. d. Gesichts*, p. 60, note 3.

(as a comparison with the Diadumenos and the Doryphoros clearly shows): the undulations of surface are, it is true, softer and rounder, but the forms of breast, stomach, navel, etc., are those characteristic of Polykleitan figures.

We have already become acquainted (p. 248, n. 4) with a direct predecessor of the Lansdowne Herakles, in a terminal statue of the Museo Boncompagni-Ludovisi, and a torso at Dresden, in which we likewise detected a Polykleitan structure of body combined with an older, Attic type of head, approximating in character to Kresilas. The motive—the shouldering of the club—is the same, but the position of the arms is reversed. It is obviously more natural to shoulder the club with the right hand, but the position of the arms in the Lansdowne statue is more rhythmical, and moreover follows the Polykleitan model—the Doryphoros—more closely.

The Lansdowne Herakles does not stand alone. Among analogous works may be cited a torso from the Villa Borghese,[1] representing—as the long fillet-ends on the shoulder prove—either a Herakles or a victorious athlete, and another torso in the Museo Torlonia.[2] Of still greater interest is a splendid bronze Herakles in the Jacobsen collection ; it repeats the motive of the Lansdowne figure, except that the left arm holds the bow and arrow instead of the club ;[3] the head shows the same fourth-century Attic type, and the body is again Polykleitan in its forms. Nor must we forget another beautiful bronze Herakles from Dalmatia, now in Vienna,[4] carrying the club on the right shoulder ; here again the slightly drooping head is thoroughly Attic, and recalls the Florentine athlete (p. 261), while the body shows the influence of Polykleitos. This same combination appears in a superb bronze statuette of Zeus at Munich, while in a bronze Zeus in the British Museum (Fig. 127)[5] the Polykleitan influence extends from the bodily forms to the whole attitude, which is closely copied from the Doryphoros ; the head, however, with the short locks brushed up from the forehead, is the exact counterpart of the Lansdowne Herakles, thoroughly Attic in its Skopasio-Praxitelean character. Further, a noble bronze statuette of Zeus in Munich[6] manifests, although less clearly, Polykleitan influence in the body, combined with an Attic position of the legs, and an Attic type of head.

Fig. 127.—Statuette of Zeus (British Museum).

The Lansdowne Herakles, owing to likeness of the head to the later Skopasian

---

[1] Torso in front porch of the villa ; the forms allied to the Doryphoros, but rounder ; veins on the abdomen. The left leg was somewhat advanced as in the Lansdowne statue, and the head was turned to the left. Good workmanship.

[2] Museo Torlonia, 5 ; allied to the Doryphoros, but rounder ; head turned to the left.

[3] Ny Carlsberg Glypto. *nyt tyllaeg* 1892, No. 1039 a. The type is that of Herakles ; remains of the quiver strap on the breast ; the position of the fingers of the left hand is characteristic for holding the bow and arrow (cf. the statuette mentioned in the following note, the 'Paris' of the Aegina marbles, and *Berlin Skulpt.* No. 51). The statue is an admirable work, but the form and ornamentation of the basis prove that it is not an original of the fourth century, but a more recent repetition of such an original. The bronze statuette from Thessaly (*Oesterr. Mitth.* iii. Taf. 7, 8), with Polykleitan forms, is an analogous work.

[4] R. v. Schneider in *Jahrb. d. Kunsts. d. Oesterr. Kaiserh.* ix. p. 135 *seq.* Taf. 1, 2.

[5] Payne Knight, xlvi. 16 ; Clarac, 802 G, 1917 D. Good execution, but from the colour of the metal evidently not a Greek original. Right hand lowered and holding something, left hand pierced. Copper nipples inlaid. [6] Friederichs-Wolters, 1750.

type of Herakles, may not impossibly be copied from an early work of Skopas himself.

A statue of the youthful Asklepios, which must have been celebrated in its day, has been preserved in a copy on a medallion of M. Aurelius,[1] and in a beautiful bronze statuette of the Roman period (Fig. 128),[2] in which we have to supply the serpent-wreathed staff which supported the right hand. In this bronze the bodily forms here again betray Polykleitan influences; further, the 'walking' motive and the sharp inclination of the head towards the side of the free leg recall creations of the Polykleitan school, such as the Pan (p. 269 *seq.*) and the works allied to it, while the position of the hands—the one leaning on a support, the other resting on the hip—very closely resembles that of the so-called Narkissos (p. 273). The statuette, however, avoids all sharp transitions, and has a grace of movement and a suppleness of modelling such as we seek for in vain in those heavier Argive works. The head, with its charming short locks brushed up from the brow, is genuinely Attic. A beardless Asklepios is actually known to us from tradition by Skopas. Pausanias saw it in the god's temple at Gortys.[3]

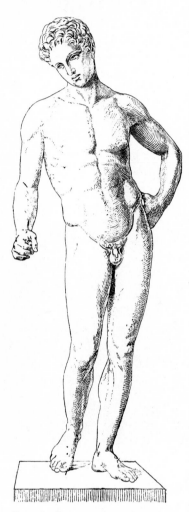

FIG. 128.—Bronze statuette of Asklepios (Carlsruhe).

There once stood on the Palatine a beautiful and interesting statue of Hermes (Fig. 129),[4] which has now been removed to the Terme Museum. The alert grace of the god's pose already suggests the Apoxyomenos of Lysippos; just as in the latter statue the right leg, which is free, is placed well to the side and slightly drawn back; and the youth balances himself on his hips while the gaze is directed to the side of the free leg; the right forearm was held sideways[5] from the body; it doubtless grasped the herald's staff, if not so energetically, yet much in the same manner as a technically exquisite bronze Hermes in Berlin,[6] which is also quite Lysippian in style. Further, the great depression of the left shoulder—while the right is raised and thrust forward—is already suggestive of that fine swing which marks not a few of the creations which

---

[1] Cf. von Sallet's *Zeitschr. f. Numis.* ix. 140 ; *Numis. Chron.* ser. iii. vol. ii. Pl. 14, 3 ; Wieseler, *Götting. Nachr.* 1888, p. 152 *seq.* Wieseler very plausibly maintains the interpretation as Asklepios, against Wroth, who had suggested Apollo.

[2] At Carlsruhe, found at Speier : Schuster, *Bronzen,* Pl. 27; Friederichs-Wolters, 1758. Roman work, probably made in Gaul. Ring on finger of left hand. Back specially good.

[3] It is possible, however, that a beardless Asklepios in the Braccio Nuovo (Helbig, *Museums,* 6), with a head of later Skopasian type, reproduces this statue.

[4] Matz-Duhn, 1046. The body has suffered severely through long exposure. The head has been broken off, but is undoubtedly authentic ; it alone is very well preserved. The legs are ancient. Replica of head in Catajo (Arndt-Bruckmann, *Einzelv.* 52, 53).

[5] The stump of the arm is placed backwards and to the side, and there is no puntello on the right side of the body.   [6] Antiquarium, *Inv.* 6505 ; from Athens.

can be traced back to Lysippos.[1]   Now the Herakles of Skopas—at any rate in
the statue of which a copy exists in the
Louvre,[2] and which has the type of head
assigned to Skopas—has this same movement of the upper part of the body, and
likewise rests one hand (the left) on the hip.
The extraordinary thing, however, about the
Hermes of the Terme is that the bodily forms
and the hair are still treated in the manner of
the fifth century; the hair lies close to the
skull, and is divided into fine locks, pointed at
the ends in true Polykleitan style;[3] yet the
forms of the face are purely Attic, and show
that the original cannot be earlier than the
fourth century.   The head fascinates by its
exquisite charm and subtle refinement; the
eyeball is slightly turned both inwards and
upwards; it is the beginning of that formation of the eye so characteristic of Skopasian
heads; the bridge of the nose is rather broad,
as in the Hermes of Praxiteles, but in spite
of this the work is undeniably somewhat older
than any of the works hitherto acknowledged
to be by Skopas or than the Hermes of Praxiteles.   The motive of the statue has been
shown to be one of the prototypes that inspired Lysippos, and previous to him it seems
to have been employed only by Skopas.
Therefore, may not the Hermes of the Terme
also be an early work by this artist?

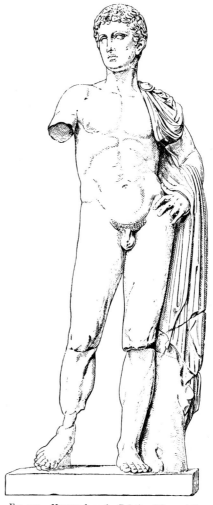

FIG. 129.—Hermes from the Palatine (Muse delle
Terme).

There is other authentic evidence to prove
that, during the middle of the fourth century,
the school of Skopas not unfrequently followed fifth-century models in its treatment of
the hair and of the bodily forms.   The Hermes
on one of the sculptured drums from Ephesos[4] is as closely connected with the

[1] Particularly the one called Alexander, and the youthful warrior in the Louvre, which may also represent Alexander (Clarac, 264, 2100); further, the Herakles type of which a bronze (Brit. Mus.) is a specially
good example (Clarac, 785, 1966).   Cf. Roscher's *Lex.* 2172.   The position of the legs is that of the
Apoxyomenos.

[2] In the Salle des Caryatides, No. 1524 (published by Gräf, *Röm. Mitth.* iv. 1889, p. 193).   The type of
head on Pl. 8, 9 (*ibid.*) belongs to this statue, and this only.   The existence of so many copies of the head and of
only one of the statue is explained by its frequent adaptation as a term (cf. p. 66, note 5, p. 235), and this also
explains the fact that so many of the heads are reversed from right to left.   The Paris head is an inferior but
an authentic copy of the same original as the single heads, and is unbroken.   The original certainly wore the
poplar-wreath.   No copies of the Paris statue have come under my notice, but the coin of Sikyon (Gräf, *loc. cit.*
213) probably reproduces the original of the Paris statue.   The head is differently placed, but in so rough a coin
that means little.

[3] This is probably what Matz-Duhn means by the 'reminiscence of Doric types' in the head.

[4] Friederichs-Wolters, 1242.   The burning of the temple in 356 forms the *terminus post quem*.   The relief
is probably near this in date.   Skopas himself made a pillar relief (Pliny, xxvi. 95).   As no other artists are
named in connexion with the other reliefs, these were probably made by his colleagues and pupils.

Hermes of the Terme in the treatment of the close-lying hair and the broad well-defined surfaces of the body as it is with Polykleitan models ; at any rate, every-thing about it differs entirely from the youth on the Ilissos relief, from the Meleager, or from the Hermes of Praxiteles. Even the 'walking motive,' with the arm hanging idly on the side of the supporting leg, recall Polykleitos. Thus everything conspires to commend the view that the works we have grouped together are connected with Skopas, and testify to a phase in which the artist was influenced by Polykleitan models.

He was, as has been very plausibly conjectured,[1] the son of Aristandros of Paros, who, since he worked with the younger Polykleitos on a votive offering set up at Amyklai by the Spartans after the victory at Aigospotamoi, must have been connected with the Argive school. Thus Skopas would naturally be early imbued with the traditions of that school, and the peculiarities of the works enumerated above, some of which may possibly be ascribed even to Aristandros, can be easily accounted for.

Archaeologists have tried to trace this Polykleitan influence in the works of Skopas, but by looking for it in the head they have gone completely astray. Only in the hair does a Polykleitan touch sometimes occur, otherwise the contour of the head and the shape of the face are absolutely the reverse of Polykleitan, and are invariably, as was remarked in the case of the Lansdowne Herakles, dependent on the purest Attic types.

From the Polykleitan school the young Skopas appropriated quite a number of formal elements, but in that spiritual conception which finds expression in the pose and the presentment of a figure, and in the forms of the head, he was entirely under Attico-Ionian influence, thus reproducing in the fourth century a phenomenon that had its counterpart in the fifth. The Parians to whom we owe the Olympian sculptures had likewise been influenced by the Argive school in formal matters, though in their spiritual conceptions they had remained genuine Ionians.[2] What at that period must still be called Ionian was afterwards entirely absorbed into Attic art. We may therefore consider Skopas also as an Attic master.

By far the most novel and audacious of the works which we attributed to his early period is the Hermes of the Terme. It introduces a rhythm full of restless energy, hitherto utterly unknown to statuary, and which prepares the way immedi-ately for Lysippos. In this statue the individuality of Skopas bursts forth in a most decided manner.[3] Yet as if to set a check on his own audacity he shows himself here rigidly conservative in matters of form. The Hermes exhibits a singular com-bination of fire and grace, and, though Lysippos eventually surpassed Skopas in the expression of nervous tension and excitement, the internal tenderness and warmth of his predecessor were always lacking in him.

Skopas, by representing figures with one foot raised on an elevation, once again forestalled Lysippos[4] in another motive full of restlessness and of broken outlines.

[1] Böckh on *C. I. G.* 2285 b. ; cf. Löwy, *I. G. B.* 287.

[2] Cf. *Archäol. Stud. H. Brunn dargebr.* 1893, p. 69 *seq.*

[3] A statuary composition which is known to me in two torsos seems to be an older, hesitating attempt in the direction of the Palatine Hermes. A youth of delicate form (which however shows Polykleitan influence) is leaning his weight on his left leg, his left hand rests on his hips, the head is turned to the right like the Hermes, but unlike it the right leg is not drawn back, and the right arm hangs by the side (torso in Vat., Gall. Lapid. 87, and another less well preserved in Museo Torlonia, 38, Pl. 10). An inferior replica reduced in size (Vat., Gall. dei Candel. 24) gives the boy a Satyr's tail. Closely related is one of the small athlete statues, Braccio Nuovo (97). Torso only ancient. Head plaster.

[4] According to the extant dates, the activity of Lysippos extends from 350—300 (King Seleukos after 306, cf. Löwy, 487), so that the period of Alexander marks the middle of it. Winter (*Jahrb. d. Inst.* 1872, 169) is

The attitude had been common in relief and painting from the time of Polygnotos onwards, but it scarcely seems to have been adopted for the round previous to Skopas.[1] Thus he represented his Apollo Smintheus[2] resting his right foot on an elevation and bending forward, laurel-branch in hand, as if to play with the mouse below, while his left hand rests on his side according to a favourite Skopasian scheme already noticed. This same attitude reappears in a statue of the youthful Pan— (except that in this case the head is raised and the eyes look straight out)—which presumably stood at Heraia in Arkadia, as it is reproduced on a silver coin[3] of that town (Plate VI. 35), and in a statuette found in the neighbourhood.[4] We may surmise that this Pan also is an earlier work of Skopas, or perhaps even a work by his father, since it must have been executed at the beginning of the fourth century.[5] Two marble copies[6] have perhaps preserved for us a later creation of Skopas; they represent a delicate boy with forms allied to those of the statue of the striding Hypnos, which we shall later recognize to be Skopasian, and with his left foot placed upon an elevation; the left arm rests on the thigh, but the body is turned somewhat to the right, producing soft lines on the whole abdominal region, and giving a momentary character to the movement. We get an analogous though far tamer and quieter conception in a well-preserved statue of the Capitol.[7] A youth, with his cloak round his lower limbs, raises his right hand to emphasize some quiet impressive harangue, and lets the left one rest on his leg, which is well raised. In style and conception this figure resembles Praxiteles rather than Skopas; the left hand hangs at the side, and presents a striking similarity to that of the Hermes at Olympia, and the head is also related. We may conjecture that here too Hermes is represented as *Logios* or *Agoraios*, and that the sculptor, follower of Praxiteles though he was, copied Skopas in the motive of the raised foot.[8]

wrong in placing Lysippos at the beginning of the seventies. In editing the inscription of Troilos (*Arch. Ztg.* 1879, 146) I conjectured that his second victory fell in the Olympiad after Ol. 102, but it may also have been considerably later; and above all the wording of the inscription, as Löwy points out (*I. G. B.* p. 76), makes it probable that the statue was erected long after the victory. The statue of Pulydamas by Lysippos was certainly set up long after the victory of 408 B.C. (Cf. Urlichs, *Kunstschriftsteller*, p. 26.)

[1] Cf. *Samml. Sabouroff*, to Taf. 114; 50th *Berl. Winckelmannsprogr.* p. 161. K. Lange (*Das Motiv des Aufgestützten Fusses*) maintains that it was introduced by Lysippos. Köpp (*Bildnis Alexanders des Grossen*, p. 18) rightly states that it was known to art long before Lysippos, but he does not distinguish between sculpture and painting. Many motives existed in painting long before they were introduced into free sculpture in the round, *e.g.* recumbent sleeping figures certainly do not appear in statuary before the Alexandrine period.

[2] The statue of Apollo Smintheus found on the coins of Alexandria Troas from the second century B.C. down to late Imperial times is not the statue by Skopas which Strabo mentions, but an earlier one with a different motive and of much severer style (Roscher's *Lexikon*, i. 457, Z. 53 *sqq.*) A coin-type which appears only under Commodus and Caracalla may reproduce the statue of Skopas (Plate VI. 34, 36). Weil, in Baumeister's *Denkm.* p. 1669, agrees with me. Overbeck (*Apollo*, p. 92 *sqq.*: cf. *Coin Plate* 5, 25, 27—33, also 5, 10, and p. 314) is opposed to my view. According to Strabo, the mouse was in a hole under the round pedestal on which the right foot rests, and in a coin of Apollonia ad Rhyndacum, recently discovered (Imhoof, *Gr. Münzen Abh. bayr. Akad.* I Cl. xviii. 3, Pl. 6, 20, p. 609, No. 156), there is something undistinguishable, which may be a mouse, in front of the pedestal. [It seems more likely, however, that this object is a raven: cf. Warwick Wroth, Brit. Mus. *Catal. Troas*, Introd. p. xvii.; the raven is quite distinct *supra*, Plate VI. 36 = Wroth, Pl. vi. 2; the Skopasian character of the statue remains none the less indisputable.—E. S.]

[3] Small silver coin about 417—370 B.C. Brit. Mus. *Catal. Pelop.* Pl. 34, 12.

[4] Berlin, *Inv.* 7486, from Andritsena (*Arch. Ztg.* 1881, p. 251). Simple, spare bodily forms, certainly from the first half of the fourth century. [5] Because of the coin and the style of the bronze statuette.

[6] Louvre, Rotonde d'Apollon, Nos. 3065, 3066. Clarac, Pl. 271, 2193, 2194. Life-size. Head of No. 3065 antique; neck, chin, and lower jaw restored. Interesting type, with brushed-back hair and fillet. Head possibly does not belong to body. 3066, head modern, support of left foot restored as a rock.

[7] Helbig, *Museums*, 509; Clarac, 859, 2170. The left hand and most of the right hand are antique. The 'Sandal-binder' is quite a different type. I know no replicas.

[8] More Skopasian is a small bronze in Berlin (Friederichs, *Kl. Kunst*, 1850), representing the youthful Herakles, or an athlete with a fillet. The right leg is raised in the act of striding, the head looks outwards. Its excited expression recalls the Skopasian Herakles.

There was yet another energetic system of broken lines, produced by representing a figure with both hands clasped round one knee, which Skopas seems to have been the first to transfer from painting to statuary in the round. The earlier conjecture, which referred the Ares Ludovisi to Skopas, seems perfectly reasonable. The statue is certainly a reduced copy of the *Mars sedens colossiaeus in templo Bruti Callaeci* (Plin. xxxvi. 26). The figure on the arch of Trajan, in which Stark thought he could identify a copy of the *Mars*, has turned out to be more probably a Herakles type borrowed from a cult instituted by Trajan.[1] A seated Ares is, however, something so curious and unique that we are predisposed to imagine a connexion between the Skopasian statue known to have been in Rome and the Ares Ludovisi. The style settles the question. To begin with, it is not in the least Lysippian, as is now generally supposed.[2] Let the head of the Apoxyomenos be compared to that of the Ares—and if there is any one whom the totally different spiritual conception of the two works should fail to convince, let him compare the foreheads. The Apoxyomenos is the earliest statue of a youth that can be dated in which the horizontal modulation of the forehead is represented as a wrinkle; in the Ares, as in all pre-Lysippian works, the modelling of this part is smooth. If it be correct, as I believe it is, to attribute the Meleager to Skopas[3] (it also passed till lately as Lysippian), then the Ares must also be by this artist. In both the heads the powerful framing of the eyes, which are deep-set and peer eagerly into the far distance, the quivering mouth and nostril,[4] are as thoroughly like each other as they are genuinely Skopasian. The Ares Ludovisi cannot be an exact copy, partly because it is a reproduction on a reduced scale of a colossal statue, partly because the workmanship is hurried and superficial; further, the little Eros between the feet of the god clashes with the style of the statue, inasmuch as it is of Graeco-Roman type, and, like a second Eros[5] that has now disappeared, is an addition made by the copyist. We have already seen (p. 89, note 8) how fond the Roman artists were of representing Ares as a lover, and how they introduced this suggestion into the older Greek works by some trifling additions. Skopas certainly did not intend to pourtray a lover lost in dreams, but a war god, of his essence restless, who when he pauses gives no thought to his personal dignity or to the outer world, but sits as he likes to ponder over fresh feats of arms. On the Parthenon frieze Pheidias had already chosen this attitude as characteristic of Ares; but it was Skopas who first had the courage to work out the idea in a colossal work in the round.

The Meleager takes rank, it is true, among the usual statuary themes, yet it also is genuinely Skopasian, fraught with fire and energy. The inclination of the left shoulder, the energetic turn of the head towards the side of the free leg, and the bend of the arm which rests on the hip, have already been often noticed in Skopas, though

---

[1] Petersen, *Röm. Mitth.* iv. 1889, p. 330 *sqq.*

[2] Friederichs, *Bausteine*, 436=Wolters, 1268; Schreiber, *V. Ludov.* 63; Helbig, *Museums*, 883; Roscher's *Lexikon*, i. 490 *seq.* M. Mayer (*Arch. Anz.* 1889, p. 41), arguing from the supposed Lysippian character, suggests Piston's Mars in Rome.

[3] Gräf, *Röm. Mitth.* 1889, 218 *sqq.* In addition to the replicas mentioned by him there are: Torso in Pal. Torlonia (restored as Hermes); torso in Louvre (from Rome), 1884; replica in Pal. Doria (no chlamys, head poor, neck new, boar's head old, wrongly adjusted on restored trunk); head in Jacobsen collection, 1071, mediocre. The Meleager of Skopas probably once stood in Tegea. [For the superb head of the Meleager placed on the torso of a Praxitelean Apollo (*infra*, p. 338, note 3), in the Villa Medici, see Plate XV.; Petersen (*Röm. Mitth.* iv. 186) was, I believe, the first to recognize this head as an original.—E. S.]   [4] At least the right nostril is ancient.

[5] More probable than the other restorations. M. Mayer's suggestion (*loc. cit.*) is the least fortunate of all. A replica (torso) in Naples (Flasch, *Verhandl. d.* 41. *Philologen. Versamml. in München*) has no puntello on the left shoulder, hence no Eros was added. The god in this replica was seated on a pillar, not on a rock. Shield missing, but it may have been fastened on separately, as there is a contact-surface on the right side of the drapery.

Fig. Q1 - Diadumenos, late Hellenistic copy of the Polykleitan
original, New York, Metropolitan Museum of Art,(cf.
p. 241, Fig. 98, Plate R, Figs. XXXV, XXXVa)

Fig. Q2 - Amazon once in Lansdowne House, London, Hellenistic copy of the Polykleitan original, New York, Metropolitan Museum of Art (cf. p.135, Fig.55, p. 139, →
Fig. XXIa)

PLATE Q

Fig. R1 – Head of a Diadumenos, New York, Metropolitan Museum of Art
(See Plate Q)

PLATE R

Fig. S1 – Head of an Athlete, considered to be one of the best copies of the Polykleitan Kyniskos, Possession of Lady D'Abernon, Stoke D'Abernon, Surrey, England

Fig. S2 – Mutilated copy of the Kyniskos of Polykleitos, Baltimore, Walters Art Gallery

Fig. S3 – Plaster reconstruction of the Kyniskos of Polykleitos, Munich, The Royal Museum of casts of Classical Statues

Fig. S4 – The Kyniskos of Castelgandolfo, Rome, National Museum

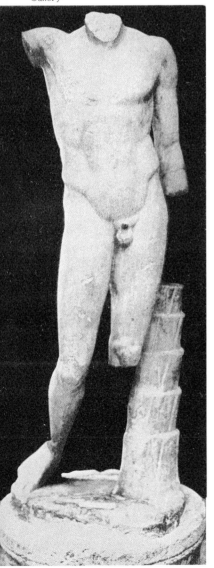

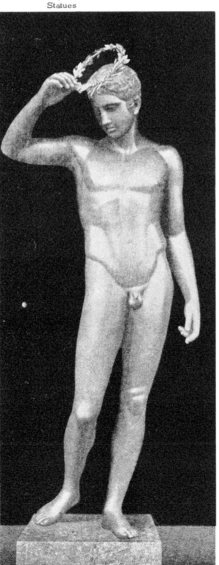

PLATE S

Fig. T1 - Venus "Genetrix". A late Hellenistic copy of an original of the 5th century B.C. Left hand is a modern restoration. Paris, Louvre

Fig. T2 - Aphrodite "Genetrix," Late Hellenistic copy. Left hand is a modern restoration. Naples, National Museum

PLATE T

U1 – Statue of a boy, part of Attic grave relief, original work of 4th century B.C., Chicago, Art Institute

Fig. U2 – Sculptured base of column from the Temple of Artemis at Ephesus, original work of 4th century B.C., London, British Museum

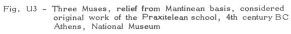

Fig. U3 – Three Muses, relief from Mantinean basis, considered original work of the Praxitelean school, 4th century BC Athens, National Museum

Fig. U4 – Priestess or adorant from large relief dedicated to Brauronian Artemis, New York, Metropolitan Museum of Art (cf. Fig. XLVI, p. 324)

217

PLATE U

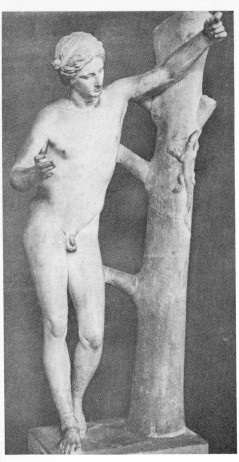

Fig. V1 - Apollo Sauroctonos, late Hellenistic copy of Praxitelean work, Paris,
Louvre

Fig. V2 - Eros, Rome, Vatican Museum

Fig. V3 - Hermes of Praxiteles, original
work, Olympia, Olympia Museum

Fig. V4 - Bronze statue, the so-called boy
of Marathon, original of 4th century BC,
Athens, National Museum

Fig. V5 - Apoxyomenos, copy of a work by
Lysippus, Rome, Vatican Museum (cf.
p. 403, Fig. LXXI)

Fig. V6 - Apoxyomenos athlete, bronze o-
riginal from Ephesus, Vienna

PLATE V

Fig. W1 - Bearded head, copy of an original
by Lysippus, Copenhagen, Ny Carlsberg
Glyptotek

Fig. W2 - Portrait head of Alexander the
Great, considered to be an original of
Lysippus, Athens, Acropolis Museum

Fig. W3 - Head of a bronze statue of a Muse
or Goddess. Original of 4th century BC,
Piraeus, City Museum

Fig. W4 - Artemis of Versailles, copy of an
original of 4th century BC, Paris, Louvre

Fig. W5 - Bronze statue of Artemis of Brauron,
early Hellenistic copy of Praxitlean original
Piraeus, City Museum

Fig. W6 - Artemis from Gabii, copy of an
original of 4th century BC, Paris,
Louvre

PLATE W

Figs. X1,2 & 4 – Goddess, Scopasian head from south slope of the Acropolis, original of 4th century B.C., Athens, National Museum

Fig. X3 – Roman copy of original (Figs. X1,2 & 4) Berlin, National Museum

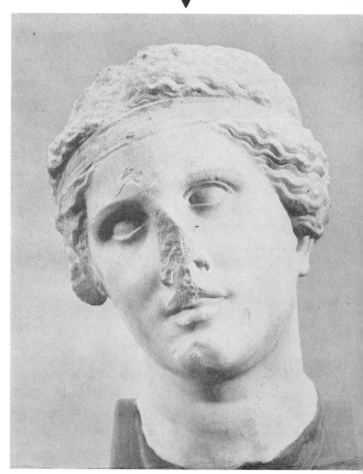

PLATE X

in the Meleager the restless vitality is intensified to a degree which makes the Lansdowne Herakles and the Palatine Hermes appear simple and even tranquil by comparison.

The motive of the Meleager reminds me of a remarkable type of Athena, which arose I incline to think from the fiery genius of Skopas. The goddess is conceived somewhat like a Joan of Arc, in the semblance of a young, still undeveloped girl; her mantle is wrapt about her in manlike fashion, her left hand is firmly placed on her hip, while with her right she grasps the spear; vibrant with courage and enthusiasm, her face slightly upturned, she looks out into space (Fig. 130).[1] The deep-set eyes and their well-defined cavity, the open mouth, and the whole expression recall the Skopasian manner. An external circumstance confirms the conjecture. Beside the goddess on her right hand may be seen a Triton; the figure does not serve as a support, still less can such an unusual attribute be a copyist's addition. Now we know that near the ancient sanctuary of Athena at Alalkomenai there was a brook called Triton, where, according to the Boeotian legend, Athena was born and brought up.[2] To this story the statue obviously refers,[3] and therefore Athena is represented as still quite a young girl. Skopas made a marble statue of her to stand in front of the temple of the Ismenian Apollo at Thebes.[4] At a time when that city was making an energetic claim to the leadership of Boeotia, it would be only natural to lay stress on the legend of neighbouring Alalkomenai, and to represent the goddess as the maiden born and brought up on the stream Triton, in that Boeotian land over which Thebes was to rule. Of course Skopas may also have worked for Alalkomenai, and, as we know that the shrine was plundered by Sulla, the statue might have been taken to Rome and copied there.[5] The somewhat spare forms and the treatment of the drapery suggest that the statue is one of the master's earlier creations. His later treatment of drapery is exemplified in his Apollo Kitharoidos, of which a copy has been preserved to us in the famous Vatican statue,[6] and which is another example of the vigour of Skopasian conception.

If we consider the treatment of the nude, we find that in this respect the Ares and the Meleager are again intimately connected; the forms show, moreover, that (supposing our attribution of them to Skopas be correct) both statues can only belong to the artist's later works, so entirely does the treatment of the body differ from that observed in those statues which we ascribed to his earlier period, and which show dependence upon Polykleitos. A great revolution has taken place: instead of being

[1] Statue in Casino Rospigliosi, Matz-Duhn, 621; Müller-Wieseler, ii. 233; Arndt-Bruckmann, *Einzelwerk.* No. 111. Replicas: (*a*) Florence, Uffizi, Dütschke, iii. No. 152. Very good workmanship; the head is genuine, the neck and upper part of the breast restored. Photo. ed. Alinari, 1295. (*b*) Berlin, *Skulpt.* 73; *Bull. Comm. di Roma*, 1887, p. 169; *Mon. d. Inst.* Supp. 27, 1. The head alone in (*c*) Glienecke (Friederichs-Wolters, *Gipsabg.* 1438), (*d*) Museo Chiaramonti, 558 (Helbig, *Museums*, 107), and (*e*) Berlin, No. 80. It is purely arbitrary and unscientific to make out the head to be Hellenistic, as is usually done. [2] Paus. ix. 33, 7; Strabo, p. 413.
[3] As the Triton beside an Aphrodite in Dresden refers to her birth from Ocean. *Arch. Anz.* 1894, p. 29.
[4] Paus. ix. 10, 2. Opposite a Hermes by Pheidias. Brunn (*Bayr. Sitzungsber.* 1880, p. 459) refutes Klein's hypothesis that the two statues (called *Pronaoi*) were necessarily contemporary in date.
[5] The original was, to judge by the replicas, probably bronze.
[6] Cf. Hoffmann, *Philologus*, 1889, 678 *seq.*; *Arch. Anz.* 1889, p. 147; Roscher's *Lex.* i. 463. The Palatine Apollo singing appears on the coins of Nero, not those of Augustus. (Overbeck, *Apollon*, Münztafel v. 47, 48, 50, 51). The Apollo with the kylix on coins of Augustus (*ibid.* v. 43) was probably the original of the Barberini statue in Munich, which has been (p. 88) referred to Agorakritos (cf. Studniczka, *Röm. Mitth.* 1888, 296, who starts from the untenable premise that the coins of Augustus reproduce the Apollo of Skopas).—The Vatican statue (Helbig, *Museums*, 267) is a poor copy, much worked over, mouth and chin restored.—A replica in Stockholm (Overbeck, *Apollon*, p. 186, 2). The beautiful head in the British Museum (Newton, *Guide Gr.-Rom. Sculpt.* ii. 99) is a better copy of the head. The hair is waved differently. Pathos is expressed by the movement of the eyebrows.—Overbeck, *loc. cit.* 186, No. 3, 1, is an older type of the late fifth century.

R R

FIG. 130.—Statue of Athena in the Uffizi.

divided into clear, sharply defined planes, the various surfaces melt insensibly into
each other ; the chest is narrower, the navel is no longer flat as in Polykleitan works,
but it is indicated by a soft depression, and the hard modulation of the abdominal
muscles has disappeared.

This treatment of the nude is still quite foreign to the sculptures of the Mausoleum or to the great sculptured column of Ephesos. The change cannot therefore
have. taken place before the middle of the fourth century ; it is however complete
in the youth on the Ilissos relief (in this respect it entirely accords with the
Meleager), and in the Hermes of Praxiteles. These works must be about contemporary with the Meleager and the Ares. The Skopasian Herakles in the Louvre is
somewhat older, and is more nearly akin to the earlier group, and forms a kind of
mean between the two series.

The same revolution of the treatment of the nude makes itself felt in the work of
Praxiteles, where its various stages can be far more easily traced. There will be
more to say about Skopas in another connexion, but for the present it seems best to
pursue further the point of view suggested by the treatment of the male nude.

II. *Praxiteles.—Date of the Hermes.—Works of the Artist's Early and Middle
Period.—Figures leaning on a support ; the Satyr and the Eubouleus.—Works
of the Artist's Later Period ; the Hermes and Kindred Statues.*

Our knowledge of the art of Praxiteles rests primarily on the extant original
statue—the Hermes of Olympia. It is of the very highest importance to obtain a
more definite date for this work, and to find out whether it belongs to the youth of the
artist, as Brunn asserts,[1] or to his later period.

It has just been remarked that the Hermes is connected stylistically only with
the later works of Skopas, and that therefore it must belong to the second half of
the fourth century. This can be confirmed by another most convincing, although
external, piece of evidence derived from the actual basis of the statue. All its
essential parts have been recovered and used for the reconstruction in the Museum
at Olympia.[2] It entirely differs from the ordinary Greek basis of the fifth and early
fourth century in height, in both the upper and lower mouldings, and in material.
The high moulded shape of the Hermes basis occurs in Olympia and elsewhere
only on bases which cannot be dated earlier than the Alexandrine period. Such
are the three bases of the artist Sophokles in Olympia,[3] which correspond to the
Hermes bases, except that their lower moulding is richer (the cornice blocks are
missing). Others are the basis of a statue by Sthennis[4] dedicated by King
Lysimachos (306—281), and the basis of one of the works of Xenokrates,[5] both in
the Amphiareion at Oropos. In the Graeco-Roman period this form of basis
became quite common in Olympia as in other sanctuaries. As regards material, the
Hermes basis is made of white limestone, only the lower block being of grey lime-

[1] Brunn, in *Deutsche Rundschau*, viii. 1882, p. 188 *seq*. Kekulé was formerly the only opponent of this view.
He saw in the Hermes 'no youthful work, but an example of the full maturity of his (Praxiteles's) powers of conception
and execution' (Baedeker's *Greece*, p. 97). Of late Overbeck has published a more detailed refutation of Brunn's
opinion (*Sächs. Ber.* 1893, p. 46 *seq*.), but adds no positive information about the date of the Hermes.

[2] Cf. *Ausgrab. v. Olympia*, Bd. v. 9.

[3] Löwy, *I. G. B.* 123—125. According to Löwy's very probable hypothesis (*I. G. B.* p. 384), this artist was
mentioned by Pliny among the contemporaries of Alexander in the 121st Olympiad, in Bk. xxxiv. 51, where his
name should probably be restored from the corrupt *fucles* of the MSS.

[4] Löwy, *I. G. B.* 103 *a* (p. 384); Ἐφημ. ἀρχ. 1885, p. 102, 3 ; *C. I. Gr. Sept.* 279.

[5] Löwy, 135 *b* (p. 387); Ἐφημ. ἀρχ. 1886, p. 55, 17 ; *C. I. Gr. Sept.* 332.

stone with round dark spots on the surface. Several varieties of this white and grey limestone occur on the bases of Olympia, but only from the time of Alexander downwards. The limestone of the earlier bases in Olympia is always of that dark black sort which already occurs at an early period, and was subsequently much affected in the circle of Polykleitos.[1] The earliest dated analogies in Olympia are afforded by the bases of the six Zeus statues called Zanes, which were erected out of the fines which the Athenians paid, Ol. 112 (B.C. 332), for the misdemeanours of one of their citizens.[2] These bases follow the earlier shape without moulding, which was chosen because the statues continued a series of six earlier Zanes, erected Ol. 98 (B.C. 388). On the other hand, the material differs from that of the preceding Zanes; it consists of white limestone alternating with blue-black and with white conglomerate. Besides these there is a red and white conglomerate, never seen in earlier times, but to be found in the bases of the statues by Sophokles.[3]

These facts point to the second half of the century as the date of the Hermes, so that the statue cannot be, as some maintain,[4] a record of the peace concluded after the events of the Anolympiad and the combat between the Arkadians and the Eleians in the Altis in B.C. 363. Nor was there any inherent probability in this date, seeing that the reconciliation between the two states was a hollow one, arranged by the aristocratic party in Mantineia: the suggestion, however, that Hermes the god of Arkadia was represented as nursing Dionysos the god of Elis, in token of the union of these two districts, is certainly correct. I accordingly incline to refer it to a period twenty years later (B.C. 343), when the aristocratic party in Elis, in league with the Arkadians,[5] won a decisive victory over the democratic party, and then formed an alliance with Philip for their own protection. This was a suitable occasion for fresh Eleian dedications at Olympia,[6] and the Hermes represented as nursing the Eleian Dionysos might well be set up as a thank-offering to the Arkadians for their aid. At the same time that he made the Hermes at Olympia[7] Praxiteles must have certainly made a Dionysos for this god's temple at Elis; the reproduction of the statue on a coin of Hadrian[8] shows that in design it was very closely akin to the Hermes.

[1] Quite different from the dark blue-black limestone, out of which so many bases in Olympia in the fifth or fourth centuries are made (also those from the circle of Polykleitos, Naukydes, Daidalos, Kleon).

[2] Paus. v. 21, 5 *seq.*

[3] All the Zanes set up in Ol. 112 (Nos. 7—12) had one kind of basis, made of three superimposed cube-shaped blocks. The lowest block is always of poros; the middle one of white limestone (yellow and of finer texture, like giallo antico in No. 10, missing in No. 12; cf. *Arch. Ztg.* 1879, p. 45 *seq.*); the upper block is black limestone with white veins in 8, 9, 10, 12; it is missing in 7; red-white conglomerate in No. 11. Two blocks of the same material belonged to the Sophokles bases.

[4] Purgold, in *Histor. u. philol. Aufsätze E. Curtius gew.* p. 233 *seq.* Dörpfeld's recent investigations have shown (*Olympia, Textbd.* ii. 33, 36) that the alteration in the Heraion assumed by Purgold never took place. Sal. Reinach, *Gaz. Archéol.* 1887, p. 282, note 9; *Revue Arch.* 1888, i. *sqq.*

[5] Ἀρκάδων συναγωνισαμένων τοῖς Ἠλείοις, Diod. 16, 63. Cf. Curtius, *Griechische Geschichte*, iii. (6th edit.) p. 623.

[6] Several larger buildings in Olympia belong to the same period, *e.g.* the Leonidaion, the great rebuilding of the east porch, the so-called Echo portico, which is approximately dated by its similarity with the Philippeion (cf. *Olympia, Textbd.* ii. 72, 92).

[7] This statue was certainly made on the spot, for it is executed with regard to the position it was to occupy in the Heraion.

[8] Weil, in Sallet's *Numism. Ztschr.* xiii. 384; Postolakkas, *Catalogue* 1883—84, Taf. 2, 9; Imhoof-Blumer and Gardner, *Num. Comm.* p. 74. The left forearm was supported, the figure rested on the right leg; the right arm was raised high; the Dionysos resembles the Hermes in every particular, except that he is looking up towards the rhyton. It is not certain that the legs were crossed. The Berlin and Athens copies are too much defaced to afford exact evidence on this point. If the legs were crossed, it would be another reason for placing the statue in the later period of Praxiteles (cf. *Samml. Sabouroff*, Text to Pl. 77, 78).

The period (*circa* B.C. 340) to which we accordingly assign the Hermes belongs however to the master's later period : he was already an artist of repute some thirty years earlier. His two great groups at Mantineia must be closely connected with the rebuilding of the city. The date assigned by Pliny to Praxiteles (Ol. 104) probably refers to the artist's activity in that city in so far as it is the date of the battle of Mantineia (B.C. 362).[1] Beyond this the only other dates we possess for Praxiteles are derived from the fact that he worked on the Mausoleum at Halikarnassos (begun B.C. 353), and also on an altar at Ephesos, of course after the fire of B.C. 356. There is absolutely nothing to prove that he was still working in the time of Alexander. The date assigned by Pliny to his sons (Ol. 121) is obviously incorrect, and too late. The date is that of the sons of Lysippos, who come first in the list, and Pliny, according to his custom,[2] included within the period other artists who did not strictly belong to it. The sons of Praxiteles are connected with Lykurgos and his family ; the statue of Menander, who died in 291, may very well have been erected in his lifetime ;[3] and the palaeographic character of the inscriptions[4] shows that the sculptors lived well within the fourth century. Pliny's date therefore could only apply to the end of their career, and involves no contradiction of our assumption that the father's activity extended from *circa* B.C. 370—330.

The following observations further confirm our dating of the Hermes : the hair of the god is fashioned with a free use of the drill—one main effect of the head being due to its employment—the hair left rough upon it with the tool-marks has a look of rich profusion, and rises very effectively above the smoothly polished flesh of the face. This technical refinement is yet foreign to the Skopasian heads from the pediments of Tegea, and to the head, probably also Skopasian, found on the south slope of the Akropolis ;[5] nor do we find it in the great number of grave-reliefs of the first half of the fourth century ; a few only, which from their style belong to the last reliefs before the reorganisation by Demetrios the Phalerean, show this use of the drill in the hair.

Lastly, the drapery of the Hermes is treated with a degree of subtlety absolutely without parallel among the works of the first half of the fourth century. The drapery of the Muses on the Mantineian reliefs, which belong to the artist's earlier period, appears, in spite of the wealth of folds, quite simple by comparison. The system of enlivening the smooth surfaces between the large folds by breaking them up by small curving or broken lines is in the Hermes carried out to the greatest and most lifelike perfection. Only among the later grave-reliefs of the fourth century is

[1] Cf. p. 295, note 1. As Praxiteles's name is the first under the date, this passage must have reference to him (cf. *Plinius und seine Quellen*, in *Fleckeis. Suppl.* Bd. ix. p. 21 *seq.*), and is not to be lightly set aside.

[2] Cf. p. 41. *Plinius und seine Quellen*, p. 22 *seq.* Only a complete ignorance of the character of Pliny's dating can have caused Overbeck (*Sächs. Ber.* 1893, 45 *seq.*) to assume that Ol. 121 was the 'Blüthezeit' of Kephisodotos II., when he was forty years old, and to found on this the date of Praxiteles. Pausanias's vague statement that Praxiteles was three generations later than Alkamenes gives no help, for it leaves a margin of years greater than the number about which the controversy exists.

[3] The statue in the Vatican (Helbig, *Museums*, 201), called Menander since Visconti's time, and supposed to be an original work, cannot be taken into consideration. The name was based on one medallion in relief which had already disappeared in Visconti's time ; moreover, the drawing of it (*Icon. Grecque*, Pl. 6) is very unlike the head of the statue. The dress is against the identification as Menander ; the chiton with short sleeves had not come into fashion in the fourth century ; it points to a personage of later date—a contemporary of the Poseidippos and of the fine-seated statue in the Capitol (Helbig, *Museums*, 499). The head of the double term at Bonn (Friederichs-Wolters, 1311) is again quite different from the Vatican head. It may be remarked incidentally that the other term at Bonn (F.-W. 1310), the so-called 'Sophokles,' has nothing in common with the portrait of this poet. The head united with the Euripides probably represents Aischylos.

[4] Cf. Löwy, *I. G. B.* 112 and 111 ; Köhler's remarks, *ibid.* 109, and *C. I. A.* ii. 1377.

[5] Cf. B. Gräf, in *Röm. Mitth.* 1889, p. 216.

this treatment found now and again. The next stage to the style of the drapery of
the Hermes is found in the Nike of Samothrace.

Against these facts and considerations, which all show the Hermes to belong
to the artist's later period, the arguments advanced by Brunn[1] to prove that it
belongs to his youth can scarcely hold. For instance, we cannot admit that 'in
the Hermes the artist has not yet attained absolutely to that perfect security of
execution which can only be the result of long practice.' There is not in all
antiquity a work showing more subtle finish or more intimate mastery of all the

FIG. 131.—Satyr in Dresden.

secrets of marble technique than the Hermes. Brunn would scarcely have passed the
verdict he did had he seen the original at Olympia.

The main point is, however, that we still possess a series of copies after Praxiteles
of a style so different and so much older than the Hermes that we are compelled to
assign them to his earlier period.

Above all there is the Satyr pouring wine (Figs. 131 and 132)[2] extant in so many

[1] *Deutsche Rundschau,* viii. 188 *sqq.*

[2] List of replicas (Schreiber, *Villa Ludovisi,* p. 93): the Ludovisi copy, a torso of the Capitol, a torso and a
head in the Vatican are published by Gh. Ghirardini in *Bull. della Comm. Arch. di Roma,* 1892, Taf. 11—14;
the Ludovisi copy also in Brunn-Bruckmann, *Denkm.* No. 376. From Schreiber's list should be omitted g, Mus.
Torlonia 35; there should be added to it a head in Mus. Chiaramonti, 367 (made into a terminal bust, neck very

copies. It is true that it cannot be identified with absolute certainty with any one of the Praxitelean Satyrs recorded by tradition. The much-vexed passage in Pausanias,[1] where he speaks of the works of art in the street of the Tripods and of the cunning by which Phryne contrived to make Praxiteles confess that he esteemed the Satyr and the Eros his finest works, is so obscure, either owing to the author's perverse manner of writing or to the unsatisfactory condition of the text, that we are not certain whether the boyish Satyr mentioned as acting as cupbearer was by Praxiteles or not. Either interpretation of the passage causes difficulties, which can, it is true, be easily solved by emending the text or by assuming the existence of a lacuna, but we can never hope to come to any incontrovertible conclusion. Our reason for believing that this particular Satyr goes back to Praxiteles does not, however, rest on the passage in Pausanias, but on other circumstances. An original of which so many copies exist

FIG. 132.—Head of Satyr in Dresden.

must have been one of the most famous statues in antiquity. Now Praxiteles was famous for his Satyrs, and, even without entering into detailed analysis, it is obvious that the work has a thoroughly Praxitelean grace and charm. The original must have been of bronze; the Satyr of Praxiteles, which Pliny mentions as the *periboëtos*, or 'far-famed,' was bronze; this statue, and, as it seems, the one in the street of the Tripods also, was grouped with a Dionysos and a third figure.[2] Such a combination would suit the 'Cup-bearer' very well, for it insures the presence of another figure for whom

thick, a ribbon hanging down each side, called 'Herakles'), and a head in the Gall. dei Candelabri, 45. Both are inferior copies.

[1] For the most recent discussions see Wolters, *Arch. Zeitg.* 1885, 82; Reisch, *Weihgeschenke*, p. 111; Gherardo Ghirardini, *Bull. della Comm. Archeol. di Roma*, 1892.

[2] Pliny, xxxiv. 69: *Liberum patrem, Ebrietatem nobilemque una Satyrum, quem Graeci periboeton cognominant.* Paus. i. 20, 2: Σάτυρος ἐστι παῖς καὶ δίδωσιν ἔκπωμα. Ἔρωτα δ' ἑστηκότα ὁμοῦ καὶ Διόνυσον Θυμίλος ἐποίησεν. In the group mentioned by Pliny, perhaps Praxiteles repeated the same Satyr which he had placed in the group which he made together with Thymilos. It appears to me quite certain that the figures named by Pausanias formed a group. The Dionysos with Eros, by Thymilos, may survive in the Naples group (Gerhard, *Neapels ant. Bildw.* p. 30, No. 96), where Dionysos leans on Eros (the antique basis shows that the figures belong together). The Eros had right supporting leg, and the Satyr on the other side of Dionysos had left supporting leg. In the group mentioned by Pliny the young Satyr must have occupied the centre between Dionysos and Methe (*Ebrietas*).

the cup is to be filled.[1] Certainly the Satyr is not filling it for himself; no Satyr would use so much ceremony on his own behalf.   He is here fashioned after the pattern of the mortal youths in attendance at feasts.   Thus also the youthful cup-bearer on the so-called funeral banquet reliefs of the fourth century appears frequently in the motive of our statue.[2]

We may therefore assume, with that degree of certainty that can be attained in matters of this kind, that this Satyr is a creation by Praxiteles.   Yet how different is this work to the Hermes!

The Satyr is still constructed on the traditions of the fifth century, and, with regard to form at any rate, betrays a strong Peloponnesian influence.   In fullest contrast to the Hermes, the body viewed from the front presents as far as possible quiet, vertical, unbroken planes.   This in itself is a mark of the same tendency so strongly imprinted on Polykleitan figures.   The abdomen and the chest are still flat, the nipples far apart, the front of the body seems to pass into the sides almost at a right angle, as in the fifth century, while in the Hermes a wealth of soft undulations insensibly carry the eye on, so that there is no sharp separation between sides and front.   Then the depression between the straight and the oblique abdominal muscles is emphasized as in Polykleitos.   The boyish figures by that artist, particularly the 'boy crowning himself' and statues akin to it like the Pan and the 'Narkissos,' are the immediate predecessors of this Satyr.   The legs are in that attitude of 'arrested motion' which Polykleitos gave to his chief works.   The head is turned and inclined to the side of the supporting leg—the left; the left forearm is stretched out horizontally, just as in that old Peloponnesian type whose influence we have traced down throughout the whole fifth century.   Moreover, the figure has the self-contained bearing of the series of Argive statues extending from Hagelaidas to Polykleitos. The Satyr has been compared to the 'oil-pourer' at Munich,[3] and has even been taken as derived from it.   The comparison is instructive, if only because it emphasizes the difference between the two figures.[4]   The 'oil-pourer' shows lines recklessly broken up, an oblique position of the body, and a sturdy attitude with legs well apart; everything is so arranged as to give a true rendering of the intention and the action, while in the Satyr the action is a matter of indifference.   The sole object of the artist is to produce a restful, pleasing design.   In this too he followed Polykleitos, who always paid most attention to that point.

To turn now to the head. The structure of the skull differs totally from that of the Hermes, and closely recalls the Polykleitan manner.   In place of the round Attic skull of the Munich 'oil-pourer' and of the Hermes, we find a close approach to the square Argive type.   The skull is also considerably deeper and higher behind the ears than in the Hermes.   The difference in the hair does not arise merely from the difference of material; it is a real difference of treatment.   The hair still lies close to the head, so as to show the shape.   The form of the separate locks (especially of the intertwining ends in front of and behind the ear), the symmetrical parting in front, and the small pointed locks hanging over the forehead, are all evidence of the influence exerted by the later Polykleitan works.

[1] From the Berlin copy (*Skulpt.* 257) it has been assumed that the vessel in the original was a drinking-horn, but the kylix of the Palermo copy is more probably correct.   In the Ludovisi statue there is preserved the end, not of a twisted horn, but of a twisted support which connected forearm and leg; these sort of supports are common in the age of Hadrian and the Antonines.   It seems to me that in the original the left hand more probably held a cup; pouring from a height seems to me more natural when the liquid falls on a broad surface, rather than into a narrow vessel.

[2] *e.g.* Friederichs-Wolters, *Gipsabg.* Nos. 1058, 1059, 1063, 1066.

[3] Ghirardini, *loc. cit.*   [4] Thus rightly Michaelis, *Ann. d. Inst.* 1883, 140, note 1.

Beyond these formal elements, however, the Argive influence does not extend. The spirit and expression of the head, nay, even the formation of the forehead, which though sparer in treatment yet shows the same shape as the Hermes, the round, soft, tender grace and kindly cheerfulness of the small mouth and cheeks, are thoroughly Attic, and entirely in the spirit of the Hermes. Marked as is the resemblance of the body to the Peloponnesian prototypes, the deviations from it are no less noticeable. The navel is sunk deeper, and below it there is no trace of the *linea alba*; the division between the abdomen and thighs is no longer marked with the old conventional hardness; the gluteus of the free leg has no depression; the flesh is softer and fuller, and the best copies show that in the original the delicate play of the muscles under the firm flesh must have been a special charm of the statue.

FIG. 133.—Eros from the Palatine (Louvre).

Hence it is clear that the Satyr is of an earlier date than the Hermes, and it is as a youthful work of Praxiteles that we must consider it. We learn from it that the work of the Polykleitan school exercised a lasting influence on the young artist—an influence we can well understand with a youth so alive to beauty and grace of form. He had opportunities enough of studying the work of Peloponnesian artists at Athens (we still have an inscription from a work by Naukydes on the Akropolis), and he soon went himself to the Peloponnesos, where he worked for Mantineia.[1] The date of the Satyr lies between 370 and 360 B.C.

To the same period belongs a second work by the same artist like at all points to the preceding. It is an Eros, of which we have a good copy in a torso from the Palatine, which has been restored and is now in the Louvre (Fig. 133).[2] That an Eros should be the nearest counterpart to the Satyr is a

[1] The group of Apollo, Leto, and Artemis in Megara must have been one of the artist's early works. Imitations of it on coins (Imhoof-Blumer and Gardner, *Num. Comm.* Pl. A, x.; FF, i. ii.) seems to point to a group of severe character in the style of the fifth century. The work might be by the elder Praxiteles.

[2] Fröhner, *Notice*, p. 311, No. 325; Brunn-Bruckmann, *Denkm.* No. 378. Fig. 133 leaves out the restored head and left arm. Left forearm, right leg, left knee, and right foot are restored. The beautiful large left wing is antique. A cast of the torso, unrestored, was formerly in the small museum of the Palatine, and was there drawn by Eichler, 1876—77, for the Institute. Steinhäuser's restorations are hideous. The antique

S S

confirmation of the Praxitelean origin of both, for Praxiteles is the very artist who was as famous for his Erotes as for his Satyrs. This Eros torso is extraordinarily like the Satyr both in the attitude of the body and in the system of forms. The only difference is that the head is turned, not to the side of the supporting leg,

FIG. 134.—Eros in Naples.

but somewhat to the right, thus sacrificing the tranquil absorption of the figure. What the hands held is uncertain; possibly a wreath or a fillet, as attributes of the god;[1] at any rate the right arm was held very high; the tree-trunk with the quiver and bow is merely an addition by the copyist. The formation of the body, though still on the same basis as in the Satyr, goes further in the direction of softness and roundness. The abdomen is less flat, the soft layer of flesh over the muscles is more clearly indicated; the depression above the navel is deeper; what remains of the hair shows a fuller, freer treatment, from which we may infer that the Eros is a later work of the youth of Praxiteles.

In close connexion with both the preceding creations are two others of less importance, which are possibly only the work of a contemporary imitator. These two statues, both under life-size, represent respectively Apollo[2] and Dionysos,[3] and correspond in attitude and bodily forms to the Satyr, except that the right hand rests quietly on the head. In the Apollo the head has been preserved; it agrees in pose and inclination with the Satyr, and, like it, bears witness to Polykleitan influence, in having the parted hair growing closely to the skull and hanging down over the forehead in symmetrical curls.

On the other hand, there is a second Eros, which must have been another creation

parts are also somewhat worked over in parts. For sketch of the antique parts and description, see Roscher's *Lexikon*, i. 1360, 1361, Z. 18 *seq.* Milani (*Mus. Ital.* iii. p. 767) and R. Förster (*Eros, Rede*, 1893, p. 10) agreed with me in referring it to Praxiteles. Weil, in Baumeister's *Denkm.* p. 1401, with fig. 1551. There is a replica in the museum at Parma (Arndt-Bruckmann, *Einzelverk.* No. 74).

[1] Cf. Roscher's *Lexikon, loc. cit.* Milani (*loc. cit.*) thought he had found an imitation of the statue on an Athenian coin: Beulé, *Monn. d'Ath.* p. 222 (= Brit. Mus. *Catal. Attica*, Pl. 12, 3; p. 39). But the motive is not the same. The figure on the coin represents a palaestric Eros (cf. Roscher's *Lex.* i. 1344, Z. 7), or another palaestric Daemon, possibly Agon, according to Weil's hypothesis (*Arch. Ztg.* Bd. xxxiii. 164). The Eros of Kallistratos, with which Milani identifies it, must have been quite different, and is, I think, reproduced in a small bronze (cf. *Jahrb. d. Ver. v. Alterthums-Fr. im Rheinland*, Heft 90, p. 63, Taf. 3, 3).

[2] In the Louvre. Fröhner, *Notice*, No. 74; Clarac, Pl. 269, 912; photo. édit. Giraudon, No. 1202. Poor. The stem with the tripod is only a technical support; the left forearm does not really lean on it. This work is quite distinct from the later Praxitelean 'Resting Apollo.'

[3] In Tarragona, Hübner, *Bildw. in Madrid*, No. 672; Friederichs-Wolters, *Gipsabg.* 1488.

of the sculptor's youth, and which, to judge from the number of extant copies, must have been far more celebrated. I know of seven copies of this Eros, of presumably the same size as the original (about life-size), and four statuettes. The best-known replica is the torso from Centocelle (head in Fig. 135)[1] in the Vatican; the statue at Naples (Fig. 134)[2] is better preserved, and the work, though hasty, is fresh, and probably dates from the first century B.C. The main effect is faithfully reproduced, but little attention is paid to such details as the hair. On the support near the left leg are seen the remains of a bow, once held in the left hand. This accessory is more correctly reproduced in a third copy at Turin.[3] In it one end of the big bow rests on the ground, and the left hand holds the upper end of the weapon. A tree-trunk

FIG. 135.—Head of Eros of Centocelle (Vatican).

which serves as support has a quiver hanging from it; but it is evident that it was only added by a copyist, for it has nothing to do with the design, and is differently treated by the several copyists. In the original the bow stood clear of the statue. A piece of the bow is also preserved in a replica in Russia.[4]

[1] Helbig, *Museums*, 185 ; Friederichs-Wolters, 1578. Holes for wings on the back.

[2] Clarac, 649, 1487 ; Roscher's *Lexikon*, i. 1359. Right arm, left forearm, and left leg restored ; wings mostly antique. The front of the body is somewhat worked over. The head is much more lifelike than the one in the Vatican.

[3] Dütschke, *Oberital.* iv. No. 49. The statue is well preserved ; the head (except the ends of the curls on the neck) is restored ; the basis is antique, so are both legs, though broken. The right foot is drawn back, and the heel raised. The left arm and hand are antique, though broken ; the hand rests on the end of the bow. The bow is carved in relief in a vertical position on the front of the trunk, the upper part of which is restored. The right upper arm is antique, and separated from the body.

[4] Stephani, *Die Antikensamml. zu Pawlowsk* (*Mém de l'Acad. de St. Petersb.* xviii. 4), p. 8, No. 6. From Stephani's description I gather that it is a genuine replica. The bow is introduced as it is in the Turin statue ; it is important to note that, according to Stephani, the right arm and the open empty hand are antique : also the large wings seem to be antique. I have already (*Bull. d. Inst.* 1877, 153) refuted Stephani's assertion that the figure formed a group with Psyche. Overbeck shares Stephani's opinion (*Plastik*, 3rd ed. ii. 34).

The fifth replica, recently found in Rome, is only a torso (Terme Museum);[1] the sixth has neither head nor arms;[2] the seventh (Palazzo Conserv.)[3] is distinguished from all the others through the absence of wings, and moreover it is by far the worst and obviously quite the latest of the copies. In the right hand may be seen the remains of some attribute, apparently a small torch, which, on the analogy of a small replica, was held reversed upon an altar. The statuette,[4] however, is of very late and poor workmanship, and is also wingless.[5] The question now arises whether the torch reversed upon the altar—an emblem of funereal import[6]—together with the winglessness which marks the figure as a kind of genius of death,[7] are, on the ground of those two poor and late replicas, to be ascribed to the original statue. The answer must be in the negative. We merely have here one of those transformations, effected by some trifling external additions, such as Greek originals not unfrequently underwent at the hands of later Roman artists; besides, in one, or perhaps even in two copies,[8] the right hand still exists, and has no such attribute. Further, a decorative stucco at Pompeii,[9] which truthfully reproduces the main points of the statue, shows the left hand supporting the large bow placed on the ground, and the right hand hanging down empty. Of course there is no support for the left leg, any more than there can have been in the original; the wings, as in the Palatine Eros, are very large. All the evidence tends to prove that the right hand was empty, yet in the original it may not impossibly have held an arrow, which might easily be omitted by the copyist.

The original must go back to Praxiteles. I once thought that we only had late adaptations of it,[10] because I wrongly believed that all the copies should be restored with the inverted torch on the altar, and because I followed the commonly received opinion that the plait of hair worn by the Eros belonged to the Roman period. This was a mistake, for practically the same fashion of hair occurs in a boy's head of the fifth century—probably also an Eros.[11] My next view was that the original of the statue should be sought for in the Peloponnesian school of the fourth century,[12] because of the intimate connexion between this statue and the later Polykleitan works. But I have since found all these characteristics in the early work of Praxiteles, and various considerations will eventually show that he was the artist. Thus the old conjecture of E. Q. Visconti seems likely to prove true.

---

[1] The torso has suffered by water; the ends of the curls are preserved; large holes in the back for the wings.

[2] Rome, Coll. Monteverde (Arndt-Bruckmann, *Einzelverk.* No. 141).

[3] Discussed by me in *Bull. dell' Inst.* 1877, 151 *seq.* Published in *Bull. delle Comm. Arch. di Roma*, 1877, Tav. 16; 17, 1. Cf. Helbig, *Museums*, 569. The head is wrongly put on.

[4] Vatican, Gall. dei Candel. 203; Gerhard, *Ant. Bildw.* Taf. 93, 2; Helbig, *Museums*, 393. For the restorations, cf. *Bull. d. Inst.* 1877, 152, No. 2.

[5] The three other statuettes are: Berlin, 139. Torso with wings.—Copenhagen, Jacobsen collection, 1051, headless, bronze wings fastened on by two cramps. Quiver hangs on the trunk, on the top of which are traces of the attachment of the bow as on the Naples replica. Remains of a spiral puntello on the right thigh to join it to the wrist.—Turin. Head only. Fair work.　　　　[6] Cf. *Bull. d. Inst.* 1877, 154 *seq.*

[7] Helbig (*Bull. d. Inst.* 1885, 71) and Führer (No. 183) called it Thanatos. [His view is now modified; cf. *Museums*, 185.—E. S.]

[8] On the copy of Pawlowsk (p. 315, note 4), and perhaps on the one at Turin (p. 315, note 3).

[9] *Mus. Borbonico*, ii. 53; Brulloff, *Thermes de Pompeii*, Pl. 4. In *Bull. d. Inst.* 1877, 160, I pointed out the differences between these two publications. Brulloff gives the right hand empty, in *Mus. Borb.* it holds an arrow. The original is in Pompeii, on the wall of the Tepidarium of the *Thermae* of Fortuna. It is clear that the hand was empty, although only the thumb and forefinger remain. The stucco relief corresponds with the statue in attitude, turn of head, etc., but the head is not bent, and the plaits of hair are not exactly reproduced.

[10] *Bull. dell' Inst.* 1877, 160; where stress is yet laid on the fact that an original of the best period is its origin. Stephani (*loc. cit.*) also assigns the motive to the Roman epoch. Wolters does this still more definitely in *Gipsab.* p. 634.

[11] *Archäol. Studien H. Brunn dargebr.* 1893, p. 88 *seq.* Taf. 3.　　　　[12] Roscher's *Lex.* i. 1362.

It is the obviously great reputation of the work which tells most in favour of Praxiteles, the most celebrated pourtrayist of Eros. In the second place, the bodily forms present great similarity to the Satyr and the Palatine Eros, though the age represented is certainly somewhat more advanced, since the muscles are more powerfully developed.

The motive, like that of the Satyr, is connected with the series of Argive types. The attitude of the body and the turn and bend of the head agree with the Polykleitan 'boy crowning himself' and the Ildefonso figure; the motion of the arms, however, is different, and the upper part of the body is slightly twisted, the right shoulder being slightly thrust forward. Even this attitude, though reversed, is found in the Polykleitan 'Dresden boy' (Plate XII.), who is almost identical with our Eros; even the arms correspond—one hanging down beside the body, the other being outstretched; and if the Eros held, as we conjectured, an arrow in his right hand, the analogy with the Polykleitan boy, who also held something in the hand towards which the head is turned, becomes so much the closer.

It is evident that the youthful Praxiteles had fallen under the charm of those Polykleitan figures, and his Eros shows an admirable adaptation of their chief characteristics. For Praxiteles, as for Polykleitos, the rhythmic grace of the whole motive depends very largely on the bend of the head. But this bend of the head has also been used by both sculptors for the purposes of characterization: in one case it serves to emphasize the modesty of the boy victor; in the other, a slight change of attitude has sufficed to produce a very different effect: it is the demoniac nature of Eros which is expressed in that bent head, in that face peering up from amid its profusion of locks.[1]

This is no longer the joyous, innocent Eros with wreath and fillet, as we can imagine him to have been represented in the Palatine torso: he has become the bewitching daemon, the captivating, irresistible god, ἀπάντων δαιμόνων ὑπέρτατος, glorified in the poetry of Euripides,[2] who gave him as symbols of his all-powerful sway the bow and arrow[3] which he carries here. We can now understand why Praxiteles gave to this Eros more developed forms than to the other.

The god holds his bow (and arrow?) ready for immediate use, yet the artist only intends them as an outward symbol, for he has essayed the difficult task of giving visible expression to the inward might of the god: he does not allow him to use his weapons, his Eros is irresistible through his upward glance and bewitching charm. . . . We have thus unconsciously arrived at a presentment of the god which agrees strictly with a well-known ancient epigram on the Thespian Eros of Praxiteles, to the effect that he excited the transports of love by hurling not darts but glances, φίλτρα δὲ βάλλω οὐκ᾿ ἔτ᾿ οἰστεύων, ἀλλ᾿ ἀτενιζόμενος.[4] Further, since this statue was, as we saw, an early work of Praxiteles, made at the same time as the Satyr; and

---

[1] That the bent head means grief is a modern misunderstanding of Friederichs (*Bausteine*, 448). His earlier opinion (expressed in his exquisite monograph on Praxiteles, p. 22), that the head is bent in a dreamy mood, and is characteristic of Praxiteles, is more correct.

[2] Cf. Roscher's *Lex*. i. 1348.   [3] Cf. *ibid*. 1348, and *Arch. Anz.* 1890, p. 89.

[4] For the epigram, cf. Benndorf, in *Bull. della Comm. Arch. di Roma*, 1886, p. 69 *seq*., who shows that ἀτενιζόμενος is in the middle voice. His proofs seem to me absolutely convincing, and Robert's arguments (*Arch. Märchen*, p. 167) are powerless to refute them. By the basis in the theatre, however, on which, according to Athenaeus, the epigram was inscribed, I incline to understand, not as Benndorf does, the original basis in Thespiai (for Athenaeus does not mention this city at all), but a basis of later date supporting a replica in Athens. Near the theatre was found a torso of an Aphrodite which appears to be an admirable replica of the Aphrodite in Thespiai (cf. *supra*, p. 319, n. 1) I have already shown (p. 271, note) that Benndorf is wrong in referring to the Eros of Thespiai a statue of Ares in the Capitoline Museum.

since in the story of Phryne's stratagem the Thespian Eros actually figures in
company with a famous Satyr; and, finally, since a statue preserved in so many
copies must have been one of the sculptor's masterpieces—there can be hardly any
doubt that we are right in identifying it with the Thespian statue.

What dates we have of Phryne's life agree very well with the conjecture that the
Eros which she dedicated at Thespiai was one of the works of the earlier period of
Praxiteles, between 370 and 360 B.C.   The only reliable chronological information we
have about her, beyond her connexion with the artist, is that she inspired the 'Anadyomene' of Apelles, and there is nothing to prevent our placing this about 350.[1]
When Phryne offered to rebuild Thebes in 335 B.C., after its destruction by Alexander,
she may very well have been advanced in years, for this was an enterprise for which
only money was needed.   The lawsuit, in which she was defended by Hyperides,
cannot be closely dated.[2]   Writers of the Middle Comedy speak of her as a
contemporary,[3] while in the New Comedy she is alluded to as a *hetaira* of the
previous generation.[4]   It has been plausibly suggested that it was not till after the
destruction of her home, Thespiai, by the Thebans that she came to Athens, at a time
when her countrymen were turning to Athens for succour (probably B.C. 373—372).[5]
At any rate, in order to be known as a Thespian, she must have been born before
that date, and need no longer have been a child[6] at the time.   Her connexion with
Praxiteles, which anyhow belongs most naturally to the artist's youth, would take
place in the period immediately following.   The temple at Thespiai was of course
spared by the Thebans,[7] and Phryne, in recognition of her successes in Athens, sent a
handsome votive offering to the god of her native town, though its walls were razed
and the town itself had passed into the power of Thebes.[8]   The Thebans, however,
would certainly not interfere with private piety or dedications in the temple, their
only object being to destroy the political existence of the community.

Phryne's offering apparently consisted of three statues, for beside the Eros stood
a statue of herself, and one of Aphrodite, both by the hand of Praxiteles: the Eros
probably stood between the two,[9] and the group was analogous to that of the Satyr
between Dionysos and Methe (p. 311).   This presentation of her own portrait by
the *hetaira* was simply in accordance with an old custom.   We are expressly told that[10]
her gilded portrait at Delphi, also by Praxiteles, was dedicated by the *hetaira* herself.
The material of this statue and the place where it was set up mark an advance

---

[1] Owing to his relations with Philip, Apelles must have been active at this time.

[2] Sal. Reinach points out (*Rev. Crit.* 1894, p. 110) that Hyperides was very little older than Phryne was
according to our assumption.   I see in this no reason against the dating proposed above.

[3] Timokles, *apud* Athen. p. 567 e.   In Aristoph. *Eccles.* 1101, Phryne is only a name given to any
courtezan.   [4] Poseidippos, *apud* Athen. p. 591 e.

[5] Xenoph. *Hell.* 6, 3, 1.   Cf. Von Stern, *Gesch. d. spartan. u. theban. Hegemonie*, p. 119.

[6] As Sal. Reinach (*Gaz. Archéol.* 1887, 283) assumes, by placing her birth about B.C. 375.   In 335 she may
just as well have been fifty as forty.   Overbeck (*Sächs. Ber.* 1893, p. 40 *seq.*) places Phryne's birth (in connexion
with his wrong late dating of Praxiteles) after B.C. 372, assuming that Thespiai was recolonized again immediately, a view that cannot be reconciled with tradition.   (Cf. *infra*, note 8.)

[7] In the similar case of Plataia, this is expressly stated.   Paus. ix. 1, 8.

[8] As Thespiai seems, like Plataia, not to have been rebuilt till after Chaironaia—for that this had not yet
taken place in 343 is proved by Demosthenes (F. L. 111, 325)—Phryne's votive gift must fall in the time when the
walls were in ruins and the citizens scattered.   For to place her gift after the rebuilding would contradict all we
know for certain about Praxiteles.   And why should Phryne have delayed her gift to her ancestral god till the
Thespians had rebuilt these walls and were again politically independent?

[9] When Alkiphron (Overbeck, *S. Q.* 1271) makes Phryne say that she stood in the middle between Eros and
Aphrodite, he is evidently merely indulging in a rhetorical period.

[10] Paus. x. 15, 1.   The statements that the περικτίονες (Athenaeus) or the Ἕλληνες (Aelian) had dedicated
the statue are in each case due to misunderstanding.

upon the Thespian offering, so that it must have been the later work.   We now have
to consider whether there exist any copies of these statues.

The well-known 'Vénus d'Arles' (Fig. 136)[1] is certainly to be referred to
Praxiteles.   This is mainly proved by the extraordinary likeness of the head to the
authentic copies of the Knidian Aphrodite (*infra*, p. 322).   The arrangement of the
hair with its double fillet, the forehead, the contour of the face—and we may
add the bracelet on the left upper arm—all correspond perfectly.   It is only in
details that the forms of the head are harder and more constrained ; the eye is
less deeply set, the eyelids are rendered in the old manner, and the drawing of the
mouth is more severe.

An examination of the body confirms the impression that the Venus of Arles
belongs to the early period of Praxiteles.   The attitude is very like that of the
Eirene and of the 'Satyr pouring out wine' : the left leg bears the weight of the body,
the left forearm is outstretched bearing some object towards which the head is turned
and inclined, and the right arm is raised.   As in the Eirene the right foot is not drawn
behind the other, but only placed to the side in Pheidian fashion with the heel off the
ground.   One of the muses on the Mantineian relief—the one playing the flute—is
also closely related in the whole rhythm of her attitude.   The simple broad treatment
of the drapery corresponds to that of the Eirene and to the relief just mentioned,
which is a work of Praxiteles's youth.   Specially characteristic is the treatment of the
nude, which so far as youth and maiden can be compared is closely related to that of
the Satyr ; for the abdomen is still flat, and the whole front of the body is still treated
in great broad planes, ending in a harsh line at the side ; the thorax is broad, and the
breasts, very youthful in form, are far apart ;[2] the undulation of the hip above the
supporting leg is as yet only slightly indicated.

There can be little doubt as to the motive of the Venus of Arles : the left hand
held a mirror ; the right was raised towards the head.   An engraved gem[3] of the early
fourth century shows a woman, doubtless an Aphrodite, with a mantle wrapped in
the same way round the lower part of the body and a mirror in her left hand.   The
terra-cottas of that period frequently reproduce the same design.[4]   The partial nudity
of the figure is explained by the fact that the goddess is at her toilet.

The statue belongs to the period of the Satyr and the Thespian Eros ; therefore
it probably represents the Aphrodite which stood beside the latter at Thespiai.

A statue in the British Museum from Ostia (Fig. 137)[5] is in close connexion with
the one just described ; it is a variant of the same motive, with the sides reversed.   The
head is again so like the Venus of Knidos that we must refer this work also to

[1] Fröhner, *Notice*, No. 137.   'Thasian' marble.   Right arm and left hand new.   Drapery worked over, head
well preserved (cf. *supra*, vignette on title-page).   Cf. Bernouilli, *Aphrodite*, p. 182 ; Brunn-Bruckmann, *Denkmäler*,
No. 296.   An excellent replica (torso) was found in Athens near the theatre (Friederichs-Wolters, 1456).   Cf.
Roscher's *Lex.* i. 415, Z. 30.   Brunn-Bruckmann, *Denkm.* No. 300 A.   The workmanship of this torso (in the
finest Parian Lychnites) is so wonderful that it is impossible to resist the notion that it is a replica from the studio of
Praxiteles himself or of one of his sons.   (For a replica of the Thespian Eros in the theatre at Athens, cf. *supra*,
p. 317, n. 4.)
[2] The breasts are much more lifelike in the Athens torso than in the Paris statue.   The Athens torso gives a
much better idea of the original.
[3] In Berlin, 4631 ; scaraboid from Sparta ; judging from style certainly not later than the first half of the
fourth century ; even the attitude of rest on the left leg corresponds ; the right hand moves towards the head, but
does not hold anything.   The hair is bound with three fillets like the statue.   Broad chest.
[4] Cf. *e.g.* Dumont-Chaplain, *Céramiques*, ii. Pl. 28, 1 ; here the raised right hand holds a band for the hair.
The style shows that this figure must be dated in the first half of the fourth century.   The attitude of rest on the
left leg and the wide flat chest are very like the Arles statue.
[5] Friederichs-Wolters, 1455.   The head is unbroken ; the left arm is restored, but it was raised ; the right
hand is new.   Fröhner, *Notice*, p. 180, calls the statue an 'imitation' of the Arles statue.

Praxiteles.   But the original must have been a later work than the Venus of Arles.
The attitude and action are less constrained, the free leg is drawn more back, and,
above all, the head, which is relatively smaller, is turned towards the side of the free
leg, and raised, thus destroying all the repose and tranquillity of the earlier conception.
The drapery is richer and more agitated, and falls down lower on the one side; the

FIG. 135.—'Vénus d'Arles' (Louvre).

bodily forms are rounder and closely related to the Knidian statue, the chest is no
longer so broad and flat, the breasts are closer together, the navel is sunk deeper,
and the lower abdominal line is treated precisely as in the Knidian statue.

The motive also was certainly identical with that of the Venus of Arles; the left
hand held up the mirror, and the right may have held some other toilet requisite. The
whole conception lacks the dignity and repose of the other statue; this maiden has a
questioning, self-conscious look; rejoicing in her beauty she raises the mirror—and
cares not if her mantle slips down a little lower.

It seems to me that a Phryne by Praxiteles must have looked just like this—ideally
beautiful and noble, yet different enough from a goddess.   The statue of Phryne so

famous in antiquity was the one at Delphi; as we saw, it was later than the
Thespian offering. It is this statue that I'should like to imagine as the original of
the 'Townley Venus.' Of both the portraits, also, between which she was placed—

Fig. XLV—Resting Satyr, Rome, Vatican Museum (See
    p. 329)

Fig. 137.—The 'Townley Venus' (Brit. Mus.)

King Archidamos of Sparta and Philip of Macedon—copies seem to exist, found in
that villa at Herculaneum whose owner was so devout an admirer of Greek philosophy.

¹ An Archidamos is preserved, as Wolters (*Röm. Mitth.* 1888, 113 *seq.*) has shown, in a terminal bust of the
Herculaneum Villa. Wolters remembers only the two Archidamos statues of Olympia, and not the Delphi
portrait, which is much more renowned; he concludes from the style that the terminal bust represents
Archidamos III., but admits the similarity of the portrait to that of Euripides. The resemblance is indeed so
strong that we may assume the same artist for both portraits. The stylistic treatment of the hair in the Archidamos points to the period of the Peloponnesian war, therefore the statue presumably represents the Archidamos
by whose name the first period of the war was designated. It is not impossible that Demetrios, who belonged to

T T

After the Cynic Krates had mocked at this juxtaposition of a courtesan and a king, later ages cited it as a typical instance of Greek licence.[1]

The Aphrodite of Knidos must, from the preceding considerations, be assigned to the middle period of the career of Praxiteles.[2]   This conjecture is strengthened when we remember that works executed for three towns so near each other, and so far from home as Knidos, Kos, and Halikarnassos, must needs be of about the same date.   The Mausoleum was begun in 353 B.C., so that the statue for Knidos should be dated about 350 B.C.   It has been preserved in a series of copies presumably of the original size, and also in statuettes.   All these doubtless reflect the style and design of the statue, but can give us no idea of its subtler qualities.   We must be careful, however, not to reckon among the copies, as has been done hitherto, works which are really later independent adaptations, such as the Munich statue and the little head at Olympia.[3]

Praxiteles has represented the goddess disrobed for the bath, in the act of laying aside her last covering.   She turns her head quickly round in the direction of the free leg,[4] an attitude only comprehensible if we imagine her as looking about her to make sure her privacy is not threatened.   This also explains the instinctive movement of the right hand.   The dominating note of the expression is its absolute freedom from any stronger emotion—from any yearning or languishing.   It was only in later adaptations that voluptuous suggestions [5] were introduced, but the goddess of Praxiteles produced her effect by the purity and innocence of her expression, by her simple grace and noble naturalness.   As regard bodily forms, the statue stands about midway between the older type of the ' Venus of Arles ' and the later Medicean Venus.   Much as she differs from the former, she yet also differs from the latter, especially in the breadth of the chest and in the modelling of the contours, which are far less full and rounded.

In addition to the nude Aphrodite of Knidos, an entirely draped Aphrodite by Praxiteles—probably the one described as *velata specie* at Kos—is known to us in a poor and late reproduction, which however has the advantage of being attested by docu-

that period, might be the artist (cf. p. 122, n. 2).   The Archidamos was found in the Villa Ercolanense in the great peristyle as a companion piece to a term representing a beardless man, who, judging from style and type, might very well be Philip of Macedon, who stood beside the Archidamos at Delphi.   Gercke (*Bonner Studien*, p. 141) suggests Philhetairos, instead of Philip, but the lower part of the face, which deviates from the fixed type of the coins, speaks against this assumption.

[1] Τῆς τῶν Ἑλλήνων ἀκρασίας ἀνάθημα, Krates, *apud* Athen. p. 591 b.

[2] Our dating of Phryne does not clash with this in the least, as Sal. Reinach asserts (*Rev. Crit.* 1894. 110), for of course no reliance can be placed on the anecdote that Phryne sat as a model to the sculptor.

[3] As Michaelis has done in his last treatise on the statue (*J. H. S.* 1887, 324 *seq.*) Cf. my remarks in *Arch. Anz.* 1891, p. 140 *seq.*   Michaelis's list of copies is in need of revision.   The following are true copies of the Venus of Knidos, and correspond in their measurements :   (1) = Mich. A, in the ' Magazino ' of the Vatican ; bronze cast in the Louvre (cf. *Arch. Anz.*, *loc. cit.*); head unbroken ; best preserved copy ; workmanship good.—(2) = Mich. D ; Helbig, *Museums*, 316 ; head wrongly adjusted ; modern neck.   Poor, leathery work.—(3) and (4) Museo Torlonia, No. 106, 146 (but *not* No. 26, which Mich. reckons with the others) ; both much restored.—(5) = Mich. C ; Pal. Pitti ; body good ; head wrongly adjusted, but genuine.—(6) Villa Ludovisi, Helbig, *Museums*, 869 ; head readjusted according to the line of breakage ; fair copy, which passes incorrectly as modern.—(7) Torso in Kaufmann Coll. (Berlin) from Tralles ; the head (*Ant. Denkm.* i. 41) is the best copy of the head.—(8) Torso, Louvre, No. 2885.—(9) Torso in Villa Medici, wrongly restored.—(10) Bust in Louvre = Fröhner, 164 ; neck unbroken.—(11) Head in Louvre, wrongly given to a reclining nymph (Fröhner, 454).—(12) Head in Museo Chiaramonti, No. 254 ; fair work, but much rubbed over.—(13) Head in Capitol, Gal. No. 39.—(14) Head, Mus. Boncompagni-Ludovisi, No. 21.—Among the statuettes there is one very good and well-preserved copy in the Museo Chiaramonti, No. 119 c ; an inferior one in Potsdam in the picture gallery.   A bronze not quite exact in detail, Fröhner, Coll. Gréau, *Bronzes*, Pl. 26, No. 927.

[4] The turn has been kept especially well in 1, 6, 7, 10, 11.

[5] Especially in the Munich statue, where the thighs are pressed together.

mentary evidence.   It is a statue in the Louvre (Fig. 138),[1] round whose plinth runs an ancient inscription, Πραξιτέλης ἐποίησεν, dating from late Imperial times.   Until a short time ago this inscription was only known from a notice in Visconti, and had disappeared because the ancient plinth had been let in or sunk in such a manner that the inscription was supposed to be lost.[2] Lately the edge of the plinth has been set free, and the inscription is again legible.[3] According to every analogy, the inscription can only mean that the work is a copy after Praxiteles, and the style certainly confirms this view.   The goddess wears a long thin chiton, girded deep about the hips ; the right shoulder is lowered, allowing the garment to slip slightly off, but not so as to expose the bosom.   The attitude is as simple as that of the Knidian statue ; the weight of the body is thrown on to the right leg, the left shoulder is much raised, the right hip curved outwards.   In the copy the left hand rests on the head of a little Eros obviously of late Roman origin, which cannot possibly have belonged to the original ; it doubtless replaces some accessory which was not to the liking of the copyist ; but if the hand be imagined to have rested on a terminal figure or an idol, we obtain a motive especially popular in the time of Praxiteles.   The head is unfortunately missing.[4]

Fig. 138.—Statue in Louvre. (From Clarac, *Mus. de Sc.* Pl. 341.)

The main charm of this statue must have resided in the natural treatment of the thin semi-transparent drapery.   The copy at any rate still allows this to be felt, and shows how differently the artist solved the problem which Alkamenes had essayed before him (*Venus Genetrix*, p. 82).   Those clinging wet draperies, those beautifully arranged if conventional folds of the earlier artist, are quite abandoned in the Praxitelean period, which condemned them as untrue ; thus here also Praxiteles, in the multitude of fine flowing folds, is striving entirely after truth of effect.   The lines of the folds are not beautiful in themselves, as they were in the older system, but they are charming (or were so in the original), because they reflect the rich abundance of nature.   The same drapery, treated in the same way, as well as the deep girdle and the slight displacement of the drapery on one shoulder, is seen in another Praxitelean work, in the chiton of the Artemis Brauronia, a statue which I agree with Studniczka in thinking we have a copy of in the 'Diane de Gabies' (Louvre).[5]   Further, many a work of later times (like the celebrated Flora Farnese)[6] was evidently inspired by the Aphrodite of Kos.

According to Studniczka's very probable suggestion, the Brauronia of Praxiteles was set up on the Akropolis, in B.C. 346.   It therefore belongs to the later period of his artistic activity.   He must evidently have returned from Asia Minor about

---

[1] Published Bouillon, t. iii. *Statues*, Pl. 6, 7.   Clarac, *Musée*, Pl. 341, 1291 (= our Fig. 138, which omits the restored head). Cf. Bernouilli, *Aphrodite*, p. 111, No. 2.

[2] Cf. Fröhner, *Notice*, 151 ; Löwy, *I. G. B.* 502.

[3] The epigraphy is of the later Imperial period.   Sal. Reinach (*Gaz. Arch.* 1887, 259, note 5) called attention to the inscription.   The statue is not, as R. supposes, a replica of the 'Genetrix.'

[4] Head and right shoulder are modern, not ancient and readjusted as Clarac and Fröhner assert.

[5] Studniczka, *Vermut. z. Kunstgesch.* p. 18 *seq.*   Robert (*Arch. Märchen*, p. 144 *seq.*) has adduced nothing decisive against this supposition ; cf. p. 102, note 3.   To the known replicas of the statue should be added a head in Berlin, *Skulpt.* 625.   The Praxitelean Dionysos, in the Hope Coll. at Deepdene (Surrey), is analogous to this Artemis in the drapery (Clarac, 695, 1614; Roscher's *Lex.* i. 1133).

[6] Clarac, 438 B, 795 D ; cf. 437, 792 (Munich Glyptothek, 298).

Fig. XLVI—Artemis of Brauron, New York, Metropolitan Museum of Art (See Notes)

this time. Shortly before this
he had brought to a close his
work in Ephesos, Halikarnassos, Knidos, and Kos.

Belonging apparently to
the earlier part of his career
is another statue of Artemis,
of which the best copy is the
one at Dresden[1] (Figs. 139,
140). It represents the goddess as a quite young, still
undeveloped girl, wearing a
long ungirt tunic, and standing in a simple, tranquil attitude, her bow in her left
hand, while the right feels for
the quiver at her back. The
Praxitelean authorship is
proved by the type of the
head, which corresponds in
contour and arrangement of
hair with the Venus of Arles
and the Knidian Aphrodite,
and merely introduces into
the type a maidenly, almost
childish element. It is above
all the attitude and drapery
of the Dresden statue which
clearly prove its early origin.
The attitude, with the un-
weighted foot placed to the
side, is that of the Eirene and
of the Venus of Arles. Like the
Eirene, too, the drapery falls
in straight folds from the

[1] Dresden, Becker, *Augusteum*, 45;
Clarac, 569, 1214 A; Müller-Wieseler,
ii. 162; Roscher's *Lex.* i. 606, No. 2.
Excellent preservation. Faithful but
rather coarse copyist's work. P. Herrmann and P. Arndt have recognized the
Praxitelean character (cf. Arndt-Bruckmann, *Einzelverk.* to No. 133).—Three
replicas in Cassel, heads not authentic;
in one (ii. 19) a piece of the raised right
arm is antique.—A good replica in Berlin, *Skulpt.* 60 (remains of the raised
right arm antique).—Good statue in
Villa Borghese (Arndt-Bruckmann,
Einzelverk. No. 133; head foreign).
An Ionic under-chiton is added. The
drapery is finer and better executed than
in the Dresden statue.

right knee, but whilst the Eirene seeks to imitate the large simple folds characteristic
of Pheidian drapery, the Munich Artemis shows a wealth of charming detail carefully studied from nature.   There is an astonishing similarity, except that the sides
are reversed, between the drapery falling from the knee and the corresponding portion
on one of the Muses, leaning on her right arm, of the Mantineia relief.

This statue was afterwards slightly altered and turned into an Isis-Tyche, by
lowering the right arm, and by doing away with the quiver, which was no longer
needed to explain the action of the hand, though the quiver-strap was retained

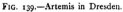

FIG. 139.—Artemis in Dresden.   FIG. 141.—Statuette of Artemis from Kition in Cyprus (Vienna).

because it gave a special charm to the drapery ; the bow in the left hand was replaced
by a cornucopia, and an Ionian under-chiton, visible at the shoulders, was sometimes
added.   The best copy of this variant is at Munich.[1]   Perhaps the basis of this conception was a Tyche by Praxiteles himself, with features borrowed from his Artemis.

[1] *Glypt.* 113.   Brunn-Bruckmann, *Denkm.* No. 123.   The ends of curls on the shoulders are antique.
Thorwaldsen rightly restored a horn of plenty in the left hand.   The replica noted by Winter in the Pal. Sciarra
(Berlin, *Skulpt.* p. 529) gives the true interpretation.   The goddess holds a horn of plenty and a snake ; the child
Harpokrates below.   Replicas, known as such by the lowered right arm, the Ionic under-garment, and the
absence of quiver, are : Clarac, 410 H, 837 A (with horn) ; Museo Torlonia, Taf. 64 and 251 (wrongly restored
in a group) ; Louvre, 1910 (Fröhner, *Notice*, 390), etc.   The type referred to on p. 60, note 1, is related to
this one.

The later Orphic identification of Tyche and Artemis[1] may be derived from an earlier, presumably Eleusinian conception.

The same type was adopted, actually by Praxiteles, for an Athena.[2] A small transverse aegis now takes the place of the quiver-strap; the right arm is raised and rests upon a lance, the left upon a shield. The goddess is conceived as a graceful girl, bright and gentle, but not quivering with excitement, like the youthful Athena attributed to Skopas (*supra*, p. 305). A head in Berlin,[3] belonging to a large statue now lost, bears so marked a likeness to the Knidian Aphrodite that its original must have been a Praxitelean work.

We must not pass over a remarkable statuette of Artemis from Kition in Cyprus (Fig. 141).[4] Here also the goddess is conceived as a graceful but quite young girl in a long chiton. She is leaning against an idol.[5] The folds of drapery round the lower part of the body are quite in the style of the Dresden Artemis. The head likewise resembles that of the Dresden statue, save that the knot of hair is rather different. But this Cypriote statuette has the freshness and bloom of a work which, however slight, is yet an original. It is so thoroughly Praxitelean that we would gladly call it a παρέργον by the master himself, made perhaps when he was in the neighbourhood of Cyprus, at Kos or at Knidos.

In addition to what has been described, a good deal of Praxitelean work might certainly be recovered from the statues and heads of other female divinities.[6] But this master's creations have given rise to such countless variants and adaptations that it is difficult to pick out what was originally his. Such an inquiry would lead us too far from our immediate object, which is to trace the main points in the successive developments of the artist's style. One example however of what is meant may be given. Praxiteles certainly also pourtrayed older, more dignified goddesses, such as Leto for example. Some such type it is that underlies the famous so-called 'Hera Ludovisi.'[7] The arrangement of the front hair, the forehead, and also the lower part of the face clearly show Praxitelean forms. In spite of this, the work is only a Roman creation based on a Praxitelean model; for we must not attempt to deceive ourselves; this famous 'Hera,' which passes for a type of ideal beauty, is in reality only a Roman empress or a lady of the Imperial family, represented as a goddess, as a Ceres or Fortuna. There is external evidence to prove this. The arrangement of the hair at the back, with the typical plait on the nape, is never given to goddesses. It is the special fashion of the Claudian age, and, so far as we know, it occurs at no other period, either before or after.[8] Further, the knotted fillet that

---

[1] *Orph. Hymn.* 72.

[2] Statue of the Villa Borghese, Helbig, *Museums*, 935; *Berichte d. Sächs. Gesell.* 1861, Taf. 1, 2; 1865, Taf. 1, 2, 3. The head is foreign. The right arm was certainly raised. The drapery corresponds in all essentials with the Artemis; on the shoulders an Ionic chiton is visible. Poor work. Replica in Turin, staircase to the *Armeria*; right arm raised; the neck new, but the head seems genuine: Corinthian helmet, hair simply taken back; general Praxitelean character.—Museo Chiaramonti, No. 403; right arm raised, head foreign. In the later statues of Athena, all sorts of Praxitelean influences may generally be distinguished.

[3] Berlin, *Skulpt.* No. 78.—A head in the Vatican (Helbig, *Museums*, 229; *Mus. Pio Clem.* vi. 2, 2) is similar, but differs in the proportions and in the turn of the head.

[4] In Vienna, *Jahrb. d. Kunsts. d. Oesterr. Kaiserh.* v. 1887, Taf. i. ii.; p. 1 *sqq.* (*v.* Schneider). Ohnefalsch-Richter, *Kypros, the Bible and Homer*, Pl. 203, 5; p. 318 *sqq.*

[5] Cf. the Dionysos at Deepdene mentioned p. 323, note 5.

[6] Note especially a Kore statue (head preserved) in Vienna, quite lately publ. by Rob. v. Schneider (*Jahrb. d. Kunsts. d. Oesterr. Kaiserh.*)

[7] Schreiber, *Villa Ludovisi*, 104; Friederichs-Wolters, 1272; Helbig, *Museums*, 872; Roscher's *Lex.* i. 2122 (Vogel); Brunn, *Götterideale*, p. 9.

[8] Cf. Bernouilli, *Röm. Ikonogr.* ii. 1, 181, 193, 182, Fig. 27, 190, Fig. 30. Taf. 14, 15, 21. The elder Agrippina has on her coins just such stiff locks as the 'Hera.' In the Ludovisi inventory for the year 1633

Fig. XLVII—Hermes of Praxiteles, Olympia, Olympia
Museum (See pp. 307 sqq., 337 sqq.)

passes in front of the diadem and falls down at the sides is certainly not the attribute of any goddess, but it is characteristic of the Imperial ladies during the early Empire, and marked them as priestesses,[1] and it is precisely in authentic heads of the Claudian age that we find this same combination of diadem and sacerdotal fillet.[2]   There are various degrees of idealization in these portraits of deified women.   In the Hera Ludovisi it is strongly emphasized, and so is the imitation of Praxitelean style.   But a careful copy from any Greek original the ' Hera ' is not,[3] and the additions in Roman taste are clear enough to be unmistakable to us, though a former school of art criticism might fail to distinguish them.

But to return to the statues of Artemis.   If we assign the Diana of Gabii to Praxiteles, then the ' Diane de Versailles ' cannot be very far removed from him.   For the types of head are nearly related.   Above all, there is nothing in this celebrated statue which could not belong to the master's later period.   Judging from coins, his Artemis at Antikyra [4] must have been very similar.   The ' Diane ' is certainly not, as was formerly believed, a creation of the Hellenistic age.   No such invention remained for that age, for all these types of divinities had been created long before.   Even the Belvedere Apollo has lately been shown to be a fourth-century creation.[5]   The Diana may well be derived from a work by the master of the Apollo—a point to which we shall have to return.

Still more closely related to Praxiteles and to his Artemis of Antikyra is a torso in the Jacobsen Collection.[6]   It is very like the Diana of Versailles, though it is simpler, with less of a gliding gait and a more decided stride ; the garment is open at the side and clings closely to the figure, like the drapery of the Aphrodite of Kos.

Another Artemis type also belongs to the later period of Praxiteles, and is the creation of the master himself.   It shows the goddess arrayed as in the Versailles statue, with a scarf twisted round the short chiton ; in an easy unstudied pose Artemis is leaning her left elbow on a tree-trunk, while her right arm rests on her hip.   A picturesque negligence of dress and of attitude and a certain genial natural-

the head is called ' Giulia ' ; the headdress, characteristic of a portrait-head, had evidently been noticed at that time. Since Winckelmann, the interpretation as Hera has been accepted, and sanctioned by Goethe, Schiller, and Humboldt.   Only Conze (*Familie d. Augustus*, p. 15) doubted the Hera interpretation, and suggested Venus Regina.   From the work on the diadem he ascribes the head to the early Imperial period.

[1] Cf. *e.g.* the Livia from Pompeii, Bernouilli, *loc. cit.* Taf. 5 ; the Roman lady from the Heraion in Olympia, *Ausgrab.* ii. Taf. 30, etc.   The knotted fillet is known to be a priestly attribute ; cf. *e.g.* the Archigallus relief, Schreiber, *Kulturhist. Bilderatlas*, Taf. 16, 9.

[2] Cf. especially the Munich head in Bernouilli, *loc. cit.* 193, where diadem, fillet, and the knot in the neck correspond with the ' Hera,' but the front hair and face are like a portrait.   The head of the Berlin colossal statue (*Skulpt.* 587) is closely related to the ' Hera,' though it is a very inferior work ; it has never been separated from the statue.   The Ludovisi statue probably, like this one, had a horn of plenty on the left arm.   Perhaps it represented Antonia, the consort of Nero Drusus.   She appears on the reverse of her gold and silver coins as Constantia Augusti in chiton and mantle, with horn of plenty on the left arm, with torch raised aloft in her right hand, and wearing a diadem and side curls.   The head on the obverse always has the knotted hair in the neck.

[3] The head with diadem and tied fillet, which is placed on the statue of the Villa Albani, 711 (Helbig, *Museums*, 844), is much more markedly Praxitelean (photo. Bruckmann).

[4] Imhoof-Blumer and Gardner, *Numism Comm.* Pl. Y 17 ; Bauermeister, *Denkm.* p. 1405 ; *Ath. Mitth.* xiv. 229, Taf. 7.   The hair seems to have been dressed in the same way as that of the Versailles statue.   For head-type cf. the coins of Ephesos of the third century, Brit. Mus. *Catal. Ionia*, Pl. x. 4, xi. 1, 2.

[5] Winter in *Jahrb. d. Inst.* 1892, p. 164 *sqq.*   Cf. *infra.*

[6] Ny Carlsberg Glypt. No. 1048 ; no drapery round the hips ; where the quiver-band and girdle meet, a ram's head serves as buckle ; this, the arms of Delphi, would be specially appropriate in the statue of Antikyra. The statue has the same turn of the head as the one in Versailles.   The coin gives the head in profile simply because the full face is not suitable to a coin.   The more marked stride is clearly rendered on the coin.   The left hand must have carried the torch, the right the bow.   On the left knee and behind on the torso are protuberances of uncertain purport.   The Jacobsen torso, No. 1049, is of Pergamene style, and quite different from No. 1048.

ness of treatment show us the sculptor in his later development. This work is preserved in a marble torso of the Museo Chiaramonti.[1] It is highly probable that a marble bust in the Hermitage [2] belongs to this type, and affords an idea of the lofty beauty of the head. The hair is combed back as in the Brauronia, but coiled round at the back in a plait. The head is bent, and has a gay, gracious expression. This pose of the head and the facial forms resemble the Hermes of Olympia as nearly as may be, considering the different personalities represented. The composition as a whole appears to be preserved only on a Greek votive relief, which itself is probably a fourth-century work.[3] A Tanagra terra-cotta gives a later adaptation of the design.[4]

With this statue and the statuette from Cyprus, mentioned above, we come to another group of Praxitelean figures—those which lean with one arm on some support. In his first period the artist does not seem to have been attracted by this attitude, which we meet for the first time in his middle and later period; it is coincident with a broader, more pictorial style, as opposed to the more studied, almost constrained motives of his earlier works. Peloponnesian influence has now fallen into the background, and the artist follows only his own natural bent.

The motive was specially curious in the case of Artemis, for it seems unsuited to her active energetic personality. So much the more clearly does the artist's tendency declare itself. The same remark is true of the Satyr, that frolicsome creature whom Praxiteles yet presents to us in a graceful, contemplative attitude. After he has shaken himself free from the older, more conventional statuary themes the master gives the fullest expression to his own longing for cheerful realism and repose—as contrasted with the Skopasian love of violent movement and excitement. In the 'resting Faun' [5] we have a work belonging to his middle period. Its Praxitelean origin can hardly be doubtful, although the statue cannot be identified with any Satyr handed down by tradition. (It certainly is not the *periboëtos*, which was part of a group.) The Praxitelean authorship is not proved merely by the evident renown of the work and by the gentle grace of the figure: another and more definite reason lies in the likeness of the head to that of the Eubouleus (Plate XVI.) [6] The breadth of the face, due to an exclusive attention to the front view, the shape of the forehead—with its well-marked horizontal modulations, the luxuriant crown of hair confined by the

[1] No. 122. Clarac, 573, 1228. Good workmanship, badly restored. Drapery specially lifelike. The raised left shoulder shows that the forearm was raised and supported.

[2] 188 B. Made into a bust in ancient times. The breast shows the chiton and the mantle on the left shoulder, but the folds are not the same as in the torso, and the quiver band is absent.

[3] In Villa Albani, against the wall in the garden, No. 295. To the left three worshippers, to the right Artemis in the type described (head broken off); below a dog. Drapery and attitude correspond with the Chiaramonti torso.   [4] *Samml. Sabouroff*, Pl. 125, 126.

[5] Cf. Friederichs-Wolters, 1216; Helbig, *Museums*, 525; Berlin, *Skulpt.* 258, 259; Brunn, *Glypt.* 105. Among the replicas note the Capitoline statue, smooth and elegant, apparently of the period of Hadrian. The copies of Villa Borghese (Helbig, *Museums*, 943), of Villa Albani, No. 110, and of Museo Torlonia, No. 113, are very good. The two in the Vatican (Helbig, 211, 55), and that of the Lateran (Helbig, 639), are inferior; on the Braccio Nuovo copy the antique fragment of a pedum on the right upper arm is an addition of the copyist. The best copy of the body is the Palatine torso in the Louvre. Among the heads, one in Vienna is to be noted, because the beautiful nose is antique. There is a celebrated head in the Hope collection at Deepdene, in Surrey (cf. Michaelis, *Anc. Sculpt.* p. 270), but I have unfortunately never seen it. [I was enabled to see this beautiful head in the summer of 1893: every effort, however, made to obtain a photograph of it for the English edition of this book has proved of no avail.—E. S.] Of smaller replicas we may mention the one in Museo Chiaramonti, 582, and the one in Tripolitza (cf. *Ath. Mitth.* 1879, p. 144, 1). The owner told me in 1878 that it came from Sparta; it is a good copy; the part under the eyes is more hollowed out than usual.

[6] Benndorf (*Anz. d. Wiener Akad.* 1887, Nov. 16) laid stress on the rounded form of the skull, the full hair, and the fillet that presses into it as points of resemblance between the Satyr and the Eubouleus.

U U

chaplet, and the way it falls at the sides and on the nape of the neck, are strikingly alike in both heads.   We must mention, too, one special point of likeness to the Hermes—in the form of the foot, which has the characteristic great toe, slender above and broadening at the end, separated from the others by a wide interval.

If we compare the body, on the one hand, to the works of the early period, and, on the other, to the Hermes, we shall find that this Satyr comes between the two. In the body the artist has certainly not attained[1] to the same degree of roundness as in the Hermes : on the contrary, the older manner is still quite evident in the broad planes, in the harsh depression between the straight and the oblique abdominal muscles, and, above all, in the flat form of the abdomen itself.   The treatment of the body is still far removed from the stage reached in the Hermes ; still it is more advanced than in the Satyr pouring wine ; the pubic region, for instance, is enlivened by little furrows treated with great delicacy.   In the unconstrained easy design, in the picturesque draping of the panther-skin, which lies across the figure, in the exclusive attention paid to the front view, and above all in the whole formation of the head, Praxiteles has given unrestrained expression to his own new method, and thrown aside all that had bound him to older models ; but in the formation of the body he had not yet gone quite so far.

With this conclusion it is, however, impossible to reconcile Brunn's view, founded on generalizations, that the Hermes is an early work, the Satyr a mature one.[2]   Brunn even thought that he had found the original of the Satyr in a torso from the Palatine in the Louvre.   The torso however is unfortunately only a copy—a good one, it is true, but no better than other good copies ; even the material, a coarse-grained marble cold and white in tone, and possibly Thasian, but certainly not Parian, is never found in Greek works of the good period, though it is common in later copies.   The work too is in many places quite lifeless, and the modelling lacks the finer touches ; it is only necessary to compare the part round the collar-bone and the shoulder with the corresponding portion of the Hermes in order to grasp thoroughly the difference between an original and a copy.

The blithe beauty of the conception and the entrancing sweetness of the head, with the delicate smile on its lips, easily explain the reputation of the statue. Protogenes, a painter whose originality was in inverse proportion to his admirable technique, early utilized the design for a picture,[3] and there are still later adaptations in marble which give to the Satyr coarser forms, a prominent abdomen, and crossed legs, and make him play the flute.[4]

We have already reckoned with the Eubouleus (Plate XVI.) as with an authentic work of Praxiteles, for such we must maintain it to be, in spite of a contrary opinion[5] that has lately been gaining ground.   The Roman copyists, as an inscription tells us, copied the head of the 'Eubouleus of Praxiteles.'   Now, to assume with Kern that this Praxiteles may be any other artist who bore the name[6] would be as perverse as if

---

[1] The copies all agree in this particular.   [2] *Deutsche Rundschau*, viii. 200.

[3] Strabo, 14, p. 652 ; Plin. 35, 106.   Stephani (*Compte Rendu*, 1870—71, p. 99) wished to refer to this statue the marble figures of the resting Satyr, which is impossible.   The painter made use of the sculptor as Eupompos made use of Polykleitos.

[4] *e.g.* Berlin, *Skulpt.* 260, 261 ; *Samml. Sabouroff*, Text to Plate 77, 78, p. 2, note 6.

[5] Kern, in *Ath. Mitth.* xvi. 1 *sqq.*, also Helbig, *Führer*, ii. p. 413.   Sal. Reinach expresses doubt in *Chronique d'Orient*, xxiv. 21, and in Daremberg et Saglio, *Dict. d'antiqu.* ii. 850 ; Rubensohn differs, with good grounds, *Die Mysterienheiligtümer in Eleusis und Samothrake* (1892), p. 10, 36 *sqq.*, 197 *sqq.*   Kalkmann (*Prop. d. Gesichts*, p. 82) cites the Eubouleus as non-Praxitelean.

[6] *Loc. cit.* 20, with reference to the Praxiteles inscriptions of Roman times, Löwy, *I. G. B.* 318, 319 (to which should be added Δελτίον ἀρχ. 1888, 177 ; 1889, 32).   These, however, all come from Greece, and were written on bases not of copies but of original works, mostly portraits, and are worded like original inscriptions. The wording Εὐβουλεὺς Πραξιτέλους proves that the work was a copy.

in the case of an inscription from a copy of a 'Madonna by Raphael' we chose to doubt whether the celebrated Raphael or some other artist of the same name were intended. The Eubouleus in question must have been by the celebrated Praxiteles, whose works were so popular among the Roman copyists, and, since Eleusis is the only place where we know of an independent cult of Eubouleus without the addition of some other name, it is at Eleusis that the original of the Roman copy must have stood. There are two extant copies of the work,[1] in addition to which the original itself has been found at Eleusis. The identification of this head, which evidently represents an Eleusinian divinity and is eminently Praxitelean, with the Eubouleus of the inscription, suggests itself at once, and is confirmed by subsequent evidence.

The identification has lately been opposed on mythological grounds, and it has been assumed that the 'Euboulos,' or 'Eubouleus,' of Eleusis was only a surname of Zeus. But it will be seen that the Eubouleus of Eleusis is neither Pluto nor Zeus, nor any other divinity, but Eubouleus himself.

An inscription of the fifth century[2] shows that he was worshipped with Kore, Demeter, Triptolemos, and two divinities called ὁ θεός and ἡ θεά, who are represented on a votive relief;[3] and a later inscription[4] gives the names of the priests of this divine couple and of Eubouleus. This 'Eubouleus' was also worshipped independently at Eleusis,[5] where he must have been regarded as an under-world divinity, since the pig and the serpent are known to have entered into his ritual;[6] but he had a separate existence, just like the couple θεός and θεά, who were probably akin to Pluto and Persephone, though at Eleusis they had their own independent cult,[7] even as Klymenos and Pluto[8] existed side by side at Hermione. The name Eubouleus, whatever its meaning, be it the wise counsellor, the well-disposed or well-intentioned, or a combination of both,[9] belongs to that series of euphemistic names given in shuddering propitiation to the powers of the under-world,[10] in order to induce them to exert only the beneficent side of their natures.

The tendency to connect and identify separate divinities with one or other of the great canonical gods was at work from the earliest days, and is assuredly a main factor in the progressive simplification of the primitive complexity. But the individual, the special, the living elements peculiar to a cult are always there from the beginning, and it is only later on that they get incorporated into another cult and eventually absorbed. 'Eubouleus,' who in the conservative ritual of Eleusis retained his individuality, is older than the 'Zeus Eubouleus' of the islands, where the male divinity worshipped with Demeter and Kore was affiliated to Zeus, who in his character of Chthonios was also a deity of the under-world. There are countless examples to show that the lesser

[1] So-called Virgil in the Capitoline Museum (Helbig, *Museums*, 463) and in Mantua (Arndt-Bruckmann, *Einzelverk*. No. 17), both recognized by Benndorf as exact replicas of the Eleusinian head. The head published by Heydemann (*Marmorkopf-Riccardi*, Taf. 1) is of a different type.   [2] Dittenberger, *Syll*. 13.

[3] Ἐφημ. ἀρχ. 1886, Taf. 3, 1. The relief belongs to the late fourth or third century B.C.

[4] *Ibid*. Taf. 3, 2 (relief of Lakrateides).   [5] *Ibid*. p. 262.

[6] Cf. Kern, *loc. cit*. 11.

[7] In *Sammlung Sabouroff*, i. *Einl. Skulpt*. p. 22, note 1; p. 29, I pointed out that θεός and θεά cannot be identified with Pluto and Persephone, and that it is futile to try to name them at all. Töpffer (*Attische Geneal*. p. 33) and Rohde (*Psyche*, i. 196) express the same opinion. It is retrogression to identify them again as Kern does (*loc. cit*. p. 6) with Pluto and Persephone. On one relief Demeter and Persephone are seated beside the θεά, and on the other Persephone was represented in addition to the θεά, as the complementary fragment found through Heberdey and Reichel proves (*Ath. Mitth*. xvii. 127): θεός and θεά are here an absolutely separate pair beside Persephone and Pluto.   [8] Paus. ii. 35, 10. Cf. Rubensohn, *loc. cit*. 198.

[9] Sal. Reinach in Daremberg et Saglio (*Dict*. ii. 849) lets both interpretations stand.

[10] Cf. *Sammlung Sabouroff*, *loc. cit*. 22. Cf. *ibid*. note 2, where Kern could have seen that the inscription from Lebadeia (mentioned by him, p. 10), which seems to prove that the name Eubouleus was applied also to Trophonios, was already quoted.

deities partly retained their original individuality, and partly became annexed to some
one of the greater gods ; for instance, one of the mother goddesses was worshipped
in Attika separately as Kourotrophos,[1] and also as one with Ge or Demeter ; the same
is the case with Pandrosos and Athena Pandrosos, Hygieia and Athena Hygieia,
Erechtheus and Poseidon Erechtheus, Peitho and Aphrodite or Artemis Peitho,
Hekate and Artemis Hekate, Eileithyia and Artemis or Hera Eileithyia, Iphigeneia
and Artemis Iphigeneia, Eukleia and Artemis Eukleia,[2] Aristaios and Zeus Aristaios
(in Keos), Asklepios and Zeus Asklepios, Maleatas and Apollo Maleatas, etc.

Legend, which is wont to enter into facts of belief and ritual as a secondary
element, called forth into existence the distinct mythological personality of Eubouleus
in the ritual of Eleusis.   The story grew out of the customary offering and burial of
young pigs, and Eubouleus was made into a swineherd, whose swine had been swallowed
up in the chasm when the earth opened at the rape of Kore.   Kern has well shown how
the myth arose from the ritual,[3] but it is purely arbitrary to call the myth late, and
to assume without the slightest foundation an older stage in which the swineherd of
Eleusis was no other than Zeus himself.   Legends that arise out of rituals are by no
means usually of late origin.[4]   On the other hand, Triptolemos the neatherd is only a
later duplicate of Eubouleus the swineherd.[5]   Now, as legend could find no place for
Eubouleus as a god of the under-world, it accordingly changed him into an heroic
attendant on the great goddesses ; he became brother to Triptolemos, and also the
son of Demeter, and as such he came, even as Triptolemos, to be conceived of as
youthful.   The monuments will now show that this aspect of Eubouleus is familiar
in the fine period of art.

On one of those Attic statuette vases (Fig. 142) on which the boy Iakchos appears
so often there is a youth with thick locks of hair, high diadem and wreath, standing like
a god, his mantle draped about his lower limbs, holding a sucking-pig in his right
hand, and in his left a bundle of the twigs or the ears of corn [6] used in the mysteries
of Eleusis.[7]   The same figure, only represented in movement, appears on the celebrated Attic hydria,[8] decorated with a frieze in relief of the Eleusinian gods ; here
the youth stands close to the great goddesses.   The statuette vase is sufficient to
show that he is not a mere sacrificial attendant ; he must be a divinity, and as a fact
the figure can only be satisfactorily and fully explained by reference to the myth of
Eubouleus, which must accordingly have been current in the fourth century, the
period to which the vases belong.

[1] A votive relief from Athens in Dresden shows the goddess as Kourotrophos with a torch (in the Hekate
type), conjoined with Apollo, Leto, and Artemis (*Jahrb. d. Arch. Inst. Anz.* 1894, p. 26).   Dedication to the
goddess Kourotrophos on a cup from the Peiraieus, Ἐφημ. ἀρχ. 1884, p. 194, 6.   Sacrifice to her, *C. I. A.* ii.
481, 59.   Prayer in Aristoph. *Thesm.* 299.

[2] Cf. the interesting passage in Plut. *Aristeid.* concerning Eukleia at Plataia ; some identified her with
Artemis, others not.   [3] *Loc. cit.* 16.

[4] After the publication of O. Müller's *Prolegomena*, it should no longer be necessary to say that the fact of a
legend only appearing in later sources proves nothing against its antiquity.

[5] As Kern shows (*loc. cit.*), Triptolemos the neatherd is connected with Alexandria and Osiris.   This
naturally proves nothing with regard to the swineherd.

[6] For its use in the Eleusinian cultus, see *Arch. Anz.* 1892, p. 106, notice to No. 19.   Of great importance
in this connexion is a fragmentary B. F. vase in the Museum at Eleusis.   It represents a procession of men and
women, all bearing the bundles of twigs which belong to the mystic cultus.

[7] The vase is published in Fröhner's *Catalogue of the Piot Collection*, Paris 1890, No. 153, p. 42 (= our
Fig. 142).   Fröhner mistakes the pig for a hare.   A replica of the figure was in the Coll. Gréau (Fröhner, *Coll.
Gréau, Terrescuites Gr.* 1891, Pl. 40, No. 462) ; the form is founded on the Piot example, but the bundle on the
left arm (it was put on separately) is missing ; the pig is better preserved.

[8] Stephani, *Compte Rendu*, 1862, Taf. 3 ; Gerhard, *Ges. Akad. Abh.* Taf. 78 ; Heydemann, *Marmorkopf
Riccardi*, p. 14 *seq.*   The vase is certainly Attic.

A striking confirmation of this Eubouleus type is afforded by a marble statuette at Eleusis [1] which corresponds with the terra-cottas in all essentials. The boy, whose soft round face and luxuriant hair resemble the marble head, carries on the left arm the bundle of ears,[2] and in the right hand may be seen the fragments of a small pig.[3] Here too he wears the mantle, as befits a god. The workmanship shows the figure to belong to the fourth or third century B.C. Another Eleusinian monument represents a different type of Eubouleus; it is the newly reconstructed relief of Lakrateides.[4] The boy at the end on the right, with long hair and short-sleeved chiton, who holds a torch, can scarcely be other than Eubouleus, whose priest Lakrateides is. He stands beside the pair, θεός and θεά, as Triptolemos stands beside Demeter and Kore. Triptolemos wears the same sleeved chiton as he, and high boots, which we may also assume for Eubouleus (the legs are missing). This type, established for Eubouleus by the Lakrateides relief, occurs on five Attic vases in conjunction with the divinities of Eleusis.[5] It is a youth who appears, either alone or with Triptolemos and Dionysos, as a companion of the two great goddesses. Like Iakchos in the group of the elder Praxiteles, he is their torch-bearer, or he holds the sceptre, like the Iakchos issuing from the earth, on another vase.[6] He usually wears an embroidered festal robe with tight sleeves, and high boots. This type is influenced by the type of Iakchos, but the former one was created for Eubouleus.

FIG. 142.—Attic statuette vase.

Finally, we must mention another Eleusinian monument which represents Eubouleus, this time shortened into a bust [7] like the Praxitelean work. It appears in relief on a tablet set up within an aedicula which is supported on a pillar, just the arrangement which I imagined we must assume for the Praxitelean head.[8] The head has again the full soft features and almost feminine neck, also long shoulder-curls like the Eubouleus of the Lakrateides relief.

[1] Noted by me in 1894 in the Eleusis Museum.

[2] The lower part of the bundle shows plastic stripes, above it is painted red.

[3] The forelegs are still recognizable.   [4] In the Museum at Eleusis.

[5] Gerhard, *Ges. Akad. Abh.* Taf. 77 (youth with two torches). *Ibid.* Taf. 71, 1 (youth to the left of Demeter with one torch). Hydria in Athens, Coll. of the Arch. Society, No. 2722 (youth, with sceptre, short-sleeved chiton, and high boots, beside Demeter, Kore, and the bull-horned Dionysos. Style of fourth century, polychrome and gilt). Hydria of the same style from Coll. Castellani (Fröhner, *Coll. Cast.* Rome, 1884, Pl. ii.), now in the Tyszkiewicz Coll. (youth in long chiton and mantle, with twisted curls, carrying a sceptre). Vase in Athens, Arch. Soc. No. 2382, fine fifth-century style; three figures separated by palmettes and the handle: Demeter, Kore, and youth wearing boots and an embroidered garment. This vase alone refutes the assumption that the figure is a priest, for it undoubtedly represents a triad of divinities. I have already explained the figure as Eubouleus in *Arch. Anz.* 1889, p. 47; Roscher's *Lex.* i. 2185.

[6] Tischbein, i. 39; *Jahrb. d. Inst.* 1891, p. 12   *eq.*

[7] Relief in the Museum at Eleusis (Photogr. in German Ath. Institute, Eleusis, 29).

[8] Cf. *Arch. Anz.* 1889, 147. Even after J. P. Meier's remarks in the *Jahrb. d. Inst.* 1890, 209, I still think this hypothesis the most likely. The side wall of the aedicula probably joined on to the left shoulder, as is shown by the perpendicular contact-surface. The left shoulder was free. Perhaps there was a second bust on the left side of this one, which would explain the turn of the head of Eubouleus.

But replicas of the Praxitelean head itself have been found in Eleusis. The only complete one, now in the Museum at Athens,[1] is neither poor nor late, but is evidently only a copy from the Praxitelean original which has been preserved to us. In the original we can trace the master's touch, in the copy we only get a spiritless and tame imitation. This contrast is specially noticeable in the hair. The amazing mastery of the Praxitelean head lies in the indefiniteness of the hair, in its curling disarray and shimmering undulations, qualities which the copyist was powerless to catch, although he imitated the technique of the drill. In the Eleusinian copy, just as in the Roman, the lines of the hair are arranged more according to scheme and rule, a process in which all the original charm is lost. So, too, the fresh untrammelled hair of the superb Skopasian head from the south slope of the Akropolis[2] lost all spontaneity in the Roman copy. The existence of replicas at Eleusis affords a proof of the canonical value attached to the original, by showing that whoever in later times desired to set up an image of Eubouleus at Eleusis only required to have a copy made of the head by Praxiteles.

The Eubouleus presumably belongs, like the 'Satyr at rest,' to the artist's middle period. In it he made free use of the drill—as he must have done in the original of the Satyr—to make the hair look loose and lifelike. Two other technical peculiarities show that it is somewhat earlier than the Hermes: the lower eyelid is not treated with the characteristic delicacy,[3] but its hard and clearly marked outline is more like what we notice in the original heads attributed to Skopas. Further, the corners of the mouth are not as in the Hermes worked with the drill, but, like the Skopasian heads (where the drill is not employed even for the hair), they show no traces of its use. Since Praxiteles did not employ all the technical resources of his later style in the Eubouleus, it follows that the work must be earlier than the Hermes. We are actually watching the growth of that refinement in the working of marble which distinguishes Praxiteles even from Skopas.

There is a Roman copy of a superb head (Fig. 143)[4] so like Praxitelean work, and more especially the Eubouleus, that we must needs be referred to an original of the master. The breadth of the full delicate face, the cut of the eyes, the chin with the shallow dimple, and the broad fleshy neck resemble the Eubouleus; so does the thick loose hair, which is worked with the drill, and was of course still more effective in the original. The two heads, however, also offer marked contrasts to one another. The short locks are parted in the middle and fall evenly and simply down on either side of the face, but not over the forehead. The head is thrust somewhat forward, and the expression is not in the slightest dreamy; rather is it energetic and expectant. The personage is more youthful than the Eubouleus, and the forehead is smoother; but the way of wearing the hair and the muscular neck show without a doubt that the head is male.

I think that no name seems to fit this head so well as Triptolemos, the brother of Eubouleus, whom Praxiteles had, according to Pliny, represented in a group (*Flora, Triptolemus, Ceres in hortis Servilianis*). A comparison of the Triptolemos on the

---

[1] *Ath. Mitth.* xvi. Taf. 2. (The other replica is only a fragment.) The eyes were inserted; this was enough to make the Praxitelean refinement in the rendering of the eye impossible. Kern claims the head of a statue in Rome (*loc. cit.* Taf. 1) as a repetition of the same type, but the resemblance is only general. The symmetric fall of curls over the forehead, characteristic of an under-world god, is absent.

[2] *Ath. Mitth.* i. Taf. 13, 14; *Skulpt.* Berlin, 610; *Röm. Mitth.* 1889, p. 216.

[3] Cf. Gräf. in *Röm. Mitth.* 1889, 204.

[4] Pal. Pitti, Dütschke, ii. 27. Nose and lips restored. Length of face 0·17. Arndt and Amelung also thought of Praxiteles as the author.

FIG. 143.—Head in Pal. Pitti (Florence).

FIG. 140.-—Head of Artemis (Dresden).

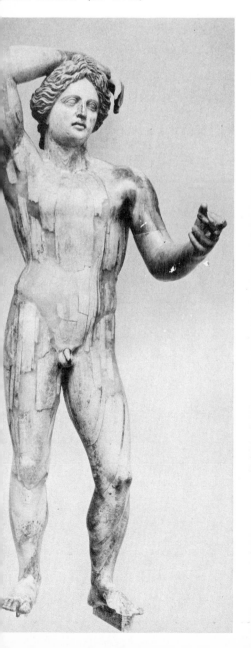

LVIII—Apollo Ivory Statuette, Athens, Stoa of
ttalos Museum (See Notes)

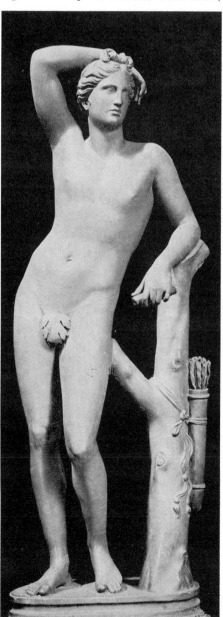

Fig. XLIX—Apollo, Florence, Uffizi Gallery

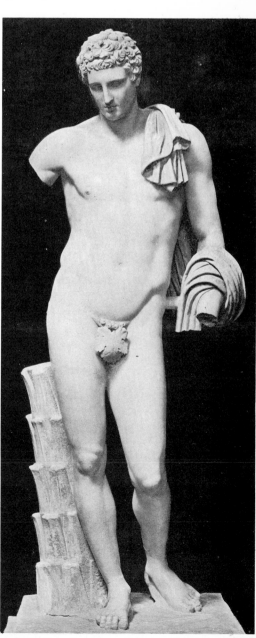

Fig. L—Hermes Belvedere, Rome, Vatican Museum (See
p. 338)

great Eleusinian relief,[1] which belongs to the period and the school of Pheidias, shows that his hair was parted in the middle and fell on either side, and that even the attitude and expression of that head (after making all due allowance for difference of style) are extraordinarily like this one. Praxiteles must have taken that older type of Triptolemos as the basis of his creation.

The Sauroktonos can be but very slightly older than the Hermes.[2] The body comes appreciably nearer to it than did the 'Satyr at rest.' The rich round modelling of the abdominal region and the rendering of the navel with a fold of skin above it are already quite in the style of the Hermes, and absolutely different from the Satyr pouring wine and the Eros; though the chest with its quiet broad surfaces passes without much transition into the sides, still somewhat after the older method. The copies do not allow us to judge of the subtler beauties of the head; the face with its soft setting of hair recalls the Aphrodite of Knidos; yet the forehead broadens considerably at the base in order to characterize Apollo, in accordance with a type elaborated, as we have already seen, as early as the fifth century (p. 194).

The statue possesses a wonderful charm, which is due entirely to the attitude, on which the artist has expended all his skill. It would have been more natural had the right hand with the arrow been nearer to the object aimed at, but this would have spoilt the beautiful front view of the body.

The true interpretation of the attitude seems to lie about midway between the fluctuating theories which have been propounded on the subject—*i.e.* the action is a playful one without any mantic meaning, yet the lizard was probably an attribute of Apollo, in the ritual for which this statue was made; and the Sauroktonos is playing with a lizard, just as the Smintheus of Skopas was playing with a mouse.

The Eros of Parion, which as I had already shown from coins[3] was leaning on his left arm, has been happily identified[4] in the so-called 'Genius Borghese' in the Louvre.[5] This statue is of course a very poor copy, but it enables us to assign to the original its place in the Praxitelean series. The hair with the loop tied up above the ears is very like the Sauroktonos; yet the little knot of hair over the forehead, and the symmetrical division of the locks just at that spot, recall the Thespian Eros. However, even the chest no longer shows any trace of the earlier type, for it is as softly rounded in every direction as that of the Hermes. There is a wide gap between it and the master's earlier statues of Eros. This difference is not merely a difference of form but also one of expression. The whole effect conveyed by every detail of attitude, form, and face is soft and round, and the feeling excited in us by this 'Genius' is one of voluptuous delight.[6] On the other hand, the Thespian Eros, with

---

[1] I consider Gräf's attempt (*Ath. Mitth.* xv. 36 *seq.*) to see in this relief Boeotio-Peloponnesian style to be completely mistaken.

[2] Replicas, Overbeck, *Apollon,* 235 *seq.* In judging of the style we should study the marble copies executed on the scale of the original, not the reduced and less faithful Albani bronze (whose Roman origin is sufficiently proved by the technique, especially by the inlaid band of silver).

[3] Roscher's *Lex.* i. 1358.

[4] By Benndorf in *Bull. della Comm. Arch.* 1886, p. 74.

[5] Fröhner, *Not.* 326. Photo. éd. Giraudon, 1201. So-called Thasian marble. The connexion between the figure and the antique stem and drapery is new; the stem probably stood rather nearer. The head is unbroken. The workmanship is poor, flat, and spiritless, yet the beauty of the original shines through. The motive of the Eros of Parion recurs on a Greek mirror and gem (cf. Roscher's *Lex.* i. 1359).

[6] Winckelmann (*Hist. of Art,* bk. v. ch. 1, § 12 = tr. Lodge, vol. i. p. 325) felt deeply the beauty of the work. In saying that it was 'fashioned after the beauty of angels' he was evidently influenced by the voluptuous angel of seventeenth- and eighteenth-century art.

its well-knit forms, is still under the spell of the constrained rhythm of Peloponnesian creations,[1] and seems consumed with repressed longing.

We have now arrived at that period of the artist's life to which the Olympian Hermes belongs. Many monuments can be grouped about this statue, but only the more important need be mentioned here. First of all comes an 'Apollo at rest' with his right arm over his head—a famous work, to judge by the many copies and later adaptations.[2] Both the attitude and figure are extraordinarily like the Hermes, and the spirit of the work is so thoroughly Praxitelean in the quiet beauty of its flowing lines, so radically different from the work of Skopas for instance,[3] that we naturally assign it to the master of the Hermes. The position of the head is like that of the Aphrodite of Knidos; the eyes gaze into the distance, and even the features show such a family likeness to the Aphrodite that the authorship of Praxiteles cannot be doubted. The hair is a fresh example of the master's skill in inventing rich and characteristic coiffures. The god is only lightly leaning on his left arm, for the left leg is not absolutely free and drawn behind the other as in the Hermes, but is planted flat on the ground, so as to give the figure more dignity of bearing.

A Dionysos, of which copies likewise exist, corresponds so closely to this[4] Apollo that it must be the work of the same artist. The attitude and the bodily forms are identical; on the left shoulder a nebris is knotted, and clings closely and softly to the figure so as to reveal its shape. The bacchic mitra is fastened into the hair, which falls in long curls over the shoulders. The type of face also, with the far-off look, is very like the Apollo, though it is modified to characterize a more effeminate, sensuous nature.

There is another Dionysos at Madrid,[5] which is certainly Praxitelean, and belongs

---

[1] I may just mention at the close of this section that a series of Kanephoroi is preserved to us as Caryatids in copies which must go back to originals from the circle of Skopas and Praxiteles. Three types may be distinguished: (a) Villa Albani, 725; Friederichs-Wolters, 1557; Helbig, *Museums*, 837; Clarac, 444, 814 B; left supporting leg, head related to Knidian Aphrodite. A replica without head in Athens, found near the Metropolitan Church. (b) Villa Albani, 628; Friederichs-Wolters, 1556; Helbig, 834; Clarac, 444, 814. Rests on left leg. Hair in furrows. Replica in Athens found with replica of a. (c) British Museum, Newton, *Guide Graeco-Rom. Sculpt.* 1, 126; Clarac, 444, 813. Rests on right leg. Hair in furrows. The types are magnificent and worthy of the greatest artists. The replicas in Athens were perhaps made to replace the originals which the Romans took away. According to a suggestion kindly communicated to me by Bulle, these types can be traced back to the Triopian sanctuary of the Chthonic divinities near Knidos. This would answer admirably to our assumption of a Praxitelean origin, for Praxiteles worked in Knidos. There was a Kanephora by Skopas in *Asini Monumentis*; the Kanephora of Praxiteles, Plin. xxxiv. 69, is, however, only a conjecture, the reading *oporan* of the cod. Riccardianus being very probably the correct one. [Cf. now Bulle's article, *Röm. Mitth.* ix. p. 134 *sqq.* His own view is that the Roman statues belonged to a sanctuary of the Triopian Demeter on the Via Appia dedicated by Herodes Atticus in memory of Regilla, and that the Athenian copies possibly belonged to the sanctuary of Serapis and Isis, in the neighbourhood of the Metropolitan church. Neither series stood free, according to Bulle, but were placed pillar-wise against a wall.—E. S.]

[2] For the type and its Praxitelean origin see my *Satyr von Pergamon*, p. 21, A, 2; Roscher's *Lex.* i. 460—462; *Samml. Sabouroff*, to Taf. 36. Collection of replicas (including some wrong material), Overbeck, *Apollon*, 209 *seq.* Good copies are Berlin 44 and 512; Louvre, Fröhner, 75, 76, and a torso, No. 3013; a torso in Palazzo Mattei. A good copy of the head is falsely placed on a seated statue of Apollo in the Museo Boncompagni-Ludovisi (Helbig, *Museums*, 877). Schreiber (*V. Lud.* 116) wrongly explains it as modern; another copy is in the Conservat. Pal. Salone, No. 31, placed on a female statue. Two replicas of the head in the Brit. Mus., Friederichs-Wolters, 1292—93. One in the Coll. Barracco (*Coll. B.* Pl. 59, 59 a). Kalkmann, misled by his measurements (*Prop. d. Gesichts*, p. 62), places this Apollo in the fifth century, and, on the other hand, calls a late Roman copyist's modification (in the Brit. Mus. from Kyrene) Praxitelean! Cf. my remarks in the *Berl. Philol. Wochenschrift*, 1894, p. 109. [3] Birch and Wolters, *loc. cit.*, thought of Skopas.

[4] The so-called Bacchus de Versailles in the Louvre, Fröhner, *Notice*, 218; photo. éd. Giraudon, 1189. Well preserved, with head. *Ibid.* Fröhner, 216.

[5] Friederichs-Wolters, 1485. I know no replicas; the bronze Dionysos published by Milani (*Museo Ital.* iii. 752 *seq.*) as Praxitelean has no connexion with Praxiteles. Cf. *infra*, p. 353.

X X

to the same period of the artist's life.   In conception it most resembles the Eros of Parion.   The god is resting his arm on an archaic terminal figure.

But belonging to this later period there are also figures standing free without any support.   First of all comes, as was noticed immediately on the discovery of the Olympian Hermes, the so-called Antinous (Hermes) of the Belvedere.[1] The head and the bodily forms, even down to minute details like the hair over the forehead, correspond most closely to the Olympian statue.   Still there are differences which cause one to suspect that this work is a still later development of the Praxitelean manner, and may be by one of his sons; these differences are the modelling of the chest, the greater curve of the hips, and the smallness of the head, which however seems to have lacked the ideal grace and refinement of the Olympian Hermes.   The right arm is placed on the hip—an attitude often found in statues by Skopas; here however it assumes a different character.   Skopas made it express fierce impatience and restlessness, but here it conveys an idea of graceful nonchalance. Compare for instance the Meleager of Skopas.   It is untrue to say that the difference arises from the subject-matter; for the Hermes belonging to the earlier works of Skopas was, as we saw, represented in like unrest (Fig. 129).   This again is a point in which Lysippos is linked to Skopas; a beautiful bronze statuette from Athens[2] gives us a Hermes of purest Lysippian style, in the swinging posture of the Apoxyomenos, the left arm placed behind the back, the right holding the kerykeion sideways, the head jerked impatiently to one side.   How totally different is the thoughtful, quiet Praxitelean figure!

Of another Praxitelean Apollo[3] we get at least a glimpse in a torso (*supra*, Plate XV.)   Like the Belvedere Hermes, he rests full on the right leg, with the hip curved outwards, and does not lean against any support; the right arm is raised to feel for the quiver at his back.   The head is turned towards the side of the free leg. The contours agree with those of the 'Apollo at rest' and the Hermes of Olympia, but they are somewhat softer.

There is another statue, a Hermes (Fig. 144),[4] which is particularly interesting owing to the novelty and originality of the motive.   The artist has for once broken through his practice of only representing figures at rest, and has attempted something more vigorous.   Even here however the master's bent is unmistakable, for the design is a model of perfectly rounded beauty and internal repose.

Besides a full-sized copy in Florence, there are two statuettes, which however are not quite exact in details.[5]   The attitude is the same as that of the 'Apollo at rest' and of the Dionysos, except that there is no support for the left arm.   However,

---

[1] Treu, *Hermes mit dem Dionysosknaben* (1878), p. 8 *seq*.   Cf. Friederichs-Wolters, 1218—20; Helbig, *Museums*, 145.   The replica from Andros is not faithful stylistically, but mixes in Lysippian elements; the Roman copies are more faithful.   A good one in the Lansdowne Collection (Michaelis, *Anc. Sculpt.* p. 454, 65), and one in the Pal. Vecchio in Florence (Dütschke, ii. 511; the head antique, but foreign).   Amelung (*Florentiner Antiken*, p. 37) mentions replicas of the head.

[2] Berlin, *Inv.* 6305; cf. *supra*, p. 300.   The bronze corresponds very closely with the Apoxyomenos in proportions and details of form.   It appears to be an original of the same school.

[3] In Villa Medici, Matz-Duhn, 215.   This is the torso on which has been placed the beautiful Meleager head published in *Ant. Denkm.* i. Taf. 40.

[4] Uffizi, Dütschke, 98; *Gall. di Firenze*, Ser. 4, 135; Clarac, 666 C, 1512 A.   Cf. *Arch. Anz.* 1889, 147. The drawing by Heemskerk, mentioned by Michaelis, *Jahrb. d. Inst.* vi. p. 140, 26, C, seems to represent this statue.   The left arm and the beginning of the right upper arm are antique; the kerykeion is restored; head unbroken; nose, lips, and edge of petasos restored; legs, wings on feet, and plinth are antique.

[5] *a*. Marble statuette, Gall. dei Candelabri, 17; only the torso antique; the chlamys is fastened on the right shoulder.   *b*. Bronze statuette in Naples, No. 5208.   No chlamys; the right hand, bent and empty, seems to grasp the hat.   The left hand is held as in the Florentine statue.   No kerykeion.

since in those other two statues the support is almost without influence upon the position of the body, seeing that the left foot is planted flat to the front, while the left arm is only slightly supported, the actual difference is very slight. The close connexion of the Uffizi Hermes with the Apollo, the Dionysos, and the Olympian Hermes is proved above all by the correspondence of the bodily forms, somewhat

Fig. 144.—Hermes in the Uffizi.

Fig. LP—Herakles and Telephos, Paris, Louvre

hard and dry though the copyist's work was. In this case too the right arm is raised; unfortunately only the stump is left in the large statue, but the bronze statuette shows that the hand was empty. The left one holds a kerykeion like the Belvedere and the Olympian Hermes; the chlamys falls over the arm as in the latter, an arrangement which we sometimes find on fourth-century Attic grave-reliefs.

The head reminds us of the 'Satyr at rest' and of the Eubouleus, for the hair grows
thick and full on the crown of the head, then falls away on either side of the face,
and there is the same breadth of forehead, while face and neck agree completely.
There are traces of a growth of beard on the cheeks — he is πρῶτον ὑπηνήτης,
as Homer represents him (Il. xxiv. 38).

In fact, the whole conception is Homeric—this Hermes is no longer the youth
trained in the palaestra, with close shorn hair and ephebic type of face; he is a free

FIG. 145.—Herakles in Villa Albani.

child of nature, a young
man in the prime of his
strength and beauty, a
ruler's son, κούρῳ αἰσυμνη-
τῆρι ἐοικώς, a son of Zeus,
as we are reminded by the
typical growth of the hair.
The Hermes is the messen-
ger between gods and men,
rejoicing in his strength as
he lifts his arm and looks
upwards, and we feel that
his winged feet are about
to bear him and his mes-
sage to Olympos.

This Hermes recalls
the Eros described by
Kallistratos, as about to
cleave the air with his
wings. I believe I have
discovered a reproduction
of this statue in a small
bronze,[1] which shows Eros
with both arms raised preparing to soar upward.
This audacious conception
would of course belong to
the artist's later period.

In close connexion
with this Florentine Hermes comes a statue of Herakles in the Villa Albani (Fig.
145).[2] The attitude is identical, and the statue has the typical late Praxitelean
forms. The hero holds his club in the left hand just as the Hermes holds his
kerykeion, and the right hand too is upraised; the restorer has put a cup into it,
and it is not improbable that it actually once held a drinking-vessel. Unfortunately a portion of the neck is new, but the head itself is genuine, and its turn
to the right is shown by what remains of the neck to be accurate. The paws
of the lion-skin are knotted together on the right shoulder so as to produce

[1] *Jahrb. d. Ver. f. Alterth.-Fr. im Rheinland*, Heft 90, p. 61 *sqq.* Taf. 3, 3. Cf. p. 314, note 1.
[2] Clarac, 804 B, 2007 A ; Helbig, *Museums*, 840. The front of the right leg above the knee, the front of the
foot, the left right arm (except at the shoulder, where sufficient remains to show that the arm was raised), the left
hand, and most of the club, except a small piece in the middle, are restored. The neck is partly restored. The
body has suffered much from exposure. The support with the quiver is antique. Emil Braun (*Ruinen und
Museen*, p. 706 *seq.*) well appreciated this little-known statue.

the effect of a chlamys, and the head of the animal falls over the breast; this is an innovation, for it is usually either drawn over the hero's head or hangs over his arm. On the other hand, it is easy to see that this draping of the skin, with the head in front, is dictated by the same taste as the panther-skin of the 'Satyr at rest.' All these points justify us in assigning this work also to Praxiteles. Like the Hermes of the Florentine statue, Herakles is gazing up brightly and cheerfully, his victories won.[1] He is the hero, who by sheer prowess has attained Olympos, and with conscious pride looks upwards to the heaven where eternal youth and happiness await him. How different to that restless hero thirsting for new feats whom Skopas conceived!

A well-known statue in the Museo Chairamonti (Fig. 146)[2] is a modified replica of the one in the Villa Albani; the bodily forms are considerably altered; a Pergamene layer has been superadded to the Praxitelean substratum. The superficial realism, the turgid manner of the Pergamenes, has obscured the beautiful simplicity of the original design; even the lion-skin has become more effective and pathetic. The attitude is changed—the club is transferred to the right hand, and held down, not up, and therefore the head is less raised. The child Telephos, about whom his father is but little concerned, is awkwardly adjusted on the left arm. The addition of Telephos shows that we have to

FIG. 146.—Herakles with Telephos (Mus. Chiaramonti).

do with a Pergamene adaptation—that is to say, with a Roman copy of such an adaptation.[3]

The head of the statue (Fig. 147, from a cast) shows, as compared with the Albani head, some traces of later modification, though mainly in externals; the beard is less full and deeply undercut, after the Pergamene fashion, and the twisted fillet is an addition. However, in its main lines the head does not differ

---

[1] A bearded Herakles, looking up, but more pathetic than the Albani one, is in Dresden (*Augusteum*, Taf. 91); skin over the head; in bodily forms rather older than the Albani statue. Beardless Herakles (excellent) with the same motive in the Coll. Jacobsen in Copenhagen (No. 1050). The attitude and build of the body are very similar to the Apoxyomenos of Lysippos, but the head is like the Skopasian type. One hesitates whether to call Lysippos or Skopas the author. The composition is far more pathetic and restless than the Praxitelean.

[2] No. 636. Helbig, *Museums*, 113. Very well preserved. Unimportant restorations. The upper end of the club with the right hand is antique. Head unbroken, only the point of the nose restored. I can see absolutely no grounds for connecting the statue with the Munich Diomede, as Brunn has done (*Bayr. Sitzungsber.* 1892, 662).

[3] For Telephos with Herakles, cf. Roscher's *Lexikon*, i. 2246 *seq.*

appreciably from the Albani Herakles, and its presupposed Praxitelean model ; for instance, it is quite uninfluenced by the exaggerated Lysippian ideal of Herakles. Therefore we may believe that the main points of the Herakles of Praxiteles are faithfully reproduced in the Chiaramonti head.   For even the system of forms corresponds throughout with the Hermes of Olympia ; the modelling of the forehead is strikingly similar, though rather more powerful ; further, the eyes and their surrounding parts, the ancient portion of the nose and the profile completely correspond.   It is only in details, like the hair and the lower eyelid, that those differences of treatment appear which always distinguish a copyist's work from an original.

In presence of this profoundly felt conception of Herakles, undoubtedly the most beautiful image of the hero that exists beside the beardless Skopasian type,

FIG. 147.—Head of Herakles Chiaramonti.

many will feel reminded of another famous ancient type—the 'Zeus of Otricoli.' There is an undoubted resemblance in the system of forms, but the likeness is due to their being not the work of one master but of one development and age.   It has recently been more than once suggested that this famous head is a specimen of the work of the second Attic school, and the suggestion is correct.[1]   It is now possible to conjecture what the statue which belonged to this head was like.   At Constantinople there is a bronze statue of Zeus (one third life-size)[2] whose head exactly reproduces the Otricoli type.   The powerful nude figure has nothing Lysippian about it, and is connected rather with the Praxitelean manner.   The figure is in the walking motive, with all the weight thrown on the right leg, and the left

[1] Löschke, *Jahrb. d. Ver. v. Alterth.-Fr. im Rheinland*, Heft 88, p. 266 ; Helbig, *Museums*, 294.
[2] Found at Janina.—*B.C.H.* 1885, Pl. 14.

hand raised aloft. According to the marks on the basis, this was precisely the attitude of the six Zanes which the Athenians erected at Olympia (B.C. 332). These Zanes must assuredly have resembled the Constantinople figure in style as well as in motive, and the Otricoli mask may very possibly go back to one of them.

We have reserved for the end a very beautiful and interesting work. This is, as I hope to be able to prove, a real original by Praxiteles himself, a head of his favourite goddess Aphrodite, belonging to his later period (Plate XVII. and Fig. 148). The head, which belongs to Lord Leconfield, was till lately in the Petworth collection, but has now been removed to the owner's London house.

This superb life-size head[1] was found last century. When I saw it for the first time in 1888[2] I was absolutely enraptured with its beauty. Unfortunately the head is somewhat damaged, the nose and part of the upper lip being restored, and, worse than this, the whole face, except for a few small portions, having been rubbed smooth, so that the freshness of the ancient surface is lost. The corners of the mouth and the adjacent parts seem to have suffered most from the polishing process, hence we may suppose that the drill-marks in the mouth were originally less conspicuous than they are now. Still, it is only the last delicate touches that have disappeared, and in all essentials the head is well preserved. Even the antique polish survives uninjured in some parts. Originally the whole neck was polished, but the hair left rough—the Hermes of Olympia being another instance of the same method. The marble is Parian, of that fine variety known as *lychnites*, which was also employed for the Hermes. As the block was not large enough, the back of the head with the bunch of hair was made separately and joined on. The join is straight, and so neatly effected that it is to-day as good as ever, and must have been quite invisible when the hair was painted. It is well known that in the Hermes several pieces—not, however, parts of the head—are put on in the same way, with straight surfaces. The head is intended for insertion into a statue, which we may suppose was draped and made of marble less fine in quality.

In *Specimens of Ancient Sculpture* (i. 45, 46) there are engravings from the head. The editor, by suggesting that it may be 'a relique of the parent statue from which so many have been derived,' shows that he looked upon it as a Greek original. Ottfr. Müller (*Handbuch*, § 375, 3) classes it among the older and more majestic types of Aphrodite.[3] It seems to have disappeared from the collection after this. Michaelis did not see it,[4] nor did Conze.

We are now able, in the light of recent discovery, to say with certainty that this is a real original work by one of the first fourth-century artists. The very best copies of Praxitelean heads—even, for example, the good copy of the Aphrodite of Knidos in a private collection in Berlin[5]—seem lifeless empty masks beside it. Nothing is worthy to be compared with it except an original such as the Hermes of Olympia. There is only one period of Greek art to which the hair technique of this head can be assigned, and that is the period of Praxiteles. I am speaking now not of the arrangement of the hair, though that too is purely Praxitelean and corresponds in essential

---

[1] Length of face, 0·21 ; brow, nose, and lower part of the face each measure 7 cm. Distance between outer corners of the eye, 0·115 ; length of mouth = 0·056.

[2] *Arch. Anzeiger*, 1890, p. 164.

[3] Mentioned again by Ottfr. Müller in *Kunstarch. Werken*, ii. 89.

[4] He is mistaken in mentioning it as a replica of the Venus of Medici (*Anc. Marb.* p. 616, No. 73), from which it differs in size and pose.

[5] *Antike Denkm.* i. 41. Cf. p. 322, note 3.

features with the Aphrodite of Knidos, but of the manner of execution. The roots of the hair are rendered with marvellous delicacy, and the loose waving locks produce a wonderfully natural effect, much more so even than does the hair of the fine Skopasian head from the southern slope of the Akropolis. This difference in effect is due to the use of the drill, which was not employed either in tho Skopasian work mentioned above, in the Tegea heads, or in any other original sculptures related to Skopas.[1] On the other hand, the hair of the Praxitelean Hermes and of the Eubouleus

FIG. 148.—Profile of Aphrodite in the collection of Lord Leconfield.

Plate *XVIII—"Aberdeen Head", London, British Museum (See pp. 346 seq.)

is very deeply drilled, a process to which is partly due the effect of life and vigour. The same method has been employed for the Aphrodite, except that in accordance with the different character of the hair the tool has been used more sparingly, but the masterly lightness and sureness of touch are the same.

The hair at the back of the head is, as in the Hermes, indicated rather than worked out. A breakage behind each ear shows perhaps where the ends of a fillet hung down, as in the Venus of Arles.

[1] Such as the grave-relief from the Ilissos and the sculptures of the Mausoleum. Cf. p. 309 seq.

The whole contour of the face, a long oval with harmoniously rounded lines and high triangular forehead, is at once recognized as Praxitelean by its resemblance to the Knidian Aphrodite. The round skull and the ear, with its long lobe well detached from the cheek, its wide opening, and the narrow fold of the cartilage, exactly resemble the Olympian Hermes.

But the master hand is above all manifest in the surpassing beauty of the eyes, which are a veritable mirror of the soul. In this respect too only the Hermes can stand comparison. In both we find the same rounding of the ball and the same treatment of the lids, which are not sharply detached from the eyeballs; the under lid is peculiarly characteristic in its exquisite delicacy, being almost imperceptibly defined against the ball and the cheek (cf. p. 334). It is drawn slightly upwards, thus giving to the eye that essentially Aphrodisian expression which, from the evidence of copies, we already know to have been one of the charms of the Aphrodite of Knidos. Imitators of Praxiteles carried this tendency to excess—witness the small head from Olympia (which however, being only a small, slight decorative work, comes under another category), with lower lids that appear almost swollen.[1]

Again, the mouth of the Petworth Aphrodite finds its closest analogy in that of the Hermes, especially in the delicate transition between the lips and the surrounding surfaces, which is an unmistakable mark of late Praxitelean art. The fascinating dimple in the chin reminds us further of the Hermes, while the Eubouleus is recalled not only by this charming trait but more especially by the treatment of the neck, the flesh of which is rendered with the softness of nature, but without a trace of feeble-ness. It is so real and living that we are almost inclined to call it the best part of the bust.

Although we can bring forward no literary witness to help in the identification of this head, we are, I think, completely justified on technical and stylistic grounds in maintaining that it is a real Greek original by the artist of the Hermes. We cannot for an instant suppose that Praxiteles made no statues of Aphrodite besides those handed down by tradition, or that Pliny gives even an approximately complete list of the many works by the master which Roman spoliation brought to Italy. From the carriage of the head and the slight elevation of the shoulder I imagine that the right arm was raised and supported. The statue was probably draped, and perhaps it lost popularity and fell out of notice on this very account. Yet it seems to have been copied; a head in the Giardino Boboli, Florence,[2] and another in Dresden,[3] seem to be replicas, though very poor ones, of the Petworth head.

How strong was the influence exercised by this work of Praxiteles on his successors is shown in an interesting manner by the Venus of Medici. This type is merely a translation of the magnificent Praxitelean ideal into a languishing and coquettish form. The original of the Medici type must have taken an amazingly firm hold of popular fancy, to judge by the great number of copies and variants in existence. I think we may safely assign it to the generation after Praxiteles, perhaps to his sons Kephisodotos and Timarchos.

In proving that the Petworth head is an original we have at the same time ascertained its date: its special correspondence with the Hermes shows that it belongs to the artist's later period. That it is somewhat later than the Eubouleus (cf. p. 334) seems evident from the fact that it shows the technical peculiarities which

[1] As remarked above (p. 322), this little head is not a copy of the Aphrodite of Knidos.
[2] Dütschke, ii. 80. Has been wrongly placed on a Hera statue.
[3] Wrongly attached to the so-called Urania. Hettner, No. 228 (Becker, *Augusteum*, Taf. 69).

distinguish the Hermes from the Eubouleus, such as the use of the drill for the corners of the mouth and the 'liquid' treatment of the lower eyelid.   Side by side with the youthful Hermes we may now claim to have an original female head from that later period of Praxiteles in which his chisel had attained to the highest mastery.

At this point it is necessary to suspend our inquiries about Praxiteles, which only profess to lay down the main lines of his artistic development, and to turn our

[To the Hermes of Olympia, the one authenticated original from the hand of Praxiteles, and to those other two works which on every analogy of form, of style, and of technique—the Eubouleus (Plate XVI.) and the Leconfield Aphrodite (Plate XVII.)—may also be attributed to the master, I now wish to add a fourth, a head in the British Museum (Plate XVIII.), known as the 'Aberdeen head,' from the collection to which it once belonged.   The stages by which its Praxitelean authorship has come to be recognized are sufficiently instructive for a brief account of them to be in place here.   The head is described in the British Museum Guide to the *Graeco-Roman Sculptures,* Part II. 1876, p. 44 (97), as 'Head of young Hercules'—'the type is probably one which prevailed in the Macedonian period.' It was Dr. Wolters who, in 1886, had the signal merit of redeeming the head from its obscurity, by adequately publishing it in the *Arch. Jahrbuch*, i. Pl. v., and by calling attention (*ibid.* p. 54) to its Praxitelean character.   It may, however, be added, if only as proof of the rapid progress which archaeological criticism has made within the last few years, that in 1886 Wolters still showed that same lack of discrimination between Skopas and Praxiteles as, to Pliny's bewilderment, did the ancient critics, since along with the Aberdeen head he published as equally Praxitelean the fine terminal bust of Herakles from Genzano which Gräf, and others after him (*supra*, p. 296), have since shown to be a copy of a Herakles by Skopas.   In 1891, when on my return from Greece I first turned to the comparative study of form, my attention was attracted by the essential similarity which the hair and the eyes of the Aberdeen head offered to the hair and eyes of the Hermes.   In the course of my demonstrations at the British Museum I pointed to the head, timidly at first, as to an original, probably by Praxiteles. It was not however till, for lecturing purposes, I had this head and that of the Hermes photographed side by side on a lantern-slide that I was able definitely to make up my mind.   When the two heads, much enlarged, were projected on the screen, the agreement between them of form and technique was exact beyond all expectation; the indubitable likeness made it at once clear to me that the alternative which I had at times contemplated—namely, that the head might merely be a studio work, traceable to a pupil of Praxiteles—must be abandoned; the head could only be by the master himself. Subsequently I found that this was also the opinion of Professor Klein of Prague (whose book on Praxiteles will, I have reason to believe, throw much light on this magnificent work) and of Professor Furtwängler, at whose suggestion I now publish the head afresh, in connexion with his own researches.   Further, Dr. Kalkmann (as I lately learnt in conversation with him) inclines to the same view.

Turning to a comparative analysis of the forms, it is at once obvious that though the hair in the Aberdeen head is conceived as a lighter, less abundant mass than in the Hermes, the form of the curls that play about the forehead, especially in the region of the temples, is identical in both heads, while on the top it is treated in the same broad masses, calculated to produce impression, rather than to render formal detail.   One point, however, should be noted to which, at present, I can instance no parallel : it is the deeply scooped-out grooves which separate the masses of hair, and which are doubtless intended to help out the effects of light and shade.   In both heads the structure and modelling of the forehead correspond in their every part ; further, the nose, with the great width between the eyes, the form of the eyeball, and the modelling of both upper and lower lids, are precisely similar, even the little furrow indicated between the eyebrow and the eyelid being rendered in both heads with identical personal touch.   Although the cheeks of the Aberdeen head are fuller than those of the Hermes, the depression in the fleshy region between cheek-bone and jaw-bone is rendered precisely in the same manner as in the Hermes, where the treatment of the cheek contributes in so high a degree to the dreamy grace and spiritual delicacy of the face (well seen in the fine photograph of the profile by Rhomaïdes).   The Aberdeen head has fuller, more sensuous lips than the Hermes, but their form is the same, and the corners of the mouth are, like those not only of the Hermes but also of the Leconfield Aphrodite, worked with the drill, the marks of which are quite distinct.   The chin has the same full rounded character as the lips ; it is shorter, and has a more marked dimple than that of the Hermes.   Finally, the close correspondence in the measurements of the two heads cannot

attention to one of his contemporaries, who is an imposing figure in the traditions of the time, though we have so far been unable to obtain a distinct picture of his art.

be without significance : these have been lately accurately taken and published by Dr. Kalkmann in his *Proportionen des Gesichts in der Griechischen Kunst* (53rd *Winckelmannsfestprogramm*, 1893), on p. 98, under Nos. 123 and 124, as follows : —

	Hermes.		Aberdeen head.
Distance between [outer corners of the] eyes . .	112 mm.	. . . .	108 mm.
Eye to chin	129 ,,	. . . .	127 ,,
Height of face	196½ ,,	. . . .	194½ ,,
Distance between ears	165 ,,	. . . .	162 ,,
Nose to neck	210 ,,	. . . .	202 ,,

(Cf. also *ibid.* p. 109 and text p. 41.)

In looking at the silhouette of the two heads, it must however be owned that the Aberdeen head presents a much broader outline at the top than does the Hermes. This divergence is, I think, only superficial, and is solely due to the difference alluded to above in the conception of the hair as a mass. The ears of the Aberdeen head are much knocked about, which makes comparison difficult, still the cartilage seems flattened, or rather as it were folded back, and kept close to the head, thus presenting a variation from the treatment of the ears in the Hermes. The lobe too is rather larger than in the latter, though the drawing about the hollow of the ear and the large hollow itself are points of resemblance. Only a small portion of the neck is preserved, but this suffices to show a breadth and strength which are eminently Praxitelean. The head has a slight inclination to the left, on which side the muscles are relaxed. The marble of the Aberdeen head is the finest Parian ; in the hair are holes for the attachment of a metal wreath.

The great likeness notwithstanding, a glance at the Aberdeen head shows that the hero or god it represents is of a different nature to the Hermes. Kalkmann (*loc. cit.*) calls the head a 'Praxitelean Herakles,' while we have seen that in the British Museum guide-book it was called a 'young Hercules.' Such in effect I believe it to be. The greater emphasis laid on the sensuous physical side suits this interpretation. Nor is it, I think, fanciful to detect a likeness between this youthful beardless Herakles and the bearded Herakles Chiaramonti (*supra*, Fig. 147). When Dr. Wolters considered that, in spite of resemblances, the 'Aberdeen head' only proved after all 'wie unendlich hoch der Hermes in der feinen Durchbildung aller Teile über den anderen Werken derselben Zeit steht'—the difference he detected was, I believe, not one of quality but of conception.

The technique, the slight working of the under lid, the use of the drill for the corners of the mouth, show that the work belongs to the artist's later period. At the back, on the right-hand side, a portion of the head has been cut away in a slanting direction ; we have there a tooled surface showing that the head probably underwent this maltreatment in order to be fitted into a pediment or some other architectural frame. As regards the *provenance* of the head, Wolters had well pointed out (*loc. cit.*) that from what we knew of the Aberdeen collection it was likely the original had come straight from Greece ; it is probable that by gaining access to the still unpublished Journals kept by Lord Aberdeen during his tour in Greece (cf. *Life of the Earl of Aberdeen*, by the Hon. Sir Arthur Gordon, p. 10) interesting facts with regard to this head might come to light. Its significance for our present purpose, however, lies not so much in its provenance or in its interpretation (two points on which Professor Klein, it can hardly be doubted, will have much to say) as in its formal and stylistic kinship to the series of Praxitelean works discussed above by Professor Furtwängler.— E. S.]

III. *Euphranor.—Imitation of Polykleitos and of the older Argive Types.—Bonus Eventus ; Dionysos ; Apollo Patroos ; Paris and Aphrodite ; Athena.—Lysippos.*

Tradition names Euphranor as a celebrated painter as well as sculptor. His versatility is especially praised, for he distinguished himself in every branch of the plastic arts, and moreover busied himself with their theory as well as with their practice. Still, nothing is ever said to lead one to suppose that he had a pronounced individuality. Here, however, as elsewhere, we must guard carefully against trying to extract too much definite criticism from the statements made by ancient writers on art. For instance, when Pliny says that in looking at the Paris by Euphranor the spectator could realize all at once ' the judge of the goddesses, the lover of Helen, and even the murderer of Achilles,' he is evidently merely quoting a neatly turned epigram. Critics ambitious to shine have ever shown themselves adepts at reading the most incredible meanings into works of art ; but their utterances are of no value for the objective understanding of the subject, and we need not conclude that the Paris was a psychological conception.[1] Nor, again, when a saying by Euphranor himself is quoted to the effect that his Theseus was fed on meat, but that of Parrhasios on roses, should we be justified in assuming any special realistic tendency in the artist.[2] The saying possibly arose from some comparison of the two pictures : in the one the flesh-tints may actually have been rosier, in the other duskier and less transparent. Pliny, however, makes one significant criticism, belonging to that series which is almost certainly borrowed from Xenokrates,[3] to the effect that the bodies of Euphranor's figures were too slight, while the heads and limbs were too large, a fault which he also attributes to Zeuxis. The criticism, like all those of Xenokrates, refers probably only to some one principal work of the artist, and is made from a Lysippian standpoint, according to which the heads of all earlier statues appeared too large for the bodies. It teaches us this much only, that Euphranor, like Zeuxis, adopted the older, pre-Lysippian proportions. On the other hand, the disparaging statement about the disproportionate slightness of the body is of greater importance, for it implies that the figures of Euphranor's statues must have had something spare and hard about them, since no critic of the Lysippian school could ever consider actual slightness of figure as a fault. The statement at any rate contradicts most emphatically the modern conception of the figures of Euphranor, which—on the ground of that saying concerning the Theseus, and also because the artist was said to have well expressed the ' worth of heroes '—have been imagined as powerful and of imposing proportions.[4] On the contrary, we should rather imagine the bodies of his statues to have been spare.

Ancient writers date Euphranor by the battle of Mantineia (362 B.C.), an episode of which—the famous Athenian cavalry engagement—he had painted in the *Stoa Basileios* at Athens (Paus. i. 3, 4). It is of course unlikely that so considerable a public commission would be intrusted to a very young artist, and, since among Euphranor's bronze works mention is made of figures of Alexander and of Philip *in quadrigis,* for which no more suitable occasion could be found than the battle of Chaironeia (where Alexander had distinguished himself by the side of Philip), it seems likely that Euphranor's artistic activity lies between 375 and 330 B.C., and that

[1] Cf. Brunn, *Bayr. Sitzungsber.* 1892, 663.   [2] Brunn, *loc. cit.,* and *K. G.* ii. 187 *seq.*
[3] Cf. Robert, *Arch. Märchen,* p. 68 *seq.*   [4] Brunn, *K. G.* ii. 189 *seq.*

he was thus throughout his career a contemporary of Praxiteles. His son Sostratos, according to extant inscriptions,[1] worked in Athens and the Peiraieus, and he is mentioned by Pliny among the artists of the epoch of Alexander.

Euphranor was a native of the Isthmos, *i.e.* of Corinth. Considering the intimate relations of Corinth and Athens at the beginning of the fourth century, it is not surprising that a Corinthian should settle for a time at Athens. Nevertheless, he was a pupil of the Peloponnesian school. His master was Aristeides, not, as Pliny incorrectly states, the celebrated painter, but the bronze-worker, himself a pupil of Polykleitos.[2] Therefore Euphranor too belongs to the outer circle of the Polykleitan school.[3]

One—and only one—work by him, the Leto carrying her children in her arms, has so far been doubtfully recognized in copies.[4] But it has lately been shown on convincing grounds[5] that the two statuettes in which archaeologists saw copies after Euphranor really reproduce a work of the severe style of about the middle of the fifth century, and that Euphranor's Leto consequently still awaits discovery. We are not, however, entirely without any landmarks to enable us to get some idea of his style. Among his bronze statues Pliny mentions a *Bonus Eventus*, holding a patera in his right hand and ears of corn and poppies in his left. From this description it has been rightly conjectured that the statue originally represented Triptolemos, and was therefore of necessity a youthful figure.[6] Since it bore the name of a Roman god, the statue had evidently been brought to Rome.[7] A *Bonus Eventus* by Praxiteles was also at Rome, together with a *Bona Fortuna*.[8] In this case the original Greek names must certainly have been *Agathodaimon* and *Agathe Tyche*, and the former, judging from his received Attic type[9] such as we see it on an Attic votive relief when he appears in company with *Agathe Tyche*,[10] must have been represented something in the manner of Pluto, as a draped bearded figure holding a cornucopia.

Roman Imperial coins, however, from Galba onwards, and likewise gems,[11] very frequently bear the figure of a youth described in the coin legend as a *Bonus Eventus* (*supra*, Plate VI. 37; *infra*, Fig. 149). Now, since this figure corresponds strictly with the description of Euphranor's work, and is obviously copied from a statue made to stand alone—a statue moreover which must have been celebrated and in Rome, and the main points of which are always carefully reproduced—it becomes as certain as

---

[1] Löwy, *I. G. B.* 105, 106.

[2] Kroker, *Gleichnamige Künstler*, p. 25 *sqq.*; Robert, *Archäol. Mär.* p. 83.

[3] It is uncertain whether Sostratos, who is mentioned as the sixth successor of Aristokles of Sikyon, was the father of Euphranor. In that case, Pantias the Chian, who made statues of Olympian victors, must have been his brother. This would not be impossible. Löwy on *I. G. B.* No. 105 also suggested a family connexion between the elder Sostratos and Euphranor.

[4] Schreiber, *Apollon Pythoktonos*, pp. 70, 88; Overbeck, *Gesch. d. Plastik*, 3rd ed. ii. 86; *Apollon*, p. 371; Helbig, *Museums*, 421.

[5] E. Reisch, 'Ein vermeintliches Werk des Euphranor,' in *Festgruss aus Innsbruck an die Philologenversamml. in Wien*, Innsbruck 1893.   [6] Cf. Kern, *Ath. Mitth.* xvi. 25 *seq.*

[7] In Pliny's account it stands between two works whose position in Rome is accurately given.

[8] Plin. xxxvi. 23. On the Capitol.   [9] Cf. Kern, *Ath. Mitth.* xvi. 24 *seq.*

[10] *Anc. Marbles of the Brit. Mus.* xi. 47. The beardless figure carrying a horn of plenty on a votive relief from Kyrene (*Archaeologia Scotica*, iv. Pl. 17; *J. H. S.* v. 157, 3) is closely analogous.

[11] Some of the more important gems are: carnelian in the British Museum (our Fig. 149), *Catal.* 929, already given by Natter, *Traité*, Pl. 23, also Cades, cl. ii. G, 57, 58. Several instances in Vienna and in Copenhagen (*Abdr. der Dän. Samml.* in Berlin 295—297), a good emerald-plasma in the Thorwaldsen Museum, No. 610, several stones in St. Petersburg (*Abdr. in Berlin*, 20, 16; 26, 14; 32, 86; 35, 47; 44, 59), Coll. Schönberg (*Abdr.* 127), etc. Coins: cf. the index of Cohen, *Méd. Impér.* 2nd ed. viii. p. 365, *Bonus Eventus*. In the Berlin collection I have compared pieces of Titus, Hadrian, and Antoninus; they continuously show exactly the same type as the gems.

such things can be that this statue was actually the work of Euphranor.   This is
of the highest importance, for an examination of the figure shows that Euphranor
followed that Argive type of which we found the Idolino to be the finest example.
The youth rests on his right leg, and places the other to the side without drawing it

Fig. 149.
Carnelian in the
British Museum.

back ; he bends his head to the right, holds the cup in his right hand,
while in the left, which hangs down, he holds a bunch of ears of
corn, or of poppies and corn mixed.   The better reproductions reveal
a certain spareness of form which is specially conspicuous in the
Idolino, so that the *Bonus Eventus* has all the characteristics of style
which tradition ascribes to Euphranor.

Taking this *Bonus Eventus* as a basis from which to recover the
standing male figures of Euphranor, we may now venture further, and
turn our attention to a small group of figures which reproduce the
Idolino type so popular, as we have seen, in Argive circles of the
fifth century, in a style which savours more of the fourth.   Among these by
far the most important is a statue of Dionysos (Fig. 150),[1] found at Tivoli.   A
number of traits combine to suggest that it must be taken as a copy after
Euphranor.   It may even be the very statue of Dionysos by him which epigraphical evidence shows to have been at Rome, or at any rate to have been copied
there.[2]   The god stood exactly in the attitude of the Idolino.   The left leg has been
wrongly restored ;[3] it originally was planted sideways with the foot flat on the
ground.   The right hand held a cup, the left hangs empty by the side.   Immediately on its discovery the connexion of the statue with Polykleitos was noticed,[4]
but too much was made of it,[5] and those who attributed it to Polykleitos himself
wandered far from the truth.   On the other hand, Michaelis, to whom we are indebted
for an excellent analysis of the statue, has made too little of this Polykleitan influence,
and has certainly not hit on the right solution when he talks of late eclecticism.   It is
to be hoped that this is only a last flicker of that unfortunate theory, now practically
extinct, of an independent ' Pasitelean school'—a theory by whose delusive light it
was formerly hoped to illumine all dark places.

The close connexion of this statue with the works of the Polykleitan circle is
absolutely unmistakable, especially in the forehead, eyes, mouth, and profile, and in
the nebris, which is disposed precisely as in the Dionysos of the Polykleitan school
mentioned on page 272.   But a comparison with the Polykleitan Dionysos and with
the other undisputed works of the same school shows that we have before us no
production of the actual inner Polykleitan circle.   The Dionysos of Tivoli can only
belong to the fourth century,[6] for its refined, delicate, and natural modelling is not
found in earlier works.   Compare, for instance, the formation of the toes (Michaelis
has already drawn attention to their Praxitelean quality) or the richly and softly
modelled knee with that of the Polykleitan Amazon, where this part is harder and
more simple, or the hair, which in this statue has a much more natural effect than in
the more severely stylistic works of the fourth century.   Further, in that Polykleitan
Dionysos there is not the slightest admixture of those feminine forms which, as

---

[1] *Mon. d. Inst.* xi. 51 ; *Ann.* 1883, 136 *sqq.* (Michaelis) ; Thrämer in Roscher's *Lex.* i. 1138 ; Friederichs-
Wolters, 520 ; Helbig, *Museums*, 967.   Good copyist work of Hadrian's period.

[2] Löwy, *I. G. B.* 495.   It seems to me likely that the inscription stood under a copy rather than under the
original.

[3] First pointed out by Petersen, *Röm. Mitth.* 1891, 238.

[4] Robert, *Arch. Ztg.* 1882, 137.   [5] See Wolters, *loc. cit.*

[6] Helbig (*loc. cit.*) is of the same opinion.

Michaelis has shown, are so noticeable a feature in the Dionysos of Tivoli—as, for instance, in the glutei and the upper arm.

Notwithstanding this, the bodily formation is still that of the Polykleitan circle, with which the artist must be connected. Apart from the attitude, the Dionysos resembles the Idolino in having a less rounded lower abdominal line than is usual in Polykleitan statues. The way too in which the hair lies close to the skull, and allows its shape to be seen, is Polykleitan. A resemblance to the Electra at Naples has been noted in

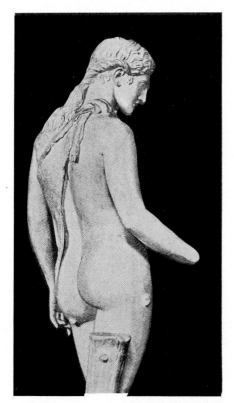

FIG. 150.—Dionysos from Tivoli (Museo delle Terme).   FIG. 151.—Bronze statue of Apollo (Brit. Mus.)   FIG. 152.—Statue in Dresden.

the method of dressing the hair: the likeness consists in the employment of the roll of hair so characteristic of earlier Argive art.[1] In the Electra, however, the roll is arranged in front of the ears according to the older fashion, while in the Dionysos it passes behind them, in an original manner. In this hair-roll we can anyhow recognize the influence of early Argive art.

All these facts fit in admirably with what we have ascertained about Euphranor, and, supposing we place the Lysippian Apoxyomenos beside this statue, have we not the best possible illustration of the criticism passed by Xenokrates on Euphranor?

[1] Cf. 50th *Berl. Winckelmannsprogr.* p. 128 *sqq.*

As a matter of fact, beside the Apoxyomenos the Dionysos looks as if he were all head and limbs, while in the former the first thing which catches the eye is the torso, and then the small head and nervous limbs as mere appendages. If traces of Euphranor are anywhere to be found—and he must be represented among our copies —this Dionysos is by him.

By its means several other statues are drawn into the group of works by this master. I formerly thought that the beautiful bronze representing a youthful Apollo

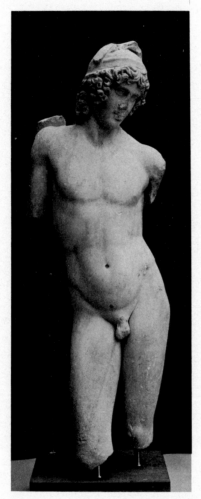 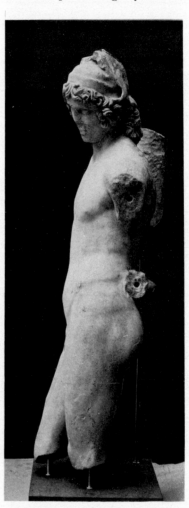

Fig. LII—Paris, Copenhagen, Ny Carlsberg Glyptotek
(See pp. 359 seq.)

in the Sabouroff Collection[1] was a Peloponnesian work of the fourth century, which, starting on the lines of the Idolino, was closely connected with the Dionysos of Tivoli. We can now recognize in it an original work in the style of Euphranor; attitude and position are the same, except that the left leg is drawn slightly back so that the heel is somewhat raised. The Apollo is appreciably younger and more boyish than the Dionysos, and naturally shows absolutely no admixture of feminine forms. With these exceptions the likeness of the two figures is remarkable;

[1] Head unfortunately missing; *Samm. Sabouroff*, Pl. 8—11 ; *Skulpt. in Berlin*, No. 1 ; Overbeck, *Apollon*, p. 227 ; Brunn-Bruckmann, *Denkm.* No. 278.

the Argive substratum pierces through in every part: the torso, especially the front view of it, is rather flat, spare, and dry ;[1] and the lifelike, finely formed limbs are in strong contrast with it. The fingers, toes, and the modelling round the knee recall the Dionysos, and are also related to Praxitelean work. Now that we have brought the Dionysos into connexion with Euphranor, the historical position of the Apollo also becomes intelligible.

A bronze statuette, formerly in the collection Gréau,[2] seems to go back to the same original as the Sabouroff Apollo, and can thus afford a notion of the face and hair. A Hellenistic imitation of an original closely connected with the preceding is preserved in a large bronze statue from Lower Egypt in the British Museum (Fig. 151).[3] The attitude and the position of the arms are like the Sabouroff bronze ; the bodily forms resemble the Dionysos, though the copyist has very much weakened his model: the head is not bent, the eyes gaze straight in front of them, the hair is very individual ; it lies close to the skull ; it is confined by a twisted fillet, whence it falls in loose curls all round the head. A work by Euphranor must have been the basis for this statue also.

With these is connected a statue at Dresden (Fig. 152),[4] with sufficient remains of the arms and legs to show that the attitude was analogous. It is the figure of a boy, similar in form to the Sabouroff bronze. In this case too the front of the figure is rather flat and spare, although remarkable for its softly blended transitions of surface. The head, which is unbroken, turns naturally to the right, and is slightly bent ; the hair, which lies close to the head, has something Polykleitan in its arrangement over the forehead, and at the back escapes in short twisted curls. The interpretation of this figure is uncertain, since it belongs to no known type. From what has been said, however, it is a natural step to conjecture in it the Triptolemos (*i.e. Bonus Eventus*) of Euphranor, shown to exist on coins and gems, and to restore it with a cup in the right hand and ears of corn and poppies in the lowered left ; at any rate, it will be difficult to find a better explanation for this remarkable type.

Further, we now perceive that it was on prototypes in Euphranor's style that the artists of Hadrian's day based certain portraits of Antinous, which are among the most celebrated of those extant.[5]

In this connexion must be mentioned a bronze statuette of Dionysos which

---

[1] Cf. the fuller analysis in the text of *Samm. Sabouroff*, p. 3 *seq.*

[2] Fröhner, *Coll. Gréau, Bronzes Ant.* No. 913, Pl. 20. Now in Berlin ; cf. *Jahrb. d. Inst.* 1886, p. 157 ; *Samm. Sabouroff*, vol. ii. *Nachträge*, p. 1 ; Overbeck, *Apollon*, p. 229. Mention must be made of a statue in Cassel, under life-size (ii. 12), in attitude and bodily forms remarkably like this Apollo ; no remains of curls on the shoulders ; the neck restored ; the head antique but foreign ; the latter is copied from an interesting older Argive work, with a roll of hair in front and behind. Closely allied to the Sabouroff bronze is another marble statue, with foreign head and no curls on the shoulders, in Catajo (Arndt-Bruckmann, *Einzelverk.* No. 59).

[3] *Anc. Marbles of the Brit. Mus.* xi. 33 ; Clarac, 482 C, 929 B. From the Coll. Mimaut. Mentioned by Michaelis, *Ann.* 1883, 141. The legs are restored, left leg too far drawn back ; the attitude was that of the Sabouroff bronze, to which the hanging left hand corresponds exactly ; thumb and forefinger, little finger, and hand are fastened together for security by bars (*not* the remains of an attribute) ; the right hand differs somewhat from the Sabouroff bronze ; it appears to have held something upright (perhaps a laurel-twig). The loose curls are made separately and put on. Eyes of silver.

[4] *Cat.* Hettner, 89 ; Becker, *August.* Pl. 87 ; Clarac, 809, 2026. The restorations (legs from above the knees, both arms from the middle of the upper arm) have been removed ; the left arm was lowered, the right probably extended outwards. Length of face, 0·152 ; distance between the nipples, 0·194 = height of head. Our illustration (Fig. 152) shows the statue in the same characteristic half-back view as the London bronze and the Tivoli Dionysos.

[5] The Capitoline (Friederichs-Wolters, 1659 ; Helbig, *Museums*, 524) and the Farnese statue in Naples (*Mus. Borb.* 6, 58). The former most certainly represents Antinous as Hermes.

Z Z

has been referred to Praxiteles.[1] Though different in conception, and more full of action than the works just described, it is yet connected with them first of all by a coiffure similar to that of the small bronze replica of the Sabouroff Apollo, and secondly by the clear reminiscences of Polykleitos in the formation of the face, the arrangement of the nebris, which is merely knotted on the one shoulder, like the one worn by the Tivoli Dionysos, and lastly also by the essential qualities of the bodily forms. For the rest, the statuette is of Roman workmanship, and is in no sense an exact copy.[2]

So far all the male statues referred to Euphranor and to his influence have been based on the scheme of the Idolino. There exist however copies of a remarkable work which at first sight seems strange when seen among the preceding ones, but which is nevertheless closely connected with them, except that it is based on another and older Argive type, which is no other than the one created by the school of Hagelaidas, and which, as we saw, was also used in the Polykleitan circle (p. 287 *sqq.*)

The figure in question represents a youthful nude Apollo ; the best-known copy is the so-called ' Adonis ' of the Vatican (Fig. 153).[3] The identification as Apollo is confirmed by a number of other copies[4] which have preserved undoubted Apolline attributes. The god, in complete harmony with the Argive scheme, stands on the left leg, with the right foot placed with full sole to the side and somewhat in advance of the other ; he looks with bent head towards the left, and stretches his left forearm horizontally in front of him, while letting the right hand hang straight down. The left hand probably held a bow. In one copy the right holds the remains of a strap, which can only have belonged to a quiver which was dangling from it ; in another copy the quiver hangs on the tree-trunk beside the left leg, and in yet another the quiver-strap passes round the chest. From these variations we may safely conclude that the quiver was not a feature of the original. The notion of making the right hand hold the quiver by the strap was introduced by the copyist from another older statue of Apollo[5]

[1] By Milani in *Museo ital. di antich. classica*, iii. Tav. 7, p. 753 *sqq.*; Sal. Reinach (*Gaz. des Beaux-Arts*, 1891, ii. 265) follows him ; Héron de Villefosse, *Bulletin des Musées*, 1892, p. 29 ; Michon, *Mon. Grecs*, 1891—92, p. 2. Cf. p. 337, note 5.

[2] In the Louvre, from Italy, supposed to have been found on the Akropolis. The appearance of the bronze is against this view. The metal has the yellow colour peculiar to the Roman bronzes, more especially to those found in Gaul. It never occurs, to my knowledge, on Greek bronzes. The patina is, moreover, quite different from that of the Akropolis bronzes, and the workmanship is of Roman style ; the hair is bluntly worked, the superficial modelling of the bodily forms lacks insight and refinement. The statuette has altogether been much overvalued.

[3] Helbig, *Museums*, No. 255, and vol. i. p. 545, for the literature of the subject.

[4] Lansdowne House, in the dining-room ; Clarac, 906 C, 476 A. The head is genuine, and wears a laurel-wreath and the loop of hair which designates Apollo ; the wreath is of course merely an addition of the copyist. The right leg is wrongly restored, set back.—St. Petersburg, Hermitage, 340 ; D'Escamps, *Marbres Campana*, Pl. 36. Head well preserved ; inferior work. In the antique right hand is a fragment of a strap (wrongly restored as a taenia), which must belong to the quiver-band ; puntelli on the thigh show its continuation ; both legs are restored. The left forearm, stretched straight out, is antique, the hand with the diskos lately restored.—Richmond, in possession of Sir Francis Cook ; noted by me in 50th *Berl. Winckelmannsprogr.* 1890, p. 152, note 92. Trunk with quiver partly antique ; head preserved ; right hand and left forearm new ; feet antique ; mediocre work.—Rome, Pal. Chigi : *Guattani*, 1785, p. 7 ; Clarac, 489, 947 ; Matz-Duhn, 184 ; Overbeck, *Apollon*, p. 135, 13. Quiver-band round the breast, not continued over the back. Trunk with snake, feet and forearm new, the rest antique. Very poor copy, inexact in the hair, effeminate expression. Torso in Berlin, No. 511, good copy. Torso restored as Hermes, formerly in Villa Casali, now in the Jacobsen Coll. in Copenhagen, No. 1059 ; right shin wrongly restored, as if drawn back ; good copy. Head without fillet, placed on the Munich 'Jason' (Brunn, *Glypt.* No. 151).

[5] The Mantua Apollo (cf. 50th *Berl. Winckelmannsprogr.* p. 141 *seq.*) and the later modification in the Museo Torlonia (Taf. 32, 126 ; Overbeck, *Atlas d. K.* Taf. 23, 24 ; *Apollon*, p. 225, 1), and the coins there referred to.

very like this one; in the original of the Adonis-Apollo, however, the right hand most probably held a laurel-branch.

This statue again is entirely built up on the lines of a fifth-century creation; nay, the artist has been so penetrated with the popular canon of Hagelaidas that he has imported into his own work some slight reflex of its proportions: for example, he has made the chest too broad for the narrow hips. But above all he has everywhere retained the practice of treating the front of the body in simple, broad planes. The work cannot however belong to the fifth century. The transitions from plane to plane are soft and smooth, and the formation of particular parts such as breast or knee find their closest analogy in works belonging—like the Thespian Eros and the 'Satyr pouring out wine'—to the early period of Praxiteles. The relation of the head to this series is likewise manifest—its likeness to that of the Thespian Eros being specially striking. All this is of weight so far as the date of the statue is concerned; but now, passing to the more delicate personal traits, we find they all speak for Euphranor. In common with the bronze Apollo in the British Museum, the 'Adonis' has hair lying close to the skull and then escaping in a rough tangle of short curls— a peculiar and original arrangement, not met with elsewhere in statues of Apollo. Some copies, though certainly not all, even have the twisted fillet. Here too, as in the Dionysos of Tivoli, earlier Peloponnesian influences are at work. With the customary type this Apollo has as little in common as the Dionysos. Both however are closely related in their facial forms; they both aim at typical beauty rather than at spiritual characterization. Both have the same heavy eyelids, treated after the earlier fashion, and similar ends of hair falling about the nape. In face and figure, and even in hair, the 'Adonis-Apollo' resembles the curly-headed Dresden youth (Fig. 152) still more strongly. Finally, if we survey the composition as a whole, we recognize in the Apollo that self-

FIG. 153.—Apollo ('Adonis'), Vatican.

same spirit and temper which pervades the works grouped round Euphranor's name. The spirit of the old Argive creation lives again, rendered in the softer manner of a later age. Unoccupied, unconcerned by any inward and personal emotion, these figures stand absolutely at rest, with heads gently bent, basking as it were in their own beauty.

The early works of Praxiteles—the Thespian Eros and the Satyr pouring wine[1]—

---

[1] In proportions, especially the small head, these are closely related to the Apollo.

are, as already stated, specially related to this Apollo, and we may conclude that the two artists were closely connected. Both were influenced by Peloponnesian models. But the active emotional Attic spirit in Praxiteles can never be disguised ; in spite of their tranquil motive, those Praxitelean statues are all doing something, even down to the Thespian Eros, employed in spreading the meshes of his glances.

If the Apollo of the so-called Adonis type belongs to Euphranor, as everything seems to indicate, it must, like those works of his contemporary Praxiteles, be placed in his earlier period, so that the difference between the Apollo and those other works which form a group with the Dionysos becomes explicable as a difference of time. In his early period the artist was permeated by the old types created by Hagelaidas, and fashioned his genius after them. Later, he gave the preference to the Idolino type, and developed its bodily forms in the direction of softness and roundness, as shown in the Dionysos and the Sabouroff Apollo.[1] The criticism passed by Xenokrates deals only with these later works.

The Apollo of the ' Adonis ' type must, to judge from the replicas, have been a well-known and celebrated work. A similar figure resting on the left leg, the right somewhat advanced, the bow in the left hand, a twig in the right, appears on later Athenian coins,[2] whence it is safe to conjecture that it is a reproduction of one of the principal statues in the city, such as for instance the statue of Apollo Patroos, the special god of the Attic race, in his temple on the Agora.[3] Now, since the cultus-statue of the Patroos actually was the work of Euphranor,[4] it seems not impossible that our copies reproduce that very statue.

The style of the Corinthian Euphranor must have been much appreciated in Athens, since he was commissioned to execute the Patroos. The fact testifies to the enthusiasm for Peloponnesian art which must have reigned in Athens at that time, and which enables us to understand still better the early work of Praxiteles. It certainly must have been a great surprise to the Athenians to see Euphranor represent their Patroos almost as a boy with a round curly head, and in a tranquil attitude. Yet the creation found favour and reflected the more effeminate spirit of the age, even as the powerful, virile Apollo of Kalamis and Myron had reflected the spirit of theirs.

An original work from the Akropolis, unfortunately only a torso,[5] bears witness to the influence of Euphranor on contemporary Attic artists. It too is an Apollo, with soft, boyish forms, showing in attitude and conformation the influence of the figure surmised to be the Patroos;[6] yet the artist has, in Attic fashion, replaced the spareness and flatness affected by Euphranor by more softly rounded flesh, and he has obviously been influenced not only by this master but by Praxiteles. He was, however, one of the lesser artists; his work must be dated at about 360 B.C.

The Apollo has its exact counterpart in a Dionysos,[7] evidently belonging to the

---

[1] The Adonis-Apollo is flatter in breast and abdomen than these. The fold which separates the pubic region from the abdomen is carried directly into the *sulcus inguinalis* as in the Polykleitan statues of boys. In those later works this is no longer the case.

[2] Imhoof-Blumer and Gardner, *Num. Comm.* Pl. CC. xv. xvii. (= our Plate VI. 31) ; Overbeck, *Apollon*, Münztaf. 4, 33. Cf. p. 196, note 2.

[3] Cf. Wachsmuth, *Stadt Athen*, ii. 418 ; Aristot. 'Αθ. πολ. c. 55, 3 ; Beulé (*Monn. d'Ath.* p. 271 connected the Patroos with these coins.

[4] Statues by Kalamis and Leochares stood outside the temple : Paus. i. 3, 4.

[5] So-called Elgin ' Eros ' in the British Museum ; Friederichs-Wolters, 1291. With quiver-band ; of course Apollo, not Eros, who is excluded by the absence of wings.

[6] Weight on the left leg, right foot a little drawn back.

[7] It is the type of the horned Dionysos, discussed by Amelung, *Florentiner Antiken*, p. 15 *sqq.* I had always supposed the head in Florence (Amelung, pp. 16, 17) to be a variant of the ' Adonis,' but the replicas enumerated

same period of Euphranor's activity, and of which the head, at any rate, has been preserved in several copies. We may venture to restore the body on the analogy of that of the Apollo, to which it must have offered a complete resemblance. Like the Apollo, this Dionysos differs from the received types in that his thick, short, curly hair, in which we again find a twisted fillet, lies close to the skull. The modelling of the face and the self-absorbed expression are extraordinarily like the Apollo. The earlier works of Praxiteles are also akin to it; but this master always makes the features less massive and simple, and gives them a more delicately emotional grace.

It further appears that we possess copies of yet another work by Euphranor, in which he clung close to the Hagelaidas types. On a term found in Rome in the seventeenth century, and which afterwards disappeared, ran the inscription Ἡρακλῆς Εὐφράνορος.[1] This proves that a terminal Herakles by Euphranor was well known at Rome through copies. In the Villa Ludovisi there is a series of terminal figures which must once have adorned a gymnasium of some kind, and which are copies of works in divers styles.[2] Among them is a Herakles holding a cornucopia, in which I had already recognized a later adaptation of the Alexikakos of Hagelaidas.[3] Since then a statuette has been found in Rome which in all main points corresponds to the idea which one would naturally form of the Herakles by the early Argive master, except that the copyist seems to have replaced the cornucopia on the left arm by the more familiar lion-skin.[4] The Ludovisi term repeats the main features of this type, but in a later style, which manifests itself less in the body than in the head, and which seems to correspond to the artistic stage reached by Euphranor. The skin is here slung round the figure, and knotted on the shoulder just as in the Praxitelean Herakles.

Finally, it is an important confirmation of our results that the only head of Paris, which judging from copies and later adaptations enjoyed a great reputation, fits so admirably into our sketch of Euphranor's art—nay, belongs so entirely to the series of works we have been discussing, that we are justified in thinking that it goes back to Euphranor's celebrated work. The youthful face in the Phrygian cap[5] has a convincing likeness to the Adonis-Apollo; and here again the Peloponnesian influence makes itself felt even in the symmetric arrangement of the curls on the forehead. At the back the curls are twisted, and specially resemble those of the Dresden Triptolemos. The original underwent adaptations and alterations, but was apparently rarely copied,

by Amelung make it quite certain that it is Dionysos. The variations in the Lateran head (Amelung, p. 22) are probably assignable to the copyist. Amelung suggested Praxiteles, but the illustrations he gives are peculiarly instructive, as showing the finer points of difference from Praxiteles.

[1] Löwy, *I.G.B.* 501. Several such inscriptions are known : there is therefore no reason for doubting the genuineness of this one.

[2] *Mon. d. Inst.* x. 56, 57. Cf. Helbig, *Museums*, 861—865; Brunn, *Bayr. Sitzungsber.* 1892, 660. These terminal figures are of different date and style (cf. p. 248, note 4), but mostly early. Cf. a similar term from Rhamnus, Ἐφημ. ἀρχ. 1891, Taf. 7.

[3] In Roscher's *Lexikon*, i. 2158 *seq.*

[4] Marble statuette (in the Roman market) preserved intact (only known to me from the photograph) ; attitude like the Stephanos athlete ; the lowered right hand rests the club on the ground, as in the term ; bearded head bent to the left ; hair like the Stephanos figure and the Olympian sculptures ; lion-skin on the outstretched forearm. The skin was probably absent in the original.

[5] As the style of this work fixes its date, we can hardly be at a loss about the interpretation. Ganymede was as yet not represented as a Phrygian, nor presumably was Attis (cf. *Samml. Sabouroff*, Text to Taf. 137, p. 4 and Supp.), but Paris was. A statue in Rome which may be reckoned among the free later modifications shows by the attributes that it was meant for the shepherd Paris (*Bull. della Comm. Arch.* 1887, Taf. 2, p. 27). The seated Paris in the Vatican, conjectured by Helbig (*Museums*, 188) to be after Euphranor, is in conception and form of Hellenistico-Roman origin. The figure seems to have been adapted from a painting or a relief. There are no replicas of it.

which accounts for the lack of unanimity shown by the extant examples in the hair
and even in the position of the head.   The most complete reproduction of the original
composition seems to be the statue in Lansdowne House (Fig. 154).[1]   The youth
stands just like the Polykleitan 'Narkissos' (*supra*, Fig. 115), except that the sides are
reversed and the legs crossed.   The right hand is supported on a tree, the left placed
behind the back ; the head looks downwards to the right.   The same pose appears in

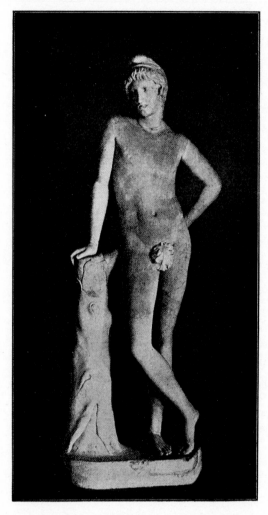

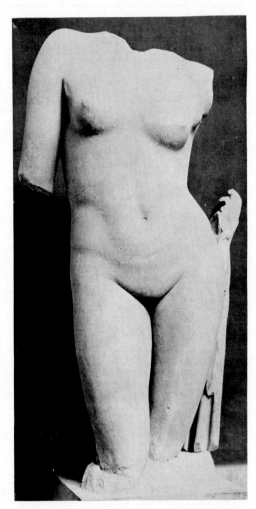

FIG. 154.—Paris in Lansdowne House.   FIG. 155.—Torso of Aphrodite (Naples).

a head at Munich,[2] a really good copy ; a head in the Villa Albani[3] differs somewhat
in the hair.   On the other hand, there is a statue at Copenhagen[4] with a beautiful
head that corresponds fairly closely to the Munich head, though it is inclined in the
opposite direction,[5] while the attitude of the body is unaltered, and only a tree-stem is

[1] Clarac, 396 E, 664 L ; Michaelis, p. 447, 39.   Head broken, but genuine. [Photographed for this edition
by kind permission of Lord Lansdowne.—E. S.]

[2] Glyptothek, 135 ; Lützow, *Münchner Antiken*, 27.

[3] No. 218.   The head is placed on a statue foreign to it.   Photo. by Bruckmann.

[4] Jacobsen Collection, No. 1052, head unbroken.

[5] Also the head in the British Museum (*Specimens*, ii. 17 ; Friederichs-Wolters, 1580) is bent to the left ; this
agrees in the hair most nearly with the Albani head,

introduced at the back. The pose of the head of the Lansdowne statue is the more
natural, and certainly more likely to be the original one. The body, at any rate in
the Copenhagen copy,[1] is closely related to the Apollo, and shows the same characteristic broad smooth masses. The attitude, while influenced by that Polykleitan
prototype, has gone beyond it in the direction of pictorial *nonchalance*. The complete
self-absorption of the figure would encourage any one with a turn for epigram to find
all possible contrasts united in the figure.

A feminine counterpart of the Paris exists in a nude female torso at Naples
which must have stood precisely in the same attitude (Fig. 155).[2] As far as a
comparison of the figures is possible, the stylistic treatment of the body is in all main
points that of the Apollo and the Paris.

A strong family likeness unites with the preceding works another beautiful head,
which has already called forth many a modern psychological description : I refer to the
so-called 'Faun' (Pan) of Winckelmann (Fig. 156), to whom it once belonged (No. 102
Munich Glypt.) The likeness of the features to the Adonis-Apollo and the youth at
Dresden is most striking. Remains of Polykleitan rendering of form are also plainly
to be seen—for instance, in the close-lying hair, and in the incision at the nape of the
neck. The figure which must have belonged to this enchanting head should be conceived after the fashion of the Dresden youth ; the head should be more inclined to
the front ; the eyes look to the right, doubtless to the side of the supporting leg. The
expression of the head, as Brunn rightly states, is one of still unconscious but awaken-
ing desire—'a soft entrancement,' as Winckelmann calls it. Brunn considers the
'Faun' to be a pendant to the Praxitelean Eros, and as a work by Euphranor this is
actually its historical position.[3]

Moreover, we can, I think, also distinguish among our copies a dignified goddess
by Euphranor. None among the extant types of Athena has been more difficult
to explain than the so-called Athena Giustiniani (Fig. 157), of which several replicas
exist.[4] It contains a host of peculiarities which at first seem to indicate a fifth-
century work,[5] side by side with others which point to the fourth.[6] The solution is
easy now that we have learnt to recognize Euphranor's style ; for this statue also
belongs to the series of his works.

Once more the attitude is influenced by the early Hagelaidas type, and is like
the Adonis-Apollo, except that the right foot has less weight thrown on it and is
somewhat drawn back, while the right hand is supported on the lance. The steady

[1] Not on the Lansdowne copy, where the forms are rounder and softer.

[2] Friederichs-Wolters, 1468. Cf. Bernouilli, *Aphrodite*, p. 279 *sqq.* ; Roscher's *Lex.* i. 415, Z. 62 *sqq.* The
left hand was supported against the side, not raised as in the paste compared by Friederichs.

[3] Closely analogous to the Pan is a head of a youth in the Jacobsen Collection, No. 1095. Finally, the
so-called Theseus of Ince Blundell Hall should also be mentioned in the present connexion (*Spec. of Anc. Sculpt.*
ii. 19 ; *Arch. Ztg.* 1874, Taf. 1; Michaelis, *Anc. Marbles*, p. 351, 43 ; cf. p. 94, note 1), the body of which
seems to me very like the Adonis. The attitude is the same. I have, however, not seen the original.

[4] I know the following copies : (*a*) Vatican, Braccio Nuovo, 114 ; Helbig, *Museums*, 51. Aegis on the breast,
and snake below ; remains of the sphinx on the helmet are antique. Aegis, snake, and sphinx are copyist's additions, and are absent in *b.* (*b*) Capitol, Helbig, *Museums*, 438. (*c*) Museo Torlonia, 298. The head and the left hand
with the shield are modern ; with aegis ; an interesting copyist's addition is the olive-tree with the snake (which
here replaces the lance and is mostly antique) touching the sleeve ; the right upper arm is raised higher than in
a and *b*, the forearm restored. Very late work. Cf. the similar copyist's invention of the laurel-trunk beside the
Mantuan Apollo. (*d*) Palazzo Pitti, Dütschke, ii. 28. Head modern ; aegis ; poor work. (*e*) Naples, *Inv.* 6399 ;
no aegis ; head modern, restored as 'Talia.' (*f*) Good copy of the head in Berlin, 77. (*g*) Head in St.
Petersburg, Hermitage, 325 ; much worked over ; poor. (*h*) Head in the Terme in Rome. Poor. (*i*) Head on
the Cassel replica of the Lemnia (*supra*, p. 5).

[5] Hence my dating in Roscher's *Lex.* i. 702, l. 5.

[6] Helbig (*Museums*, 51) refers to an Attic relief of 375—374, which, however, bears only a superficial
resemblance to the statue.

FIG. 156.—'The Faun of Winckelmann' (Munich).

Fig. LIII—Bonus Eventus, London Museum

Fig. LIV—Apollo Patroos, Athens, Stoa of Attalos Museum (sf. Fig. 36, p. 87)

pressure on the left foot, the turn of the head to this side, and the horizontal projection of the left forearm are all part of that early scheme. No convenient attribute could be found for the left hand, for it would have been unsuitable and clumsy to place something in it when the right hand was already holding the spear; it only remained to make it play with the edge of the cloak.[1] The holding up of the lance involved a variation from the Argive scheme which required the arm to be held downwards; the artist managed it by raising the arm as quietly and slightly as possible, and he arranged the wide sleeves of the Ionic chiton so as to fill the whole of the triangle between the elbow and the body with vertical lines. Thus the variation from the pattern type is compensated for and passes almost unnoticed. The uniform large surface which the broad folds of the Ionic chiton form over the breast is thoroughly intentional, and contributes to the impression of dignified repose. The aegis, shown in some copies, is a disturbing addition made by the copyist; it is absent in other copies whose evidence should be insisted on; for copyists, while apt to introduce popular and typical attributes,[2] never left them out if they were to be found in the original. By leaving out the aegis the artist seems to recall that earlier type[3] of peaceful Athena which so often appears without this attribute. The folds of the chiton, on the other hand, only superficially resemble the fifth-century manner; their real likeness is to the drapery of the Praxitelean Aphrodite of Kos (*supra*, Fig. 138). The folds of the cloak are treated in a simple and dignified fashion; there is even a severe touch about the straight fall of the drapery over the left shoulder. Still there is nothing clear-cut or large about them, and we feel that they are somewhat conscious and intentional in arrangement.

While all this fits in admirably with the works already referred to Euphranor, the accordance of the head is still more conclusive. It too has a purely superficial resemblance—due mainly to the low forehead—to the types of severer style; but it has none of their harsh strength, and it finds its real analogy in the Adonis-Apollo and kindred works, except that it is less kindly in expression, owing to the air of dignified severity produced by the slightly drooping corners of the mouth. The treatment of the hair, which contrasts with the strongly stylistic methods of the fifth century, is related in principle to the Dionysos of Tivoli; but in arrangement it is almost identical with that of the Athena we assigned to Skopas (*supra*, Fig. 130); the same arrangement, in conjunction with the ram's head on the helmet, was seen in an Athena head of Praxitelean style (p. 326). Another detail too which definitely shows the head to belong to this later period is the soft leathern lining showing under the helmet at the sides and at the back, and which makes its first appearance on Corinthian coins of the end of the fifth century.[4] Lastly, a good extrinsic support to our statement that this statue is referable to a Corinthian artist, *i.e.* to Euphranor, is afforded by the tiny roll-shaped attachments which form the uncommon decoration of the plumeless helmet;[5] they are exclusively a characteristic of Athena's helmet on Corinthian coins of the fourth century, and hardly ever appear elsewhere. Thus

---

[1] This motive, as also the attitude and fall of drapery, has been used by the artist who made the statue of Antinoos in the Eleusis Museum.

[2] Like snake and olive-tree in *a* and *c*.

[3] Cf. Roscher's *Lex.* i. 697, l. 6 ; Preller-Robert, *Griech. Mythol.* i. 191, note 3.

[4] First in the new, quite free style, Brit. Mus. *Catal. Coins, Corinth*, Pl. 2, 21 ; Pl. 3 *sqq.*

[5] In the Berlin copy of the head they are preserved on both sides, just in the place where they appear on the Corinthian coins. In the original, as the coins show, there must have been a similar roll on the top of the helmet. The sphinx, shown in the Vatican copy, is certainly an addition of the copyist ; in the Capitoline and Berlin heads the helmet is smooth above.

Fig. 157.—Athena Giustiniani (Braccio Nuovo, Vatican).

Euphranor took his native Corinthian type of Athena with all its details as the basis of his creation.

Finally, when we call to mind that there was a celebrated statue of Athena by Euphranor dedicated below the Capitol[1] which must certainly have been copied, we shall have no hesitation in considering it to have been the original of the Giustiniani type.

This Athena, like the Apollo Patroos, would belong to Euphranor's earlier period, even as the Dionysos and the works akin to it belong to the later. The older group is intimately connected with the earlier works of Praxiteles and also of Skopas. But Euphranor never got beyond that clinging to the types of the Argive school which with his two contemporaries was only a transient phase. He was obviously a man of formulas ; not a strong, fiery nature, but thoughtful and quiet, *docilis ac laboriosus,* active and versatile—doubtless capable of exquisite invention, in dependence upon older types, but evidently lacking the freshness of inspiration or the inexhaustible fantasy of a Skopas or a Praxiteles.[2]

It would be interesting to know whether Euphranor ever adopted that roundness of modelling and that expressive formation of the eye and its adjacent parts which mark the style of Skopas and Praxiteles in their later period. It seems probable that Euphranor remained conservative, and it is not likely that he assimilated much of this newer method. A statue of a youth in the Capitoline Museum[3] is of interest in this connexion. It is most closely and indubitably connected with the later creations of Euphranor, such as the Sabouroff Apollo and kindred works. The attitude is the same (*i.e.* it is that of the Idolino), so is the position of the arms and of the head. But the body is modelled in a perfectly round, smooth manner, with soft undulations of surface ; the head is appreciably smaller, and shows in forehead, eyes, and the whole formation of the face and hair a style similar to that of the later Praxitelean or even of Lysippian heads. It is quite plain that we have before us the last outcome of Euphranor's art, though it is uncertain whether the artist himself lived to accomplish this progress. The small head makes this improbable, but his son Sostratos, a contemporary of Lysippos, might very well have worked in this manner. A youthful Hermes (Dresden),[4] with wings fastened to his fillet, is related to the Capitoline statue.

The coming dominion of the Lysippian style soon pushed to one side these offshoots of Euphranor's art. While Euphranor clung to the old Argive types, and to the less intense Polykleitan creations, Lysippos broke away entirely from these traditions. He certainly studied the old masters to a certain extent—nay, he called the Doryphoros his master, and how he adapted it we may still conjecture from the monuments[5]—yet by giving himself up entirely to the novel, energetic motives which Skopas had introduced he infused new blood into the stagnating Peloponnesian art.

---

[1] Plin. xxxiv. 77. The statue was called the *Minerva Catuliana,* as it was set up by A. Lutatius Catulus, who after the fire of 83 B.C. dedicated the newly rebuilt Capitoline temple with great splendour.

[2] Plutarch's information that Euphranor painted the cavalry engagement at Mantineia in a very lifelike manner is naturally quite reconcilable with this view.

[3] Salone 12. Photographs of the head by Bruckmann. Head unbroken ; right arm, left hand, legs, and support restored. Right supporting leg, left thigh turned slightly out ; the head, with short hair, looks out quietly towards the right.

[4] Hettner, 151 ; Becker, *August.* Pl. 42. Poor execution. Attitude as in statues discussed above ; chlamys on left shoulder ; head with short hair turned to right ; fillet supporting *antique* small wings.

[5] The Herakles statue of the Museo Chiaramonti, No. 294, shows an interesting combination of the proportions and forms of the Doryphoros with the Lysippian realistic rendering of form. The pose of the head just differs slightly, inasmuch as it is turned a little toward the other side (the neck seems to be rightly restored) ; the head

It is interesting to compare with the aforementioned Capitoline statue a Lysippian statue of a youth, at Berlin,[1] that tallies with it exactly as regards age and pose. Although it is in more complete repose than any other Lysippian figure known to me, yet the comparison forcibly brings out the stronger stir of life in head and limbs. How much stronger therefore will it not appear in those Lysippian figures, whether of gods or athletes,[2] which are represented in active movement.

Still we must confess that Euphranor infused an inner meaning into the old Peloponnesian types, whilst Lysippos externalized the inner conceptions of Skopas. In the art of Lysippos lay the beginning of the pathetic style, which spread to such an extent in Hellenistic times.

is of the bearded Lysippian type. It seems to me not improbable that Lysippos himself used the canon of Poly-kleitos in this way, adapting it in his own manner. His procedure would be the same as when Rubens copied an older work.

[1] *Skulpt.* 471. The body, without pubes, is analogous to the youth of the Capitol. The attitude and head are quite Lysippian. This is doubtless a copy of an athlete by Lysippos.

[2] The majestic motive of resting the hand high on the sceptre, seen in the greater gods, was invested with a pathetic character by Lysippos, who made the hand grasp the staff higher up. Cf. the rock-relief from Alyzia, where Lysippos worked, Heuzey, *Olympe et Acarnan.* pl. 12, p. 412 (cf. Roscher's *Lex.* i. 2173, line 33), and the same figure used as a symbol on an Athenian coin, Imhoof-Blumer and Gardner, *Num. Comm.* pl. EE. 13. The same motive is shown in the large bronze statue (*Ant. Denkm.* i. 5; Helbig, *Museums*, 965), which, as Rossbach has recognized, represents Alexander Balas; I think, however, that the motive of this statue is only borrowed from the famous Alexander with the spear by Lysippos. As regards athletes in motion by Lysippos, the two statues in Dresden (Hettner, 245, 246) are worthy of special notice. The beardless head is surprisingly similar to that of the sandal-binder of the Akropolis (*Ath. Mitth.* 1886, Taf. 9, 1). A head analogous to the bearded one, but much more beautiful, is in the Jacobsen collection at Copenhagen (No. 1072); it belongs to an athlete in similar motion, and is one of the finest and most purely Lysippian works in existence. It probably belongs to an earlier period of the artist than the Apoxyomenos, for the hair is flatter, and worked in an older manner.

Fig. LV.—Hermes of Andros, Athens, National Museum (See p. 338)

*Plate XVII—Aphrodite, Collection of Lord Leconfield (See pp. 343 sqq.)

Fig. LVI—Poseidon from Melos, Athens, National Museum (See p. 376)

Fig. LVII—Venus of Milo, Paris, Louvre (See pp. 367 sqq.)

THE VENUS OF MILO

BY subjecting the famous statue from Melos in the Louvre to a fresh critical examination, we shall, at the same time, have occasion for enlarging and extending in more than one direction the knowledge we have gained in the preceding essay of the art of Skopas and Praxiteles.

The 'Venus of Milo' is still a centre of eager controversy, and only recently a distinguished archaeologist pronounced the whole question to be an insoluble riddle.[1] Before resigning myself to this conclusion, I should like to be sure that no means of solution has been left untried. Since questions of very great interest in the history of art arise in connexion with this statue, it will be well to see what further light can be obtained from a sober and unbiassed examination both of facts and of tradition.

I. *The Lost Inscribed Fragment: Discussion of the Statue's Provenance.*

Our first inquiry must be concerning the fragments belonging to the statue. It is now almost universally acknowledged that a left upper arm and a hand holding an apple, which were found with the Venus, really belong to it. Even F. Ravaisson, the author of the most recent reconstruction, admits this fact, although

---

[1] Sal. Reinach, in the *Gaz. des Beaux-Arts*, 1890, i. 376 *sqq.* Among the more recent literature on the subject the following may be mentioned : F. Ravaisson, in the *Revue Arch.* 1890, t. xv. p. 145 *sqq.* ; criticism of the same by Sal. Reinach in the *Chronique des Arts*, 1890, p. 294 ; F. Ravaisson, *La Vénus de Milo* (extract from *Mém. de l'Académie des Inscr. et Belles-Lettres*, tome xxxiv. 1), Paris 1892 ; my review of the same in the *Berliner Philol. Wochenschrift*, 1893, 1107. Less recent works are : Saloman, *Die Plinthe der Venus von Milo*, 1884 ; Löwy, *I. G. B.* (1885), p. 209 *sqq.* ; Wolters, *Gipsabg.* (1885), p. 560 *sqq.*; W. Henke in Lützow's *Zeitschr. f. bild. Kunst*, 1886, p. 194, 222, 257 ; Overbeck in the *Renuntiationsprogramm der Phil. Facultät*, Leipzig 1887, *Archäol. Miscellen.* vi. 'Die Plinthe der A. v. M.'; Heydemann, *Pariser Antiken* (1887), p. 5 ; Sal. Reinach, *Esquisses Archéol.* 1888 ; *Chron. d'Orient* (1888), p. 465 *sqq.*, 699 *seq.* ; 1893, p. 35 ; Schreiber in *Litter. Centralblatt*, 1888, 1687 ; Valentin, *Kunst, Künstler, und Kunstwerke* (1889), p. 219, 313 ; Häberlin, *Studien zur Aphr. von Melos*, 1889 ; Kroker in *Festschrift für Overbeck*, 1893, p. 45 ('Die linke Hand der A. v. M.') Finally, my own short discussion of the question written in 1882 for Roscher's *Lexikon*, i. 414 *seq.*, embodying part of the material of the present chapter, but requiring correction in some points. The theory recently put forward by Mironoff, that the Venus of Milo was a Victory, has been thoroughly disproved by Petersen, *Röm. Mitth.* 1894, p. 91 *seq.*

it is unfavourable to his theory that the figure formed part of a group.[1] The left upper arm must belong to the statue, for it contains a dowel-hole exactly corresponding to one in the torso. The hand with the apple matches the fragment of arm in scale, material, and technique, in the traces of weathering, and in the marks of breakage:[2] evidently it must belong to the same figure as the arm. These facts may be regarded as settled on technical grounds apart from any aesthetic considerations. It is true that the two fragments show poorer workmanship than the main parts of the statue,[3] but this must not be taken as contrary evidence, for in ancient marble statues the extremities are not unfrequently neglected, especially if they were to be as distant from the spectator's eye as the left hand of this statue.

The fragment of plinth with the artist's inscription offers a much more difficult problem, because, as is well known, the original has disappeared. It is not, however, by ignoring or by concealing it that we can make good this loss, the sin of an earlier generation. Indeed, the evidence, if fairly weighed, leads inevitably to the conclusion that the lost inscribed fragment originally belonged to the plinth—a view recently maintained by Overbeck, by Geskel Saloman, and by H. Heydemann. One ascertained fact must be borne in mind: when the statue and the separate pieces were brought to the Louvre and the first attempts (quite unbiassed by preconceived theories) were made to put them together, it was at once noticed that the inscribed fragment exactly fitted the breakage on the right side of the plinth, nor did any of the witnesses present —savants like Clarac, Quatremère de Quincy, and Saint-Victor among them—ever express the smallest doubt as to this, or suggest that the inscribed fragment did not fit. It must therefore have appeared quite obvious that the inscribed piece belonged to the statue. Another question, however, was immediately raised: Did it form part of the original work, or was it an antique restoration? They decided for the latter, but were not agreed as to how this restoration had come about. Clarac believed quite simply that the inscription gave the name of the real artist, while Quatremère de Quincy conjectured that the plinth had been mended with a chance piece of marble which happened to be inscribed.[4] Quatremere could not bring himself to believe that the inscription was that of the real artist, and therefore invented this far-fetched hypothesis. He would never have done this had he been able to discover the least imperfection in the fit of the two pieces. Therefore the theory lately urged, that if the inscription had really fitted it would have been fastened on and would be there to this day, is absolutely unwarrantable.[5] But it is very easy to see why the piece was not fastened on, and why it disappeared. In the first place, since it was believed to be merely a later addition, it was neglected as of no consequence for the original composition. Secondly, the late obscure artist named in the inscription could not possibly, it was supposed, have made the statue. Thirdly, since the statue was to be presented to the king as a work of Praxiteles (see

---

[1] Ravaisson makes the hand rest on the shoulder of a male figure grouped with the Venus. If this were so, the short muscle in the palm of the hand would appear flattened by the contact, which is not the case.

[2] The restorer Lange's remark (quoted by Ravaisson, *V. de Milo*, 1892, p. 55) is specially important. He notices that the traces of weathering on the upper side of the hand are a continuation of those on the upper side of the arm.

[3] Besides this, Henke (*loc. cit.*) has shown that there are parts of the torso which are not worked any better than the hand. So Ravaisson and Kroker (*loc. cit.*)

[4] F. Ravaisson has lately repeated this conjecture (*Vénus de Milo*, 1892, p. 52), therefore he too must believe that the piece belongs to the statue. He does not, however, deign to explain how it happened that the Mars or Theseus grouped with the Venus came to disappear (without however the hand with the apple that rested upon his shoulder also disappearing !), and to be replaced by a little terminal figure with an inscribed basis picked up anywhere.   [5] Sal. Reinach, *Gaz. des Beaux-Arts*, 1890, i. 384.

Adr. de Longpérier's famous letter on the subject in Friederichs, *Bausteine*), it would naturally be inconvenient to have to affix to it the name of an unknown sculptor.

The disappearance of the inscription, in my opinion, is only a proof of its genuineness.[1] It was an awkward witness, and had to be quietly got out of the way. A letter from Clarac to Forbin, published by Ravaisson (*Vénus de Milo*, 1871, p. 22), throws a startling light on the state of affairs in the Louvre at that time. Clarac, although 'Conservateur du Musée Royal des Antiques,' was excluded from the consultation that took place concerning the setting up of the figure, his 'notice' on the statue never reached the king, the statue was set up clandestinely and hastily[2]—all this doubtless to suppress Clarac's unwelcome opinion that the inscription, although added later, gave the real name of the artist.

Now this theory of an antique restoration, which alone prevented Quatremère and Clarac from seeing that the inscription had belonged to the statue from the beginning, was quite arbitrary, and undoubtedly false. It arose solely from ignorance of the technique of ancient marble statuary. Nowadays everybody knows that Greek originals may often be distinguished from Roman copies by the very fact that they *are* pieced together. In the best period artists were very economical with their marble. The practice of accurately piecing marble together was already very general among the artists of the second half of the sixth century B.C. At a later date it may be observed in the Hermes of Praxiteles, and it was still more widespread in the period after Alexander; instances are the Nike of Samothrake, some of the Pergamene figures, the Belvedere torso, and other works of the first and second centuries B.C., mentioned by Tarral (*apud* Göler von Ravensburg, *Venus v. Milo*, p. 37).[3] It is among the last-named works that the technique of the Aphrodite of Melos finds its nearest parallel.[4] Not only were the upper and lower parts of the torso made separately and then put together, but also the left arm, the left foot, and a piece of the right hip.[5]

To reject any one of these pieces because it does not suit our theories or taste is purely arbitrary, and if we carried the method to its logical conclusion we should accept only one piece as original, while all the rest would be put down as later additions, a manifest absurdity that no one has yet ventured upon.[6] Knowing, then, that the original statue was made of different pieces, we shall require definite proof before allowing that any one of the pieces is a restoration.

It is true that the various pieces of marble are not all of the same quality, but this is no proof that they did not originally belong together. In other statues made up of several blocks it is not unusual to detect strong differences in the marble, especially between head and torso. Therefore Clarac's assertion that the inscribed fragment is of a marble 'un peu différent'—'d'un grain un peu plus gros' than the rest of the basis is no argument against its genuineness, especially as it has been observed that the upper part of the body is made of a different marble from the lower.[7]

---

[1] This is rightly emphasized by E. Robinson, *Catalogue of the Casts from Greek and Roman Sculpture*, Boston 1887, p. 92; 1891, p. 253.

[2] Ravaisson, *loc. cit.*

[3] Cf. also Saloman, *Plinthe*, p. 17.

[4] Cf. *Arch. Ztg.* 1881, p. 306, and Collignon in *Rev. Archéol.* 1888, i. p. 294.

[5] The joined piece of the right hip can be clearly seen on the new casts, and in Ravaisson's *Vénus de Milo*, Plates I. and II. 1871. Clarac (*Vénus Victrix*, p. 23) and Ravaisson (*loc. cit.* p. 10) are wrong in supposing it a restoration.

[6] Clarac (*Vénus Victrix*, p. 13) was at first inclined to consider the lower half of the body as a restoration, but on closer examination he changed his view.

[7] Des Cloiseaux *apud* Ravaisson, *Vénus de Milo*, 1871, p. 67.

3 B

On the other hand, although the inscribed fragment is lost, the part of the plinth still extant shows that a piece is missing to which the lost inscribed block exactly corresponds. There is therefore not the smallest ground for doubting the testimony of those first eyewitnesses who, in spite of their preconceived theories, accepted the inscribed block as part of the plinth.

Since casts have recently been taken of the 'Venus' without the restorations (Fig. 158), any one can easily convince themselves that the plinth, like the whole statue, was put together out of different pieces.[1] The block of marble was insufficient, and the plinth had to be continued to the right by joining on a piece. To the right of the existing plinth there is a slanting contact-surface worked smooth at the upper edge, and it is plain also that the piece adjusted to the right must have been higher than the rest of the plinth. Now those first eyewitnesses, and Debay's drawing, which we still possess (Fig. 159), prove that the lost piece of marble had a slanting surface to its left, exactly corresponding to the surface on the existing plinth, and that it was of the desired height.

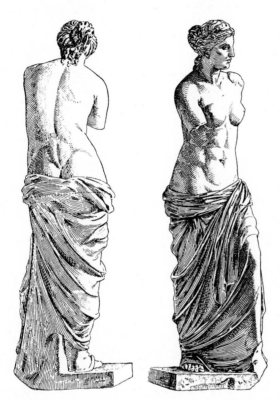

FIG. 158.—Venus of Milo (with plinth unrestored).

Geskel Saloman, in his treatise on the Plinth of the Venus of Milo (p. 30), described carefully and in detail the marks on the existing portion of the plinth, and my own examination confirms his results in all essential particulars. Yet his exposition does not quite account for certain difficulties which arise on closer consideration. I therefore consulted the sculptors who have been working at the reconstruction of the Pergamene frieze—MM. Possenti and Freres—in Berlin, and with their help arrived at the following results.

Needless to say that Overbeck's restoration, made before the real shape of the plinth was known, must be wrong,[2] because it gives a false distorted turn to the left foot; this foot must have projected beyond the edge of the plinth. Tarral's restoration (Göler von Ravensburg, pl. 4) is also wrong, because it contradicts Debay's drawing (Fig. 159) by placing the inscribed piece too far to the right. Saloman, Overbeck, and Ravaisson[3] maintained, but incorrectly, that the existing plinth was let into a second plinth. This was often done in the case of marble statues, but not in this particular instance. There could not have been a plinth at the back, because the perpendicular surface of the existing plinth is neatly finished off, and the folds of drapery

---

[1] The supposition of Valentin (*Kunst, Künstler, und Kunstwerke*, p. 321), that the plinth was put together for the first time in modern times—actually in the Louvre—is refuted by the appearance of the plinth.

[2] *Gesch. d. Plastik*, 3rd ed. vol. ii. p. 331.

[3] Saloman, p. 36; Ravaisson, *V. d. M.* 1892, p. 54.

on the left (of the spectator) are worked right down to the ground. The left perpendicular face (looked at from the front), like the back of the plinth, is smoothly finished, and therefore also intended to be visible. For it is well known that the faces of plinths intended for insertion were left rough. But the front face appears not to correspond; it cannot possibly have been visible, nor can the front of the inscribed block have formed a continuation to it. Something must have been fastened on in front of it. The manner in which it is prepared with a smooth edge, top and bottom, is precisely that of a tooled contact-surface, and excludes every other interpretation.[1] To complete the rectangular plan, as Possenti showed me, the lost piece must have been wedge-shaped (Fig. 160).

The inscribed block need not have stood more than a very little farther forward ($\frac{1}{2}$ cm., according to Possenti, meets the technical requirements) than the existing plinth. Clarac's statement (*Vénus Victrix*, p. 49), that the fragment lay 'bien juste dans l'alignement de la surface antérieure' de l'ancienne plinthe,' is therefore not quite correct, but the mistake is easily understood. The deviation of plane is so slight as to be easily passed over; indeed, the left-hand edge of the inscribed block on which the thin wedge-shaped piece joined on in the front abutted, seems, as Debay's drawing shows, to have been injured. Besides, Clarac's remark is not made in the course of a scientific description, but in a rhetorical period in which he is

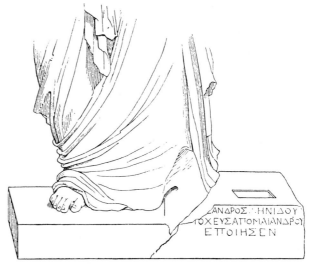

ΛΑΝΔΡΟΣ ΗΝΙΔΟΥ
ΤΟΧΕΥΣ ΑΠΟΜΑΙΑΝΔΡΟΥ
ΕΠΟΙΗΣΕΝ

FIG. 159.—Drawing by Debay, showing the inscribed block adjusted to the plinth.

attempting to prove, not that the inscribed piece fitted, which nobody doubted, but that the inscription was there not by accident but by intention, and that it really gave the artist's name. Clarac's inexactness of wording is shown by another undoubted instance in the very same sentence. What he called 'fractures' are really, as Quatremère and Saint-Victor rightly maintained, contact-surfaces. Debay's drawing does not show the front of the plinth as a junction-surface. It has been drawn smooth, possibly because it looked better so; hence it is not surprising that Debay also overlooked the divergence in plane between the two front surfaces.

If, as seems likely, the wedge-shaped piece put on in front was of the same marble as the inscribed block, then the whole front of the plinth was originally uniform in material. Therefore there is nothing in the condition of the extant fragments against the genuineness of the inscribed block. On the contrary, several circumstances afford proof positive that the missing piece of plinth must have been

---

[1] Overbeck's assumption (*Leipz. Renuntiationsprogr.*, *loc. cit.*), that the plinth was sunk in another up to the smoothed edge of the front surface, is contradicted by the fact that the back and left side are smoothly finished. Ravaisson (*V. d. M.* 1892, p. 54) recognized the original existence of a separate piece of marble in front of the plinth, but by his hypothesis of a large 'fausse plinthe' he completely ignored the finished state of the back and left side.

just such a piece as Debay's drawing and the evidence of the eyewitnesses attest the lost inscribed block to have been.

We have already pointed out that the missing piece had a slanting contact-surface, and must have been higher than the existing plinth.   This extra height may be calculated from the remaining portion.   On the outer side of the left foot of the figure are to be seen (*a* on Figs. 161, 162) the remains of a small horizontal plane surface hitherto unnoticed, which must have been continued in the piece of plinth added on.   Now this plane is exactly level with the height of the inscribed block in

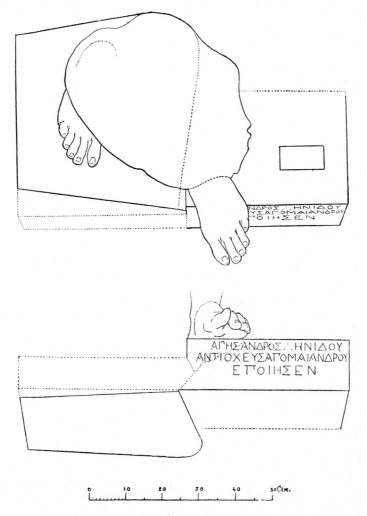

Fɪɢ. 160.—Ground-plan and projection of the plinth, with restorations indicated.

Debay's drawing; it is considerably lower than a horizontal plane at the level of the heel of the left foot would be, as may be easily calculated from the remains of the ankle visible through the drapery.   Hence the foot, the front and larger portion of which was, as is well known, made of a separate piece, must have sloped downwards in a slanting direction.[1]   The small fragment of flat surface *a* gives the level where the foot rested, and this is the level of the inscribed block.   The ends of the folds of drapery behind the foot turn up just at the same level, showing that at that

[1] Cf. Saloman, *Plinthe*, 37 ; Overbeck, *loc. cit.*

point they touched the ground. The actual edge of the drapery is not preserved, but the smoothly worked contact-surface *b* shows that the missing edge of drapery was made of a small piece of marble inserted between the torso and the additional piece of basis. This was done, Possenti informs me, because the edge of the drapery worked in one piece with the torso would not have afforded a solid enough termination to the block.

The lost portion of the plinth cannot possibly have formed the support for a male figure grouped with Aphrodite, as Ravaisson has again recently suggested—first, because it was higher than the part which supports the female figure, and the man could not possibly be placed on a higher basis than the woman ; and, secondly, because it did not reach to the back of the existing plinth, and was therefore only large enough for a smaller object. This is evident from the appearance of the contact-surface, which comes to an end before it reaches the back of the plinth (cf. the side view of the plinth, Fig. 161, where the slanting hatchings mark the smoothly worked portion of the contact-surface).

Again, the drapery at the back does not turn up as in front, where it met the higher additional piece of plinth, but falls right down to the lower edge of the plinth. The inscribed piece drawn by Debay satisfies these conditions in so far that the rectangular hole visible on the upper surface shows distinctly that it was only destined to support some small pillar-shaped object. On the other hand, Debay has placed the line terminating the plinth at the back too high, probably with the intention of improving the appearance of the whole plinth : evidently for the same reason he also, as is well known, drew the existing plinth considerably higher than it really is.[1] In our Fig. 160 the added piece is made to end at the back where the smoothed edge of the existing plinth ceases completely ; the end must have sloped down somewhat at the back, as shown in Fig. 161.

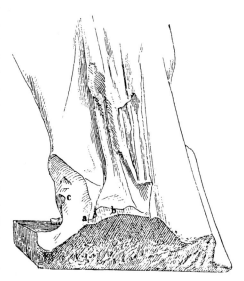

Fig. 161.—Side view of the extant plinth.

Finally, the ends of folds turning up behind the foot, the remains of the horizontal surface *a*, and the vertical surface on the inner side of the left foot[2] make it absolutely certain that the left foot was placed not on a round object but on a flat tectonic surface like the fragment sketched by Debay.

Since, then, the extant remains of the basis point quite positively to a continuation shaped precisely like the inscribed fragment drawn by Debay, it becomes impossible even for the most sceptical to doubt the original authenticity of this fragment, whose exact correspondence, at the time when it was still extant, was not disputed even by those who would have welcomed every opportunity for doubt.

The front of the plinth thus consisted of two parts—the longer and lower to the left, the shorter and higher to the right. On either of these the artist could have cut

[1] The correction of this error naturally brings the inscription somewhat nearer the lower edge.

[2] Saloman, *Plinthe*, p. 37, and Overbeck, *loc. cit.* I should like to add further that the rounded hollow (*c* on our sketch) above this vertical edge, which must necessarily have belonged to a tectonic member, is not part of the horizontal surface of that member, but merely belongs to a fold of drapery.

his inscription.   He chose the right-hand surface, probably because it was of a more convenient shape, and because it formed the front of a solid block instead of being merely a thin added piece like the left-hand wedge.   As a rule, inscriptions which are cut not on the pedestal but on the work of art itself (as in this case) are found to be written in a small space in several lines, and are not conspicuously placed.   In this instance the inscription is under the foot, and yet is easily read from below if the statue be placed at the height that was customary in the third and second centuries B.C. The Belvedere torso is inscribed between the legs of the figure on the marble seat.

How completely our restoration harmonizes on the one hand with the existing remains, and on the other with Debay's drawing, can be so easily ascertained by a comparison of Figs. 158 and 159—161 that it need not be further emphasized.

We cannot follow the fortunes of the inscribed block from the time it left Melos till its arrival in the Louvre, but this is immaterial.   The fact is enough that it was brought to the Louvre with the other pieces of the statue ostensibly from the same provenance, and that it was at once adjusted to the plinth.   It must not, however, be

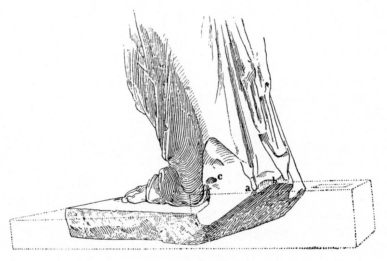

FIG. 162.—Side view of the plinth. (Restoration indicated by dotted lines.)

forgotten that the suggestion (afterwards so often reiterated as a fact) put forward by the Vicomte de Marcellus, to the effect that the inscribed fragment was only brought from Melos by the Marquis de Rivière in November 1820, remains a pure conjecture. Although years later M. de Marcellus professed to have no recollection of receiving the inscribed block in May 1820, this is no proof that he did not take it away. Supposing the lettering to have been much effaced, the Vicomte might very well mistake the block for a mere shapeless fragment ; and he himself asserts that he brought away everything that was found with the Venus except the large exedra inscription.   The block in question may very well have been among the 'quelques socles' which he received.   That the Marquis de Rivière brought it later is a pure supposition.   Dumont d'Urville immediately after the discovery stated, as is well known, that an illegibly inscribed fragment was found with the statue, and describes it as the pedestal of one of the terminal figures discovered at the same time.   This means that it had a hollow as if for the support of a term, thus corresponding to the piece we are now examining.   We can hardly doubt, therefore, that the fragment mentioned by Dumont d'Urville is identical with ours.   Again, Voutier's drawing published by Ravaisson,[1] and said to have been made in Melos before the statue was shipped, *i.e.* before May 24, 1820, contains the inscribed piece under discussion. It is drawn as 'piédestal d'un des hermès.' It is evident that Voutier's drawing represents the same fragment as that described by Dumont, and that this fragment is the inscribed block drawn by Debay.[2] To connect the inscription with a terminal figure is, of course, a purely arbitrary hypothesis, suggested at the time of the discovery, and adopted by Dumont and Voutier. We shall attach but little value to Voutier's evidence if we bear in mind that he restored the plinth of the Venus as a complete rectangle. He also drew an inscribed basis[3] under the second term, but this basis plainly shows by its section of profile that it could have had nothing to do with the term. It was simply a stray fragment of pedestal with a hole for insertion. Voutier's drawing, then, is valuable only as evidence that the inscription was found with the statue, but his combinations of inscriptions and terminal figures are quite arbitrary.

A few words must here be added about the character of the spot where the statue was found, though this is really a minor consideration. According to Salomon Reinach,[4] this was a limestone-burner's kiln or workshop (*magasin de chauxfournier*), where bits of refuse marble of all kinds were collected for burning. If this statement were correct, it would still be no evidence against the genuineness of the inscribed block. But I cannot admit that it is correct. Dumont d'Urville, an eyewitness, speaks of 'une espèce de niche,'[5] and of hewn stones found first by a peasant. He also says that an inscribed marble block was found over the opening to the niche (*entrée de la niche*). Clarac speaks of a 'niche carrée d'environ quatre pieds de large.' In Olympia I have often helped to excavate limestone kilns where had been burnt precious works of statuary, which however had always been previously broken up into small pieces. But not even the most ignorant person could ever mistake such a limekiln for an architectural 'niche.' Reinach's supposition has no foundation in fact. The contents of the 'niche' consisted, not of a mass of odd fragments of a number of different statues, but simply of the pieces of the Venus and of the small terms (such terminal figures being, as is well known, a favourite decoration of niches) and of an odd hand. A foot 'chaussé d'un cothurne' was found, according to Dumont, 'en même temps,' but, according to Marcellus, not in the same place, but lower down near the sepulchral caves. This foot is identical with the left foot with a sandal, of smaller proportions than the Venus mentioned by Clarac on p. 24 of his work.[6] In November two clumsy arms were brought to the Marquis de Rivière, as coming from the spot where the statue lay—a statement which is naturally not very reliable. It is evident that these premises are insufficient to warrant the theory of 'un magasin de chauxfournier.'

My own opinion is that the statue was found *in situ*. I base it solely on the evidence of the earliest informants as given above, leaving entirely out of the question the statement made long after the discovery, and already disproved by Ravaisson, that the statue was found intact.[7] A square niche with an inscribed block over it was evidently what the discoverers saw. The niche

[1] *V. de M.* 1892, Pl. 2 ; p. 10, 51. Cf. *Berl. Phil. Wochenschr.* 1893, 1108.

[2] Löwy's objections (*loc. cit.* p. 112) are not serious. Debay may have drawn the inscription from a transcript, and the original may very well have been illegible to the unpractised.

[3] Mentioned nowhere else. [4] *Gaz. d. Beaux-Arts, loc. cit.* p. 382.

[5] Brest (20 Nov. 1820) also calls the spot a 'niche.'

[6] The foot must still be in the Louvre, though Ravaisson (*V. de M.* p. 54) says it cannot be found there.

[7] Cf. Ravaisson, *V. d. M.* 1892, p. 26 *sqq.* It is needless to discuss the foolish nonsense contributed by H. Rochefort to the *Art Français* of Jan. 21, 1893, and quoted *in extenso* in *Arch. Anz.* 1893, p. 27 (cf. Sal. Reinach, *Chronique d'Orient*, 1893, p. 35 ; *Berl. Phil. Wochenschr., loc. cit.*)

contained the statue and two terminal figures,[1] and, as far as is known, no other
fragments of sculpture. Clarac says (p. 25) that the block, from its dimensions, seemed
to have been placed above the niche. He evidently considered Dumont's statement
about the position of the block an inference, but a correct inference, and we have no
reason for holding a different opinion. Morey's assertion that the statue was found in a
sepulchral grotto partly hewn out of the rock[2] found great favour, but had no foundation
other than statements of the Melos peasants, who were only too ready to show the
English traveller (who visited the island eighteen years after the discovery) any
cave which they thought would satisfy his curiosity. The real niche in question,
being in their arable land, was probably destroyed very soon after its contents were
removed. It is not the late statement of Morey, but the first authentic records,
which can serve as evidence, for we know how quickly ancient remains disappear if
the ground where they lie is cultivated. Now the place where the statue was found
was in cultivated soil, *above* the caves. These are hewn in the rocks of the valley
called *Klima*, which slopes down towards the sea. Ross has given a vivid description
of these in his *Inselreisen* (3, p. 9). No trustworthy record exists of any remains of
sculpture which the caves may have contained. The higher ground, on the other
hand, especially the site of the ancient town of Melos, was peculiarly rich in remains.
In the immediate neighbourhood of the place where the Venus was discovered there
were found some years later a statue of Hermes bearing the artist's inscription, seven
fragments of another statue, and the inscription C. I. G. (Böckh) 2431, to which I shall
have to refer again.[3] Recently the statue of a boxer has been discovered at the same
spot as the Venus.[4] In a 'grotte' within the town ruins, but not localized more
accurately, has been found, along with innumerable votive gifts to Asklepios and
Hygicia, the superb Asklepios head now in the British Museum.[5] In the lower
part of the city near the sea, 'dans la localité dite Klima,'[6] several well-preserved
statues now in the Central Museum, Athens, recently came to light.[7] These probably
stood in a sanctuary of Poseidon, to whom one of them bears a dedicatory inscription. Another is a colossal figure of the god himself,[8] of peculiar interest as affording
the closest analogy to the Venus. It is nude above and draped below, and consists
of two blocks of slightly different marble joined just within the upper roll of drapery,
exactly as in the Venus. The treatment of the folds, especially on the right leg, which
supports the weight of the body, is strikingly similar. No one has ever maintained
that the Poseidon is earlier than the Hellenistic period.

The inscription on the block above the niche reads[9] :—

Βάκχιος Σατίου[10] ὑπογυ[μνασιαρχήσ]ας τάν τε ἐξέδραν καὶ τὸ / ...Ἑρμᾶι Ἡρακλεῖ.

[1] Two according to Dumont, Brest, and Voutier, yet three came to the Louvre, and Marcellus also speaks of
three ; the third was probably found later. Cf. *infra*, p. 377, and Ravaisson, *V. de M.* p. 38.

[2] The assumption so often repeated latterly, that the statue was found in a hiding-place, is purely arbitrary.
Even Ravaisson (*loc. cit.*) speaks of a 'cachette.' It is true that Le Blant (in *Mélanges d'Archéologie et d'Hist.* x.
(1890) p. 389 *sqq.*) had shown from literary sources that in the fifth century A.D. statues of the gods were sometimes
concealed from the Christians. That the Hercules Mastai and the Capitoline Venus were found in such hiding-
places seems certainly correct, but it is quite false to assert this of the Venus of Milo. Le Blant himself (p. 394)
seems to doubt it. The original report on the find of the Melian statue makes it quite impossible ; a niche with
a dedicatory inscription above the entrance, and adorned with terms, is scarcely a 'hiding-place.'

[3] Brest in *Ann. d. Inst.* 1830, 195. The Hermes is now in Berlin. For the inscription belonging to it see
Löwy, *I. G. B.* No. 354.　　　　　[4] *Rev. des Études Grecques*, 1891, 192.

[5] *Annali*, 1829, p. 341. Cf. Wolters, *Ath. Mitth.* xvii. p. 7.　　　[6] *Bull. de Corr. Hell.* 1889, p. 498.

[7] Kabbadias, γλυπτὰ τοῦ ἐθν. μουσείου, Nos. 235—238.

[8] *Bull. de Corr. Hell.* 1889, Pl. 3 ; Kabbadias, No. 235.

[9] Clarac, *Inscript. du Louvre*, Pl. 54, 441 (No. 802), p. 853 ; Böckh, *C. I. G.* 2430.

[10] Clarac's reading is Σ(έξτου) 'Ατίου.

The 'exedra' is doubtless the niche itself, dedicated by a sub-gymnasiarch to the special divinities of the palaestra, Hermes and Herakles. καὶ τὸ / ... (the slanting stroke belongs to an A or Λ) is most naturally restored as καὶ τὸ ἄ[γαλμα —, and this can only refer to the Venus. The name of the goddess may have followed the word ἄγαλμα. It would be quite in accordance with usage [1] for a gymnasiarch on leaving office to dedicate a niche to Herakles and Hermes, the two patrons of gymnasia, but there was no reason why he should not include among his votive gifts images of other divinities. We have already noted that in the immediate neighbourhood of the niche were found the inscription (*C. I. G.* 2431)—again a dedication to Hermes and Herakles—a statue of Hermes, and the fragments of another figure of which nothing is known: the recently discovered boxer also comes from the same spot. All this points to the conclusion that we have here remains of the decorations of a gymnasium, and not a chance heap of marble fragments.[2] The small terminal figures found with the Venus, and which, according to Clarac (*Vénus Victrix*, p. 6), were leaning against the posterior wall of the niche, are quite in place here. At first only two were found, one bearded and one beardless. These were drawn by Voutier, and described by Fröhner (*Notice de la Sculpture Antique*, Nos. 194 and 209). The shafts are in good preservation. A third (Fröhner, 195) was found later, and was also brought to the Louvre. The shaft was broken and is restored. All three are of somewhat different proportions;[3] but in general decorative effect,[4] in marble, and in style, they harmonize so closely that it seems reasonable to suppose that they ornamented one and the same enclosure. No. 209 represents the old bearded type of Hermes, No. 194 presumably Hermes as a youthful athlete, No. 195 the young Herakles. Probably there were originally more of these decorative terms, but their importance as votive gifts must have been small compared to that of the large statue. The workmanship is poorer than that of the Venus, but may easily be of the same date: it is certainly pre-Imperial.[5]

We are, however, justified in asking whether the dedicatory inscription may not belong to a later date than the artist's signature. The block with the dedicatory inscription has likewise disappeared (another inconvenient witness hushed up !), but we fortunately have a fairly exact copy by Clarac. Both inscriptions are written in the same characters, except that the dedicatory inscription has *Pi* with the second stroke long, a form which we know from the Pergamon inscriptions to have been in use at the end of the third century B.C. along with the older form with the shorter second stroke.[6] We therefore have no reason for dating the dedicatory inscription later than the artist's. The character of the epigraphy allows us to place either inscription anywhere between 200 B.C. and the Christian era, but their nearest

---

[1] Cf. *Pergamon*, viii. *Inscr.* No. 9, dedication to Hermes by a gymnasiarch, *C. I. A.* iii. 105. Do. 123 to Hermes and Herakles. Also *Bull. Corr. Hell.* 1891, p. 251 *sqq.* for several similar inscriptions from the gymnasium in Delos. The usual votive offering seems to have been a terminal figure.

[2] Cf. Saloman, *La Statue de Milo*, p. 20 *seq.*

[3] The exact measurements, communicated to me by M. Michon, are as follows: No. 194: whole height (exclusive of the modern basis) = 1·153. Height of bust = 0·30, of head = 0·17; breadth of shaft = 0·17, depth = 0·14.—No. 209: whole height (exclusive of the modern basis) = 1·26; height of bust = 0·31, of the head down to the (modern) point of the beard = 0·24; breadth of the shaft = 0·195; depth = 0·16.—No. 195: whole height of *ancient* portion = 0·745; height of bust = 0·32; of head = 0·185; breadth of shaft = 0·175, depth = 0·145. The phallos was attached somewhat differently in each.

[4] The height of the arm-holes (7 cm.) and the distance from the head to the terminal shaft is the same in all three.

[5] The edge of the eyelids is smoothed off, the eyeball is almost concave instead of convex—peculiarities which no longer occur in Imperial times.

[6] See *Pergamon*, viii. *Inscr.* Nos. 33—37 (Attalos I.), 47, 51, 53 (about 200 B.C.), 58, 169, 236, 239, 240–2 (end of empire). For the different forms of *pi* in Attic records see Dittenberger, *Arch. Ztg.* 1876, p. 139.

parallels are found from 150 to 50 B.C. For more exact dating we must rely on a
comparison of styles.

It is interesting to compare the quadrangular niche in which the Venus was discovered with the remains of niches found ranged round a court which served as the
place of assembly for the Italic colony on the Island of Delos. These niches[1] contained either benches—in which case they were genuine ἐξέδραι—or statues offered
by various persons at different times, and the whole building was dedicated to Hermes-
Mercury, the patron of the colony. The building with its sculpture may be dated
about the end of the second century B.C., the very period to which we have assigned
the exedra of the Gymnasium of Melos.

That court in Delos had probably been copied from a gymnasium. Several
constructions of this kind serving as gymnasia or palaestrae, and dating from
Hellenistic or Roman times, have been preserved. The characteristic portion of the
design is a square, pillared courtyard surrounded by a wall containing rectangular or
rounded niches (exedrai) once adorned by statues. Such are the Gymnasium of
Hadrian in Athens (Πρακτικὰ τῆς ἀρχ. ἑταιρίας, 1885, πιν. i.), the Gymnasium in
Delos (Bull. de Corr. Hell. 1891, p. 238), and the Palaestra at Olympia. For others
in Perge, Side, and elsewhere see Petersen in Lanckoronski, Städte in Pamphylien
und Pisidien, i. p. 41, 134. It is obvious how excellently the Melian finds fit into
this series; the further fact that the theatre is close to the spot accords admirably
with our theory (cf. Petersen, loc. cit. p. 134 seq.)

It has been a somewhat difficult task to work our way back to the actual circumstances of the discovery of the 'Venus of Milo.' The facts themselves are so
simple that it is astonishing they should ever have been misunderstood. It was the
blind and prejudiced notion of the time that this statue was a unique and unrivalled
treasure, the work of Pheidias or of Praxiteles, something quite isolated from, and
independent of, historical limitations. Ignorance of marble technique fostered this
fancy, for the separate pieces which did not tally with a preconceived ideal were
ruthlessly rejected as later additions. When an opinion has once taken hold it is
extraordinarily difficult to eradicate it, however flatly an unprejudiced examination
of fact may contradict it.

II. *Restoration of the Statue.*

Having ascertained what parts of the statue are in existence, we must now proceed to restoration of the missing parts. The square hole in the inscribed piece of
plinth evidently held something like a pillar. This object must have stood fairly high,
for the left side of the figure is less carefully worked than the right, evidently because
it was to be partially concealed. Dumont d'Urville and Voutier, as we have seen,
supposed the inscribed block to be the pedestal of one of the terms. Quatremère de
Quincy says that the hole in the block corresponded in width to the socket of one of
the three terms, and Clarac remarks (Vénus Victrix, p. 38) that possibly this figure
may have been set in the block on the occasion of a restoration. Nothing is said to
show that it fitted exactly, hence there is no evidence for the view, upheld chiefly
by Tarral and G. Saloman, that one of the beardless terms belonged to the inscribed block. The approximate correspondence in size might be purely accidental,
and there are various circumstances that tell directly against the Tarral-Saloman
theory; for instance, the workmanship of the terminal figure is much poorer than that

---

[1] Homolle in *Bull. de Corr. Hell.* v. 390 *sqq.* viii. 113.

of the statue, and the material, a common bluish marble, is inferior. The artistic effect produced by a conjunction of statue and term is distinctly unpleasing, as has sufficiently been pointed out by others,[1] and as Tarral's restoration shows at a glance. It would moreover be not only a hideous but an unparalleled device to place a term as support to a figure with which it had no definite connexion.[2] Overbeck's notion of a pillar on which the shield stands must be rejected, because we know that the left hand held an apple. The same fact speaks against Heydemann's hypothesis,[3] that the goddess is decking a trophy. For such an occupation she must have both hands free, and not be negligently holding the apple with her left : besides, the ancient *tropaion* was always round, not rectangular, as must have been the shaft inserted in this hole.

Let us for once simply follow the clue given by the shape of the hole : we shall immediately see that a pillar must be restored here. We must, however, find a motive for this pillar. This motive could only be to serve as a support : Aphrodite was resting the elbow of her left arm on a pillar. This is, in fact, the solution of all the difficulties. Others[4] have already observed that the whole attitude demands a support on the left side. The biceps of the left arm is not tense, as it would be were the arm held freely. For the rest, it can easily be gathered from the restorations that show the arm raised free into the air how constrained and unnatural, how ugly and angular, this position would be.

Owing to the fact that in both torso and arm there are distinct traces of the hole for the large dowel which once connected the two, the position of the upper arm can be settled beyond dispute.[5] The arm ought to be moderately raised to the side ; this is proved by the edge of the fracture on the left armpit. The convexity below prevents the arm being lifted higher. The direction of the forearm is absolutely certain from the direction of the dowel-hole in the upper arm. Possenti's attempt at restoration proves that if the dowel-hole in the upper arm be rightly connected with that in the body, the biceps of the upper arm would be turned not upwards but forwards, and that the forearm, which, as the muscles of the upper arm show, was bent nearly at a right angle,[6] would also be directed not upwards but forwards. Earlier attempts at restoration have all been incorrect, because they did not take into account the direction of the dowel-hole. Lastly, the position of the left hand must be fixed. It did not hang down, but was turned upwards, as Possenti rightly remarks, because the swelling on the upper arm at the elbow points to this position of the lower arm. This also explains the position of the apple, which was held by the thumb, the third and the fourth finger, while the first and second fingers were gracefully extended.[7] Now, if the hand had hung down, the apple must have been grasped more firmly. This position of the apple is natural only if it rested on the upturned palm of the hand. It is easy to see why the back of the hand is so roughly worked. It

---

[1] Cf. Heydemann, *Pariser Antiken*, p. 7.

[2] Certain terra-cottas derived from pictures (e.g. *Samm. Sabouroff*, Taf. 84) fall under a different heading from large statuary compositions.

[3] Other archaeologists take no account of the hole in the basis, though Fried. Kiel, to be sure (*Die Venus von Milo*, Hanover 1882, p. 32) imagines a lance fixed in the hole and held by the goddess with both hands—*i.e.* Venus as giantess with a spear as thick as a tree !

[4] Cf. Ravaisson, *Rev. Arch.* 1890, xv. 148 ; *Venus de Milo*, p. 56.

[5] A portion of the smooth surface of junction may still be seen on the fragment of arm. On the torso the corresponding surface has been broken away, but the piece may be restored with absolute certainty by aid of the dowel-holes.   [6] Cf. Henke in *Lützow's Zeitschr. f. Bild. Kunst*, 1886, p. 198.

[7] Cf. Kroker, *loc. cit.* Kroker's notion that the first and second finger must have held something—and that this was the edge of the shield—is in itself sufficiently unsatisfactory. It will be seen to be quite impossible, from the proofs adduced above as to the real position of the arm.

was turned downwards, and was therefore not much seen. Fig. 163 gives a sketch of a restoration proposed by Possenti, which is carried out in plaster, and illustrates what I have just said.

FIG. 163.—Proposed restoration of the Venus of Milo.

The arm thus raised and supported under the elbow forms a not ungraceful motive—at any rate, it has many analogies. A figure of Hermes on a vase (Millin, *Vases Peints*, ii. 20) may first be mentioned ; it is evidently influenced by sculpture, and the arm is supported on a tall slender pillar in the way supposed for the Venus.[1] The vase appears to be of fourth-century Attic manufacture. Still more instructive is a series of terra-cotta statuettes of the fourth century B.C. representing Aphrodite half-draped like the Melian statue, the elbow supported on a pillar and the left arm raised. Further, Aphrodite in a similar attitude often occurs on gems of the Hellenistic period (Fig. 164).[2] A beautiful bronze statuette of the nude Aphrodite (Dresden, Fig. 165)[3] reproduces a motive which is still commoner in terra-cottas. The forearm is not raised,[4] but bent forward in the position proved for the Aphrodite of Melos. The left hand—and this is specially interesting in the present connexion—hangs loosely from the wrist holding an apple. The support was in a separate piece and has disappeared, but the whole attitude makes it quite certain that it was originally there.[5] Pillar supports are of very common occurrence in ancient statuary. Pheidias himself had given one to the Parthenos, though it was purely technical, and not, as here, part of the composition..

In further confirmation of our restoration we may note two late Roman marble variants of the motive of the Melian statue, in both of which are to be seen traces of a support under the left arm. These are a statuette in Trèves, and another in Dresden. The traces are less distinct in the Trèves statuette,[6] but in the Dresden example[7] (Fig. 166) is still to be seen the end of a rectangular pillar on a low base. This statuette is, however, in no sense a replica of the Venus of Milo. Probably the pillar supported an attribute—possibly a lyre[8]—with which the left hand was occupied, and towards which the right hand also was directed.

FIG. 164.—Aphrodite on a gem (Berlin).

---

[1] Published examples : Dumont-Chaplain, *Céramique Gr.* ii. 28, 2, apparently identical with *Arch. Anz.* 1891, p. 121, 10. See also *Arch. Anz., loc. cit.* p. 22, 6, and *Samm. Sabouroff*, Taf. 132 below, to the left.

[2] Brown convex paste (Berlin, *Inv.* p. 581). The gem belongs to a distinct class, which is most certainly Hellenistic. In the right hand is a leaf-fan, the left hand seems to have held the end of the cloak (Fig. 164). For an analogous Hellenistic gem cf. King, *Ancient Gems and Rings*, ii. Pl. 23, B. 5.

[3] Basis and pillar modern. Pre-Roman.

[4] Berlin Antiq. TC. 7794. Half-nude Aphrodite ; left upper arm raised and supported on pillar, forearm hanging down.

[5] Cf. the Apollo bronze, *Arch. Anz.* 1889, p. 105, where the left arm is held as in the Melian statue, and presupposes a similar support.

[6] Flasch, *Jahrb. d. Ver. v. Alterthumsfr. im Rheinl.* Heft 62, Taf. 2, p. 74 *sqq.*; Hettner, *Die Röm. Steindenkmäler in Trier*, No. 684. Flasch's interpretation of the figure as a Hygieia seems very uncertain to Hettner, who inclines to think it represents a Victory setting up a trophy.

[7] Half life-size figure, Hettner, No. 174 ; published with the old restorations (now removed), Le Plat, 124, and Clarac, 595, 1301. Poor, late workmanship.

[8] Hettner suggests Terpsichore. Cf. Clarac, 481, 959 B.

I had carried my inquiry to this point, when I first noticed what is the strongest proof of my restoration, and what at the same time seems to place it beyond all uncertainty—namely, that the highly revered cultus-statue of Melos, the Tyche of the island, was represented in the same attitude as the one which we are compelled to suppose was that of the Melian statue. This type is known to us from Imperial bronze coins of the island, of which there are three examples in Berlin (see Fig. 167, with the legend ΤΥΧΗ),[1] and from a relief on the drum of a column found, along with its counterpart which reproduces an archaic cultus-image of Athena, in Melos,

Fig. LIX—Aphrodite. Copenhagen. Ny Carlsberg Glyptotek (See p. 385 i)

FIG. 165.—Bronze Aphrodite (Dresden).

Fig. LVIII—Artemis (?). St. Louis. City Art Museum

near the theatre (Fig. 168).[2] The goddess supports her right arm on a simple pillar or column in the position ascertained for the left arm of the Aphrodite, except that in the Tyche the forearm too is raised, in keeping with the solemn attitude of the goddess. It is not impossible that, like our Venus, the original statue held the apple, which as the symbol of the island would be a singularly appropriate attribute.

It is at once obvious that the motive of the supported arm must have been transferred from the Tyche to the Venus, and that the reverse was not the case,

[1] The three examples in Berlin all have the pillar as support and the child raising its arms to the right. The description in Imhoof-Blumer, *Griech. Münzen* (*Abh. Bayr. Akad.* i. Cl. xviii. 3), p. 547, should be rectified accordingly. [2] Cf. Wolters in *Ath. Mitth.* xv. 248.

for the position is quite in harmony with the calm dignity of Tyche; she holds
the infant Ploutos on her left arm, and with a festal, solemn air rests her left elbow

FIG. 166.—Statue in Dresden.

upon the pillar. On the other hand, the motive is so
little suited to the animated pose of the Aphrodite that
it must have been borrowed. The statue of Tyche,
although, to judge by the drapery, not earlier than
the middle of the fourth century B.C., is most probably older than the Aphrodite. Hence we may conclude that the motive belonged originally to Tyche,
and was transferred to Aphrodite, although the artist
altered the forearm and did not represent it raised.
This transference seems only natural when we remember
the close connexion of the two divinities in Hellenistic
times, especially among the Asiatic Greeks.[1] In my
view, the artist wished to characterize the Aphrodite
of the Gymnasium as goddess of Good Luck, and
therefore gave her the pose of the Tyche of the
city. If, as I suppose, Tyche held the apple, the transference was still more fitting, for the apple was the
peculiar attribute of Aphrodite.[2] A remarkable coin
of Melos of Imperial date proves that the Tyche type
was used even for a male figure personifying the Good
Luck of the city.[3]

The preceding considerations not only justify our restoration of the left arm
with the support, but have given us fresh material for deciding the question of
'originality.' Our statue cannot be an 'original' in the usual sense of the word, since
the artist who designed it borrowed, for purely external and
not artistic reasons, a motive foreign to the central conception.
It is necessary to bear this in mind in our attempts to restore
the right arm. We shall no longer demand (as those critics
have done who took it for granted that they were dealing with
an absolutely original work) a perfect correspondence between
the motive of right and left hand. The discovery of the left
hand holding the apple was in itself enough to exclude the
idea of such correspondence.

FIG. 167.—Bronze coin of the
island of Melos (Berlin).

The strong tension of the upper part of the right arm
can be explained only by supposing that the hand was extended
downwards across the body towards some point a little distance from it. This point
can only be the drapery on the left thigh. Most restorations make the arm too
short.[4] The hand could easily reach the lower edge of the mantle falling about

[1] Cf. *Samm. Sabouroff*, Text to Taf. 25, p. 3 *seq.*

[2] In Magnesia accordingly she was called Ἀφρ. Μηλεία, as we know from a coin (Imhoof-Blumer, *Monnaies
Grecques*, p. 292; cf. Herakles Μήλειος). This Aphrodite has naturally nothing whatever to do with Melos (in
which case the adjective would be Μηλία). Ravaisson, however (*Vénus de Milo*, p. 109), quoted this coin
(without giving the reference), and translates ' Vénus des Méliens !'

[3] The coin is published by Imhoof-Blumer, *Griech. Münz.* Taf. 2, 9. The figure, which is bearded, is,
regardless of sex, designated as Τύχη. I cannot agree with Imhoof's view that this is due to mere carelessness;
it seems to me more likely that the image refers to a benefactor of the island who was represented as her *Tyche*,
holding the infant Ploutos.

[4] So in Tarral and Hasse. The correct length is given in Valentin's restoration (*Kunst und Künstler*, plate
to p. 240).

the thigh. All this portion is unfortunately much worn away, yet the lie of the folds is still sufficiently clear to show that the hand was busied here. Possenti, who is of the same opinion, has also pointed out to me that the right arm, like the left, must have been joined on, because the block of marble of which the upper torso was made was not large enough to include the whole of the arm. The existing arm-stump shows evident marks of breakage, hence the contact-surface was probably lower down, as indeed we should expect from the size of the block, which is large enough to have included the upper arm.

The right arm was not fastened on in the same way as the left arm. It was not supported, but hung down, therefore it needed a more solid attachment. It was connected with the body of the statue by a strong side dowel. Under the right breast is a large

FIG. 168.—Relief from a column in Melos.

square hole two inches deep, for the dowel which supported the arm.[1] In the front view, this dowel was, as Possenti's restoration shows, not visible, and in the side view which our figure gives it is covered by the arm. The explanation of the right arm already given by Dumont d'Urville—namely, that it was feeling for the drapery—turns out, therefore, to be correct, as must strike any careful observer unprejudiced by aesthetic theories. The mantle is but loosely thrown round the body, and the action of pulling it closer by the end which falls over the left thigh is a very natural one, requiring no special intention to account for it. The folds over the left thigh are somewhat displaced and drawn up, and this can only be due to the action of the right hand. We should note, however, that the motive of the left hand, which was supported and held an apple, is comparatively independent.

It is clear that the two arms thus restored lend neither unity nor harmony to the composition; in short, their loss is one less to be deplored than might at first appear. But since we are now

FIG. 169.—Aphrodite with the apple. Terra-cotta from Myrina (Berlin).

[1] I am now convinced by Signor Possenti's arguments that the hole belongs not to a later restoration (as I formerly believed), but to the original fastening of the arm, which was very firm and solid.

trying to find out, not what the statue ought to have been or how it would answer best to our preconceived notions, but what it actually was, we shall not allow this discovery to affect our results.

We may reasonably ask at this point : If the goddess is leaning on her left arm and calmly holding her attribute, whence comes the agitated position of the upper part of the torso, and why is the left foot raised ? Why has she put on the mantle in such a way that she must grasp it with the right hand ? What is the meaning of the motive ?

An exquisite terra-cotta statuette from Myrina, of Hellenistic date (Berlin, Fig. 169),[1] gives a variant showing the harmonious grace of which the subject was capable. In this figure we have again an Aphrodite with the upper part of the body undraped, the left arm leaning on a pillar, the right leg supporting the weight of the body, and the head turned to the left. But the motive is vigorous and concentrated. The figure seems to be one of the few terra-cottas which really reflect the spirit of statuary. It is an old type effectually made new by the upward turn of the head and the spread of drapery arranged to form a background to the nude torso. A specially interesting feature of the conception is the animated manner in which the right hand holds up the attributive apple.[2]

How was it that the artist of the Melian statue failed to round off and harmonize his work in some such way ? The answer to this question demands a separate chapter.

III. *Influences that affected the Artist of the ‘ Venus.’—Skopas.—Historical Position of the Venus.*

The artist of the Venus of Milo took two entirely independent traditional types, and tried to combine them by means of partial modification. The result, as might have been imagined, was not altogether happy. We have already seen that the motive of the left arm was taken over from the Tyche of Melos. But it can also be ascertained whence the artist borrowed the main design : it can be traced back to an original, the best-known copy of which is the well-known *Venus of Capua* (Fig. 170).[3]

The usual theory, that this figure is a weak Roman variant of the Venus of Milo, is singularly perverse, and can be easily disproved by external evidence alone. The Venus of Milo is unique, and no replicas of it exist.[4] Of the Capua Venus there are not only several exact replicas[5] but sundry Roman variants, showing that this statue, and not the Venus of Milo, was the one renowned in antiquity.

The Capuan type several times appears grouped with Ares,[6] but that this was

---

[1] In the Berlin Antiquarium, TC. *Inv.* No. 8151. Height 0·29.

[2] Cf. another statuette from Myrina in Karlsruhe. (Sal. Reinach, *Chronique d' Orient*, p. 325.) The right hand holds the apple, while the left draws up the cloak.

[3] For literature see Friederichs-Wolters, *Gipsab.* 1452. Both arms are restored from just below the shoulder. The basis in the original is about 35 cm. broader to the right of the helmet. This surface (left out in the cast, cf. Fig. 170) would not be large enough for an Ares, and probably supported an Eros, a favourite addition of the copyists. Good illustration in Brunn-Bruckmann, *Denkmäler*, No. 297.

[4] The supposed replicas are really copies of the Venus of Capua.

[5] e.g. (a) ‘Venus Torlonia’ in Villa Albani, No. 733 (Valentin, *Hohe Frau von Milo*, Taf. 4, 10 ; cf. Helbig, *Museums*, 838). The head does not belong to the statue. (b) Torso from Smyrna in Vienna (Göler von Ravensburg, *Venus v. Milo*, p. 173 ; Benndorf, in *Arch. Epigr. Mitth. aus Oesterr.* 1880, p. 72, note).

[6] In the Florentine group (Clarac, 634, 1430, phot. Alinari) the Venus, both in body and drapery, is an exact copy of the Capuan statue. The small poor group in the Villa Borghese agrees in this respect with the Florentine ; the goddess sets her foot on a pair of greaves (group given by Nibby in *Mon. Scelti d. Villa*

not the original intention is plain from the circumstance that the figure of Ares is now of one type now of another. If these groups could all be referred to one original, the type of Ares would always be the same. The composition of the groups is so poor and clumsy that it is impossible to refer it to an earlier period than that in which the extant monuments were actually executed.

The Capuan type occurs with the addition of an under-garment, not only as a single figure,[1] but also grouped with Ares[2] or Asklepios.[3] The chiton differs so much

Fig. 172.—Head in Palazzo Caetani (Rome).

in the various examples that it cannot have formed part of the original design. It seems clear that it was added because the type had to be used for portraits of

Borghese, Tav. 44 ; more lately by Ravaisson, *loc. cit.* Pl. 7, 1. Ravaisson is unaware of the former publication, and has left out the head of Ares, which although broken and wrongly set is yet genuine). In the Capitoline group (Clarac, 634, 1428 ; Helbig, *Museums*, 502), the Venus, being turned into a portrait-statue, has been given a chiton. The same is the case in the Paris group (Clarac, 326, 1431), where the arrangement of the mantle is likewise altered. Cf. the sarcophagi, and the relief from Side in Lanckoronski, *Pamphyl. u. Pisid.* i. p. 147 ; Reinach, *Chron. d'Or.* p. 701 ; Ravaisson, *loc. cit.* Pl. 7, 3 ; the fragment of a terra-cotta relief from Locri published by R. *ibid.* Pl. 7, 4, and on which he lays great stress, has absolutely nothing whatever to do with the group. It is the remains of a fifth-century group, similar to the one which I described in the 50th *Berl. Winckelmannsprogr.* (see also Herzog, *Stud. z. Gesch. d. Gr. Kunst*, p. 12).

[1] (*a*) 'Venus Falerone' in the Louvre (No. 1737), *Mon. d. Inst.* iii. 2, 1 ; Göler v. Ravensburg, *V. v. M.* 178. Left foot on helmet. (*b*) Statue in Madrid, cast in Paris (Göler, p. 179 ; Ravaisson, *V. de M.* Pl. 6, 3, 4). Chiton added after the model of the Venus of Kos of Praxiteles. Replica in the Vatican, Giardino della Pigna. (Ravaisson, *loc. cit.* Pl. 6, 1, 2.) (*c*) Statue in the Louvre (No. 1733) restored as a Muse. (*d*) Cast of a torso said to have been found in the Giardino Boboli, Ecole des Beaux-Arts, Paris. (*e*) Coll. Jacobsen, Copenhagen. A good copy without head or arms. (*f*) Statuettes in Trèves and Dresden (see *supra*, p. 380).

[2] Cf. p. 384, note 6.

[3] Group in Turin, Dütschke, iv. 312 ; pub. by Ravaisson (*V. de M.* Pl. 7, 2).

distinguished Roman ladies,[1] represented as Venus Victory,[2] Hygieia, or a Muse, and in all such cases a fuller costume was naturally indispensable.

In Imperial times, as I have already said, the type is adopted for a figure of Victory writing a list of victories on a shield. This idea seems to have been first conceived by some artist of Vespasian's reign, for the type—in various trifling variants —suddenly appears on the bronze coins of Vespasian;[3] we next find it on the silver money of Trajan,[4] on his triumphal column,[5] and on later coins,[6] but there is no instance earlier than Vespasian.[7] The famous statue of Brescia[8] is known from its provenance to have belonged to the same reign. Its artist did not care to make an exact copy of the Aphrodite. Not only did he add the chiton, but he altered the folds of the upper garment to suit the petty taste of his day. The nature of the alterations, however, plainly shows that the original on which he founded his work was—not the Venus of Milo, but—the Venus of Capua. The hypothesis that the Brescia statue is the original type is completely excluded not only by the presence of the chiton but by the fact that it stands alone, while the Capua type is represented by numerous replicas. A very small alteration was enough to transform the Capuan Venus into a Victory, for the Venus, as we shall learn presently from Corinthian coins, was herself originally represented with a shield.

By the restitution of the shield in the Capuan type, the unusual motive, which in the Melian statue remained obscure, becomes clear and intelligible throughout. The goddess has placed her left foot on a support[9] in order to rest the shield on her sloping left thigh.[10] The shield was placed sideways so as not to cover the front of the statue, consequently the body is turned towards the left. The right shoulder is lowered and the right arm pressed close to the breast, because the right hand held the lower edge of the shield. The left arm is raised horizontally, because the left hand held the upper edge of the shield. The head is bent to look into the reflecting surface, and the upper torso is nude, because it is just this part of the body that the goddess wishes to see reflected. The mantle is high on the left hip, because the weight of the shield held it firm on that side. On the right side it slips lower down.

A comparison with the Melian statue shows at once that its motive is derived from the Capuan type. The main lines of the composition—the raised foot, the turn of the nude torso to the left, the gesture of the arms—are all meaningless when the shield is removed, and are adopted here only because they form a graceful pose. Yet the artist was no slavish imitator, like those Roman copyists who grouped together at random and without alteration traditional types of Ares and Aphrodite. He was one who knew how to subject the composition to a thorough remodelling for a definite purpose. All the movements which had the shield for centre might be made less pronounced now that the shield was removed. Thus the inclination of the body

---

[1] All copies with chiton where the heads are preserved are Roman portraits. To the same series belong also the sarcophagi where the dead woman appears as Venus.

[2] The late Roman figure on a cinerary urn from Lykia is half Venus half Victory (*Ath. Mitth.* ii. Taf. 10).

[3] Shield supported on the thigh or hanging on a palm. Upper part of the body nude.

[4] Shield on a pedestal. Upper part of the body nude.

[5] Shield on a pedestal. Upper part of the body draped.

[6] Cf. Fröhner, *Méd. de l'Empire Romain*, p. 163 (Caracalla).

[7] The Nike writing on a shield on coins of the gens Egnatuleia and on some pre-Imperial gems is a different type altogether.

[8] Friederichs-Wolters, *Gipsabg.* 1453.

[9] The helmet under the left foot, which appears in several replicas, was most likely a feature of the original.

[10] The shield, which was most certainly made of metal, has naturally left no traces on the drapery.

and head to the left and forward being lessened, the whole figure becomes more erect, and the eyes look straight into space. The right shoulder droops less and the right arm falls more perpendicularly—all this evidently because the goddess is no longer looking at her image in the bright surface. These variations alone should have sufficed to warn those who wished to restore the Venus of Milo with a shield. But the drapery too has been altered. As the shield is not there to keep up the left side of the cloak, and there is accordingly no reason why one side should be higher than the other, both sides have been allowed to slip down as far as they can without falling off. The torso, especially from a back view, gains in sensuous charm by the change, but the drapery would always produce an impression of insecurity even were the right hand still intact to keep it in place.

With the rejection of the shield as mirror the meaning of the drapery and the naturalness of the pose are lost. In the original type the goddess, who is wont to be draped, has partly disrobed for a definite reason, in order to contemplate her own beauty undisturbed. In the Melian type she displays her charms apparently with no object at all, and one does not see why she does not disrobe altogether. When we remember that our modern notions of the 'ideal nudity' appropriate to Aphrodite were quite foreign to Greek artists of the best period,[1] and that in the fourth century, when Aphrodite began to appear undraped, there was at first always some definite motive to account for her doing so, it must be still more plain to us that the Capuan is the older motive, the Melian the later variant. Not till after the period of Alexander did it become customary to represent Aphrodite nude without any special reason, as in the well-known Medici and Capitoline types. Praxiteles made his Venus of Knidos nude because she was just stepping into the bath, and the Venus of Arles, which we have traced to Praxiteles, is partly undraped because she is at her toilet and holds a mirror. The Aphrodite looking at herself in a shield is analogous to these, and would admirably suit the period in which Praxiteles created a *pseliumene*. A well-known passage in the *Argonautica* of Apollonios (i. 742) proves that the motive was invented before the middle of the third century B.C. The poet is describing a piece of embroidery, part of which represents the goddess looking at her own reflection in the shield of Ares :—

ἐξείης δ᾽ ἤσκητο βαθυπλόκαμος Κυθέρεια
Ἄρεος ὀχμάζουσα θοὸν σάκος. ἐκ δέ οἱ ὤμου
πῆχυν ἔπι σκαιὸν ξυνοχὴ κεχάλαστο χιτῶνος
νέρθεν ὑπεκ μαζοῖο· τὸ δ᾽ἀντίον ἀτρεκὲς αὔτως
χαλκείη δείκηλον ἐν ἀσπίδι φαίνετ᾽ ἰδέσθαι.

The poet seems to have the Capuan type before his mind's eye. He too thinks of the goddess as fully draped and loosening her chiton on one side in order to see herself in the mirror. We have here literary evidence for our view that the disrobing required a motive to account for it. The chiton, which takes the place of the mantle of the statuary composition, is clearly only an effective poetic invention, and must not be referred to another definite artistic prototype.

---

[1] The few examples of the nude Aphrodite in archaic art (cf. Körte in *Arch. Studien H. Brunn dargebr.* 1893, p. 24) are influenced by foreign types ; the nude figures supporting mirrors seem to have been borrowed direct from Egypt. Other nude female figures (not to be confused with Aphrodite) represent attendants or priestesses : *e.g.* archaic bronzes with cymbals (Körte, p. 28), flute-player (*Röm. Mitth.* 1892, p. 54), and probably also the original of the Esquiline Venus (Helbig, *Museums*, 566). The latter statue has been most improbably interpreted as Atalanta, for the resemblance of the motive naturally proves nothing.

It would only be natural to suppose that it was the shield of Ares which Aphrodite was choosing as her mirror, seeing that the two divinities are often closely united in one cultus,[1] were it not that the evidence of Corinthian Imperial coins seems to point another way. The cultus-image reproduced by these coins stood in a small temple [2] on the Akrokorinthos, and corresponded in attitude to the Capuan type, except that the sides were reversed (*supra*, Plate VI. 38).[3] Now in Corinth Aphrodite was worshipped with Helios, not with Ares. Pausanias calls the image of Aphrodite on the Akrokorinthos 'armed' (ὡπλισμένη). Of late it has been assumed that the goddess on the coins is the armed Aphrodite of Pausanias.[4] But the goddess on the coins holds the shield alone, which she is using as a mirror, and no other weapons of any kind. To call such a figure 'armed' would surely be far-fetched. It is much more likely that the image seen by Pausanias was an ancient idol. If this be so, there must have been two images in the sanctuary of the Akrokorinthos—one ancient and armed, mentioned by Pausanias, and a later statue, reproduced on the coins, but ignored by Pausanias. Similar instances are not unfrequent. The old image of Artemis Laphria seen by the periegete at Patrai is not reproduced on coins,[5] while the later cultus-statue appears on coins but is passed over by Pausanias. An old idol of this kind, if we may assume its existence at Corinth, would find an analogy in the armed figures of Aphrodite in Cyprus, Kythera, and Sparta,[6] especially as the Corinthian worship was derived from Kythera [7] and closely connected with the Peloponnesian pre-Dorian cultus of the armed goddess in Sparta. We conclude, then, that the shield is not derived from Ares, since the goddess is not worshipped with Ares in Corinth, but that it is a survival of the old tradition of an armed image. The notion of an armed Goddess of Love being unintelligible to a younger generation, it had to be modified and humanized as in our statue.

: The same change is to be noticed in other representations of divinities in the Praxitelean period. Apollo Sauroktonos plays with the lizard which in some older conception we may suppose to have been his attribute. The Artemis Brauronia, as she puts on her upper robe, delicately reminds the spectator of the ritual presentation of garments. The Apollo Smintheus of Skopas, which replaced an older image, sports with the mouse which in older days was sacred to him. So our Aphrodite lays aside her heavy armour, but keeps the shield to mirror her loveliness.

We shall not be far wrong if we assume that the original of the Capuan type was made for Corinth in the fourth century, that it disappeared when the city was sacked (while the old idol, valuable only in a religious and not in an artistic sense, may have been spared),[8] and that at the time of the new colonization its place was supplied by a copy which, to judge by the coins, reproduced the original, only with reversed sides. It is just possible, but less likely, that the original existed in Roman times in some locality where Aphrodite was worshipped in conjunction with Ares, and that the

---

[1] Cf. Preller-Robert, *Gr. Myth.* i. 340, and Paus. iii. 17, 5.

[2] ναΐδιον, according to Strabo, viii. p. 379. The coins differ greatly in the reproduction of the temple.

[3] Imhoof-Blumer and P. Gardner, *Num. Comm.* Pl. G, 121 *sqq.*, p. 25 *seq* ; Pl. D, 63 (with Poseidon). All the coins with one exception have the sides reversed as compared with the Capuan statue, hence they probably reproduce the attitude of the Corinthian cultus-image. In the one exception, Imhoof-Gardner, Pl. FF xiii. (coin of Commodus in Berlin), the change is probably necessitated by the grouping of the figure with Herakles.

[4] Imhoof-Blumer and Gardner, *loc. cit.* ; Head, *Hist. Num.* p. 340.

[5] Studniczka, *Röm. Mitth.* iii. (1888), 297 *seq.*

[6] Cf. Preller-Rober`, *Gr. Myth.* i. 357. Aphrodite is called ἀρεία and ἐνόπλιος in Sparta, ἔγχειος in Cyprus, and στρατεία in Caria.

[7] Cf. Alkiphron *apud* Preller-Robert, i. 350, A, 2.

[8] We learn from Pausanias that several archaic idols had been preserved in Corinth. Cf. Imhoof-Gardner, *loc. cit.* p. 10.

Corinthians of the time had a copy made from it without reference to their own local cultus. The older armed image, to which, as I believe, Pausanias refers, is decided evidence in favour of the first view.

However that may be, it is certain that the original of the Capuan statue belonged to the fourth century. This is plain from the reasons already adduced, and from the style, notably of the head (Fig. 171).

The Capuan statue, which was found in the amphitheatre renewed under Hadrian, had been correctly assigned to this Emperor's period,[1] and bears every mark of the time in its style. The cold elegance of the workmanship, the dry mannerism with which the hair is treated, the plastic indication of the pupils, the dead smoothness of the flesh, even the profile of the plinth are characteristic, and for some time prevented due appreciation of the value of the figure. Fortunately however we possess in a marble bust in the Palazzo Caetani at Rome an earlier and more lifelike copy at any rate of the head (Fig. 172).[2] Careful comparison will show that this head must be referred to the same original as the Capuan statue. The only variations are a fillet instead of a diadem, and the absence of the small ends of hair on the back of the neck. The diadem is a usual Roman adornment of Venus, and is

FIG. 171.—Head of Venus of Capua.

probably added by the copyist. The simple fillet, on the other hand, belongs to Aphrodite in Praxitelean art, and is therefore likely to be an original feature. The Victory of Brescia affords another proof that the fillet is correct; she wears a similar one (except that a laurel-wreath is engraved on it), and it can be derived only from the original, which is identical with the original of the Capuan statue. That the Caetani head is not a copy of the Victory of Brescia (as I stated in Roscher's *Lexikon*, i. 414), and, in fact, does not belong to a Nike statue at all, is plain not only from an accurate comparison of the two, but also from the measurements. The Caetani head corresponds in proportions to the Capua type, the Brescia statue stands alone. The latter is an independent Roman modification of the Aphrodite, as we have seen from the drapery. The artist kept fairly near his original in the workmanship of the head, but did not attempt to make an

---

[1] Bernouilli, *Aphrod.* p. 161.

[2] Matz-Duhn (*Zerstr. Bildw. in Röm.* 797). Von Duhn was the first to call special attention to the head; Friederichs-Wolters, *Gipsabg.* 1454. Said to be intact; I have not seen the original. From the shape, probably a bust, and not intended for insertion into a statue (in which case the piece to be let in would be longer in front, and narrower on the shoulders).

FIG. 170.—Venus of Capua (Naples).

exact copy.   The face is shorter and broader, and by making the lips thinner he has omitted a distinctly Aphrodisian trait.   He probably added the little curls in front of the ear.   The empty soulless expression of the face shows how totally unable this Roman artist was to impart to his work any quality corresponding to the spirituality of the Greek original.   In studying the Capuan type, then, we had better leave the Victory out of the argument, and keep to authentic copies.[1]   Of these the Caetani bust seems to be the most faithful; although a coarser version of the original, it yet is uniform in style, and nothing extraneous has been added.   This style, as need scarcely be remarked, is that of the circle of Praxiteles and of Skopas.   This is especially marked in the simply parted hair, which forms an angle over the forehead, is confined by a smooth band, and worked without deep shadows.[2]   In the facial forms, moreover, it is impossible not to recognize the character of that period.

In judging of details it is necessary to inquire whether we have to imagine an original of marble or of bronze.   The question of material is more important in connexion with the fourth than with the fifth century B.C.   In the fifth century marble and bronze were similarly worked (cf. p. 7); in the fourth century, with Skopas and Praxiteles, was developed a technique peculiar to marble.   The wonderful freedom in the treatment of masses of hair and the delicate indication of roots, to cite only one point, which we see in extant originals such as the Hermes, the Eubouleus, the Petworth Aphrodite, the head from the south slope of the Akropolis, and the Demeter of Knidos, and which we can divine from copies such as the Aphrodite of Knidos, would be impossible in bronze.   Copies of the Sauroktonos show how Praxiteles treated bronze hair.   Our Aphrodite is evidently derived from bronze, not from marble, and is analogous to the Sauroktonos, not to the Aphrodite of Knidos and other works whose originals are to be imagined as marble.   The hair is not loosely massed, but defined from root to point in separate locks that show great variety of form.   On the knot of hair at the back and on other parts of the head are marks of incision, evidently an imitation of bronze technique.   The motive of the statue, an extended arm holding a shield, is much more appropriate to bronze than to marble.

It is instructive to compare with the Caetani head similar conceptions as treated by Praxiteles.   The Aphrodite of Knidos (p. 322) is a good instance for our purpose, and the Venus of Arles (p. 320) a still better one, because the pose of the head is similar to that of the Caetani Aphrodite, and the motive, a mirror, is probably the same.   The Caetani Aphrodite differs materially from both these types.   At the first glance we notice the absence of the long regular oval face so characteristic of the Praxitelean school, we miss the marvellous harmony and calm conveyed by the gentle and even balance of the face-curves from centre to sides and from sides to centre.   Here the lines are restless and broken, and seem to crowd to the front.   The hair forms a less regular angle on the forehead, which is wider, especially at its base, the eyebrows are thicker, the cheek-bones broader, the setting of the eyes more marked.   The inner corners of the eyes are deeply sunk—almost drawn into the head—and at a higher level than the outer corners.   The nose projects more, making a less perpendicular profile.   The nostrils swell as if breathing.   But the mouth shows the most decided difference of all. The lips are fuller and more animated, the raised upper lip is strongly curved, the lower one has a strong dent in the middle.   The ear, too, has its own peculiar form,

---

[1] The marble head worked into a bust in the possession of Count Stroganoff in St. Petersburg is a replica of the Capuan statue.   Another is in the Coll. Barracco, Rome ; *Coll. Barracco*, p. 60, 60 a.   Helbig (text, p. 46) does not recognize it.   A much-restored head in the Louvre known to me only from Ravaisson, *V. de M.* Pl. 5, 3, is possibly a copy.   [2] Cf. *Samm. Sabouroff*, i. *Skulpt.* Introd. p. 11 *sqq.*

unlike that observed in those two Praxitelean heads. Instead of standing upright it lies over towards the back. The hollow is small, the cartilaginous part broader with decided protuberances, the lobe is small and delicate, and completely joined to the head in front. What we lose in grace, harmony, and repose by comparison with Praxiteles we gain in a more individual expression, in a more vigorous life, and in the fiery energy of mouth and eye.

Now the contrasts noted above are practically the very same that mark off the works of Skopas from those of Praxiteles.[1] The Caetani head possesses, in common with Skopasian heads, not only expression and structure, i.e. the short broad face, but even details such as the shape of the ears, the breathing nostrils, and the raised upper lip. The few points of difference are not noticeable enough to warrant us in ascribing the work to any other artistic individuality. We must remember, too, that this is only a copy, and that the subject is a new one in the Skopasian school. The head is looking down instead of up; hence the upper eyelids are plainly seen, instead of nearly disappearing as they do in those other heads to which an upward gaze has been given.

The Skopasian type represented by the Caetani head is not isolated. Several other monuments are closely analogous to it. The head of a Leda[2] in Florence shows great similarity in hair, fillet, forehead, and eyes, and although of poor workmanship it must be referred to an original by the artist of the Caetani head or by one of his imitators. More significant is a head of rich, strong beauty, adjusted to a statue called 'Giunone,' in the Capitoline Museum; it bears unmistakable analogies to fourth-century types (Fig. 173);[3] in the forehead, eyes, and breathing nostrils it recalls the Caetani head; at any rate, it comes nearer to the Skopasian than to the Praxitelean school. We must of course beware of imagining that all Skopasian heads must have the intense upward look to be seen in many works of the school.[4] Further, in the Jacobsen collection, in Copenhagen, there is a head of Aphrodite which, though a poor and much-defaced copy, shows the distinguishing marks of the style of Skopas.[5] A colossal head in the Hermitage may, on the other hand, be a Hellenistic adaptation[6] of the Caetani type.

We have seen that the head of the shield-bearing Aphrodite should be ascribed to the school of Skopas. Turning now to the body, and comparing it with that of the Knidian Aphrodite for instance, we shall be struck by the elasticity and vigour of our statue, due to the greater spareness and slenderness of hips and breasts, while the heavier build of the Knidian goddess seems to betoken easy negligent repose. This distinction is in keeping with what we know of the different tendencies of Praxiteles and of Skopas. Specially peculiar to the Capuan type[7] are the sloping shoulders and

---

[1] Botho Gräf, *Röm. Mitth.* 4, 1889, p. 189 *sqq.* Cf. Von Sybel in *Lützow's Zeitschrift für bild. Kunst*, N. F. ii. 249 *sqq.*

[2] Dütschke, *Uffizien*, 192; Overbeck, *Zeus*, p. 514; Müller-Wieseler, *Denkm.* 2, 44. Cast in Dresden. A replica in the courtyard of the Naples Museum.

[3] For literature cf. Helbig, *Museums*, i. 532. The head is inserted into the statue, not broken. It is of different marble, still it might belong to the statue, were not the style so different. It is of fourth-century style, while the body is Hellenistic and Pergamene. Cast of the head in Dresden, from the Mengs collection.

[4] Gräf (*loc. cit.* p. 218) admits that the female head of the Capitol (cf. also Helbig, *Museums*, i. 445), which he classifies as Skopasian, has been worked over and intensified. I should go further, and say that it is a decidedly Hellenistic development, a long way removed from Skopas.

[5] Ny Carlsberg Glypt. 1073. Mouth, nose, and other portions are restored. The hair is simply arranged in a knot, without fillet. Already Helbig had with fine insight recognized an Aphrodite in this work.

[6] D'Escamps, *Marbres Campana*, Pl. 38; Guédéonow, *Ermit.* 175.

[7] In this respect the replica grouped with Ares in the Florentine copy agrees with the Capuan statue.

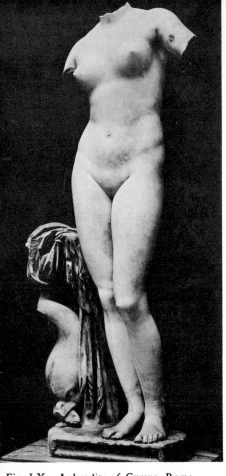

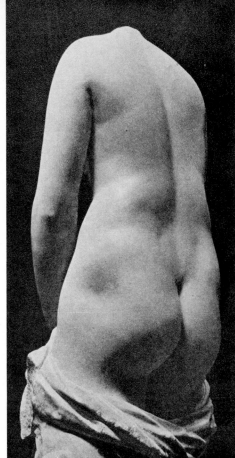

Fig. LX—Aphrodite of Cyrene, Rome, National Museum (See Notes)

Fig. LXI—Aphrodite of Knidos, Rome, Vatican Museum (See pp. 322, 3)

Fig. LXII—Aphrodite of Syracuse, Sicily, Syracuse Museum

LXIII—Venus Capitoline, Rome, Capitoline Museum (See pp. 322, 3)

Fig. LXIV—Aphrodite-Bronze Statuette, St. Louis. City Museum

Fig. LXV—Aphrodite Medici. Florence, Uffizi Gallery (See p. 345)

the rounded breasts, which are more globe-shaped than in the Praxitelean Aphrodites.

In the drapery, again, fourth-century taste is conspicuous.[1] The rolled drapery about the hips is peculiarly characteristic, and is found on countless Attic grave-reliefs of the period. The Ludovisi Ares—an invention, as we have seen, of Skopas—wears drapery similarly treated, and so do the Niobids. In the latter connexion, the Florentine Niobids should be specially studied,[2] for, though poor copies, they faithfully reproduce fourth-century style, while the famous 'Chiaramonti' Niobid[3] is really not a copy at all, but a free translation of one of the original figures into Hellenistic forms. But to resume—the drapery of our Aphrodite well illustrates the tendency of Attic art in the Praxitelean period to despise decorative effect and aim straight at truth of nature.[4]

In the agitated pose and slim proportions of our type scholars thought to detect the Lysippian manner. But we have everywhere recognized in Skopas the precursor of Lysippos, the artist whom Lysippos most closely followed. Of those works which have been attributed to Lysippos the one most similar to the Aphrodite is the 'Eros stringing a bow';[5] the movement—except that it is directed to the other side—is almost identical, a correspondence which makes it probable that the two compositions are related. The position of the Aphrodite, however, although full of energy, is yet tranquil and firm, while the Eros has that sway of the torso which is so distinctive a mark of the Apoxyomenos. Now, as the Palatine Hermes (*supra*, Fig. 129) which we referred to Skopas had precisely the same motive, we are bound to consider whether the Eros also may not be traceable to Skopas. This, however, seems to me improbable, owing to the insignificance of the type of head.

We have assumed that, like that of the 'Eros stringing a bow,'[6] the original of the Capuan Aphrodite was of bronze. This does not invalidate the Skopasian attribution, for not only does Pliny mention Skopas among the bronze-workers, but we know for certain that his Aphrodite Pandemos at Elis riding the goat was of bronze, and there may have been many other bronzes among the works by him whose names have been handed down to us without mention of the material in which they were executed. We have no reason to suppose that Skopas, any more than Praxiteles, worked solely in marble. Among the works which we have already brought into connexion with Skopas, some may have been of bronze—for instance, the youthful Athena (*supra*, Fig. 130).

There are still a few more statues which we venture to refer to Skopas because of their resemblance to the Aphrodite ; chief among them is the Leda in Florence (for discussion of the head-type see p. 392). The torso and drapery are allied to the Aphrodite, the shoulders and the rounded but less developed breasts are similar.[7] The motive, which has been often misunderstood, is free from any voluptuous suggestion.[8] The frightened bird has flown to the girl for protection ; she is bending over it and wrapping it in the folds of her garment. The swan is small in scale, as in

---

[1] Much restored in the Capuan statue.   Better preserved in the Florence group.

[2] Cf. the hanging drapery of the 'Son of Niobe,' Overbeck, C.

[3] Helbig, *Museums*, 73.

[4] Cf. *Samm. Sabouroff*, i. *Skulpt*. Introd. p. 14.

[5] Cf. Roscher's *Lex*. i. 1362.

[6] Cf. Helbig, *Museums*, i. 429.   The Thespian Eros of Lysippos was of bronze.

[7] Note also the bracelet on the *right* upper arm corresponding to the Florentine replica of the Capuan type. The Praxitelean Aphrodite wears it on the *left* arm.

[8] Such as Overbeck, *Zeus*, p. 514.   O. Jahn (*Arch. Beitr*. p. 4) appreciated the group much more correctly.

the earlier 'Leda' monuments, and the whole conception is that of the Greek terracottas of the fifth and fourth centuries B.C., and of a statue which I have discussed elsewhere.[1] In this case too the figure should be interpreted rather as Nemesis than as Leda. It is interesting to compare this Skopasian 'Leda' with that older oft-copied Leda, which, like the Barberini 'Suppliant,' to which it is allied, must be referred to the fifth century, and to an artist nearly connected with Pheidias.[2] It is more dramatic and effective than our Skopasian statue, which is simpler, more natural, and deeper in feeling.

A second not less interesting work of the same series is the Psyche of Capua (Naples),[3] which has so often been called Praxitelean,[4] but is really a very good copy after a purely Skopasian work, with the characteristic sloping shoulders and globe-shaped breasts. The latter have, it is true, been somewhat worked over, but the essentials of the form remain unchanged: it is the same flat, youthful breast that we noticed in the Nemesis-Leda.[5] There is a bracelet on the right arm.[6] Marks of the Skopasian Aphrodite type in the face are seen in the peculiar mouth, the dilated nostrils, the ear set slanting back with small opening, the strongly marked ear cartilage uneven in outline, and in the lobe growing close to the head. Such cumulative evidence leaves no room for doubt that we have here a work by the artist of the Caetani head. But the interpretation of the figure is not so easy. It is certain, however, that it does not represent Psyche, as was formerly supposed. Aphrodite would be nearer the truth. The figure obviously leaned its weight on the right leg, and the left hand drew over the left shoulder the drapery which shrouded the lower part of the body.[7] The head was turned to the right and bent down. Perhaps the goddess was grouped with an Eros holding a mirror. The 'melancholy character' of the work cannot be urged against this interpretation, for it is easy to imagine melancholy in a bowed head when we know nothing of the motive. The head is posed as in the Capuan Venus, only more inclined. This inclination doubtless formed the principal charm of the figure in the eyes of the artist, who in this instance has with characteristic boldness gone beyond his prototype. One step more, and we should have the 'Kallipygos' motive of the succeeding generation.

A third beautiful plastic conception, which we may refer to a bronze original by Skopas, is the Hypnos, represented by a marble copy in Madrid and a bronze head in the British Museum.[8] It has long been acknowledged that the original must have been in bronze. This is proved not only by the extant remains of a bronze copy, but by the vigour of the action, which, when represented in marble, necessitates the presence of a meaningless and disfiguring support. The style of this work,

---

[1] *Samm. Sabouroff*, i. *Vases*, Introd. p. 8 *sqq.*   [2] *Ibid.* p. 9 *seq.* 12.

[3] Friederichs-Wolters, 1471. The piecings are original, and not, as was formerly believed, due to restorations. Date first century B.C. The figure is analogous to the Ares of the Conservatori Palace (Helbig, *Museums*, 568) (see *supra*, p. 271), which is also made up of several pieces. Neither figure had wings. The working over is by no means as bad as had been supposed : it can be detected on the breast in the region of the collar-bone, but the head has been left absolutely untouched.

[4] So lastly by Benndorf, *Bull. della Comm. Arch. di Roma*, 1886, p. 73.

[5] Cf. for the breasts of the Psyche, E. Brücke, *Schönheit und Fehler der Menschlichen Gestalt*, p. 67.

[6] Cf. p. 394, note 7.

[7] E. Wolff recognized this (*Bull. d. Inst.* 1833, 134) ; also Stark (*Sächs. Ber.* 1860, 90). An examination of the original will show Kekulé's supposition (*Annali*, 1864, 145), that the left upper arm was wrongly set on, and had originally been drawn back, to be quite false. His further hypothesis, that Psyche was tied to the tree, naturally becomes untenable.

[8] Friederichs-Wolters, *Gipsabg.* 1287, 1288. For list of small bronze replicas see Winnefeld, *Hypnos*, p. 8. Of these, the Turin figure is published in *Atti della Soc. di Archeol. e Belle Arti di Torino*, iv. 1883, Tav. 15, p. 113, and the two Lyons copies in *Gaz. Archéol.* 1888, Pl. 6. See also Sauer in Roscher's *Lex.* i. 2849, and Brunn, *Götterideale*, p. 26, Taf. 3.

rightly attributed to the Praxitelean epoch, has been likened to that of the Sauroktonos,[1] but the more closely we look at the head the more clearly we shall see that its resemblance to the Sauroktonos is merely superficial, while it is closely analogous to the Skopasian Aphrodite—in a word, it offers the same contrast to the Sauroktonos that the Aphrodite of Skopas does to the Aphrodite of Praxiteles. We find in the Hypnos a broad type of face and a pronounced bony structure, quite different from the graceful elongated oval of the Sauroktonos. The forehead of the latter, and the wavy hair that frames it, correspond closely to the Venus of Arles and the Knidos Aphrodite, while in the Hypnos the forehead and the hair growing back from it so strongly resemble the Caetani Aphrodite that we are justified in referring the two conceptions to the same artist. The dilated nostrils of the Hypnos are characteristically Skopasian, but the protuberance in the middle of the forehead, which, as Brunn showed, is definitely necessitated by the wings, is individual to the divinity represented. Finally, the swinging stride, recalling the Palatine Apollo,[2] and the chiastic disposition of the limbs are much more appropriate to Skopas than to Praxiteles, while, to pass to the treatment of the nude, the modelling of the abdomen and the navel with its little furrow are details more nearly related to the Skopasian Meleager than to the Sauroktonos or the Hermes.

This magnificent invention, then—the work of an artist who went straight to the heart of his subject—must be assigned to the later period of Skopas's activity. Unlike the Kairos of Lysippos, a composition carefully built up by an effort of activity, this conception flowed warm and living from the soul of the artist. With gliding gait and quiet pulse of wings the god of sleep sinks down upon a weary world. It was a happy inspiration of Skopas to place the wings on the head instead of on the shoulders, as in the earlier representations of Hypnos.

The original of the statue must surely have been intended for one of the few shrines where Hypnos was worshipped. We only know of three such in Greece. There was an ancient altar in Troezene which Hypnos shared with the Muses (Paus. ii. 31, 3); statues of Hypnos and Thanatos (to which a cult was probably attached) stood near the Chalkioikos in Sparta (Paus. iii. 18, 1); in the Hieron of Asklepios at Epidauros Hypnos was worshipped, at least in later times;[3] and finally the front chamber of an οἴκημα in the peribolos of the sanctuary of Asklepios at Sikyon (Paus. ii. 10, 2) was consecrated to him.[4] As Asklepios was wont to manifest himself to his suppliants in sleep, and Sleep might easily be personified as a daemon favourable to recovery, the connexion of the two divinities seems natural enough. Pausanias states that only the head of the figure was in existence in the cella.[5] Possibly the original statue had been stolen, and if so the head Pausanias saw must have been a copy, for whoever took the statue would not leave the head behind. We know that Skopas worked in Sikyon, for Pausanias refers to a Herakles there made by him (probably reproduced on Imperial coins).[6] Hence it is not impossible that the statue in the cella was also a work by Skopas.

Other coins of the Imperial times seem to show that a third famous work of the same artist, not assigned by tradition to any special place, may have belonged to

[1] Cf. Murray, *Hist. of Gr. Sculpture*, ii. 259, where Benndorf is quoted.
[2] Cf. p. 305, note 6.
[3] Cf. Blinkenberg in *Nord Tid-Skrift f. Filol. ny Ränke*, x. 270, 8 ; 273, 20.
[4] The back cella was consecrated to Apollo Karneios.
[5] In the Stoa which was naturally attached to the Asklepieion, Pausanias saw another statue of Hypnos—κατακοιμίζων λέοντα ; Pausanias may be here inaccurately referring to the type (known by later copies) of Hypnos sleeping on a lion. (*Bull. d. Inst.* 1877, 122 *seq.*) [6] Cf. p. 301, note 2

Sikyon. I refer to the Maenad, known to us through two epigrams and a passage of Kallistratos.[1] On the coins of Julia Domna in Sikyon there occurs the type of a frenzied Bacchante which agrees with the description in the epigrams,[2] and which Imhoof-Blumer and Gardner[3] have pointed to as reproducing one of the marble βάκχαι seen by Pausanias (ii. 7, 5) in the temple of Dionysos at Sikyon beside the gold and ivory image of the god. Pausanias, as often, has omitted to name the artist, but it seems to me highly probable that this Bacchante, celebrated enough

FIG. 173.—Head in the Capitol. (From the cast.)

FIG. 174.—Head from Tralles, in Smyrna. (From the cast at Bonn.)

to be reproduced on coins, was actually the Bacchante of Skopas. The flying drapery, floating gait, and rapturous attitude show that the original statue must have borne a strong resemblance to the Apollo Kithairoidos.

But we must return from this digression to our special subject, the Venus of Milo. Enough has been said to prove that it was based on a work presumably by Skopas ;

[1] Kallistratos himself is probably dependent on the epigrams (cf. *Jahrb. d. Ver. d. Alterthums-Freunde im Rheinland*, Heft 90, 1891, p. 66).

[2] As χιμαιροφόνος she must have held a sword ; no such weapon can however be distinguished on the coins.

[3] *Num. Comm.* p. 29, Pl. H. vi. v.

thus it was a right instinct which induced scholars who could not bring proofs to
confirm their impression to bring it into connexion with this artist.[1]   In spite of the
numerous modifications, the Skopasian groundwork is manifest not only in external
details, such as the arrangement of the fillet and of the hair (which is however
effectively modernized by the addition of the loosened strands falling on the neck),

FIG. 175.—Statue in Pal. Valentini (Rome)

but in the attempt to impart fire and vitality to
the expression.   The artist sought to heighten
this Skopasian quality.   In his desire to bring into
the conception something of dignity and elevation, he lengthened the lower part of the face,
thus returning to the older manner.   The successors of Praxiteles, in the same way, tried to
outdo him in grace.   The result in each case is a
slight exaggeration of the master's peculiarities.
The Aphrodite of Skopas becomes the Venus
of Milo, the Aphrodite of Praxiteles becomes
the Venus of Medici.

It is characteristic of a later development
that the firm, well-knit forms of the original
Skopasian head have undergone in the Melian
statue a certain relaxation, threatening to become
almost fluid in their lack of compactness and
definition.   The same tendency may be observed
in other heads of Hellenistic date, notably in
the much-admired head from Pergamon,[2] so
often compared with the Melian Aphrodite.
This head, though doubtless considerably older
than our Venus, shows the laxity of the
forms carried to such a point that an expression of weakness, almost amounting to
vacancy, is the result.   On the other hand, the
beautiful head from Tralles, now in Smyrna
(Fig. 174),[3] belongs to the beginning of the
series, and is not far removed from Skopas in
general character, betraying Hellenistic taste
only in the treatment of the hair.

Mention must also be made here of a smaller and more widely known head from
Tralles which has been brought into close connexion with the Melian statue, and even
referred to the same original,[4] although it has in common with it only quite general
traits.   Its artist evidently imitated Praxiteles, from whom he may have been
separated only by a generation or two.   It cannot be said that he made a definite
copy, but he followed that master's characteristic rendering of form, such as the delicate

[1] *e.g.* Waagen, Welcker (*Ant. Denkm.* i. 445),   Stark (*Sächs. Berichte,* 1860, p. 51),   Urlichs (*Skopas,*
p. 122), and B. Gräf (*Röm. Mitth.* iv. 217) have all in a more or less degree pointed to the Skopasian
characteristics.   [2] Lützow's *Zeitschrift f. Bild. Kunst,* 1880, xv. 161.

[3] In the Mus. of the Evang. School.   Badly published in *Bull. Corr. Hell.* 1882, Pl. III.   Cast at
Bonn (Fig. 174).

[4] Benndorf in *Oesterr. Mitth.* 1880, Taf. 1, 2 ; p. 66 *sqq.* ; Overbeck, *Gesch. d. Plastik,* 3rd ed. ii. 342 ;
Friederichs-Wolters, *Gipsabg.* 1451 ; R. v. Schneider, *Uebersicht der Wiener Kunsthistor. Samm.* 1891, p. 78,
interprets the head as an Artemis.

oval of the face, the dimple on the chin, the sweet expression ; but the whole conception has become small, not to say trifling.

We have seen (p. 377) that the epigraphy of the inscription allows us to date the Venus of Milo as early as the end of the third century B.C., though the period between 150 and 50 B.C. was more probably that in which the Venus was made. The stylistic peculiarities now confirm this later date. The hair is arranged, as we have already said, in the fourth-century manner, but the treatment is in marked contrast to fourth-century work. What hard rendering of the roots of the hair on the forehead, what lifeless parallel grooves in the strands that are combed back ! The above-mentioned head from Pergamon, which belongs probably to the third century, illustrates the exact reverse of this procedure. The artist has arranged the hair according to the fashion of his time, but in the delicate indication of the growth of the hair and in the light treatment of the region round the eye he preserves the best traditions of fourth-century work—traditions which seem to have been unknown to the artist of the Melian statue.

FIG. 176.—Statue in Pal. Valentini.
(Restorations omitted.)

In determining the style of our Aphrodite, the drapery is also of very great importance. Here the artist has definitely altered his Skopasian model. He has rejected the treatment which aims at simple truth of nature, and has chosen instead—not the usual Hellenistic manner, as shown in the marbles of Pergamon—but, strangely enough, the manner of the Parthenon pediment figures.[1] The stuff lies in large unbroken masses, with sharp edges and no cross folds, and it clings to the nude parts as if moistened. Only on the right thigh does it show a touch of Hellenistic taste. To this large massive treatment of drapery we owe the theory, not without adherents even at the present day, that the statue is by a successor of Pheidias. In my view this imitation is precisely what shows the statue to belong to that Renascence which, about the middle of the second century B.C., embodied a reaction against the extravagance of the Hellenistic school. The Belvedere Herakles torso is a work of kindred tendency. Here the nude is treated according to Pheidian tradition,[2] and without any of the realism in which the art of Pergamon excelled. A comparison of the Venus of Milo with the Venus of Medici will convince us that the Melian figure shows a return to Pheidias not only in the draped but also in the nude parts.[3] The impression of grandeur of style which the statue has always made was intentionally aimed at by the artist. It is probable also that the statues of the Pheidian school which gradually lead up to this motive were not unknown to him. Perhaps the statue of Aphrodite

[1] Cf. Overbeck, *Gesch. d. Plastik*, 3rd ed. ii. 341.
[2] Roscher's *Lex.* i. 2182, 20.
[3] Cf. Waagen, *Kunstwerke und Künstler in Paris*, p. 108.

Ourania, in Elis, by Pheidias, with the left foot on a tortoise, was the origin of the whole series.[1]

An excellent work of art belonging to the generation after Pheidias, probably an Aphrodite, is preserved to us in two copies in the Palazzo Valentini [2] and the Palazzo Odescalchi at Rome (Figs. 175, 176). This figure shows so many points of analogy to the Venus of Milo, more especially in those particulars where the latter differs from its Capuan original, that we may very well imagine that the artist in his adaptation of the Aphrodite of Skopas consciously emulated the style of some such Pheidian prototype.

Aphrodite here, as always in the Pheidian period, wears the chiton under the mantle. It clings closely to the body, thus forming an almost transparent covering, in the manner of the sculptures on the Nike balustrade and of the Aphrodite of Alkamenes. The left foot is advanced but not raised, and the form of the left leg is distinctly seen through the mantle, just as in the case of the Aphrodite of Melos. The sharply defined curves of the mantle wrapped round the body and enveloping the right leg, on which the weight of the body is supported, show the breadth of conception, the combined wealth and animation of forms which characterize the school of Pheidias from the epoch of the Parthenon pediments onwards. The Hera of Ephesos (p. 84, note 4) and the so-called Barberini Hera (p. 82) are similar works, but the Aphrodite Valentini far surpasses them in beauty and richness of drapery. One of the fragments of the reliefs by Agorakritos [3] is very closely related to the Valentini figure. Again, the head of the figure, with its large full forms, its forehead high in the middle, and its delicate roots of hair, finds its nearest analogies in two statues which we have already ascribed to Agorakritos (p. 88), i.e. the Barberini Apollo and the Athena of the Capitol, and this circumstance gives some weight to the belief that the Valentini Aphrodite is to be referred to Agorakritos. There is the same dignity and majesty of pose, the same expression of frank victorious pride, that we saw in other works by the same hand.

The artist of the Melian Aphrodite has tried to catch at least a ray of inspiration from Agorakritos, but his work, as we have shown, must be dated not earlier than the Renascence of the second century B.C. This chronology is confirmed by a purely external circumstance—the appearance of the inscription on an integral part of the statue. This is without any analogy before the end of the second century B.C.[4] Previous to that time, with the exception of course of the archaic period, it was the invariable custom of artists to sign their statues on the pedestal ; after this date, probably in order to insure permanence in case the statue should be removed, signatures were placed on some block—such, for instance, as the supports—which was intimately connected with the statue.

The Venus of Milo, then, belongs to a series of works executed in the latter half of

---

[1] Cf. p. 72 seq. In a recently acquired statue in Berlin, see p. 73, note (Arch. Anz. 1893, p. 74, and Kekulé, Weibliche Gewandfigur, etc.), the left foot is placed higher. In Stackelberg's terra-cotta (Gräber, Taf. 69) the foot is only slightly raised, and in the terra-cotta (Rev. Arch. 1891, i. Pl. 6, p. 289; Th. Reinach) from the Troad, probably a copy of a statue, it is raised extraordinarily high.

[2] Pal. Valentini : Guattani, Mon. Ant. ined., 1788, Tav. 2 ; Clarac, 698, 1655 ; Matz-Duhn, Zerstr. Bildwerke, No. 606 ; Roscher's Lex. i. 414. The left arm and lower right arm and the cymbals are restored. The copyist has neglected to give the Ionic sleeve on the left arm. The head is broken, but belongs to the figure. The left hand evidently drew the mantle up over the shoulder. Thick sandals on the feet. Large eyes. Good, intelligent workmanship.—Poorer replica in Pal. Odescalchi. Head, lower right arm, and left arm are restored (Matz-Duhn, 605).

[3] Ἐφημ. ἀρχ. 1891, Taf. 9, 1. Cf. p. 85.

[4] The earliest examples are the Borghese Gladiator by Agasias (Löwy, I. G. B. 292 ; ibid. 293, 343) and the Belvedere torso (cf. Löwy, p. 350).

the second and first century B.C., and many of which are of considerable excellence. The artist took his motive from a creation of Skopas, which he modified considerably, and contaminated, not altogether happily, with the type of the Tyche of Melos. At the same time he strove to impart to it something of Pheidian grandeur. So far then he showed independence in his modification of the style, inasmuch as he drew his inspiration from older Attic art, and sought to emulate it. Call him 'eclectic' if you will, he was at least a man who could make a traditional type his own, and reproduce it with all the freshness of a new conception. The pleasure arising from this quality in his work should not be lessened by the scientific analysis to which we have subjected the statue.

Fig. LXVI—Pediment head, Temple of Athena Alea: Tegea. Athens. National Museum (Possibly original work of Skopas: See Notes)

Fig. LXVII—Head of a Youth. New York. Metropolitan Museum of Art (See Notes)

Fig. LXVIII—Head of a Youth from Antikythera. Athens National Museum (See Notes)

Fig. LXIX—Meleager. Copenhagen. Ny Carlsberg Glyptotek (See pp. 184, 304, 307)

Fig. LXX—Statue of Agias. Delphi, Delphi Museum (See Notes)

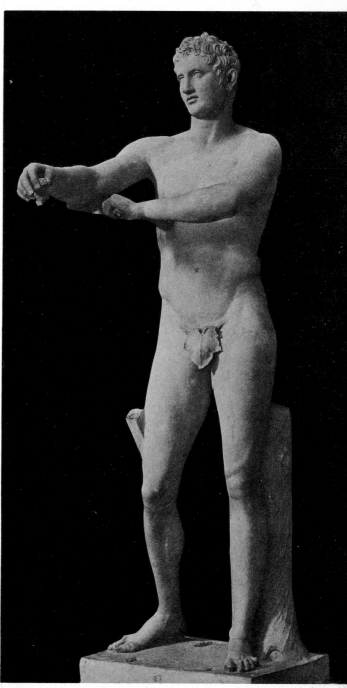

Fig. LXXI—"Apoxyomenos" Athlete, Rome, Vatican
Museum (See pp. 300 seq., 304, 308, 341, 351)

Fig. LXXII—Apollo Belvedere, Rome. Vatican Museum
(See pp. 328, 405 sqq.)

THE APOLLO OF THE BELVEDERE

SELDOM has any archaeological hypothesis met with such enthusiastic and universal approval as did the famous contention published by Stephani in 1860 concerning the Apollo of the Belvedere. Ever since that time it has been considered practically certain that the god bore an aegis in his left hand. This view soon made its way into every popular handbook as an ascertained result of modern archaeology,[1] although the only evidence for it was a doubtful fragment in the hand of a bronze replica of the Apollo belonging to Count Stroganoff in St. Petersburg. Not only was Stephani's identification of this fragment accepted almost without dissent, but confidence was carried to such a pitch that his further vague and entirely unfounded supposition, that the statuette was part of the great bronze find made at Paramythia in 1792—a statement evidently intended to increase the value of the statuette—was accepted as a proven fact even in scientific circles.[2] In reality, the statuette had been traced back to Italy, and no further.

When for the first time I saw the Stroganoff bronze in 1882, I was to my astonishment at once convinced that, whatever might be the meaning of the fragment in the left hand, it had never formed part of an aegis.[3] In 1883, however, Kieseritzky defended Stephani's view,[4] which henceforth passed almost unchallenged. I made no answer at the time, as I wished first to examine the bronze again; accordingly, in the article 'Apollo' written in 1883 for Roscher's *Lexikon*, I stated circumspectly that the fragment of the attribute had not yet been fully explained.[5] This reserve was, to my regret, misunderstood in some quarters: I was supposed to be incapable of acknowledging an error,[6] and faith in Stephani remained unshaken.

---

[1] See Helbig, *Führer*, No. 158; Friederichs-Wolters, *Gipsabg.* 1523; Preller-Robert, *Griech. Myth.* i. 295.

[2] Overbeck, *Apollo*, p. 248; Helbig, *Führer*, i. 106. The figure resembling the Apollo Belvedere—of which we know neither the material nor the provenance—given by Veli Pasha to Dr. Frank cannot have been one of the exquisite bronzes found at Paramythia in 1792, and may easily have been a forgery. This is again a perfectly arbitrary and improbable conjecture of Stephani. The Pasha was not such an ignorant fool as to present an object of such value, even supposing him to have had it to give, to a person like Dr. Frank.

[3] *Arch. Ztg.* 1882, 247.   [4] *Arch. Ztg.* 1883, 27.   [5] Roscher's *Lex.* i. 465.

[6] Studniczka, *Wiener Zeitschrift für Gymnasialwesen*, 1886, p. 682.

Opposition was silent till 1887, when almost simultaneously two scholars, A. Gercke and O. A. Hoffmann, showed by a number of incontrovertible proofs derived from ancient literature that the notion of Apollo bearing the aegis and victorious over the Gauls was simply an erroneous modern fancy.[1] In 1889 O. A. Hoffmann proceeded to an investigation of the Stroganoff bronze, and maintained that Kieseritzky's defence of the aegis theory was self-contradictory and out of harmony with facts.[2] Gherardo Ghirardini followed him on the same lines, and in an elaborate treatise emphatically denied the existence of the aegis.[3] He deplored that the arguments adduced by me in 1882 had hitherto met with so little notice, and hoped for a speedy change of opinion. Nevertheless Helbig, in his *Führer durch die Sammlungen Roms*,[4] 1891, set aside as unimportant every objection to the prevailing theory. On the other hand, F. Winter, in his admirable treatise on the Belvedere statue, published in 1892,[5] decided to leave the bronze statuette and its would-be aegis entirely out of the discussion.

In the spring of 1891 I carefully examined for the second time the Stroganoff bronze, which was then accessible to the public on certain days. All at once the scales fell from my eyes: the solution of the problem was infinitely simpler than had ever been imagined—*the bronze is nothing but a poor and absolutely valueless modern forgery*.[6]

Since the year 1882, when I first saw the statuette, I had had every opportunity of training my eye to appreciate the distinctions between real and false bronzes, in the course of my work at the Berlin Museum, where a great number of forged bronzes from different collections have been specially brought together for purposes of study. In 1882 I failed to detect the forgery, partly from lack of practice, and partly because the trammels of authority were too strong to allow of doubt where a figure so famous was in question.

The statuette—which however is not small, but one third life-size—shows not a trace of the genuine patina which appears on all antique bronzes that have really been excavated.[7] This is alone sufficient to prove the modern origin. There is another point which any one can appreciate without having seen the original. A support under the raised left heel exactly corresponds to a similar support in the Belvedere statue. Now this detail is throughout antiquity specially characteristic of marble work. When one foot of a statue was set back with raised heel, it was usual to leave under the foot the piece of marble connecting it with the plinth. This was done to afford support to the foot and to prevent it from breaking. In a metal figure, which is cast separate from the base, such a support is absolutely meaningless. It is therefore never found in real antique bronzes, and its presence here satisfactorily shows that the statuette is a copy of the Vatican figure.

Again, the statuette is very badly cast and full of small holes.[8] These are not repaired in the usual antique way, *i.e.* with small rectangular patches, but roughly filled

[1] A. Gercke, *Jahrb. d. Inst.* 1887, 260 ; O. A. Hoffmann, 'Aegis oder Bogen ?' *Jahresber. d. Lyceums zu Metz*, 1887.   [2] *Herm-Apollo Stroganoff*, Marburg 1889.

[3] *Bulla della Commiss. Arch. Com. di Roma*, 1889, 407, 451.

[4] Vol. i. p. 110. [For Helbig's latest views see *Museums*, 160.—E.S.]

[5] *Jahrb. d. Arch. Inst.* 1892, p. 164.

[6] I at once communicated this discovery to Kieseritzky, who later passed it on to Conze. In a note in *Jahrb. d. Inst.* 1892, p. 164, Conze pronounced my view to be worthy of consideration, but did not express any decisive opinion of his own.

[7] Had the bronze been found at Paramythia, as Stephani contended, one would expect to find on it the specially beautiful patina of those bronzes. Its patina is not only not antique, it is merely counterfeit modern.

[8] Cf. the forged Amazon bronze in Verona. See p. 137, note 1.

up from inside with molten lead, according to a favourite method of modern forgers. Not long ago there was offered to the Berlin Museum a forged Herakles bronze, showing similar holes filled up with lead. The Stroganoff statuette was apparently broken and carelessly put together with lead, but the parts—including the left arm— are of the same date, and evidently belong together. The mantle was never better finished than it is now ; on the arm there is only a small fissure patched up with lead, but no traces of solder to show that the mantle once covered it. The original intention probably was to cast the mantle with the forearm separately and fasten them on, but this intention was never carried out, no doubt because the crowded thin folds of the mantle were difficult to render. In the sixteenth-century bronze copy in the Louvre of the Belvedere statue (by Durant), the left arm with the whole front part of the drapery is separately cast.[1] The so-called 'aegis' in the left hand of the statuette is cast to imitate a breakage, and the patina is false. The piece is slightly scolloped out at the edge, but otherwise there are no traces of chisel work. The head, also unchiselled, is poor and common, and like the body bears every trace of being only a slavish copy by a mediocre workman. What he meant by the fragment in the left hand we do not know, and need hardly inquire ; it is evident that by this divergence from the original the forger, who knew quite well the hand of the Apollo to be restored, intended to make the statuette more interesting. And in this he has doubtless succeeded, since for over thirty years scholars have been mystified by his bronze.

Another forged copy, or rather variant, of the Vatican statue is to be seen at Saragossa.[2] I know it only from illustrations. The left arm is raised with a dramatic gesture ; the drapery on the arm is omitted, but hangs down over the body as in the Stroganoff figure. The chlamys (here with a fringed edge) is drawn across so as to cover the pubes—a trait which alone suffices to betray the modern origin. The fingers are cast to imitate breakages.

Having now disposed of the Stroganoff figure, we need have no doubt whatever that the Belvedere Apollo with the quiver on his back held the bow in his left hand, possibly also the end of an arrow grasped in one finger. But neither was his right hand empty : it bore an attribute, a portion of which is still to be seen at the upper end of the antique part of the tree-stem, although oddly enough this has not been noticed.[3] The right arm is broken, once in the upper arm and once at the elbow. The upper arm is antique, the forearm, as marble and workmanship show, is restored.[4] To the same restorer is to be traced the piece which unites the tree-stem with the hand (the fingers of which are restored in plaster). A large rectangular puntello on the thigh shows that the lower part of the right arm was originally somewhat more raised and more to the front. The connexion between the tree-trunk and the hand was effected by the attribute held in the hand ; the end of this attribute may be seen worked in relief on the tree-trunk ; it consists of a few laurel-leaves[5] pointing downwards, and four ends of the peculiar knotted woollen fillets which formed the usual adornment of

---

[1] Here, as in the Stroganoff bronze, the support under the left foot is cast with the figure.

[2] Gascón de Gotor, *Zaragoza* (1891), pl. to p. 56.

[3] Except by K. Bötticher (*Erklär. Verzeichniss der Abgüsse in Berlin*, 1872, p. 323) who was, however, mistaken in supposing the right hand genuine. My own observations were made on the original, and are quite independent of his. The tree-trunk, although broken, was in one piece with the round plinth and the right foot. It has been fastened on again, not quite accurately. Freerichs (*Apoll. v. Belvedere*, Paderborn 1894) is mistaken in believing that the plinth, the tree-stem, and the feet do not belong to the statue.

[4] Proved by Petersen, *Jahrb. d. Inst.* 1890, 51. In the small catalogue of the Vatican, ed. 1875, p. 236, the lower arm is already noted as a restoration.

[5] In the Apollo statue, Berlin, No. 51, a laurel-branch likewise formed the connexion between hand and tree-trunk.

Apollo's Omphalos and Tripod.[1] Doubtless, then, the right hand bore a laurel-branch with *stemmata*, the well-known Apolline symbol which the archaic Apollo on early coins of Kaulonia raises in his hand, and which, together with the bow in the left hand, continued to be frequently given to the god during the severe period, and right down into late antiquity.[2] The knotted fillets also occur frequently on coins. Apollo holds them in his hand, sometimes with the laurel-branch, sometimes without.[3] The meaning of this attribute is always the same ; it symbolizes the cleansing, healing, and expiating function of the god, just as the bow designates him as ' Far-darter.' The two attributes in conjunction characterize him as the god who wards off darkness and evil disease. So Herakles, in the Orphic hymn,[4] scares away[5] with his branch and his arrows evil spirits—the κακὰς ἄτας and the κῆρας χαλεπάς. The motion of the god indicates his passage through his realm, and the turn of his head signifies that he is ever on the alert, ready to bring protection and succour wherever the oppressed call him. Thus on Persian coins the Great King appears armed with the arrow and striding swiftly like a divinity bringing help to his subjects.

In a previous treatise[6] I tried to show that no definite ' situation ' is expressed in the statue (a view now further substantiated by the discovery of the laurel-twig), and that an older, possibly a fifth-century, type underlies this conception. Since then Winter has published his theory—in my eyes absolutely convincing—that the statue is a copy of a work by Leochares.[7] It is in the Ganymede of this artist that the unusual gliding gait of the Apollo, the rhythm in the movement of the limbs, as well as the bodily forms, have their nearest analogy ; the resemblance between the two is so strong and so personal that we are justified in referring them to the same artist.[8] Further, there is also a type of Alexander, which has been recently shown to be probably derived from Leochares,[9] and which manifests a decided likeness to the Apollo Belvedere in the form of the neck, the curls behind the ear, and above all, as it seems to me, in the shape of the eye and the pressure of the eyeball against the outer corner.

In any case I agree with Winter in separating the Apollo from Hellenistic work and in placing it in the Attic school of the fourth century. This is a conclusion which cannot be disputed. Even details like the hair tied in a bow,[10] the feet and the sandals,

---

[1] Cf. tripod on coins of Kroton. The kerykeion is also found with these knotted fillets. See *Wiener Vorlegeb.* 1890—91, Taf. 10, also the holy tunny-fish from Kyzikos, *Brit. Mus. Cat. of Coins, Mysia*, Pl. 3, 20, and other sacrificial animals and utensils.

[2] Cf. in particular the fine coin of Side, of severe style, Gardner, *Types*, Pl. 10, 6 ; Oberbeck, *Apollo*, Coin-plate 3, 52 ; coins of Metapontum (Overbeck, *loc. cit.* 3, 9) and of Athens (*ibid.* 3, 29, 33), *Samml. Sabouroff*, Text to Taf. 8—11, p. 3, and the Berlin statue, 51.

[3] See Overbeck, *Apollo*, Coin-plate 3, 48 (Magnesia), 49 (Aegae), and 51 (Myrina). Eros on a gem (motive similar to the statue of Parion) carries in his right hand a twig with knotted fillets. (Cades, *Amore*, 55. Cf. Roscher's *Lex.* i. 1359.)

[4] *Orph. Hymn*, 12, 5. Cf. Rohde, *Psyche*, i. 219, note.

[5] An interesting R.F. vase from Greece (in Berlin, recently acquired) shows Herakles seizing a *ker*, represented as a small winged daemon, by the throat and threatening it with his club.

[6] *Arch. Ztg.* 1882, p. 251.

[7] *Jahrb. d. Arch. Inst.* 1892, p. 164. Overbeck's answer in *Sächs. Berichte*, 1892, p. 34, is not of much consequence, seeing that O. considers the Apollo to be standing much in the same way ('nicht viel anders') as the Doryphoros of Polykleitos.

[8] The head of the Ganymede (quoted as an additional proof by Winter, p. 176) must be left out of the argument, as its genuineness is by no means certain.

[9] Köpp, *Bildniss Alexanders des Grossen*, p. 18, Taf. ii. Head of Munich statue.

[10] For undoubted examples on originals of the fourth century, see *Samml. Sab.* Text to Taf. 22 ; *Ath. Mitth.* 1885, Taf. 8 and 9. This fashion of hair will be seen from those instances to be peculiarly characteristic of the Praxitelean epoch. Also on a head from Aegion in the Nat. Mus., Athens (Kabbadias, No. 192), on an Attic

resembling those of the Olympian Hermes,[1] and the conformation of the body,[2] all point to the later period of Skopas and Praxiteles or to the earlier period of their successors (Leochares was a somewhat younger contemporary of those artists, seeing that he worked with Lysippos on the ' Lion-hunt' of Alexander). The strong resemblance between this Apollo and the Diana of Versailles (p. 328), which once led scholars to the false assumption that the two statues formed a pair,[3] is now explained by the fact that they belong to the same period—*circa* 330 B.C.—and to the same artistic school. We have already shown that the ' Diane' has many features in common with the later Praxitelean statues of Artemis. The rhythm of the figure and the gliding gait are so closely related to the Apollo that she too may not impossibly be a creation of Leochares.

The Belvedere statue is a careful and evidently a faithful Roman copy ; the presence of the tree-stump, which jars on the eye, makes it reasonable to suppose that the original was of bronze.[4] The copyist seems to have done his best to reproduce the details of this original, and after the experience we have gained of ancient copying there is no reason to doubt his trustworthiness. A second replica exists in the so-called ' Steinhäuser' head,[5] one of those hasty and inexact marble copies from bronze which only reproduce the essential features. The copyist has in this case treated the hair very cavalierly, merely inadequately indicating it on the top of the head and leaving it as a solid mass behind.[6] So too he has omitted all the finer modelling of the features, and confined his chisel to the principal forms ; and yet, like many copyists of the good, *i.e.* the Augustan, period, he has succeeded in reproducing the expression of the face and the characteristic light and vigour in the eye, so that, before the technical methods of antique copying were as well understood as they are at present, this head was supposed, especially from the characteristic although sketchy [7] treatment of the eye, to represent an older variant of the Belvedere Apollo type, while in reality it is simply another copy of the same original, executed in a different manner.[8] We must do our best to imagine the original with the help of both replicas. For the eyes we should rely on the Steinhäuser head, at the same time neglecting its lifeless mouth, empty forms, and clumsy hair in favour of the more exact rendering to be found in the Belvedere statue.

So far we possess no good second copy of the torso, though I hold it not impossible that some day a replica will turn up without the chlamys. I cannot help suspecting that this drapery is an addition made by the copyist, like the chlamys

grave-relief, seated female figure (Coll. Jacobsen, Ny Carlsberg Glypt. 1060 a), and on two of the Muses on the Chigi reliefs, Petersen (*Röm. Mitth.* 1893, Taf. 2, 3 ; p. 73).

[1] Cf. Winter, *loc. cit.* The formation of the toes should also be noticed. The sandals do not, as I formerly quite erroneously supposed (*Arch. Ztg.* 1882, p. 251), indicate Hellenistic origin.

[2] I also associated the bodily forms quite incorrectly (*loc. cit.*) with the Pergamene Apollo. On a closer comparison one recognizes the strong difference between them ; the Pergamene work bears traces everywhere of a common external naturalism.   [3] A mistake in which I also shared (*loc. cit.*)

[4] The whole polish of the flesh, however, seems modern ; on the right side the original surface is better preserved ; hair and drapery are not polished.

[5] For literature see Friederichs-Wolters, *Gipsabg.* 1525.

[6] This kind of careless copying must not be confounded with that broad touch of genius which often ignores details, and which may be observed on many original works. The difference in the hair, however, had formerly made me suppose, though quite incorrectly (*Arch. Zeitg.* 1882), that the Steinhäuser head must be the copy of a different original.

[7] The left tear-gland, for instance, has come out abnormally large ; at the same time, the part below the left eye is very good.

[8] The difference in scale, so much emphasized by Kekulé (*Arch. Ztg.* 1878, p. 9), is slight. The ' Steinhäuser' copyist worked hastily, and may have cut too deep into the marble, thus making a reduction of all the measurements necessary. Winter still overestimates the Steinhäuser head.

of the Meleager, which it resembles in style and treatment: it neither harmonizes with the quiver on the back, nor do its petty folds and its artificial stillness suit the splendid swing of the whole conception. In turning from the question of copies back to the original, we next have to consider whether this Apollo descending like the storm and vigorously turning his head to the side was a new creation now for the first time finding expression in art.

It was, as I have already shown,[1] from a pictorial composition that Leochares derived the idea which he worked out so boldly and skilfully in his Ganymede. True, he had to give up the beautiful and natural motive in which the boy's arms are clasped round the eagle's neck, and, though the motive he chose was less appropriate, it yet afforded a fine rhythmic motion, essentially the same as that of the Apollo, and still more similar to the dancing Satyr, which is possibly by Leochares, and certainly of his school.[2]

Now coin-types, and notably those of Amphipolis,[3] make it evident that, like his Ganymede, the Apollo of Leochares also was inspired by an older model. The beautiful silver coinage of Amphipolis with the Apollo head facing is comprised within the period between the foundation of the city in B.C. 437 and its capture by Philip in B.C. 358. Among these coins the latest and softest in style (they are further characterized by the inscription Ἀμφιπολιτῶν and the symbol of a Boeotian shield) have been assigned, with much probability, to the period of the Theban hegemony (371—362).[4] On the other hand, the coins of severe style bearing the shortened inscription Ἀμφι should be dated during the first years of the city's existence.[5] Here the head of Apollo is in a tranquil attitude, and there is no indication of any chlamys. A third series of coins, still more beautiful and varied than the other two, are inscribed Ἀμφιπολιτέων,[6] and probably belong to the period between 370 and 430—420 (Plate VI. 24, 25). Here the Apollo head, also facing, is turned decidedly to the left, and on some examples the chlamys is indicated. Practically the same type, with the head turned to the side, the floating curls, and the chlamys, appears on some magnificent coins of Klazomenai (Plate VI. 27, 28, 29)[7] of the same date, and again on coins of Miletos (Plate VI. 26).[8] This was the type which influenced the heads of Helios on the earliest coins of Rhodes, struck, as we must suppose, soon after the founding of the colony in 480 B.C.[9]

The head of Apollo on the coins seems based upon a statuary type representing the god in a vigorous, striding attitude, and with head turned to the left—a figure corresponding in all essentials to the statue of Leochares. Now there was a prototype for this statue, actually among the works of the later Pheidian epoch; the Apollo of the coins belongs to that series of heads, also represented facing and with streaming

---

[1] *Samm. Sabouroff*, Text to Taf. 147, p. 5.

[2] I have dwelt on the connexion with the Ganymede, *loc. cit.* For replicas (a statue in Naples and two statuettes from Thessaly and Pompeii respectively), see *Satyr von Pergamon, Berliner Winckelmannsprogram*, 1880, p. 14, Taf. 3, 2.   [3] *Arch. Ztg.* 1882, p. 252.

[4] De Witte, *Rev. Numism.* 1864, p. 100. Von Sallet (*Beschr. d. Ant. Münzen in Berlin*, ii. 34) disputes this chronology, and dates the coins among the earliest. But the recent style speaks for De Witte's view.

[5] In this case also the style is quite decisive. The shortened inscription corresponds to the older custom. Von Sallet (*loc. cit.* p. 36) recognizes the severity of the style, without however drawing the right conclusion. Specially severe are the small coins with the head in profile and the legend Ἀμφι. Nor can I agree with Head's supposition (*Hist. Num.* p. 190), that the coinage only began after the town was taken by Brasidas: like the similar colony of Thurii, the city must have had the right of striking its own coinage from the first.

[6] Good reproductions in Percy Gardner, *Types*, Pl. 7, 11; Head, *Guide*, Pl. 21, 7, 8; *Berliner Cat.* ii. Taf. 3, 22—25. A beautiful example, newly acquired, in London, *Num. Chron.* 1892, Pl. 2, 6.

[7] Head, *Guide*, Pl. 19, 24—26; *Hist. Num.* p. 491.

[8] Brit. Mus. *Catal. Ionia*, Pl. 21, 8. Chlamys indicated.   [9] Head, *Guide*, Pl. 20, 37, 38.

hair, in which we have already recognized dependence upon the style of Pheidias and his contemporaries (*supra*, p. 105 *sqq.*) Since Amphipolis was founded under the auspices of Perikles, it is not surprising to find Athenian artists of the school of Pheidias cutting Athenian types for her coinage.

But we also possess marble copies of a work, or at any rate of the head of a work, which was a prototype of Leochares's conception. Two copies of this earlier work exist, one in the British Museum (Fig. 177)[1] and one in Naples, where it is wrongly placed on the torso of a wounded hero and misnamed a *gladiatore*.[2] The work is

FIG. 177.—Head of Apollo (Brit. Mus.)

Fig. LXXIII—
Terracotta head based on the Apollo Belvedere, from Charsada, North-West Frontier Province. India.

in reality a youthful Apollo, well characterized by the full hair and the forehead broadening at the base. The analogy to the Belvedere statue consists not only in these general features but specially in the animated turn of the head to the left and the bright steady gaze of the eyes, which almost seem to emit rays of light. But a long interval of time separates the two conceptions. The London and Naples heads have the firm simple planes, the large and sharply defined forms of the older style ; the Belvedere head shows richer modelling and smoother transitions. In the

---

[1] I noticed the resemblance of this head to the Belvedere Apollo on my first visit to London in 1881 ; Fig. 177 is from a photograph taken at that time. Köpp has since published (*Bildniss Alexanders des Grossen*, p. 24) two other views of the head.

[2] *Museo Borbon.* v. 7 ; Clarac, 865, 2203 ; Photograph Sommer, 1582. A portion of the neck is also preserved.

earlier head the mouth seems to be put on from outside, in the later it is well knit with the rest of the face, and its edges melt impalpably into the surrounding surfaces. Again, the eyes of the earlier head show no trace of the careful modelling of the region around the eye, so telling as a vehicle of expression; there is no indication of the lower edge of the eye-socket, but the cheek continues unbroken up to the groove below the eyeball; the lower lid is broad and hard, and the part between the upper lid and the upper edge of the eye-socket is modelled according to old convention. Instead of swelling out gradually towards the temple, it is represented as a compact roll of flesh separated by a slight depression from the eyebrow, which continues in a hard sharp ridge as far as the temple. All these are marks which distinguish Pheidian from Praxitelean work.

But the type of this British Museum Apollo is not unfamiliar to us, for it is closely connected with a series of heads which we have previously discussed (p. 99 *sqq.*); the whole expression of the head and its turn, the form of the open mouth with the powerful curve of the lips, recall the Dioscuri of Monte Cavallo and the works related to them. Above all, the analogy which the hair presents in its forms and its peculiar *asymmetria* to the heads ascribed to the Elder Praxiteles (*supra*, Figs. 42, 1; 43, 44) seems to me so personal and individual as to warrant us in attributing the London head to the same artist.

Doubtless the whole movement of the statue had nothing of the gliding grace of the Belvedere figure. We may imagine a motive more in the manner of the Monte Cavallo Dioscuri, though not so violent. The right knee was probably more bent, and a real stride represented. An Athena of the Pheidian school, copied in a statuette of Epidauros,[1] very well shows how artists of that time conceived of a divinity hastening to give succour and aid. The head is turned with an animated gesture, the knee of the striding leg is bent and well advanced; it was the singular merit of Leochares to impart to the attitude grace, lightness, and elasticity.

In this Apollo of the Pheidian circle—presumably by the Elder Praxiteles— the god is represented as Healer and Saviour, striding like the Athena Hygieia of Epidauros,[2] or like that earlier Apollo of Kaulonia who waves the laurel-twig in token of expiation. On the Akropolis of Athens stood a bronze statue of Apollo, called 'Parnopios' because the god had saved the land from a plague of grasshoppers. The figure was 'said to be' by Pheidias (τὸ ἄγαλμα λέγουσιν Φειδίαν ποιῆσαι, Paus. i. 24, 8). That it was certainly not signed we may conclude from Lucian's remarks on the Athena Lemnia.[3] Like other works attributed by Pausanias to the master, it may have been by one of his pupils or colleagues; for instance, like the Promachos, which Pausanias also attributed to Pheidias, it may possibly have been a work of the elder Praxiteles, and be identical with the statue of 'Apollo the Saviour' by that master. Some hundred years later, when Leochares had a similar commission to execute, he adopted the Pheidian type; an Apollo by him at Athens formed, we know, a pendant (of like significance, probably) to the *Alexikakos*, the warder of evil, by Kalamis, in front of the temple of the Patroos.

---

[1] Ἐφημ. ἀρχ. 1886, Taf. 12 (left hand); *Ath. Mitth.* 1886, p. 309 (Petersen). Not only the helmet but the hair and type of face are Pheidian.

[2] Petersen's explanation (*loc. cit.*) seems far-fetched. The goddess is simply hastening to help in need. For the torch on the basis of the relief, see Friederichs-Wolters, 1176.

[3] Cf. *supra*, pp. 10, 32, 62. The λέγουσιν of Pausanias (on the strength of which Michaelis in *Ath. Mitth.* ii. p. 1, note 2, reckons the Parnopios as doubtful) does not in itself necessarily imply anything at all, as Gurlitt (*Pausanias*, p. 193) has shown, for even when he is quoting an inscription Pausanias not unfrequently introduces it by φασίν.—*e.g.* in the case of the Aphrodite by Kalamis, i. 23, 2.

EUGENIE SELLERS STRONG

The original translator and editor of the first English edition of this book. Eugenie Sellers Strong, was born in England in the late nineteenth century. Early in her career as a classical scholar she met Adolph Furtwängler and worked closely with him in the preparation of that volume which was published in London in 1895.

She lectured on Greek art and architecture at the British Museum, the Victoria and Albert Museum and in Rome, before becoming librarian to the Duke of Devonshire from 1904—1910.

At that time she became a Cambridge Fellow and the Assistant Director of the British School of Archaeology in Rome, a post she held until 1925. Two years later she was made Commander of the Order of the British Empire.

In addition to her work on this book, Mrs. Strong was the author of the basic reference book *Roman Sculpture*, as well as *Art in Rome* and *Art in Ancient Rome*. She was also a frequent contributor of many valuable articles in periodicals. She died in Girton, California in 1943.

EDITOR'S PREFACE

THE task of editing a book like the present, which has been received almost with acclamation by scholars of all schools, has been a responsible one, and I am quite conscious that I may have succeeded after all in satisfying neither the student nor the general reader. The one, preoccupied with detail, will perhaps complain of the omissions, while the other, in search only of a vivid impression, may be repelled by the length and depth. Two main alterations in the plan of the book must be noted at once: the two passages treating of archaic art (pp. 675—732, pp. 250—257) have been omitted, partly owing to their fragmentary nature, and partly because the author contemplates the publication of a series of essays upon the archaic art of Greece in which these his first sketches will be worked up and expanded. In the second place, the long and difficult chapter on the temples of the Akropolis (for the scholarly translation of which I am indebted to Miss Margaret Alford) has been printed as an Appendix, for it seemed best not to interrupt the sequence of the artistic inquiry with an Essay which, though it bears closely upon Pheidias, is mainly of historical and topographical interest. For the rest, I have made it my aim, as far as possible, to disengage the author's arguments from all such controversial matter as might cumber or obscure them. For instance, it seemed to me that the claims of scholarship would be fully satisfied if the numerous theories put forward from time to time to discredit the Pheidian authorship of the Parthenon sculptures, or the fluctuations of opinion with regard to the Kresilaian Diomede or the Myronian Perseus, were relegated to footnotes which should provide the learned and the curious with all necessary references. On the other hand, when Professor Furtwängler crosses swords with champions like Dörpfeld on the subject of the 'Opisthodomos,' or Löschcke on the date of the Trial and Death of Pheidias, we feel that contact with such opponents' arguments strikes fire from his own, so that all passages of this kind have been faithfully preserved. The same may be said of the chapters on the 'Venus of Milo' and the 'Apollo of the Belvedere,' and above all of the whole Essay on the Akropolis temples, for here

again argument and controversy are so closely interwoven that to shorten the
latter would be materially to weaken the former. In these chapters, therefore, the
only alterations are those that have been introduced by the author himself. These
and a number of smaller omissions and additions made by him throughout the whole
of the book call for no special comment ; they will be easily detected and appreciated by the reader acquainted with the original. The majority were necessitated
either by subsequent literature or by subsequent discovery. The portions of the
German edition that were printed as ' Nachträge ' have been inserted in their proper
place in the text, while every effort has been made to give references to the literature
that has appeared since the publication of the German book a year ago. In my
revision of the translation generally, I have ventured upon compression wherever this
was possible without injury to the sense, while in one or two instances I have left
rather more to the imagination of the reader than is usual in a German work of this
nature. Thus, after the exhaustive analysis of the forms peculiar to Myron given
on pp. 165—202, it seemed unnecessary to repeat them in detail, in the case of each
single statue or head which the author in a concluding section (XIII.) has grouped
about this artist. Professor Furtwängler has himself found time in the midst of his
various occupations to bestow a general supervision upon the English edition ; nor is
it necessary to say that no editorial alterations have been introduced without his
express sanction, while not a few have been planned in consultation with him.

The number of illustrations, which in the portion chosen for translation was
only 162 (including the plates), has been raised to 207. These 45 fresh illustrations
have been selected on the same plan as that already pursued by the author, to bring
into notice new or almost forgotten monuments. In their arrangement I have tried
to convince the reader of what great results might be achieved with the help of a
collection of casts, comprising not merely a few representative works, but all or nearly
all the extant products of classical art whatever their period, and supplemented by a
complete series of photographs. From the three statues reproduced side by side on
page 87, it must surely appear that their attribution to one and the same artist is no
matter of guess-work or of facile intuition, but the reasoned result of such a comparative study of form as is possible only in some comprehensive collection of casts as at
Dresden or Munich. In like manner I trust that the full illustrations in the chapter
on the Amazons (pp. 128—141) will enable the reader to take in at a glance less obvious
but essential differences which, when we have only memory to trust to, are apt to
become merged and hidden in external resemblances of type and dress. In this
connexion my thanks are due to the Marquis of Lansdowne and to Mr. Astor for
allowing the finest copy in existence of the Polykleitan Amazon to be worthily
published (Plate VIII.)

The very few illustrations which in the German edition were still repeated from
former publications have now been replaced from photographs—of the originals,
wherever this was possible, or at any rate of casts when, as in the case of so many
Italian galleries, bad lighting and other causes often make photography impossible.
The Bologna head (Plate III.) has again been reproduced only from the cast, for in
spite of the trouble so courteously taken by the Director of the Museo Civico, Professor
Brizio, the stained condition of the marble has made it impossible to obtain a negative

sufficiently good for reproduction in photogravure. I had also hoped to replace the poor illustration of the once celebrated Hope Athena at Deepdene by a plate from the original. Having failed, however, to obtain from the present occupant of Deepdene so much as an answer to my applications for permission to photograph the statue, there was nothing for it but to repeat the illustration taken from the *Ancient Specimens* (Fig. 27). In the matter of illustration generally, I have to thank Mr. A. S. Murray for the special facilities accorded to me for photographing in the British Museum, Mr. Barclay V. Head for his assistance in the preparation of the plate of coins (VI.), Dr. Paul Herrmann of Dresden for the fine new negatives of the Lemnia (Plates I., II.*, and III.) In addition, Herr F. Bruckmann of Munich and M. A. Giraudon of Paris have generously allowed me to reproduce a number of their photographs. Of the new plates there are three to which I should like to call special attention: the superb head from Beneventum in the Louvre (Plate XIV.), which should rouse us to a sense of what precious relics of the ancient *statuaria* may still lie hidden in our museums; the 'Aberdeen head,' that exquisite fragment in our own British Museum which escaped so curiously long the eye of both connoisseurs and archaeologists, and in which I think it not too bold to recognize an original from the hand of Praxiteles (Plate XVIII.); finally, the grand and presumably original head of the Skopasian Meleager, which, though it has already been well reproduced in the *Antike Denkmäler*, deserves to become known amid the grace of its Roman surroundings (Plate XV.)

By the courtesy of the author and of his English translator, Mr. James F. Muirhead, I have been enabled to refer throughout to the English edition of Professor Helbig's *Museums of Classical Art in Rome*, and I trust that this book, which will appear almost simultaneously with the present one, will give a fresh impulse to the unprejudiced study of the treasures of those Roman galleries to which, as Professor Furtwängler shows, we must still go if we would find or restore the ancient 'master-pieces.' The late Bishop Wordsworth, during his travels in Greece, likened the country, from the point of view of what remained and did not remain, to a manuscript torn indeed and defaced, but 'not yet, like Rome, a palimpsest.' Now it is precisely this fact that it is a palimpsest that still secures to Rome its archaeological pre-eminence, for, with the exception of a fragment recovered of late years here and there, the record which we are trying to decipher has been forgotten or destroyed in its native land. The very beauty and uniqueness of these fragments as works of art blind us to their incompleteness as evidence, but if we wish to gain some idea of the whole story it is to Rome that we must go, and there accustom ourselves to spell it out through the mistaken interpretations and ignorant glosses of the copyists.

Per casus varios, per tot discrimina rerum
Tendimus in Latium.

But it would be an error to suppose that Italy, *la mère savante de toute Renaissance*, is only fruitful in copies. There is the Ludovisi throne—in which the infant art of relief seems to have reached at a bound the limit of its accomplishment—and now at last we are in a position to place side by side with the Hermes itself an original from the hand of the master whom the consent of ancient connoisseurs ranked with Praxiteles. In archaeology, unfortunately, we cannot pick and choose;

all that we can do is to make the most of what has been thrown up from the wreck of Time, but 'where are they painted that are lost?' It was therefore only natural that for a time at least we should regard the Hermes as supreme, if only because he was solitary; yet whoever will compare him—soft, self-involved, with lips just parting as vague voluptuous languors steal over him—and the Meleager of Skopas, with that look all outward and upward of some inspired 'pilgrim of eternity,' will gain some idea of what we must have lost through the accidental eclipse of this great genius.

Lastly, it is hoped that this book, as it exhibits a picture, will also discover a process. Of the exact nature of that process it would hardly be necessary to speak, but for the fact that the copiousness and brilliancy of the achievements of a single critic in the more popular field of Italian art have thrown us in England into a state of naïve commotion akin to that of the ancient Mexicans, when, having never seen a horse, they mistook the troopers of Cortés for a new species of animal. For, as the critic in question never appears without his hobby, the two coalesce, as it were, in our imagination, until we think and speak of that which is nothing but the course and condition of all fruitful inquiry as if it were the honorific appendage of a particular name and the abnormal product of a particular field. On the contrary, the present book is from first to last an example of the inductive method, which, though it has never been applied before on so extensive a scale to the art of Greece, is, in principle at least, as old as Winckelmann. But here observation and comparison do not end in themselves; they rest upon a basis of history and philology, and the result is that we have the reproduction of a development, not merely the recension of a catalogue.

It cannot be denied, however, that the strength and flexibility of our instrument are often strained to the full by the very nature of the material it works in. That material is, as we have seen, not only fragmentary but secondary, while the limitations of sculpture as an art betray themselves in an external uniformity which always impedes, and sometimes baffles, our analytic research of variety. If observation comes upon a gap, theory leaps ahead, like a man's shadow that gets in front of him as soon as he begins to move away from the light. Then there is the constant temptation to explain too much, to impose a large significance upon minute features, as to which we might say in words borrowed from Johnson, 'the dull utterly neglect them, the acute see a little, and supply the rest with fancy and conjecture.' So much for the defects of our 'method.' They know them best who use it most diligently and most skilfully; nor would there be any occasion to insist upon them at all, were it not for the numbers of those to whom, if we may judge from their attitude of barren negation, 'willing to wound but yet afraid to strike,' it would seem as if discretion were the better part of discovery.

It is therefore in a double aspect as matter and method that these Essays are now offered to the English reader, in confidence that what is not final will yet be found fruitful; and—

Was fruchtbar ist, allein ist wahr.

E. S.

November 19, 1894.

APPENDIX: EDITOR'S NOTES

The purpose of these notes is twofold: to supplement the information given by Furtwaengler, especially concerning things unknown to him in 1895, and secondly to comment on the changes in, and addition, of, certain photographs. As one can readily understand from reading Miss Sellers' notes, the acquisition of photographs was very difficult. Added to this was the problem of quality reproduction since the photographic process was still in its infancy so to speak before the turn of the century. Wherever possible the original photographs have been replaced. In addition, many have been added, particularly to illustrate new finds, or to illustrate statues mentioned by Furtwaengler, but not previously shown. Certain other photographs have been added to permit comparative study, in keeping with Furtwaengler's own methods.

ATHENA LEMNIA

Plates I, II and *II of the earlier edition have been combined on Page 2. Fortunately I was able to replace the profile of the Bologna head on Page 18 with a more detailed photograph, but on Page 28, for lack of anything better, I used Plate III of the original edition, a photograph from a cast. Two new photographs (Figs. LXXIV, a & b) from the Museo Civico in Bologna, published here for the first time to my knowledge, give the necessary details for study according to the observations of the author (Pages 4 sqq.). The study of Athena Lemnia is most necessary in order to follow Furtwaengler's thoughts on this most important sculptor, Pheidias.

Furtwaengler used the discovery of the Athena Lemnia as the basis for his discussions on the style of Pheidias. The main arguments against Furtwaengler's theories on the Lemnia were expressed by W. Amelung who pointed out (Jahrbuch ix, 169) that there was no evidence that the Lemnia was bronze. To support this statement, he used later references in the text of Ailios Aristeides which refer to the three Athenian Athenas as the ivory, the bronze and the Lemnia. (Overbeck, SQ, 639). Using this text, Amelung deduced that the Athena Lemnia, being neither ivory or bronze, was acrolithic, but it is my belief that this reference is a weaker foundation for argument than the stylistic observations by Furtwaengler. I believe that possibly Aristides noted the Lemnia in a separate category, not due to her being made from a different material, but rather due to the departure from the more well known forms of Athena, i.e. the helmet held in her hand rather than worn, and the simple coiffure, etc. (Cf. p. 14).

As a matter of fact, the Athena Areia of Plataea, mentioned by Pausanias (IX, 4, 1) as the work of Pheidias, was an acrolithic statue, but as we have no proof that it was ivory and gold, it may be suspected that it was of marble and gilded bronze instead. We do not know whether the Athena Areia was seated or standing, but it may, in any case, be considered a stylistic ancestor of the golden and ivory Athena Parthenos. Still, there is no evidence that it is related to the Lemnia. As A. S. Murray observed, while Amelung's reconstruction of an Athena resulted in a work with definite Pheidian characteristics, it was apparently not the Athena Lemnia. Thus, it would seem that the most valid and best treatment of the problem of Athena Lemnia still belongs to Furtwaengler, although definite conclusions have not yet been reached.

ZEUS OLYMPIOS

Furtwaengler's theory that Pheidias must have had a workshop at Olympia has since been confirmed in the recent excavations of 1959. At that time, the German Archaeological Institute had the good fortune to discover the bottom of a black kylix inscribed Φειδίο εἰ | μί. (= I belong to Pheidias) not far from the place where the molds were found for some of the golden parts of the statue of Zeus Olympios (Figs. LXXXV, a & b).

The obverse of the bronze coin of Elis (Fig. B1) depicting the head of the Pheidian Zeus Olympios can be seen to compare almost exactly to the head of Zeus in Boston (Fig. B3). The head of the statue on the reverse of the Eleian coin and on the Macedonian coin (Fig. B2) minted by King Philip in celebration of his victory in the Olympic games (356 B.C.) also bear this resemblance.

The two panel reliefs (Figs. C1 & C2) closely resemble the others in a group of marble reliefs found in the harbor of Piraeus in 1931. The latter have been identified as Amazonomachia from the Parthenos shield by a copyist of Pheidias. Since these two are also Amazonomachia figures, but not traceable to the Parthenos shield, we may assume that the copyist used as his model the Amazonomachia figures from the pedestal of Zeus Olympios, the only other known possible source for such Pheidian subject matter.

The figure of the wounded bearded warrior (Fig. C2) is better known in an earlier and more complete copy in Rome (Helbig, Antiq. I, 722), but it would seem that the Chicago copy is closer to the original. A comparison of this warrior's head (Fig. F1) with the head of the Anakreon Borghese (Fig. F2), considered by many to be an excellent example of Pheidian style, results in the discovery of Pheidian elements in the former as well.

THE OLYMPIAN ZEUS CULT STATUE IN THE ATHENIAN OLYMPIEION

The pictures of Plates A and B have been selected to show Pheidian style and especially works of art echoing the famous cult statue of Zeus Olympios at Olympia. Plate A illustrates the close connection between the well-known Zeus Otricoli (Fig. A2) and a bronze statuette of Zeus in the British Museum (Fig. A1). Both are related to the same original, but apparently not to the Pheidian Zeus of Olympia as seen on the bronze coin in Fig. B2. (A. S. Murray, "Greek Bronzes," 1899, pp. 63-64). Therefore, we may reasonably suspect that these are copies of the cult statue erected at the Olympieion in Athens during the Hadrianic era.

Certain scholars have identified the cult statue of Zeus Olympios of the Athenian Olympieion on the reserve side of a bronze Athenian coin (Fig. LXXIV), but a figure of Zeus recently discovered on a relief from Brauron (Fig. LXXV, early 4th century B.C.) indicates that the type of Olympian Zeus illustrated on the coin antedates the Hadrianic era (117-138 A. D.). As a result, we must accept the existence of a pre-Pheidian Athenian cult statue of the Olympian Zeus which was copied by the

sculptor of the Brauronian. 4th century B. C. relief and which was illustrated again centuries later
on an Athenian coin as a famous relic of the past,
as was done with many other famous statues and
groups. This same Brauronian relief has been valuable in the reidentification of the so-called statue
of Ceres in the Vatican (Fig. 35). This statue
corresponds exactly to the relief figure of the female to the left of Zeus. From the mythological
subject matter depicted in this scene (Dexiosis of
Apollo and Artemis by Leto and Zeus) we may
positively conclude that the original was a statue
either of Hera or Leto, and that the Vatican statue
and the Brauronian relief are two copies of another
famous original antedating the early fourth century B. C.

ATHENA PARTHENOS

Plates D, E and H show various replicas of
the Pheidian gold and ivory cult of Athena Parthenos in the Parthenon. The Varvakeion statuette
(Figs. E1 & E4) shows a close connection to the
Leningrad (Kertsh) medal, the Aspasios gem and
the bronze Athenian coin (Fig. E2). The Lenorman Athena (Fig. E3) indicates that the golden
shield of the original was decorated with an em-
bossed relief (Cf. Pliny, N. H. 36, 18) and this
unfinished copy has provided a basis for the identification of the Strangford Shield (Figs. D1 and
D2) as a major copy of the same theme. The figures of the Strangford Shield made it possible to
identify the scenes of several late Hellenistic panel
reliefs found in the Piraeus harbor, as mentioned
earlier, as copies of Amazonomachia motifs from
the shield of the Parthenos (Cf. Stavropoulos, Ph.,
"The Shield of Athena Parthenos", Athens—Bibliography in Hill, Ancient City of Athens, pp.
240-241 Notes 6-7).

The Borghese statue in the Louvre (Fig. E6)
and the British Museum bronze statuette (Fig. E5)
are two Hellenistic adaptations of Athena Parthenos. The Jacobsen and Copenhagen heads (Figs.
H1 & H5) may also be considered to be echoes of
the Parthenons. The 4th century coin (Fig. H6)
shows the oldest known replica of the Pheidian
statue, giving evidence that by that time a support
had become necessary for the right hand of Athena
which held the Nike statuette. Later, in the Roman
period, this support became a permanent element
in the form of a column (Fig. E4).

PHEIDIAS AND HIS PUPILS

The stylistic relation   between the Pheidian
school and that of Alkamenes is illustrated in
Plate F. At the time of Furtwaengler's studies of
Alkamenes, there were no definite identifications of
that sculptor's work, but in 1903 a terminal statue
of Hermes Propylaios was discovered at Pergamon
bearing the inscription (Fig. #1, p. 87):

εἰδήσεις Ἀλκαμένεος περικαλλὲς ἄγαλμα
Ἑρμᾶν τὸν πρὸ πυλῶν· εἵσατο Περγάμιος.

Many museums possess copies of this original.
Two. from an Athenian workshop, are considered
the best of these. They were discovered in 1959
with the group of bronzes at Piraeus and one is
shown in Fig. F4 together with the Metropolitan Museum copy (Fig. F3).

There is also a relationship between the works
of Pheidias and those of his pupil Agorakritos.

The Pheidian Apollo Bargello in Florence
(Fig G1) and the deLaborde head (Fig. G2)
are shown in relation to the fragmentary sculptures

by Agorakritos from the pedestal of the statue of
Nemesis at Rhamnus (Fig G3 and G4).

The sculptor of the Erechtheion was also a fol-
lower of Pheidias as may be seen in Plate H. The
Elgin Caryatid from the British Museum (Fig.
H4) is shown in parallel with the torso of the
Massarenti copy of the Parthenos (Fig. H5) and
the coin of Aphrodisias (see above). The Vatican
Caryatid (Fig. H7) indicates a case of free copying during the Roman phase of Hellenistic sculpture and fairly accurate copying is illustrated in
the case of the head of one of the Caryatides from
Hadrian's Villa (Fig. H2). The Jacobsen and
Copenhagen heads of Athena (Figs. H1 & H5)
can be compared readily with the Elgin and Vatican Caryatides, thus showing their stylistic relationship to the Athena Parthenos as well. The
terra-cotta head from the Stoa of Attalos Museum
(Fig. H3) is illustrative of the pre-Pheidian type
of Athena statue.

MASTERS BEFORE AND AFTER PHEIDIAS

Plates I through P are arranged to enable the
reader to compare the works of Pheidias and his
school with his predecessors as well as to observe
his influence on the masters of the early forth
century B. C. The most famous work of Athenian
sculpture prior to the time of Pheidias is the group
of the Tyrannicides (Harmodios and Aristogeiton)
by Nesiotes and Kritios. In Fig. I1. the group
appears as reconstructed in the New York Metropolitan Museum. The photographs of the New
York copy of the head of Harmodios (Figs. I,
2 & 3) show a hair treatment reminiscent of the
archaic period. It may be supposed that the sculptors wished to retain the more obvious characteristics of the original statue by Antenor which
was carried away by the Persians in 479 B.C., while
improving upon the anatomy of the figures according to the later style. The young boy (Fig. J2)
found in the excavations of the Acropolis of
Athens is an original work of Kritios and the
plastic form has been vastly improved compared
to the "Strangford Apollo" (Fig. J1) which has
a remarkably advanced anatomical structure, although a late archaic work. The statue of a boy
is dated before the years 480-479 B.C.. whereas
the group of the Tyrannicides is dated circa 477-
476 B.C. The helmeted warrior relief (Fig. K2)
shows the archaic anatomical style typical of Athenian works prior to Kritios. The feeling of motion introduced by Kritios and Nesiotes had its
effect on provincial architectural sculpture and is
reflected in the terra-cotta group of Zeus and
Ganymede (Fig. K1). Although the latter was
created a decade later. the movement is very similar to that of the Tyrannicides.

The inscribed portrait of Themistocles from
Ostia (Fig. L1) is one of the few portrait sculptures which can definitely be connected with the
pre-Pheidian Athenian works. Its strong analogies
with the pediment sculptures of Olympia, both in
features and in technique. indicate its genuineness
which has recently been questioned. (P. Amandry
in Bull de la Faculté de Lettres de Strasbourg 38,
1961, 413-435).

SCOPAS

The fragments of the pedimental sculptures
from the temple of Athena Alea at Tegea form
a very important addition to our knowledge of
Scopasian style. Pausanias mentions that the archi-
tect of the temple was Scopas himself, and this

Fig. LXXIV a & b — Athena Lemnia, Museo Civico, Bologna (From the original).

Fig. LXXV a & b — Molds for casting golden parts of statue of Zeus Olympios, found in workshop of Pheidias, Olympia Museum.

Fig. LXXVI — Bottom of Attic kylix with owner's inscription: Φειδίō εἰμί. (I belong to Phei-dias), found in excavations of the workshop of Pheidias at Olympia Olympia Museum.

statement guides us to the logical conclusion that even if the pedimental sculptures were not chiselled by the master himself, they must be considered as the best known examples of his original style as it influenced his assistants and followers who would have had the best opportunity for the assignment.

The heads shown (Figs. XLIII, LXVI) are remarkable for their vital style and intensity of passion. The deeply sunken eyes, the primary characteristic of Scopasian sculpture, leave no doubt that we have something original of the Parian master's work.

LYSIPPOS

The famous bearded Copenhagen head of an Apoxyomenos by Lysippos (Fig. W1) is shown with a head of Alexander the Great from the Acropolis, and now, for the first time, both of these works can be compared with the bronze head of a Muse (Fig. W3) found in Piraeus and which shows definite Lysippian characteristics. The statue of Agias by Lysippos (Fig. LXX) can be compared to good advantage with Scopasian Meleager (Fig. XLIV) and it is also interesting to note the comparative features of the Apoxyomenos (Fig. V5), the Praxitelean boy of Marathon (Fig. V4) and the bronze Apoxyomenos from Ephesus (Fig. V6).

THE PRAXITELEAN ARTEMIS BRAURONIA

Pausanias I, 23, 7. *"There is also (Sc. on the Acropolis of Athens) a sanctuary of Artemis Brauronia, the cult statue in which is by Praxiteles. The surname of the goddess is derived from the sanctuary of Brauron and the ancient wooden image is actually there, the 'xoanon' of the Tauric Artemis itself, as they say."*

This once-mentioned and literally unknown Praxitelean work, which several scholars have tried in vain to identify from later copies of statues and statuettes of Artemis, recently identified itself, thanks to a dedicatory relief found in the excavations at Brauron (Fig. LXXXIV). In it the cult statue of Artemis appears standing behind an altar towards which moves a procession of adorants ready to sacrifice a bull.

The cult statue of the goddess represented on this relief is clearly a statue of the Praxitelean style. Artemis holds a phiale in her left hand and a bow in her right. The distinctive coiffure of the statue may be recognized as an influential element in later dedicatory statues of "arktoi" found in the sanctuary of Brauron.

By a happy coincidence, we can now immediately recognize three copies of this Praxitelean statue. One of them, if not the original itself, is the bronze statue of Artemis found in Piraeus in 1959 (Fig. LXXXVI). Another is the figure from a large relief, definitely Attic, in the Metropolitan Museum of Art (Fig. LXXXV). The third is a head from a statuettte also found in the excavations at Brauron (Fig. LXXXVII).

The bronze statuette from Piraeus bears a stiking resemblance to the cult statue shown on the relief from Brauron, which is the key to the identification of the Praxitelean Artemis Brauronia. The same can be said for the marble copy of the Brauronia in New York which definitely belongs to the small closely related group of Attic copies from the same original. The accompanying smaller figure can now be positively identified as a priestess or adorant (Fig. U4) and it provides us with one more piece of evidence of the Praxitelean style, due to its close resemblance to the figures of the Muses (Fig. U3) on the Mantinean basis.

Due to the untimely death of Dr. John Papademetriou, director of excavations at Brauron, it is unknown who will publish the finds of sculpture located there, or when. But as a contribution to his memory, I wish to add at least one identification connected with one of his finds. It is intended to provide enlightment on the problem of the sculptural type adopted for the warlike and armed Tauric Artemis, as opposed to the benign Praxitelean Brauronia.

In the area of the Temple of Artemis at Brauron, the torso of a marble statuette representing an armed Artemis was found in 1959 (Fig. LXXXV. a). According to Papademetriou, this was one of the akroteria of the temple. But the cuirass, the movement of the figure and the positioning of the arms indicate that we have surviving in Brauron an excellent example of the belligerent type of Tauric Artemis which later became, in the Brauronia of the Athenian Acropolis, the sweet and beautiful representative of feminine Attic beauty, through the chisel of Praxiteles.

THE PRAXITELEAN APHRODITE THESPIA

With the restoration of a dedicatory inscription from a bronze vase (Platon 7, 1955, pp. 342-344) the information that Aphrodite, as protectress of the Beotian city of Thespiai, was called "Aphrodite Thespia" became an epigraphically documented fact.

Thus we know that the cult of Aphrodite Thespia, the main deity of Thespiai, cannot be identified with the chthonic cult of Aphrodite Melainis, to whom, according to Pausanias (IX, 27, 1), was dedicated a sanctuary in the city. But this was difinitely far from the temple housing the cult of the city protectress and her child Eros.

From the time of this restoration, the representations of heads of Aphrodite on Thespian coins must be called Aphrodite Thespia, and some of the types of the fourth century B.C. might be considered as echoing the features of the Praxitelean statue. But the most striking discovery becomes possible thanks to the reverse of a bronze Thespian coin of the Roman period. The statue thereon, identified as "Aphrodite Melainis" by Imhoof-Blumer and P. Gardner (Num. Comm. to Paus., p. 117, Pl. X, No. XIX), has been overlooked as a possible copy of the cult statue of Aphrodite Thespia by Praxiteles. This coin replica indicates very clearly that Furtwaengler's suggestion that the Praxitelean Aphrodite in Thespiai must be identified with the original represented by the Venus d'Arles (Fig. 135) can now be justified by means of a coin unknown to him.

The same coin showing the replica of the Aphrodite Thespia also has a small feminine figure standing to the right of Aphrodite. It is not difficult to identify this figure with the statue of Phryne, which according to literary evidence, stood "between the Praxitelean cult statues of Aphrodite and Eros in the Thespian sanctuary," (Alkiphron, Fr. 3. Ed. Schepers 1905).

Another unpublished Thespian coin representation in the Numismatic Museum of Athens shows a different view of the group of Aphrodite and Phryne in Thespiai, which, until now, has not been considered as a Praxitelean group (Cf. L. Lacroix, *Les repr. des st. sur les mon. gr.*, pp. 302-305).

Fig. LXXVII (a)— Relief from Brauron, 4th century B.C., Eclectic composition depicting Zeus Olympios, Leto, Apollo and Artemis, Athens, National Museum. (b) Statue of Hera, Vatican Museum. (c) Bronze Athenian coin depicting Zeus Olympios.

Fig. LXXVIII — Fragment of a marble grave stele, Attic, Ca. 400 B.C., St. Louis, City Art Museum.

Fig. LXXIX — Detail of a bronze statue of Athena found in Piraeus, Ca. 4th century B.C., City Museum.

Fig. LXXX — Nike of Paionios, Olympia, Olympia Museum, (Cf.p.41,6).

Fig.LXXXI— Hermes of Praxiteles, Olympia, Olympia Museum, (Cf.p.327, Pl.V).

Fig.LXXXII — Hermes of Andros, Athens, National Museum (Cf.fig.lv, p.364).

Fig.LXXXIII — Diadumenos of Delos, Athens, National Museum.

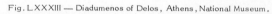

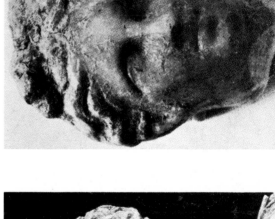

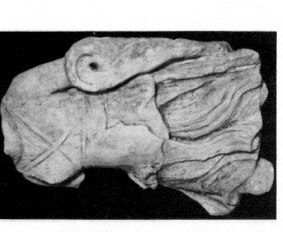

Fig. LXXXIV — Relief from Brauron representing the cult statue of the Goddess Artemis standing behind an altar and a procession of adorants preparing to sacrifice a bull, Athens, National Museum.

Fig. LXXXV — (Right) Artemis Brauronia statue, New York Metropolitan Museum of Art, (Cf. p. 324, Pl. U, 4).→

Fig. LXXXVa–Tauric Artemis found at Brauron.

Fig. LXXXVI—Head of bronze statue of Artemis, Piraeus, City Museum (Cf. Pl. W5).

Fig. LXXXVII—Head of statuette of Artemis found in Brauron, Athens, National Museum.

ADDITIONAL NOTES.
by EUGENIE SELLERS STRONG

I. P. 95 *sqq.*: *Dioscuri of Monte Cavallo.* In a letter which I received a few days ago, Professor Furtwängler quotes an interesting statement made by Julius Lange (*Thorwaldsen, Fremstilling af Mennesket*, p. 9), to the effect that Canova said of the Elgin marbles in 1803 that only one single antique in all Rome was conceived in their grand style—namely, *the finer of the two Colossi of Monte Cavallo.* I also find it stated by Memes, *Memoirs of Canova* (Edinburgh 1825), p. 291, that 'of the latter (*i.e.* the Colossi), even at a subsequent period of life, he (Canova) made a constant morning study for years, in relation to his own improvement, *and to establish the style of Phidias in the Elgin Marbles.'*—E. S.

II. P. 132, 1. To the replicas of the Kresilaian Amazon should be added a head in the Jacobsen Collection (1073 *a*), poor and much restored, but of value as having on the right side, in the line of the ear and near the crown, the remains of a rectangular support, which once connected the head with the right wrist ; this confirms the restoration proposed on p. 132. The head may possibly be identical with Michaelis *o.*

III. P. 346 *seq.*: *The Aberdeen Head.* Lord Stanmore has the kindness to inform me that it is *certain* the head came direct from Greece, and adds : ' All the fragments my father brought with him from thence were placed together by themselves, and this head was among them.'—E. S.

ILLUSTRATIONS

My thanks are due to the fellow-members of the ''Polemon'' Archaeological Association of Athens, and especially the secretary. Miss Theophano Arvanitopoulou and the president. Mr. Andrew Papagianopouloc-Palaios who gave me permission for the use of photographic reproductions of sculptures in the museums of Europe from prints dated at the end of the ninteenth century. Thanks to these. I have been able to replace many illustrations of the first edition with new photographs of the same period. Where original photographs were not available the printed reproductions were used again. and for some of these. the reader deserves my apologies.

In addition my thanks go to the following sources (alphabetically) :

American School of Classical Studies at Athens: Figs. liv. xlviii. H3.
Art Institute of Chicago: C1. C2. F1. U1.
Bologna Museo Civico: Figs. lxxiv and lxxiv. a.
British Museum: Figs. xiii. A1. M2.
City Art Museum of St. Louis: Figs. lviii. lxiv. ixxviii. L79.
Alison Frantz: Figs. lxx. K2. O1.
German Archaeological Institute. Athens: Figs. lxxv, a & b. lxxvi. lxxx. lxxxi. lxxxii. lxxxiii. K1.
J. Paul Getty Museum. Malibu. California: Frontispiece. Fig. xliv. a.
London Museum: Fig. liii.
Metropolitan Museum of Art. New York: Figs. 55. xxxv. xxxv. a. xxxvii. xxxix. lxxxv. 1 1. 2. 3. P3. Q1. Q2. R1. U4.
Ny Carlsberg Glyptotek. Copenhagen: Figs. 17. xxi. a. lii. lix. lxix. F2. H1. W1.
Dr. J. Papademetriou: Figs. iv. v. v. a. vi. viii. ix. xi. xii. xviii. xxx. a. xlvii. lxxvii. a. lxxix. lxxxiv. lxxxvii. E1. F4. L2. W3.
Dr. John Threpsiades: Figs. 33. xv. xxxi. xxxviii. xli. E5. E6. J2. M1. N1. X1. 2. 4.
Thanks. too. to Mr. Flemming Johansen of the Ny Carlsberg Glyptotek. Mrs. Anne Jones of the J. Paul Getty Museum. Fotofast. Bologna. Mrs. Nada Saporiti of the Metropolitan Museum of Art. Mr. Meritt S. Hitt of the St. Louis City Art Museum. Mr. Gerhard Neumann of the German Archaeological Institute and to members of the staff of the Art Institute of Chicago for their special assistance in helping to prosure the above mentioned photographs.

BIBLIOGRAPHY

THIS BIBLIOGRAPHY IS NOT INTENDED TO BE
IN ANY SENSE EXHAUSTIVE; IT INCLUDES ONLY
THE MORE IMPORTANT BOOKS OF INTEREST
TO THE GENERAL READER.

Ancient Authorities

Overbeck, J.: Die antike Schriftquellen zur Geschichte der bildenden Künste bei den Griechen, 1868, (Rp. 1959).

Jones, H. Stuart: Select Passages from Ancient Writers Illustrative of the History of Greek Sculpture, 1895, (with translations).

Jex-Blake, K. & Sellers, E.: Pliny's Chapters on the History of Art, 1896.

Gallet de Santerre, H. & H. LeBonniec: Pline l'ancien: Histoire Naturelle, *livre xxxiv*, 1959.

Sillig's Dictionary of the Artists of Antiquity, (tr. H. W. Williams in Coll of Suppl. to Lempriere's Classical Dictionary), 1837.

Inscriptions Relating to Sculptors and Sculpture

Loewy, E.: Inschriften griechischer Bildauer, 1885.

Marcadé, J.: Recueil des signatures de sculpteurs grecs, i, 1959, ii.

Raubitschek, A.: Dedications from the Athenian Akropolis, 1949.

Woodhead, G.: The Study of Greek Inscriptions, 1958.

Archaeological Discoveries and Excavations

Frazer, G.: Pausanias' Description of Greece, *vols. i-vi* 1898.

Reinach, S.: Repertoire de la statuaire greque et romaine, *vols. i-vi*, 1906-30.

_____: Repertoire de reliefs grecs et romains, *vols. i-iii*, 1909-12.

Michaelis, A.: A Century of Archaeological Discoveries, translated by B. Kahnweiler, 1908.

Marshall, F. H.: Discovery in Greek Lands, 1920.

Reproductions of Statues on Coins

Ashmole, B.: "The Relation Between Coins and Sculpture" in *Trans. Intern. Numism. Congr. 1936*, 1938.

Bieber, M.: "Representations de statues sur des stateres de Corinthe," in *Revue Num.*, 1907, pp. 317-323.

Gardner, P.: "Copies of Statues on Coins" (in *New Chapters on Greek Art*), 1926.

Hill, G. F.: L'Art dans les monnaies grecques, 1927.

Imhoof-Blumer, F. & Gardner, P.: Numismatic Commentary on Pausanias, 1887 (Rp. *JHS, 6-8, 1885-87.*

Lehman, P. W.: Statues on Coins of S. Italy...etc., 1946.

Lacroix, L.: Les reproductions de statues sur les monnaies grecques, 1949.

Seltman, C. T.: Masterpieces of Greek Coinage, 1949.

Dictionaries and Encyclopediae

Roscher, -: Ausfürliches Lexicon der Griechischen und Römischen Mythologie, *vols. i-vi, A-Z + Nachtrage,* 1884-1937.

Daremberg, Ch. & Saglio, E.: Dictionnaire des antiquités grecques et romaines d'après les textes et les monuments, 5 vols., 1877-1919 (Rp., 1962-).

Pauly-Wissowa: Realencyclopädie der Classichen Altertumswissenschaft 1894-1963, 75 vols. publ. to date, (in progress).

Encyclopedia dell'Arte Antica, 1960-, *vols. i-v* publ. to date.

Thieme, U. & Becker, F.: Allgemeines Lexicon der bildenden Kunstler, von der antike bis zur Gegenwart, 1907-1950, 37 vols.

Larousse Encyclopedia of Prehistoric and Ancient Art, 1962.

Oxford Classical Dictionary, 1949.

Specialized Bibliographies

Marouzeau, J.: Dix années de bibliographie classique (1914-24), 2 vols.

 I. Auteurs et textes, ed., rev. & corr., 1957

 II. Matières et disciplines, 1928

_____ & Ernst, J.: L'*Année philologique*, 1924-1963, *vols. i-xxxiv* publ. to date.

Matz-Mau: Katalog der Bibliothek des Deutschen Archaeol. Instituts in Rom, 1913-32, (supplements issued irregularly).

Vermeule, C.: A Bibliography of Applied Numismatics in the Fields of Greek and Roman Archaeology and the Fine Arts, 1956.

"Fasti Archaeologici" Annual volume, bibliography and summaries of publ. articles and books, 1946-, *vols. i-xiv* publ. to date.

"Lustrum", vol. vi, 1961. A bibliography of Greek Archaeology and Literature by D. Webster, (1956-1960).

General Reference

Alscher, L.: Griechische Plastik, 4 vols, 1954-. (Vol. ii in preparation).

Arvanitopoulos, A.: Greek Sculptors, 1931, (in Greek).

Beazley, J. D. & Ashmole, B.: Greek Sculpture and Painting to the End of the Hellenistic Period. 1932.

Bianchi-Bandinelli, R.: Storicità dell'arte classica, 1950.

Bieber, M.: Antike Skulpturen und Bronzen in Kassel, 1915.

_____: Griechische Kleidung, 1928.

_____: The Sculpture of the Hellenistic Age, rev. ed. 1961.

Bielefeld, E.: Amazonamachia. Beiträge zur Geschichte der Motivwanderung in der antiken Kunst, (*Hallische Monographien nr. 21*), 1951.

Blümel, C.: Antike Kunstwerke, 1953.

_____: Griechische Bildhauerarbeit, 1927.

_____: Greek Sculptors at Work, 1955.

Bothmer, D. von: Amazons in Greek Art, 1957.

Brunn, H.: Geschichte der Griechischen Künstler, vol. I, 2nd ed., 1889.

Buschor, E.: Das Porträt. Bildniswege und Bildnisstufen in funf Jahrtausenden, 1960.

_____: Die Plastik der Griechen, 1940.

_____: Technisches Sehen. Festrede gehalter in deroffentlichen. (*Sitzung. der Bayer Ak. der Wiss, Münch*), 1952.

_____: Vom Sinn der griechischen Standbilder, 1942.

Carpenter, R.: The Esthetic Basis of Greek Art, rev. edtn. 1959.

_____: Greek Sculpture: A Critical Review, 1960.

_____: The Sculpture of the Nike Temple Parapet, 1929.

Charbonneaux, J.: La sculpture grecque au musee du Louvre, 1946.

_____: Greek Bronzes, 1961.

Chase, C. H.: Greek and Roman Sculpture in American Collections, 1924.

_____: Greek & Roman Antiquities, Boston Museum of Fine Arts, 1950.

Curtius, L.: Die antike Kunst, vol. ii, Die Klassische Kunst Griechenlands, 1938, (rp. 1959).

Dickins, G.: Hellenistic Sculpture, 1920.

Fowler, H. N. & Wheeler, J. R.: Handbook of Greek Archaeology, 1909.

Fowler, H. N.: A History of Sculpture, 1916.

Gardner, E. A.: Six Greek Sculptors, 1910.

_____: Handbook of Greek Sculpture, 2nd ed., 1915.

Gardner, P.: The Principles of Greek Art, 1914, (Rp. 1926).

Johansen, K. F.: The Attic Grave Reliefs of the Classical Period, 1951.

Kavvadias, P.: History of Greek Art, 1924, (in Greek).

Kekule von Stradonitz, R. K.: Die griechische Skulptur, in *Handbucher der Königlicher Museen zu Berlin*, 1907.

Laurenzi, L.: Ritratti Greci(*Quaderni per lo st. dell'Archeol. Fasc. 3-5*), 1941.

Lechat, H.: Phidias et sculpture grecque au Ve siecle, 1924.

Lippold, G.: Kopien und Umbildungen Griechischer Statuen, 1923.

_____: Die griechische Plastik, in *Handbuch der Archaeologie, iii, 1*, 1950.

Lullies, R. & Hirmer, M.: Greek Sculpture, rev. ed., 1960.

Moebius, H.: Die Ornamente der griech. Grabstelen. 1929.

Murray, A. S.: A History of Greek Sculpture, 1890.

Muthmann, F.: Statuenstützen und dekorative Beiwerk an griechischen und römischen Bildwerken, 1951.

Picard, Ch.: Manuel d'archeologie grecque. La Sculpture, vols. i-iv, 1935-1954.

Richter, G.: Animals in Greek Sculpture. 1930.

_____: Greek Portraits, *i-iv, Coll. Latomus, 20, 36, 48, 54,* 1955-1962.

_____: A Handbook of Greek Art, 2nd ed. rev., 1960.

_____: Handbook of the Greek Collection, Metropolitan Museum of Art, 1953.

_____: The Sculpture and Sculptors of the Greeks, 3rd ed. 1950.

_____: Three Critical Periods in Greek Sculpture, 1951.

Schuchhardt, W. H.: Die Epochen der griechischen Plastik, 1959.

_____: Griechische Plastik der Klassischen Zeit. (Die Sammlung Parthenon), 1954.

Svoronos, J. N.: Das athener Nationalmuseum, 3 vols., 1908-1913.

Tsountas, Ch.: History of ancient Greek Art, 1929, (rp. in 2 vols., 1959), (in Greek).

Waldmann, E.: Griechische Originale, 2nd ed., 1923.

426 BIBLIOGRAPHY

AGORAKRITOS

Rubensohn, O.:"Parischer Künstler," in *JDAI 50*,1935,pp. 46-69.

Schefold, K.: Agorakritos als Erbe des Pheidias, 1957(in *Robert Böhringer-Eine Freundesgabe*).

Schweitzer, B.: "Dea Nemesis Regina," in *JDAI 46*,1931, pp. 175-246.

ALCAMENES

Langlotz, E.: Alkamenes-Probleme, (108 Winckelmannspr.) 1952.

Papaspyridi, S.: In *Ath. Mitt. 69/70*, 1954-55, pp.67 seq.

Schroeder, B.: Alkamenes-Studien, (79 Winckelmannspr.) 1921.

Stevens, G.Ph.: In *Hesperia 19*, 1950, pp. 149-57.

Walston, C.: Alkamenes and the Establishment of the Class - ical Type In Greek Art, 1926.

Wroth, W.: "Asklepios and the Coins of Pergamon," in *Num. Chron.*, 1882, pp. 1-51.

ANTENOR

Becatti, -:"I Tyrannicidi di Antenore," in *Archeol. Classica 9* 1957, pp. 97 seq.

Jongkees, J.H.: "Notes on the Coinage of Athens; vii,'O Δῆμος Antenor's Tyrannoktones," in *Mnemosyne 13*, 1947, pp. 145-160.

ARKESILAOS

Bieber, M.: "Die Venus Genetrix des Arkesilaos," in *Röm. Mitt., 48*, 1933, pp. 261-276.

Borda, M.: "Arkesilaos," in *Bull. Com., 73 (1949- 1950)*, 1953, pp.189- 204.

Elderkin, G.W.: "The Venus Genetrix of Arcesilas," in *AJA 42*, 1938, pp. 371-74.

Harcum, C.G.: "A Study of the type called Venus Genetrix," in *AJA 42*, 1927, pp. 141-52.

EUPHRANOR

Thompson, H.A.: "Apollo Patroos," in Ἀρχ.Ἐφ.*1953/54*, vol. iii, pp. 30 ff.

KALAMIS

Cahn, H.A.: "Zu Kalamis," in *Studies Pres. to D.M. Robinson, I*, 1951, pp. 559-567.

Orlandini, P.: Calamide, Bibliografia e Sviluppe della Questione dalle Origini ai Nostri Giorni, 1949.

Reisch, A.: "Kalamis," in *JOAI, 9*, 1906, pp. 199-268.

Studniczka, E.: Kalamis, 1907.

Svoronos, J.N.: "Un groupe inconnu de trois statues a Sicyone," in *Journ. internat. d'arch. num., 14*, 1914, pp. 71-80.

KRESILAS

Orlandini, P.: "I donari firmati da Kresilas e Dorotheos a Hermione," *Arch.classica, vol.iii,fasc1*,1951,pp. 94-8.

_____ : "Kresilas," in *Atti della Accad. dei Lincei, Memorie, Ser.viii-iv, fasc. 5*,1952,pp.273 - 335.

Pfuhl, E.: "Der Raub des Palladions," in *Röm. Mitt.*, *14*, 1901. pp. 33-41.

KRITIOS AND NESIOTES

Beyen, H.G.: La Statue d'Artemision, 1930.

Brunnsåker, -: The Tyrant Slayers of Kritios and Nesiotes, 1955.

Buschor, E.: Die Tyrannen-Mörder(*Sitz.Bay.Akad.Wiss.*) 1940, No. 5.

Cardara, C.: "On Theseus and the Tyrannicides," in *AJA 55*, 1951, pp. 293-300.

Raubitschek, A.: See Inscriptions Relating to Sculptors, etc.

Walter, O.: "Zur Tyrannenmörder-gruppe," in *JOAI, 40*, 1953, pp. 126-43.

Wycherley, R.E.: Literary and Epigraphical Testimonia, *Athenian Agora, vol.iii*, 1957, pp. 93-98.

LYSIPPOS

Collignon, M.: Lysippe, 1905.

Johnson, F.P.: Lysippos, 1927.

Loeffler, E. "Lysippos' Labors of Herakles," in *Marsyas 6*, 1954, pp. 8-24.

Maviglia, A.: L'Attività artistica di Lisippo, 1914.

MYRON

Andrén, A.: "Der Lateranische Silen und die Gruppe von Athena und Marsyas," in *Opuscula Archaeologica iii*, 1944, pp. 1-36, pls. i-vii.

Arias, P.E.: Mirone, 1940.

Bulle, H.: "Die Samische Gruppe des Myron," in *Festschrift P. Arndt*, 1925, pp. 62-86.

Carpenter, R.: Observations on Familiar Statuary in Rome, (*Mem. Amer. Acad.*, *xviii*, 1941).

Hommel, H.:"Domina Roma," in *Die Antike,18*, 1942, pp. 127-158.

Mirone, S.: Mirone d'Eleutere, 1921.

Schröder, B.: Zum Diskobol des Myron, 1913.

PAIONIOS

Harder, P.: Paionios und Grophon: Zwei bildhauermschriften, in *Festschrift für B. Schweitzer*, 1954.

Schröder, B.: Mikon und Paionios," in *JDAI 29*, 1914, pp. 123-168.

Studniczka, F.: Die Siegesgöttin, 1898.

PHEIDIAS

Amelung, W.: "Athena des Phidias," in *JOAI 11*, 1908, pp. 169-211.

Arias, P.E.: Pheidias, 1944.

Arvanitopoulos, A.: Pheidias, 1935, (in Greek).

Becatti, G.: Problemi Fidiaci, 1951.

Beyen, H.G.: La Statue Artemision, 1930.

Blümel, C.: Phidiasische Reliefs und Parthenonfries, 1957.

Buschor, E.: Phidias der Mensch, 1948.

_____ : Pferde des Pheidias, 1948.

Cook, A.B.: Zeus, *vol. i-iii*, 1914-1940.

Dimitrov, D.P.: "Bronze Statuette eines sitzenden Zeus aus Stara-Zagora," in *Arch. Anz*, 1937. cols. 310-35.

Eichler, F.: "Thebanische Sphinx. Ein Bildwerk aus Ephesos," in *JOAI*, *30*, 1937, pp. 75-110.

Evelyn-White, H.G.: "The Throne of Zeus at Olympia," in *JHS 28*, 1908, pp. 49-55.

Goethert, F.W.: "Zur Athena Parthenos," in *JDAI*, *49*, 1934, pp. 157-161.

Hekler, A.: Die Kunst des Phidias, 1924.

Herington, C.J.: Athena Parthenos and Athena Polias, 1955.

Hill, D.K.: "A Copy of the Athena Parthenos," in *Art Bulletin 18*, 1936, pp. 150-167.

Jenkins, R.J.H.: "The Bronze Athena at Byzantium," in *JHS*, *67*, 1947, pp. 31-33.

Kavvadias, P.: The Statuette of Athena from Varvakeion & its Relation to the Cult Statue in Parthenon (in Greek), 1881.

Lange, K.: "Die Athena Parthenos," in *Ath. Mitt. 6*, 1881, pp. 56-94.

Langlotz, E.: Phidiasprobleme, 1948.

Laurenzi, L.: Umanità di Fidia, *(Studia Archeologica, 3)*, 1961.

Lehmann-Hartleben, K.: "Die Athena Parthenos des Phidias," in *JDAI 47*, 1932, pp. 12-46.

Lermann, W.: Athenatypen auf griechischen Münzen...etc.,' 1900.

Liegle, J.: "Der Zeus des Phidias im Lichte einer Neuer - werbung des Berliner Münzkabinetts," in *Bericht ü.d vi. Int. Kongress f. Arch*, 1940, pp. 653-660.

Matz, F.: "Zeuskopf in Villa Borghese," in *JDAI, 46*, 1931, pp. 1=31.

Mustilli, D.: "Studi fidiaci," in *Bull. Com.*, *61*, 1933, pp. 7-24.

Pagenstecher, R.: "Zur Athena Parthenos des Phidias,"in *Ath. Mitt., 33* 1908, pp. 113-134.

Pfuhl, E.: "Die grosse Eherne Athena des Phidias," in *Ath. Mitt., 57*, 1932.

Pick, B.: "Die 'Promachos' des Phidias und die Kerameikos Lampen," in *Ath. Mitt., 56*, 1931, pp. 59-74, pl. i.

Poulsen, V.H.: "Phidias und sein Kreis," in *Coll. of Ny Carlsberg Glyptotek, iii*, 1942, pp. 33-92.

Rizzo, G.E.: "Conosciamo noi Fidia...," in *Dedalo, yr. vii, vol.ii*, 1926-27, pp. 273-294.

Santangelo, M.: "Una terracotta di Falerii e lo Zeus di Fidia," in *Boll. d'Arte*,1948, pp.1-16.

Schrader, H.: "Das Zeusbild des Pheidias in Olympia," in *JDAI,56*, 1941, pp. 1 ff.

Winter, Franz: "Der Zeus und die Athena Parthenos des Phidias," in *JOAI, 18*, 1915, pp. 1-16.

POLYKLEITOS

Anti, C.: "Monumenti Polycletei," in *Mon. Ant. 26*, 1920, pp. 501-792.

Bandinelli, R.: Policleto, (*Quaderni per lo studio dell'archeologia, i*) 1938.

Blümel, C.: Der Diskosdräger Polyklets, (90 Winckels - mannpr.). 1930.

Brueckner, A.: Polyklets Knöchelwerfer, (77 Winckels - mannpr.), 1920.

Mahler, -: Polyklet und seine Schule, 1902.

Paris, P.: Polyclète, 1895.

Robinson, D.M.: "The Cyniskus of Polyclitus," in *Art Bul. 18*, 1936, pp. 133- 149.

POLYKLEITOS (continued)

Wolters, P.: "Polyklets Doryphoros in der Ehrenhalle der Münchner Universität, " in *Munch. Jahrb. der bild. Kunst 11*, 1934, pp. 1-25.

PRAXITELES

Amelung, W.: "Die Basis des Praxiteles aus Mantinea, " in *Archaeol. Studien*, 1895.
Antonsson, O.: The Praxiteles Marble Group in Olympia, 1937.
Bieber, M.: "Die Koische Aphrodite des Praxiteles, " in *Zeitscher f. Num. 34*, 1924, pp. 315-320.
Blinkenberg, C.: Knidia Beiträge zur Kenntnis der Praxitelischen Aphrodite, 1933.
Blümel, C.: Der Hermes eines Praxiteles, 1948.
Carpenter, R.: In *AJA 58*, 1954, pp. 1-12.
Charbonneaux, J.: "L'Aphrodite de Cnide de la collection Kaufmann, " in *Revue des arts*, 1951, pp. 175 ff.
Collignon, M.: Scopas et Praxitèle, 1907.
Ducati, P.: Prassitele, (without date).
Hege, W.: Olympia, 1937, pp. 50 ff, Pls. 85-91.
Klein, W.: Praxiteles, 1898.
Mirone, S.: "Les Éros de Praxitèle et en particulier l'Eros des Mamertins, " in *Revue Num*, 1921, pp. 23-37.
Oikonomides, Al. N.: "Aphrodite Thespia, " in Πλάτων 7, 1955, pp. 342-46.
_____: "Kritika eis Pausanian, "in Πλάτων 12, 1960, pp. 52-4.
Perrot, G.: Praxitèle, 1905.
Rizzo, G.E.: Prassitele, 1932.
Robinson, C.A.: "The Zeus Ithomatas of Ageladas, " in *AJA 49*, 1945, pp. 121-27.
Ruzicka, L.: "Zwei Statuen des Praxiteles auf Münzen von Pautalia, " in *Strena Buliciana*, 1924.
_____: "Die Münzen von Pautalia, " in *Bull. Inst. archeol. bulgare, 7*, 1932-33, pp. 27 ff.
Savignoni, L.: See Scopas.
Weege, F.: Der kinschenkende Satyr aus Sammlung Mengarini, (89 Winckelsmannpr.), 1929.
Weil, R.: "Der Dionysos des Praxiteles in Elis, " in *Zeitschr. f. Num. 13*, 1885, pp. 384-88.
Wolters, P.: "Der Eros des Praxiteles in Parion, " in *Sitzungsber. d. bayer. Ak. d. Wiss., Philios.-philil. u. hist., K1*, 1913.

SCOPAS

Arias, P.E.: Skopas, (*Quaderni e guida di arch., 1*), 1952.
Collignon, M.: See Praxiteles.
Grace, V.R.: "Scopas in Chryse, " in *JHS 52*, 1932, pp. 228-232.
Neugebauer, K.A.: Studien über Skopas, 1913.
Riis, P.J.: "The Pedigree of Some Herakles Figures from Tarsus, " in *Acta. Arch., 23*, 1952, pp. 152-54.
Savignoni, L.: "Apollo Pythios, " in *Ausonia, ii, 1*, 1907, pp. 16-66, pls. iv-x.
Schober, M.A.: "Zu den elischen Bildwerke der Aphrodite, " in *JOAI, 21- 22*, 1922-24, pp. 225-228.
Six, J.: "Die Mänaden des Skopas, " in *JDAI 33*, 1918, pp. 38-48.
Urlich, -: Skopas, 1863.

TEMPLE SCULPTURES

Alscher, L.: Kompositionsgesetze der Olympianmeister, in *Mitt. d. D.A.I, 4*, 1951, pp. 65 ff.
Becatti, G.: Il Maestro d'Olimpia, 1943.
British Museum: An Historical Guide to the Sculptures of the Parthenon, 1962.
Buschor, E. & Hamann, R.: Die Skulpturen des Zeustempel zu Olympia, 1924.
Buschor, E.: "Die Olympiameister, "in *Ath. Mitt., 51*, 1926, pp. 163 ff.
Collignon, M.: Le Parthenon. L'histoire, l'architecture et la sculpture, 1914.
Corbett, P.E.: The Sculpture of the Parthenon, 1959.
Dinsmoor, W.B.: The Architecture of Ancient Greece, 1950.
_____: "The Sculptured Frieze from Bassae, " in *AJA 60*, 1956, pp. 401-452.
_____: "The Temple of Ares at Athens, " in *Hesperia 9, 1940*, pp. 1-52.
Gardner, E.N.: Olympia, Its History and Remains, 1925.
Hill, I.T.: The Ancient City of Athens, 1953.
Jeppesen, K.: "The Pedimental Compositions of the Parthenon, "in *Acta Archaeologica 24*, 1953, pp. 103 ff.
Kahler, H.: Das griechische Metopenbild, 1949.
Kunze, E.: Neue Meisterwerke griech. kunst aus Olympia,, 1948.
_____ & others: Olympia Berichte, vols. ii-vi, 1938-58.

Michaelis, A.: Ancient Marbles in Great Britain, trans. by C.A.M. Fennell, 1882.
_____: Der Parthenon, 1871.
Miltner, F.: Ephesos, Stadt der Artemis, 1958.
Morgan, C.: "Pheidias and Olympia, " in *Hesperia 21*, 1952, pp. 295-339.
Paton, J.M. & others: The Erectheum, 1927.
Oikonomides, Al. N.: The Akropolis of Athens, 1958.
Rodenwaldt, G.: Kopfe von den Sudmetopen des Parthenon, 1948.
_____: Das Relief bei den Griechen, 1923.
Smith, A.H.: Sculptures of the Parthenon, 1910.
Schweitzer, B.: "Pheidias der Parthenonmeister, " in *JDAI 55*, 1940, pp. 170-241.
Stevens, G. Ph.: Restorations of Classical Buildings, 1955.
Yalouris, N.: Les Sculptures du Parthenon, 1960.

VENUS OF MILO

Charbonneaux, J.: "La Venus de Milo et Mithridate le Grand", in *Revue des Arts*, 1951, pp. 8-16.
_____: "La Venus de Milo, " (*Opus Nobile 6)*, 1958.

APOLLO BELVEDERE

Amelung, W.: "Zum Apollon vom Belvedere, " in *Ath. Mitt., xxv*, 1900, pp. 286-291.
Deubner, O.: Hellenistische Apollogestalten, (*Diss. Munich)* 1934,
Neugebauer, K.A.: "Der Apollon vom Belvedere und sein Meister, " in *Arch. Anz.*, 1946-57, pp. 1-36.

ZEUS OF ARTEMISION

Arvanitopoulos, A.: In Πολέμων 1, 1929, pp. 88-94.
Beyen, H.G.: La Statue d'Artemision, 1938.
Casrouge, Chr.: In Ἀρχ. Δελτίον 13, 1930-31, pp. 41 ff.
Curtius, L.: Interpretation von sechs griech. Bildwerken, 1947.
Elderkin, G.W.: "Bronze Statuettes of Zeus Keraunios, "in *AJA 44*, 1940, pp. 225-233.
Mylonas, G.E.: "The Bronze Statue from Artemision, " in *AJA 48*, 1944, pp. 143 ff.
Oikonomos, G.: "Le nouveau 'Zeus' du Musée d'Athenes, " in *Monuments Piot 30*, 1929, pp. 15-24.
Robinson, C.A.: "The Zeus Ithomatas of Ageladas, " in *AJA 49*, 1945, pp. 121-127.

Reproductions of Statues on Vases, Lamps and Gems

Beazley, J.D.: Attic Red-Figure Vase Painters, 2nd ed. in 3 vols, 1963.
_____: Attic Black-Figure Vase Painters, 1956.
_____: The Lens Collection of Ancient Gems, 1920.
Bothmer, O. von: "Enkaustes Agalmaton, " in *N.Y. Metr. Bulletin*, 1950, pp. 156-161.
Broneer, O.: Terracotta Lamps, *Corinth, vol. iv*, 1930.
Furtwängler, A.: Die Antike Gemmen, 3 vols., 1900.
_____: Konigliche Museen zu Berlin, Beschreibung des geschnittenen steine in Antiquarium, 1896.
Grandjouan, C.: Terracottas and Plastic Lamps of the Roman Period, in *The Athenian Agora, vol. vi*, 1961.
Lippold, G.: Gemmen und Kameen, 1922.
Perlzweig, J.: Lamps of the Roman Period, in *The Athenian Agora, vol. vii*, 1961.
Richter, G.: Catalogue of engraved Gems Greek-Etruscan und Roman in the Metropolitan Museum of Art-N.Y., 1956.
Schefold, K.: "Statuen auf Vasenbildern, " in *JDAI 52*, 1937, pp. 30-75.
Vermeule, C.: Aspects of Victoria on Roman Coins, Gems, and in Monumental Art, *Numismatic Circular*, 1958.
Walters, H.B.: Catalogue of the Engraved Gems and Cameos Greek, Etruscan and Roman, in the British Museum, 1926.

RELIGION, MYTHOLOGY AND ART

Apollodorus: The Library, (Greek text, Engl. translation & comm. by Sir J.G. Frazer), 2 vols, Loeb, 1921.
Collignon, M.: Manual of Mythology in Rel. to Greek Art, 1890.
Graves, R.: The Greek Myths, 2 vols, 1955.
Grimal, P.: Dictionnaire de la Myth. Gr. et Romaine, 1958.
Harrison, J.: Prolegomena to Hist. of Gr. Religion, Rp. 1960.
_____: Themis and Epilegomena, Rp. 1962.
Harrison, J.E. & Verall, M.: Mythology and Monuments of Ancient Athens, 1890.
Kerenyi, C.: The Religion of the Greeks & Romans, 1962.
_____: The Heroes of the Greeks, 1960.
Larousse Encyclopedia of Mythology, 1960.
Meautis, G.: Mythologie grecque, 1959.
Nilsson, M.P.: Geschichte der griech. Religion, 2 vol. 1950-1955, *(Handbuch des Altertumswissenschaft v, ii)*.
Scully, V.: The Earth, the Temple & the Gods, 1962.

INDEX

(Numbers following after a comma refer to the notes.)

I. HISTORICAL

II. MUSEUMS

ENGLAND

Private Collections: BLACKER : Diadumenos, terra-cotta 239, 8.

BROADLANDS (Hampshire) : Athena of Velletri, replica 141, 2 (*a*). Head of Hermes 57 ; of Herakles, Polykleitan 234, 1.

DEEPDENE in Surrey (Hope collection) : Athena 73, 4. 76 *sqq.* Dionysos 323, 5. Resting Satyr after Praxiteles, head 329, 5.

INCE BLUNDELL HALL (Lancashire) : Head of athlete 172. Dionysos, Polykleitan school 272, 1 (*c*). 'Theseus' 94, 1. 359, 3.

LANSDOWNE HOUSE (London) : Amazon 134 *seq.* Apollo, 'Adonis' type 354, 4. Athena of Velletri, replica 141, 2 (*d*). Statue of athlete 171. Marcus Aurelius 92, 4. Boxer 245, 3. Statue of Herakles 296 *sqq.*; of Hermes, Polykleitan 288 *sqq.* Head of Hermes 290. Belvedere Hermes, replica 338, 1. Paris 358 *seq.*

PETWORTH HOUSE (Sussex) : Amazon 130, 138. Head of athlete with fillet 161 *sqq.* Oil-pourer 257 *seq.* Aphrodite, Praxitelean 343 *sqq.* (removed to Lord Leconfield's London residence).

RICHMOND (Collection of Sir Francis Cook) : Apollo, 'Adonis' type 354, 4. Hermes bronze 233, 1. Vase with Blinding of Polyphemos 109.

Belonging to A. H. SMITH, ESQ.: terra-cotta relief with figs. 133, 134 of north frieze of Parthenon, 431, 5.

Presumably in England: Diomede 148. Athena 73, 4. Polykleitan boy 266, 1.

FLORENCE

UFFIZI : Aphrodite and Ares 384, 6. 392, 7. 394, 1. Asklepios, severe style 205 *sqq.* Athena 305, 1 (*a*). Athlete (*apoxyomenos*) 205. 260, 3. 261, 1. 515. 519. Doryphoros, statue 228, 1 ; torso 228 ; head 229, 1. Boxer (?) 247, 1. Hermes, Praxitelean 338, 4. Leda 392, 394. Niobids 394. Venus of Medici 345.

MUSEO ETRUSCO : Chimaira 134, 5. Idolino 283 *sqq.* 290. 350 *sqq.*

PALAZZO PITTI: Aphrodite, Knidian 322, 3 (5). Apollo, severe style 81. Athena, Giustiniani type 359, 4 (*d*). Doryphoros head 229. Herakles 296, 3. Hermes 289, 2. Praxitelean head (Triptolemos ?) 334, 4. Oil-pourer 259, 9. Supposed 'Sappho' 69, 7.

GIARDINO BOBOLI : Aphrodite head 345. Athlete ('Harmodios') 171. 'Hera,' replica of Capitoline type (= Ov. K. M. 461, 6), cf. p. 82. Hermes and Dionysos 230. Female head, Myronian 202. Motive of Venus of Capua 385, 1 (*d*).

PALAZZO CEPPARELLI : Draped female statue 69.

PALAZZO RICCARDI : Anakreon 60, 7 (*b*). So-called 'Eubouleus' 331, 1. Bust of hero, Myronian 165 *sqq.* 'Sappho' head 66, 2 (*e*). Head of victorious athlete with fillet 161, 3 (*c*). 169, 5. Head of Zeus 190, 2.

PALAZZO VECCHIO : Hermes, Belvedere type 338, 1.

GENEVA.

Ares, bronze 230. Vase from Magna Graecia, after prototype of Pheidian style 109, 5.

GENOA.

PALAZZO REALE : 'Narkissos' 272, 4 (*i*)

HANOVER.

KESTNER MUSEUM : Pan 270, 1 (*i*)

LEYDEN.

Pan 270 *seq.*

LONDON.

BRITISH MUSEUM : Apollo statue, bronze from Lower Egypt 353 ; head, of Pourtalès 165, 1 ; do. from Baths of Caracalla *ibid.* ; do. ('Alexander') 411 ; do. resting 337, 2. do. Kithairoidos 305, 6. Ares, bronze 230. Aristaios (?) statue from Kyrene 277. Athena, bronze of severe style 16, 1 (1). 23, 11; head of Velletri type 141, 2 (*c*). Athlete, Westmacott 250 *sqq.* Athlete statuette, Polykleitan 265. Diadumenos, Vaison 238 *sqq.* 242 *sqq.*; Farnese 244. Diskobolos 161, 4. Eros, so-called Elgin 256. Sculptured drum from Ephesos 301 *seq.* Herakles bearded, Myronian 178. Aberdeen head, Praxitelean 346 *seq.* Hero, statue of 298. Kanephoros, Praxitelean 337, 1 (*c*). Bearded head (Asklepios ?) 210; another 205. Mercury, bronze from Gaul 232. Disc with relief of the Niobids 43, 4. Female statue from Ostia ('Townley Venus') 319 *seq.* Two statues of Pan 270, 1 (*b*), (*c*). Perikles, terminal bust 177 *sqq.* Pheidias's portrait on shield 48. 'Sappho' head 66, 2 (*c*). Xanthos, three torsos of severe style 23, 5. Nereid monument 450. Zeus, bronze statuette 299.

PRIVATE COLLECTIONS : *supra,* ENGLAND.

LYONS.

Hypnos, two small bronze replicas 395, 8.

MADRID.

Athena, statue related to Lemnia 27.
Athena head, Velletri type 141, 2 (*f*).
Birth of Athena, relief 463 *seq.* Diadumenos 240 *seq.* Diomedes (?), head 149, 3. Dionysos 337. Ildefonso group 257. Female head 60. 'Sappho-Phaon,' terminal bust 66, 2 (*p*). Venus of Capua motive 385, 1 (*b*).

MANTUA.

Apollo 19. 25. 52 *seq.* 194. 197. 354, 5. 359, 4 (*c*). Eubouleus 331, 1. Narkissos 272, 4 (*e*), (*h*).

MUNICH.

GLYPTOTHEK : Aphrodite 322 and note 5. Apollo, Barberini 88. 305, 6 ; head of, 'Adonis' type 354, 4 (placed on the 'Jason'). Artemis of Gabii 52, 4. 439 *seq.* 'Artemis' (Tyche) 325. Athena 60 and note 6; Albani 141, 2 *sqq.* Athlete, black marble 264, 1 (*B*). Diomedes 146

III. GENERAL

Al. N. Oikonomides was born in Athens, Greece. He studied Archaeology and classical languages at the University of Athens and later at the University of Chicago. He has participated in several expeditions and excavations and has published numerous articles in scholarly journals. For a time he worked as Assistant Curator in the museums of the Acropolis and Epidaurus and later traveled throughout Europe to complete a research program in the major museums, thereby gaining the necessary background knowledge which has enabled him to prepare this revised edition of *Masterpieces of Greek Sculpture*, already considered by several specialists in the field to be a valuable contribution to the reference library on Greek sculpture.

In 1960 Oikonomides left London where he had been doing research at the British Museum and came to the United States. He now lives in Chicago and is preparing a new book *The City of the Owl*, a study of the mythology history and monuments of his native city, Athens.